Concepts and Applications
Fourth Edition

David J. Anspaugh, PED, EdD, CHES

Michael H. Hamrick, EdD, CHES

Frank D. Rosato, EdD

ALL OF THE UNIVERSITY OF MEMPHIS
Memphis, Tennessee

Boston   Burr Ridge, IL   Dubuque, IA   Madison, WI   New York   San Francisco   St. Louis
Bangkok   Bogotá   Caracas   Lisbon   London   Madrid
Mexico City   Milan   New Delhi   Seoul   Singapore   Sydney   Taipei   Toronto

We dedicate this book to

Susan H. Anspaugh   *Dorothy Hamrick*   *Patricia Rosato*

McGraw-Hill Higher Education

*A Division of The **McGraw-Hill** Companies*

WELLNESS: CONCEPTS AND APPLICATIONS, FOURTH EDITION

This book is printed on acid-free paper.

1 2 3 4 5 6 7 8 9 0 VNH/VNH 0 9 8 7 6 5 4 3 2 1 0

ISBN 0–07–039329–X

Vice president and editorial director: *Kevin T. Kane*
Publisher: *Edward E. Bartell*
Executive editor: *Vicki Malinee*
Senior developmental editor: *Melissa Martin*
Senior marketing manager: *Pamela S. Cooper*
Project manager: *Sheila M. Frank*
Production supervisor: *Enboge Chong*
Designer: *K. Wayne Harms*
Senior photo research coordinator: *Carrie K. Burger*
Senior supplement coordinator: *David A. Welsh*
Compositor: *Shepherd, Inc.*
Typeface: *10/12 Sabon*
Printer: *Von Hoffmann Press, Inc.*

Interior/cover design: *Becky Lemna*
Cover photograph: *© Ken Reid/FPG International*
Photo research: *LouAnn K. Wilson*

The credits section for this book is on page 497 and is considered an extension of the copyright page.

www.mhhe.com

Concepts and Applications

Preface

Wellness: Concepts and Applications assumes that health is not a destination but a journey. Wellness is not a static condition but a continual balancing of the different dimensions of human needs—spiritual, social, emotional, intellectual, physical, occupational, and environmental. Because we are all responsible for our own growth in these areas, this book strives to emphasize the importance of self-responsibility. And because we know that knowledge alone stimulates change for very few people, the reader is challenged to be actively involved in the learning process by constantly assessing how the information presented affects lifestyle from a personal perspective.

Wellness: Concepts and Applications is neither a fitness book nor a personal health text. Instead, this text is designed to help students gain knowledge and understanding in a variety of areas, with the goal of taking that information and using it to make behavioral changes that will have a positive impact on their lives. In many cases these changes are necessary if people are to develop the skills, attitudes, beliefs, and habits that will ultimately result in the highest possible level of health and wellness.

Audience

When the fitness and wellness concept appears in university courses and programs, it is usually a scaled-down model of the traditional personal health course or an upscale version of physical fitness courses. In some cases it is a hybrid of personal health and fitness courses, with emphasis on self-participation in the medical marketplace. *Wellness: Concepts and Applications* is a hybrid because the physical components of wellness are blended with its many other components. The primary objectives of this text are to present cogni-

tive health and wellness information appropriate for today's college students and to offer suggestions for their application. These suggestions relate to lifestyle behaviors over which people can exert some control. The emphasis is on self-responsibility, and this theme is implemented through a strong self-analysis and assessment component.

Approach

Important features unique to *Wellness: Concepts and Applications* distinguish it from other texts.

Balanced approach: Unlike other approaches that emphasize only physical fitness as a route to wellness, *Wellness: Concepts and Applications* provides a balanced presentation of the health benefits of exercise, diet, and cardiovascular wellness, along with the management of lifestyle change and consumer responsibility to achieve lifetime wellness.

Complete lifestyle decision-making information: Along with Goals for Behavior Change, Real-World Wellness boxes, Wellness on the Web Behavior Change Activities, and Assessment Activities that help apply the content, coverage of substance use, sexually transmitted diseases, cancer, and chronic health conditions is provided to enable and encourage responsible student decision making.

Consumer-oriented: Chapter 15, "Becoming a Responsible Health-Care Consumer," offers information to help students become wise consumers.

Interdisciplinary author team: Two health educators and a fitness educator currently teaching wellness courses have combined their expertise to provide the most balanced presentation possible.

Full-color: A full-color format is used in the photographs, line drawings, and design of the text to increase visual appeal and to enhance the teaching-learning process.

Highlights of This Edition

Every chapter of *Wellness: Concepts and Applications* has been carefully updated. New chapters, features, and issues found in this edition are highlighted here.

New Design and Illustrations

The fresh look, appealing colors, and exciting graphics in this new edition will draw students in with every turn of the page. The illustration program has been completely revised: The many new photographs reflect the diversity of college students of all ages, and the all-new drawings are attractive and informative.

Separate Chapters on Cancer and Common Conditions

In this edition of *Wellness: Concepts and Applications*, separate chapters are devoted to cancer and common conditions. To prevent and manage conditions such as colds, diabetes, and osteoporosis, students want and need basic, accurate information. In addition, rapid developments in cancer prevention, diagnosis, and treatment warranted a separate, more comprehensive chapter on cancer, in which the latest research and information are presented.

HealthQuest Activities

The HealthQuest CD-ROM that accompanies each new copy of *Wellness: Concepts and Applications* contains many useful health and wellness self-assessments. The software is organized into nine modules: Stress Management and Mental Health; Fitness; Weight Control; Communicable Diseases; Cardiovascular Health; Cancer; Tobacco; Alcohol; and Other Drugs. The modules are based on Prochaska's stages of change model, which is presented in Chapter 1 of the text. The HealthQuest Activities complement the Assessment Activities in the text, and they help students get the most from the book and the software.

Goals for Behavior Change

Goals for Behavior Change, listed at the beginning of each chapter, give students objectives that help them apply what they learn in the text. These objectives reinforce the concept of self-responsibility on which the text is based.

Wellness on the Web Behavior Change Activities

The text includes activities in every chapter that take students to quizzes, questions, and self-assessment activities that make surfing the web more interactive and fun for students. Completing these activities will help them assess their current practices and design a more wellness-oriented lifestyle.

Wellness Across the Generations

Many students who take a wellness course are returning to school after some time in the work force. Many of them are raising children or caring for aging parents. Younger students are concerned about how their health will change as they age. New Wellness Across the Generations boxes address wellness concepts throughout the life span by looking at issues such as childhood origins of heart disease, alcohol and drug use among young women, and strength training for older adults.

Nurturing Your Spirituality

Spirituality has become an important focus of the wellness movement. Nurturing Your Spirituality boxes highlight the spiritual dimension of wellness and its effect on overall wellness. The boxes cover topics such as living well with cancer, making decisions about sex, and enjoying healthy pleasures, showing students that wellness goes beyond the physical dimension.

Real-World Wellness

These unique question-and-answer boxes show students how to put wellness concepts into practice. Helpful tips give students practical advice for initiating behavior change and staying motivated to follow a wellness lifestyle. For example, students will learn how to exercise safely in the city, how to decide which smoking cessation aid to use, and how to choose satisfying, nutrient-dense snacks.

Just the Facts

In every chapter, special material in Just the Facts boxes encourages students to delve into a particular topic or closely examine an important health issue.

Complete, Current Coverage of Nutrition and Weight Control

Chapter 6, "Forming a Plan for Good Nutrition," and Chapter 8, "Achieving a Healthy Weight," have been completely revised to include the latest, most comprehensive information available on nutrition and diet. See the next section for a detailed list of new topics.

New or Expanded Topics

We are committed to making this textbook the most up-to-date wellness text available. Following is a sampling of topics that are either completely new to this edition or are covered in greater depth than in the previous edition:

Chapter 1: Wellness and Fitness for Life

- New presentation of the Prochaska stages of change model
- Updated information on the leading causes of death
- New information on the importance of choosing a wellness lifestyle regardless of age and health history
- Greater emphasis on the spiritual dimension of wellness
- New introduction to the benefits of a wellness lifestyle

Chapter 2: Preventing Cardiovascular Disease

- Simplified terminology and more accessible language
- New information on the childhood origins of heart disease
- Greater emphasis on heart disease risk factors and prevention
- New assessment that focuses on CVD risk factors that can be changed
- New discussion of obesity as a major risk factor that can be changed (new AHA classification)
- New information on emerging risk factors for heart disease
- New discussion of heart disease risk among post-menopausal women
- Expanded coverage of stress and personality type
- New discussion of hypertension among African Americans

Chapter 3: Increasing Cardiorespiratory Endurance

- New discussion of managing exercise-related problems
- New information on maintaining cardiorespiratory endurance as we age
- New section on exercising safely in an urban environment
- New tips on choosing home fitness equipment
- New information on ergogenic aids
- Updated information on VO_2 max based on the new ACSM guidelines
- Updated discussion of the health-related and performance-related components of fitness

Chapter 4: Building Muscular Strength and Endurance

- Expanded presentation of the benefits of training
- New discussion of the benefits of strength training for older adults
- Updated recommendations that reflect the 1998 ACSM guidelines

- New discussion of slow-twitch and fast-twitch muscle fibers, myofibrils, and motor units
- New section on ergogenic aids other than steroids, such as vitamins, sports drinks, weight-gain products, creatine, protein supplements, and herbal products
- Updated examples of exercise equipment

Chapter 5: Improving Flexibility

- Expanded coverage of low-back pain, upper-back pain, and neck pain
- New information on exercise to improve flexibility, including among children and the elderly
- New discussion of the emotional and physical benefits of yoga and tai chi
- New explanation of the principles of conditioning as they apply to flexibility
- New discussion of how flexibility exercises should be used during warm-up and cool-down

Chapter 6: Forming a Plan for Good Nutrition

- New food safety tips
- New tips on choosing healthful ethnic foods
- New section on vegetarianism
- Expanded coverage of the importance of water intake
- New section on botanicals, herbs, and phytomedicinals
- Expanded coverage of snacking, fast food, and other convenience foods
- Expanded coverage of vitamins
- New assessment on dietary fat intake
- New section on nutrition and disease prevention
- New section on nutrition during pregnancy
- New discussion of portion sizes
- New coverage of nutrition for activity
- Updated references, with 86 new citations from 1996 to 1999

Chapter 7: Improving Body Composition

- New coverage of body composition of children and adolescents
- New discussion of the importance of setting realistic fitness goals
- New section on subjective ways of determining overweight and body composition
- New information on the latest measurement devices
- New explanation of the margin of error of various measurement techniques
- Coverage of the new BMI guidelines
- New explanation of how to determine a realistic body fat percentage
- Presentation of a new technique used for bioelectrical impedance
- Updated discussion of height-weight tables
- New discussion of the importance of waist circumference alone as a risk for heart disease

Chapter 8: Achieving a Healthy Weight

- New illustration showing locations of body fat deposition
- Updated information on the latest fad diets, including herbal weight loss aids
- New discussion of preventing weight gain and body composition changes as you age
- New information on body image and self-esteem
- New section on recognizing signs of an eating disorder and getting help
- New discussion of exercise as the key to weight maintenance
- New tips for coping with supersize portions
- New tips for evaluating weight-loss schemes
- New section on weight-loss drugs and fasting

Chapter 9: Coping with and Managing Stress

- New "how-to" tips for dealing with stress
- New information on how spirituality affects stress and reduces the likelihood of illness and disease
- New coverage of work-related stress, including a discussion of child-care issues
- Expanded coverage of stress, the immune system, and illness and disease, including an explanation of the term *psychoneuroimmunology*

Chapter 10: Taking Charge of Your Personal Safety

- Updated death rates for motor vehicle accidents
- New information on medication overdoses among elderly adults
- New discussion of fostering healthy relationships, including a list of the characteristics of healthy relationships
- Greatly expanded coverage of recreational safety, including skateboarding, rollerblading, boating, jet-skiing, bicycling, and using trampolines
- Greatly expanded section on motor vehicle safety, including sport utility vehicles, use of cell phones while driving, road rage, drowsy driving, seat belts and airbags, and motorcycle safety
- New section on homicide
- New section on domestic violence, including partner abuse, child abuse, and elder abuse
- New section on hate crimes
- New discussion of the connection between alcohol and violent acts, such as rape

Chapter 11: Taking Responsibility for Drug Use

- New discussion of the genetic basis of addiction
- New presentation of alternatives to drug use
- New information on the dangers of alcohol use, drug use, and smoking during pregnancy
- New section on prescription and OTC drug abuse
- New assessment on drug use

- Expanded coverage of the dangers of secondhand smoke, smokeless tobacco, and cigars
- New coverage of drinking among college students, including binge drinking
- New section on drinking and driving
- New coverage of the resurgence of heroin use among young people

Chapter 12: Preventing Sexually Transmitted Diseases

- New section on communicating with your partner about STDs
- New discussion of assessing your own values about sex
- Greater emphasis on prevention and safer sex practices
- New information on hepatitis B and pelvic inflammatory disease
- Updated information on the newest drugs for treating HIV/AIDS
- New discussion of anonymous and confidential HIV testing, including home test kits
- New assessment that focuses on prevention

Chapter 13: Reducing Your Risk of Cancer

- New chapter that presents information on different types of cancer, including risk factors, risk reduction, early detection, treatment, and management
- New information on childhood cancers
- New discussion of living well with cancer
- New assessment on evaluating preventable risk factors
- New section that introduces the ABCD rule for detecting skin cancer

Chapter 14: Managing Common Conditions

- New discussion of chronic disease and aging
- New section on preventing common conditions
- New tips for living well with a chronic condition
- New assessment activity on managing asthma
- Updated treatment options for arthritis, headaches, and other conditions
- New coverage of inflammatory bowel disease

Chapter 15: Becoming a Responsible Health Care Consumer

- New tips for safe medication use among older adults
- New information on support groups, including on-line chat rooms, for various health conditions
- New section on complementary (alternative) medicine
- New tips for communicating with health care providers
- New section on evaluating health information on the internet

- New list of reliable on-line health and wellness newsletters
- New section on health care quackery

Successful Pedagogical Features

Wellness: Concepts and Applications continues to use a variety of learning aids to enhance student comprehension.

Key Terms: The most important terms for student retention have been set in boldface type in the text for easy identification.

Chapter Objectives: These are introduced at the beginning of each chapter. They help the student identify the chapter's key topics. Accomplishing the objectives indicates fulfillment of the chapter's intent.

Chapter Summaries: These identify the main parts of the chapter and reinforce the chapter objectives.

Review Questions: Questions are provided to help students review and analyze material for overall understanding.

References: Accurate and current documentation is given at the end of the chapters.

Suggested Readings: Additional current resources are provided for students to obtain further information.

Assessment Activities: Each chapter concludes with at least two Assessment Activities to help students apply the content learned in the chapter to their own decision making. The text is perforated for easy removal of the Assessment Activities.

Appendix: Food Composition Table—More than 1200 common foods and fast foods are analyzed. This comprehensive table will help students complete Assessment Activities in Chapter 6.

Glossary: A comprehensive glossary is provided at the end of the text that includes all key terms, as well as additional terms used in the text.

Supplements

An extensive package is available to adopters of *Wellness: Concepts and Applications*. The package has been developed to help the instructor obtain maximum benefit from the text.

Instructor's Manual and Test Bank

Each chapter begins with a brief overview of the content followed by a list of the objectives for that chapter. Detailed lecture outlines and additional class activities have been developed for each chapter, and each chapter concludes with a resource section, including relevant media, software, organization sources, and additional recommended readings. The test bank includes more than 1400 questions. The manual concludes with

65 full-page transparency masters of helpful illustrations and charts.

Computerized Test Bank

This software provides a unique combination of user-friendly aids that enable the instructor to select, edit, delete, or add questions as well as construct and print tests and answer keys. The computerized test bank package is available to qualified adopters of the text in Windows and Macintosh formats.

Overhead Transparency Acetates

A total of 60 of the text's most important illustrations, diagrams, tables, and charts are available as full-color transparency acetates. These useful tools facilitate learning and classroom discussion and were chosen specifically to help explain difficult concepts. This package is also available to qualified adopters of the text.

Fitness and Wellness Supersite

www.mhhe.com/hper/physed/fitness-wellness

At our Fitness and Wellness Supersite, you can find information about our books and telecourse, learn what conventions we plan to attend, and get updates to *Health Net* and *The AIDS Booklet*. The password-protected section of the site includes fitness and wellness news, downloadable personal assessments and lab activities, digitized still images, and a PowerPoint presentation created especially for *Wellness: Concepts and Applications*.

McGraw-Hill Online Learning Center

www.mhhe.com/anspaugh

The Online Learning Center for *Wellness: Concepts and Applications* is a great resource for you and your students. It offers downloadable ancillaries, such as a PowerPoint presentation that corresponds to each chapter in the book. Students can take on-line quizzes, find updated health information, and log on to interactive web links.

McGraw-Hill PageOut: The Course Web Site Development Center

PageOut is a program that enables you to easily develop a website for your course. The site includes a course home page, an instructor home page, a customizable syllabus, web links, discussion areas, an on-line grade book, student web pages, and sixteen design templates. This program is now available to registered adopters of *Wellness: Concepts and Applications*. If you adopt 200 or more copies per year of a McGraw-

Hill text, our technology experts will create your website for you in 30 minutes or less. For more information, log on to www.pageout.net/pageout.html.

FitSolve Software

This networkable software program helps students design and implement a personalized fitness program based on their unique needs. The program's colorful graphics and easy data entry system let students focus on content and concepts. It includes cholesterol measurement options, treadmill protocols for cardiovascular assessment, the 1.5-mile run test, the Rockport Fitness Walking Test, muscle endurance and flexibility tests, and a variety of body fat measurement options.

NutriQuest™ Software and Diet/Fitness Log

Available for Windows and Macintosh, this nutrient-analysis software allows easy analysis of dietary intake, using an icon-based interface and on-screen help features. Foods for breakfast, lunch, dinner, and snacks can be selected from more than 2250 items in the database. Records can be kept for any number of days. The program can provide intake analyses for individual foods, meals, days, or an entire intake period. Intake analyses can compare nutrient values to RDA or RNI values and to the USDA Food Guide Pyramid and can provide breakdowns of fat and calories sources. An accompanying diet and fitness log motivates students to track their progress. This software can be packaged with the text for a nominal fee.

TestWell: Making Wellness Work for You

TestWell is a self-scoring, pencil-and-paper wellness assessment booklet developed by the National Wellness Institute and distributed exclusively by McGraw-Hill. It adds flexibility to any personal health or wellness course by allowing instructors to offer pre- and post-assessments at the beginning and end of the course, or at any time during the semester.

Diet and Fitness Log

This log helps students assess their diet and physical activity habits. Week-long diet and fitness logs and ten workout strength logs invite students to develop life-long wellness programs by recording and evaluating their daily choices. Each log offers a brief introduction, followed by an evaluation section in which they can assess their improvements and setbacks.

Health Net: A Health & Wellness Guide to the Internet

This up-to-date booklet is your navigational tool for exploring the vast array of health and wellness resources on the internet. A helpful introduction provides general information about the internet. Each of the following sections in the booklet contains an annotated list of websites to supplement those given in the text.

Video Library

Choose from McGraw-Hill's videotape library, which includes selected Films for Humanities and all videos from the award-winning series *Healthy Living: Road to Wellness.*

The AIDS Booklet

This booklet, by Frank D. Cox, offers current, accurate information about HIV and AIDS: what it is, how the virus is transmitted, how the disease progresses, its prevalence among various population groups, symptoms of HIV infection, and strategies for prevention. Also included are discussions of the legal, medical, and ethical issues related to HIV/AIDS. This booklet ensures that your students have the most current information possible about this important topic.

Berkeley Wellness Letter

Available to qualified adopters, this highly regarded wellness newsletter keeps you informed of the latest developments in the field.

Acknowledgements

We wish to thank the reviewers, whose contributions have added significantly to the text. To the following, a grateful acknowledgement of their expertise and assistance:

For the Fourth Edition

Robbi Beyer
University of Wisconsin (Oshkosh)

Evonne Bird
Truman State University

Rochelle Caroon-Santiago
McNeese State University

Linda Crawshaw
Kutztown University

Randy Deere
Western Kentucky University

Judy Dittman
Dakota State University

Millard Fisher
DeKalb College

Charles Goehl
Elmhurst College

Stephen Horowitz
Bowling Green State University

Tammy James
West Chester University

Cathy Kennedy
Colorado State University

Rebecca Rutt Leas
Clarion University

David Moates
Manatee Community College

Sandi Morgan
San Jacinto College

Gary Oden
Sam Houston State University

Michael Paul
County College of Morris

Brian Pritschett
Eastern Illinois University

DawnElla Rust
Stephen F. Austin State University

Steve Sansone
Chemeketa Community College

Sue Stindt
Jackson Community College

Frederick Surgent
Frostburg State University

Beverly Zeakes
Radford University

For the Third Edition

Kathie Garbe
Kenesaw State College

William Huber
County College of Morris

Margaret Hughes
College of St. Benedict

Ken Owen
Manatee Community College

Edith Thompson
Rowan College of New Jersey

Judith Walton
The University of Texas of Brownsville

Randye Williams
Missouri Western State College

For the Second Edition

Joel Barton III
Lamar University

Mary Eagan
University of Illinois at Chicago

Mimi Frank
California State University at Dominguez Hills

Rick Guyton
University of Arkansas at Fayetteville

Vicki Kloosterhouse
Oakland Community College

Rebecca Rutt Leas
Clarion University

John McIntosh
Shoals Community College

Kenneth Sparks
Cleveland State University

Laurel Talabere
Capital University

For the First Edition

Pat Barrett
Radford University

Wilson Campbell
Northeast Louisiana University

Arlene Crosman
Linn-Benton Community College

Betty Edgley
Oklahoma State University

Mary Mahan
Miami-Dade Community College

Eva W. McGahee
North Georgia College

Brenda Obert
University of Maine–Farmington

Glen J. Peterson
Lakewood Community College

Russell F. Smiley
Normandale Community College

John G. Smith
Long Beach City College

Rod Smith
Clark College

James A. Streater, Jr.
Armstrong State College

Michael L. Teague
University of Iowa

Luke E. Thomas
Northeast Louisiana University

Gary L. Wilson
The Citadel

David J. Anspaugh

Michael H. Hamrick

Frank D. Rosato

Brief Contents

1 Wellness and Fitness for Life   1

2 Preventing Cardiovascular Disease   33

3 Increasing Cardiorespiratory Endurance   65

4 Building Muscular Strength and Endurance   97

5 Improving Flexibility   131

6 Forming a Plan for Good Nutrition   153

7 Improving Body Composition   213

8 Achieving a Healthy Weight   233

9 Coping With and Managing Stress   273

10 Taking Charge of Your Personal Safety   305

11 Taking Responsibility for Drug Use   331

12 Preventing Sexually Transmitted Diseases   357

13 Reducing Your Risk of Cancer   377

14 Managing Common Conditions   403

15 Becoming a Responsible Health Care Consumer   421

Appendix: Food Composition Table   453

Glossary   489

Credits   497

Index   499

Contents

Preface   v

1 Wellness and Fitness for Life   1

Components of Wellness   2

The Wellness Challenge   7

Achieving Lifestyle Change: A Self-Help
Approach   11

Assessment Activities

1-1   Lifestyle Assessment Inventory   23

1-2   Health Locus of Control   29

1-3   Assessing Your Health Behavior   31

2 Preventing Cardiovascular Disease   33

Circulation   34

Cardiovascular Disease: A Twentieth-Century
Phenomenon   36

Risk Factors for Heart Disease   38

Prevention of Heart Disease   53

Medical Contributions   54

Assessment Activities

2-1   What's Your Heart Attack Risk?   61

2-2   A Case Study of Bill M.   63

**3 Increasing Cardiorespiratory
Endurance   65**

The Components of Physical Fitness   66

Cardiorespiratory Endurance   67

Cardiorespiratory Endurance and Wellness   70

Principles of Conditioning   70

Other Exercise Considerations   76

Environmental Conditions   79

Assessment Activities

3-1   The Rockport Fitness Walking Test   85

3-2   The 1.5-Mile Run/Walk Test   89

3-3   The Bench Step Test   91

3-4   Calculating Target Heart Rate   93

3-5   Design an Exercise Program   95

**4 Building Muscular Strength
and Endurance   97**

The Health Benefits of Resistance Training   98

Anaerobic Exercise   99

Muscular Strength   99

Muscle Contraction and Resistance Training   100

Muscular Endurance   111

Principles of Resistance Training   112

Ergogenic Aids   113

Keeping a Daily Training Log   115

Assessment Activities

4-1   Calculation of Strength (Selected
Muscle Groups)   119

4-2   Muscular Endurance   121

4-3   Abdominal Muscular Endurance—the Canadian
Trunk Strength Test   123

4-4   Assessing Muscular Strength and Endurance with
Selected Calisthenic Exercises   125

4-5   Resistance Training Log   129

5 Improving Flexibility   131

Flexibility and Wellness   132

Developing a Flexibility Program   132

When to Stretch   132

Types of Stretching   133

Flexibility Assessment   139

Preventing Back and Neck Pain   139

Assessment Activities

5-1   Sit-and-Reach Test   145

5-2   Shoulder Flexion Test   147

5-3   Sling Test   149

5-4   Trunk Extension   151

6 Forming a Plan for Good Nutrition   153

Nutrition and Health   154

Essential Nutrients   154

Other Nutrients with Unique Health Benefits   170

Putting Nutrition to Work   174

Other Nutrition Issues of Concern   185

Food Labels   190

Changes in American Eating Patterns   192

Planning a Nutrition Strategy for Wellness   193

Assessment Activities

6-1   Assessing Your Carbohydrate
and Protein RDA   199

6-2   Assessing Your Maximum Fat and Saturated
Fat Intakes   201

6-3   Nutrient Intake Assessment   203

6-4   How Does Your Diet Compare
with the Recommended Diet?   207

6-5   Do You Have Fatty Habits?   209

6-6   Eating Behaviors to Consider   211

7 Improving Body Composition   213

Obesity   214

Overweight   214

Regional Fat Distribution   216

Methods for Measuring Body-Weight Status   218

Measurement of Body Fat   219

Selected Methods for Measuring
Body Composition   219

Assessment Activities

7-1   Using BMI to Estimate Body-Weight Status
and Calculate Desirable Body Weight   229

7-2   Calculating Desirable Body Weight from Percent
Body Fat   231

8 Achieving a Healthy Weight   233

Americans' Obsession with Body Weight   234

Defining the Problem   235

Health Aspects of Obesity   236

Weight Loss: A New Attitude Emerges   237

Development of Obesity   237

Causes of Obesity   238

Dieting and Exercise: Strategies for Weight
Maintenance or Weight Loss   243

Regular Exercise Is the Key to Weight Management:
Make It Fun   254

Eating Disorders   255

Principles of Weight Management: Putting It
All Together   258

Assessment Activities

8-1   Assessing Your Body Image   265

8-2   Calculating Caloric Expenditure Through
Exercise   267

8-3   Estimating Your Basal Metabolic Rate   269

8-4   Assessing Calorie Costs of Activities   271

9 Coping with and Managing Stress   273

What is Stress?   274

Sources of Stress and Warning Signs   276

Factors Generating a Stress Response   277

Physiological Responses to Stress   277

Self-Esteem and Stress   280

Personality and Stress   282

Dealing with Stress   283

Relaxation Techniques   283

Selecting a Stress-Reducing Technique   288

Assessment Activities

9-1   Life Stressors   291

9-2   How Stressed Are You?   293

9-3   Stress Style: Body, Mind, Mixed?   295

9-4   Identification of Coping Styles   297

9-5   How Hardy Are You?   299

9-6   Time-Management Worksheet   301

9-7   Analyzing Your Use of Time   303

10 Taking Charge of Your Personal Safety   305

Home Safety   306

Recreational and Outdoor Safety   307

Vehicle Safety 311

Violence and Intentional Injury 315

Assessment Activities

10-1 How Safe Is Your Home? 323

10-2 Recreational Safety—How Safe Are You? 325

10-3 Road Rage and You 327

10-4 Encounters of the Dangerous Kind 329

11 Taking Responsibility for Drug Use 331

Reasons for Drug Use 332

Drug Classification 333

Commonly Abused Substances 335

Illegal Drugs 345

Other Drugs of Concern 347

A Final Thought 349

Assessment Activities

11-1 Do You Have a Drinking Problem? 353

11-2 What Are Your Reasons for Drug Use? 355

12 Preventing Sexually
Transmitted Diseases 357

Safer Sex 358

Sexually Transmitted Diseases (STDs) 360

Viral Diseases 361

Bacterial Diseases 367

Other Common STDs 369

Assessment Activities

12-1 Are You at Risk for a Sexually Transmitted
Disease? 373

12-2 Making a Decision 375

13 Reducing Your Risk of Cancer 377

Causes and Prevention 379

Cancer Site 382

Exercise and Cancer Prevention 382

Cancers of Concern to Everyone 384

Treatment 394

Assessment Activities

13-1 Cancer Early Detection Inventory 399

13-2 Are You Practicing Cancer Prevention? 401

14 Managing Common Conditions 403

Diabetes Mellitus 404

Arthritis 407

Osteoporosis 408

Asthma 410

The Common Cold 411

Influenza 411

Headaches 412

Inflammatory Bowel Disease 412

Assessment Activities

14-1 Are You at Risk for Diabetes? 417

14-2 Managing Your Asthma 419

15 Becoming a Responsible Health Care
Consumer 421

Understanding Health Information 422

Guidelines for Evaluating Health Information 422

Managing Health Care 428

Alternative Medicine 434

Assessing Your Health 438

Paying for Health Care 443

Assessment Activities

15-1 Are You Communicating with
Your Physician? 447

15-2 Assessing the Results of Diagnostic Tests 449

15-3 Self-Care Inventory 451

Appendix: Food
Composition Table 453

Glossary 489

Credits 497

Index 499

Spirits
Socialize
Physically write
emitting
intellectual
occupations in
environments

Wellness and Fitness for Life

Key Terms

contracting
countering
health-behavior gap
health disparities
lifestyle diseases
locus of control
psychosomatic diseases

risk factor
self-help
self-efficacy
shaping up
transtheoretical model of
 behavioral change
wellness

Goals for Behavior Change

- Implement four new health-promoting behaviors.
- Increase physical activity to improve overall wellness.
- Choose and implement three countering strategies.
- Formulate a self-help plan for lifestyle change.

Objectives

After completing this chapter, you will be able to do the following:

- Discuss the wellness approach to healthy living.
- Identify benefits of living a wellness lifestyle.
- Describe the dimensions of wellness.
- Cite evidence of the relationship between physical health problems and social, emotional, and spiritual stressors.
- Identify health disparities that exist in the United States.
- Compare and contrast the major influences on the health of Americans today with those of Americans of the past.

- Identify and discuss the main wellness challenges for Americans.
- Identify obvious and subtle factors that help shape behavior.
- Discuss some of the underlying assumptions of lifestyle change.
- Identify and describe the six stages of change.
- Describe strategies that can be useful in designing and implementing an action plan for change.

 ood health is one of our most cherished possessions, one that is often taken for granted until it is lost. Some people convincingly argue that everything else in life is secondary to good health. For many, it is not difficult to recall instances when life's goals, whether academic, career, or family, small or large, immediate or long-range, seemed unimportant because of sudden illness or a long-term debilitating health crisis.

Fortunately, the prospects of good health for Americans have never been better. The extent to which good health is realized is contingent on many factors. Chief among these factors are our actions and the choices we make. We can make choices that will promote health and well-being, prevent or delay the premature onset of many chronic illnesses, and improve our quality of life (see Real-World Wellness: Benefits of Living a Wellness Lifestyle). Staying healthy is not just a matter of common sense. Rather, it is a lifelong process that requires self-awareness, introspection, reflection, inquiry, accurate information, and action. This process relies on the concept of wellness and implies that each of us has the opportunity and the obligation to assume responsibility for factors that are under our control and to shape our health destiny. The wellness approach represents a formidable challenge because the processes leading to today's serious health threats are insidious, often originate in childhood or adolescence, flourish throughout adulthood, and finally culminate in full-blown disease in middle age or later. Lifestyle interventions that are initiated late in life produce limited success, but begun early in life they have maximum effect.

Components of Wellness

Wellness is defined as the continuous, active process of becoming aware of the different areas in one's life, identifying the areas that need improvement, and then making choices that will facilitate attainment of a higher level of health and well-being.[1] Wellness is a process rather than a goal. It means developing attitudes and engaging in behaviors that enhance quality of life and maximize personal potential. Although wellness implies working toward a highly developed level of health, it does not imply making the best choice in every situation or achieving "perfect wellness."

Consider the brief profiles of David, Susan, Carlos, and Maria. How would you rate each of them in terms of health and wellness?

David is physically active, places a high priority on his social life, barely makes passing grades in school, and engages in binge drinking almost every weekend. Susan is a perfectionist and her grades reflect it. To her, a B means

Real-World Wellness

Benefits of Living a Wellness Lifestyle

I am a full-time student, work twenty plus hours a week, and help with family responsibilities. At the same time, I'm trying to maintain my academic scholarship. There just isn't enough time in the day to be concerned about health and wellness. What am I to gain from a wellness lifestyle?

A wellness lifestyle offers the following benefits:

- Increases energy level and productivity at work and school
- Decreases absenteeism from school and work
- Decreases recovery time after illness or injury
- Supplies the body with proper nutrients
- Improves awareness of personal needs and the ways to meet them
- Expands and develops intellectual abilities
- Increases the ability to communicate emotions to others and to act assertively rather than aggressively or passively
- Promotes the attitude that life's difficulties are challenges and opportunities rather than overwhelming threats
- Acts from an internal locus of control
- Increases ability to cope with stress and resist depression
- Improves the cardiorespiratory system
- Increases muscle tone, strength, flexibility, and endurance
- Improves physical appearance
- Helps prevent or delay the premature onset of some forms of chronic disease
- Regulates and improves overall body function
- Promotes self-confidence
- Delays the aging process
- Promotes social awareness and the ability to reach out to, understand, and care about others

failure. She spends an inordinate amount of time studying, regularly skips meals, has no physical activity outlet, and rarely socializes. Her family tells her to "get a life." She needs the entire weekend to recover from the stress of academics. Carlos runs 3 miles every day, works out with weights 3 times a week, eats a balanced diet almost every day, has a close circle of friends, refuses to use his seat belt when driving, and smokes an average of two packs of cigarettes daily. Maria is a worrier. She makes good grades but is rarely satisfied. Her eating practices are exemplary, but she is constantly counting fat grams and calories and rarely looks forward to mealtime. She is self-conscious about her weight and occasionally engages in bulimic practices.

Figure 1-1 depicts how health moves along a continuum from optimal health to premature death. Your position on this continuum is always subject to change and is affected by many factors, including physical health, activity level, nutritional patterns, personal demands, career goals, time of year, and effectiveness in managing stress. The direction you move on the continuum and your place on the continuum at any given time are largely determined by the activities you pursue and your attitudes toward these activities. These activities and attitudes can prevent illness and promote health or can destroy peace of mind and physical well-being. Because your behaviors are intrinsic to your health, you must learn to assume responsibility for your health by developing the skills and acquiring the knowledge to improve it.

In the past, medicine approached wellness from a different perspective. It emphasized the treatment of diseases rather than their prevention. It demanded no more than passive participation by the patient in the decision-making process. Now people are encouraged to become active participants in their health care, to exercise control over wellness **risk factors** (factors or conditions that threaten wellness and increase the chances of developing or contracting disease), to shape

Heal_th_**Que**_st_ **Acti**_viti_es

- Use the Wellboard to report your life score (number of years out of 114) and the score percentages for each of the eight health areas.
- Fill out the Wellboard using data from a fictional college student. On the first assessment screen, change the demographics to show how gender, ethnicity, age, marital status, and community affect average life expectancy.

their lifestyles to promote health, and to serve as partners with health care providers in making medical decisions. This approach places the responsibility for wellness on the individual.

Achieving a high level of wellness requires constant balance and maintenance of certain components (figure 1-2): spiritual, social, physical, emotional, intellectual, occupational, and environmental.

Spiritual

Spirituality is a belief in a source of value that transcends the boundaries of the self but also nurtures the self. Everyone has a personal perception of spirituality. The spiritual component provides meaning and direction in life and enables you to grow, learn, and meet new challenges. Spiritual wellness includes developing a strong sense of values, ethics, and morals. It overlaps

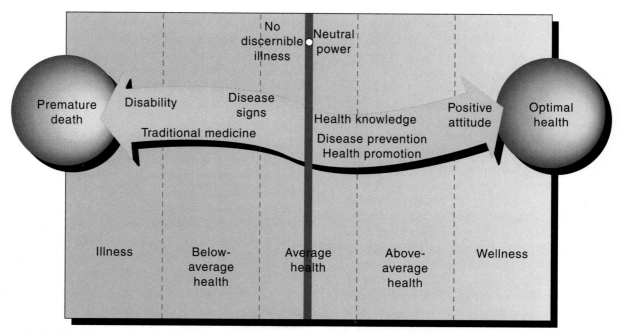

Figure 1-1 The Health Continuum

Figure 1-2 The Seven Components of Wellness

with the emotional component of wellness (described later). While spirituality may relate to religious precepts, it does not necessarily adhere to any particular religious structure (see Nurturing Your Spirituality: Can Spirituality Improve Your Physical Health?).

Social

Being social means having the ability to interact successfully with people and one's personal environment. Social health is the ability to develop and maintain intimacy with others and to have respect and tolerance for those with different opinions and beliefs. Numerous studies report on the advantage patients who are surrounded by a network of family and friends have over patients without a social support system in recovering from surgery or coping with chronic conditions. Social contacts are even being studied in terms of communicable diseases. Researchers from Carnegie Mellon University gave 276 healthy volunteers nasal sprays containing one of two cold viruses. Volunteers with large relationship networks developed fewer cold symptoms and infections than did people with smaller networks. Researchers pointed out that what mattered was not the total number of friends, but the number of types of

relationship. People with six or more relationship types (parents, siblings, schoolmates, coworkers, roommates, and community acquaintances) had 4.2 times fewer colds than did those who had one to three types. The study defined a relationship as speaking with a person at least every two weeks.[2] The investigation revealed that a lack of diverse social contacts is a stronger risk factor for colds than is smoking, low vitamin C intake, or elevated stress hormones.[3]

Physical

The physical component of wellness involves the ability to carry out daily tasks, develop cardiorespiratory and muscular fitness, maintain adequate nutrition and a healthy body fat level, and avoid abusing alcohol and other drugs or using tobacco products. In general, physical health is an investment in positive lifestyle habits. Separate chapters in this text are devoted to many of these physical dimensions of wellness.

Emotional

Emotional wellness is the ability to control stress and to express emotions appropriately and comfortably. Emotional health is the ability to recognize and accept

Nurturing Your Spirituality

Can Spirituality Improve Your Physical Health?

It's all in your mind. Or is it in your body? Or both? The interconnections between mind and body are the bases for many types of alternative health practices. Spirituality is believing in a source of value that transcends the boundaries of the self but also nurtures the self. Mind-body medicine builds upon spirituality, encouraging methods for improving the body by altering the mind. The National Institutes of Health (NIH) suggests the following spiritual practices:

- *Psychotherapy* focuses on the mental and emotional health of the patient and has been proven to reduce the amount of time required to recover from an illness.

- *Support groups* give patients the consolation that others have endured similar health challenges and survived, instilling hope.

- *Meditation,* formerly associated solely with religious practice, is a self-governed exercise for relaxation. Regular practice of meditation is recommended for reducing blood pressure and anxiety and increasing the quality of life and longevity.

- *Imagery* includes use of all the senses to encourage attitude change, behavior, or physiological responses. Uses of imagery include pain control in cancer patients and increasing immunity in elderly patients.

- *Hypnosis* is an ancient practice molded to fit modern needs. Today physicians, dentists, psychologists, and other mental health professionals utilize hypnosis to help people overcome addictions, control pain, and deal with phobias.

- *Biofeedback* provides patients with a picture of what is occurring physiologically in their bodies and an understanding of how trial-and-error adjustments of mental processes can affect these physiological behaviors. This technique is used in treatment for a wide variety of disorders, such as epilepsy, respiratory diseases, migraines, vascular disorders, and hypertension.

Enjoyable physical activity improves wellness inside and out.

- *Yoga* is a disciplined practice of altering mental and physiological processes previously thought to be outside an individual's control. These alterations, performed on a regular basis, can reduce anxiety, lower blood pressure, treat arthritis, and increase the efficiency of the heart.

- *Dance therapy* uses body movement for therapeutic purposes. It is proven effective for achieving such goals as improving self-concept and self-esteem, minimizing fears, reducing bodily tension, improving circulatory and respiratory functions, promoting healing, and reducing depression.

- *Music therapy* puts to good use the power of music on the psyche. Do you ever listen to music to make you feel better? So do stroke, Parkinson's, brain-injury, cancer, anxiety, cerebral palsy, and burn patients.

- *Art therapy* uses self-expression through art to enhance healing. Art therapy is used with patients who are being treated for burns, emotional problems, chemical addictions, and sexual abuse.

- *Prayer and mental healing* involves communication with some form of higher power. A wide variety of healing techniques fall within this category. Examples are being physically touched by a religious healer or experiencing healing through personal prayer or attendance at church. Studies link regular church attendance with reduced chance of dying from stroke or heart disease, lower blood pressure, lower suicide rates, and reduced depression.

feelings and not be defeated by setbacks and failures. Achieving emotional wellness allows you to experience life's ups and downs with enthusiasm and grace and maintain satisfying relationships with others.[4]

Many studies report on the connection between wellness and emotional health. Anger, for example, is a powerful emotion that has consistently been found to increase the risk of heart attacks. In a recent study of 1305 men, those men who had high anger scores on a personality test were 2.5 times more likely to suffer heart attack symptoms as were their peers with low anger scores.[5] In another study of 1623 patients, 8 percent of heart attack victims had experienced episodes of anger within one day of their heart attacks. Researchers concluded that episodes of anger more than doubled the risk of a heart attack.[6] Irritable bowel syndrome, sometimes referred to as *spastic colon,* is another physical problem thought to have emotional ties.

People with this condition experience various abdominal symptoms ranging from severe cramping to diarrhea and are often subjected to countless diagnostic tests. While traditional treatments include diet therapies and medications, recent studies have shown that treatments aimed at reducing emotional stressors are much more successful.[7]

Many other health problems are rooted in emotional stressors. Health conditions ranging from hives to cancer may have as their origin a breakdown in the body's immune system caused by the body's response to emotional stressors. These stressors, by disrupting the body's delicate balance of powerful hormones, may serve as the triggering mechanism for myriad health problems. The growing acceptance of stress-coping techniques, like those presented in Chapter 9 of this text, is evidence of the trend toward nonphysical strategies for preventing and treating many health problems.

Intellectual

The intellectual component of wellness involves the ability to learn and use information effectively for personal, family, and career development. Intellectual wellness means striving for continued growth and learning to deal with new challenges effectively. It means acting on accepted principles of wellness and assuming responsibility for eliminating the discrepancy between knowledge and behavior, often referred to as the **health-behavior gap.** For example, people know that they should wear their seat belts and that they should not smoke, yet many people do not buckle up and continue to use tobacco products. For wellness to occur, people must internalize information and act on it.

An intellectually well person understands and applies the concepts of locus of control and self-efficacy. **Locus of control** refers to a person's view or attitude about his or her role in wellness and illness. A person's locus of control may be either internal or external. When people view problems concerning their health or other parts of their lives as generally out of their control (when they view themselves as being at the mercy of other people, places, and events), they have an external locus of control. On the other hand, people who have an internal locus of control view their own behaviors as having significant effects, feel that they are at least partially the masters of their fate, and recognize that they can change the course of their health. People with an internal locus of control are more likely to succeed in wellness activities, because they assume the necessary responsibility for their actions. Assessment Activity 1-2 at the end of this chapter will help you determine whether you have an internal or external locus of control.

Another influence on intellectual wellness is self-efficacy. **Self-efficacy** refers to a person's belief in his or her ability to accomplish a specific task or behavior. Perhaps the most important influence on the achievement of a wellness goal is the perception that it can be accomplished. Although the support of others is a source of encouragement, success is likely to require generating a personal sense of competence. Self-efficacy is not earned, inherited, or acquired; it is something you bestow on yourself.

For high-level wellness to be achieved, people must see themselves as successful and believe that they can accomplish a task. Although locus of control establishes an attitude toward one's role in achieving wellness, self-efficacy establishes behavior. Self-efficacy links knowing what to do and actually accomplishing the task. Together, an internal locus of control and a strong sense of self-efficacy are powerful tools in promoting wellness and coping with illness. Evidence of this connection is apparent in a countless number of scientific studies. For example, in a thirteen-year study of 2832 Americans, researchers at the National Center for Health Statistics found that heart disease patients with a more internal locus of control coupled with a strong sense of self-efficacy were 12 times less likely to die of heart disease than were their peers with an external locus of control or a poor sense of self-efficacy or both.[8]

Occupational

Occupational wellness is the ability to achieve a balance between work and leisure time. Attitudes about work, school, career, and career goals greatly affect work or school performance and interactions with others. Striving for occupational wellness adds focus to your life and allows you to find personal satisfaction in your life through work.

Environmental

Environmental wellness is the ability to promote health measures that improve the standard of living and quality of life in the community, including laws and agencies that safeguard the physical environment.

To illustrate the impact of environment on wellness, consider the differences in mortality (incidence of deaths) and morbidity (incidence of sickness) between earlier times and today. At the beginning of the twentieth century, the average life span of Americans was 47 years. Today, at the end of the twentieth century, it is 76.5 years,[9] an all-time high. In 1900, communicable or infectious diseases (diseases that can be transmitted from one person to another) were the major causes of death. Influenza, pneumonia, tuberculosis, smallpox, polio, diphtheria, and dysentery were often fatal and were greatly feared. Only 50 percent of children were expected to reach their fifth birthday. Environmental conditions were appalling; water was dirty and food was often unsafe for consumption. People generally had little control over their health, and prospects for a long life were greatly influenced by fate and circumstance. By comparison, children born today have a 99 percent rate of survival to their fifth birthday. Governmental agencies at the federal, state, and local levels now assume responsibility for protecting health and preventing infectious diseases. Vaccinations have eradicated many dreaded diseases. The world food supply has more than doubled.[10] Adult literacy has increased. Mind-boggling advancements in medical technology have given rise to diagnostic and surgical procedures far beyond the wildest imaginations of early–twentieth–century physicians. Still, even with all of the discoveries of modern medicine, the greatest improvement in the health of Americans is due to a much more basic element of the environment: safe water. No other factor, not even vaccinations or antibiotics, has had as significant an impact on mortality reduction and population growth as safe water.[11]

Today, environmental influences include more than safe water, food, and air. Recent developments in countries such as Russia, where the death rate in 1995 outstripped the birth rate by 1.6 times and the mortality rate was as much as 77 percent higher than it was in 1990,[12] are grim reminders of the effect of the political environment on health and wellness. Here in the United States, subtle influences such as the socioeconomic factors of income, housing, and education play a critical role in the health status of various population groups.

Health disparities (health differences), a term that refers to the disproportionate prevalence of diseases and health problems among certain population groups, have had an important impact on the incidence and severity of many health conditions. The Surgeon General of the United States has identified ninety-three health areas that are related to these disparities (see Just the Facts: Eliminating Health Disparities—Goals for *Healthy People 2010*).

An important assumption of the wellness approach to living is that good health is best achieved by balancing each of the seven components. The body, mind, and spirit are inseparably linked. When they work together in a fully unified, integrated biological system, the body can ward off or overcome many diseases. When any of these components breaks down, wellness is threatened. Although the association between disease and physical causes (such as pathogens) is obvious, some people are reluctant to accept the association between illness and its mental, social, and spiritual aspects.

Nonphysical causes of illness are intangible and difficult to assess. Many people experience poor health because of guilt, anger, hostility, poor interpersonal skills, loneliness, anxiety, and depression. Any of these factors can interfere with the body's immune system and lay the foundation for the disease process. Medical records are replete with examples of **psychosomatic diseases,** in which physical (soma) symptoms are caused by mental and emotional (psycho) stressors. Such symptoms are just as real as if caused by disease-producing germs. Virtually every disease involves interplay among the components of wellness. Fortunately, after a long-standing obsession with medical technology, many health care providers are beginning to focus on treating the whole person, and more people are demanding more than test-tube medical care.

Assessment Activity 1-1 at the end of this chapter provides an evaluation of various aspects of wellness.

The Wellness Challenge

The most serious health problems of today are largely caused by the way people live and are referred to as lifestyle diseases. The leading causes of death in the United States among all age groups are heart disease, cancer, and stroke; they account for almost two-thirds of all deaths (table 1-1).[13] These are chronic diseases that are often caused by behaviors established early in life. *Chronic diseases* are health conditions that often begin gradually, have multiple causes, and usually persist for an indefinite time. Heart disease, diabetes, arthritis, and hypertension are examples of chronic illnesses. By contrast, *acute illnesses* come on suddenly, often have identifiable causes, are usually treatable, and often disappear in a short time. Appendicitis, pneumonia, and influenza are examples of acute illnesses.

Diseases are, of course, not the only causes of death. Accidents, homicide, and suicide are the leading killers of Americans between the ages of 15 and 24. Most (77 percent) accidental deaths among this age group involve motor vehicle accidents, many of which are alcohol related. For young adults 25 to 44 years old, accidents, cancer, heart disease, suicide, human immunodeficiency virus (HIV) infection, and homicide are the leading causes of death.

For too many Americans these conditions reflect the dangers of negative lifestyle choices. In spite of this fact, much of Americans' health-related anxiety involves exotic diseases. The current fear that some sort of strangely mutated disease will soon pose the greatest threat to life on Earth ironically coincides with a reduction in attention to chronic diseases that do kill in large numbers. The fear of bizarre pathogens leading to

Just the Facts

Eliminating Health Disparities—Goals for *Healthy People 2010*

Healthy People 2000 is a document that was issued in 1990 by the U.S. federal government. Its purpose was to establish national health goals to be reached by 2000. The document set goals for eliminating disparities (differences) in health status and health risks among population groups. Health objectives were established for racial and ethnic minority groups, women, people with low incomes, people with disabilities, and specific age groups, such as children, adolescents, and the elderly. However, few of these target objectives set out to achieve equity by the year 2000. *Healthy People 2010*, on the other hand, is setting the goal of eliminating these disparities during the next decade.

Despite notable progress in the overall health of the nation, African-Americans, Latinos, American Indians, Alaskan Natives, and Pacific Islanders continue to shoulder more of the burden of illness and death compared with the U.S. population as a whole. These disparities are even greater if comparisons are made between each racial and ethnic group and the Caucasian population:

- Infant mortality rates are 22 times higher for African-Americans and 12 times higher for Native Americans.
- African-American men under 65 suffer from prostate cancer at nearly twice the rate of other men.
- Vietnamese women suffer from cervical cancer at nearly 5 times the rate of other women.
- African-American men suffer from heart disease at nearly twice the rate of other men.
- Native Americans suffer from diabetes at nearly 3 times the average rate, African-Americans suffer 70 percent

higher rates, and the prevalence of diabetes among Latinos is nearly double.

- Racial and ethnic minorities constitute about 25 percent of the total U.S. population, yet they account for nearly 54 percent of all AIDS cases.

The demographic changes anticipated over the next decade magnify the importance of addressing health disparities. Groups that currently have poorer health status are expected to grow as a proportion of the total U.S. population; therefore, the future health of the United States as a whole will be influenced by our success in eliminating health disparities. *Healthy People 2010* identified ninety-three health areas in which the disparity is 25 percent or greater between the general population and at least one select population. Following are some of these disparities classified by age, disability, socioeconomic status, geographic location, and race and ethnicity:

Age
- Sedentary lifestyle
- Alcohol-related motor vehicle deaths
- Homicides
- Fall-related deaths
- Motor-vehicle crash deaths
- Drowning deaths
- Residential fire deaths
- Hip fractures among adults 65 years old and older

continued

---

runaway deaths in the United States has been fueled primarily by newspaper headlines, fictional books, and movies. Four recent headlines serve as examples:

- Mad cow disease "jumps" to humans.
- "Bird flu" causes Hong Kong to slaughter every chicken.
- Kenya disease killing humans, animals.
- Fatal, no-name virus leaps from animals to humans.

Although the appearance of an unstoppable, overwhelming disease is possible and the spread of new viruses in a global community is a genuine concern, the real threats to Americans are mundane and are less likely to be featured as the lead stories in the

evening news. These threats to health have been the focus of the Public Health Service of the Department of Health and Human Services (DHHS) for more than a decade and are published as objectives in the landmark document *Healthy People 2000: National Health Promotion and Disease Prevention Objectives*. These objectives, which are now being updated, serve as reminders of the health threats most likely to affect Americans.

Healthy lifestyles that involve diet, physical activity, and personal health habits offer the most potential for preventing health problems or delaying them until much later in life. More specifically, the following twelve steps-for-life,[14] developed by the internationally

Just the Facts

continued

- Nonfatal poisoning
- Asthma hospitalizations
- Cervical cancer screenings
- Gonorrhea infection screenings
- Tetanus boosters in the last ten years
- Pelvic inflammatory disease

Gender

- Smokeless tobacco use
- Suicides
- Diagnosis/treatment of depression
- Homicides
- Unintentional injury deaths
- Drowning deaths
- Hip fractures among adults 65 years old and older
- Nonfatal spinal cord injuries
- Oral cancer deaths

Disability

- Sedentary lifestyle
- Overweight

Socioeconomic status (related to income, education, and employment)

- Vigorous physical activity
- Cigarette smoking
- Smoking cessation during pregnancy
- Diagnosis and treatment of dental caries (cavities)

- Complete tooth loss among those 65 years or older
- Breast cancer screenings

Race/Ethnicity

- Coronary heart disease
- Sedentary lifestyle
- Cancer deaths
- Overweight
- Prevalence of diabetes
- Cigarette smoking
- Smokeless tobacco use
- Stroke deaths
- Drug-related deaths
- Teen pregnancies
- Suicides
- Homicides
- Firearm-related deaths
- Residential fire deaths
- Asthma hospitalizations
- Dental caries
- Gingivitis
- Oral cancer deaths
- Infant deaths
- Fetal deaths
- Low birth-weight incidence
- Prenatal care in the first trimester
- HIV infection incidence
- Influenza, pneumonia, tetanus vaccinations

renowned Cooper Institute for Aerobics Research, provide the framework for promoting health and improving the quality of life:

1. Exercise regularly.
2. Eat more fresh vegetables and fruit, high-fiber foods, and whole grains and drink more water.
3. Limit animal fat, cholesterol, and sodium in the diet.
4. Supplement the diet with calcium and antioxidant vitamins.
5. Pursue and maintain ideal body weight.
6. Stop illegal drug use and abstain from or limit alcohol consumption.
7. Terminate smoking and use of smokeless tobacco.
8. Avoid excessive sun exposure or wear sunblock.
9. Fasten seat belts.
10. Obtain good prenatal health care.
11. Regularly have medical checkups and perform self-exams.
12. Keep immunizations up-to-date.

Many experts emphasize, in addition to the twelve steps just listed, the need to practice safe sex habits. HIV infections are a serious health problem and one of the leading causes of death in young people. The dramatic drop in the death rate from complications of HIV infections, a nearly 50 percent drop in 1997, has led to a false sense of optimism about the spread of this disease. Most of the drop in HIV-related deaths is due

Table 1-1 Leading Causes of Death for All Ages and for Ages 25–44

Cause	All ages		Ages 25–44	
	Number	Rank	Number	Rank
All causes	2,314,729		133,602	
Heart disease	725,790	1	15,800	3
Cancer	537,390	2	21,555	2
Stroke	159,877	3	3,358	8
Chronic obstructive lung disease	110,637	4	—	—
Accidents	92,191	5	25,477	1
Motor vehicle accidents	42,420	—	13,837	—
Other accidents	49,772	—	11,640	—
Pneumonia and influenza	88,383	6	1,933	10
Diabetes mellitus	62,332	7	2,405	9
Suicide	29,725	8	12,008	4
Nephritis (kidney disease)	25,570	9	—	—
Chronic liver disease and cirrhosis	24,765	10	3,890	7
Septicemia (blood poisoning)	22,604	11	—	—
Alzheimer's disease	22,527	12	—	—
Homicide and legal intervention	18,774	13	8,287	6
Human immunodeficiency virus infection	16,685	14	11,166	5
All other causes*	345,791		27,733	

*Figures are based on weighted data; categories may not add to totals.

SOURCE: Ventura, S. J., R. N. Anderson, J. A. Martin, and B. L. Smith. 1998. Births and deaths: Preliminary data for 1997. *National Vital Statistics Report* 47(4).

to the availability of powerful new drug treatments. Sexual habits remain a serious concern. People must consider the impact of their personal health behaviors on their health, life expectancy, and quality of life.

The risk factor most strongly associated with premature death and chronic disease is cigarette smoking. In studies that try to pinpoint the actual cause of death, tobacco use is responsible for 20 percent of all deaths. Experts state that it is the single most preventable cause of death and disease in the United States. It is followed in descending order by poor diet and lack of exercise, alcohol, infectious agents, pollutants, firearms, risky sexual behavior, motor vehicles, and illicit drug use (see figure 1-3). Donna Shalala, Secretary of the U.S. Department of Health and Human Services, described the seriousness of tobacco use in testimony before the Senate:

Today, nearly 3,000 young people across our country will begin smoking regularly. Of these 3,000 young people, 1,000 will lose that gamble to the diseases caused by smoking. The net effect of this is that among children living in America today, 5 million will die an early preventable death because of a decision made as a child.[15]

For the smoker, his or her primary wellness challenge is to stop smoking; if that proves impossible, sig-nificant reduction in the frequency and duration of smoking will attenuate some of the risk factors that threaten health.

Second in importance to the smoker and first in importance to the nonsmoker as a wellness challenge are improvements in diet and an increase in physical activity. The medical research community has directed considerable attention to the benefits of a diet that conforms to the latest *Dietary Guidelines for Americans,* which were issued in 1995 by the United States Department of Agriculture (USDA). Few diseases escape the influence of nutrition. Evidence is growing that the major threats to wellness are related to dietary habits. Chapter 6 documents the health benefits of diets low in saturated fat and high in fruits, vegetables, and grain products.

The most formidable wellness challenge for Americans of all ages, however, is neither smoking cessation nor improvements in dietary habits. It is related to sedentary lifestyles. More people are at risk due to physical inactivity than to any of the other risk factors.[16] Less than 10 percent of the U.S. adult population reports regular, vigorous physical activity for twenty minutes or longer three or more days per week. Only about 25 percent of adults report physical activity on five or more days per week for thirty

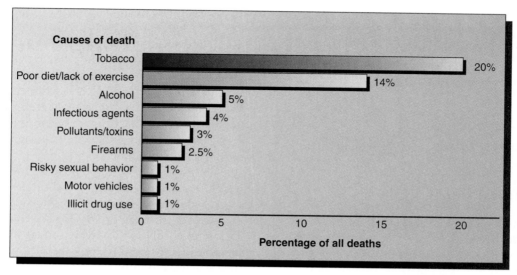

Causes of death

Cause	Percentage
Tobacco	20%
Poor diet/lack of exercise	14%
Alcohol	5%
Infectious agents	4%
Pollutants/toxins	3%
Firearms	2.5%
Risky sexual behavior	1%
Motor vehicles	1%
Illicit drug use	1%

Percentage of all deaths

Figure 1-3 Causes of Death in the United States

Running is a challenging activity that builds cardiorespiratory endurance.

minutes or longer, and another 25 percent of adults do not participate in any regular physical activity.[17] Americans' propensity for sedentary lifestyles comes at a time when evidence of the benefits of an active lifestyle is compelling. Physically active people outlive those who are inactive, and physical activity enhances the quality of life for people of all ages. Physical inactivity is regarded by many respected researchers as a risk factor for heart disease that is comparable to cigarette smoking, high blood pressure, and high blood cholesterol.

The Surgeon General's hallmark report *Physical Activity and Health*[17] brought a historic new perspective to exercise, fitness, and physical activity by shifting the emphasis from intensive aerobic exercise to a broader range of health-enhancing physical activity regardless of age (see Wellness Across the Generations: It's Never Too Late for Wellness!). For those who are inactive, even small increases in physical activity are associated with measurable health benefits (see Just the Facts: Physical Activity and Health—Selected Highlights). The benefit of physical activity is the underlying theme of this text and, ideally, will serve as an impetus for you to establish an active lifestyle.

Achieving Lifestyle Change: A Self-Help Approach

A fundamental assumption underlying lifestyle-change programs is that behavior is a learned response. For example, we are not born with a taste for some foods and a dislike for others. And using seat belts is not a function of heredity. Like most other behaviors, health behaviors are learned responses to both obvious and subtle influences. This learning begins at birth and continues throughout life. It is important to remember that this is just as true for behaviors that promote wellness as for behaviors that diminish it.

Wellness Across the Generations

It's Never too Late for Wellness!

"Well, I've been living this way for forty years. I'm too old to change my ways. Why change now?" Does this sound familiar? Do you feel that taking steps toward wellness is only for those younger than you? If so, think again. It is never too early or too late to begin improving your wellness. You can begin changing your behavior today and reap the benefits within a very short amount of time.

If you are a smoker, quitting smoking creates immediate positive results and lasting improvements in your health status. Within twenty minutes of smoking your last cigarette, your blood pressure will drop to its normal level. After eight hours, the amount of carbon monoxide in your blood will return to normal. Within five years, the risk of dying from lung cancer will be cut in half. In fifteen years, your risk of dying from cardiovascular disease will be as low as that of someone who does not smoke.*

People of all ages fall victim to violence and accidental injury. Taking steps to protect yourself from rape, homicide, sexual harassment, and injury caused by car accidents, fires, and falls is a critical part of maintaining your health. These steps are not just for children and young adults; they are for all of us.

Leotards and "meat market" exercise gyms not your style? You might want to consider just going for a walk or riding a bicycle. These wide-ranging benefits of aerobic fitness might persuade you to put on your walking shoes: reduction of the risk of heart disease, prevention of hypertension, strengthening of lungs, control of weight, warding off of infections, improvement of bodily functions, and increase in longevity.

With the average life expectancy reaching well into the 70s, wouldn't you like to still be enjoying life thirty or forty years from now? Making some basic changes in your daily life today will greatly improve your chances of being around for a much longer time. It's never too late to improve your wellness!

*1996. Quitters do win. *Mayo Clinic Health Letter* 14(6):2.

Examples of obvious influences that help shape behavior include parents and family, role models, advertising, and social norms. In many instances these influences are combined to form a single powerful influence on behavior, such as exemplified by an advertisement for cigarettes using "ideal" masculine or feminine models, depending on the brand of cigarettes and the target population. Advertisers are successful not only at marketing products but also at influencing people to think they need those products.

Subtle forces also shape behavior. A good example is *subliminal advertising,* a technique in which messages, words, and symbols are embedded or hidden in the pictures, sounds, or words used in advertisements. Theoretically these messages, though not directly observable, can be perceived by the subconscious mind in such a way as to influence behavior.

Much of our behavior is also motivated by psychological needs. An infant whose main source of attention and stimulation comes during feeding time may learn to associate food with the deeper psychological needs of love and affection. A parent who consistently uses food to appease an unhappy child may be inadvertently establishing a preoccupation with food that will endure far beyond childhood.

Sometimes, behavior is motivated in response to force or coercion. *Reactance motivation,* a theory of behavior that has been associated with drinking among college students, suggests that telling people to abstain completely from doing something often produces the opposite reaction. For many people it isn't difficult to recall instances in their own lives in which they behaved a certain way primarily because they were told that they could not or should not behave that way. Coercion in particular leads to the arousal of reactance, which in turn tends to reduce compliance.

These examples help to explain the myriad complex forces that contribute to behavior and illustrate why successful lifestyle change is so difficult to achieve. The hope and promise of any lifestyle-change program is that, while easier said than done, bad habits can be unlearned and new habits can be learned.

A Self-Help Plan

A **self-help** approach assumes that individuals can manage their lifestyle changes and can learn to control those features in the environment that are detrimental to health. In other words, expensive, long-term, professional help is not a prerequisite for everyone trying to make a lifestyle change. The self-help approach puts you in control of your health, requires your involvement, and permits you to determine what to do and how and when to do it. However, to be successful, this

Just the Facts

Physical Activity and Health—Selected Highlights

Here are selected highlights from the Surgeon General's Report:

- *Mortality:* Higher levels of physical activity are associated with lower mortality rates. Those who are moderately active on a regular basis have lower mortality rates than do those who are least active.

- *Cardiovascular disease:* Regular physical activity decreases the risk of cardiovascular disease. Regular physical activity is comparable to not smoking in decreasing risk of heart disease.

- *Cancer:* Regular physical activity is associated with a decreased risk of colon cancer.

- *Non–Insulin-Dependent Diabetes Mellitus:* Regular physical activity lowers the risk of developing non–insulin-dependent diabetes mellitus.

- *Osteoarthritis:* Weight-bearing physical activity is necessary for maintaining normal muscle strength, joint structure, and joint function.

- *Falling:* Promising evidence suggests that strength training and other forms of exercise in older adults preserve their ability to maintain independent living status and reduce the risk of falling.

- *Obesity:* Low levels of activity, resulting in fewer kilocalories used than consumed, contribute to the high prevalence of obesity in the United States. Physical activity may favorably affect body fat distribution.

- *Mental health:* Physical activity appears to relieve symptoms of depression and anxiety and improve mood. Regular physical activity may reduce the risk of developing depression, although further research is needed on this topic.

- *Health-related quality of life:* Physical activity appears to improve the health-related quality of life by enhancing psychological well-being and by improving physical functioning in people compromised by poor health.

- *Adverse effects:* Most musculoskeletal injuries related to physical activity are believed to be preventable by gradually working up to a desired level of activity and by avoiding excessive amounts of activity. Serious cardiovascular events can occur with physical exertion, but the net effect of regular physical activity is a lower risk of mortality from cardiovascular disease.

Source: U.S. Department of Health and Human Services. 1996. *Physical Activity and Health: A Report of the Surgeon General.* Atlanta, Ga.: U.S. Department of Health and Human Services, Centers for Disease Control and Prevention, National Center for Chronic Disease Prevention and Health Promotion.

---

approach requires considerable time and thought devoted to planning. Successful lifestyle change is almost impossible to achieve without a plan.

The self-help approach that follows is based on the **transtheoretical model of behavior change.**[18] This model of lifestyle change is presented in six stages (figure 1-4), as described next along with recommended strategies. In applying this model of change, it is helpful to remember several important assumptions:

1. Each of the six stages is well defined and entails a series of tasks that need to be completed before moving to the next stage.

2. A linear progression through the stages of change, although possible, is rare. Most people lapse at some point, and it is possible to get stuck at one stage or another. However, the important thing is to formulate a plan and act on it. Even if a relapse takes you back temporarily to an earlier stage, you are twice as likely to succeed during the next six months as a person who never tried at all.[19]

3. A key to successful change is knowing what stage you are in for the health issue or behavior at hand. Behavioral research reveals that people who try to accomplish changes they are not ready for set themselves up for failure. Similarly, too much time spent on a task already mastered—such as understanding your problem—may result in an indefinite delay in taking action.

4. Although nearly all change begins with precontemplation, only the most successful ends in termination. But you cannot skip stages. Most people who succeed follow the same road for every problem. However, you may be at different stages of change for different problems.

5. Successful behavior change does not typically happen all at once; it takes time.

Wellness On the Web
Behavior Change Activities

The Health-Behavior Gap
The discrepancy between knowing what behavior is good for your health and actually doing it is called the *health-behavior gap*. The key to striving for high-level wellness is motivation, since no single principle or incident can provide the stimulus necessary to institute change and maintain positive lifestyle habits. Dr. Michael Arloski shares ten suggestions, or tenets, that have emerged from his twenty years of work as a wellness professional. He attempts to answer the critical question, "Why don't people do what they know they need to do for themselves?" Go to www.healthy.net/Library/articles/arloski/tentenets.htm. Read each of the ten tenets, choose five of them, and complete the brief self-evaluation activity for the items you selected.

Your Wellness Profile
An important first step in any lifestyle-change program is to evaluate your health history. For your personal health and wellness evaluation, visit the Wellness-Sources website at www.wellness-sources.com/eval/history.html. Answer all questions using your mouse. It is very important to answer the questions thoroughly and completely. When you're finished, click the Submit button. Then click the Back button of your browser to get to the Test Results Page for your completed evaluation.

Your Life Expectancy
The Longevity Game identifies factors that can help you lead a healthier, longer, more productive life. The game is based on information gathered by the life insurance industry, public health organizations, and scientific studies. Go to the Northwestern Mutual Life website at www.northwesternmutual.com. Scroll down and click on the Longevity Game. After completing the list of questions, click the Submit button to calculate your life expectancy. What lifestyle factors increase your life expectancy? What lifestyle factors decrease your life expectancy? What specific behaviors could you change to increase your longevity?

Stage	1. Precontemplation	2. Contemplation	3. Preparation	4. Action	5. Maintenance	6. Termination
Characteristic	Lack of awareness Denial	Awareness of the need to change Thinking about changing	Planning to change within a month Thinking about the future	Engaging in strategies Commitment to change	Greater difficulty than action stage Duration from six months to a lifetime	Problem behavior no longer an issue
Goal	Feedback on need to change Consciousness raising	More consciousness raising Emotional arousal	Public affirmation of change Development of a plan	Application of strategies Changes in environment Forming of or joining support groups Establishment of rewards Countering	Application of same strategies as in action stage	Exit from cycle of change
Stage	1. Precontemplation	2. Contemplation	3. Preparation	4. Action	5. Maintenance	6. Termination

Figure 1-4 Stages, Characteristics, and Goals of Lifestyle Change

Precontemplation stage

In this stage, individuals have no intention of changing in the near future. Precontemplators may be unaware of the health risks associated with their behaviors. Or they may feel a situation is hopeless; maybe they've tried to change before without success. They often use denial and defensiveness to keep from going forward. They feel safe in precontemplation because they can't fail there.

Strategies. Consciousness raising is a key strategy. Sometimes it comes from a visit to the doctor, a health-threatening diagnosis, a headline news story, or simple feedback from others. One way to encourage consciousness raising is to take an inventory of personal health habits and practices. A good way to start is simply to make a list of your health-promoting behaviors, practices you engage in to maintain or improve your level of wellness (see Just the Facts: Examples of Health-Promoting Behaviors). Make another list of health-inhibiting behaviors, practices that may be detrimental to your health (see Assessment Activity 1-3). If your lists are specific and identify behaviors that relate to wellness in its broadest sense (that is, the physical, social, emotional, and psychological aspects of health), comparing the two should give you insight into and information about your lifestyle.

Detailed, comprehensive lifestyle questionnaires, such as in Assessment Activity 1-1, can provide even more information about specific health practices and behavioral tendencies that can be targeted for change. Many of these questionnaires are similar to those you might complete for your physician. Regardless of the tool you use, remember that the goal is to learn more about yourself.

Contemplation stage

Contemplators have a sense of awareness of a problem behavior and begin thinking seriously about changing it. However, it is easy to get stuck in the contemplation stage for years. Perhaps making a change requires more effort than someone is willing to expend or the rewards or pleasures of the current behavior seem to outweigh the benefits of change. Traps[20] include the search for absolute certainty (nothing in life is guaranteed); waiting for the magic moment (you need to make the moment); and wishful thinking (hoping for different results without changing your behavior).

Strategies. Contemplators need more consciousness raising. Reading, studying, and enrolling in courses are good ways to promote an awareness of the potential problems associated with certain behaviors. (One goal of this text, for example, is to increase your conscious-

Just the Facts

Examples of Health-Promoting Behaviors

Specific Behaviors Conducive to Good Health

- I avoid the extremes of too much or too little exercise.
- I get an adequate amount of sleep.
- I avoid adding sugar and salt to my food.
- I include 15 to 20 g of fiber in my diet each day.
- I plan my diet to ensure consumption of an adequate amount of vitamins and minerals.
- I brush and floss my teeth after eating.
- I avoid driving under the influence of alcohol or drugs.
- I drive within the speed limit.
- I wear my seat belt whenever traveling in an automobile.
- I avoid the use of tobacco.
- I consume fewer than two alcoholic drinks per day.
- I know the instructions provided with any drug I take.
- I do my part to promote a clean and safe environment.
- I feel positive and enthusiastic about my life.
- I can express my feelings of anger.
- I can say "no" without feeling guilty.
- I engage in activities that promote a feeling of relaxation.
- I am able to develop close, intimate relationships.
- I am interested in the views of others.
- I am satisfied with my study habits.
- I am satisfied with my spiritual life.
- I am tolerant of the values and beliefs of others.

ness of habits and practices that promote wellness and of risk factors that may threaten your health.) Getting involved in activities that expose you to information about various aspects of health and wellness allows you to focus on the negatives of your current health practices and to imagine the consequences down the line if your behavior doesn't change.

Cognitive dissonance, the internal conflict that occurs when people feel that their behavior is inconsistent with their intentions or values (such as exhibited by a smoking parent who doesn't want his or her child to smoke), helps in this stage. Also, *emotional arousal,* sometimes accomplished by watching a movie or news story on the subject in question (such as about the sudden death of a child caused by drunken driving), spurs someone to action. Social strategies also help. For example, a problem drinker might attend an Alcoholics Anonymous meeting as a way of experiencing social support for behaving differently.

Preparation stage

Most people in this stage are planning to take action within a month. They think more about the future than about the past, more about the pros of a new behavior than about the cons of the old one. Many people motivate themselves by making their intended change public rather than keeping it to themselves. This stage involves developing a plan that is customized to a person's unique circumstances and personality.

Most people make two serious mistakes when starting a lifestyle change. First, they expect miracles and set unrealistic goals. Setting goals that are too ambitious often guarantees failure. For many people the fear of failure easily discourages future efforts at a lifestyle change.

Second, people often view lifestyle change as a temporary goal rather than as a lifetime change. Perhaps more than anything else, this attitude accounts for the

Behavior change, such as following a healthier diet, should be viewed as a lifetime goal, not a temporary fix.

high *recidivism* (the tendency to revert to the original behavior) rate of many programs. One of the best examples is weight-loss programs. In weight-loss programs, for example, people typically set a goal, diet until they reach their goal, revert to their original eating habits, and invariably regain the lost weight. The proper way is to change eating habits so that they will endure for a lifetime. When people try to change some aspect of behavior, they have to deny themselves something that feels comfortable or that provides some source of enjoyment or pleasure. Denial often triggers a preoccupation that worsens the health behavior being changed. This is the reason dieters often become more interested in food during a diet. It is important to remember that the real test of a program's success is not how many people reach their goals but how many people successfully maintain that goal for at least two years (see Real World Wellness: Are You Ready for a Lifestyle Change?).

No single strategy for lifestyle change is right for everyone. The key is to get involved in planning your personal program and to use your imagination to create the most suitable plan.

Strategies. In this stage a firm, detailed plan is developed that involves (1) assessing behavior and (2) setting specific, realistic goals.

Assess behavior. Behavior assessment, the collection of data on target behaviors, is the lifeline of any lifestyle-change plan. It involves the process of counting, recording, measuring, observing, and describing. Any behavior that can be qualified is assessed.

Assessment tools are usually daily logs, journals, and diaries. Data should be collected long enough to note behavioral trends, usually for a minimum of one to two weeks.

Sometimes a behavior assessment will prompt a change in behavior without any other action. In most lifestyle-change programs a plan of action is not started until it is clear that assessment alone will not be enough to alter the behavior completely. Bootzin [21] illustrates this point by citing the experience of a friend:

A friend of mine discovered that he was interspersing the phrase "you know" in almost every sentence he spoke. He decided to try to suppress that behavior. The first step he took—as it turned out, the only step that was required—was to record the number of times he said "you know." Each day that he recorded, his frequency of emitting that phrase decreased. Recording served as a sufficient intervention to bring that verbal behavior under control.

The assessment phase also provides clues to a person's commitment to making a change in lifestyle. A thorough, detailed log is a good sign that a person has the motivation to carry out the plan.

Real-World Wellness

Are You Ready for a Lifestyle Change?

I've started an exercise program four times during the past two years. Each effort resulted in failure. I don't want to start again until I know I'm ready. How will I know that I'm ready to begin a lifestyle-change program?

If you can answer "yes" to the following questions, you are ready to begin a lifestyle-change program:

- Do you view lifestyle change as a lifetime goal rather than as a temporary, short-term goal?
- Are you willing to get personally involved in planning a lifestyle-change program?
- Are you prepared for some disappointments?
- Are you willing to experiment with different ideas?
- Do you have the patience to accept success in small increments stretched over a long period?
- Are you willing to set modest, realistic goals?
- Are you willing to establish some time benchmarks for success?
- Are you willing to make some changes in the way you live?
- Are you willing to tell others about your goals?
- Can you accept a relapse as a temporary setback rather than as a full-blown failure?
- Are you willing to formulate a plan that makes provisions for countering, avoidance, contracting, shaping up, reminders, and support?

When the assessment phase is finished, there should be sufficient information to form a behavioral profile, state specific goals, and customize an intervention program that matches goals and strategies to a person's unique circumstances and personality.

Set specific, realistic goals. Setting specific goals means setting goals that focus on concrete, observable, measurable behaviors. A behavioral goal to overcome shyness is very different from a goal that requires someone to initiate a conversation with a different person each day for the next week. If goals are specific, you know precisely what you are trying to accomplish and where, when, and how often. By using specific goals, you get instant feedback on your progress. Another way to increase specificity is to establish a timetable for achieving goals. A timetable adds structure to the plan and provides a way to evaluate progress.

Realistic behavioral goals are reasonable and relate to personal circumstances. Setting realistic goals also means forming them in the context of correct information. For example, an informed dieter knows that setting a goal to lose 10 pounds in a week is not reasonable. A more achievable goal is 1 to 2 pounds.

When setting goals, starting off small is best. Setting a modest goal initially facilitates some degree of success, which increases confidence. For complex lifestyle changes, behavioral psychologists recommend breaking down an ambitious, long-range goal into a set of intermediate goals, beginning with the easier ones and then moving gradually to more difficult ones. Goals should be structured in moderation. Extreme goals promote the erroneous attitude that lifestyle change is temporary. They create a strong sense of denial, encourage preoccupation with target behaviors, and invariably lead to failure. Exceptions include cigarette smoking, alcoholism, and drug dependence, for which abstinence is still the primary treatment.

Action stage

In this stage a person overtly makes changes in behavior, experiences, or environment. This is the busiest stage of change. It's also the stage most visible to others. New behaviors, such as exercising, not smoking, or actively changing a dietary pattern, can be observed.

Strategies.   People in the action stage implement their plan for change. In doing so, they apply their sense of commitment to the change. Rewards and incentives are important elements of this stage. **Countering,** or behavior substitution, in which a new behavior is substituted for the undesirable one, is the most common and one of the most powerful strategies available to people trying to make a change. When this technique is applied, the goal is to think of a behavior that is incompatible with the one being altered. Examples include chewing gum to suppress the urge to smoke, substituting diet colas for sweetened colas, and going for a walk instead of watching television. Some effective countering techniques are summarized in Just the Facts: Countering Strategies.

Making changes in the environment is another key element of the action stage. Avoidance, or the elimination of the circumstances associated with an undesirable behavior, is a fundamental technique of the control process. A smoker cannot smoke if there are no cigarettes, an ice cream binge is not possible if there is no ice cream parlor, and loud music cannot interfere with studying if the radio is put away.

Avoidance is not limited to objects. It may also include jobs, school, and even people. If taking eighteen hours of coursework while working twenty hours per

Just the Facts

Countering Strategies

Here are some countering strategies you can use to replace problem behaviors:

- Exercising
- Cooking
- Playing a musical instrument
- Relaxing (see Chapter 9)
- Cleaning
- Doing crossword puzzles
- Walking
- Reading a book
- Calling a friend
- Going to a movie
- Keeping busy
- Learning to be more assertive
- Learning a new skill
- Joining a fitness club
- Organizing
- Playing a game
- Surfing the internet
- Learning to use new software
- Watching a favorite television show
- Practicing thought stopping (counterthinking) by substituting positive thoughts for negative ones

week is compromising your academics, you may feel justified in dropping several courses or withdrawing from school altogether if a reduction in your workload isn't possible. By the same token it may be necessary to associate less often with people who contribute to a problem behavior.

The use of reminders is also a key element of an action plan. These may be in the form of a daily planner, calendar, clocks, sticky notes, signs on a door, or a to-do list. During times when behavior change is not an issue, the list might read, "call home, library, 2:00–4:00 PM, racquetball, 4:30–5:30, dinner date, 6:00–8:30, study time, 9:00–11:00. If you are working on an action plan for lifestyle change, adding action

goals is a natural extension. If, for example, you are working on social skills, you might simply add, "initiate a conversation with a classmate," or "eat lunch with someone different." A positive benefit of reminders, in addition to their reinforcement of positive behaviors, is the satisfaction that results from checking something off a list.

Contracting is another common action strategy. Written contracts tend to be more powerful than spoken ones. They usually include a statement of long-range and intermediate health goals, target dates for completion of each goal, intervention strategies, and rewards and incentives, such as "I will deposit five dollars in my new car savings account for every day that I attend all of my classes between now and the end of the semester." These contracts are not legal documents, so simplicity and creativity are in order.

Shaping up is an another essential part of lifestyle change. It requires a person to allow him- or herself opportunities to practice desired behaviors, usually in small increments. The saying "Behavior begets behavior" is the essence of shaping up. This is also true for harmful behaviors. For example, cigarette smokers rarely enjoy their first cigarette; they learn to enjoy smoking by smoking. The same is true for most beer drinkers. Typically, shaping up occurs gradually until it becomes fully integrated into one's behavioral repertoire.

The acquisition of positive health behaviors occurs the same way. A step-by-step approach, with reinforcement following each successive movement, promotes success. In overcoming a fear of flying, a person might first visit the airport; the next step might be to tour an airplane; next the person may take a seat, fasten up, and visualize flying. Each step brings the person closer to flying, each step is reinforced, and any feelings of anxiety are countered with relaxation. People forget that problem behaviors are formed cumulatively and reflect many years of conditioning. It is only reasonable to expect that acquiring a preference for a new behavior will also require considerable time, thought, and reinforcement.

Another good strategy in an action plan is the formation of a support group, which may include a roommate, family, friends, classmates, or someone who can identify with the lifestyle goal. Dieting may be easier and more tolerable when done with a friend. Two people may accomplish their goals more effectively than either can alone. For example, two roommates may be more successful at maintaining their exercise regimen together than separately. Involving someone else in the process of change makes it easier to stick to your action plan, provides a source of encouragement, and holds you accountable for your goals.

Maintenance stage

The goal in this stage is to retain the gains made during the action and other stages and to try hard to prevent a relapse. Change never ends with action. Although people tend to view maintenance as a static stage, it is actually a continuation of the action stage and can last six months to a lifetime. Programs that promise easy change usually fail to acknowledge that maintenance is a long, ongoing process. This is why trendy, extreme programs, such as many diet programs, have a high recidivism rate. People may achieve their weight-loss goal, but they cannot maintain their strategy for losing weight for life. When this happens, a person may erroneously view the action plan as a temporary strategy. This is the opposite of maintenance and lifestyle change.

It is important to remember that most people experience a relapse and return to the precontemplation or contemplation stage of change, maybe several times, before eventually succeeding in maintaining the change. People move through the change process at different paces, and relapse is simply a part of behavior change. It is important to learn from any relapse instead of reacting to it by giving up.

Strategies. Strategies used in the action plan should be continued in maintenance. Provisions for avoidance, reminders, contracting, countering, shaping up, and support groups apply during maintenance just as they do during the action stage.

Termination stage

The termination stage is the ultimate goal for people trying to make a lifestyle change. In this stage the problem behavior is no longer tempting. A person becomes confident that his or her problem behavior will never return; it becomes a nonissue. The cycle of change is exited.

Strategies. Some experts believe that termination is impossible, that the most anyone can hope for is a lifetime of maintenance. The key strategy is to be aware of early warning signs of relapse, such as overconfidence, that can recycle the problem behavior.

Regardless of the results, maintaining the proper perspective about success and failure is important. Many people have the attitude that they either completely succeed or completely fail. This way of thinking can be devastating to a person's motivation. When goals are not fully realized, the proper attitude is to view the shortcoming as justification for making adjustments in the program. The goals may have been too general or unrealistic. The intervention strategies may have lacked relevance. Reshaping goals, setting a more realistic schedule, changing the rewards and penalties, or formulating different intervention strategies may be necessary.

Above all, you should maintain a healthy perspective about yourself and not burden yourself with guilt if you fall short of your goals. What seems important now becomes insignificant when viewed within a broader context. You may consider how significant this event is likely to be to you two years from now. Doing this helps establish the right perspective on your progress. More important than total success are the answers to the following questions: What did you learn from this experience? What did you learn about yourself? What can you do differently? Lifestyle change is a lifelong project that requires insight, skillful planning, and plenty of practice.

Summary

- Wellness is a lifelong process that requires self-awareness, introspection, reflection, inquiry, accurate information, and action. It means assuming attitudes and engaging in behaviors that promote health and well-being.
- Health is a constantly changing state of being that moves along a continuum from optimal health to premature death and is affected by an individual's attitudes and activities.
- Lifestyle diseases represent the major threat to the health and quality of life of Americans.
- Wellness requires the consistent balancing of physical, emotional, spiritual, intellectual, social, occupational, and environmental dimensions.
- An internal locus of control is the attitude that a person is in control of his or her life. An external locus of control is the belief that factors affecting health are outside one's control. An internal locus of control is consistent with the principles of wellness.
- *Self-efficacy* refers to the beliefs people have in their ability to accomplish specific tasks or behaviors. A strong sense of self-efficacy is consistent with the principles of wellness.
- The mind, body, and spirit are inseparably linked. A breakdown in any one of these can threaten health and wellness.
- Psychosomatic diseases occur when physical symptoms are caused by psychological, social, spiritual, or emotional stressors.
- *Healthy People 2010* has as one of its goals the elimination of health disparities that exist among population groups.
- Lifestyle diseases are those that are caused by the way people live. The major lifestyle diseases are heart disease,

cancer, and stroke. Together these account for almost two-thirds of deaths among Americans.
- Chronic diseases are those that persist for an indefinite time.
- Accidents are the leading cause of death among Americans between 15 and 44 years of age.
- The risk factor most strongly associated with premature death and chronic disease in the United States is cigarette smoking.
- The risk factor that is most prevalent among Americans is physical inactivity.
- Physical inactivity as a risk factor for heart disease is comparable with cigarette smoking, high blood pressure, and high blood cholesterol.

- Lifestyle change is one of the most pervasive human endeavors.
- A fundamental belief in lifestyle-change programs is that health behavior is a learned response and therefore can be changed.
- Health behavior is influenced by many complex forces, including family, role models, social pressure, advertising, and psychological needs.
- The six stages of change are precontemplation, contemplation, preparation, action, maintenance, and termination.
- Action strategies include countering, avoidance, reminders, contracting, shaping up, and support groups.

Review Questions

1. How are the health problems of today different from those of fifty years ago? One-hundred years ago?
2. This book suggests that wellness is a process rather than a goal. What does this mean? What are the implications of this statement?
3. What are the components of wellness? How are they similar? Dissimilar?
4. Define *psychosomatic diseases.* Cite four examples of psychosomatic conditions.
5. Cite some data that confirm the relationship between physical health problems and the spiritual, social, and emotional dimensions of wellness.
6. What are the differences between an internal locus of control and an external locus of control? Which of the two is more consistent with the principles of wellness?
7. Define the concept of self-efficacy. What is the relationship between the concepts of locus of control and self-efficacy?
8. How does the impact of environmental improvements compare with advancements in medical technology in terms of increasing health and longevity among Americans?
9. To what does the concept *health disparities* refer? Give five examples.
10. How do the leading causes of mortality among all Americans compare with those of young adults between the ages of 15 and 24? Between 25 and 44?

11. What do medical experts consider the risk factor most strongly associated with premature death and chronic disease?
12. This book suggests that the most formidable wellness challenge for Americans of all ages is overcoming a sedentary lifestyle. What is the rationale for identifying physical activity as more important than diet or cigarette smoking?
13. Identify six benefits of physical activity as cited in the Surgeon General's Report *Physical Activity and Health.*
14. Identify and briefly describe the six stages of change as presented in the transtheoretical model of behavior change.
15. What are some common mistakes people make in trying to change or modify some aspect of their health behavior?
16. What is a major reason for the high recidivism rate in many lifestyle-change programs?
17. If a college student wants to use countering strategies as a way to cope with compulsive eating, what can he or she do or use?
18. Your roommate wants to improve his or her study habits. Identify for your roommate four strategies that apply the techniques recommended in the action stage of lifestyle change.
19. Give an example of a specific and realistic lifestyle goal.

References

1. National Wellness Institute, Inc. 1997. *Testwell: Making Wellness Work for You,* Madison, Wis.: WCB Brown and Benchmark.
2. New England Journal of Medicine. 1997. Can social contacts prevent colds? *Healthnews* 3(9):7.
3. Harvard Medical School. 1998. Emotions and health: Can stress make you sick? *Harvard Health Letter* 23(6):1.
4. National Wellness Institute, *op. cit.*
5. New England Journal of Medicine. 1996. Grumpiest men have greater risk of heart disease. *Healthnews* 2(17):6.
6. Harvard Medical School. 1996. Anger and heart attacks revisited. *Harvard Heart Letter* 6(6):4.
7. Tufts University. 1997. Irritable bowel syndrome: Treating the mind to treat the body. *Tufts University Health and Nutrition Letter* 15(7):4.
8. Editors of *American Health.* 1996. Pessimism may be hazardous to your health. *American Health* 15(3):54.
9. Ventura S. J., R. N. Anderson, J. A. Martin, and B. L. Smith. 1998. Births and deaths: Preliminary data for 1997. *National Vital Statistics Reports* 47(4).
10. Plotkin S. L., and S. A. Plotkin. 1998. A short history of vaccination. In *Vaccines,* eds. S. A. Plotkin and E. A. Mortimer, Jr. Philadelphia: WB Saunders.

11. Knox, R. 1998. Longevity reshaping the globe. *The Commercial Appeal* 159(132):2.
12. Associated Press. 1997. Racked with ill health, Russia shrinks. *The Commercial Appeal* 158(159):2.
13. Ventura S. J., et al., *op cit.*
14. American Alliance for Health, Physical Education, Recreation, and Dance. 1995. Cooper delivers stirring convention address. *Update* May/June:1–4.
15. U.S. Department of Health and Human Services. 1998. *Targeting tobacco use: The nation's leading cause of death, at a glance—1998.* Atlanta: Center for Disease Control.
16. U.S. Department of Health and Human Services. 1998. *Healthy People 2010 Objectives—Draft for Public Comment.* Washington: U.S. Government Printing Office.
17. U.S. Department of Health and Human Services. *Physical Activity and Health: A Report of the Surgeon General.* Atlanta: U.S. Department of Health and Human Services, Centers for Disease Control and Prevention, National Center for Chronic Disease Prevention and Health Promotion.
18. Prochaska, J. 1994. *Changing for Good.* New York: William Morrow and Company.
19. Prochaska, J. 1996. Just do it isn't enough: Change comes in stages. *Tufts University Diet and Nutrition Letter* 14(7):4–6.
20. Ibid.
21. Bootzin, R. 1975. *Behavior Modification as Therapy: An Introduction.* Cambridge, Mass.: Winthrop Publishers.

Suggested Readings

Rippe, J. M. 1996. *Fit over Forty.* New York: William Morrow and Company.

James Rippe, once an obsessive marathon runner, presents a revolutionary plan to achieve lifelong physical and spiritual health and well-being. It is based on a landmark study that established the first-ever fitness standards for people over 40 and features ten self-tests for evaluating your personal fitness level. It provides the tools needed to custom-design a lifelong fitness program that will enhance total wellness.

Prochaska, J. O., J. C. Norcross and C. C. Diclemente. 1994. *Changing for Good.* New York: Avon Books.

Three acclaimed psychologists studied more than 1000 people who were able to positively and permanently alter their lives without psychotherapy. They discovered that change does not depend on luck or willpower. It is a process that can be successfully managed by anyone who understands how it works. This book offers simple self-assessments, informative case histories, and concrete examples to help clarify the six stages of change.

Benson, H., and M. Stark, 1997. *Timeless Healing—the Power and Biology of Belief.* New York: Fireside.

Drawing on twenty-five years as a physician and researcher, Dr. Benson reveals how affirming beliefs, particularly belief in a higher power, make an important contribution to physical health. This book explains how anyone, with the aid of a caring physician or healer, can use beliefs and other self-care methods to heal many medical problems.

Name _____ **Date** _____ **Section** _____

Assessment Activity 1-1

Lifestyle Assessment Inventory

Directions: Wellness involves a variety of components that work together to build the total concept. Following are some questions concerning the different aspects of wellness. Using the scale, respond to each question by circling the number that best represents you at this point in time. At the end of each section, add up your response numbers and transfer the total to the appropriate section in the Wellness Assessment Summary. Save your results. Your instructor may ask you to complete this assessment again toward the end of the semester.

10 Yes, almost always (at least 90% of the time)
7 Very often (more than 50% but less than 90% of the time)
5 Sometimes (about 50% of the time)
3 Occasionally (less than 50% of the time but more than 10% of the time)
1 No, almost never (less than 10% of the time)

Physical Assessment

	Yes/Almost Always	Very Often	Sometimes	Occasionally	No/ Almost Never
1. I get at least thirty minutes of moderately intense physical activity most days of the week.	10	7	(5)	3	1
2. When participating in physical activities, I include stretching and flexibility exercises.	10	7	(5)	3	1
3. I include warm-up and cool-down periods when participating in vigorous activities.	10	(7)	5	3	1
4. I engage in resistance-type exercises at least two times per week.	10	7	(5)	3	1
5. My physical fitness level is excellent for my age.	10	7	(5)	3	1
6. My body composition is appropriate for my gender (men, 10%–18% body fat; women 17%–25%).	10	7	(5)	3	1
7. I have appropriate medical checkups regularly and am able to talk to my doctor and ask questions that concern me.	(10)	7	5	3	1
8. I keep my immunizations up-to-date.	(10)	7	5	3	1
9. I keep up with the medical history of close relatives.	(10)	7	5	3	1
10. I keep records of the time, date, and results of medical tests.	10	(7)	5	3	1

Physical assessment score _____

Alcohol and Drugs Assessment

	Yes/Almost Always	Very Often	Sometimes	Occasionally	No/ Almost Never
1. I avoid smoking.	(10)	7	5	3	1
2. I avoid using smokeless tobacco products.	(10)	7	5	3	1
3. I avoid drinking alcohol or restrict my consumption to two drinks or fewer per day.	10	7	5	3	1
4. I avoid drinking alcohol to the point of intoxication.	10	7	5	3	1
5. I do not drive when drinking alcoholic beverages or taking medicines that make me sleepy.	10	7	5	3	1
6. I avoid using mood-altering substances.	10	7	5	3	1
7. I follow directions when taking medications.	10	7	5	3	1
8. I thoroughly read labels before taking a nonprescription drug.	10	7	5	3	1
9. I ask about warnings and side effects of prescription drugs before taking them.	10	7	5	3	1
10. I keep in my wallet or purse a record of drugs to which I am allergic.	10	7	5	3	1

Alcohol and drugs assessment score _____

Nutritional Assessment

	Yes/Almost Always	Very Often	Sometimes	Occasionally	No/ Almost Never
1. I eat at least three to five servings of vegetables and two to four servings of fruits each day.	10	7	5	3	1
2. My daily diet includes at least six to eleven servings from the bread, cereal, rice, and pasta food group.	10	7	5	3	1
3. I limit my daily intake of dairy products to two to three servings.	10	7	5	3	1
4. My daily intake of meats, eggs, and nuts is two to three servings.	10	7	5	3	1
5. I make a conscious effort to choose or prepare foods low in saturated fat.	10	7	5	3	1
6. When purchasing a food item, I read the labels to identify foods high in salt, hidden sugars, tropical oils, and saturated fat.	10	7	5	3	1
7. I avoid adding salt to my food without first tasting it.	10	7	5	3	1
8. I avoid eating unless I'm hungry.	10	7	5	3	1
9. I stop eating before feeling completely full.	10	7	5	3	1
10. I avoid binge eating.	10	7	5	3	1

Nutritional assessment score _____

Social Wellness Assessment

	Yes/Almost Always	Very Often	Sometimes	Occasionally	No/ Almost Never
1. I have at least one person in whom I can confide.	10	7	5	3	1
2. I have a good relationship with my family.	10	7	5	3	1
3. I have friends at work or school from whom I gain support and with whom I talk regularly.	10	7	5	3	1
4. I am involved in school activities.	10	7	5	3	1
5. I am involved in my community.	10	7	5	3	1
6. I do something for fun and just for myself at least once a week.	10	7	5	3	1
7. I am able to develop close, intimate relationships.	10	7	5	3	1
8. I engage in activities that contribute to the environment.	10	7	5	3	1
9. I am interested in the views, opinions, activities, and accomplishments of others.	10	7	5	3	1
10. I provide social support to others.	10	7	5	3	1

Social wellness assessment score _____

Spiritual Wellness Assessment

	Yes/Almost Always	Very Often	Sometimes	Occasionally	No/ Almost Never
1. I know what my values and beliefs are.	10	7	5	3	1
2. I live by my convictions.	10	7	5	3	1
3. My life has meaning and direction.	10	7	5	3	1
4. I derive strength from my spiritual life daily.	10	7	5	3	1
5. I have life goals that I strive to achieve every day.	10	7	5	3	1
6. I view life as a learning experience and look forward to the future.	10	7	5	3	1
7. I have a sense of peace about my life.	10	7	5	3	1
8. I am tolerant of the values and beliefs of others.	10	7	5	3	1
9. I am satisfied with the degree to which my activities are consistent with my values.	10	7	5	3	1
10. Personal reflection is an important part of my life.	10	7	5	3	1

Spiritual wellness assessment score _____

Emotional Wellness Assessment

	Yes/Almost Always	Very Often	Sometimes	Occasionally	No/ Almost Never
1. I feel positive about myself and my life.	10	7	5	3	1
2. I am able to be the person I choose to be.	10	7	5	3	1
3. I am satisfied that I am performing to the best of my ability.	10	7	5	3	1

	Yes/Almost Always	Very Often	Sometimes	Occasionally	No/Almost Never
4. I can cope with life's ups and downs effectively and in a healthy manner.	10	7	5	3	1
5. I am nonjudgmental in my approach to others.	10	7	5	3	1
6. I feel there is an appropriate amount of excitement in my life.	10	7	5	3	1
7. When I make mistakes, I learn from them.	10	7	5	3	1
8. I can say "no" without feeling guilty.	10	7	5	3	1
9. I find it easy to laugh.	10	7	5	3	1
10. I avoid blaming others for my failures or problems.	10	7	5	3	1

Emotional wellness assessment score _____

Stress Control Assessment

	Yes/Almost Always	Very Often	Sometimes	Occasionally	No/Almost Never
1. I am easily distracted.	1	3	5	7	10
2. I tend to be nervous and impatient.	1	3	5	7	10
3. I prepare ahead of time for events or situations that cause stress.	10	7	5	3	1
4. I schedule enough time to accomplish what I need to do.	10	7	5	3	1
5. I set realistic goals for myself.	10	7	5	3	1
6. I can express my feelings of anger.	10	7	5	3	1
7. I avoid putting off important tasks to the last minute.	10	7	5	3	1
8. I participate in activities that provide relief from stress.	10	7	5	3	1
9. When working under pressure, I stay calm and patient.	10	7	5	3	1
10. I can make decisions with a minimum of stress and worry.	10	7	5	3	1

Stress control assessment score _____

Intellectual Wellness Assessment

	Yes/Almost Always	Very Often	Sometimes	Occasionally	No/Almost Never
1. I believe my education is preparing me for what I would like to accomplish in life.	10	7	5	3	1
2. I am interested in learning just for the sake of learning.	10	7	5	3	1
3. I like to be aware of current social and political issues.	10	7	5	3	1
4. I have interests other than those directly related to my vocation.	10	7	5	3	1
5. I am able to apply what I know to real-life situations.	10	7	5	3	1
6. I am interested in the viewpoint of others, even if it is very different from my own.	10	7	5	3	1
7. I seek advice when I am uncertain or uncomfortable with a recommended health or medical treatment.	10	7	5	3	1

	Yes/Almost Always	Very Often	Sometimes	Occasionally	No/ Almost Never
8. I ask about the risks and benefits of a medical test before its use.	10	7	5	3	1
9. When seeking medical care, I plan ahead how to describe my problem and what questions I should ask.	10	7	5	3	1
10. I keep abreast of the latest trends and information regarding health matters.	10	7	5	3	1

Intellectual wellness assessment score _____

Occupational Wellness Assessment

	Yes/Almost Always	Very Often	Sometimes	Occasionally	No/ Almost Never
1. I am aware of my own skills, strengths, and weaknesses as they relate to possible occupational choices.	10	7	5	3	1
2. I have a good work ethic at school, home, and work.	10	7	5	3	1
3. I look for opportunities to learn about careers that may be of interest to me.	10	7	5	3	1
4. I am aware of the demands that future occupational choices may make on my personal life.	10	7	5	3	1
5. I am aware of the demands that future occupational choices may make on my family life.	10	7	5	3	1
6. I try hard to connect academics to the needs and demands of occupational choices.	10	7	5	3	1
7. I view occupational choices as a source of personal growth and fulfillment.	10	7	5	3	1
8. I do not consider money the only criterion for choosing a career.	1	3	5	7	10
9. I am aware of the need for continuing education in various careers of interest to me.	10	7	5	3	1
10. I am willing to spend extra personal time acquiring skills and knowledge required for occupational success.	10	7	5	3	1

Occupational wellness assessment score _____

Environmental Wellness Assessment

	Yes/Almost Always	Very Often	Sometimes	Occasionally	No/ Almost Never
1. I try to conserve energy by turning off lights and electrical appliances when they are not being used.	10	7	5	3	1
2. I repair or report leaking faucets.	10	7	5	3	1
3. I avoid littering.	10	7	5	3	1
4. I avoid disposing of toxic chemicals or petroleum products illegally.	10	7	5	3	1

5. I look for recycled materials when purchasing products.	10	7	5	3	1
6. I store toxic chemicals in their original containers and out of the reach of small children.	10	7	5	3	1
7. I make sure that smoke detectors are in use and working properly.	10	7	5	3	1
8. I make sure that carbon monoxide detectors are in use and working properly.	10	7	5	3	1
9. I check for or inquire about radon concentrations when moving into a new house or apartment.	10	7	5	3	1
10. I wash my hands with soap for at least 10 seconds after using the bathroom.	10	7	5	3	1

Environmental wellness assessment score _____

Wellness Assessment Summary

Transfer the total score for each section to the following spaces. Add the scores and divide by 10 to determine your average wellness score.

Physical assessment	_____
Alcohol and drugs assessment	_____
Nutritional assessment	_____
Social wellness assessment	_____
Spiritual wellness assessment	_____
Emotional wellness assessment	_____
Stress control assessment	_____
Intellectual wellness assessment	_____
Occupational wellness assessment	_____
Environmental wellness assessment	_____
Total	_____
Average wellness score	_____
(Divide total score by 10)	

90–100—Excellent. You are engaging in behaviors and attitudes that can significantly contribute to a healthy lifestyle and a higher quality of life. If you scored in this range, you are an example to many.

75–89—Good. You engage in many health-promoting attitudes and behaviors that should contribute to good health and a more satisfying quality of life. However, there are some areas that could use some upgrading to provide optimal benefits. If you are at this level, you are showing how much you care about yourself and your life.

65–74—Average. You are typical of the average American who tends to act without really considering the consequences of behaviors. Now is the time to consider your lifestyle and the ramifications it is having on you now and will have in the future. Maybe there are some positive actions that you could consider taking to improve your quality of life.

45–73—Below average. Perhaps you lack current information about behaviors and attitudes that can enhance your health and quality of life. Now is the time to begin to learn about positive changes that can improve your life.

0–44—Needs improvement. It's good that you are concerned enough about your health to take this test, but indications are that your behaviors and attitudes may be having detrimental effects on your health. You can easily begin to take action now to improve your prospects for the future.

Follow-Up

Complete the following statements: In completing this wellness assessment,

1. I was surprised to learn that I _____

_____

2. I was disappointed that _____

_____

3. I have learned that the concept of wellness _____

_____

Name _____ Date _____ Section _____

Assessment Activity 1-2

Health Locus of Control

Locus of control is an important component of individual wellness. This activity will assist you in identifying your locus of control and its ability to affect your health. This rating scale is an adaptation of the Multidimensional Health Locus of Control Scales. The test is composed of three subscales:

1. The *Internal Health Locus of Control Scale (I)* measures whether you feel that you have control over your own health.
2. The *Powerful Others Health Locus of Control Scale (P)* measures whether you feel that powerful individuals, such as physicians or other health professionals, control your health.
3. The *Chance Health Locus of Control Scale (C)* measures whether you feel your health is due to luck, fate, or chance.

Directions: For each answer, choose a number from 1 to 5 that best describes your feelings.

5 = Strongly agree
4 = Agree
3 = Neither agree nor disagree
2 = Disagree
1 = Strongly disagree

Subscale 1: Internal Health Locus of Control (I)
_____ If I get sick, my behavior determines how soon I get well.
_____ I am in control of my health.
_____ When I get sick, I am to blame.
_____ If I take care of myself, I can avoid illness.
_____ If I take the right actions, I can stay healthy.
_____ Total

Subscale 2: Powerful Others Health Locus of Control (P)
_____ Having regular contact with my physician is the best way for me to avoid illness.
_____ Whenever I don't feel well, I should consult a medically trained professional.
_____ My family has a lot to do with my becoming sick or staying healthy.
_____ Health professionals control my health.
_____ When I recover from an illness, it's usually because other people, such as doctors, nurses, family, and friends, have been taking good care of me.
_____ Regarding my health, I can only do what my doctor tells me to do.
_____ Total

Subscale 3: Chance Health Locus of Control (C)
_____ No matter what I do, if I am going to get sick, I will get sick.
_____ Most things that affect my health happen to me accidentally.
_____ Luck plays a big part in determining how soon I will recover from an illness.
_____ My good health is largely a matter of good fortune.
_____ No matter what I do, I am likely to get sick.
_____ If it is meant to be, I will stay healthy.
_____ Total

To obtain your score for each subscale, add the numbers you chose.

1. A score of 23 to 30 on any subscale means you have a strong inclination toward that particular subscale. For example, a high C score indicates you hold strong beliefs that your health is a matter of chance.
2. A score of 15 to 22 means you are moderate on that particular subscale. For example, a moderate P score indicates you have moderate belief that your health is due to powerful others.
3. A score of 6 to 14 means you are low on that particular subscale. For example, a low I score means you generally do not believe that you control your own health.

Assessment Activity 1-3

Assessing Your Health Behavior

Before planning a lifestyle-change program, you should take an inventory of your health behaviors. This reveals important information about your lifestyle and should also help identify areas in need of improvement.

Directions: In this assessment, you are asked to make two lists. In the left column, list the things you do to maintain or improve your level of health. These are your health-promoting behaviors. In the right col-

umn, list the things you do that may be detrimental to your health. These are your health-inhibiting behaviors. Try to be specific. Include the things that affect your mental, emotional, social, spiritual, and physical health. If you have a difficult time thinking of specific activities, you can refer to Assessment Activity 1-1.

Health-promoting behaviors	**Health-inhibiting behaviors**
1. _____	1. _____
2. _____	2. _____
3. _____	3. _____
4. _____	4. _____
5. _____	5. _____
6. _____	6. _____
7. _____	7. _____
8. _____	8. _____
9. _____	9. _____
10. _____	10. _____
11. _____	11. _____
12. _____	12. _____
13. _____	13. _____
14. _____	14. _____
15. _____	15. _____

Which health-inhibiting behavior would you be willing to change right now? _____

_____

(handwritten notes)

7 components of
wellness
Spirit
Say
People
Eat
Into
Obesity
Everyday

(handwritten notes)

Precontemplation
Contemplation
Preparation
Action
Maintenance
Termination

(handwritten notes)

Frequency
Intensity
Duration
Overload
Progression
Specificity

(handwritten notes)

Intensity
Duration
Frequency
Overload
Progression
Specificity

(handwritten notes)

Don't
Fuck
On
People's
Stuff

2

Preventing Cardiovascular Disease

Key Terms

aneurysm
atherosclerosis
cerebral hemorrhage
cholesterol
embolus
hypertension

ischemia
lipoprotein
myocardial infarction
sedentary
thrombus

Objectives

After completing this chapter, you will be able to do the following:

- Describe the gross anatomy and function of the heart.
- Trace the development of cardiovascular disease during this century in the United States.
- Identify and differentiate among several types of cardiovascular disease.
- Identify the risk factors for coronary heart disease and discuss ways to reduce them.
- Explain the lifestyle behaviors that contribute to health and longevity.

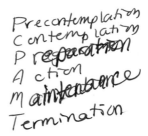

Goals for Behavior Change

- Choose three high-fat foods that you regularly eat and replace them with low-fat healthier foods.
- Find out what your total cholesterol, LDL cholesterol, and HDL cholesterol are. Select three or four lifestyle behaviors to change to improve your cholesterol profile.
- Find out what your blood pressure is. Select two or three behaviors to change (excluding taking medication) to lower it.
- If you use tobacco products, devise a plan for quitting the tobacco habit.
- If you are not currently active, make a list of physical activities to improve your health status and level of fitness. Determine how many calories you would attempt to expend per week.
- Plan and implement three strategies to help you deal with chronic stress.

ardiovascular disease encompasses a group of diseases that affect the heart and blood vessels. Cardiovascular disease—the leading cause of death in the United States—accounts for 42 percent of all deaths.[1] About 25 percent of Americans (approximately 59 million people) have one or more forms of heart or blood vessel disease. Approximately 1.5 million heart attacks have occurred every year in the last few years, and about 500,000 of these end in death each year. At least 250,000 heart attack victims die within the first hour following the onset of symptoms. They fail to reach a hospital before death occurs. A significant number of these premature deaths could have been prevented with early recognition and treatment.

Of heart attack victims, 50 percent wait an average of two hours before seeking medical attention. Denying the possibility that a heart attack is occurring is the primary reason for the delay. The situation is complicated because the symptoms of a heart attack are similar to those of other physical ailments, and people are more prone to believe that it is one of the other problems than that it is a heart attack.

Although the figures are foreboding, substantial progress has occurred during the last forty-five years. The death rate for cardiovascular diseases has declined by more than 50 percent since 1950.[1] Although an impressive accomplishment, it is somewhat diminished by the fact that cardiovascular diseases remain by far the leading cause of death in the United States. Two types in particular, coronary heart disease and strokes, are the first and third leading causes of death. More than 50 percent of the premature deaths in our society are attributed to lifestyle habits.

Authorities agree that preventive measures emphasizing risk-reduction strategies that involve lifestyle changes will produce the most dramatic benefits in the fight against heart disease.[2] Also contributing to the downward trend in the death rate from cardiovascular disease are more sophisticated diagnostics, improved treatment, and prompt recognition of impending heart attacks.

Circulation

You can understand circulation better if you are familiar with the basic anatomy and function of the heart. The heart consists of cardiac muscle and weighs between 8 and 10 ounces. It is about the size of a fist and lies in the center of the chest. The heart is divided into two halves, or pumps, by a wall (the septum), and each half is subdivided into an upper chamber (the atrium) and a lower chamber (the ventricle). The right heart, or pulmonary pump, receives deoxygenated blood from the tissues and pumps it to the lungs so that carbon

dioxide can be exchanged for a fresh supply of oxygen. From the lungs, the oxygen-rich blood is sent to the left heart, or systemic pump, so that the oxygenated blood can be pumped to all the tissues of the body. Both pumps work simultaneously. The systemic pump carries the heavier workload of the two and thus has a more muscular ventricular wall. Figure 2-1 illustrates the circulatory system.

The arteries carry oxygenated blood away from the heart while the veins carry deoxygenated blood to the heart. There are two exceptions, one in the arterial system and one in the venous system. First, the pulmonary artery carries *deoxygenated* blood from the right heart to the lungs to exchange carbon dioxide for a fresh supply of oxygen. Second, the pulmonary vein carries *fully oxygenated* blood from the lungs to the left heart for distribution throughout the body.

The primary function of circulation is to provide a constant supply of blood and nutrients to the cells while removing their waste products. Under ordinary circumstances, the interruption of blood flow for as little as four to six minutes can result in irreversible brain damage due to oxygen deprivation.

The average heart beats seventy to eighty times per minute at rest. Endurance athletes often have resting heart rates in the thirty and forty beat range, whereas

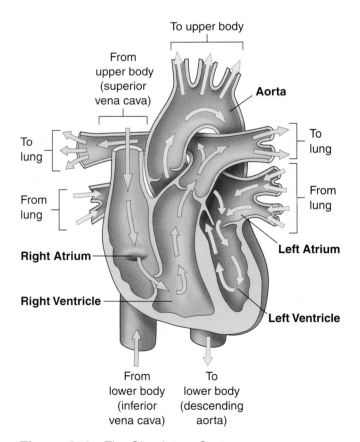

Figure 2-1 The Circulatory System

some overweight and sedentary smokers have resting heart rates in the nineties. The low heart rates of endurance athletes reflect physiological adaptations to training that represent normal values for this group. The Framingham Heart Disease Study showed that a rapid resting heart rate increased the risk of death from heart attack. Mortality increased progressively with higher resting heart rates, especially among men.

The heart is self-regulating; that is, it contains its own conduction system that is fully capable of establishing and maintaining the heart beat without outside neural stimulation. The heart's beating rate and rhythm are established by the sinoatrial node (SA node, or pacemaker), which is located in the right atrium, as shown in figure 2-2. The atria contract, forcing blood into the ventricles as the electrical impulse travels from the SA node to the atrioventricular node (AV node), which is located between the right atrium and right ventricle. The electrical impulse pauses for one tenth of a second at the AV node to allow the ventricles to fill with blood and then resumes down the system and spreads throughout the ventricular walls. The ventricles contract during this time, ejecting blood from these chambers.

Blood that enters the chambers of the heart does not directly nourish the heart muscle because there are no direct circulatory routes from the heart's chambers into its muscular walls. Instead, blood must first be ejected from the heart to the aorta (the largest artery in the body) and then to the coronary arteries that supply the myocardium (heart muscle) with blood and oxygen. The majority of blood is received by the myocardium during diastole (between beats) because the blood vessels dilate during this time, increasing their capacity to accept and deliver blood.

Coronary circulation is illustrated in figure 2-3. The left coronary artery supplies a major portion of the myocardium with blood, whereas the right coronary artery serves less of it. Both vessels divide and subdivide downstream and eventually culminate in a dense network of capillaries (the smallest blood vessels in the body). Blood supply to the myocardium is so important that every muscle fiber is supplied by at least one capillary. The coronary veins return deoxygenated blood to the right atrium so that it can enter pulmonary circulation. The veins bring deoxygenated blood from all tissues back to the right atrium.

Blood plasma is a clear, yellowish fluid that carries approximately 100 chemicals. Plasma represents 55 percent of the blood content. The remaining 45 percent consists of blood solids—the erythrocytes (red blood cells), the leukocytes (white blood cells), and the blood platelets. The red blood cells are the most abundant of the blood solids, composing about 99 percent of the total. These cells carry oxygen and carbon dioxide attached to hemoglobin, which is an iron-rich protein pigment and a main component of red blood cells. The white blood cells are an important part of the body's defense system against invading microorganisms and other foreign substances. The blood platelets are involved in the complex processes that lead to the formation of clots for repairing damaged blood vessels.

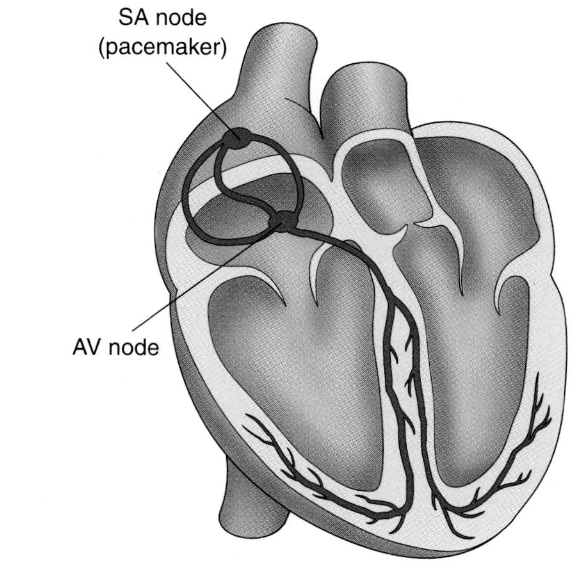

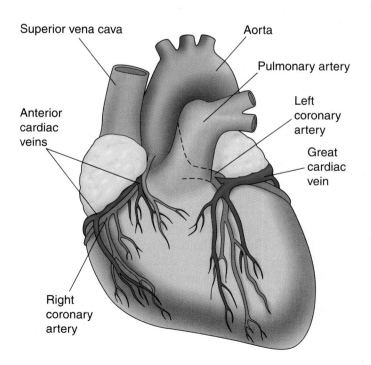

Figure 2-2 Electrical Conduction System of the Heart

Figure 2-3 Coronary Circulation

Cardiovascular Disease: A Twentieth-Century Phenomenon

Cardiovascular disease, a relatively rare event 100 years ago, reached epidemic proportions during the middle of the twentieth century. The term *angina pectoris* (chest pain) was introduced into the medical literature by William Heberden, a British physician, in the latter part of the eighteenth century. He was unable to offer any treatment for this strange malady. It was not until 1910 that physicians made the connection between recurrent episodes of angina pectoris and heart disease. Chest pain and other manifestations of a heart attack were not identified with obstructions of the coronary arteries until the early 1900s. An American physician gave the first accurate description of the events associated with a heart attack in 1912. The illness he described, which afflicted a 55-year-old man with no previous evidence of disease, is now a common occurrence in American life. The man died three days after the onset of symptoms. A postmortem examination of the heart revealed that a clot had occluded, or blocked, one of the major coronary arteries. In 1912, this was a medical rarity.

Coronary heart disease is responsible for the majority of heart attack deaths, but other forms of heart disease contribute to disability and death. Congenital heart defects, which exist at birth, affect approximately 32,000 newborns annually. Approximately 5400 of these infants die from their defects. Rheumatic heart disease, caused by a streptococcal infection of the throat or ear, is virtually 100 percent preventable. Antibiotic treatment during the infection stage arrests the processes that could lead to rheumatic heart disease. Congestive heart failure occurs when the heart muscle is so damaged that it can no longer contract with sufficient force to pump blood throughout the body. The leading causes of congestive heart failure are poorly controlled or uncontrolled long-standing hypertension or a history of previous heart attacks or both.

Coronary Heart Disease

Coronary heart disease (also known as *coronary artery disease*) is actually a disease of the arteries that supply the heart with blood and nutrients. A diagnosis of coronary artery disease is made if any artery is narrowed by 60 percent. A heart attack, or **myocardial infarction** (death of heart muscle tissue), occurs when an obstruction or spasm disrupts or blocks blood flow to a portion of the heart muscle. The amount of heart muscle damage is determined by the location of the obstruction or spasm and the speed with which medical intervention is begun. Heart attacks of any magnitude produce irreversible injury and myocardial tissue death. It usually takes five to six weeks to form a fibrous scar around dead cardiac tissue. This area of dead tissue can no longer contribute to the pumping of blood, resulting in a less efficient heart. Massive heart attacks that cause extensive muscle damage result in death.

Although most heart attacks occur after the age of 65, the dysfunctions leading to them often begin before adolescence. These processes occur most often without symptoms and often go undetected until, without warning, a heart attack occurs. The attack is sudden, but the circumstances leading to it develop over many years. In fact, there is considerable evidence that the silent phase of coronary heart disease begins as early as childhood.[3,4]

Risk factors are genetic predispositions, lifestyle behaviors, and environmental influences that increase one's susceptibility to disease. Elevated blood pressure and blood fats (cholesterol and triglycerides) that occur during adulthood can often be traced back to childhood. See Wellness Across the Generations: Childhood Origins of Heart Disease for more information about this connection.

The ongoing Framingham Study, which began in 1949, identified the risk factors connected with heart disease.[9] Cigarette smoking, high blood pressure, elevated cholesterol levels, diabetes, obesity, stress, physical inactivity, age, gender, and family history were found to be highly related to heart attack and stroke. As the risks were discovered, the realization evolved that heart disease was not the inevitable consequence of aging or bad luck but an acquired disease that was preventable. After a few years, researchers realized that preventive efforts should begin in childhood.

Autopsy studies of 18-year-olds who died in accidents have shown a positive relationship between blood cholesterol levels and the prevalence of fatty streaks on the walls of the coronary arteries and aorta. The evidence indicates that the average cholesterol level in children in overfed, underexercised societies such as the United States is too high.

Autopsy studies of American combat battle casualties, whose average age was 22 years, in the Korean and Vietnam wars showed obstructions in the coronary arteries. These obstructions are caused by **atherosclerosis**, which is a slow, progressive disease of the arteries that can originate in childhood.[4] It is characterized by the deposition of plaque beneath the lining of the artery (figure 2-4). Plaque consists of fatty substances, cholesterol, blood platelets, fibrin, calcium, and cellular debris. The atherosclerotic process is responsible for 80 percent of the coronary heart disease deaths in the United States. The lipid oxidation theory, which is the current theory of the development of atherosclerosis, is explained in the section dealing with cholesterol as a risk factor.

Wellness Across the Generations

Childhood Origins of Heart Disease

Behavior patterns established during childhood that increase the likelihood of coronary heart disease may and often do persist into adulthood. A physically inactive child is likely to become a physically inactive adult.[5] Only 50 percent of young people in the United States (ages 12 to 21 years) regularly participate in vigorous physical activity, and one-fourth report no physical activity at all.[4] Fifteen to 25 percent of children and adolescents are obese.[6] An estimated 6 million teenagers and 100,000 youngsters under the age of 13 are regular smokers.[7] Smoking rates among high school students rose from 27.5 percent in 1991 to 34.8 percent in 1995.[8] These are major risks that begin in childhood and continue into adulthood.

Attempts to prevent heart disease need to begin in childhood. Knowledgeable parents can serve as role models who practice, rather than just talk about, healthy behaviors. Active parents should be the strongest influence, but they are not the only influence. Schools need to offer quality physical education programs throughout the twelve years of precollege education, and communities should offer opportunities and provide facilities for active participation in games and recreational play.

As many as one-third of all heart attacks are silent; that is, they have no obvious signs or symptoms. Three to four million Americans experience cardiac **ischemia** without knowing it. Ischemia (reduced blood flow) occurs as the result of arterial disease or arterial spasms that restrict blood flow to any part of the body, including the heart.[1] Silent ischemia can and does initiate heart attacks without prior warning. However, the typical heart attack is obvious, and the symptoms are pronounced. See Just the Facts: Heart Attack: The Warning Signs.

Stroke (Brain Attack)

The majority of strokes (cerebrovascular accidents, or brain attacks) follow the same sequence of events that results in coronary heart disease. A stroke is essentially the result of diseased blood vessels that supply the

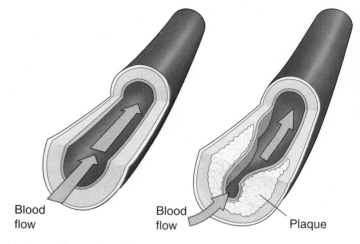

Figure 2-4 Progressive Narrowing of a Normal Coronary Artery (Atherosclerosis)

Just the Facts

Heart Attack: The Warning Signs

The Warning Signs

- Uncomfortable pressure, fullness, a squeezing sensation as if a band were being tightened around the chest, pain in the center of the chest lasting longer than 2 minutes

- Pain that spreads to the shoulders, arms, or neck

- The above warning signs accompanied by dizziness, fainting, sweating, nausea, and shortness of breath.

What to Do If These Signs Appear

If you have chest discomfort lasting more than 2 minutes:

- Do not deny what may be occurring

- Call the emergency service or have a friend or family member drive you to the nearest hospital that has 24-hour emergency cardiac care

- Know in advance which hospitals have such service

- Prominently display in your home the telephone number of the emergency rescue service and also carry a copy with you.

brain. It shares the same risk factors as coronary heart disease, and it takes years to develop.

Strokes are caused by a **thrombus** (a clot that forms and occludes an artery supplying the brain) or an **embolus** (a clot that forms elsewhere in the body and fragments, dislodges, and is transported to one of the cerebral blood vessels that is too small for its passage). **Cerebral hemorrhage** (the bursting of a blood vessel in the brain caused by trauma, arterial brittleness, or aneurysm) is also a cause of stroke. An **aneurysm** is a weak spot in an artery that forms a balloonlike pouch that can rupture. It may be a congenital defect or the result of uncontrolled or poorly controlled hypertension.

Between 70 and 80 percent of all strokes are due to a thrombus or an embolus. Brain cells that were once supplied by these blood vessels die and do not regenerate. As a result, the functional losses that occur (e.g., paralysis on one side of the body, difficulty speaking) cannot be fully recovered. The fact that brain cells die also means that treatment will not be very effective. Many stroke victims are unable to return to a normal lifestyle unless the stroke was mild, in which case a full recovery is possible.

Strokes that are caused by hemorrhages result in a 50 percent mortality rate. Victims die from the pressure imposed by blood leaking into the brain. Those who survive this type of stroke are likely to recover more of their normal functions than are those whose strokes were caused by a blood clot. The blood that spills in and on the brain during a hemorrhagic stroke produces pressure that gradually abates as the blood is absorbed by the body. Function is regained as the pressure relents.

On many occasions a stroke is preceded by warning signs and signals days, weeks, or months before a major stroke. These must be recognized and then acted on so that prompt medical and lifestyle interventions may be instituted to prevent or delay a stroke.

Just the Facts

Stroke: The Warning Signs

The American Heart Association suggests that people be familiar with the following warning signs:

- Temporary loss of speech or difficulty in speaking or understanding speech
- Unexplained dizziness, unsteadiness, or sudden falls
- Temporary dimness or loss of vision, particularly in one eye
- Sudden, temporary weakness or numbness of the face, arm, and leg on one side of the body
- Occurrence of a series of minor strokes, or transient ischemic attacks (TIAs)

Preventing a stroke is similar to preventing coronary heart disease. Both involve blood pressure and cholesterol control, smoking cessation, weight management, exercise, and proper nutrition. See Just the Facts: Stroke: The Warning Signs, which identifies the major warning signs.

Risk Factors for Heart Disease

The risk factors for cardiovascular disease have been categorized by the American Heart Association (AHA) as follows: (1) major risk factors that cannot be changed (increasing age, male gender, and heredity), (2) major risk factors that can be changed (elevated blood cholesterol levels, high blood pressure, cigarette smoking, physical inactivity, and obesity), and (3) other contributing factors (diabetes and stress) (figure 2-5).

These risk factors account for the majority of cardiovascular disease in the United States. However, there are many other factors that can be involved, some of which are backed by a sound and growing body of evidence. These include high serum homocysteine, lipoprotein (a), high blood fibrinogen, and high blood insulin levels. Other possible risk factors, supported by inconclusive evidence, include short stature, baldness, ear lobe creases, high serum uric acid level, and others. A few of the more important of these risk factors are covered later in this chapter.

Major Risk Factors That Cannot Be Changed

Age

Approximately 55 percent of all heart attacks occur in people who are 65 years of age or older. This age group accounts for more than 80 percent of fatal heart attacks.[1]

Male Gender

Until recently, the incidence of coronary heart disease among women was largely unexplored. Men have been the primary subjects in coronary heart disease and risk factor studies because of the high incidence of both among men. However, coronary heart disease is also the leading cause of death and disability among women, accounting for almost 250,000 deaths annually.[1] Women have less heart disease than men, particularly before menopause. See Wellness Across the Generations: Women and Coronary Disease: Pre- and Postmenopause.

An alarming trend in recent years is the increased incidence of heart attacks in premenopausal women

Risk factors that cannot be changed

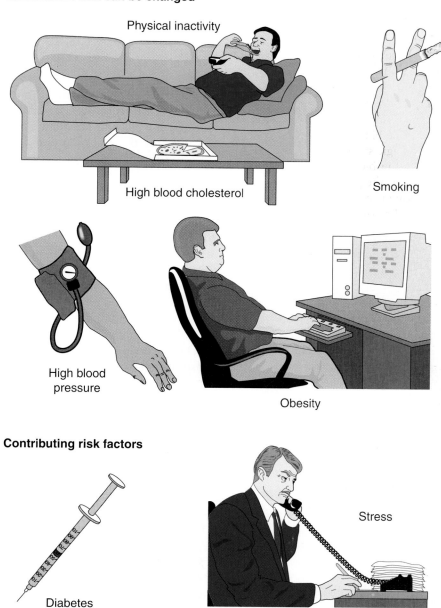

Increasing age   Male gender   Heredity

Risk factors that can be changed

Physical inactivity

High blood cholesterol   Smoking

High blood
pressure

Obesity

Contributing risk factors

Stress

Diabetes

Figure 2-5 Cardiovascular Disease Risk Factors

Wellness Across the Generations

Women and Coronary Heart Disease: Pre- and Postmenopause

Heart attacks are relatively rare among premenopausal women because of the production and presence of estrogen (the female sex hormone responsible for the development of secondary sexual characteristics and the various phases of the menstrual cycle and essential for bone formation). Estrogen is also protective in that it lowers LDL cholesterol (the harmful form), raises HDL cholesterol (the protective form), and may increase blood flow to the heart.

During and after menopause, the production of estrogen decreases and eventually stops, and the protection from heart disease diminishes. Women tend to develop coronary heart disease about ten years later than men. By age 65 the risk for men and women equalizes.[10]

To maintain a lower risk after menopause women should consider estrogen replacement therapy (ERT), because this form of therapy can cut the risk of coronary heart disease in half. ERT is particularly beneficial for women who have had a previous heart attack or for those who are at high risk because of cigarette smoking, high blood pressure, high cholesterol, obesity, or physical inactivity. However, ERT may not be appropriate for all postmenopausal women because it increases the risk for breast cancer.

Women should make the decision regarding ERT replacement in consultation with their physicians who are aware of their heart disease risk and who know their family histories of breast cancer.

who have been smoking cigarettes long enough for it to affect their health, especially when combined with oral contraceptive use.

Heredity

According to the American Heart Association, "A tendency toward heart disease or atherosclerosis appears to be hereditary, so children of parents with cardiovascular disease are more likely to develop it themselves."[1] A history of first-degree male relatives (father, grandfather, and brothers) who have coronary heart disease or who died of coronary heart disease before the age of 55 or first-degree female relatives (mother, grandmother, and sisters) who have coronary heart disease or who died of coronary heart disease before the age of 65 indicates a strong familial tendency.[2] If the family history is positive, the modifiable risk factors must be controlled.

Although age, male gender, and heredity are major risks that are not under our direct control, we can modify their effects by living a wellness lifestyle. Abstaining from tobacco products; exercising regularly; controlling blood pressure, cholesterol, and body weight; managing stress; and maintaining a social support system can lessen the impact of these unchangeable risk factors.

Major Risk Factors That Can Be Changed

Cholesterol

Cholesterol is a steroid that is an essential structural component of neural tissue; it is used in the construction of cell walls and for the manufacture of hormones and bile (for the digestion and absorption of fats). A certain amount of cholesterol is required for good health, but high levels in the blood are associated with heart attacks and strokes.

The American Heart Association suggests that Americans reduce cholesterol consumption to less than 300 milligrams per day (300 mg/day), that fat intake be reduced to a maximum of 30 percent of the total calories consumed, and that saturated fat be reduced to no more than 10 percent of the total calories. Many authorities are convinced that limiting total fat and saturated fat is more important than being overly restrictive of cholesterol.

Data from 1987 to 1992 indicate that total fat consumption in the United States decreased by 6 percent, whereas saturated fat intake decreased by 11 percent. This parallels the decline in consumption of animal flesh and animal products.[11] Although this is a small step in the right direction, the fact is that the dietary intake of saturated fat remains too high, at 12 percent of total calories.[12] Many authorities recommend that saturated fat consumption make up no more than 8 percent of total calories. They also suggest that the most effective approach to lowering serum cholesterol is to reduce the intake of saturated fat in order to slow down the liver's production of cholesterol. At the same time, it is also a good idea to lower dietary cholesterol.

Americans have made substantial progress in reducing cholesterol consumption. The average cholesterol consumed by men and women respectively in 1960 was

704 mg/day and 493 mg/day.[13] By 1994, cholesterol intake had dropped to 376 mg/day for men and 259 mg/day for women.

Cholesterol is consumed in the diet (exogenous, or dietary cholesterol), but it is also manufactured by the body from saturated fats (endogenous). A normally functioning adult liver manufactures 1500 to 2500 mg of cholesterol daily.[14] The cells lining the small intestine provide another 500 mg daily, so the body is manufacturing up to 3000 mg/day.

If you add the typical dietary intake of 259 to 376 mg/day to this total, you can see that the body must process, use, or remove considerable amounts of cholesterol to prevent it from accumulating and clogging the arteries. The liver alone produces enough cholesterol to meet the body's needs. Therefore, consuming cholesterol is not necessary to maintain health. Table 2-1 lists some common foods that contain cholesterol and saturated fat.

A number of population studies during the last twenty years have indicated a positive relationship between serum cholesterol (the level of cholesterol circulating in the blood) and the development of coronary heart disease. The National Heart, Lung, and Blood Institute reviewed this evidence and concluded that high circulating levels of serum cholesterol cause heart disease.

Values of serum cholesterol above 200 milligrams per deciliter (mg/dl) of blood are higher than the average risk. Table 2-2 (on p. 45) shows the values of risk associated with total cholesterol (TC), LDL and HDL cholesterol (to be discussed shortly), and another serum lipid (blood fat), the triglycerides.

An important collaborative study involving twelve research centers throughout the United States provided clinical evidence implicating cholesterol as a culprit in coronary heart disease.[15] Half of a group of 3806 subjects was given a cholesterol-lowering drug, and the other half was given a placebo (a substance that looked like the drug but had no medicinal properties). The subjects were followed for approximately 7.4 years, at which time the data indicated that the drug group reduced their cholesterol levels by 13 percent, suffered 19 percent fewer heart attacks, and experienced 24 percent fewer fatal heart attacks. The incidence of coronary bypass surgery and angina were also significantly reduced. The researchers concluded that each 1 percent reduction in cholesterol level results in a 2 percent reduction in the risk of coronary heart disease.

A later follow-up of this study indicated that the reduction in coronary heart disease is probably closer to 3 percent for every 1 percent that cholesterol is lowered.[16] The strategies for lowering cholesterol in the blood are presented in Real-World Wellness: Strategies for Lowering Cholesterol.

The cholesterol carriers. The amount of cholesterol circulating in the blood accounts for only part of the total cholesterol in the body. Unlike sugar and salt, cholesterol does not dissolve in the blood, so it is transported by protein packages, which facilitate its solubility. These transporters are the lipoproteins that are manufactured by the body. They include the chylomicrons, very low-density lipoprotein (VLDL), intermediate-density lipoprotein (IDL), low-density lipoprotein (LDL), and high-density lipoprotein (HDL). Dietary cholesterol enters the body from the digestive system attached to the chylomicrons. The chylomicrons shrink as they give up their cholesterol to the cells of the body. The fragments that remain are removed by the liver and used to manufacture and secrete VLDLs, which are triglyceride-rich lipoproteins. The triglycerides represent 99 percent of the stored fats in the body. The VLDLs are degraded as their cargo of triglycerides is either used by the cells for energy or stored in adipose cells. The VLDL remnants may be removed by the liver or converted to LDLs (figure 2-6).

Table 2-1 Sources of Dietary Cholesterol and Saturated Fat

	Cholesterol (mg)*	Saturated Fat (g)**		Cholesterol (mg)*	Saturated Fat (g)**
Meats (3 oz.)			**Seafood (3 oz.)**		
Beef liver	372	2.5	Squid	153	.4
Veal	86	4.0	Oily fish	59	1.2
Pork	80	3.2	Lean fish	59	.3
Lean beef	56	2.4	Shrimp (6 large)	48	.2
Chicken (dark meat)	82	2.7	Clams (6 large)	36	.3
Chicken (white meat)	76	1.3	Lobster	46.4	.08
Egg	274	1.7			
			Other items of interest		
Dairy products (1 cup; cheese, 1 oz.)					
Ice cream	59	8.9	Pork brains (3 oz.)	2,169	1.8
Whole milk	33	5.1	Beef kidney (3 oz.)	683	3.8
Butter (1 tsp.)	31	7.1	Beef hot dog (1)	75	9.9
Yogurt (low fat)	11	1.8	Prime ribs of beef (3 oz.)	66.5	5.3
Cheddar	30	6.0	Doughnut	36	4.0
American	27	5.6	Milk chocolate	0	16.3
Camembert	20	4.3	Green or yellow vegetable or fruit	0	Trace
Parmesan	8	2.0	Peanut butter (1 tbsp.)	0	1.5
			Angel food cake	0	1.96
			Skim milk (1 cup)	4	.3
Oils (1 tbsp.)			Cheese pizza (3 oz.)	6	.8
Coconut	0	11.8	Buttermilk (1 cup)	9	1.3
Palm	0	6.7	Ice milk, soft (1 cup)	13	2.9
Olive	0	1.8	Turkey, white meat (3 oz.)	59	.9
Corn	0	1.7			
Safflower	0	1.2			

*There are 1000 mg in a gram.

**There are 28 g in an ounce and 454 g in a pound.

Real-World Wellness

Strategies for Lowering Cholesterol

My doctor told me that my cholesterol level is too high. How can I lower it to reduce my risk of having a heart attack or stroke?

First, establish a realistic goal, such as about how much you think you can lower your cholesterol. Second, identify the lifestyle changes that can lower cholesterol. Third, attempt to do all of the following that apply to you:

- Reduce your fat consumption to less than 30 percent of total calories (25 percent would be better).

- Reduce your saturated fat consumption to less than 10 percent of total calories (8 percent would be better).

- Reduce your dietary cholesterol to less than 300 mg/day (less than 200 mg/day would be better).

- Lose weight if you are overweight.

- Stop smoking cigarettes and/or stop using other tobacco products.

- Increase your consumption of soluble fiber, found in fruits, vegetables, and grains.

- Do aerobic exercise at least three to four times per week for at least 30 minutes each time.

If these strategies fail to normalize your cholesterol level in six months, you may have to consider taking cholesterol-lowering drugs.

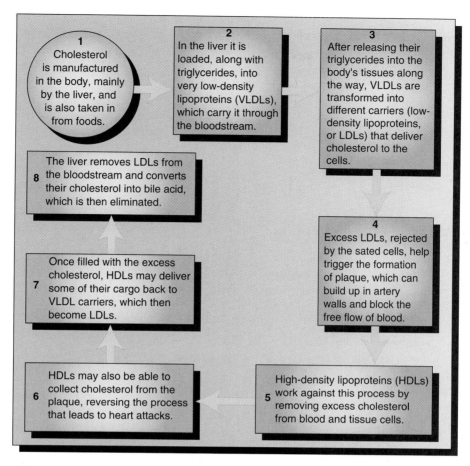

1. Cholesterol is manufactured in the body, mainly by the liver, and is also taken in from foods.

2. In the liver it is loaded, along with triglycerides, into very low-density lipoproteins (VLDLs), which carry it through the bloodstream.

3. After releasing their triglycerides into the body's tissues along the way, VLDLs are transformed into different carriers (low-density lipoproteins, or LDLs) that deliver cholesterol to the cells.

4. Excess LDLs, rejected by the sated cells, help trigger the formation of plaque, which can build up in artery walls and block the free flow of blood.

5. High-density lipoproteins (HDLs) work against this process by removing excess cholesterol from blood and tissue cells.

6. HDLs may also be able to collect cholesterol from the plaque, reversing the process that leads to heart attacks.

7. Once filled with the excess cholesterol, HDLs may deliver some of their cargo back to VLDL carriers, which then become LDLs.

8. The liver removes LDLs from the bloodstream and converts their cholesterol into bile acid, which is then eliminated.

Figure 2-6 Cholesterol Carriers

LDLs are the primary transporters of cholesterol and the most capable of producing atherosclerosis. Michael S. Brown and Joseph L. Goldstein won a 1985 Nobel Prize in medicine and physiology for discovering that the liver and the cells of the body have receptor sites that bind LDLs, removing them from circulation. The liver contains 50 to 75 percent of these sites; the remainder are in other cells of the body. When LDL concentrations are excessive, the liver sites become saturated, and further removal of them from the blood is significantly impeded. As a result, plasma levels of cholesterol rise, leading to the formation and development of atherosclerotic plaque.

The development of atherosclerosis in the coronary arteries is very complex. The *lipid oxidation theory* represents the latest thinking of the scientific community regarding the formation of plaque and therefore the growth and progress of atherosclerosis. This theory proposes that the initial event in the atherosclerotic process is an injury (lesion) that occurs to the inner lining of the arteries. Such injuries occur because of prolonged exposure to tobacco smoke, high blood pressure, elevated LDL cholesterol, diabetes mellitus, high amounts of serum homocysteine, and viral and bacterial infections.[3] These injuries, which occur at multiple sites, allow LDL cholesterol to infiltrate under the artery lining, where they become oxidized (come in contact with oxygen). Oxidized LDLs become toxic and trigger the body's immune system to destroy them. The process of destroying oxidized LDLs contributes to the formation of plaque. Generally, two to three decades after the atherosclerotic process begins, plaque has progressed to the point that one or more arteries become so narrowed that a blood clot or spasm occurs, shutting off blood supply to a portion of the heart muscle. The result is a heart attack. See figure 2-7 for an illustration of this process.

Heart attacks are rare when LDL values in the blood are below 100 mg/dl. A national panel of experts has developed guidelines for safe and unsafe levels of LDL, and these appear in table 2-2. A high circulating level of LDL cholesterol is positively related to cardiovascular disease. Weight loss, a diet low in saturated fat and total fat, exercise, and medication (if needed) will lower LDL levels in the blood.

HDLs are involved in reverse transport; that is, they accept cholesterol from the blood and tissues and transfer it to VLDLs and LDLs for transport to the

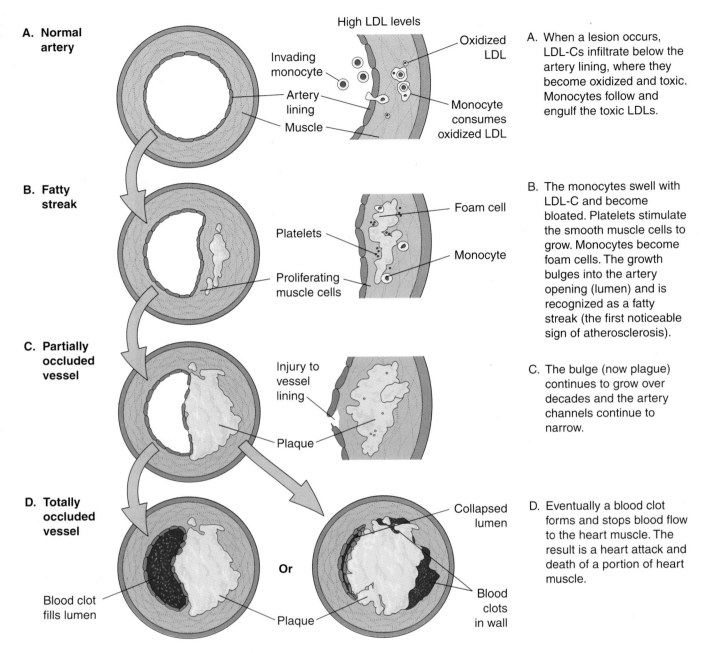

A. Normal artery

High LDL levels

Invading monocyte

Oxidized LDL

Artery lining

Muscle

Monocyte consumes oxidized LDL

A. When a lesion occurs, LDL-Cs infiltrate below the artery lining, where they become oxidized and toxic. Monocytes follow and engulf the toxic LDLs.

B. Fatty streak

Platelets

Foam cell

Proliferating muscle cells

Monocyte

B. The monocytes swell with LDL-C and become bloated. Platelets stimulate the smooth muscle cells to grow. Monocytes become foam cells. The growth bulges into the artery opening (lumen) and is recognized as a fatty streak (the first noticeable sign of atherosclerosis).

C. Partially occluded vessel

Injury to vessel lining

Plaque

C. The bulge (now plague) continues to grow over decades and the artery channels continue to narrow.

D. Totally occluded vessel

Blood clot fills lumen

Or

Plaque

Collapsed lumen

Blood clots in wall

D. Eventually a blood clot forms and stops blood flow to the heart muscle. The result is a heart attack and death of a portion of heart muscle.

Figure 2-7 Progression of Atherosclerosis and Coronary Artery Disease

liver, where it can be degraded, disposed of, or recycled. HDLs protect the arteries from atherosclerosis by clearing cholesterol from the blood. Cardiovascular health depends greatly on low levels of total cholesterol and LDLs and a high level of HDLs. Cigarette smoking, diabetes, elevated triglyceride levels, and anabolic steroids lower HDL, whereas physical exercise, weight loss, and moderate alcohol consumption raise it.

Moderate alcohol consumption (two drinks or less per day) increases HDL cholesterol levels. An alcoholic drink is defined as a 5-ounce glass of wine or a 12-ounce beer or 1½ ounces of 80-proof spirits. How-

ever, alcohol is a depressant that impairs judgment and removes inhibitions so that people under its influence behave in ways they ordinarily would not while sober. Alcohol consumption is not an acceptable way to raise HDL cholesterol. (See Chapter 10 for a more complete discussion of the effects of alcohol.)

Table 2-2 presents the current guidelines for HDL cholesterol levels in the blood. The higher the HDL, the greater the protection from cardiovascular disease. The average value for men is 45 mg/dl, and for women it is 55 mg/dl.[17] This biological difference in HDL levels between genders partly explains the lower incidence of

Table 2-2 Risk Profile—Lipid and Lipoprotein Concentrations

	Total Cholesterol (mg/dl)	LDL Cholesterol (mg/dl)	HDL Cholesterol (mg/dl)	Triglycerides (mg/dl)
High risk	≥245*	≥190	≤35†	≥1000
Moderate risk	221–244	160–189	36–44	500–999
Mild risk	201–220	130–159	45–54	250–499
Average risk	182–200	100–129	55–65	151–249
Low risk	<182‡	<100	≥65	≤150

*≥ Equal to or greater

†≤ Equal to or less

‡< Less than

Data are from a variety of sources, including the MRFIT study, NIH Consensus Conference, National Cholesterol Program, and Framingham Heart Study, as compiled by Goldberg, L., and D. L. Elliot. 1994. The use of exercise to improve lipid and lipoprotein levels. In *Exercise for Prevention and Treatment of Illness*, eds. L. Goldberg and D. L. Elliot. Philadelphia: F. A. Davis Co.

Table 2-3 Ratio of Total Cholesterol to HDL Cholesterol

Risk	Men	Women
Very low (one-half average)	<3.4	<3.3
Low risk	4.0	3.8
Average risk	5.0	4.5
Moderate risk (two times average)	9.5	7.0
High risk (three times average)	>23	>11

heart disease in premenopausal women as compared with men. After menopause, HDL levels in women begin to decrease, as does their protection provided by this subfraction of cholesterol. The ratio between total cholesterol (TC) and HDL (TC/HDL) should also be considered when the risk is interpreted. This ratio is determined by dividing TC by HDL (table 2-3).[17]

Another blood fat, the serum triglycerides, is involved in the development and progression of atherosclerosis. Average serum triglycerides, depending on age and gender, range from 50 mg/dl to 200 mg/dl. Table 2-2 identifies the risk associated with various serum triglyceride levels.

High serum triglycerides usually coexist with low HDL cholesterol, a proven risk factor for cardiovascular disease. Teasing out the independent effect of serum triglyceride levels has been difficult. But recent evidence has shown that high levels are a modest independent risk factor for heart disease and a very reliable predictor when coupled with low HDL cholesterol.[18]

Serum triglycerides greater than 190 mg/dl increase blood viscosity (blood thickness), resulting in sluggish blood flow. Viscous blood is more difficult to circulate, so oxygen and nutrients are not delivered as efficiently to the body's tissues, and these include the heart muscle.[19]

Table 2-2 shows the relative risk posed by high serum triglycerides. Levels below 150 mg/dl are in the low-risk category, but newer evidence suggests that an optimal level is below 100 mg/dl.[20]

A number of studies have shown that sedentary people with high triglycerides can reduce serum triglycerides by as much as 45 percent when they participate regularly in moderately intense exercise. Physically fit people metabolize serum triglycerides more effectively than do sedentary people and are able to clear these triglycerides from the blood more rapidly after a high-fat meal.[20]

Other strategies for lowering serum triglycerides include weight loss; reductions in dietary sugar, fat, and alcohol; and the substitution of fish for meat a couple of times during the week. Increasing fish consumption, as long as it is not fried, lowers the dietary intake of calories and saturated fat and increases the intake of omega-3 fatty acids, which tend to lower serum triglycerides.

Blood pressure

Blood pressure, which is recorded in millimeters of mercury (mmHg), is the force exerted against the walls of the arteries as blood travels through the circulatory system. Pressure is created when the heart contracts and pumps blood into the arteries. The arterioles (smallest arteries) offer resistance to blood flow, and if

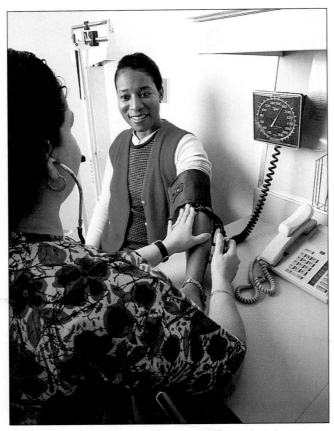

Keeping your blood pressure under control helps keep your heart healthy.

Table 2-4 Classification of Blood Pressure for Adults Age 18 Years and Older

Category	Systolic (mmHg)	Diastolic (mmHg)
Normal	<130	<85
High normal	130–139	85–89
Hypertension		
Stage 1 (mild)	140–159	90–99
Stage 2 (moderate)	160–179	100–109
Stage 3 (severe)	180–209	110–119
Stage 4 (very severe)	≥210	≥120

the resistance is persistently high, the pressure rises and remains high. The medical term for high blood pressure is **hypertension.**

Hypertension is a silent disease that has no characteristic signs or symptoms, so blood pressure should be checked periodically. Blood pressure can be measured quickly with a sphygmomanometer. A cuff is wrapped around the upper arm and inflated with enough air to compress the artery, temporarily stopping blood flow. A stethoscope is placed on the artery below the cuff so that the sound of blood coursing through the artery can be heard when the air is released. The first sound represents the systolic pressure (the maximum pressure of blood flow when the heart contracts), and the last sound heard is the diastolic pressure (the minimum pressure of blood flow between heart beats). A typical pressure for young adults is 120/80. Pressures of 140/90 or greater are considered to be hypertensive.[1] The lower limit of normal is 100/60. From a health perspective, having a low to normal blood pressure and maintaining it as long as possible is advantageous.

Standards for classifying blood pressure in adults appear in table 2-4. This table represents the latest thinking among medical researchers about the stages of

blood pressure values. All hypertensive values in the table represent an increased risk for cardiovascular and kidney disease. The higher the blood pressure, the greater the risk. The lower the blood pressure (within normal range), the better. For example, a 2 mmHg decrease in systolic blood pressure is estimated to reduce the risk of mortality from stroke by 6 percent and from coronary heart disease by 4 percent.[21]

Approximately 50 million American adults and children have high blood pressure, and 35,130 people die of its complications annually.[1] The cause of high blood pressure is not known in 90 to 95 percent of the cases. This is referred to as *essential hypertension. Essential* is a medical term that means "of unknown origin or cause." Essential hypertension cannot be cured, but it can be controlled. The other 5 to 10 percent of the cases of hypertension have a specific cause. If the cause can be determined and eliminated, blood pressure will return to normal.

The heart is adversely affected by uncontrolled or undiagnosed hypertension of long duration. Pumping blood for years against high resistance in the arteries increases the workload of the heart, and it becomes enlarged in response to the strain. The heart receives inadequate rest because the resistance to blood flow is consistently high, and this produces overly stretched muscle fibers. They progressively lose the ability to rebound. The result is that they contract less forcefully. At this point the heart loses its efficiency and weakens. If intervention does not occur early, congestive heart failure is inevitable. Hypertension also damages the arteries and accelerates atherosclerosis.

Hypertension is the most important risk factor for brain attacks (strokes) as well as a major risk for heart disease. More than 500,000 brain attacks occur every year. Certain segments of the population are at higher

risk, such as African-Americans, who have more than a 60 percent greater risk of death and disability from stroke than do whites; this is a direct result of pervasive hypertension.[22] Stroke mortality is highest in African-American females who were born before 1950 and in African-American males born after 1950.

Treatment for hypertension. Treatment for hypertension may include all or some of the following: weight loss, salt and alcohol restriction, calcium and potassium supplementation, voluntary relaxation techniques, exercise, and medication. Excess body weight increases the work of the heart because it must meet the nutrient demands of the extra tissue.

High salt intake increases the blood pressure in those who are salt sensitive. Estimates indicate that at least 30 percent of Americans are salt sensitive, but the actual number is probably higher. Salt is an acquired taste that can be modified. Curbing salt consumption while blood pressure is still normal cannot hurt and it may help.

Some calcium-deficient hypertensive people may normalize their blood pressure by taking calcium supplements. However, calcium supplementation does not work for all calcium-deficient hypertensive people, and it does not work for hypertensive people who are not calcium deficient.

Yoga, meditation, hypnotherapy, biofeedback, and other relaxation techniques can lower the pressure of hypertensive people. They can also reduce the pressure of normotensive people (those with normal blood pressure).[23] Meditating hypertensive people lowered their systolic pressure by 11 points and their diastolic pressure by 6 points more than did people in a control group who were counseled on the importance of losing excess weight, exercising regularly, cutting salt consumption, and drinking less alcohol.

Many people drink alcohol because it relaxes them, but ingestion of more than 2 ounces of alcohol per day raises blood pressure in some people. The same precautions regarding the use of alcohol and HDL cholesterol apply for hypertension.

The American College of Sports Medicine (ACSM) has developed a position paper on the relationship between exercise and hypertension.[24] Some of the more important conclusions follow:

1. Endurance exercises can reduce both systolic and diastolic pressures by 10 points each in people with mild essential hypertension (with systolic pressures between 140 and 180 mmHg and diastolic pressures between 90 and 105 mmHg).
2. Moderately intense endurance exercises lower the blood pressure as much as or more than vigorous exercise.
3. Endurance exercise training delays or prevents the onset of hypertension in people who are at high risk.

4. By itself, resistive or strength training does not seem to lower the blood pressure unless it is accompanied by aerobic training and is done in a circuit (circuit training is explained in Chapter 4).

5. Physically fit hypertensive people have a lower mortality rate than do physically unfit normotensive people.

The mechanisms through which exercise lowers blood pressure in hypertensive individuals are not fully understood. The probable mechanisms include the following:

1. Exercise contributes to weight loss, which in turn lowers blood pressure.

2. Aerobic training reduces resistance to blood flow in the arteries and at rest, lowering the force required to circulate blood.

3. Many hypertensive people have elevated levels of hormones that constrict blood vessels. Exercise metabolizes these, which results in less resistance to blood flow.

4. Exercise training sensitizes the cells to insulin, so less circulates in the blood. The kidneys respond by excreting sodium, which reduces the blood pressure.

Medications that control blood pressure have been developed. However, they have side effects that include weakness, leg cramps, stuffy nose, occasional diarrhea, heartburn, drowsiness, anemia, depression, headaches, joint pain, dizziness, impotence, and skin rash. The side effects are unique to the drugs being used to control blood pressure. Despite these side effects, many people find it easier to take the medicine than to make the difficult lifestyle changes that lower blood pressure. However, the effort to control blood pressure with medication should not negate the importance of controlling lifestyle factors that contribute to hypertension. Medicine and lifestyle efforts are not mutually exclusive— each contributes to blood pressure management.

Cigarette smoking/tobacco use

Many medical authorities consider cigarette smoking the most harmful of the preventable risk factors associated with chronic illness and premature death.[25] The American Cancer Society estimates that approximately 419,000 annual deaths are related to cigarette smoking.[25] In 1987, lung cancer became the leading cause of cancer death among women, replacing breast cancer. In 1997, 66,000 women died of lung cancer compared to 44,000 who died of breast cancer. Eighty-seven percent of all lung cancers in both sexes are directly related to cigarette smoking. Additionally, smoking accounts for 29 percent of all cancer deaths. Further, it is a major cause of heart disease and is associated with chronic bronchitis, emphysema, strokes, and other diseases.

Harmful products in cigarettes. Nicotine, carbon monoxide, and other poisonous gases, tars, and chemical additives for taste and flavor are the hazardous products in cigarettes. Carbon monoxide and nicotine have a devastating effect on the heart and blood vessels. Nicotine is an addictive stimulant that increases the resting heart rate, blood pressure, and metabolism. For this reason, it should be reclassified as a drug and placed under the jurisdiction of the Food and Drug Administration (FDA).

A brief summary of nicotine's effects on the cardiovascular system is found in Just the Facts: Nicotine. Carbon monoxide, a poisonous gas that is a by-product of the combustion of tobacco products, displaces oxygen in the blood because it has a greater attraction to hemoglobin. The diminished oxygen-carrying capacity of the blood is partly responsible for the shortness of breath that smokers experience with mild physical exertion.

Cigarettes and other tobacco products are not regulated by the FDA because tobacco is not classified as a food or drug. The tobacco industry is under no mandate to disclose the nature and type of chemicals that are added to tobacco products. Some of these additives are harmful. The public has a right to know, but the tobacco industry has successfully resisted attempts by government agencies and consumer groups to force disclosure.

The harmful effects of cigarette smoking are insidious and take time to appear. The medical profession measures the damage from smoking in pack years. Smoking one pack of cigarettes per day for fifteen years is equal to 15 pack years (15 years × 1 pack per day =

Just the Facts

Nicotine

Nicotine is a powerful stimulant that does the following:

- Increases LDL and lowers HDL levels
- Causes the platelets to aggregate, increasing the probability of arterial spasms
- Increases the oxygen requirement of cardiac muscle
- Constricts blood vessels
- Produces cardiac dysrhythmias (irregular heart beat)
- Is a causative agent in the 30% of coronary heart disease deaths related to smoking
- Increases the viscosity of the blood

15 pack years). Two packs per day for fifteen years is equal to 30 pack years ($15 \times 2 = 30$). Medical problems become evident after 25 to 30 pack years.

The challenge of quitting. To quit the tobacco habit, you have to simultaneously break the addiction to nicotine and the psychological dependence on smoking. This involves changing behavior and effectively dealing with the social and situational stimuli that promote the desire to smoke. In a survey in 1984, 69 percent of smokers reported that they wanted to stop smoking.[26] Since 1964, more men than women have quit, more whites than African-Americans, and more non-Hispanics than Hispanics. More elderly people and more educated people also have higher quit rates.[27]

Complicating the effort to quit, particularly among young women, is the fear of gaining weight. Approximately 65 percent of those who quit do gain weight, but the physiological adaptations that occur may only account for a 7- to 8-pound weight gain. The physiological mechanisms responsible are probably associated with a slowing of metabolism, a slight increase in appetite, and slower transit time of food in the digestive system so that more is absorbed by the body. Weight gain beyond 8 pounds is probably caused by altered eating patterns rather than physiology. Food smells and tastes better when a person is not smoking. Food may substitute for a cigarette, especially during social activities. It may provide some of the oral gratification previously obtained from smoking, and it may relieve tension. Weight gain can be avoided by eating sensibly and exercising moderately and frequently.

As a group, smokers are 7 percent thinner than nonsmokers, but smokers tend to distribute more fat in the abdominal area.[28] The waist-to-hip ratio (WHR) is greater in smokers even though they are thinner. This fat distribution predisposes smokers to coronary heart disease, diabetes, stroke, and some forms of cancer.

Passive smoking and smokeless tobacco. Involuntary or passive smoking (inhaling the smoke of others) is associated with premature disease and death. Estimates indicate that 38,000 to 43,000 nonsmokers who are regularly exposed to environmental smoke die annually from smoking-related causes.[25] The majority of these (35,000 to 40,000) die from heart disease, and 3000 die from lung cancer. There is a dose-response effect. The more the nonsmoker is exposed to environmental smoke, the greater his or her risk for premature morbidity (illness) and mortality (death).

Children of smoking parents are more likely to experience a higher incidence of influenza, colds, bronchitis, asthma, and pneumonia. The impact of passive smoking on them can last a lifetime and may range from delayed physical and intellectual development to the hazards associated with prolonged exposure to carcinogenic substances.

An alarming trend is the escalating sale of smokeless tobacco products. Chewing tobacco and dipping snuff have become popular among high school and college men. The World Health Organization (WHO) has described the growing use of smokeless tobacco as a new threat to society. Nicotine is an addictive drug regardless of the method of delivery, and its effects are similar whether it is inhaled, as in smoking, or absorbed through the tissues of the oral cavity, as in dipping and chewing. The incidence of oral cancer may be 50 times higher among long-term users of smokeless tobacco products than among nonusers. Smokeless tobacco is addictive and deadly, and its use is rising among adolescent males.

Cigar sales in the country had been flat for twenty-five years until 1994, when sales began to increase as the result of a marketing campaign by the magazine *Cigar Aficionado,* cigar invitation-only dinners, and celebrity endorsements of cigar smoking, characterizing it as sophisticated and glamorous. Cigar smoking is no longer looked upon as the sole dominion of males; many women have taken up the habit. Cigar sales increased from 3.4 billion in 1993 to 5.1 billion in 1997.[29]

Cigars were not specifically included in the 1984 law that required tobacco companies to place labels on packages of cigarettes warning that they were hazardous to health. As a result, cigars carry no such warning label. This does not mean that cigar smoking is not harmful to health. See Just the Facts: Cigar Smoking—a Hazard to Health for the facts on cigar smoking.

Physical inactivity

Physical inactivity is finally being officially recognized as a major risk factor for cardiovascular disease by the American Heart Association.[1] The upgrading of physical inactivity, which appeared in the AHA's 1993 report, reflects the importance of participating in physical activities regularly. The AHA made the upgrade because the weight of the evidence that has been accumulating in the last few decades shows that exercise produces many important health benefits. This is good news for those who have been physically active, and it may motivate some sedentary people to become active.

Physical inactivity (hypokinesis) is debilitating to the human body. A couple of weeks of bed rest or chair rest produce muscle atrophy, bone demineralization, and decreases in aerobic capacity and maximum breathing capacity. Your body was constructed for and thrives on physical exertion.

Just the Facts

Cigar Smoking: A Hazard to Health

A common assumption is that cigar smoking is not as hazardous as cigarette smoking, because people usually don't inhale cigar smoke. The facts regarding the dangers of cigar smoking are as follows:

- Cigars contain nicotine, carbon monoxide, tars, and poisonous gases.

- Nicotine reaches the brain by being absorbed through the lining of the mouth rather than from the lungs, but the effect is the same. See Just the Facts: Nicotine for a summary of nicotine's harmful effects on the heart and blood vessels.

- Most of the same cancer-producing substances found in cigarettes are also present in cigars.

- Overall cancer deaths are 34 percent higher for men who smoke cigars than for men who do not.

- Cigar smokers have 4 to 10 times more risk of dying from mouth and throat cancers than do nonsmokers.

Two major reviews have shown that physical inactivity poses a significant risk for developing heart disease. In one review, the researchers critiqued forty-three studies and concluded that physical inactivity increased the risk for coronary heart disease by 1.5 to 2.4 times.[30] The risk associated with physical inactivity is similar to that of the other major risk factors. According to the Centers for Disease Control and Prevention, the need for regular exercise by the general public should be promoted as vigorously as efforts to control blood pressure, lower cholesterol, and stop smoking. A later review by another team of researchers concluded that inactive people have a 90 percent greater risk for developing coronary heart disease than do active people.[31]

With few exceptions, the results of later studies are consistent with the results of these two reviews. Some of the more recent studies have indicated a dose-response relationship between level of physical activity and cardiovascular disease.[32] This means that (1) men at high risk who regularly participate in light- to moderate-intensity physical activity expending about 1500 calories per week will likely lower their risk for coronary heart disease by about 25 percent to 50 percent, and (2) men who engage regularly in more intense physical activity (above the moderate level) lower their risk for coronary heart disease by 60 to 70 percent and experience greater longevity.

Several studies examined the effect on coronary heart disease of level of physical fitness rather than of total numbers of calories expended per week in physical activity. These studies corroborated the results of the calorie expenditure studies that physically fit people are less inclined to develop coronary heart disease than are unfit people. (Thus far, only one long-term study has included women in the subject population.[33])

In summary, people who are actively engaged in leisure-time or occupational physical activity as well as those who participate in physical activities for the purpose of developing fitness are at a lower risk of death from cardiovascular disease and all-cause mortality. Other major studies have supported the view that people who regularly engage in physical activities of moderate intensity have significantly fewer heart attacks and experience fewer deaths from all causes than do people who exercise little or not at all. Moderate activity was described as the equivalent of walking 1 to 2 miles per day for a total of 5 to 10 miles per week. The greatest health benefits were gained by those who expended 1500 to 2000 calories per week (15 to 20 miles of walking) in physical activity. A total of 17,000 men were followed for more than thirty years. Those who regularly walked, climbed stairs, or participated in sports activities decreased their risk from all causes of mortality. Those who expended a minimum of 500 calories per week (5 miles of walking or its equivalent) to a maximum of 3500 calories per week (35 miles of walking or its equivalent) experienced a progressive increase in longevity.

Investigators at the Cooper Institute for Aerobics Research[33] studied the relationship between physical fitness and mortality from all causes. The uniqueness of this study was twofold: first, the researchers measured the physical fitness levels of all subjects by treadmill testing, and second, more than 3000 of the 13,344 subjects were women. Because of their lower risk for cardiovascular disease, women have essentially been neglected as subjects in heart disease studies.

The results of this study indicated that a low physical fitness level increased the risk for both men and women of death from cardiovascular disease, cancer, and all other forms of disease. The difference in all-cause mortality was greatest between those who were in the moderately fit category and those in the low-fit category. The difference between the moderately fit and the highly fit was insignificant. For people who exercise regularly, the risk of dying from a heart attack is 35 to 55 percent less than it is for sedentary people.[34]

A study using only women as subjects investigated the physical fitness benefits versus the health benefits of three levels of walking intensity.[35] One group walked at 5 MPH, a second group walked at 4 MPH, and a third group walked at 3 MPH. The results showed that physical fitness improved on a predictable dose-response basis. The fastest walkers improved the most and the slowest walkers improved the least, but the cardiovascular risk was reduced equally among the three groups. Low-level exercise was as effective as the highest level in promoting cardiovascular health. Exercise for health does not have to be as strenuous as exercise for physical fitness.

The American College of Sports Medicine and the Centers for Disease Control and Prevention reacted to the results of these studies by jointly issuing a new recommendation for exercise for Americans. The new guideline states that "every U.S. adult should accumulate 30 minutes or more of moderate intensity physical activity on most, preferably all, days of the week."[36] This is a minimum guideline for exercise and was not intended to replace previous recommendations regarding more vigorous exercise for the purpose of improving physical fitness. Instead, the recommendation is directed at that 60 percent of our population who are sedentary or marginally active. Health professionals hope that the new recommendation will motivate physically inactive and underactive Americans to participate in a more active lifestyle.

The term *physical activity* refers to any physical movement that results in energy expenditure. Physical activity includes but is not limited to walking, climbing stairs, mowing the lawn (using a riding mower does not count), raking leaves without a blower, mopping and vacuuming floors, washing and waxing the car (by hand), dancing, and playing with children and grandchildren. Moderate intensity physical activity can be achieved by walking 3 to 4 miles per hour or through any other activity that burns as many calories as walking at those speeds.

People who consistently exercise above the moderate level not only receive the health benefits but also develop a higher level of physical fitness. Those who exercise in accordance with the new guidelines gain about the same health benefits as those who are more physically active, but they will not attain the same degree of physical fitness. That 60 percent of the population who are inclined to ignore the advice to exercise regularly can become part of the estimated 250,000 premature deaths per year that are attributed to a **sedentary** lifestyle.

The health and longevity returns from exercise and a physically active lifestyle are significant. Estimates indicate that longevity is increased by 1 minute for every minute spent walking and by 2 minutes for every minute spent jogging.[37] The potential for improving the health status of Americans through appropriate lifestyle behaviors is evident from estimates indicating

that 60 percent of all deaths are premature and approximately 50 to 60 percent of all illness and disabilities are preventable.[38]

Obesity

Obesity strains the heart and co-exists with many of the modifiable risk factors that promote cardiovascular disease. Obese people who have no other risk factors are still more likely to develop heart disease or stroke. Obesity contributes to approximately 300,000 deaths annually in the United States. Not only is obesity associated with an increased risk for heart disease, but the manner in which fat is distributed in the body might also accentuate the risk.[39] Fat that accumulates in the upper half of the body (referred to as *visceral* or *central abdominal obesity*) is likely to be accompanied by high triglycerides, low HDL cholesterol, insulin resistance, and hypertension. This cluster of factors is called *syndrome X,* and it is associated with a significant increase in the likelihood of developing cardiovascular disease.

Obese people can lower their risk with a modest weight loss of 5 to 10 percent. This is a realistic, attainable goal. But the risk remains lower only if the loss of weight is maintained. Approximately 95 percent of people who lose weight regain it in a few years. Although dieting is the primary method for losing weight, regular exercise is the most effective method for maintaining the loss. Diet and exercise are not mutually exclusive; instead, they compliment each other, and both are important players in weight management.

Diabetes mellitus

Diabetes mellitus is a metabolic disorder in which the body cannot make use of sugar (glucose) as a fuel. The hormone insulin must be produced and secreted into the bloodstream so that blood sugar can be transported into the cells. The cells have receptor sites to which insulin attaches, making the cell amenable to the entrance of sugar.

In type I diabetes, no insulin is produced, and so it must be injected daily. Type I, insulin-dependent diabetes mellitus (IDDM), usually occurs early in life. Type II, or non–insulin-dependent diabetes mellitus (NIDDM), occurs in middle-aged, overweight, sedentary adults. Excessive weight is a factor because it increases cellular resistance to insulin so that more insulin than normal is required to effect the passage of sugar from the blood to the cells. In contrast, exercise decreases insulin resistance, making cellular membranes more permeable to sugar. About 90 percent of all diabetes mellitus is of the type II variety. Data indicate that at least 75 percent of new cases of type II diabetes can be prevented through regular exercise and maintaining normal weight.[40]

Nurturing Your Spirituality

Can Stress and Depression Make You Sick?

A convincing body of evidence suggests that chronic anger, anxiety, loneliness, or depression can be catastrophic for people with coronary artery disease.[42] At the same time, emerging evidence shows that these same mood states and feelings in healthy people may increase the likelihood of developing heart disease in the future.

Scientists are beginning to unravel the connection between mood states and heart disease. Consistently high levels of stress hormones circulating in the bloodstream suppress the immune system by interfering with the normal repair and maintenance functions of the body. This increases one's vulnerability to infections and disease. Continuing high levels of cortisol and norepinephrine stimulate a prolonged fight or flight response that can eventually lead to wear and tear on the heart and arteries. Frequent and prolonged periods of stress increase blood pressure, and that usually leads to injuries of the artery walls. These injuries are the first step in the development and ultimate progression of atherosclerosis.[43] Data indicate that exaggerated responses to stress may be a triggering mechanism for heart attack and stroke.

Depression (prolonged sadness beyond a reasonable length of time) also stimulates the production of stress hormones. Depression that occurs later in life increases the risk of coronary heart disease in two ways: (1) by reducing blood flow to the heart in those whose blood vessels are narrowed and (2) by causing heart rhythm disturbances.[44]

Scientists have much to learn about the relationship between the heart and mind. Physicians are beginning to acknowledge that depression is a significant factor in producing cardiovascular complications for those who already have heart disease. The good news is that depression is treatable. Mild depression responds to regular exercise and voluntary relaxation techniques, both of which reduce the production of stress hormones. On the other hand, severe depression requires psychological counseling and medication plus regular exercise and relaxation training. Eighty percent of all people with severe depression respond to treatment.

Regular exercise promotes relaxation, reduces the response to stress, enhances emotional well-being, and lowers cardiac reactivity (high heart rate, blood pressure, and resistance to blood flow). Cardiac reactivity occurs when modest stressors produce physiological responses by the heart and circulatory system that are out of proportion to the stressor. If these occur frequently, the development of atherosclerosis may well be the result.

Exercise acts as a safety valve that enables people to "let off steam" in a constructive way. Jogging, swimming, cycling, weight training, racquetball, and other exercises focus our energies in worthwhile pursuits that rid the body of stress products that have accumulated. Exercise training, which is a physiological stressor, helps build tolerance to psychological and emotional stressors. In other words, the "physiological toughness" developed through exercise training enables us to cope more effectively with other types of stressors.[45]

Do stress and depression cause heart attacks? The answer is a qualified "yes." We should have a more definitive answer after a few more years of research.

Diabetes mellitus has numerous long-range complications. These primarily involve degenerative disorders of the blood vessels and nerves. Diabetics who die prematurely are usually the victims of cardiovascular lesions and accelerated atherosclerosis. The incidence of heart attacks and strokes is higher among diabetics than nondiabetics. In fact, diabetes increases the risk of coronary artery disease by 2 to 3 times the normal rate in men and 3 to 7 times the normal rate in women.

The arteries supplying the kidneys, eyes, and legs are particularly susceptible to atherosclerosis. Kidney failure is one of the long-term complications of diabetes. Diabetes is also the leading cause of blindness in U.S. adults. Impaired delivery of blood to the legs may lead to gangrene, necessitating amputation of the affected tissues. In addition to circulatory problems, degenerative lesions in the nervous system may result, leading to multiple diseases that result in dysfunction of the brain, spinal cord, and peripheral nerves. Unfortunately, medical science has been unable to identify the biological mechanisms responsible for these long-term vascular and neural complications. However, these complications can be mitigated by leading a balanced, well-regulated life, thereby keeping diabetes under control. Control includes dietary manipulation, exercise, weight control, rest, and medication if needed.

The landmark Physician's Health Study was the first major effort to show that exercise reduced the risk of developing type II diabetes. The physicians participating in the study who exercised vigorously five or more times per week had a 42 percent greater reduction in the incidence of type II diabetes than did those who exercised less than one time per week. The reduction in risk was particularly pronounced among those at greatest risk: the obese. The researchers concluded that at least 24 percent of all cases of type II diabetes were related to sedentary living. Even high-risk men (those who were overweight and had a parental history of diabetes) benefited from regular exercise. Every 500 calories burned per week in leisure-time physical activity reduced the risk of type II diabetes by 6 percent.[41]

Stress

Stress is difficult to define and quantify. Authorities agree that distress, or chronic stress, produces a complex array of physiological changes in the body. Together, these physiological events are called the *fight or flight response*. The hormones that are released by the body during these events produce the stress response. This includes (1) increases in heart rate, breathing rate, blood pressure; (2) the tendency for blood platelets to aggregate (clump together); (3) blood sugar rushing to the muscles to provide more energy; and (4) the activation of the immune system. The stress response represents a significant strain on the body.

Stressors (events or situations that cause stress) may be acute or chronic. Acute stressors are situational and temporary. Taking a midterm exam or making an oral presentation are examples of events that provoke acute stress. When such an event is over, the body returns, within a short time, to its prior state of balance and harmony. However, chronic stress (characterized by prolonged elevations of stress hormones and a general feeling of uneasiness that permeates one's life) presents a much more serious problem. Constant worry about work, finances, or relationships or persistent feelings of anger and isolation are examples of chronic stress. Is chronic stress a causative agent in the development of chronic diseases in general and heart disease specifically? See Nurturing Your Spirituality: Can Stress and Depression Make You Sick? (p. 52)

Prevention of Heart Disease

Preventing heart disease is much preferred to treating it after the fact. Prevention includes regular exercise, maintenance of optimal body weight, sound nutritional practices, abstinence from tobacco products, nonuse of alcohol (or use in moderation), and abstinence from drugs. Dealing with stress in constructive ways, removing oneself as much as possible from destructive and disease-producing environmental conditions, and having periodic medical examinations are other aspects of prevention. It is much better physically, psychologically, and economically to make the effort to enhance health now than to reject or ignore health promotion principles and treat disease later. It is never too late to change behavior. Even patients with coronary artery disease can benefit from lifestyle changes.

Until very recently, medical thinking indicated that established atherosclerotic plaques in the coronary ar-

Stress-relieving activities, such as meditation, soothe the spirit and may even lower your risk of heart disease and other chronic illnesses. How do you manage stress?

teries were there to stay. Progression of the disease seemed inevitable unless medical corrective procedures were employed. But evidence has surfaced indicating that reversal of the disease is possible with appropriate lifestyle behaviors.

Dean Ornish showed that comprehensive behavior changes are required to reverse established coronary artery disease. Ornish devised a program that included a vegetarian diet in which only 6.8 percent of the calories came from fat; 4.4 hours of moderate aerobic exercise per week; stress-management techniques consisting of stretching exercises, practicing of breathing techniques, meditation, progressive relaxation, and the use of imagery; smoking cessation; and attendance at regular group support meetings. The subjects in this study were evaluated against a control group who received "usual and customary" care.[46]

At the end of the first year, 82 percent of the subjects in the Ornish program showed regression of atherosclerosis compared with only 10 percent of the usual care group. Over the following four years, the Ornish subjects showed further regression, whereas the usual care group experienced progression of atherosclerosis.[47]

Other investigators have examined the effect of less stringent interventions than those advocated by the Ornish program on the regression of atherosclerosis. These attempts have been less successful than the Ornish program but more successful than the usual care program.

The main criticism of the Ornish program was that lifelong compliance would be difficult. Twenty-nine percent of the study participants dropped out during the last four years of the program. It is not easy to permanently change bad habits, but the hard work associated with following a low-fat diet, exercising consistently at a moderately intense level, and giving up smoking can make people with coronary artery disease feel better and may allow them to avoid surgery.

Refer to Assessment Activity 2-1 at the end of this chapter. Respond to each of the risk questions about factors to determine your risk status.

Other Possible Risk Factors

Iron-Enriched Blood

In 1992 a study completed in Finland found that men with high levels of iron (as measured by serum ferritin) also had a high probability of incurring heart problems. Since then, a number of studies completed in the United States have failed to confirm the high iron–high heart disease connection. In fact, these American studies found quite the opposite. Women with high iron levels were found to have half the heart disease risk as women with low iron stores, and men in the high iron group were 20 percent less likely to die of heart disease than were men with the lowest levels.[48] The rationale is that low iron levels lead to a reduction in oxygen-carrying hemoglobin so that less oxygen is transported to the tissues. It is entirely possible that the decrease in oxygen transport to the cells, including the cells of the heart, is responsible for the heart problems that occur with greater frequency in those who are iron deficient.

Now that you are aware of the major risk factors for heart disease, refer to Assessment Activities 2-1 and 2-2 to test your risk and your knowledge. Be as accurate as possible when providing the necessary information for Activity 2-1. Read the case study (Assessment 2-2) and respond to all of the questions.

Homocysteine

Homocysteine is an amino acid that is derived from food. Its function is to manufacture protein to build and maintain body tissues. Homocysteine is carried through the bloodstream, and under normal conditions, it is broken down into two other amino acids.

When that breakdown does not occur, homocysteine levels rise to present a risk for heart disease. Several studies, including the Physician's Health Study and the Framingham Heart Study, showed that the probability of having a heart attack increases to 3 times the normal level in subjects with the highest homocysteine levels. This puts homocysteine on par with the other major risk factors for coronary artery disease.[49]

Homocysteine is measured in *micromoles,* which are based on molecular weight. The normal range is 4 to 15 micromoles per deciliter of blood. Heart attacks are more likely to occur to those whose levels are above 15.[50]

Homocysteine contributes to heart disease probably by damaging the inner lining of the arteries. The damage initiates the abnormal growth of smooth muscle cells, which in turn promotes the development and progression of atherosclerosis.

The good news is that homocysteine levels can be controlled with diet. The B vitamins (folic acid or folate, B_6, and B_{12}) are needed to split homocysteine into other amino acids. Folate is the most important of the three, but evidence indicates that optimal benefits occur when all three are available in appropriate amounts. The recommended daily amounts for these vitamins are 400 micrograms of folate, 6 micrograms of B_{12}, and 2 milligrams of B_6.

Lipoprotein (a) or Lp (a)

Lipoprotein (a) represents a group of particles that resemble LDL-C (the bad form of cholesterol). A high circulating level of Lp (a) in the blood may increase the risk for coronary artery disease and stroke, and although study results are not yet conclusive, they appear to be heading in that direction. Many scientists believe that high levels of Lp (a) promote the formation of blood clots and increase the ability of LDL-C to form plaque (the material that blocks arteries).

Lp (a) levels above 30 milligrams per deciliter of blood are considered high. Some medical researchers believe that high values of Lp (a) may be as dangerous to the heart as low levels of HDL-C (the good form of cholesterol).[51] Lp (a) levels are determined primarily by one's genetic composition. Low-fat diets and cholesterol-lowering drugs have little effect on Lp (a). Therefore, people with high levels of Lp (a) should concentrate on lowering LDL-C and total cholesterol, raising HDL, and keeping the other heart disease risk factors under control.

Medical Contributions

Diagnostic Techniques

Diagnosing cardiovascular disease is becoming more sophisticated. Diagnosis begins with a medical examination and patient history. This procedure may be supplemented with a variety of tests that may confirm or refute the physician's suspicions of the presence of cardiovascular disease. Exercise stress tests using a motor-driven treadmill with the patient hooked to an electrocardiogram (ECG) have gained popularity in the last ten years or so. Such noninvasive tests use surface electrodes on the chest that are sensitive to the electrical actions of the heart. Mechanical abnormalities of the heart produce abnormal electrical impulses that are displayed on the ECG strip. These are read and interpreted by the physician.

The treadmill "road tests" the heart as it works progressively harder to meet the increasing oxygen requirement as the exercise protocol becomes more physically demanding. This test is more accurate for men than women. The gender difference in response to the treadmill test is not completely understood, but it is believed that women's breasts and extra fat tissue interfere with the reception of electrical impulses by the chest electrodes.

In some cases a thallium treadmill test is required because it is more sensitive; however, it is also much more expensive. This involves the injection of radioactive thallium during the final minute of the treadmill test. Thallium is accepted, or taken up, by normal heart muscle but not by ischemic heart muscle. The absorption or nonabsorption of thallium can be seen on a television monitor. The thallium stress test increases diagnostic sensitivity to cardiovascular disease to approximately 90 percent.

Echocardiographpy is a safe, noninvasive technique that uses sound waves to determine the size of the heart, the thickness of the walls, and the function of the heart's valves. *Cardiac catheterization* is an invasive technique in which a slender tube is threaded from a blood vessel in an arm or leg into the coronary arteries. A liquid contrast dye that can be seen on X-ray film is injected into the coronary arteries. X-ray films are taken throughout the procedure to locate where and how severely the coronary arteries are narrowed.

Medical Treatment

A variety of drugs are used in cardiovascular therapies. These drugs lower blood pressure and cholesterol, minimize the likelihood of blood clotting, and dissolve clots during a heart attack.

Plain aspirin is proving to be a very effective drug in the fight against heart disease. Low-dose (one-fourth of a regular aspirin) aspirin therapy consisting of a single daily dose for those who have heart disease reduces the risk of having another heart attack or dying from a subsequent attack. Low-dose aspirin therapy is more effective when supplemented with a "booster" dose of one whole aspirin on the first and fifteenth of each month. Lastly, regular aspirin usage may prevent a first

heart attack from occurring in apparently healthy people, but no one should take aspirin or any other drug without first consulting a physician.[52]

Surgical techniques have also affected the treatment of cardiovascular disease. *Coronary artery bypass surgery* is designed to shunt blood around an area of blockage by removing a leg vein and sewing one end of a leg vein into the aorta and the other end into a coronary artery below the blockage, thereby restoring blood flow to the heart muscle (figure 2-8).

The internal mammary arteries also are used for bypass grafts. In fact, many authorities consider these to be the ideal grafts. There are two internal mammary arteries, but the one in the left side of the chest is preferable because it is nearer to the coronary arteries. Many surgeons would rather not use both arteries in the same patient because the diminished flow of blood to the chest impairs healing of the surgical wound. Also, fashioning bypass grafts out of these arteries is time-consuming precision surgery, and there are only two of them and they don't reach all parts of the heart. The advantage is that 95 percent of them remain open ten years after surgery.

Balloon angioplasty uses a catheter with a doughnut-shaped balloon at the tip. The catheter is positioned at the narrow point in the artery, and the balloon is inflated, which cracks and compresses the plaque, stretches the artery wall, and widens the blood vessel to allow greater blood flow (figure 2-9). Laser angioplasty uses heat to burn away plaque if the catheter can be maneuvered into the correct position. This technology appears to be useful for patients with certain types of

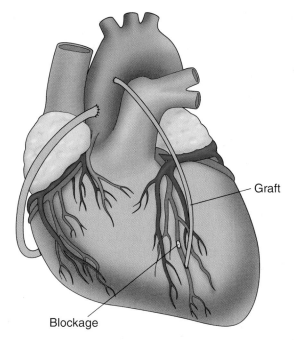

Figure 2-8 Coronary Bypass Graft

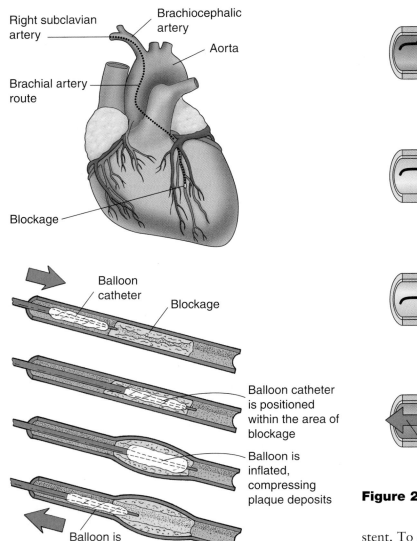

Figure 2-9 Balloon Angioplasty

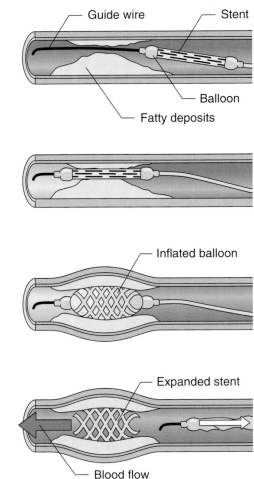

Figure 2-10 Coronary Stent

atherosclerotic narrowings or blockages. Coronary atherectomy, one of the newest techniques, uses a specially tipped catheter equipped with a high-speed rotary cutting blade to shave off plaque.

Catheterization techniques are also used to implant a coronary stent in a diseased artery. The stent is a flexible, metallic tube that functions like a scaffold to support the walls of diseased arteries, thus maintaining an open passage for blood flow (figure 2-10). Stents are positioned in such arteries by a catheter. When correctly positioned, a balloon inside the stent is inflated, causing the stent to expand. This action stretches the artery. Then the balloon is withdrawn, leaving the expanded stent behind to keep the blood vessel open.

This technique shows much promise, but there is a serious limitation associated with the procedure: It increases the risk of blood clots forming at the site of the stent. To counteract this risk, patients are given blood-thinning medications for two to three months following the stent's implantation, and then they are maintained on aspirin thereafter.

Artificial valves have been developed to replace defective heart valves, and these work quite well. Artificial (mechanical) hearts have not performed to expectation, however, because modern technology has not produced a device that can be powered internally. It appears that such a device is still a long way off.

Mechanical devices (left ventricular assist devices) have been used to aid the failing hearts of patients awaiting donor hearts. These devices take over the burden of pumping blood throughout the body and may keep patients alive for a month or more. Left ventricular assist devices suffer from the same power source problem as mechanical hearts.

Heart transplants have prolonged many lives. The outlook for patients has improved considerably because of the development and use of medicines to suppress the immune system in such patients and because of refinements in the prevention and early detection of the body's attempts to reject donor hearts. As a result, about 85 percent of transplant patients live longer than one year, and 65 percent survive for at least five years. In 1968, twenty-three heart transplants were performed; in 1995, about 2350 were performed.

Candidates for transplants are those whose hearts are irreversibly damaged with disease that does not respond to conventional treatment. Without a new heart, these people will die. The main problems associated with heart transplantation are insufficient numbers of donors, the difficulty of procuring compatible donor hearts, and the constant threat of organ rejection by the recipient.

Summary

- Approximately 1.5 million heart attacks occur each year, and 500,000 of these result in death.
- The heart is actually two pumps in one; the pulmonary pump, which sends deoxygenated blood to the lungs, and the systemic pump, which sends oxygenated blood to all tissues of the body.
- Blood plasma is a clear, yellowish fluid that makes up about 55 percent of the blood. The remaining 45 percent consists of blood solids—red blood cells, white blood cells, and blood platelets.
- Strokes are caused by a thrombus, an embolus, or a hemorrhage.
- Coronary heart disease is actually a disease of the coronary blood vessels that bring nourishment and oxygen to the heart.
- Many of the risk factors for heart disease originate in childhood.
- The treatment of heart disease includes the development of appropriate lifestyle habits and medical intervention.
- The major risk factors that cannot be changed are age, male gender, and heredity.
- The major risk factors that can be changed are elevated cholesterol levels, hypertension, cigarette smoking, physical inactivity, and obesity.
- The other contributing risk factors are diabetes mellitus and stress.
- Cholesterol is a steroid that is essential for many bodily functions, but too much circulating in the blood creates a risk for cardiovascular disease.

- Low-density lipoproteins are associated with the development of atherosclerotic plaque.
- High-density lipoproteins protect the arteries from the formation of plaque.
- Blood pressure is the force exerted against the walls of the arteries as blood is pumped from the heart and travels through the circulatory system.
- *Hypertension* is the medical term for high blood pressure.
- Cigarette smoking may be the most potent of the risk factors associated with chronic illness and premature death.
- Involuntary, or passive, smoking is associated with premature disease and death.
- Obesity is a major risk factor that often co-exists with many of the other risk factors for cardiovascular disease.
- Diabetes mellitus must be controlled to reduce the cardiovascular complications that accompany it.
- Regular exercise significantly reduces the risk for type II diabetes mellitus.
- Stress predisposes a person to illness and may hasten the disease process.
- Elevated levels of homocysteine and of Lp (a) in the blood are proving to be important risk factors for heart disease.
- Medical research has made a significant contribution to reducing the incidence of heart disease through the development of sophisticated technological advances in diagnosis and treatment.

Review Questions

1. Define *pulmonary pump* and *systemic pump* and discuss the function of each.
2. Describe the advent of heart disease in the United States.
3. Identify and describe the causes of stroke.
4. What is coronary heart disease? Discuss the treatment options that are available.
5. What are the risk factors for heart disease and how are they categorized by the AHA?
6. What is cholesterol? LDL? HDL?
7. What is the relationship between total cholesterol and HDL?
8. What is essential hypertension?
9. What ingredients in cigarettes increase the risk for cardiovascular disease? Describe their effect on the heart and blood vessels.
10. What is the risk associated with smokeless tobacco products?
11. Defend the proposition that a moderate level of exercise improves health and increases longevity.
12. What are the cardiovascular complications of diabetes mellitus?
13. How does stress contribute to cardiovascular disease?
14. Can heart disease be prevented or at least delayed? Identify the lifestyle behaviors that may be involved in the process.
15. Can atherosclerosis be reversed? Cite evidence to support your answer.
16. What contributions has the medical profession made to decreasing the death rate from heart disease?

References

1. American Heart Association: *1997 Heart and stroke—statistical update,* Dallas, 1997, American Heart Association.

2. Risk reduction, *Harvard Heart Letter* 5(11):1, 1995.

3. Squires, R. W. 1998. Coronary atherosclerosis. In *ACSM Resource Manual* (3d ed), ed. J. L. Roitman. Baltimore, Md.: Williams & Wilkins.

4. U.S. Dept. of Health and Human Services: Physical activity and health: a report of the surgeon general, Atlanta, 1996, U.S. Dept. of Health and Human Services, Centers for Disease Control and Prevention, National Center for Chronic Disease Prevention and Health Promotion.

5. Corbin, C. B., and R. P. Pangrazi. *Physical activity for children: a statement of guidelines,* NASE/AAHPERD, 1998.

6. Wardlaw G. M., P. M. Insel, and M. F. Seyler: *Contemporary nutrition: issues and insights,* St Louis, 1994, Mosby.

7. Bartecchi C. E. et al: The human cost of tobacco use, *New England Journal of Medicine* 330(13):907, 1994.

8. Up in smoke, *University of California at Berkeley Wellness Letter* 12(11):8, 1996.

9. Kannell W. B. et al: Epidemiology of acute myocardial infraction: the Framingham Study, *Medicine Today* 2:50, 1968.

10. Margolis S., S. C. Achuff. *Coronary heart disease.* Baltimore: 1998. The Johns Hopkins Medical Institutions.

11. Margolis, S., and L. J. Cheskin. 1998. *Weight Control.* Baltimore: The Johns Hopkins Medical Institutions.

12. Walsh, J. 1998. Low fat, no fat, some fat—high fat? Type of fat, not amount, may be key. *Environmental Nutrition* 21(4):1.

13. University of California at Berkeley. 1994. Fascinating facts. *University of California at Berkeley Wellness Letter* 10(6):1.

14. Lamb, L. 1992. Update on cholesterol and triglycerides. *Health Letter* 39(suppl.):1.

15. Editors. 1984. The lipid research clinics coronary primary prevention trial results. I. Reduction in incidence of coronary heart disease. *JAMA* 251:351.

16. LaRosa, J. C., et al. 1990. The cholesterol facts: A summary of the evidence relating dietary facts, serum cholesterol, and coronary heart disease: A joint statement by the American Heart Association and the National Heart, Lung, and Blood Institute. *Circulation* 81:1721.

17. Steen, S. N., and G. Butterfield. 1998. Diet and nutrition. In *ACSM Resource Manual* (3d ed.), ed. J. L. Roitman. Baltimore, Md.: Williams & Wilkins.

18. Harvard Medical School. 1998. Triglycerides emerge as a coronary risk factor. *Harvard Heart Letter* 8(11):6.

19. Tufts University. 1997. Why you know your triglyceride level. *Tufts University Health and Nutrition Letter* 15(5):3.

20. University of California at Berkeley. 1998. The ups and downs of triglycerides. *University of California at Berkeley Wellness Letter* 14(3):4.

21. National High Blood Pressure Education Program. 1993. *The Fifth Report of the Joint National Committee on Detection, Evaluation and Treatment of High Blood Pressure, National Heart, Lung, and Blood Institute, National Institutes of Health,* NIH publication no. 93-1088, Bethesda, Md.: National Institutes of Health.

22. U.S. Dept of Health and Human Services. 1988. *Healthy People 2010 objectives: Draft for public Comment.* Washington, D.C.: Office of Disease Prevention and Health Promotion.

23. Tufts University. 1997. Meditation lowers blood pressure as well as drugs. *Tufts University Diet and Nutrition Letter* 14(11):3.

24. ACSM. 1993. Physical activity, physical fitness, and hypertension. *Medicine and Science in Sports and Exercise* 25(10):1.

25. American Cancer Society. 1997. *Cancer Facts and Figures—1997,* Atlanta, Ga.: American Cancer Society.

26. Office on Smoking and Health, National Center for Chronic Disease Prevention and Health Promotion, CDC. 1996. Cigarette smoking among adults in the U.S., 1994. *MMWR* 45(27):588.

27. Centers for Disease Control and Prevention. 1994. CDC surveillance summaries. *MMWR* 43(SS-3).

28. U.S. Department of Health and Human Services. 1988. *The Health Consequences of Smoking—Nicotine Addiction, a Report of the Surgeon General.* Rockville, Md.: U.S. Department of Health and Human Services.

29. U.S. Department of Health and Human Services. 1998. *Progress Review—Tobacco, Prevention Report.* Washington, D.C.: Office of Disease Prevention and Health Promotion.

30. Powell, K. E. 1987. Physical activity and the incidence of coronary heart disease. *Annual Review of Public Health* 8:253.

31. Berlin, J. A., and G. A. Colditz. 1990. A meta-analysis of physical activity in the prevention of coronary heart disease. *American Journal of Epidemiology* 132:612.

32. Whaley, M. A., and L. A. Kaminsky. 1998. Epidemiology of physical activity, physical fitness, and selected chronic diseases. In *ACSM Resource Manual* (3d ed.), ed. J. L. Roitman. Baltimore, Md.: Williams & Wilkins.

33. Blair, S. N., et al. 1989. Physical fitness and all-cause mortality—a prospective study of healthy men and women. *JAMA* 262:2395.

34. Manson, J. E., et al. 1992. The primary prevention of myocardial infarction. *New England Medical Journal* 326:1406.

35. Duncan, J. J., et al. 1995. Women walking for health and fitness. *JAMA* 273:402.

36. Pate, R. R., et al. 1995. Physical activity and public health. *JAMA* 273:402.

37. Paffenbarger, R. S., and R. T. Hyde. 1986. Letter. *New England Journal of Medicine.* 315:400.

38. Pescatello, L. S., et al. 1994. Health care reform and the exercise professional. *ACSM Certified News* 4(2):1.

39. Gordon, N. F. 1998. Conceptional basis for coronary artery disease risk factor assessment. In *ACSM Resource Manual* (3d ed.), ed. J. L. Roitman. Baltimore, Md.: Williams & Wilkins.

40. Schardt, D., and S. Schmidt. 1996. How to avoid onset diabetes. *Nutrition Action Health Letter* 23(7):3.

41. Manson, J. E., et al. 1992. A prospective study of exercise and incidence of

diabetes among U.S. male physicians. *JAMA* 268:63.

42. Harvard University. 1998. Can stress make you sick? *Harvard Health Letter* 23(6):1.

43. Harvard University. 1998. Stress and atherosclerosis. *Harvard Health Letter* 23(4):8.

44. Harvard University. 1998. Grumpy old men: At risk for coronary disease? *Harvard Health Letter* 8(12):7.

45. Sime, W. E., R. S. Eliot, and E. E. Solberg. 1998. Stress and heart disease. In *ACSM Resource Manual* (3d ed.), ed.

J. L. Roitman. Baltimore, Md.: Williams & Wilkins.

46. Ornish, D., et al. 1990. Can lifestyle changes reverse coronary heart disease? *The Lancet* 336:129.

47. Ornish, D., et al. 1993. Can lifestyle changes reverse atherosclerosis? Four-year results of the lifestyle heart trial. *Circulation* 88(suppl.):2064.

48. Editors. 1997. Iron's link to heart disease. *Healthnews* 3(3):7.

49. Harvard University. 1997. Evidence mounts for heart disease marker. *Harvard Health Letter* 22(11):1.

50. Mayo Clinic. 1977. Homocysteine. *Mayo Clinic Health Letter* 15(12):7.

51. University of California at Berkeley. 1997. Ask the experts. *University of California at Berkeley Wellness Letter* 14(3):7.

52. Hennekens, C. H., M. L. Dyken, and V. Fuster. 1997. Aspirin as a therapeutic agent in cardiovascular disease—a statement for healthcare professionals from the American Heart Association. *Circulation* 96:2757.

Suggested Readings

Harvard University. 1998. B vitamins and heart disease. *Harvard Health Letter* 23(12):8.

This article promotes the idea that a lack of vitamin B_6 may be a more important marker for heart disease than homocysteine levels in the blood. One major study suggests the possibility that heart attacks may produce an increase in homocysteine levels rather than the other way around. More research will clarify the roles of vitamin B_6 and homocysteine.

Tufts University. 1998. Different strokes—or no strokes at all—can improve fitness. *Tufts University Health and Nutrition Letter* 16(8):7.

This article extols the virtues of water exercise as an effective and safe means of improving one's level of physical fitness. Although swimming is appropriate for those who swim, other water activities may be used in place of swimming by those who do not.

University of California at Berkeley. 1998. Exercise does the trick. *University of California at Berkeley Wellness Letter* 15(1):2.

A short synopsis that examines the roles of exercise and diet in lowering cholesterol, total and LDL-C. It provides evidence to support combining dieting and exercise.

Brehm, B. A. 1998. Six tips for helping a friend kick the habit. *Fitness Management* 14(12):28.

This article tries to sensitize nonsmokers to the difficulty encountered by smokers who are trying to quit. The author provides six ways that nonsmokers can help smokers quit.

Gower, T. 1998. Rating the cholesterol busters. *Health* 12(8):120.

This article discusses natural ways to lower cholesterol. Natural ways include soy, soluble fiber, garlic, vitamin E, cholestin, and niacin.

Name _____ Date _____ Section _____

Assessment Activity 2-1

What's Your Heart Attack Risk?

Directions: By answering questions in the 12 items below, you can calculate your odds of having a heart attack within the next 10 years. The test is based on data from four of the most extensive American studies of coronary risk. (The test is not accurate for people who already have a history of coronary disease. For definitive advice, ask your doctor.) Advice on improving your odds follows this test.

The Test

For every "yes" answer to items 1 through 9, add or subtract points as shown.

Question	Men	Women
1. Do you get little or no regular exercise?	Plus 2	Plus 6
2. Calculate your body mass index (BMI) as follows: Multiply your weight in pounds by 704. Divide the result by your height in inches. Divide that result by your height in inches again and round to the nearest whole number.		
Is your BMI from 21 to 24?	Plus 0	Plus 2
Is your BMI from 25 to 28?	Plus 2	Plus 3
Is your BMI 29 or over?	Plus 4	Plus 6
3. Do you have diabetes?	Plus 8	Plus 11
4. If you're an ex-smoker, did you quit in the past five years?	Plus 1	Plus 4
If you smoke, do you smoke fewer than 15 cigarettes a day?	Plus 2	Plus 8
Do you smoke 15 to 24 cigarettes a day?	Plus 4	Plus 15
Do you smoke more than 24 cigarettes a day?	Plus 6	Plus 18
5. Did either of your parents have a heart attack before age 60?	Plus 9	Plus 9

Question	Men	Women
6. Do you take medicine to control blood pressure? (This is a sign that your pressure was once elevated.)	Plus 1	Plus 1
7. If you are a postmenopausal woman, are you currently taking estrogen alone?		Minus 5
Are you currently taking estrogen plus progestin?		Minus 3
If you don't currently take estrogen, did you previously take it (with or without progestin)?		Minus 2
8. Do you take low doses of aspirin at least every other day? (A low dose is between one quarter and one whole 325-mg tablet.)	Minus 4	Minus 4
9. Do you drink alcohol in moderation? ("Moderate" drinking is 2 to 14 drinks per week. A "drink" is 12 ounces of beer, 5 ounces of wine, or 1½ ounches of liquor.)	Minus 4	Minus 4

Add up your points so far. SUBTOTAL _____ _____

Now calculate items 10 through 12, rounding to the nearest whole number.

	Men	Women
10. Multiply your systolic pressure (the higher number) by 0.14 if you are a man, by 0.15 if you are a woman.	Plus ___	Plus ___
11. Multiply your age by 0.51 if you are a man, by 0.8 if you are a woman	Plus ___	Plus ___

12. Multiply your total cholesterol level by 0.07 if man, by 0.06 if you are a woman. Multiply your HDL level by 0.25 if you are a man, by 0.3 if you are a woman.

Plus ___   Plus ___

Minus ___   Minus ___

If you don't know your cholesterol levels and want to assume they're about average, you could substitute 205 for total cholesterol and 51 for HDL. Adults 20 and over should have cholesterol testing at least every 5 years.

Add up your points for items 10 through 12.   SUBTOTAL _____   _____

Add the two subtotals to get your score   TOTAL _____   _____

Probability* of Having a Heart Attack

Men			
Score	1 Year	5 Years	10 Years
0–35	<0.1%	<0.4%	<1%
36–45	0.1–0.2%	0.4–1%	1–3%
46–55	0.2–0.6%	1–3%	3–7%
56–65	0.6–2%	3–8%	7–17%
66–70	2%	8–13%	17–27%
71–75	2–4%	13–20%	27–40%
76–80	4–6%	20–30%	40–56%

Women			
Score	1 Year	5 Years	10 Years
0–60	<0.1%	<0.4%	<1%
61–70	0.1–0.2%	0.4–1%	1.3%
71–80	0.2–0.5%	1–3%	3–7%
81–85	0.5–1%	3–5%	7–12%
86–90	1%	5–8%	12–19%
91–95	1–2%	8–13%	19–29%
96–100	2–4%	13–20%	29–43%

*"Probability" indicates the percentage of people like yourself who will have a heart attack during the period cited. If your probability is 7% for the 10-year column, for example, it means that out of a random sampling of 100 people with the same score as yourself, seven will have a heart attack within a decade of today.

Assessment Activity 2-2

A Case Study of Bill M.

Directions: To determine your understanding of cardiovascular health and wellness, read the following case study and answer the accompanying questions. Bill, a 38-year-old man who is 5'8" tall and weighs 205 lb, has the following history:

- His father died of a heart attack at age 48 years; his grandfather died of a heart attack at age 52 years.
- His cholesterol level is 256 mg/dl, LDL is 172 mg/dl, and HDL is 40 mg/dl.
- His blood pressure is consistently in the 150/95 range.

- He smokes one pack of cigarettes per day.
- He drinks six to eight brewed cups of coffee daily.
- He eats two eggs with bacon or sausage and buttered toast daily.
- Meat is a major part of supper; he skips lunch.
- His favorite snacks are ice cream, buttered popcorn, and salted peanuts.
- He occasionally plays tennis on Sunday afternoons.
- He owns his own business and often works 55 to 60 hours per week.

Answer the following:

What are Bill's risk factors for coronary heart disease? _____

Which of these can he control? _____

What suggestions can you give him regarding his current diet? _____

_____

What effect may a change in diet have on his coronary risk profile? _____

_____

What suggestions can you make regarding Bill's need for exercise, and how might a change in his activity level affect his coronary risk profile? _____

_____

What are the risks associated with obesity? _____

_____

Increasing Cardiorespiratory Endurance

Key Terms

aerobic
aerobic capacity
cardiorespiratory
 endurance
cross-training

health-related fitness
hyperthermia
hypothermia
performance-related fitness

Objectives

After completing this chapter, you will be able to:
- Identify and define the health-related components of physical fitness.
- Discuss the principles of conditioning.
- Calculate your target heart rate for exercise by two different methods.
- Identify and discuss the health benefits of consistent participation in exercise.
- Describe the problems associated with exercise in hot and cold weather.

Goals for Behavior Change

- List three physical activities you normally do every week (exclusive of structured, planned exercise) and find and implement ways of making them more challenging.
- If you do not exercise regularly, list several factors that will motivate you to begin a cardiorespiratory endurance program. Begin a simple walking or other exercise program with these factors in mind.
- If you are physically active, list the main factors that will encourage you to improve the frequency, intensity, or duration of your activity. To help you stay motivated, post this list in a place where you will see it every day.
- Choose a piece of home exercise equipment that seems well suited to your exercise preferences and goals.

echnology has affected the lives of Americans by increasing productivity while simultaneously reducing and in some cases eliminating the amount of physical work for the labor force. Therefore, physical fitness for most of the population can no longer be attained on the job, and leisure hours represent the only time for its development. Literally dozens of physical activities, exercise regimens, sports, games, and household and other physical chores that may contribute to health enhancement and fitness development are available. These activities are sufficiently different from each other, running the gamut from low to high skill requirement, so that almost anyone can find one or two activities that are enjoyable, fun, and challenging. This chapter focuses on the principles and concepts that have evolved for developing cardiorespiratory endurance for the purposes of health enhancement and physical fitness.

The Components of Physical Fitness

Authorities do not agree on a definition of *physical fitness,* but most have endorsed the concept of performance-related and health-related fitness. **Performance-related fitness,** or sports fitness, consists of the following components: speed, power, balance, coordination, agility, and reaction time. These are essential for sports performance, but they may or may not contribute significantly to those activities performed for health enhancement (see the Just the Facts: What's the Difference?).

Speed is velocity, or the ability to move rapidly. *Power* is the product of force and velocity and the rate at which work is performed. *Balance,* or equilibrium, is the ability to maintain a desired body position either statically or dynamically. *Coordination* is the harmonious integration of the body parts to produce smooth, fluid motion. *Agility* is the ability to change direction rapidly. *Reaction time* is the time required (usually measured in hundredths of a second) to respond to a stimulus.

The components of **health-related fitness** are cardiorespiratory endurance, muscular strength, muscular endurance, flexibility, and body composition. In this text the exercise emphasis is on health-related fitness.

Performance-related and health-related fitness, although different, clearly are not mutually exclusive. For example, competitive athletes require an abundance of the performance-related components of fitness, but the natures of their sports may also require the simultaneous development of the health-related components. Athletes who play racquetball, tennis, basketball, soccer, and handball fall within this category. Conversely, the same sports are appropriate for

Just the Facts

What's the Difference?

Components of Fitness
Health related

- Cardiorespiratory endurance
- Muscular strength
- Muscular endurance
- Flexibility
- Body composition

Performance related

- Speed
- Power
- Balance
- Coordination
- Agility
- Reaction time

Activities
Health related

- Walking
- Running
- Jogging
- Cycling
- Hiking
- Swimming
- Rope jumping
- Weight training
- Cross-country skiing

Performance related

- Racquetball
- Handball
- Squash
- Tennis
- Badminton
- Soccer
- Softball
- Basketball
- Football
- Water polo

health and fitness enthusiasts who prefer to achieve their goals through friendly competition.

However, the development and maintenance of health-related fitness do not necessarily depend on athletic ability or activities that are high in the performance components. Fitness for health purposes can be achieved with minimal psychomotor ability through activities such as walking, jogging, cycling, hiking, backpacking, orienteering, swimming, rope jumping, and weight training.

Such activities as these are self-paced; that is, the exerciser selects a pace that is relatively comfortable and that can be sustained for a minimum of 10 minutes. No competing opponent pushes the exerciser beyond his or her physiological limits.

Remember the adage "No pain, no gain"? Trying to comply with it has done more harm than good to sedentary people attempting to become physically active. The health benefits of exercise occur when exercise is somewhat uncomfortable but not painful. Only the most dedicated health enthusiasts and competitors can face exercise that constantly produces pain.

Although exercise for health enhancement should stress cardiorespiratory development, the other components of fitness should not be neglected. Flexibility exercises should be a part of warm-up and cool-down procedures. Flexibility exercises may be performed three to five times per week, and the best results occur during the cool-down period following the cardiorespiratory workout.[1] Stretching is most effective at this time because muscle temperature is elevated. Warm muscles respond well to stretching, and the likelihood of muscle injury is decreased as well. Resistance/strength training plays an important role and should be an integral part of a well-rounded fitness program.

As with all components of wellness, developing and sustaining an exercise program are the responsibilities of each individual. This text provides convincing evidence of the need for regular exercise and provides guidelines for initiating a sound program or reinforcement for those who are currently exercising.

Cardiorespiratory Endurance

Cardiorespiratory endurance is the ability to take in, deliver, and extract oxygen for physical work, that is, the ability to persevere at a physical task at a given intensity level. Cardiorespiratory endurance improves with regular participation in aerobic activities, such as speed walking, jogging, cycling, swimming, and cross-country skiing. The term **aerobic** literally means "with oxygen," but when applied to exercise, it refers to activities in which oxygen demand can be met continuously during performance. Aerobic performance depends on a continuous and sufficient supply of oxygen to burn the carbohydrates and fats needed to fuel such activities. In other words, someone performing aerobically has the capacity to sustain the intensity or the energy requirement for longer than a couple of minutes,[2] a phenomenon known as *steady state*. Steady state can be achieved only during aerobic exercise, and it represents a level of exertion that feels relatively comfortable to the exerciser. It is also referred to as a *pay as you go system* in that the oxygen cost of an activity is paid in full by the body during the activity.

Cardiorespiratory endurance is also referred to as **aerobic capacity,** or maximum oxygen consumption (VO_2 max). It is the most important component of physical fitness and is the foundation of total fitness.

The physiological changes that result from cardiorespiratory training are referred to as the *long-term* or *chronic effects of exercise*. The effects of training are measurable and predictable.

Heart Rate

A few months of aerobic training lowers the resting heart rate by 10 to 15 beats per minute (bpm).[3] It also lowers the heart rate for a given workload. For example, a slow jog may produce a heart rate of 165 beats per minute before training and 140 beats per minute after a few months of training. The trained heart is a stronger, more efficient pump that is capable of delivering the required blood and oxygen with fewer beats.

Stroke Volume

Stroke volume is the amount of blood that the heart can eject in one beat. Aerobic training increases the stroke volume by (1) increasing the size of the cavity of the ventricles, which results in more blood filling the heart, and (2) increasing the contractile strength of the ventricular wall, so contraction is more forceful and a greater amount of blood is ejected from the ventricles. The increase in stroke volume, both at rest and during exercise, is one of the primary effects of endurance training and one of the major mechanisms responsible for improvement in aerobic fitness.

Cardiac Output

Cardiac output is the amount of blood ejected by the heart in 1 minute. Cardiac output (Q) is the product of heart rate (HR) and stroke volume (SV) ($Q = HR \times SV$). Cardiac output increases with aerobic training during maximal effort—it does not increase at rest or during submaximal exercise. The reason that cardiac output does not change during rest or submaximal exercise is that the lowered resting heart rate compensates for the increase in stroke volume. What does change is the manner in which cardiac output is achieved. This is illustrated by the following example: An untrained 25-year-old man has a resting heart rate of 72 bpm and a stroke volume of 70 ml of blood per beat. His cardiac output at rest is calculated as follows:

$$Q = HR \times SV$$
$$= 72 \times 70$$
$$= 5040 \text{ ml } (5.0 \text{ L})$$

The same person after two years of aerobic training has the same cardiac output at rest, but it is achieved differently: The resting heart rate is now decreased to 55 bpm and the stroke volume is increased to 92 ml of blood per beat.

$$Q = 55 \times 92$$
$$= 5040 \text{ ml } (5.0 \text{ L})$$

The average cardiac output at rest is 4 to 6 liters of blood per minute. During maximal exertion, cardiac output reaches values of 18 to 20 liters of blood per minute for the average person but may reach as much as 40 liters per minute for large, well-conditioned athletes. What an incredible piece of work by an organ that weighs less than a pound! To put this in perspective,

imagine forty 1-liter cola bottles filled with blood. This is the amount that the hearts of some highly conditioned people can pump in 1 minute. Maximal cardiac output improves with training primarily because of the resulting increase in stroke volume.[3] Maximal heart rate is essentially unaffected by training; therefore, its influence on maximal cardiac output is relatively constant. However, maximal heart rate declines with age by about 1 bpm per year after age 20. Training cannot stop the decline; it can only slow the process somewhat.

Blood Volume

Aerobic training increases total blood volume, plasma volume (the liquid portion of the blood), and the blood solids (the red blood cells, white blood cells, and blood platelets). The increase is greatest in plasma volume, so the blood becomes more liquid. The increase in the ratio of plasma volume to red blood cell volume is an adaptation to exercise that lowers the viscosity, or thickness and stickiness, of the blood. This change decreases the resistance to blood flow, allowing it to circulate more easily through the blood vessels.

Blood is automatically shunted by the body to areas of greatest need. At rest, a significant amount is sent to the digestive system and kidneys. During vigorous exercise, as much as 85 percent of the blood is sent to the working muscles, reducing the amount sent to the digestive and urinary systems.[1]

Heart Volume

The muscles of the body respond to exercise by growing larger and stronger. As a muscular pump, the heart's volume and weight increase with endurance training. Training that lowers the resting heart rate stimulates greater filling of the ventricles, whose muscle fibers respond to the increased pool of blood by stretching. This produces a recoil effect in the muscle fibers that results in a stronger contraction with more blood ejected per beat. Continued training causes the ventricles to enlarge and grow stronger, so the weight and the size of the heart increase. The hypertrophied (enlarged) heart is a normal response to endurance training that has no long-term detrimental effects. In fact, although maintaining this effect for life is beneficial, several months of inactivity will reduce heart weight and size to pretraining levels. The atrophy (wasting away) associated with physical inactivity is inevitable.

Respiratory Responses

The chest muscles that support breathing improve in both strength and endurance with exercise. Vital capacity, which is the amount of air that can be expired maximally following a maximal inspiration, increases slightly. A corresponding decrease occurs in "dead space" air or residual volume, which is the amount of air remaining in the lungs after a maximal expiration.

Training substantially increases maximal pulmonary ventilation (the amount of air moved in and out of the lungs). Before training, the lungs can ventilate approximately 110 liters of air per minute. Pulmonary ventilation increases to about 135 liters of air following a few months of training. Highly trained athletes commonly ventilate 180 to 200 liters of air per minute.

Blood flow to the lungs, particularly to the upper lobes, appears to increase after training. This results in a larger and more efficient surface for the exchange of oxygen and carbon dioxide.

Metabolic Responses

Aerobic endurance training improves aerobic capacity by 5 to 25 percent in previously untrained, healthy adults. The magnitude of improvement is primarily dependent upon the initial level of physical fitness. The lower the fitness level, the greater the gain from aerobic training.[3] Rarely do improvements greater than 30 percent occur. When they do, they usually occur to those who also lose a large amount of body weight and fat.[4]

The improvement in aerobic capacity is the result of several physiological adaptations that increase the body's production of energy. First, adenosine triphosphate (ATP), the actual unit of energy for muscular contraction, is produced in greater quantities. The mitochondria, which are specialized organelles responsible for manufacturing ATP, respond to training by increasing in size and number to increase their output. Second, oxidative enzymes within the mitochondria that accelerate the production of ATP increase in quantity. Third, cardiac output and blood perfusion of the muscles performing the work increase. Fourth, training facilitates and increases the extraction of oxygen by the exercising muscles. These are some of the major adaptations that combine to enhance aerobic endurance.

Aerobic capacity (VO_2 max) is limited by heredity and is finite. The heredity component of VO_2 max is approximately 40 percent.[5] This represents a substantial influence on a given person's potential for aerobic performance. Therefore, the sensitivity of the VO_2 max response to aerobic training is to a significant degree dependent upon heredity. If those who inherit the genetic potential for endurance events also train diligently, they become capable of exceptionally high levels of performance. Diligent training with an average genetic potential results in average or slightly above average performance. Only a select few inherit the ability to produce world-class endurance performances. The majority of people are in the average category, but all can achieve their aerobic *potential* with training.

Aerobic capacity reaches a peak after six months to two years of steady endurance training. At this point, it levels off and remains unchanged for a number of years, even if training is intensified. However, aerobic performance continues to improve with harder training, because a higher percentage of the aerobic capacity can be maintained for a longer period. For example, six months of appropriate training may allow you to jog 3 miles at 60 percent of your aerobic capacity. Another year of harder training may allow you to run 3 miles at 85 percent of your capacity. Capacity has not changed during this time, but physiological adaptations have occurred that enable the body to function at progressively higher percentages of maximum capacity.

Aerobic capacity decreases with age. During adulthood, peak aerobic energy steadily declines by an average of about 1 percent per year between the ages of 25 and 75.[6] A significant portion of the decline is related to the lack of physical activity that accompanies aging: Those who are physically active throughout their lifetimes experience declines in aerobic capacity but not at the same rate as those who are inactive. See Wellness Across the Generations: Exercise Is for Everyone for more details about the impact of exercising on aging.

Wellness Across the Generations

Exercise Is for Everyone

The ability of the body to take in, transport, and extract oxygen for physical work and exercise declines with age. On the average, aerobic capacity declines by about 8 to 10 percent every decade after the age of 25 in both males and females. One of the major sources of this decline in the United States is the decreasing level of physical activity that tends to accompany aging. This trend toward inactivity also results in a loss of muscle weight, an increase in fat weight, and a decrease in metabolic rate, all of which contribute to the decline in aerobic capacity. Although physiological aging does lower aerobic capacity, at least 50 percent of the decline is due to "disuse atrophy" caused by inactivity.[7]

Biological aging cannot be stopped. We cannot live forever. However, exercise comes as close to an antiaging pill as anything else that is available. Even older people who have been sedentary for decades can benefit from aerobic exercise and weight training.

The beneficial outcomes of regular exercise for older people include an increase in energy, a favorable change in body composition (loss of fat, gain of muscle), an increase in muscular strength and endurance, an increase in metabolism, and significant improvements in cardiovascular and musculoskeletal health.[8] All of these changes translate into a higher quality of life and longevity.

Physically fit 60 and 70 year olds have the aerobic capacity of unfit 25 year olds.[8] All of this means that physically fit elderly people have the energy to live independently during their later years. The ability to perform the daily chores of living and to participate in an active lifestyle with energy to spare develops confidence that contributes to the enjoyment of life.

The effects of training persist as long as training continues. Training of moderate intensity may increase the VO_2 max by 10 to 20 percent. However, the VO_2 max returns to pretraining levels within a few months if training is discontinued.[9] Most of the decline occurs during the first month and slows down during the next two months. Fitness developed through years of continuous training can be lost in months if training is interrupted or discontinued. Highly conditioned athletes respond to detraining in a similar manner. In a study, subjects who suspended training for eighty-four days after ten years of active participation experienced a significant decline in aerobic capacity after three weeks of inactivity. They returned to pretraining levels in most fitness parameters by the end of the study. The exceptions to complete reversal were muscle capillary density and mitochondrial enzymes, which remained 50 percent higher than levels measured in sedentary control subjects. This study indicated that the results of inactivity are variable and affect some systems more quickly than others. Physical decline cannot be prevented with physical inactivity.

Three different methods for assessing your cardiorespiratory endurance are presented in the Assessments Activities. These include the Rockport Fitness Walking Test, the 1.5-Mile Run/Walk Test, and the 3-Minute Bench Step Test. Each is accompanied by norms, so you can compare your performance against the standards.

Cardiorespiratory Endurance and Wellness

Most Americans believe that exercise is good for them, but the majority cannot explain how or why. This section provides some of the answers

Consistent participation in exercise is necessary to improve health status. Sporadic exercise does not promote physical fitness or contribute to health enhancement. In fact, infrequent participation increases the risk of sudden death during the time of exercise.[10] Physical inactivity is a major risk for coronary heart disease. The risk is approximately equal to that imposed by cigarette smoking, high blood pressure, and elevated serum cholesterol. Sixty percent of all adult Americans are inactive or marginally active. The number of physically inactive people exceeds the combined total of those who smoke, are hypertensive, or have high serum cholesterol.[10] Based on these numbers, promoting regular exercise for the general public should be an important priority of public health policy.

Coronary heart disease is rarely responsible for sudden cardiac death during or after exercise among people under the age of 30. Congenital heart defects or other cardiac abnormalities, such as faulty valves, enlarged hearts, and heart muscle disease, are the usual culprits for this age group. Most exertional deaths occur among older Americans and are due to coronary heart disease. A study by Harvard medical researchers found that heavy physical exertion, such as shoveling snow, gardening, walking fast, jogging, playing softball, and playing tennis, could trigger a heart attack.[11] For the physically unfit, the risk of incurring a heart attack during and in the first hour after strenuous exertion increased by 107 times. The risk for physically fit

people increased only 2.7 times. These data applied equally to men and women.

The danger attributed to physical exertion is greatly diminished in people who exercise regularly. In fact, the benefits they receive from physical training far outweigh the minimal risk associated with one bout of strenuous exercise. A similar study conducted at the same time in Germany found amazingly similar results.[12]

One and one-half million heart attacks occur every year in the United States. The Harvard researchers concluded that 75,000 of these are exertional and they usually occur after strenuous exercise. Most of these heart attacks occur among those who are physically inactive and at high risk.[11] See Just the Facts: Exercise-Related Problems for some tips on reducing the hazards associated with regular exercise. Some selected health benefits of regular exercise are listed in table 3-1. If these benefits could be distilled and sold in pill form, the American public would line up to pay any reasonable price to attain them. And yet all of these benefits are readily available to anyone who is simply willing to commit the time and effort. While millions of people are exercising, 60 percent of the adult population is not.

Principles of Conditioning

Becoming familiar with the principles of exercise is necessary to maximize the results of a physical fitness program. Your objectives can be met through the appropriate manipulation of intensity, frequency, duration, overload, progression, and specificity. Setting of objectives, warm-up, cooldown, and careful selection of activity are important elements that add to the enjoyment and effectiveness of exercise.

Intensity

Intensity refers to the degree of vigorousness of a single session of exercise. In 1995, The American College of Sports Medicine (ACSM) and the Centers for Disease Control and Prevention (CDC) developed and promoted the following recommendation for exercise: Every U.S. adult should accumulate 30 minutes or more of moderately intense physical activity on most and preferably all days of the week.[13] The recommendation refers to *physical activity* rather than *exercise*. This is an umbrella term that includes many kinds of physical exertion, including structured exercise. *Moderate intensity* refers to walking at a 3 to 4 mile per hour pace (15 to 20 minutes per mile) or engaging in any activity that burns a similar number of calories at a similar rate. The 30 minutes of activity can be split up into two or three bouts of 10 to 15 minutes each throughout

Just the Facts

Exercise-Related Problems

Many health, fitness, and cosmetic benefits occur to those who exercise on a regular basis. Although they are outweighed by the benefits, risks are associated with such behavior. Despite precautions, injuries occasionally occur. Beginning exercisers are particularly susceptible to injury because of their lack of knowledge about training coupled with their misguided attempts to achieve their goals too quickly. The following suggestions should result in safer workouts:

1. Dress according to the weather: shorts, t-shirt, mesh baseball-type cap in warm weather; layers of light clothing, hat, gloves, ear protection, and windbreaker in cold weather.

2. Wear appropriate shoes for the activity in which you participate: jogging shoes, walking shoes, aerobic shoes, or cross-trainers. In general, exercise shoes should be one-half to three-quarters of an inch longer than your longest toe. There should also be room enough for the toes to spread out. The soles of most exercise shoes consists of three layers. The outer sole that contacts the floor or ground should be made of hard rubber. The next layer is the midsole, which protects the midfoot and toes. The last layer is made of a thick, spongy substance that absorbs most of the shock when the foot strikes the surface.

3. Warm up and cool down properly before and after exercise.

4. Exercise within your capacity—it should feel a little uncomfortable but not painful. According to the American College of Sports Medicine (ACSM), the initial stage of an exercise program should last four to six weeks at a low intensity (50 to 60 percent of the maximal heart rate or HR_{max}). Each exercise session should last for 12 minutes during the first week and increase by 2 minutes per week for the next 4 to 5 weeks. At this point, the exerciser is ready to increase the intensity, frequency, and duration of each session.

5. While following these simple guidelines reduces the possibility of incurring pain or injury, beginning exercisers may experience, as a result of overuse, shin splints, side stitch, blisters, chafing, muscle cramps, muscle soreness, achilles tendon injuries, and lower-back pain.

   a. Muscle soreness following exercise usually occurs among beginners who have yet to adapt to physical exertion or to those at any level of fitness who exceed their physical capabilities. Following the ACSM guidelines reduces exposure to muscle pain.

   b. Side stitches occur primarily among walkers and joggers. They consist of severe pain in the upper right quadrant of the abdomen. Side stitches may be caused by reduced blood flow to the diaphragm (a large, dome-shaped muscle that separates the abdominal cavity from the chest cavity), or they may be due to the collection of gas in the intestines. In either case, deep breathing and direct pressure applied with both hands at the site of the pain may provide relief. Sometimes, stopping the activity for a few minutes is required for the pain to subside.

   c. A common injury occurring among beginners is shin splints. Shin splints produce a burning pain that radiates along the inner surface of the large bones of the lower leg. These are nagging, painful injuries that are better prevented than treated. The causes of shin splints include training demands that exceed a person's capacity to perform. High-impact activities such as jogging or aerobics to music, poor-quality exercise shoes, hard exercise surfaces, and walking or jogging on hilly surfaces are other contributing causes. Treatment includes applications of ice, rest, wrapping or taping the affected shin, and placing heel lifts in the shoes.

the day. Table 3-2 provides a summary of the ACSM-CDC exercise principles and their application to the enhancement of health and physical fitness.

The recommendation for health enhancement is a minimum guideline designed to motivate and recruit that 60 percent of the population who are not physically active. It is not intended to lower the standard for those who currently exercise at a higher level or whose primary goal is the development of physical fitness. Programs designed primarily to improve health may not improve or may minimally improve physical fitness. It takes higher-intensity exercise to significantly improve physical fitness. Those who exercise for physical fitness purposes also derive health benefits in a two-for-one deal. It takes a slightly higher level of training to achieve both.

Table 3-1 Health-Related Benefits Associated with Regular Aerobic Exercise

Reduces the risk of cardiovascular disease

- Increases HDL cholesterol
- Decreases LDL cholesterol
- Favorably changes the ratios between total cholesterol and HDL-C and between LDL-C and HDL-C
- Decreases triglyceride levels
- Promotes relaxation; relieves stress and tension
- Decreases body fat and favorably changes body composition
- Reduces blood pressure, especially if it is high
- Makes blood platelets less sticky
- Decreases the incidence of cardiac dysrhythmias
- Increases myocardial efficiency
  1. Lowers resting heart rate
  2. Increases stroke volume
- Increases oxygen-carrying capacity of the blood
- Reduces the risk of colon cancer and breast cancer

Helps control diabetes

- Makes cells less resistant to insulin
- Reduces body fat

Develops stronger bones that are less susceptible to injury

Promotes joint stability

- Increases muscular strength
- Increases strength of the ligaments, tendons, cartilage, and connective tissue

Contributes to fewer lower-back problems

Acts as a stimulus for other lifestyle changes

Improves self-concept

Table 3-2 Summary of Exercise Principles for the Development of Physical Fitness and Health

Exercise Principles	Exercise Goals	
	To Develop and Improve Level of Physical Fitness (1998 Guidelines)	To Develop and Improve Health Status (1995 Guidelines)
Intensity	• 55/65 to 90% of HR_{max} • 55 to 64% of HR_{max} for sedentary beginners • 40/50 to 85% of the VO_2 or cardiac reserve	• Moderate (walking 3 to 4 MPH)
Frequency	• 3–5 days per week	• Most, preferably all, days of the week
Duration (time)	• 20–60 minutes at 60 to 90% of HR_{max} • 200–300 calories per exercise session	• 30 minutes or more of HR_{max}
Overload	• Should not exceed 10% of the previous workout	• NA*
Progression	• Based on physiological readiness • According to the schedule of overload	• NA
Specificity	• For competitors who are training for maximal performance	• NA

*not applicable

The intensity level recommended by the American College of Sports Medicine (ACSM) in 1990 for the purpose of developing physical fitness was 55/65 to 90 percent of the maximal heart rate (HR_{max}).[9] HR_{max} can be measured by a physical work capacity test on a treadmill or cycle ergometer. Because most people do not have access to such tests, HR_{max} can be estimated by subtracting age from 220. A 20-year-old person has an estimated HR_{max} of 200 beats per minute ($220 - 20 = 200$). This formula predicts rather than measures HR_{max}; therefore, a measurement error of approximately plus or minus 10 beats per minute is associated with its use.

After the HR_{max} has been determined, the target for exercise may be calculated. The target zone for exercise provides the desirable heart rate for the development of physical fitness. For the 20-year-old person whose HR_{max} is 200 beats per minute, the target zone for exercise is calculated as follows:

$$200 \text{ (estimated } HR_{max})$$
$$\times 0.60 \text{ (60\% of } HR_{max})$$
$$120 \text{ (lower-limit target)}$$

$$200 \text{ (estimated } HR_{max})$$
$$\times 0.90 \text{ (90\% of } HR_{max})$$
$$180 \text{ (upper-limit target)}$$

This 20-year-old person should exercise at a heart rate between 120 and 180 beats per minute, depending on objectives and level of fitness. The target for a person who has an average level of fitness is 150 to 160 beats per minute for exercise. The training effect occurs at heart rate levels below the maximum.

Another method for calculating exercise heart rate, the Karvonen formula, considers fitness level and resting heart rate. The training heart rate is calculated with this formula by using a percentage of the heart rate reserve (cardiac reserve), which is the difference between the HR_{max} and the resting heart rate. The best way to determine the resting heart rate for this method is to count your pulse rate for fifteen seconds while in the sitting position immediately after waking in the morning. You should repeat this for four to five consecutive days and average the readings for a relatively accurate representation of your resting heart rate. Next, you should estimate your level of fitness based on your exercise habits and select a category from table 3-3 to determine the appropriate exercise intensity level. If you cannot decide which category is the most appropriate, take one of the fitness tests at the end of this chapter. Your performance on these should place you in a category that reflects your physical fitness level.

The Karvonen formula is

$$THR = (MHR - RHR) \times TI\% + RHR$$

where *THR* is the training heart rate, or the heart rate that should be maintained during exercise, *MHR* is the maximum heart rate, *RHR* is the resting heart rate, and *TI%* is the training intensity (see table 3-3). Therefore the exercise heart rate for a 25 year old with a resting heart rate of 75 beats per minute and an average fitness level is calculated as follows:

$$\begin{array}{r} 220 \\ - 25 \\ \hline 195 \text{ } (HR_{max}) \end{array}$$

$$\begin{aligned} THR &= (195 - 75) \times 0.70 + 75 \\ &= 120 \times 0.70 + 75 \\ &= 84 + 75 \\ &= 159 \end{aligned}$$

The training heart rate for this 25-year-old subject is 159 beats per minute. Assessment Activity 3-4 will enable you to determine your target heart rate for exercise.

Learning to take the pulse rate quickly and accurately is necessary to monitor exercise intensity by heart rate. Two of the most commonly used sites for taking the pulse rate are the radial artery on the thumb side of the wrist and the carotid artery at the side of the neck (figure 3-1). Use the first two fingers of your preferred hand to palpate the pulse. At the wrist, the pulse is located at the base of the thumb when the hand is held palm up. To find the carotid pulse, slide your fingers downward at the angle of the jaw below the earlobe to the side of the neck. You apply only enough pressure to feel the pulse, particularly at the carotid artery. Excessive pressure at this point stimulates specialized receptors that automatically slow the heart rate, leading to an underestimation of the rate actually achieved during exercise. The wrist is the preferred site for the *palpation* (examination by touch or feel) of the pulse rate. Measure the carotid pulse if you cannot feel your pulse at the wrist.

Locate and count the pulse rate immediately after exercise stops. Count the beats for ten seconds and multiply by 6 to get beats per minute. Start the count

Table 3-3 Guidelines for Selecting Exercise Intensity Level

Fitness Level	Intensity Level (%)
Low	60
Fair	65
Average	70
Good	75
Excellent	80–90

 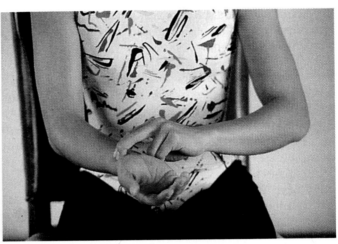

Figure 3-1 Sites for Taking a Pulse

The two sites for measuring pulse: A, location for taking a pulse at the carotid artery; B, location for taking a pulse at the wrist (radial artery).

by assigning a zero to the first beat that is felt or, as nurses do, start the count by assigning the first beat felt a value of 1. Regardless of which technique you use, be consistent in its application. Some practice is required to locate the pulse quickly and count it accurately.

Another method for monitoring the intensity of exercise is to rate your subjective perception of the effort. On some days, exercise seems easier than normal, and on other days it may seem more difficult.

Frequency

The *frequency* of exercise refers to the number of days of participation each week. The 1990 ACSM guidelines for improving physical fitness recommend that exercise be pursued three to five days per week for optimal results. Fewer than three days is an inadequate stimulus for developing fitness, and conversely, more than five days per week represents a point of diminishing returns from exercise and increases the likelihood of injury. Those who are exercising for health reasons and are following the 1995 guidelines are advised to engage in physical activities on most, preferably all, days of the week.

You can overdo exercise—too much results in staleness or overtraining. The signs of overtraining include the following:

- A feeling of chronic fatigue and listlessness
- Inability to make further fitness gains or regression of the level of fitness

- Sudden loss of weight
- An increase of 5 beats per minute in the resting heart rate
- Loss of enthusiasm for working out
- An increase in the risk for injury
- The occurrence of irritability, anger, and depression

Treatment requires that you cut back on training or stop completely for one to two weeks. When you resume exercise, it must be of lower intensity, frequency, and duration. You must rebuild and regain fitness gradually. Prevention is the best treatment for overtraining because people for whom exercise is a way of life are reluctant to discontinue training, even temporarily, for fear that they will lose their fitness edge. Convincing them that continuing to exercise is the worst possible action is extremely difficult.

Duration

Duration refers to the length of each exercise session. Intensity and duration are inversely related—the more intense the exercise, the shorter its duration. Intensity is always an important consideration for the development of physical fitness. Reducing the intensity somewhat while increasing the frequency and duration is the most beneficial method for health enhancement. In 1990, the ACSM recommended 20 to 60 minutes of continuous or noncontinuous aerobic activity.[1] The 1995 guidelines suggest the accumulation of 30 minutes or more of physical activity per day.[13]

Wellness On the Web Behavior Change Activities

How Hard Are You Training?

When you think of intensity, you think of hard work. In physical training, intensity refers to the degree of vigor you achieve in a single session of exercise. For cardiorespiratory endurance training, like running or power walking, you can measure intensity by using various heart-rate methods. One popular method is the Karvonen formula. Eoin Fahy, Ph.D., has a website dedicated to running at **www.home.connectnet.com/eoinf/ index.html.** This site contains a special section you can use to estimate your training heart-rate zone using the Karvonen formula. From Dr. Fahy's home page, select "heart rate"; fill in your age, gender, and resting heart rate, and click "calculate." You'll find three different levels of training heart-rate ranges.

Why Exercise?

How do experts define physical fitness? There's no general agreement, but most authorities endorse the concept of performance-related and health-related fitness. Like all aspects of wellness, you as an individual are responsible for developing an exercise program and sticking with it. Taking this step is much easier when you understand the importance of exercise as an integral part of a quality lifestyle. Stephen Seiler, Ph.D, is an endurance sport enthusiast and exercise physiologist who has a strong interest in the physiology of performance and in the role of exercise as "preventive medicine." To enhance your understanding of exercise physiology as it relates to wellness, go to Dr. Seiler's website at **www.krs.hia.no/~stephens/index.html.** On his home page, select "Exercise Physiology—The Big Picture." Scroll down the list of topics and read more about a specific area of exercise physiology as it relates to your wellness and fitness goals.

The Key to Your Heart

When we say someone is "heartless," we're speaking figuratively, not literally, because every person most definitely has a heart. From the moment we're conceived until we draw our last breath, our heart works tirelessly to fuel the processes that give us life. In an average lifetime, the heart beats more than two and a half billion times without ever stopping to rest. Throughout history, this life-sustaining power has created an aura of mystery around the heart. Modern science has removed much of the mystery, but we continue to be fascinated and curious about this vital human organ. To explore the heart in detail, go to **www.sln.fi.edu/biosci/heart.html.** In "The Heart: An Online Exploration," you'll discover the complexities of the heart's development and structure. You'll have the opportunity to follow the blood as it circulates through the blood vessels and the various body systems. Most important, you'll learn how to keep your heart healthy and how to monitor your heart's health.

Another way to monitor duration is to calculate the number of calories expended per exercise session. The ACSM recommends that, if you expend 300 calories per exercise session, you exercise three times per week; if you expend only 200 calories per exercise session, you exercise four times per week. These guidelines are sufficient for health benefits to accrue, but for fitness purposes, they should be viewed as a minimal level of exercise. (Table 8-5 in Chapter 8 discusses the way to determine how long you need to engage in the activities of your choice to achieve these goals.)

Progression, Overload, and Specificity

As people attain a level of fitness that meets their needs and when further improvement is not desired, the program switches from developing fitness to maintaining it. At this point the principles of overload and progression may be set aside, but both are necessary for the improvement phase of fitness. *Overload* involves subjecting the body to unaccustomed stress. Challenging the body to periodically accept a slightly increased level of work forces it to adapt by attaining a higher level of fitness. Deciding when to impose each new challenge involves the principle of progression. The workload is increased only when the exerciser is ready to accept a new challenge. For aerobic exercise, target heart rate or perceived exertion may be used to establish criteria for scheduling the progression. For example, if you jog, swim, or cycle a certain distance, the exercise heart rate will decrease over time as your body adapts to training. When the exercise heart rate drops to a predetermined level or the effort required becomes quite comfortable, you should adjust the pace or distance to return to the original target zone. However, the new physical challenge should not exceed the current amount of exercise by more than 10 percent. This should ensure that the new workload is not excessive.

The principle of *specificity* of training suggests that the body adapts according to the specific type of stress placed on it. The muscles involved in any activity are the ones that adapt, and they do so in the specific way in which they are used. For example, jogging prepares you for jogging but is poor preparation for cycling. Cycling does not prepare you for swimming. Although

Motivational Tips

Follow these tips to stay motivated to exercise:

- Exercise with a friend. Make sure both of you have compatible goals and are similar in fitness level. Friends can help each other sustain a program, particularly during busy times when the temptation to push exercise out of an already crowded schedule is quite high.

- Exercise with a group. Exchange ideas and literature about exercise with group members.

- Elicit the support of friends and family. Their support is a powerful source of reinforcement.

- Associate with other exercisers. They represent an enthusiastic, positive, and informative group—and their values are contagious.

- Join an exercise class or a fitness club. This gives you a place to go and meet people who want to exercise.

- Keep a progress chart. This will give you an objective account of your improvement.

- Exercise to music. Music makes the effort appear easier than it actually is.

- Set a definite time and place to exercise. This is particularly important during the early days of the program. Schedule exercise as you would any other activity of importance and then commit to the schedule.

- Participate in a variety of activities. Cross-training is excellent for the person who exercises for health or recreation.

- Do not become obsessive about exercise. Skipping exercise is not a good practice normally, but skipping is appropriate at times. Do not exercise when you are sick or overtired. Do not feel guilty about missing exercise for a day or two. Resume exercise as soon as you can.

these activities stress the cardiorespiratory system, they are sufficiently different that there is little fitness carryover among them.

The principle of specificity is particularly important for competitive athletes. Competitors attempt to maximize the returns from their training effort; therefore, runners must train by running, swimmers must swim, and cyclists must cycle. The focus is on maximal improvement in one activity so that the body is trained in a specific manner. This locks athletes into regimented training programs, but noncompetitors who exercise for health and physical fitness reasons are not under such constraints. They can vary activities and prevent the boredom of participating in the same activity day after day, week after week. Cycling, jogging, swimming, racquetball, cross-country skiing, weight training, and other activities may be used in any combination or order for the development of physical fitness. This is the essence of **cross-training**. Not only does cross-training relieve boredom, it may reduce the incidence of injury because it does not stress the same muscles in the same way during every workout.

Cross-training has many advantages and is an excellent technique for attaining the health benefits of exercise. Variety, the major attraction of cross-training, can also be a disadvantage, however. By participating in many different activities, you seldom become proficient in any one. However, if the objective is physical fitness or health enhancement, proficiency is incidental.

Identifying goals provides some direction for the activities selected and the way the principles of exercise are to be manipulated to increase the probability of success. Only one or two major goals should be selected, and these should be as specific as possible so that an effective exercise program may be devised. Activities, objectives, and exercise principles must match.

When you have identified the objectives and know what you wish to achieve from the exercise program, identify the means for sustaining the program. Your resolve to exercise is shakiest during the early stages of the program, usually because people push untrained bodies beyond their limits. This results in sore muscles, stiffness, and possible injury. Consequently, the dropout rate is highest in the beginning of any exercise program. The irony is that the greatest return for the effort is attained during this phase. Some tips for sustaining that effort are presented in Just the Facts: Motivational Tips.

Other Exercise Considerations

Warming Up for Exercise

Warming up prepares the body for physical action. The process involves physical activities that gradually heat the muscles and elevate the heart rate. A brisk walk, slow jog, jogging or hopping in place, rope jumping, and selected calisthenics will raise the heart rate and increase muscle temperature. A person should break out in a sweat during the warm-up. This indicates that heart rate and body temperature have increased to some extent and the person is ready for more vigorous activity. The warm-up should last 5 to 10 minutes.

Increasing the heart rate gradually during the warm-up period is most important. This allows the circulatory system to adjust to the load. If the heart rate elevates suddenly, circulation cannot adjust rapidly enough to meet the oxygen and nutrient demands of the heart muscle. The effects of this lag time are abolished in about 2 minutes, but increasing the heart rate quickly can be hazardous even during those 2 minutes, particularly for those with compromised circulation. Even the healthy heart may be affected by eliminating the gradual phase of warm-up. One study showed that every one of forty-four healthy male subjects, ages 21 to 52 years, had normal electrocardiogram (ECG) responses to running on a treadmill when they were allowed a warm-up consisting of 2 minutes of easy jogging. However, 70 percent of the group developed abnormal ECG responses to the same exercise when they were not allowed to warm up.[14]

Warm-up may be specifically tailored to the activity to be performed. For example, joggers may warm up by slowly jogging the first 0.5 to 0.75 mile, gradually speeding up to the desired pace. Cyclists, swimmers, cross-country skiers, and rope skippers may use the same approach.

Passive warm-up techniques, such as massage, sauna baths, steam baths, hot showers, hot towels, and heating pads, should not be used as substitutes for an active warm-up. These techniques may precede an active warm-up if a person feels stiff and sore from the previous workout.

Stretching exercises may be performed after the warm-up is completed. At this point, muscle temperature is elevated so that stretching is more effective and muscle, tendon, and joint injuries are less likely to occur. Stretching is most effective during the cooldown period following the workout because (1) muscles are heated and receptive to stretching, and (2) muscles that have contracted repeatedly during exercise need to be stretched. Figures 5-1 through 5-8 in Chapter 5 illustrate some typical stretching exercises that may be used before and after the workout period.

Cooling Down from Exercise

The cooldown is as important as the warm-up. Cooldown should last 8 to 10 minutes and consist of two phases. The first phase involves approximately 5 minutes of walking or other light activities to prevent blood from pooling in the muscles that have been working. Light activity causes rhythmic contractions of the muscles, which in turn act as a stimulus to circulate blood from the muscles to the heart for redistribution throughout the body. This boost to circulation following exercise, often referred to as the *muscle pump,* is essential for recovery and shares some of the burden of

circulation with the heart. The muscle pump effect does not occur if a period of inactivity follows exercise. An inactive cooldown forces the heart to work at a high rate to compensate for the reduced volume of blood returning to it because of blood pooling in the muscles. The exerciser runs the risk of dizziness, fainting, and more serious consequences associated with diminished blood flow to vital organs.

Light physical activity after exercise also speeds the removal of lactic acid that has accumulated in the muscles. *Lactic acid* is a fatiguing metabolite resulting from the incomplete breakdown of sugar. It is produced by exercise of high intensity or of long duration.

The second phase of cooldown should focus on the stretching exercises performed during the warm-up. Most participants find that stretching after exercise is more comfortable and more effective because the muscles are heated and more elastic.

Type of Activity

Many activities contribute to one or more components of health-related physical fitness. Activity selections should be based on objectives, skill level, availability of equipment, facilities, instruction, climate, and interest. Any rhythmic, continuous aerobic activity that uses large muscle groups and can be performed for an extended period of time is suitable for the attainment of health and fitness.

The President's Council on Physical Fitness and Sports (PCPFS) enlisted the aid of seven experts to evaluate fourteen popular physical activities for their contribution to physical fitness and general well-being. Although this assessment occurred several years ago, the ratings are as valid today as when they were originally conceived. A summary of these appears in table 3-4.

Selected sports have also been evaluated for their contribution to the health-related components of physical fitness. These appear in table 3-5. Lifetime sports (such as tennis, badminton, and racquetball) are more conducive to fitness development than are team sports (such as volleyball, soccer, softball, and basketball) because fewer players are needed. Ideally, fitness should be developed and maintained primarily through self-paced activities (for example, jogging, cycling, walking, and swimming), but the challenge inherent in sports may be necessary to sustain motivation for some people. Lifetime sports are challenging and fun, and they offer variety. However, fitness attained from these activities depends on skill level and a willingness to exert maximal effort in competition. The orthopedic demands of these activities may be greater than a sedentary beginner can tolerate. Quick stops and starts, bursts of high-intensity activity, sudden changes of direction, and rapid twists and turns place a great deal of

Table 3-4 Rating Fourteen Sports and Exercises

Exercise	Cardio-respiratory Endurance (Stamina)	Muscular Endurance	Muscular Strength	Flexibility	Balance	General Well-Being				Total
						Weight Control	Muscle Definition	Digestion	Sleep	
Jogging	21*	20	17	9	17	21	14	13	16	148
Bicycling	19	18	16	9	18	20	15	12	15	142
Swimming	21	20	14	15	12	15	14	13	16	140
Skating (ice or roller)	18	17	15	13	20	17	14	11	15	140
Handball/ squash	19	18	15	16	17	19	11	13	12	140
Skiing— nordic	19	19	15	14	16	17	12	12	15	139
Skiing— alpine	16	18	15	14	21	15	14	9	12	134
Basketball	19	17	15	13	16	19	13	10	12	134
Tennis	16	16	14	14	16	16	13	12	11	128
Calisthenics	10	13	16	19	15	12	18	11	12	126
Walking	13	14	11	7	8	13	11	11	14	102
Golf**	8	8	9	9	8	6	6	7	6	67*
Softball	6	8	7	9	7	7	5	8	7	64
Bowling	5	5	5	7	6	5	5	7	6	51

*The ratings are on a scale of 0 to 3; thus a rating of 21 is the maximum score that can be achieved (a score by 3 of all seven panelists). Ratings were made on the following basis: frequency, four times per week minimal; duration, 30 to 60 minutes per session.

**The rating was made on the basis of using a golf cart or caddy. If you walk the course and carry your clubs, the values improve.

Table 3-5 Rating Selected Sports

Sport	Cardiorespiratory Endurance	Muscular Strength/Endurance		Flexibility	Body Composition
		Upper	Lower		
Badminton	M-H*	L	M-H	L	M-H
Football (touch)	L-M	L-M	M	L	L-M
Ice hockey	H	M	H	L	H
Racquetball	H	M	H	M	H
Rugby	H	M-H	H	M	H
Soccer	H	L	H	M	H
Volleyball	M	M	M	L-M	M
Wrestling	H	H	H	M-H	H

*H, high; M, medium; L, low. The values in this table are estimates that vary according to the skill and motivation of the participants.

stress on the musculoskeletal system. The physically fit can handle the aerobic and musculoskeletal requirements of active sports, but attempting to "play yourself into shape" is a mistake. With knowledge of the principles of exercise, warm-up, cooldown, and the contributions of various physical activities to physical fitness, you can design an exercise program using Assessment Activity 3-5. See Real-World Wellness: Choosing Fitness Equipment for the Home for helpful advice on exercising at home.

Environmental Conditions

People work and exercise in a variety of environmental conditions. Hot and cold weather produce unique problems for people who function outdoors. Their safety and comfort depend on their knowledge of the ways the body reacts to physical activity in different climatic conditions.

Heat is produced in the body as a by-product of metabolism. Physical activities significantly increase metabolism, generating more heat than normal. Heat must be dissipated efficiently, or heat may build up, resulting in **hyperthermia,** abnormally high body temperature that can cause illness or even death. *Heat exhaustion* is also a serious condition but not an imminent threat to life. It is characterized by dizziness, fainting, rapid pulse, and cool skin. Treatment includes immediate cessation of activity. The victim should be moved to a cool, shady place, placed in a reclining position, and given cool fluids to drink.

Heat stroke is a medical emergency and a threat to life. It is the most severe of the heat-induced illnesses. The symptoms include a high temperature (106° F or higher) and dry skin caused by the cessation of sweating. These symptoms are accompanied by delirium, convulsions, or loss of consciousness. The early warning signs include chills, nausea, headache, and general weakness. Victims of heat stroke should be rushed immediately to the nearest hospital for treatment.

Mechanisms of Heat Loss

Heat is lost from the body by conduction, convection, radiation, and evaporation of sweat. Conduction, convection, and radiation are mechanisms responsible for heat loss *and* heat gain. These three depend on the difference between the temperature of the body and that of the environment. These mechanisms do not function alone to effect heat loss or gain.

Conduction occurs when direct physical contact is made between objects of which one is cooler than the other. The greater the difference in temperature between the objects, the greater the transfer of heat. An example is entering an air-conditioned room from

 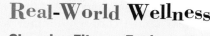

Real-World **Wellness**

Choosing Fitness Equipment for the Home

I'm a working mother with two young children. My only chance to exercise is at home after the children have been put to bed. I'm most interested in purchasing a good piece of cardio equipment that will burn calories and increase my energy level. What advice can you give me for selecting such equipment?

Here are some helpful hints:

1. Some of the most effective cardio equipment includes motor-driven treadmills, stationary exercise bikes, stationary rowers, stair climbers, cross-country skiing machines, videotape aerobic workouts (with or without stepping benches), and jump ropes.

2. Selecting the right piece of equipment is important. Many well-intentioned home exercisers become bored with the equipment they purchase or find that it is not meeting their needs, so they quit exercising.

3. Try out a piece of equipment before buying it. Make sure it feels comfortable, is easy to use, and is the right size for you.

4. Give equipment the three-week test: Before making your purchase, borrow or rent the piece of equipment and use it three to five times per week for three weeks. At the end of three weeks, you should know whether you enjoy it well enough to use it regularly and whether it will meet your needs and goals. The best equipment in the world is useless unless you use it regularly.

5. Check the construction of equipment to make sure that it is sturdy. The machine should not rock or wobble, and it should perform smoothly.

6. Equipment that is made of lightweight sheet metal or has many plastic parts may not withstand regular use.

7. Do not buy the least expensive machine. Think of this purchase as a long-term investment. Usually a middle-of-the line product will do very well. These carry a ninety-day warranty for parts, and the warranty may be extended to also include service.

8. Shop at a reputable sports equipment store that has a knowledgeable sales staff who can answer your questions and help you make the appropriate choice.

9. Make sure that the store will deliver and set up the equipment.

10. If marketing and promotional claims made for the equipment sound too good to be true, they probably are.

outdoors on a summer day and sitting in a cool leather chair. Heat is lost through contact with the cooler chair.

Conductive heat loss occurs even more rapidly in water.[2] Water is not an insulator but a conductor. It absorbs several thousand times more heat than does air at the same temperature. Air is an excellent insulator but a poor conductor. This is the reason that sitting at poolside is more comfortable than sitting in the pool, even if the temperatures of air and water are equal.

Heat loss or gain by *convection* occurs when a gas or water moves across the skin. Heat is transferred from the body to the environment more effectively if a breeze is blowing. Convective heat loss in water is increased when a person is swimming rather than floating because of the increased movement of the water across the body. The same principle applies to running outdoors because of the air flow over the body.

Humans, animals, and inanimate objects constantly transmit heat by electromagnetic waves to cooler objects in the environment. This heat loss through *radiation* occurs without physical contact between objects. Heat is simply transferred on a temperature gradient from warmer objects to cooler ones.

Heat loss by radiation is very effective when the air temperature (ambient temperature) is well below skin temperature. This is one of the main reasons that outdoor exercise in cool weather is better tolerated than the same exercise in hot weather. Temperatures in the upper 80s and 90s often result in heat gain by radiation.

Evaporation of sweat is the main method of heat loss during exercise, and this process is most effective when the humidity is low. High humidity significantly impairs the evaporative process because the air is very saturated and cannot accept much moisture. If both temperature and humidity are high, losing heat is difficult by any of these processes. Under these conditions, adjusting the intensity and duration of exercise or moving indoors, where the climate can be controlled, may be beneficial.

Heat loss by evaporation occurs only when the sweat on the surface of the skin is vaporized—that is, converted to a gas. The conversion of liquid to a gas at the skin level requires heat supplied by the body. As liquid sweat absorbs heat from the skin, it changes to a gaseous vapor that is carried away by the surrounding air, resulting in the removal of heat generated from exercise. Small amounts of evaporative sweat remove large quantities of heat. For example, each pint of sweat that evaporates removes approximately 280 calories of heat. Beads of sweat that roll off the body do not contribute to the cooling process—only sweat that evaporates does.

Exercise in hot and humid conditions forces the body to divert more blood than usual from the working muscles to the skin in an effort to carry the heat accumulating in the deeper recesses to the outer shell. The net result is that the exercising muscles are deprived of a full complement of blood and cannot work as long or as hard. Exercise is therefore more difficult in hot and humid weather.

Heat loss by evaporation is seriously impeded when a person wears nonporous garments, such as rubberized and plastic exercise suits. These garments encourage sweating, but their nonporous nature does not allow sweat to evaporate. This practice is dangerous because it may easily result in heat buildup and *dehydration* (excessive water loss), leading to heat-stress illnesses. You should dress for hot-weather exercise by wearing shorts and a porous top. A mesh, baseball-type cap is optional. It is effective in blocking the absorption of radiant heat if you exercise in the middle of the day because the sun's rays are vertical. You do not need to wear a cap when exercising in the cooler times of the day or if the sun is not shining.

Guidelines for Exercise in the Heat

Guidelines for exercising in heat and humidity have been developed for road races, but these guidelines can be applied to any strenuous physical activity performed outdoors during warm weather. Ambient conditions are considered safe when the temperature is below 70° F and the humidity is below 60 percent. Caution should be used and people who are sensitive to heat and humidity should reconsider exercising when the temperature is greater than 80° F or the humidity is over 60 percent. People who are trained and heat acclimated can continue to exercise in these conditions, but they should be aware of the potential hazards and take precautions to prevent heat illness.

The keys to exercising without incident in hot weather are acclimating to the heat and maintaining the body's normal fluid level. The main consequence of dehydration (excessive fluid loss) is a reduction in blood volume. This results in sluggish circulation that decreases the delivery of oxygen to the exercising muscles. Lowered blood volume results in less blood that can be sent to the skin to remove the heat generated by exercise. If too much of the blood volume is lost, sweating stops and the body temperature rises, leading to heat stress illness. Heat illness is a serious problem that can be avoided by following these guidelines designed to preserve the body's fluid level:

- Estimating water loss:
  - Weigh yourself nude before and after exercise.
  - Towel off sweat completely after exercise and then weigh yourself.

In hot, humid weather, drinking water and wearing loose clothing help prevent hyperthermia and heat stress illnesses.

- Each pound of weight loss represents about 1 pint of fluid loss. Be sure to drink that and more after exercise. See Just the Facts: Fluid Consumption Before, During, and After Exercise.
- Other considerations:
  - Modify the exercise program by (1) working out during cooler times of day, (2) choosing shady routes where water is available, (3) slowing the pace or shortening the duration of exercise on particularly oppressive days, and (4) wearing light, loose, porous clothing to facilitate the evaporation of sweat.
  - Never take salt tablets. They are stomach irritants, they attract fluid to the gut, they sometimes pass through the digestive system undissolved, and they may perforate the stomach lining.
  - Exercise must be prolonged, produce profuse sweating, and occur over a number of consecutive days to reduce potassium stores. For the average bout of exercise, you do not need to worry about depleting potassium or make a special

Just the Facts

Fluid Consumption Before, During, and After Exercise

The American College of Sports Medicine[15] has issued the following recommendations about fluid consumption:

1. Make a special effort to drink plenty of fluid every day so that you will be fully hydrated prior to exercise.
2. For exercise lasting 60 minutes or less:
   - Drink a minimum of 1 pint (2 cups) of water about two hours prior to exercise
   - Start drinking soon after exercise begins and continue drinking at regular intervals in an effort to replace the fluid lost from sweating
   - Drink cool fluids (59° F to 72° F) flavored for palatability, because cool fluids do not interfere with stomach emptying, they do not cause stomach cramping, and they absorb some of the body's internal heat.
3. For intense exercise lasting 60 minutes or more:
   - Drink fluids that contain a small amount of carbohydrates (sugar: glucose, sucrose; starch: maltodextrin) and sodium on a regular basis
   - Regularly ingest carbohydrates to maintain blood glucose level and delay fatigue
   - Ingest sodium in very small amounts (0.5 to 0.75 gram per liter of fluid) to enhance taste and promote fluid retention
   - After the workout, continue drinking the same beverage until your thirst is satisfied and then drink some more.
4. Most exercisers are reluctant drinkers during workouts and do not drink enough to match the fluid they lose through sweating, but they should make a conscious effort to get enough fluid during exercise.
5. The general rule after exercise is to drink until you satisfy your thirst and then drink some more. The thirst mechanism of humans is a poor index of the body's need for fluid.
6. Water is an acceptable drink, but it may blunt the thirst drive before rehydration is complete. Therefore, find a tasty beverage that is noncarbonated, nonalcoholic, and caffeine free to drink after exercise. Homemade lemonade, fruit juices cut in half with water to reduce the concentration of sugar, and commercial sports drinks fit the bill very nicely.[8]

effort to replace it. The daily consumption of fresh fruits and vegetables, as suggested by the food pyramid, is all that is needed (see Chapter 6).

- Remember to use a sunscreen lotion when the weather is sunny or hazy. Be sure that the sunscreen you select has a sun-protection factor (SPF) of at least 15, and apply it liberally over exposed skin.

Guidelines for Exercise in the Cold

Problems related to exercise in cold weather include frostbite and **hypothermia** (abnormally low body temperature). *Frostbite* can lead to permanent damage or loss of a body part from gangrene. This can be prevented by adequately protecting exposed areas, such as fingers, nose, ears, facial skin, and toes. Gloves, preferably mittens or thick socks, should be worn to protect the fingers, hands, and wrists. Blood vessels in the scalp do not constrict effectively, so a significant amount of heat is lost if a head covering is not worn. A stocking-type hat is the best head covering because it can be pulled down to protect the ears. In very cold or windy weather, use surgical or ski masks and scarves to keep facial skin warm and to moisten and warm inhaled air.

All exposed or poorly protected flesh is vulnerable to frostbite when the temperature is low and the windchill high. Air temperature plus wind speed equals the windchill index. This value will help you know how to dress appropriately for outdoor exercise.

People often experience a hacking cough for a minute or two after physical exertion in cold weather. This is a normal response and should not cause alarm. Very cold, dry air may not be fully moistened when it is inhaled rapidly and in large volumes during exercise, so the lining of the throat dries out. When exercise is discontinued, the respiratory rate slows and the volume of inhaled air decreases, allowing enough time for the body to fully moisturize it. Coughing stops within a couple of minutes as the linings are remoistened.

Hypothermia is the most severe of the problems associated with outdoor activity in cold weather. Hypothermia occurs when body heat is lost faster than it can be produced. This can be a life-threatening situation.

Exercise in cold weather requires insulating layers of clothing to preserve normal body heat. Without this protection, body heat is quickly lost because of the large temperature gradient between the skin and environment. A layer or two of insulating clothing can be discarded if you get too hot.

Real-World Wellness

Exercising Safely in an Urban Environment

I live in a large city and like to jog outdoors in my neighborhood. How can I limit the risks associated with exercising in the heart of the city?

You can start by becoming familiar with the risks in order to avoid or lessen their impact. Some of the major hazards follow:

1. Traffic volume is one of the primary risks associated with jogging in a large city. This risk can be reduced by wearing reflective clothing, jogging during daylight hours, and jogging on the sidewalks rather than the streets. The best way to handle the problem is to find a nearby park or outdoor running track.
2. A second risk comes from air pollution, primarily carbon monoxide and ozone. The Centers for Disease Control and Prevention has identified outdoor exercisers as one group at high risk for the effects of ozone, carbon monoxide, and other air pollutants. Rapid, deep breathing during exercise results in inhaling more pollutants more deeply into the lungs. Some studies have shown that 30 minutes of jogging during heavy traffic conditions increased carbon

monoxide levels in the blood to the equivalent of smoking half a pack of cigarettes.

Carbon monoxide interferes with the delivery of oxygen to the body's tissues and, when inhaled in high quantities, can cause illness and death. Carbon monoxide emissions from cars, trucks, and buses are most prevalent during rush hours, so avoid jogging on busy streets during these times.

Ozone causes lung inflammation and injury. The long-term effects of exercising in high ozone conditions are not known. Ozone tends to accumulate in the atmosphere after 10:00 A.M. It is heaviest during bright, sunny days because it is produced by the photochemical reaction of sunlight with hydrocarbons and nitrogen dioxide from motor vehicle exhaust.

Jogging before the rush hour begins will (1) help control your exposure to motor vehicle emissions and (2) allow you to exercise prior to the buildup of ozone in the atmosphere.

3. Joggers and other outdoor exercisers can be targets for crime. Carry no visible money or valuables, such as watches or jewelry. Carry an I.D. tag with your name and the telephone number of a family member or friend in case you are involved in an accident. Do not carry addresses, yours or your family's, in case you are mugged.

Hypothermia can occur even if the air temperature is above freezing.[16] The rate of heat loss for any temperature is influenced by wind velocity. Wind velocity increases the amount of cold air molecules that come in contact with the skin. The more cold molecules, the more effective the heat loss. The speed of walking, jogging, or cycling into the wind must be added to the speed of the wind to properly evaluate the impact of windchill.

You should wear enough clothing to stay warm but not so much as to induce profuse sweating. Knowing how much clothing to wear comes from experience exercising in different environmental conditions. Clothing that becomes wet with sweat loses its insulating qualities. It becomes a conductor of heat, moving heat from

the body quickly and potentially endangering the exerciser.

If you exercise or work outdoors in cold weather, you may want to wear polypropylene undergarments. Polypropylene is designed to whisk perspiration away from the skin so that evaporative cooling does not rob heat from the body. You should wear a warm outer garment, preferably made of wool, over this material, If it is windy, wear a breathable windbreaker as the third, outer layer.

If you follow the guidelines for activity in hot and cold weather, you can usually participate quite comfortably all year long. Other hazards associated with outdoor exercise are discussed in Real-World Wellness: Exercising Safely in an Urban Environment.

Summary

- *Physical fitness* is defined in terms of performance-related and health-related fitness.
- Cardiorespiratory endurance is the most important component of health-related fitness.
- The long-term effects of physical training include modifications in heart rate, stroke volume, cardiac output, blood volume, heart volume, respiration, and metabolism.
- Aerobic capacity is finite, improves by 5 to 25 percent with training, and decreases with aging; this decrease is slower in those who are physically fit.
- The training effect is lost in stages if exercise is interrupted or discontinued.
- Exercise affects cholesterol levels, blood pressure, and triglyceride levels, may reduce the risks of diabetes mellitus

and stress, and is an alternative method for quitting use of tobacco products.
- The principles of exercise can be manipulated to meet any exercise objective.
- Exercising by varying the activities per exercise session or during exercise sessions is cross-training.
- The heat generated by exercise is lost from the body by conduction, convection, radiation, and evaporation.
- Evaporation of sweat is the major mechanism for ridding the body of heat that develops during exercise.
- Hypothermia is the most severe problem associated with exercise in cold weather.

Review Questions

1. What are the physiological changes that occur from regular participation in aerobic exercise?
2. What are the health benefits that occur from regular participation in aerobic training?
3. Name and define the physiological changes that occur with exercise training.
4. Identify and define the principles of physical conditioning.
5. Define *cross-training* and give some examples.
6. Why should you warm up before exercise?
7. Identify and define the mechanisms of heat loss. Which of these is most important during exercise and why?
8. Describe fluid replacement before, during, and after exercise.

References

1. ACSM. 1998. The recommended quantity and quality of exercise for developing and maintaining cardiorespiratory and muscular fitness and flexibility in healthy adults. *Medicine and Science in Sports and Exercise* 30(6):975.
2. Foss, M. L., and S. T. Keteyian. 1998. *Fox's Physiological Basis for Exercise and Sport*. Boston: WCB/McGraw-Hill.
3. Franklin, B. A., and J. L. Roitman. 1998. Cardiorespiratory adaptations to exercise. In *ACSM's Resource Manual* (3d ed.), ed. J. L. Roitman. Baltimore, Md.: Williams & Wilkins.
4. Holly, R. G., and J. D. Shaffrath. 1998. Cardiorespiratory endurance. In *ACSM's Resource Manual* (3d ed.), ed. J. L. Roitman. Baltimore, Md.: Williams & Wilkins.
5. Blair, S. N., et al. 1995. Changes in physical fitness and all-cause mortality. *JAMA* 273:1093.
6. Williams, M. A. 1998. Human development and aging. In *ACSM's*

Resource Manual (3d ed.), Baltimore, Md.: Williams & Wilkins.

7. U.S. Dept. of Health and Human Services. 1996. *Physical Activity and Health: A Report of the Surgeon General.* Atlanta: U.S. Dept. of Health and Human Services, Centers for Disease Control and Prevention, National Center for Chronic Disease Prevention and Health Promotion.

8. Nieman, D. C. 1999. *Exercise Testing and Prescription.* Mountain View, Calif.: Mayfield Publishing Co.

9. Coyle, E. F. 1998. Deconditioning and retention of adaptations induced by endurance training. In *ACSM's Resource Manual* (3d ed.), ed. J. L. Roitman. Baltimore, Md.: Williams & Wilkins.

10. Beckman, S. 1998. Emergency procedures and exercise safety. In *ACSM's Resource Manual* (3d ed.), ed. J. L. Roitman. Baltimore, Md.: Williams & Wilkins.

11. Mittleman, M. A., et al. 1993. Triggering of acute myocardial infraction by heavy physical exertion. *New England Journal of Medicine* 329(23):1677.

12. Willich, S. N., et al. 1993. Physical exertion as a trigger of acute myocardial infraction. *New England Journal of Medicine* 329(23):1684.

13. Pate, R. R., et al. Physical activity and public health. A recommendation from the Centers for Disease Control and Prevention and the American College of Sports Medicine. *Journal of the American Medical Association* 273:402.

14. Barnard, R. J. et al. 1973. Cardiovascular responses to sudden strenuous exercise—heart rate, blood pressure, and ECG. *Journal of Applied Physiology* 34:833.

15. American College of Sports Medicine. 1996. Position paper on exercise and fluid replacement. *Medicine and Science in Sports and Exercise* 28:1.

16. Bernard, T. E. 1998. Environmental considerations: Heat and cold. In *ACSM's Resource Manual* (3d ed.), ed. J. L. Roitman. Baltimore, Md.: Williams & Wilkins.

Suggested Readings

Editors. 1998. Exercise and fracture risk. *Health News* 4(10):8.

Women who do aerobics or weight training or who play tennis at least two hours per week can expect to reduce the risk of hip and vertebral (spinal bones) fractures by one-third more than can inactive women. Exercise also helps women avoid falls by improving their strength, balance, and coordination.

Harvard University. 1998. An exercise prescription for older people. *Harvard Heart Letter* 8(5):1.

This article presents the principles of exercise and the precautions that should be taken by older people wanting to start an exercise program. It makes the case that age should not be a deterrent to aerobic and resistive exercises. Research is presented that documents the need for and the benefits that older people receive from regular participation in exercise.

Superko, H. R. 1998. The most common cause of coronary heart disease can be successfully treated by the least expensive therapy—exercise. *ACSM Certified News* 8(1):1.

Coronary artery disease is a metabolic disorder that has a strong genetic component, and its most common trait is a high amount of small LDL-C particles. This profile increases the risk three times above normal in males. But it successfully responds to regular exercise and loss of body weight.

Terbizan, D. J., and B. Straud. 1998. How Much Exercise? *Fitness Management* 14(9):32.

This article discusses the need for American adults to exercise and documents the reasons why. It also elaborates on the various goals that people attempt to meet through exercise and presents recommendations for their achievement, categorized in a five-level activity pyramid, from least intense to most intense: fat burning zone, heart healthy zone, aerobic zone, intense conditioning, and competitive zone.

Tufts University. 1998. How to stay young five years longer. *Tufts University Health and Nutrition Letter* 16(5):2.

Growing evidence indicates that middle-aged adults who exercise at least four hours per week, don't smoke, and remain lean are 50 percent more likely to live into their 70s than are sedentary, overweight smokers. Those who follow these lifestyle habits do not develop minor disabilities such as difficulty in walking or reaching for things until they reach the age of about 74. Overweight, nonexercising smokers begin experiencing these disabilities at age 69.

Assessment Activity 3-1

The Rockport Fitness Walking Test

Directions: This walking test estimates aerobic capacity based on the variables of age, gender, time required to walk 1 mile, and the heart rate achieved at the end of the test. The guidelines for taking the test are as follows:

1. Count your heart rate for 15 seconds and multiply by 4 to get beats per minute.
2. The course should be flat and measured, preferably a 440-yard track.
3. Use a stopwatch or a watch with a second hand.
4. Warm up for 5 to 10 minutes before taking the test. Preparation for the test should include a 0.25-mile walk followed by the stretching exercises.
5. During the test, walk at a brisk pace, covering 1 mile as rapidly as possible.
6. Take your pulse rate immediately after the test. Mark this rate on the chart on the following pages that is appropriate for your age and gender.
7. Draw a vertical line through your time and a horizontal line through your heart rate. The point where the lines intersect determines your fitness level (see the charts on the following pages).

Rockport provides a series of twenty-week walking-for-fitness programs that are based on the results of the walking test. These may be obtained for a nominal fee ($1 at this writing) by sending a request to Rockport Fitness Walking Test, 72 Howe Street, Marlboro, Massachusetts, 01752.

The charts on the following pages are designed to tell you how fit you are compared with other individuals of your age and gender. For example, if your coordinates place you in the "above average" section of the chart, you are in better shape than the average person in your category.

The charts are based on weights of 170 lbs. for men and 125 lbs. for women. If you weigh substantially more, your relative cardiovascular fitness level will be slightly overestimated. If you weigh substantially less, your relative cardiovascular fitness level will be slightly underestimated.

Men

20- to 29-year-old men

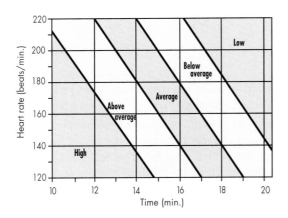

30- to 39-year-old men

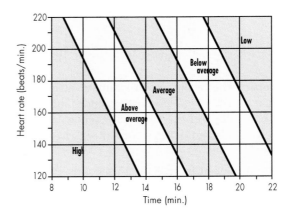

40- to 49-year-old men

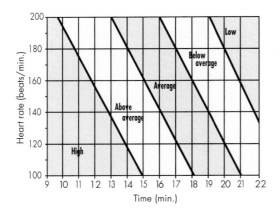

50- to 59-year-old men

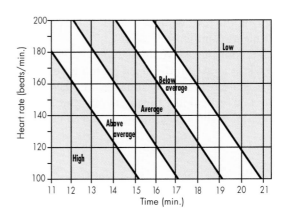

60-year-old and older men

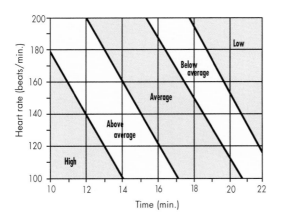

Women

20- to 29-year-old women

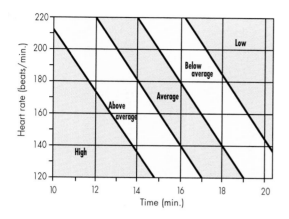

30- to 39-year-old women

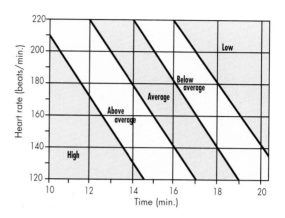

40- to 49-year-old women

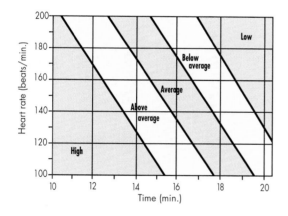

50- to 59-year-old women

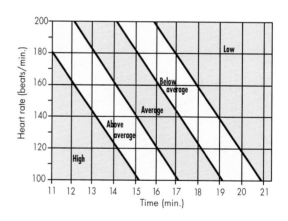

60-year-old and older women

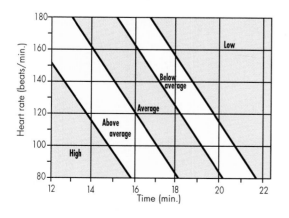

Assessment Activity 3-2

The 1.5-Mile Run/Walk Test

Directions: Select a measured course, preferably a running track, so that the starting and finishing points are at the same location for ease of timing and recording. Cover the distance as rapidly as possible to attain a realistic estimate of fitness level. You will perform better if you take the opportunity to practice running the course first so that you can learn how to pace yourself.

If you cannot run the entire distance, walk until you recover enough to continue running again. Allow a 5- to 10-minute warm-up before the test and an equal amount of time for cooling down after the test. Use the following charts to compare your performance with the norm.

Aerobic Physical Fitness Classification

Men

Fitness Category	13–19 Yrs.	20–29 Yrs.	30–39 Yrs.	40–49 Yrs.
Very poor	>15:31*	>16:01	>16:31	>17:31
Poor	12:11–15:30	14:01–16:00	14:46–16:30	15:36–17:30
Fair	10:49–12:10	12:01–14:00	12:31–14:45	13:01–15:35
Good	9:41–10:48	10:46–12:00	11:01–12:30	11:31–13:00
Excellent	8:37–9:40	9:45–10:45	10:00–11:00	10:30–11:30
Superior	<8:37	<9:45	<10:00	<10:30

*>, greater than; <, less than

Women

Fitness Category	13–19 Yrs.	20–29 Yrs.	30–39 Yrs.	40–49 Yrs.
Very poor	>18:31*	>19:01	>19:31	>20:31
Poor	16:55–18:30	18:31–19:00	19:01–19:30	19:31–20:00
Fair	14:31–16:54	15:55–18:30	16:31–19:00	17:31–19:30
Good	12:30–14:30	13:31–15:54	14:31–16:30	15:56–17:30
Excellent	11:50–12:29	12:30–13:30	13:00–14:30	13:45–15:55
Superior	<11:50	<12:30	<13:00	<13:45

Name _____ Date _____ Section _____

Assessment Activity 3-3

The Bench Step Test

Directions: The equipment needed includes a sturdy 12-inch–high bench, a metronome, a stopwatch, and, if possible, a stethoscope. The metronome should be set at 96 beats per minute for a total of 24 cycles. One cycle consists of four steps as follows: up left foot, up right foot, down left foot, down right foot.

Step up and down in time with each beat of the metronome for 3 full minutes. At the end of the 3 min-utes, sit down on the bench immediately. Start the pulse count within the first 5 seconds and continue for 1 full minute. Do not count for 15 seconds and multi-ply by 4, because the heart rate will be higher than the actual minute heart rate. The 1-minute postexercise heart rate is the score for the test. Refer to the follow-ing chart for scoring.

Postexercise 1-Minute Heart Rate (Beats per Minute)

Fitness Category	18–25 Yrs.		26–35 Yrs.		36–45 Yrs.	
	Men	**Women**	**Men**	**Women**	**Men**	**Women**
Excellent	70–78*	72–83	73–79	72–86	72–81	74–87
Good	82–88	88–97	83–88	91–97	86–94	93–101
Above average	91–97	100–106	91–97	103–110	98–102	104–109
Average	101–104	110–116	101–106	112–118	105–111	111–117
Below average	107–114	118–124	109–116	121–127	113–118	120–127
Poor	118–126	128–137	119–126	129–135	120–128	130–138
Very poor	131–164	141–155	130–164	141–154	132–168	143–152

*Count the pulse for 1 full minute after 3 minutes of stepping at 24 cycles/min. on a 12-inch bench.

Assessment Activity 3-4

Calculating Target Heart Rate

Directions: Use the Karvonen method to determine your target heart rate for exercise by filling in the following chart.

Karvonen formula: $THR = (HR_{max} - RHR)$
$$\times TI\% + RHR$$

Key

THR = target heart rate
HR_{max} = maximum heart rate ($HR_{max} = 220 -$ age)
RHR = resting heart rate
TI% = training intensity

Example

- A 23-year-old man in good condition (0.75 training intensity from table 3-3)
- RHR = 66 bpm (beats per minute)

- $HR_{max} = 220 - 23 = 197$ bpm
- THR = *164 bpm*

$THR = (197 - 66) \times .075 + 66 = 131 \times 0.75 + 66$
$= 164$ bpm

Your target heart rate:
$HR_{max} = 220 - AGE =$
$THR = (HR_{max} - RHR) \times TI\% + RHR$

$THR = (\text{_____} - \text{_____}) \times + \text{_____}$

$= \text{_____} \times \text{\_\_\_\_\_} + \text{_____}$

$= \text{_____} + \text{_____}$

$= \text{_____}$ bpm

Name _____ **Date** _____ **Section** _____

Assessment Activity 3-5

Design an Exercise Program

Directions: Design an exercise program for yourself. First, identify your goals (weight loss, health enhancement, improving your level of physical fitness, stress re-duction, etc.) and second, respond accordingly to each of the following five items.

1. Activity or activities: _____

2. Frequency of exercise:_____

3. Intensity of exercise: _____

4. Duration of exercise:_____

5. Activity schedule: Place the activity or activities in the following weekly calendar with the suggested amount of time devoted to each activity.

Sunday	Monday	Tuesday	Wednesday	Thursday	Friday	Saturday

Building Muscular Strength and Endurance

Key Terms

anaerobic
atrophy
circuit resistance training
  (CRT)
concentric contraction
eccentric contraction
hypertrophy

isokinetic
isometric
isotonic
muscular endurance
muscular strength
variable resistance

Goals for Behavior Change

- Begin a strength-training program or improve the one in which you already participate.
- Supply your close family members with at least five health-related reasons they should participate in resistance training.
- Identify the parts of your body where you would like to make the greatest physical change and explain why.
- Identify some of the tasks or sports that you perform daily, weekly, or monthly that would be easier to do if you increased your strength.

Objectives

After completing this chapter, you will be able to do the following:

- Explain the benefits of resistance training for older people.
- Define the different types of muscle contraction.
- Identify the various systems of dynamic and static exercise training.
- Describe the limitations of isometric exercise training.
- Explain the advantages and disadvantages of circuit resistance training.
- Define each of the principles of resistance training.

- Explain the differences in strength between men and women.
- Describe the short- and long-term effects of anabolic steroid use.
- Describe the health benefits of resistance training.
- Describe the progressive resistance technique that increases muscle endurance.

ver the last decade, evidence has been steadily mounting of the growing importance of muscular development for health enhancement, fitness, and aesthetic purposes. The muscular system improves through resistive forms of exercises, such as weight training and calisthenics. Resistive exercises complement aerobic forms of exercise, because each uniquely contributes to health, physical fitness, and personal appearance. Both types of exercise are required for a well-rounded conditioning program, and together they produce optimum results.

Aerobic exercises, which improve cardiorespiratory function and enhance health status in many ways, are presented in Chapter 3. Resistance exercises also contribute to physiological and psychological health. In fact, many experts are convinced that resistance training is the only type of exercise capable of slowing, and possibly reversing, declines in muscle mass, bone density, and strength. Not long ago, these negative changes were considered to be the result of the aging process.[1]

The body contains more than 600 muscles, and 65 percent of these are located above the waist. All muscles, regardless of location, respond to the physiological law of use and disuse. "Use it or lose it" is an axiom that applies to all human beings during every phase of the life cycle. Americans tend to become more sedentary as they age. The declining stimulation results in a progressive shrinking and weakening of the muscles.

With few exceptions—notably cross-country skiing, rowing, and swimming—aerobic activities provide limited stimulation of upper body musculature. Sedentary living neglects the muscular system entirely and accelerates the loss of muscle tissue and body strength. The need for resistance training was illustrated in a study of runners during a ten-year period. Runners who did no resistance training suffered muscle atrophy in their upper bodies while maintaining muscle size in their legs.[2] Their arms, which received little stimulation from jogging, decreased in circumference.

Jogging is unable to stimulate the arms at or above the threshold needed for muscular development or maintenance, but the addition of resistive exercises can. This is an example of how the two types of training complement each other.

The Health Benefits of Resistance Training

Irrefutable evidence proves that strength training produces unique health benefits for people of all ages as well as for those with various types of infirmities. The American College of Sports Medicine, The American Heart Association, and the Surgeon General's *Report on Physical Activity and Health* have all proclaimed and strongly supported the need for strength training for health enhancement and for improving quality of life. Strength training increases muscle mass and decreases the fat content of the body. The implications for weight loss and management are enormous, because muscle tissue is more metabolically active than is fat tissue. This means that the body burns more calories under any condition, including rest.[3]

An improvement in strength reduces the exerciser's heart rate and blood pressure while he or she is lifting weights. The practical application of these responses is that there is less stress on the heart when people lift or move moderately heavy objects in everyday life.[4]

Resistance training increases the strength and endurance of the antigravity muscles, improving posture and producing less stress on the lower back.[5] Stronger, more stable joints are better able to withstand physical stress or trauma.

Strength training also enables one to perform the functions of daily life with less effort. Actually, stronger muscles allow people to perform functional tasks that become more difficult as people age, such as getting in and out of a car, in and out of a bathtub, or up from an easy chair and climbing stairs. Dynamic forms of resistance training have a high degree of transferability to everyday activities.

An increase in leg strength helps those who have osteoarthritis (wear and tear arthritis) because stronger muscles absorb a greater share of the physical stress at joints. In effect, stronger muscles spare the joint structures from some of the weight-bearing activity. Rheumatologists (physicians who specialize in the diagnosis and treatment of arthritic conditions) often recommend weight training to their patients because it alleviates symptoms and strengthens the muscles, tendons, and ligaments that surround the joints.[1]

An improvement in leg strength also leads to better balance and decreases the likelihood of falling, which reduces the chances that a fracture might occur.[4] Osteoporosis is a disease characterized by the deterioration of the skeletal system. Bone mineral content decreases so that the bones become fragile and susceptible to fracture. Women are more prone to osteoporosis, but men are also affected as they age. People can protect the skeletal system by eating a nutritious diet and by participating regularly in weight-bearing and resistive exercise. Resistive exercises are versatile, having the capacity to stress all of the joints and the bones that articulate with them, and they produce lateral forces that increase the thickness and density of bones, so they have the potential to prevent osteoporosis.

The results brought about by resistance exercises allow people to live independently and with dignity as they age. Evidence indicates that Americans are living longer, and many will live with physical and functional limitations.[6] Illnesses occur with greater frequency and severity as we age, but much of the disability associated with aging is not due entirely to the aging process. Many authorities attribute at least 50 percent of these changes to "disuse atrophy."[7] The fact is that our typically sedentary lifestyles, which are more prevalent among the aging population than among any other group of Americans, are responsible for a significant number of these illnesses. Those who stimulate their muscles regularly, regardless of their age, do not experience the type of physical deterioration observed in those who are physically inactive. Recent research indicates that physical inactivity is responsible for the majority of age-related muscle loss.[1,8]

Strength training also produces an impressive array of psychological and emotional benefits, which include improvements in self-esteem and self-confidence.[3] It helps to improve the mood of mildly to moderately depressed individuals. Resistive exercise programs improve reaction time and may contribute to more restful sleep. Just the Facts: The Benefits of Resistance Training provides a summary of the positive outcomes that can be achieved through resistance training. Also see Wellness Across the Generations: Strength Training for Older Adults.

Many cardiac patients currently participate in strength development exercise. Substantial benefits may be gained at minimal risk.[9] Improving upper and lower body strength allows cardiac patients to perform everyday lifting activities with less effort and greater movement efficiency. Also, strength training may have a positive impact on cardiorespiratory endurance, hypertension, blood fat levels, and psychological well-being.

Anaerobic Exercise

Strength development exercises are **anaerobic.** *Anaerobic* literally means "without oxygen," and when applied to exercise, it refers to high-intensity physical activities in which oxygen demand is above the level that can be supplied during performance. Short-term supplies of fuel stored in the muscles provide the energy for anaerobic activities. As a result, these can only be sustained for several seconds. Sprinting 100 yards, lifting a heavy weight, and running up two or three flights of stairs are some examples of anaerobic activities.

Muscular Strength

Muscular strength is the maximum force that a muscle or muscle group can exert in a single contraction. It is best developed by some form of progressive resistance exercise, such as weight training with free weights (bar-

Just the Facts

The Benefits of Resistance Training

Resistance training produces the following positive results:

- Increases muscle mass and decreases fat mass
- Increases strength and muscle endurance
- Increases basal metabolic rate (BMR)
- Develops the antigravity muscles (abdominal, lower back, hips, front and back of the thighs, both calves)
- Increases bone density (resulting in less risk of bone fracture)
- Improves dynamic balance (resulting in less risk of falling)
- Improves mobility, such as that necessary for walking and stair-climbing
- Improves reaction time
- Contributes to more restful sleep
- Helps to elevate the mood of mildly to moderately depressed people
- Improves body image, self-esteem, and self-confidence
- Improves the effectiveness of insulin in older adults
- Aids in weight loss and weight management
- May increase HDL cholesterol (the protective form)

bells and dumbbells) or single or multistation machine weights.

Muscular strength is developed best through high-intensity exercise. Lifting heavier loads a few times to fatigue produces larger gains than does lifting lighter loads many times to fatigue. Weight trainers speak of the amount of work accomplished in high-intensity exercise repetitions, sets, and terms of percentage of 1 repetition maximum (1 RM) for each exercise. A *repetition* is one complete lift of an exercise beginning with the starting position, moving the weight through a full range of motion, and returning to the starting position. Doing this ten times in a continuous fashion is referred to as *10 repetitions* or *10 reps,* and these 10 reps represent 1 *set* of that exercise. Repeating the entire sequence two more times completes *3 sets* of the exercise. One repetition maximum (1 RM) represents the heaviest load that can be lifted one time. Ten RM is a lighter load that can be lifted ten times but not eleven. In other words, maximum fatigue occurs on repetition number 10, thereby preventing repetition number 11.

Wellness Across the Generations

Strength Training for Older Adults

One of the realities of aging is muscle atrophy (decrease in size), resulting in a loss of strength, power, balance, and coordination. However, scientists have shown that a substantial amount of muscle loss is due to lack of appropriate physical activity rather than to the aging process. Engaging regularly in resistance exercises can build muscle, maintain muscle, and limit the loss of muscle tissue.

Inactive people can expect to lose approximately 50 percent of their muscle mass between 20 and 90 years of age.[10] This loss is accompanied by a 30 percent reduction in strength between 50 and 70 years of age. Data from the ongoing Framingham Study showed that 40 percent of female subjects 55 to 64 years of age, 45 percent of female subjects 65 to 74 years of age, and 65 percent of female subjects 74 to 85 years of age were unable to lift 10 pounds. The loss of muscle strength is most pronounced after age 70. Data show that muscle strength declines by approximately 15 percent per decade during the 60s and 70s and accelerates to 30 percent per decade thereafter.[10]

Because of this limitation, everyday functions taken for granted by the young become physical challenges, including opening bottle caps and jar lids, carrying groceries, and climbing stairs. If muscle atrophy progresses unabated, walking without assistance becomes very difficult if not impossible, and the likelihood of falling increases.

The good news is that the muscles of older people respond to training in much the same way as the muscles of young adults. In fact, older people may make greater gains because of their initial level of debility (weakness). Studies have shown that the elderly can double or even triple their strength level in as little as three to four months of strength training.[10] Strength training also seems to have profound anabolic (muscle-building) effects in elderly people.

Select a weight that is 80 to 90 percent of 1 RM if strength development is the primary goal. If you are a beginner, be extremely careful in establishing 1 RM for each exercise, because your musculoskeletal system is not trained to handle such loads. It is recommended that beginners skip the 1 RM method of weight selection and instead, through trial and error, find a weight that can be lifted for at least but not more than 8 to 10 reps. One RM for each exercise may be safely established after six weeks of training.

Muscle Contraction and Resistance Training

Muscle contraction is either static or dynamic. *Static contractions* (isometric) occur when muscles exert force but do not move (shorten or lengthen). *Dynamic contractions* (isotonic and isokinetic) involve muscle contractions that are either *concentric* (muscle shortening) or *eccentric* (muscle lengthening). See figure 4-1 for an illustration of each.

Some of the exercises commonly used to develop the major muscle groups of the body are shown in figures 4-2 to 4-17. The anatomical charts in figures 4-18 and 4-19 show the location of the muscles stressed in each exercise. These exercises are demonstrated on exercise machines and free weights, methods that are equivalent and work the same muscle groups.

See Assessment Activity 4-1 for a method of determining your strength based on body weight and gender.

Static Training (Isometrics)

Isometric contractions (in which muscle length is constant) occur when muscles produce tension but do not shorten, because the resistance is beyond the contractile force that can be generated by the exercising muscles. Examples of isometric contractions are pushing against a wall, pushing sideways or upward against a door jamb, and loading a weight machine with poundage that is beyond one's capacity to lift. See figure 4-20 for an illustration.

Optimal strength development from isometric contractions occurs with 5 to 10 sets of 6-second contractions at 100 percent of maximum force.

Isometric exercises are effective for developing strength, but this approach has some important limitations. The most serious of these is a higher than expected rise in exercise arterial blood pressure and an increased workload on the heart throughout the entire contraction. All-out straining isometric contractions should not be performed by people with heart and vascular disease. A second limitation is that strength developed isometrically is joint-angle specific. Maximum strength development occurs at the angle of contraction, with a training carryover of approximately 20 degrees in either direction from that angle.[11] To develop strength throughout the muscle's range of motion, you must perform isometric contractions at three different points in the range of motion.

Figure 4-1 Contractions

The two types of contractions: *A*, a concentric contraction; *B*, an eccentric contraction.

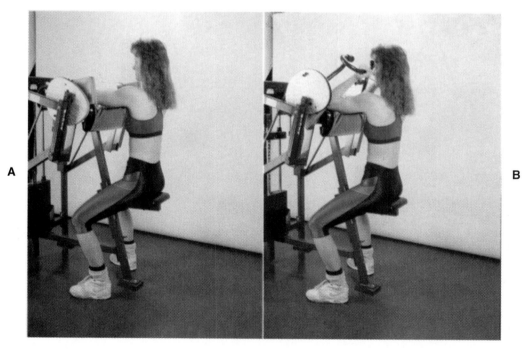

Figure 4-2 Biceps Curl

A: Start with your arms extended, palms up. *B*: Flex both arms, slowly move the weight through a full range of motion, and return to the starting position. The prime mover is the biceps brachii.

Figure 4-3 Biceps Curl (Free Weights)

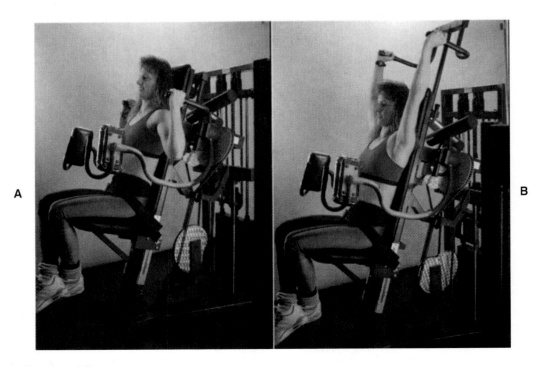

A   B

Figure 4-4 Overhead Press

A: Sit upright with your hands approximately shoulder width apart. *B*: Slowly press the bar upward until your arms are fully extended, and lower to the starting position. Avoid an excessive arch in your lower back. The prime movers are the triceps and deltoid muscles.

Figure 4-5 Overhead Press (Free Weights)

Figure 4-6 Bench Press

A: Lie on your back with your knees bent and your feet flat on the bench to prevent arching your back. *B*: Slowly press the bar forward, fully extending your arms, and return to the starting position. The prime movers are the pectoralis major, triceps, and deltoid muscles.

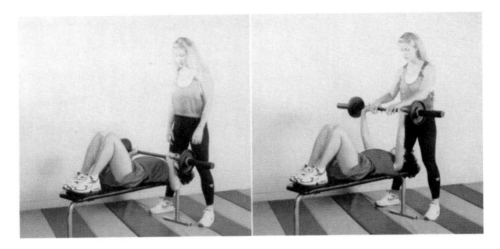

Figure 4-7 Bench Press (Free Weights)

A

B

Figure 4-8 Abdominal Crunch

A: Sit upright with your chest against the pads, hands folded across your stomach. *B*: Slowly press forward through a full range of motion, and return to the starting position. The prime mover is the rectus abdominis muscle.

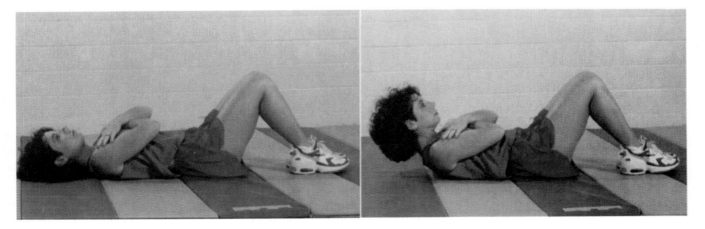

Figure 4-9 Abdominal Crunch (Mat Exercise)

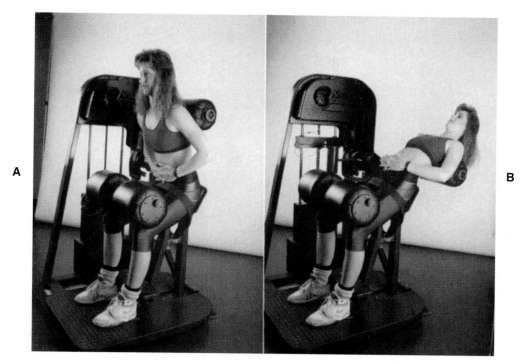

Figure 4-10 Lower Back Extension

A: Place your thighs and back against the pads. *B*: Slowly press backward until your back is fully extended, and return to the starting position. The prime movers are the erector spine and gluteus maximus muscles.

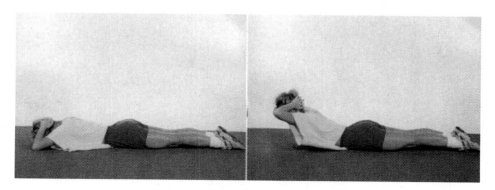

Figure 4-11 Back Extension (Mat Exercise)

Because muscles cannot overcome the resistance in isometric training, measuring improvement is difficult, constituting another limitation of this system. Improvements in strength can be measured if exercisers have access to specialized equipment, such as dynamometers and tensiometers, that record the amount of force applied. Motivation for exercise is difficult to sustain without feedback.

Research indicates that isometric exercise systems are as effective as dynamic exercise systems for developing strength. The question is not which system is better but which system best satisfies the intended use for the newly acquired strength. The transferability of strength to occupational and leisure pursuits is very relevant.

Strength developed in the muscles is highly specific to the manner in which the muscles are trained. Muscles trained isometrically perform best when stressed isometrically; muscles trained dynamically perform best when stressed dynamically. There is some transfer of isometric training to everyday life. Carrying groceries, a baby, or any object in a fixed position or pushing and pulling objects requires isometric strength, but most movements are dynamic, and transfer is more widely applicable from dynamic systems of training.

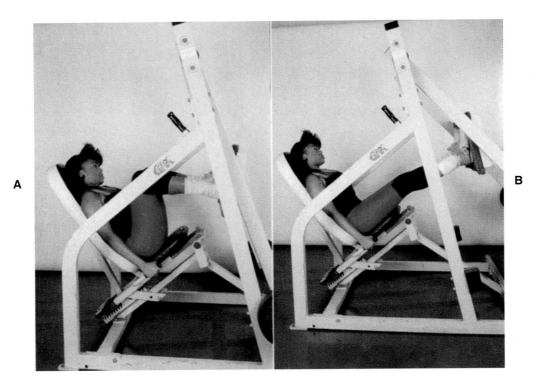

Figure 4-12 Leg Press

A: Adjust the seat so that your legs are bent at approximately 90 degrees. *B*: Slowly extend your legs fully, and return to the starting position. The prime movers are the quadriceps and gluteus maximus muscles.

Figure 4-13 Half-Squat (Free Weights)

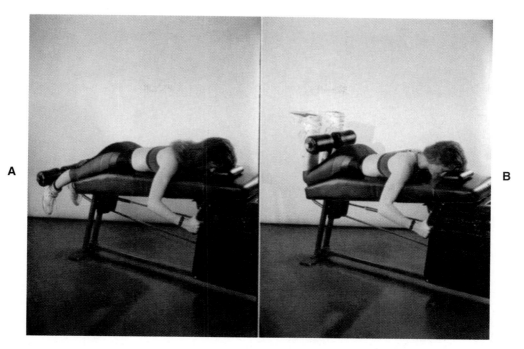

Figure 4-14   Hamstring Curl

A: Lie face down with your lower legs under the pads. *B:* Curl the weight approximately 90 degrees, and return to the starting position. The prime mover is the hamstring muscle group.

Figure 4-15   Hamstring Curl (Free Weights)

Dynamic Exercise

Dynamic exercises include **isotonic** (equal tension), variable resistance, free weights, and **isokinetic** (equal speed) exercises.

Isotonic training

Isotonic muscle contractions occur when muscles shorten and move the bones to which they are attached, resulting in movement around the joints. Isotonic movements consist of concentric and eccentric muscle contractions. The **concentric contraction** occurs when a muscle shortens as it develops the tension to overcome an external resistance. The **eccentric contraction** occurs when the muscle lengthens and the weight (resistance) is slowly returned to the starting position. When muscles contract eccentrically, they are resisting the force of gravity as they lengthen so that the weight is not allowed to free-fall. In general, muscles can produce about 40 percent more tension eccentrically than concentrically.[5] But no advantage exists for training programs that emphasize eccentric contractions. Research indicates that conventional isotonic programs develop as much strength and produce less of the delayed muscle soreness that is associated with eccentric contractions.

Figure 4-16 Chest Press
A: Keep your upper arms parallel to the floor, bend your elbows at 90 degrees, and place your hands on the handles.
B: Slowly push the bars until your elbows are pointing forward, and return to the starting position. The prime movers are the pectoralis major and deltoid muscles.

Figure 4-17 Lateral Supine Raises (Free Weights)

Isotonic exercises produce delayed muscle soreness twenty-four to forty-eight hours after a workout. Eccentric contractions cause microscopic damage to muscle fibers, their connective tissue, and the cell membranes.[12] Soreness occurs because the damaged tissues swell and apply pressure on the nerves. Delayed muscle soreness is more common among beginning exercisers, exercisers who attempt to overload too quickly, and those who change from one activity to another.

Stretching exercises, light workouts, or complete rest may be required to alleviate muscle soreness. Prevention is the best treatment. Prevention involves allowing enough time to adjust to a new routine (at least one month), overloading the muscles in small increments (not trying to do too much too fast), and exercising within capacity. Because muscle soreness may last forty-eight hours, those who use isotonic exercise systems are advised to exercise no more than every other day. This schedule ensures that the next bout of exercise will occur after soreness has abated.

Variable resistance training

Variable resistance exercise equipment was developed because isotonic exercises do not maximally stress muscles throughout their full range of motion. The maximum

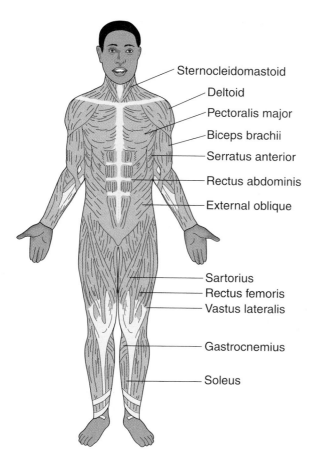

Figure 4-18 Selected Muscles of the Body—Front View

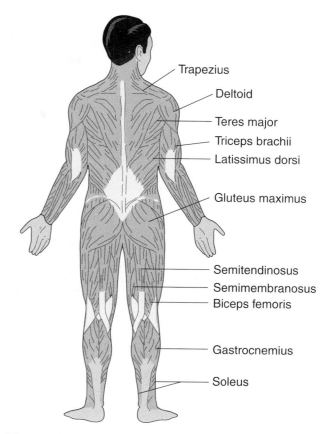

Figure 4-19 Selected Muscles of the Body—Rear View

weight lifted isotonically is limited to the weakest point in the musculoskeletal leverage system. The weight appears lighter at some points in the joint movement and heavier at others. In reality, the weight itself is constant and the human bony leverage system changes.

Variable resistance equipment is designed to provide maximum resistance through the full range of motion. Universal Gym equipment accomplishes this by altering the lifter's leverage. Decreasing the leverage increases the resistance at points in the movement where the muscles are strongest. Nautilus equipment uses a system of cams to do the same. Variable resistance training challenges people to exert more force throughout the range of motion, which should result in greater returns. Whether variable resistance weight training is more effective than conventional weight training is yet to be resolved. Evidence indicates that it is as good and may be better, even though it varies the resistance imprecisely.

Free-weight training

Isotonic training with free weights (dumbbells and barbells) continues to be an appropriate method of strength development. Free-weight training provides many ad-

vantages. For athletes, it yields some flexibility in strength development because the movements are not confined to a track. Exercises can be selected or improvised to simulate the movements required by specific sports, allowing the development of the muscles that will be used in competition. Concurrently, ancillary musculature that plays a supporting or stabilizing role for the major muscles is also stimulated and developed.

For noncompetitors, free weights have several advantages. The equipment is inexpensive and versatile. A starter set of free weights typically costs less than $150. Free weights do not require much space, so the workout can occur in the home.

The main limitation of free-weight exercise is that this system does not provide maximum resistance throughout the full range of motion. A second limitation is the need for one or two spotters to assist with exercises such as the bench press and half-squats.

Isokinetic training

Isokinetic resistance training involves dynamic movements performed on exercise devices that produce maximum resistance throughout the full range of motion. The movement speed is preselected by the exerciser and

Just the Facts

Muscle Fiber Types

In humans, it appears that the total number of muscle fibers and the fiber type are set genetically and that both are fully established at birth. Current research indicates that the number of muscle fibers probably cannot be increased and the fiber type cannot be changed. If this theory is accurate, then the increases in muscle size resulting from training must be caused by hypertrophy (increase in size) of the existing fibers. Muscle hyperplasia (an increase in the number of muscle fibers) has been shown to occur in several species of animals through heavy resistance exercise. Muscle hyperplasia has not been verified in humans, but the possibility cannot be ruled out.

Muscles consist of three types of fibers: (1) type I or slow-twitch oxidative fibers (SO); (2) type IIa or fast-twitch, oxidative glycloytic fibers (FOG); and (3) type IIb or fast-twitch glycloytic fibers (FG). Each fiber type can be identified by its speed of contraction and the primary energy source that it uses. Slow-twitch oxidative fibers rely on the aerobic or oxygen system. These fibers are responsible for exercise and activities of an aerobic or endurance nature. The fast-twitch oxidative, glycloytic fibers (type IIa) contract faster than the type I fibers and are capable of using oxygen but not as efficiently as type I fibers. These fibers support exercises that require both aerobic and anaerobic energy. The fast-twitch glycloytic fibers (type IIb) have the fastest contractile speed of the three and support high-intensity anaerobic exercises.

Muscle fibers do not cross over—type I fibers remain slow-twitch and type II fibers remain fast-twitch, regardless of the type of training to which they are exposed. To produce a change in muscle fiber type requires a structural change in the motor nerve that supplies it with electrical impulses. A motor nerve stimulates either all slow-twitch or all fast-twitch fibers, and when the electrical impulse is delivered, all fibers in the motor unit contract.

The ratio between the fiber types also appears to be set genetically. Changing one fiber type to another under normal conditions is probably impossible, because the motor nerve that innervates (supplies nerve impulses to) the muscle determines its function.

The ratio of slow-twitch to fast-twitch muscle fibers can be determined by examining under a powerful microscope muscle biopsies from selected sites in the body. The muscle composition of world-class aerobic athletes (distance runners, cyclists, cross-country skiers) is predominately slow-twitch, whereas the muscle compositions of the world-class power or anaerobic event athletes (shot-putters, sprinters, power and Olympic weight lifters) is primarily fast-twitch. Knowing the ratio of fiber type could be important for these competitors, but it is relatively unimportant when one exercises for health reasons. Health enthusiasts can participate in a variety of activities with some degree of success and satisfaction regardless of fiber type.

---

remains constant throughout the movement. Isokinetic exercise theoretically improves on traditional and variable-resistance dynamic systems.[13] Isokinetic devices adjust the resistance to accommodate the force applied by the exerciser. The greater the application of force, the greater the resistance to movement supplied by the device. Maximum force applied through the full range of motion is countered with maximum resistance at all joint angles. This activates the greatest number of motor units and should produce greater gains in strength than other dynamic systems of exercise.

Circuit Resistance Training

Circuit resistance training (CRT) is very effective for people who wish to develop several fitness dimensions simultaneously. Muscular strength and endurance,

changes in body composition, and improvement in cardiorespiratory endurance can be attained together.

A circuit usually consists of eight to fifteen exercise stations. The weight selected for each exercise station should equal 40 to 55 percent of the exerciser's capacity. The exerciser does as many repetitions as possible for 15 to 30 seconds at each station. The rest interval between exercise stations should equal the exercise time spent at each station. The circuit is repeated two to three times for a total elapsed time of 30 to 50 minutes per workout. As fitness improves, overload can be applied by (1) increasing the amount of weight at each station, (2) increasing the amount of exercise time at each station (up to 30 seconds), (3) decreasing the amount of rest between stations, or (4) any combination of these.

Figure 4-20 Isometric Contraction

An isometric contraction is a static contraction against an immovable object.

The CRT system is challenging, versatile, and fun. Exercise stations can be rearranged, exercises that develop similar muscle groups can be substituted for each other, and the order in which the circuit is traversed can be changed. Because relatively light weights are used, the likelihood of injury is reduced. Circuits can be set up in relatively small spaces. Machine weights are ideal for CRT because of the speed with which resistances can be changed, but free weights are adaptable to this system as well. The main limitation of CRT is that optimal gains in strength or cardiorespiratory endurance are difficult to achieve. Strength is most efficiently developed through lifting very heavy weights combined with a substantial rest period between sets. Cardiorespiratory endurance can best be achieved through rhythmic and continuous activities, such as jogging, cycling, cross-country skiing, and rowing, that are preformed for a minimum of 20 minutes per workout. An example of a circuit is presented in Just the Facts: Circuit Resistance Training.

Just the Facts

Circuit Resistance Training

The following is an example of a circuit. You should warm up before CRT and finish the workout with a cooldown.

Station 1	Leg presses or half-squats	15–30 secs.
Station 2	Bench presses	15–30 secs.
Station 3	Back hyperextensions	15–30 secs.
Station 4	Biceps curls	15–30 secs.
Station 5	Overhead presses	15–30 secs.
Station 6	Sit-ups or abdominal crunches	15–30 secs.
Station 7	Push-ups	15–30 secs.
Station 8	Lateral raises	15–30 secs.
Station 9	Hamstring curls	15–30 secs.
Station 10	Pull-ups	15–30 secs.

Muscular Endurance

Muscular endurance is the application of repeated muscular force against a submaximal resistance. Inflating a tire with a bicycle pump, walking up five flights of stairs, lifting a weight 20 times, and doing 50 sit-ups are some examples of activities that develop muscular endurance. It is developed by many repetitions against resistances that are considerably less than maximum.

Research has shown that the greatest effect on muscle endurance occurs with submaximal loads that can be lifted 20 or more times.[14] Programs that emphasize low resistance and high repetitions produce very limited improvement, if any, in *strength*. The primary stimulus of these programs is on the body's ability to supply blood and oxygen to the working muscles for them to contract on a repeated basis. Endurance exercises increase muscle capillarization and muscle myoglobin. An increase in muscle capillaries allows the muscles to accept more blood. The increase in oxygen carried by the capillaries is transferred to a greater quantity of myoglobin, which delivers it to the muscles. As with other types of isotonic resistance training programs, muscle endurance exercises should be performed no more than every other day.

Isometric or static muscle endurance is the ability to sustain or hold a submaximal contraction for a period of time.[5] Examples are carrying objects, such as groceries and other packages; pushing or pulling objects, such as a lawn mower; and carrying children.

Assessment Activity 4-2 presents a method of determining your muscular endurance. Assessment Activity 4-3 measures abdominal muscle endurance, and Assessment Activity 4-4 measures muscular strength and endurance with calisthenics.

Principles of Resistance Training

The principles of exercise—intensity, duration, frequency, overload, progression, and specificity—apply to resistance training as well as aerobic training. These principles were established over many years through research and experience. The current set of guidelines recommended for average healthy adults was published in 1998 by the American College of Sports Medicine (ACSM):[2]

> A minimum of eight to ten exercises involving the major muscle groups should be performed two to three days per week. A minimum of 1 set of 8 to 12 RM or to near fatigue should be completed by most participants; however, for older and more frail persons (approximately 50 to 60 years of age and above), 10 to 15 repetitions may be more appropriate.

These recommendations are minimum standards for weight training and are designed to motivate sedentary nonathletic adults to try this form of exercise. According to ACSM, more sets, heavier weights, and exercising three times per week produce greater results, but the additional time and effort required for more sets, greater frequency, and heavier weights probably exceed the interest of this population. Although this may be true, healthy American adults should be encouraged to exercise above these minimum recommendations.

Intensity

Intensity refers to the amount of weight used for a given exercise. It is probably the most important variable in resistance training, and it is the most important stimulus associated with the development of strength and muscle endurance.[14]

For muscular development and health enhancement, the intensity of resistance training may be set by selecting a weight (through trial and error) that can be lifted at least 8 times but no more than 12 times. This weight is probably 70 to 80 percent of a maximal effort.[10]

The intensity level for resistance exercise varies according to the training system used. Optimal strength development through isometrics involves maximal contractions, 5 to 10 sets with a total contraction time of 30 to 60 seconds. Optimal strength development

through dynamic systems of exercise should include 3 to 5 sets of 4 RM to 6 RM per set, with at least 2 minutes' rest between sets, and this should be performed three times per week.[5] If muscle endurance is the primary goal, the workout should consist of 3 to 5 sets of 15 RM to 25 RM per set, with approximately 1 minute's rest between sets, performed three times per week.

Duration

The duration or length of each exercise session is dependent upon the number of exercises, repetitions, and sets, the amount of rest between sets, and the time available to the performer. The ACSM estimates that its minimum guidelines require about 20 minutes to complete. Conventional resistance programs (3 sets, 10 to 12 exercises, 8 to 12 reps) take about 50 minutes. Serious bodybuilding requires two to four hours in advanced weight training systems, six days per week. Availability of time and individual goals will dictate the length of workout.

Frequency

Frequency refers to the number of training sessions per week. Dynamic resistance exercises (isotonic and isokinetic) should be performed every other day (seven training sessions every two weeks) or three times per week (six training sessions every two weeks). Near-maximum gains in strength for novice weight trainers occur with these exercise frequencies.

Isometrics can be performed every day because muscle soreness does not result. However, for physiological and psychological reasons, you should designate two to three days of rest throughout the week.

Overload and Progression

The principle behind strength increase is straightforward—the muscles must be subjected periodically to greater resistance as they adapt to the previous resistance. This overload principle applies to all muscles regardless of the system of training.

Overload may be applied by progressively increasing the amount of weight lifted or the number of repetitions performed or by decreasing rest time between sets. An increase in the number of repetitions leads to increases in muscle endurance, an increase in the amount of weight lifted leads to an increase in muscle strength, and a decrease in rest time increases muscular and aerobic endurance.

The principle of progression relates to the application of overload. It dictates how much and when an increase in resistance, reps, or sets or a decrease in rest time should occur. For example, the application of overload in a strength development program featuring

6 RM is accomplished by increasing the load when the exerciser can perform more than six reps on more than one occasion. The added weight reduces the number of reps that can be performed. Continued training improves strength and increases the number of reps. Once again, when the exerciser can perform more than six reps on more than one occasion, the weight is increased. This cycle is repeated for as long as strength development is the goal.

Specificity

The principle of specificity reflects the body's response to exercise. The type of training dictates the type of muscle development. Training programs that emphasize high resistance and low repetitions increase muscle strength and size. The gains are the result of muscle **hypertrophy,** which is an increase in the diameter of muscle fibers, and the recruitment of more motor units.

Training programs that emphasize low resistance and a high number of repetitions develop muscle endurance. The high volume of work increases the blood and oxygen supply to the muscles by increasing capillary density and muscle myoglobin concentration.

The effectiveness of resistance training programs is based on the knowledgeable use of principles that guide such programs. However, other factors contribute to program effectiveness. These are found in Real-World Wellness: Other Important Considerations for Resistance Training.

Ergogenic Aids

Ergogenic aids are substances, techniques, or treatments that theoretically improve physical performance in addition to the effects of normal training. This discussion on ergogenic aids will be limited to a few of those that are reputed to accelerate muscle and strength development.

Many athletes and nonathletes alike take supplements of various types to accelerate muscle development. This short summary of a few of the many ergogenic aids suffices to show that some of these actually have performance-enhancing qualities, but many do not.

Protein Supplementation

The adult requirement for protein is 0.8 gram (g) per kilogram (1 kg = 2.2 lbs.) of body weight. Research has shown that resistance training may push this requirement to 1.6 to 1.8 g/kg of body weight.[15] Values such as these are easily obtained with the typical American diet, particularly for active people who tend to consume more calories than does the average adult. Protein in excess of these values has resulted in no further gains in strength, power, or muscle size.[16]

Real-World Wellness

Other Important Considerations for Resistance Training

In addition to the principles of resistance exercise, what factors should I consider to ensure the effectiveness and safety of my resistance training program?

Here are some other important factors for novice weight trainers:

- *Order of exercises:* Many people believe that large muscle exercises should precede small muscle exercises. This format allows one to train at a higher intensity level. Large muscle exercises such as half-squats or leg presses should be performed prior to hamstring curls; bench presses should precede triceps extensions. If small muscle group exercises precede large muscle exercises, fatigue (preexhaustion) is carried over to the large muscle exercises, which limits their effectiveness.

  Novice exercisers should not exercise the same muscles in consecutive exercises, because they are likely then to be less tolerant to the preexhaustion phenomenon that occurs from the buildup of lactic acid resulting from the previous exercise.

- *Rest intervals between sets:* The rest period depends upon the goals of training. For example, if the goal is strength development, the rest period between sets should be 2 to 3 minutes. If body building is the goal, the rest period should be 1 minute or less. If circuit training is the system used, the rest period between exercises should be 15 to 30 seconds.

- *Speed of movement:* For the general public, speed of movement should be relatively slow and controlled. It should take 2 to 3 seconds for the concentric contraction and the same amount of time for the eccentric concentration.

- *Multiple sets versus single sets:* Although 1 set of each exercise performed two to three days per week increases strength, it is a minimal effort. Doing 2 to 3 sets three times per week is better.

- *Breathing patterns:* Most important, never hold your breath during physical exertion because this produces an extraordinary rise in blood pressure. Breathe rhythmically during exertion. The suggested pattern of breathing during weight training is to exhale during concentric contractions, while muscles are shortening, and to inhale during eccentric contractions, while muscles are lengthening and while returning weights to starting positions.

- *Spotting:* Spotters are needed for certain exercises performed with free weights. These include multijoint exercises, in which weights must be returned to a rack on completion, and exercises during which weights need to be properly positioned. Half-squats and bench presses are examples of exercises requiring assistance.

- *Safety:* The chances of sustaining an injury from resistance training are relatively small, but as with all physical activities, the chance exists. Safety is enhanced by employing correct lifting techniques, making use of spotters, breathing properly, maintaining equipment in good working order, and wearing proper exercise clothing.

- *Full range of motion:* To develop strength throughout the full range of motion, exercising muscles must produce force through complete flexion and extension. Be careful not to hyperextend or overextend, which can result in injury.

Vitamins and Minerals

Physical performance is adversely affected by vitamin and mineral deficiencies. Those who have deficiencies can supplement their diets with the missing element or elements. However, the performance of well-nourished, physically active people is not improved through vitamin and mineral supplementation.

Creatine

Many, but not all, studies show that supplementing with creatine (an amino acid) may enhance performance in short-term, high-intensity activities such as resistance training. Creatine supplementation increases skeletal muscle creatine content for most people. It is particularly advantageous for strict vegetarians who eat no animal flesh and therefore have low levels as a result. Creatine supplementation promotes faster recovery from repetitive high-intensity exercises so that users can perform a higher volume of work than normal.[5]

Current evidence indicates that creatine supplementation is safe in the short-term, but long-term data are lacking. Creatine supplementation does not benefit the casual exerciser.

Ginseng

This herb has been used for centuries as a cure-all and energizer. Theoretically, it improves physical performance by combating fatigue. No credible scientific evidence supports this contention.

Chromium Picolinate

This mineral is purported to build muscle and promote weight loss. Deficiencies of chromium in the United States are rare. No good scientific evidence exists that chromium picolinate supplementation has the capacity to build muscle or enhance weight loss, but evidence indicates that it might be harmful to human cells.

Anabolic-Androgenic Steroids

Anabolic-androgenic steroids are hormones. Their anabolic properties contribute to muscle enlargement, while their androgenic properties produce masculinizing effects. They build muscle mass and strength, and as a result, they improve, in some people's estimation, physical appearance and physical performance.

Anabolic steroid use by nonathletes is on the rise. This is particularly true for young men. A nationwide survey of 3403 male high school seniors indicated that 6.6 percent of this group were current users or had previously been users of steroids and that 25 percent of the current users showed signs of dependency. According to this report, the improvement in physical appearance reputed to occur with steroid use accompanied by peer approval of those physical changes functioned as a powerful reinforcer for continued use.

Heavy steroid users were more likely than light users to take two or more steroids simultaneously and more apt to take these drugs by injection rather than in pill form. Injection as a method of delivery is highly characteristic of drugs that involve addiction. The steroid "hook" is insidious and powerful: 30 percent of the heavy users vowed that they would not discontinue steroid use if steroids were proved to cause liver cancer, 31 percent would not stop if they proved to cause heart attacks, and 39 percent would not stop if they proved to cause infertility.[17]

Although definitive evidence of the long-term effects of steroid use is not available, the potential for long-term harm is certainly real. Predicting how and when the effects of steroids will be manifested is impossible because people respond differently to these drugs as a result of differences in body chemistry. The steroid effect is complicated further by the fact that black market preparations contain additives, and some preparations are contaminated. The potential for harm is readily discernible; 80 to 90 percent of all steroids used are purchased through the black market. Table 4-2 presents some of the known and possible effects of steroid use.

Keeping a Daily Training Log

Beginning weight trainers should keep a daily log of their training activities. The advantages of keeping such a record far outweigh the minimal amount of bother, time, and effort required to make the entries during the workout. Each entry should be recorded during the rest period between sets.

Table 4-2 Overview of Anabolic Steroid Effects

Effects Supported by Strong Evidence

In Males and Females

Stunted growth when taken before puberty	Male-pattern baldness
Coronary artery disease	Deepening of the voice
Low HDL cholesterol	Menstrual irregularities (in women)
Sterility, low sperm count (in men)	Development of facial and body hair
Liver tumors and liver disease	Decreased breast size
Death	Clitoris enlargement (in women)
Acne	Fetal damage (when taken during pregnancy)
Water retention	
Oily, thickened skin	

Possible Effects

In Males and Females

Diarrhea	Bone pains
Muscle cramps	Impotence (in men)
Breast development (in men)	Sexual problems
	High blood pressure
Aggressive behavior	Kidney disease
Headache	Depression
Nausea	

Adapted from Nieman, D.C. 1999. *Exercise Testing and Prescription.* Mountain View, Calif.: Mayfield Publishing Co.

The advantages of maintaining a daily training log include the following:
- You will always know which exercises you performed and the amount of weight that was used for each.
- You will always know the number of repetitions and sets that you performed of each exercise.
- The training log provides an objective account of your improvement. You can compare the amount of weight you are currently lifting with the amount at the beginning of your training.
- The training log provides an accurate history.
- The training log is a motivating device that provides objective feedback of performance improvement.

A sample training log is shown in figure 4-21. A blank training log is given in Assessment Activity 4-5 for you to use to document your resistance training program. It will be helpful to make additional copies of this training log.

Name ___Cathy Smith___

Program objectives ___To gain strength and muscle definition___

Starting date ___Jan. 1, 1999___

Exercise	Jan. 1			Jan. 3			Jan. 5			Jan. 7			Jan. 9			Jan. 11			Jan. 13		
	Resis. (lbs.)	Reps	Sets	Resis. (lbs.)	Reps	Sets	Resis. (lbs.)	Reps	Sets	Resis. (lbs.)	Reps	Sets	Resis. (lbs.)	Reps	Sets	Resis. (lbs.)	Reps	Sets	Resis. (lbs.)	Reps	Sets
1. Bench press	60	10	3																		
2. Biceps curl	25	10	3																		
3. Back extension	80	10	3																		
4. Leg press	150	10	3																		
5. Hamstring curl	30	10	3																		
6. Chest press	30	10	3																		
7. Abdominal crunch	—	25	3																		
8. Overhead press	35	10	3																		

Figure 4-21 Sample Training Log

Resistance (abbreviated as *Resis.*) refers to the amount of weight (in pounds) that is lifted or pressed. *Reps* (for *repetitions*) is the number of times the weight is lifted or pressed. *Sets* are the groups of reps.

Summary

- The physiological law of use and disuse applies to all human beings during all phases of the life cycle.
- The muscular systems of older adults are trainable and respond to resistance training with an increase in strength and muscle size.
- Muscular strength is the maximum force that a muscle or muscle group can exert in a single contraction.
- Dynamic exercises consist of concentric and eccentric muscle contractions.
- Isotonic exercises are dynamic in that muscles shorten and lengthen, producing movement around a joint.
- Variable resistance exercise equipment is designed to provide maximum resistance throughout the full range of motion.

- Circuit resistance training is a versatile system that allows a person to develop several fitness dimensions simultaneously.
- The principles of exercise—intensity, frequency, duration, overload, progression, and specificity—apply to resistance training. These can be manipulated to meet all muscle development objectives.
- The average man can generate 30 to 50 percent more force than the average woman.
- Anabolic steroids are performance-enhancing drugs that are harmful and illegal.
- Research in the last decade has shown that resistance training contributes to wellness in a variety of ways.
- Muscle endurance is the ability to apply repeated muscular force.

Review Questions

1. Define *muscular strength* and *muscular endurance*.
2. What are the differences among isometric, isotonic, isokinetic, and variable resistance exercises?
3. What are concentric and eccentric contractions?
4. What are the health benefits of participating in resistance exercise?
5. How do you account for the strength differences between men and women?
6. Name and define the principles of conditioning as they relate to resistance training.
7. What are the health consequences and physical performance benefits of steroid use?

References

1. Harvard University. 1998. Stay stronger longer with weight training. *Harvard Health Letter* 23(12):1.
2. American College of Sports Medicine. 1998. The recommended quantity and quality of exercise for developing and maintaining cardiorespiratory and muscular fitness, and flexibility in healthy adults. *Medicine and Science in Sports and Exercise* 30(6):975.
3. Bryant C. X., J. A. Peterson 1998. Strength for women through the stages of life. *Fitness Management* 14(7):36.
4. Bryant C. X., J. A. Peterson, and B. A. Franklin. 1998. Fountain of youth, *Fitness Management* 14(10): 44.
5. Nieman, D. C. 1999. *Exercise Testing and Prescription: A Health-Related Approach*. Mountain View, Calif.: Mayfield Publishing Co.
6. Modifica, M. 1998. Exercise and aging. *Fitness Management* 14(10):48.
7. U.S. Dept. of Health and Human Services. 1996. *Physical Activity and Health: A Report of the Surgeon General*. Atlanta: U.S. Dept of Health and Human Services, Centers for Disease Control and Prevention, National Center for Chronic Disease Prevention and Health Promotion.
8. Davis, A., et al. 1998. Strength, physical activity, and body mass index: Relationship to performance-based measure and activities of daily living among older Japanese women in Hawaii. *Journal of the American Geriatrics Society* 46:274.
9. Faigenbaum, A. D., and Y. Beniamini. 1997. The evaluation of muscular strength in cardiac patients. *ACSM Certified News* 7(2):1.
10. American College of Sports Medicine. 1998. Exercise and physical activity for older adults. *Medicine and Science in Sports and Exercise* 30(6):992.
11. Fleck, S. J., and W. J. Kraemer. 1997. *Designing resistance training programs.* Champaign, Ill.: Human Kinetics.
12. Foss, M. L., and S. J. Keteyian. 1998. *Fox's Physiological Basis for Exercise and Sport.* Boston: WCB/McGraw-Hill.
13. ACSM. 1995. *ACSM's Guidelines for Exercise Testing and Prescription.* Baltimore, Md.: Williams & Wilkins.
14. Kraemer, W. J., and J. A. Bush. 1998. Factors affecting the acute neuromuscular responses to resistance exercise. *ACSM's Resource Manual.* Baltimore, Md.: Williams & Wilkins.
15. Williams, M. H. 1998. *Nutrition for Health, Fitness, and Sport.* Dubuque, Iowa: WCB/McGraw-Hill.
16. Williams, M. H. 1998. Nutritional ergogenics and sports performances. *PCPFS Research Digest* 3(2): pp. 1–8.
17. Yesalis, C. E., S. P. Courson, and J. Wright. 1993. History of anabolic steroid use in sport and exercise. *Anabolic Steroids in Sport and Exercise.* Champaign, Ill.: Human Kinetics.

Suggested Readings

Baechle, T. R., and B. R. Groves. 1998. *Weight Training Steps to Success*. Champaign, Ill.: Human Kinetics.

This 192-page text, written by two respected authors, provides a step-by-step guide for beginning weight trainers. The text provides enough information for beginners to use to design their own valid programs of weight-training exercises. The text features more than 200 illustrations.

Westcott, W. L., and T. R. Baechle. 1998. *Strength Training Past 50*. Champaign, Ill.: Human Kinetics.

This text provides research-based guidelines, suggestions, and recommendations to help people 50 and older to develop and follow sound, effective, and safe strength-training programs.

Mann, C. 1998. *Built Hard*. Champaign, Ill.: Human Kinetics.

This text guides fitness enthusiasts who wish to enter the sport of bodybuilding. It also provides many insights for people who wish to improve their appearance. Contents include setting goals, cross-training, stretching, warming up, and developing all of the major muscles of the body.

Faigenbaum, A. D., and L. J. Micheli. 1998. Youth strength training, *The Fit Society* (spring): 1,8.

The authors provide evidence of the need for and effectiveness of weight training for adolescents. They also provide guidelines for proper resistance-training programs for this population.

Editors. 1998. Muscleing your way to independence. *Cardi Sense* 8(1): 1.

This article discusses the importance of maintaining muscle strength into our 60s, 70s, and 80s and demonstrates how elderly people can incorporate muscle-challenging activities into their daily tasks. The article also suggests how common objects in the home can be used in place of dumbbells to stimulate the muscles.

Name _____ **Date** _____ **Section** _____

Assessment Activity 4-1

Calculation of Strength (Selected Muscle Groups)

Directions: The calculation of strength by this method is expressed as the ratio of strength to body weight. The amount of weight accomplished for each lift is converted to a proportion of your body weight and is determined in the following manner:

1. Find your 1 RM for each of the following exercises: biceps curl (two arm), overhead press, bench press, half-squat or leg press, and hamstring curl.
2. Divide your 1 RM for each exercise by your body weight. For example, a 130-lb. woman performs a 1 RM bench press of 80 lbs. Her score is 80 ÷ 130 = 0.61. Turn to the chart for an interpretation of her score. Look under the Bench press column and

note that her score of 0.61 is in the Average category. In this example, the woman has the following results on the five lifts: biceps curl = 0.28 (fair), standing press = 0.26 (fair), bench press = 0.61 (average), half-squat or leg press = 1.35 (good), and hamstring curl = 0.52 (good). These data are plotted in the first strength profile chart.

3. When you have computed a score for each of your lifts, turn to the strength profile charts. Plot your data in the blank chart provided.
4. Refer to figures 4-1 through 4-16 for a refresher on how to do these exercises.

Strength/Body Weight Ratio

Women

Biceps Curl	Overhead Press	Bench Press	Half-Squat or Leg Press	Hamstring Curl	Strength Category
0.45 and above	0.50 and above	0.85 and above	1.45 and above	0.55 and above	Excellent
0.38–0.44	0.42–0.49	0.70–0.84	1.30–1.44	0.50–0.54	Good
0.32–0.37	0.32–0.41	0.60–0.69	1.00–1.29	0.40–0.49	Average
0.25–0.31	0.25–0.31	0.50–0.59	0.80–0.99	0.30–0.39	Fair
0.24 and below	0.24 and below	0.49 and below	0.79 and below	0.29 and below	Poor

Men

Biceps Curl	Overhead Press	Bench Press	Half-Squat or Leg Press	Hamstring Curl	Strength Category
0.65 and above	1.0 and above	1.30 and above	1.85 and above	0.65 and above	Excellent
0.55–0.64	0.90–0.99	1.15–1.29	1.65–0.84	0.55–0.64	Good
0.45–0.54	0.75–0.89	1.00–1.14	1.30–1.64	0.45–0.54	Average
0.35–0.44	0.60–0.74	0.83–0.99	1.00–1.29	0.35–0.44	Fair
0.34 and below	0.59 and below	0.84 and below	Less than 1.0	0.34 and below	Poor

Strength Profile Charts

Example

	Biceps curl	Overhead Press	Bench Press	Half-Squat or Leg Press	Hamstring Curl
Excellent					
Good					
Average					
Fair					
Poor					

Your Data

	Biceps curl	Overhead Press	Bench Press	Half-Squat or Leg Press	Hamstring Curl
Excellent					
Good					
Average					
Fair					
Poor					

Name _____ **Date** _____ **Section** _____

Assessment Activity 4-2

Muscular Endurance

Directions: Through trial and error, select a weight that you can use while performing 20 RM for each of the following exercises: bench press, leg extension or half-squat, biceps curl, and hamstring curl. For example, a male subject weighing 150 lbs. can perform 20 RM of 100 lbs. in the bench press. The score for this exercise is computed as follows:

Now look at the chart under Bench press and observe that a score of 67% is average. Perform each of the four exercises (20 RM) and calculate the muscle endurance scores following the example.

$$\frac{100 \text{ lbs. (20 RM)}}{150 \text{ lbs.}} = 0.67 \text{ or } 67\%$$

Muscle Endurance: Body Weight Ratio 20 RM

Men

Bench Press	Leg Extension or Half-Squat	Biceps Curl	Hamstring Curl	Strength Category
≥76%*	≥166%	≥50%	≥40%	Excellent
70%–75%	150%–165%	43%–49%	33%–39%	Good
60%–69%	133%–149%	37%–42%	27%–32%	Average
50%–59%	116%–132%	30%–36%	20%–26%	Fair
<50%	<116%	<30%	<20%	Poor

Women

Bench Press	Leg Extension or Half-Squat	Biceps Curl	Hamstring Curl	Strength Category
≥50%	≥115%	≥32%	≥38%	Excellent
42%–49%	100%–114%	23%–31%	31%–37%	Good
35%–41%	88%–99%	15%–22%	23%–31%	Average
27%–34%	77%–87%	12%–14%	15%–22%	Fair
<27%	<77%	<12%	<15%	Poor

*≥, equal to or greater than; <, less than.

Name _____ Date _____ Section _____

Assessment Activity 4-3

Abdominal Muscular Endurance—the Canadian Trunk Strength Test

Directions: The Canadian trunk strength test is an alternative to the conventional sit-up test to measure abdominal muscular endurance. It is not necessary or desirable to raise the trunk more than 30 degrees. Sit-ups beyond 30 degrees cause the abdomen to contract isometrically, so the hip flexors supply the power to raise the trunk above this level. The Canadian trunk strength test is performed in the following manner:

1. Lie on your back with knees bent 90 degrees.
2. Extend your arms so that the fingertips of both hands touch a strip of tape perpendicular to the body on each side.
3. Place two additional strips of tape parallel to the first two strips, 8 cm apart.

4. Curl up, sliding your fingertips along the mat until they touch the second set of tape strips, and then return to the starting position.
5. The curl up is slow, controlled, and continuous with a cadence of 20 curl ups/min. (3 secs./curl up).
6. A metronome provides the speed of movement. It is set at 40 beats/min. (curl up on one beat, down on the second).
7. Perform as many curl ups as you can up to a maximum of 75 without missing a beat. See figure 4-22 for a demonstration of the Canadian trunk strength test and then turn to the chart for an interpretation of your score.

Standards for the Canadian Trunk Strength Test

| | Number Completed | | | | | |
| | Men—Age | | | Women—Age | | |
Strength Category	<35	35–44	>45	<35	35–44	>45
Excellent	60	50	40	50	40	30
Good	45	40	25	40	25	15
Marginal	30	25	15	25	15	10
Needs work	15	10	5	10	6	4

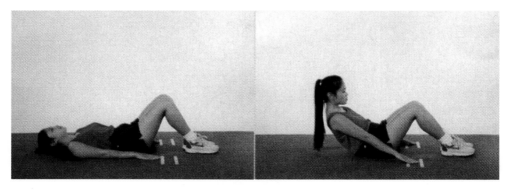

Figure 4-22 Canadian Trunk Strength Test

Assessment Activity 4-4

Assessing Muscular Strength and Endurance with Selected Calisthenic Exercises

Directions: The tests making up this assessment require minimal equipment and are easy to administer.

- *Chin-ups:* Grasp an overhead horizontal bar, hands shoulder-width apart, palms facing your body. On the upstroke your chin must go above the bar, and your arms must extend fully on the downstroke. Your legs must remain extended throughout the exercise and should not be used to thrust your body upward (figure 4-23).

- *Flexed-arm hang:* Perform this exercise if you cannot do chin-ups. Have someone assist you to the exercise position with your chin above the bar, palms facing away from your body. A stopwatch is started as soon as you assume this position and is stopped if you tilt your head back to keep your chin above the bar, if your chin touches the bar, or if your chin drops below the bar. Record the time to the nearest whole second (figure 4-24).

Figure 4-23 Chin-Ups

Figure 4-24 Flexed Arm Hang

Figure 4-25 Push-Ups

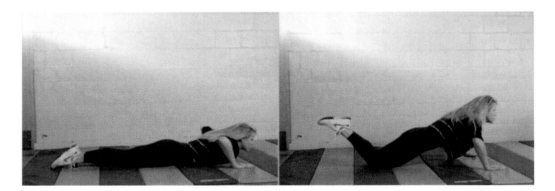

Figure 4-26 Modified Push-Ups

- *Push-ups:* Assume a prone position (face down) with your arms extended, hands on the floor under your shoulders. Keep your back and legs straight and your feet together. The person counting the push-ups should place a fist under your chest. Bend your elbows, lowering your chest until contact is made with the counter's fist, and then return to the starting position by straightening your arms. Repeat as many times as possible without resting to a maximum score of 46 push-ups (figure 4-25).

- *Modified push-ups:* Perform this exercise if you cannot do the standard push-up. The modified version is performed in the same manner as the standard push-up except that you support your body weight with your hands and knees. Do as many as you can without rest to a maximum of 24 (figure 4-26).

Muscular Strength and Endurance Standards

Chin-Ups	Flexed-Arm Hang (secs.)	Push-Ups	Modified Push-Ups	Strength Category
20 or more	30 or more	40 or more	24 or more	Excellent
15–19	24–29	32–39	14–23	Good
10–14	15–23	27–31	8–13	Average
6–9	9–14	20–26	2–7	Fair
5 or less	8 or less	19 or less	1 or less	Poor

Assessment Activity 4-5

Resistance Training Log

Directions: Keep a record of your resistance fitness activities on the form provided. Make copies of this form for repeated uses.

Daily Training Log

Name _____ Starting date _____

Program objectives _____

Exercise	Date:			Date:			Date:			Date:			Date:		
	Resis.* (lbs.)	Reps	Sets	Resis. (lbs.)	Reps	Sets	Resis. (lbs.)	Reps	Sets	Resis. (lbs.)	Reps	Sets	Resis. (lbs.)	Reps	Sets

*Resis, resistance; reps, repetitions.

5

Improving Flexibility

Key Terms

ballistic stretching
flexibility
goniometer
proprioceptive
  neuromuscular facilitation
  (PNF)

static stretching
stretch reflex

Objectives

After completing this chapter, you will be able to do the following:

- Define *flexibility*.
- Identify factors affecting flexibility.
- Distinguish among static, ballistic, and proprioceptive neuromuscular facilitation stretching.
- Assess and prescribe a personal flexibility program.
- Discuss the high incidence of neck pain, upper-back pain, and lower-back pain in the United States.
- Demonstrate proper lifting techniques for prevention of lower-back injury.

Goals for Behavior Change

- Begin participating regularly in a stretching program to improve flexibility.
- Identify some of the tasks or sports that you perform regularly for which being more flexible would be helpful.
- Practice correct lifting techniques when moving heavy objects.
- Modify your work or study area to lower the risk of neck and back pain.
- Try two safe ergogenic aids and analyze their effectiveness.

Flexibility and Wellness

Flexibility programs are planned, deliberate, and regularly performed sets of exercises designed to progressively increase the range of motion of a joint or series of joints.[1] Though often neglected, flexibility is an important component of health-related fitness.

Factors that limit joint movement include (1) the bony structure of the joints (the skeleton is established by heredity, but it can be harmed by trauma, disease, calcium deposits, etc.); (2) the amount of tissue (muscle and fat) around and adjacent to the joint; (3) the elasticity of muscles, tendons, and connective tissue; and (4) the skin (scar tissue from surgery or a laceration over a joint may limit movement). Other factors that influence flexibility are age, gender, and level and type of physical activity. Young people are more flexible than adults because tendons lose their elasticity with age. However, inactivity may play a greater role than the aging process in the loss of flexibility because muscles and other soft tissues lose elasticity when not used. Active individuals are usually more flexible than inactive people.[2] Women tend to be more flexible than men because the hormones that permit women's tissue to stretch during the childbirth process facilitate all body stretching.[3] The range of motion for most movements begins to decline in the mid-20s for men and women.[2] (Complete Assessment Activities 5-1 through 5-4 at the end of this chapter to determine your flexibility.)

Joint flexibility is important for several reasons. Inflexible muscles around the joints limit range of movement, eventually inhibiting activities of daily life. This phenomenon is most frequently seen in older people who have difficulty reaching down to tie their shoes or bending over to get a drink of water from a fountain. Lack of flexibility in the shoulders can affect performance of normal duties, such as changing an overhead light bulb or removing a can of vegetables from a cupboard.[4] Tight muscles may also contribute to joint deterioration by subjecting the bones to excessive pressure, causing pain and abnormalities in joint lubrication. Regular flexibility exercises can improve body posture. Flexibility exercises following aerobic activity reduce muscle soreness.[4]

According to the American College of Sports Medicine (ACSM), stretching exercises may prevent injuries.[5] The supporting data come primarily from observational studies, which are not as definitive as randomized, controlled clinical trials. But, even though scientific evidence does not strongly support flexibility training for injury prevention, sports medicine specialists advocate its use.[6] Based upon the available evidence as well as experience, flexibility exercises prevent injury and maintain a full range of joint motion.

Just the Facts
Benefits of Flexibility Training

Here are some of the positive outcomes of flexibility training:

- Reduction of stress and tension
- Muscle relaxation
- Improved fitness, posture, and symmetry
- Relief of muscle cramps
- Relief of muscle soreness
- Prevention of injury
- Reduced frequency of injury
- Return to full range of motion after an injury

Maintenance of flexibility is most important for the prevention of lower-back pain. For example, a sedentary lifestyle characterized by sitting for long periods leads to a loss of flexibility and increases the likelihood of lower-back injury. Flexibility of the hamstring muscles (a group of muscles in the back of the thighs) and the lower-back muscles contributes to good posture. Posture is also improved by the development of strong abdominal muscles and the maintenance of normal body weight. Extra body weight, particularly that which accumulates around the abdominal area, throws the body out of balance and applies a forward force on the lower (lumbar) spinal area, which places extra stress on the lower back.[7]

The benefits of flexibility training are summarized in Just the Facts: Benefits of Flexibility Training. See also Nurturing Your Spirituality: The Ancient Arts of Yoga and Tai Chi.

Developing a Flexibility Program

Flexibility can be improved by exercises that promote the elasticity of the soft tissues. Figures 5-1 through 5-8 demonstrate exercises that can maintain and improve the flexibility of the major body sites. These 10-minute exercises can be done every day, both before and after exercise, and also on days of rest from exercise.

When to Stretch

Stretching exercises can be included in the warm-up prior to exercise and in the cool-down period following

Nurturing Your Spirituality

The Ancient Arts of Yoga and Tai Chi

Medical health care training and delivery have been gradually adopting a more holistic view of treating patients. This holistic view recognizes the role of spirituality in the healing process. Johns Hopkins Medical School currently offers an elective course for its medical students on spirituality and healing.[12] The National Institutes of Health has awarded grants to a small number of medical schools to develop and promote courses on this subject.

At the same time that spirituality is making a medical comeback, Americans are searching for ways to alleviate stress, promote relaxation, and enhance health. Two physical arts that blend spirituality and health, tai chi and yoga, are gaining popularity.

Tai chi originated as a self-defense art, but it has evolved into a religious ritual, relaxation technique, and exercise program for people of all ages, including the very elderly. Tai chi features slow, balanced, low-impact movements that may reduce stress and improve flexibility, balance, and strength.[13] It requires concentration, controlled breathing, and balance while body weight is shifted as a person transitions from one movement to another. It is often referred to as *movement meditation,* because it promotes muscle relaxation through movement.

The potential benefits of tai chi include the following:

- Improved flexibility
- Physical therapy, because it may assist in recovery from injury
- Improved balance and coordination
- Improved strength, particularly of the lower body (buttocks, thighs, and calves)

- Improved posture
- Increased ability to relax
- Possible slight reduction in the resting blood pressure.

It takes years to become adept at tai chi, but several movements and positions can be learned with a few weeks of instruction.

Yoga originated in India about 6000 years ago. There are several types, but hatha yoga seems to be most popular among Americans. Hatha yoga features a system of exercises that promote physical fitness and mental well-being.[14]

Yoga is a Sanskrit word that means "union." Its practitioners strive for total union in experience that is, a union of physical, mental, and spiritual states. Achieving this union results in a calm, relaxed, tranquil attitude.

Research indicates that yoga's meditative characteristics may prevent or at least decrease the severity of psychosomatic illness. Psychosomatic illnesses are mind-body maladies. They are caused by negative mental states and attitudes that produce changes in body physiology that result in disease. Some common psychosomatic diseases are tension headaches, ulcers, asthma, stress, essential hypertension, impotence, back pain, and menstrual problems.

Master practitioners can, at will, influence bodily responses that are controlled by the autonomic nervous system, such as breathing rate, heart rate, and blood pressure. But it takes years of practice to achieve this level of control.

The exercises and body positions featured in yoga promote mobility and flexibility, but some of these positions are potentially unsafe. It is important to learn from an experienced instructor to minimize mistakes.

Practiced regularly, yoga may lower resting blood pressure, relieve mild depression, and contribute to strength and balance. Anecdotal evidence (evidence that comes from personal reports) also indicates that practitioners experience more energy and feel calmer and more focused.[14]

---

exercise and done on nonexercise days. Stretching prior to working out should occur only after the muscles have been warmed up with 5 to 10 minutes of brisk walking, slow jogging, riding a stationary bike, or similar activity. A gradual warm-up increases heart rate slowly and raises the temperature of muscles, tendons, and ligaments by increasing blood flow to these structures. Stretching after a warm-up is safer and more productive than stretching before: Stretching cold muscles increases the probability of incurring a soft tissue injury.[8] Warm up prior to stretching for approximately 10 minutes on the days of rest between workouts.

The highest payback from stretching comes at the end of an aerobic or resistive workout. During this time, the muscles are thoroughly warmed and capable of stretching maximally and safely. Also, the muscles that have been contracting and shortening vigorously and continuously during the workout should be systematically stretched and lengthened after the workout.

Types of Stretching

Muscles must contract for movement to occur. The contracting muscles are called *agonists* and are the prime movers. For an agonist to contract, shorten, and

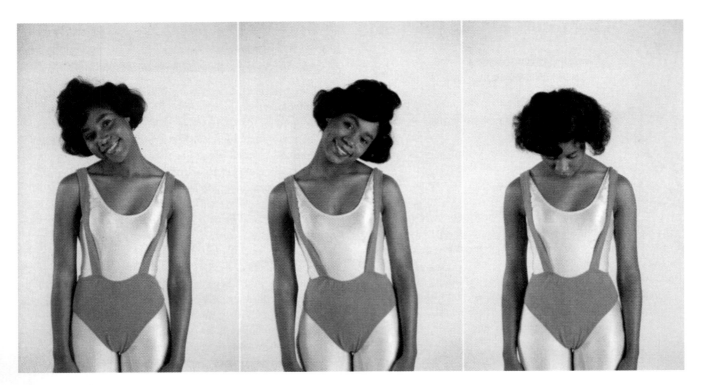

Figure 5-1 Neck Stretches

Slowly bend your neck from side to side and front to back. Do not do head circles, because these require hyperextension (excessive extension) of the cervical (neck) area of the spinal column, which produces potentially harmful compression of the intervertebral disks.

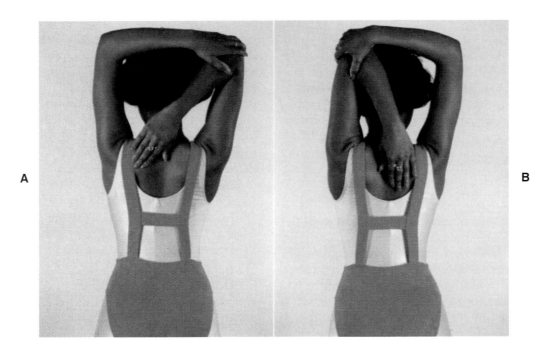

Figure 5-2 Shoulder Stretch

A, gently pull your right arm behind your head and hold for 15 to 30 seconds. *B,* repeat with the other arm.

Figure 5-3 Chest and Shoulder Stretch

Stretch your arms to full extension with both palms on the floor and press your chest down to the floor. Hold 15 to 30 seconds and slowly release.

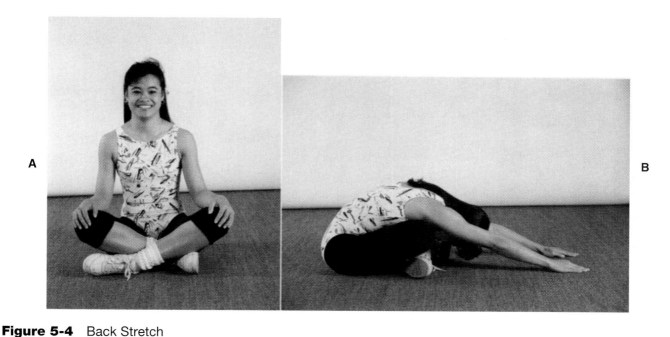

A

B

Figure 5-4 Back Stretch

A, cross your legs and lean forward, extending your arms to the front. *B,* hold for 15 to 30 seconds and slowly release.

A

B

Figure 5-5 Groin Stretch

A, place the soles of your feet together and lean forward. Hold 15 to 30 seconds. *B,* variation: push down gently on both knees and hold for 15 to 30 seconds.

Figure 5-6 Quadriceps Stretch

Lie on your side as shown. Bend the knee of your top leg, grasp your ankle with your free hand, and slowly pull your heel toward your buttocks until you feel the stretch in the muscles in the front of your thigh. Hold 15 to 30 seconds, roll over to the other side, and repeat with your other leg.

Figure 5-7 Hamstring Stretch

Place the sole of your left foot against the thigh of your extended right leg. Lean forward without bending the knee of your extended leg. Hold for 15 to 30 seconds and repeat with your other leg.

Figure 5-8 Calf and Achilles Tendon Stretch

Assume the position shown. Be sure the heel of your extended leg remains in contact with the floor and both feet are pointed straight ahead. Slowly move your hips forward until you feel the stretch in the calf of your extended leg. Hold 15 to 30 seconds and repeat with your other leg.

produce movement, a reciprocal lengthening of its *antagonist* must occur. For example, when the biceps muscle of the upper arm contracts, its opposite, the triceps muscle, must relax and lengthen. In this case the biceps is the agonist and the triceps is the antagonist, but the triceps becomes the agonist for movements that require it to contract, making the biceps the antagonist. Understanding these concepts is necessary to understanding stretching techniques.

Static stretching involves slowly moving to desired positions, holding them for 15 to 30 seconds, and then slowly releasing them. This method of stretching does not activate the **stretch reflex** (automatic or reflexive contraction of a muscle being stretched), so the muscle is essentially stretched without opposition.

The stretch reflex consists of two proprioceptors: the muscle spindle and the Golgi tendon organ. A *proprioceptor* is a sensory organ found in muscles, joints, and tendons that provides information regarding bodily movement and position. The *muscle spindle* is a receptor that is sensitive to changes in muscle length. The *Golgi tendon organ* is a receptor that is also sensitive to changes in muscle length but additionally responds to increases in muscle tension.[9]

Stretching the muscles also stretches their muscle spindles, which send volley sensory impulses, informing the brain that the muscles are being subjected to

[handwritten notes at top: 3x/7x a week, 10% more than normal, 1-3 reps. 15-30 sec, continuously]

stretch. Impulses are sent back to the muscles, which cause them to contract reflexively, thus resisting the stretch. But if a muscle is stretched statically and the position is held for at least 6 seconds, the Golgi tendon organ responds to the change in length and tension by sending a volley of signals of its own to the brain via the spinal cord. Unlike the signals from the muscle spindle, those initiated by the Golgi tendon organ cause the antagonist muscle (the muscle being stretched) to relax reflexively. This protective mechanism allows the muscle to stretch through relaxation as the Golgi tendon organ nullifies or overrides the signals of the muscle spindle. Thus, stretching positions held for at least 6 seconds and preferably for 15 to 30 seconds allow muscles to lengthen and stretch with minimal chance of injury.

Static stretching should produce a feeling of mild discomfort but not pain. Static stretching (see figures 5-1 to 5-8) results in little or no muscle soreness, has a low incidence of injury, requires little energy, and can be done alone. For these reasons, static stretching is the preferred system for increasing flexibility.

These guidelines should be followed for safe and effective static stretching:

- Warm up for a few minutes before stretching by walking, slow jogging, doing light calisthenics, or doing some similar activity.
- Stretch to the point of mild discomfort.
- Do not stretch to the point of pain.
- Hold each stretch for 10 to 30 seconds minimum.
- Do not hold your breath during a stretch; breathe rhythmically and continuously.
- Move slowly from position to position.
- Perform each stretch at least four times.
- Stretch after the workout; this actually produces the greatest benefit because the muscles are warm and more amenable to stretching.
- Perform stretching exercises five to six times per week.[10]

Deliberate attempts to improve flexibility should occur throughout the life cycle. See Wellness Across the Generations: Flexibility Guidelines for Children and Older Adults for more specific information.

Proprioceptive neuromuscular facilitation (PNF) is another effective and acceptable stretching technique. It is more complex than most methods of stretching, but it is the most effective.[5,6,9] By combining slow passive movements (the force for passive movement is supplied by a partner) with maximal voluntary isometric contractions, you can bypass the stretch reflex stimulation that accompanies changes in muscle and tendon length.

All variations of PNF stretching require a partner and some combination of passive stretching and isometric contractions. Two of the common PNF

[handwritten notes at bottom: Ballistic (active) dynamic action (bouncing); Static (passive) safest; PNF requires contraction of the muscle, assists, will help you improve stretching]

Wellness Across the Generations

Flexibility Guidelines for Children and Older Adults

Flexibility peaks in the mid- to late 20s for men and women and declines thereafter in people who are not actively engaged in physical activities that include planned exercises for the purpose of maintaining or increasing range of motion. Evidence indicates that flexibility can be increased in healthy older adults who participate in aerobic activities supplemented with stretching exercises.[2] Physical activities such as walking and aerobic dance coupled with stretching exercises increases the range of motion of older adults.

Recommendations for improving the flexibility of children are somewhat different. Because children are more flexible than adults, 5 to 9 year olds need less time devoted to flexibility exercises than do older adults.[11] However, some formal stretching is required, and activities such as tumbling and climbing are suggested. For older children, ages 10 through 12, the amount of time spent on improving flexibility should be greater than that of younger children but less than that of adults. Children, especially boys, begin to lose flexibility at this age, so regular stretching exercises and physical activities, such as tumbling, that promote flexibility are recommended.

It is important to establish the habit of regularly stretching the muscles, tendons, and joints throughout one's lifetime. Stretching becomes even more important as we become older.

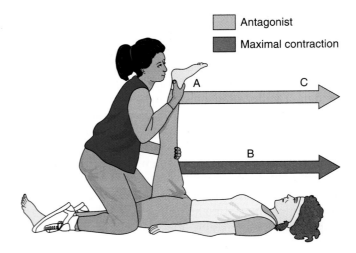

Figure 5-9 Contract-Relax (CR) Technique

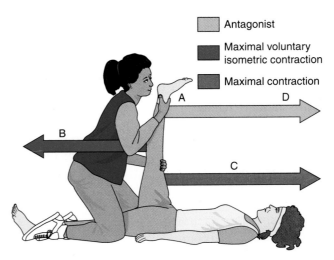

Figure 5-10 Slow Reversal-Hold-Relax (SRHR) Technique

methods, contract-relax (CR) and slow reversal-hold-relax (SRHR), are presented in figures 5-9 and 5-10. For comparison, both figures exemplify stretching the hamstring group (muscles in the back of the thigh). The hamstrings are the antagonist muscle group, and the quadriceps muscles (muscles in the front of the thigh) are the agonists. For example, the CR method is performed as follows (figure 5-9):

- A partner gently pushes the upraised leg in the direction of arrow *A*. This movement passively stretches the antagonist (hamstrings).
- The subject follows this with a 6-second maximal contraction of the agonist (quadriceps).

- This is followed by another passive stretch of the hamstrings.

This is repeated twice with a few seconds of rest between sequences.

The SRHR method is performed in the following manner (figure 5-10):

- A partner gently pushes the upraised leg in the direction of arrow *A*.
- The subject then performs a 6-second maximal voluntary isometric contraction (MVIC) of the antagonists (hamstrings) against resistance supplied by the partner.
- The subject follows this with a 6-second maximal contraction of the agonists (quadriceps).
- This is followed by another passive stretch of the hamstrings.

This sequence is repeated twice with a few seconds of rest between exercises.

Although PNF appears to be the most effective stretching method for enhancing flexibility, it has some limitations. It requires a partner, it produces more pain and muscle stiffness, it requires more time, and it increases the risk of injury, particularly when used by novices.

Ballistic stretching uses dynamic movements or repetitive bouncing motions to stretch muscles. Each time a muscle is stretched in this manner, the muscle spindle (one of two receptors that make up the stretch reflex) located in that muscle is also stretched. It responds by sending a volley of signals to the central nervous system that order the muscle to contract, thus resisting the stretch. This is not only counterproductive—the muscle is forced to pull against itself—but also can lead to injury because the elastic limits of the muscle may be exceeded. Ballistic stretching is not recommended for flexibility development.

Flexibility Assessment

Measuring flexibility is rather difficult, and several instruments have been developed for this purpose. Probably the most widely used device is the **goniometer**. This is a protractorlike device that measures the range of motion of a specific joint. This method is an accurate means of assessing flexibility.[15] However, for the average person, assessing flexibility by using the goniometer is not practical.

Several tests are suitable for measuring flexibility when more sophisticated means cannot be used. (The directions and norms for these tests are provided in the assessment activities.) You should warm up and follow the rules for general stretching before taking the assessments.

Preventing Back and Neck Pain

All people experience tense muscles and muscle soreness in various parts of the body on an occasional basis. The neck, shoulder, and back are particularly susceptible to the types of pressures that cause pain. Sedentary lifestyles contribute to back pain; unfortunately 60 percent of Americans are sedentary or marginally active. Also contributing to neck and back pain are occupations that require workers to stand for long periods or to spend a significant amount of time sitting behind a desk, in front of a computer, or behind the wheel of an automobile. According to the Bureau of Labor Statistics, approximately 92,500 cases of occupational injuries and illnesses are due to repetitive motion. Typing or key entry, repetitive use of tools, and repetitive placing, grasping, or moving objects other than tools result in such injury.[16] Musculoskeletal problems are highly associated with these work-related

physical tasks when the level of exposure is high. Performing unaccustomed physical work or engaging in unfamiliar sports also produces stress on the back and neck. Activities that require repetitive overhead reaching or extended sitting at a computer may produce pain and discomfort in the back, shoulders, and neck. The exercises in figures 5-1 through 5-4, coupled with a few minutes of moving about, may prevent or alleviate pain in these areas of the body.

These problems can be significantly lessened if (1) employers carefully design the layout of work stations, job methods, tools, and materials to reduce exposure to the physical factors related to performing repetitive tasks, and (2) employees become aerobically fit and engage in activities to promote muscle and joint flexibility.

Lower-back pain affects 80 to 90 percent of American adults at some point in their lives.[17] It is one of the main reasons people visit their primary care physicians even though 90 percent of people affected recover within a month.

The high incidence of lower-back pain is caused by the following: excess body weight, weak abdominal muscles, weak and inflexible back muscles, weak and inflexible hamstring muscles, poor posture, cigarette smoking, lifting objects incorrectly, work- or sports-related injuries, and diseases such as osteoarthritis and osteoporosis.

Excess body weight stresses the lower back by pulling the spinal column forward. This causes an excessive amount of arch in the lower back that results in poor alignment of the spine. As a result, obese people are more susceptible to lower-back problems than are normal-weight people.

Weak abdominal muscles, weak and inflexible back muscles, and tight hamstring muscles distort upright posture and tilt the pelvis forward, which increases stress on the lower back.[18] Figure 5-11 illustrates exercises that stretch the lower back and develop the abdominal muscles.

Smokers have a higher incidence of lower-back pain than do nonsmokers. Smoking appears to increase degenerative changes in the spine.

Figure 5-12 demonstrates correct and incorrect ways to lift a weight from the floor. Lifting correctly substantially lowers the risk of sustaining a lower-back injury. See Just the Facts: Tips for Preventing and Treating Back and Neck Pain.

The spinal column consists of thirty-three bones (the vertebrae) and represents the only bony connection between the upper and lower halves of the body. Although humans are born with thirty-three separate vertebrae, by adulthood five vertebrae of the sacrum fuse into one bone, and the four vertebrae of the coccyx also fuse into one bone, leaving a total of

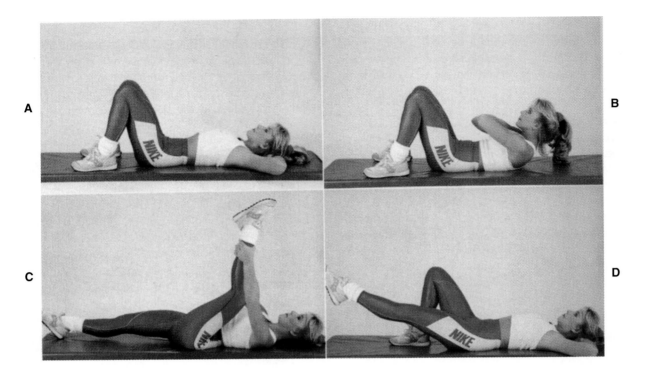

Figure 5-11 Maintaining a Healthy Back

A, to develop the abdominal muscles, lie on your back in the position shown, and contract your abdominal muscles to force the lower back against the floor. Hold for 6 to 10 seconds. Relax and repeat 5 to 10 times.

B, to develop the abdominal muscles, lie on your back, cross your arms over your chest, and raise your shoulder blades off the floor as shown. Return to the starting position. Repeat 5 times and work up to 25.

C, to stretch the hamstrings, hips, and buttocks, raise one leg and extend the other. Reach up and grasp the upright leg below the calf. Alternate legs and work up to 20 repetitions with each.

D, to develop lower abdominal muscles, keep one leg bent with that foot flat on the floor. Raise the extended leg about 6 inches off the floor, and return to the starting position. Do 10 reps and repeat with the other leg. Work up to 25 reps.

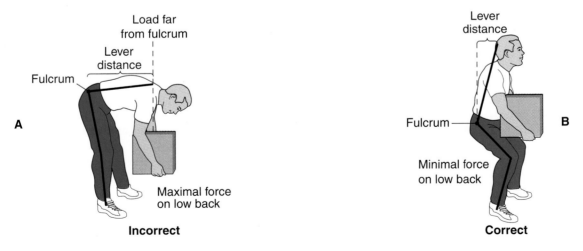

Figure 5-12 How to Lift Objects

A, lifting an object from the floor with straight legs and a bent back places significant stress on the lower back, increasing the likelihood of injury. Notice the distance between the box being lifted and the body of the lifter. *B,* lifting an object from the floor with bent legs and a straight back allows the lifter to keep the box close to the body, which places the majority of stress on the legs rather than on the lower back.

Just the Facts

Tips for Preventing and Treating Back and Neck Pain

The following behaviors may help to alleviate or prevent back and neck pain:

- If you sit, stand, or work in one place for extended periods of time, periodically walk around for a few minutes and do some simple stretching exercises.

- If your job requires long periods of standing, you can reduce the stress on your lower back by placing one foot and then the other on a small stool for a few minutes at a time. This rounds the spine and reduces lower-back stress. You can also shift your weight from one foot to the other.

- If you drive for long periods of time, sit comfortably and make sure you can easily reach the dash, pedals, and steering wheel. You can also try placing a small pillow behind your lower back. Also, stop the vehicle every two to three hours to take a short stretch break

- Exercise regularly to develop the abdominal muscles and to stretch the back muscles.

- Stretch the back muscles and hamstrings at least three times per week.

- Maintain a healthy body weight.

- Bend at the knees while lifting objects so that your legs do most of the work.

- Do not smoke cigarettes, because they contribute to the degeneration of the spine.

twenty-four vertebral bones. See figure 5-13, which illustrates the shape and bony structure of the vertebral column.

Located between the bones of the spine are rings of tough fibrous tissue, the disks, which act as shock absorbers, keeping the vertebrae from rubbing against each other. The spinal column is S-shaped and consists of naturally occurring curves. When these curves are balanced, the body weight is evenly distributed and movement occurs fluidly. Misalignment in these regions applies substantial stress to the concave, or inner, side of the curves. The more pronounced the curves, the greater the stress because of the uneven distribution of weight on the bones and disks.

Approximately 90 percent of all back problems occur in the lumbar region (lower back) of the spine because that region carries the weight of the torso (the trunk of the human body). Fatigue causes the pelvis to tilt forward when a person is standing, increasing stress on the spinal column and its supporting structures. Wearing high-heeled shoes does the same thing.

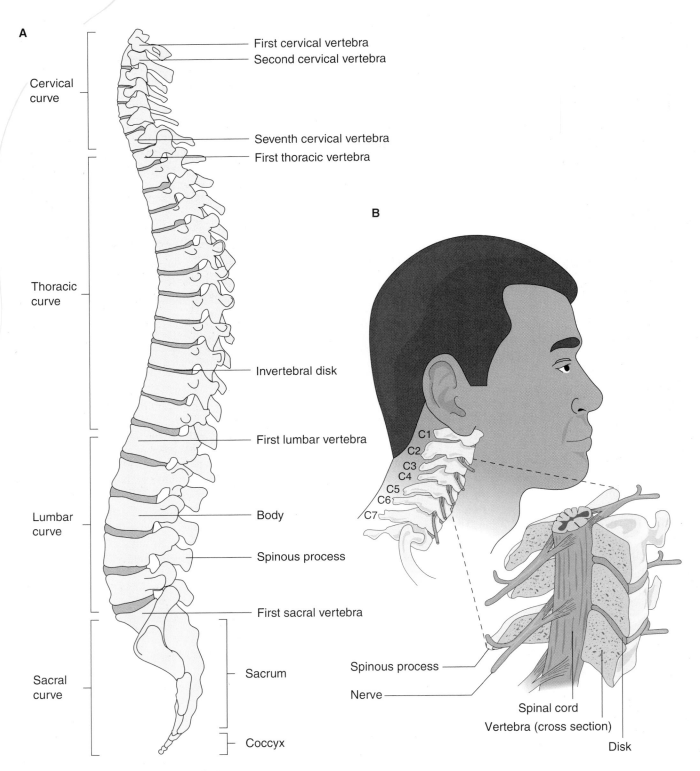

A

Cervical
curve

First cervical vertebra
Second cervical vertebra

Seventh cervical vertebra
First thoracic vertebra

Thoracic
curve

Invertebral disk

First lumbar vertebra

Lumbar
curve

Body

Spinous process

First sacral vertebra

Sacral
curve

Sacrum

Coccyx

B

C1
C2
C3
C4
C5
C6
C7

Spinous process

Nerve

Spinal cord

Vertebra (cross section)

Disk

Figure 5-13 The Vertebral Column

A, the complete column viewed from the left side. Note that the vertebrae of the sacrum are fused into one bone, and those of the coccyx have also fused into one bone. *B,* the vertebrae of the cervical curve from the right side.

Summary

- *Flexibility* refers to the range of motion at a joint or series of joints and is specific to each joint.
- Factors that influence flexibility of a joint are the bony structure, the amount of tissue at the joint, the skin, and the elasticity of the muscles, tendons, and ligaments at the joint.
- Flexibility is influenced by age, gender, and physical activity.
- The maintenance of flexibility of the hamstrings and lower back muscles is important in the prevention of lower-back pain.
- Normal body weight and good posture are also necessary for a healthy back.
- Ballistic stretching is counterproductive to improving joint elasticity and may contribute to injury.
- Static stretching is the recommended type of exercise. Stretches should be held for 15 to 30 seconds and repeated at least three times.

- Stretching should not be painful, only mildly uncomfortable.
- Stretching exercises can be performed daily.
- Proprioceptive neuromuscular facilitation is the most effective but most difficult form of stretching.
- Proprioceptive neuromuscular facilitation combines passive movement with isometric contractions.
- The goniometer is the most widely used device to measure flexibility.
- Lower-back pain is one of the most common reason for visiting a physician.
- Factors associated with lower-back and neck pain include excess weight, poor posture, inactivity, fatigue, weak abdominal muscles, wearing high heels, stress, cigarette smoking, weak, inflexible back and hamstring muscles, lifting objects incorrectly, work or sports injuries, and disease.

Review Questions

1. Explain why flexibility is such an important component of health-related fitness.
2. Discuss the steps to take when developing a flexibility program.
3. What concepts are necessary to understand about stretching?
4. Distinguish among static, ballistic, and PNF stretching.
5. Discuss the guidelines that should be followed for safe and effective stretching.

6. What factors are associated with lower-back and neck problems?
7. Describe the proper lifting technique for preventing back injury.
8. Discuss the role of repetitive movements in the development of upper-back and neck pain.
9. What can an employer and an employee do to reduce the potential for repetitive motion injuries?

References

1. Alter, M. J. 1996. *Science of Flexibility.* Champaign, Ill.: Human Kinetics.
2. ACSM. 1998. Position stand on exercise and physical activity for older adults. *Medicine and Science in Sports and Exercise* 30:6, 992.
3. Robergs, R. A., and S. O. Roberts. 1997. *Exercise Physiology.* St. Louis, Mo.: Mosby.
4. Tufts University. 1997. To stretch or not to stretch? *Tufts University Health and Nutrition Letter* 15(10):4.
5. ACSM. 1998. Position stand on the recommended quantity and quality of exercise for developing and maintaining cardiorespiratory and muscular fitness, and flexibility in adults. *Medicine and Science in Sports and Exercise* 30(6):975.
6. Nieman, D. C. 1999. *Exercise Testing and Prescription.* Mountain View, Calif.: Mayfield Publishing.
7. Bryant, C. X., and J. A. Peterson. 1998. Treating and preventing low

back pain. *Fitness Management* 14(4):52.
8. University of California at Berkeley. 1998. The home stretch. *University of California at Berkeley Wellness Letter* 15(3):4.
9. Fredette, D. H. 1998. Exercise recommendations for flexibility and range of motion. In *ACSM Resource Manual* (3d ed.), ed. J. L. Roitman. Baltimore, Md.: Williams & Wilkins.
10. ACSM. 1995. *ACSM's Guidelines for Exercise Testing and Prescription.* Baltimore, Md.: Williams & Wilkins.
11. Corbin, C. B., and R. P. Pangrazi. 1998. *Physical Activity for Children: A Statement of Guidelines.* Reston, Va.: NASPE Publications.
12. Johns Hopkins University. 1998. Can Religion Be Good Medicine? *The Johns Hopkins Medical Letter* 10(9):3.

13. University of California at Berkeley. 1998. Tai chi: Smooth, balanced, low-impact. *University of California at Berkeley Wellness Letter* 15(2):6.
14. Harvard University. 1998. The ultimate mind-body workout. *Harvard Health Letter* 24(2):4.
15. Prentice, W. E. 1999. *Fitness and Wellness for Life.* Boston: WCB/McGraw-Hill.
16. U.S. Dept. of Health and Human Services and Office of Public Health and Science. 1998. *Healthy People 2010 Objectives: Draft for Public Comment.* Washington, D.C.: U.S. Dept. of Health and Human Services.
17. Harvard University. 1999. Fact and fiction about chiropractic. *Harvard Health Letter* 24(3):1.
18. Harvard University. 1998. Exercising options for a healthy back. *Harvard Health Letter* 23(11):4.

Suggested Readings

Alter, M. J. 1998. *Sport Stretch*. Champaign, Ill.: Human Kinetics.

This complete guide to developing and maintaining flexibility is applicable for both weekend warriors and serious athletes. It features step-by-step guidelines plus photos of 311 different stretching exercises.

Alter, M. J. 1996. *Science of Flexibility*. Champaign, Ill.: Human Kinetics.

For readers who want to move beyond the basics, this book discusses the following topics in some depth: factors that limit flexibility, methods for modifying limiting factors, controversial stretching exercises, and stretching for specific sports and health conditions.

Black, S. 1997. *The Supple Body: The Way to Fitness, Strength, and Flexibility*. Indianapolis, Ind.: Macmillan General Reference.

The premise of this book is that a fit body is one that is strong, flexible, and firm. This book guides the reader through a system of gentle exercises designed to achieve strength and flexibility. It includes color illustrations and 300 photos of exercises targeted to specific areas of the body.

Verna, C., S. Hosid, and J. Smolty. 1998. *The Complete Idiot's Guide to Healthy Stretching*. Aurora, Colo.: Alpha Books.

This text features more than 250 photographs illustrating stretching exercises for all parts of the body. It is useful for inactive people and athletes.

Name _____ **Date** _____ **Section** _____

Assessment Activity 5-1

Sit-and-Reach Test

The sit-and-reach test is used to measure hip flexor, lower-back, and hamstring flexibility. It is measured with a testing box that can be purchased or built. The box should be 12 inches high and have an overlap in front so that negative (minus) readings can be obtained when subjects are unable to reach their feet (the footline). For simplicity and standardization purposes, the footline is given a value of 0, with plus and minus readings given in inches.

Directions:

1. Warm up for 3 to 5 minutes before taking this test.
2. After warming up, remove your shoes and sit with both feet flat against the end board of the box with your legs fully extended and your knees locked.
3. Extend your arms forward as shown in the photo, one hand on top of the other with your fingertips perfectly even.
4. Bend forward from the waist as far as possible while sliding your hands along the scale.
5. Hold the maximum stretch for at least 1 second.
6. Perform three trials: The final score is the best of the three.
7. Lock your knees during all trials.
8. Use the following sit-and-reach test standards to interpret your score.

Trial 1: _____ inches

Trial 2: _____ inches

Trial 3: _____ inches

Sit-and-Reach Test Standards

Classification	Distance reached in inches (footline at 0)
Excellent	≥ 7*
Good	4.0–6.9
Average	0–3.9
Fair	−3.0– −0.25
Poor	≥−3.1

*≥ equal to or greater than

Name _____ **Date** _____ **Section** _____

Assessment Activity 5-2

Shoulder Flexion Test

Directions: The objective of the shoulder flexion test is to measure the deltoids and shoulder girdle. A measuring scale and straight edge are needed to perform this assessment. Begin by assuming a prone position with your arms fully extended. Your chin should remain in contact with the floor throughout the exercise.

Grasp the straight edge with both hands and raise it as high as possible from the floor. The distance from the floor to the straight edge is measured as the height in inches. Repeat this assessment three times and record the best number in inches as the final score. See the following chart for your classification.

Trial 1: _____ inches

Trial 2: _____ inches

Trial 3: _____ inches

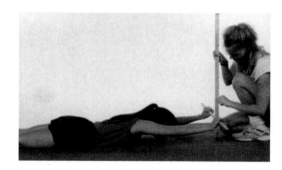

Shoulder Flexion Test Standard*

Classification	Men	Women
Excellent	26 or above	27 or above
Good	23–25	24–26
Average	18–22	19–23
Fair	13–17	14–18
Poor	12 or below	13 or below

*All scores are in inches. Use the best of three trials as the score.

Name _____ **Date** _____ **Section** _____

Assessment Activity 5-3

Sling Test

Directions: The purpose of this test is to determine the length and flexibility of your sling muscles (the extensor muscles of the back). If you have back problems or have had back surgery, consult a physician before attempting this test. This is a test and not an exercise, so it should not be used to increase flexibility.

Begin by lying on your back on the floor and bending both knees. Pull your right leg to your chest by tightly holding your knee with both hands. Straighten out your left leg and push it to the floor without letting your right leg move away from your chest.

A tester uses a ruler to measure the distance between the floor and back of the knee. Reverse your leg position and measure.

Sling Test Standards

Classification		Standard
Excellent		Able to hold one leg firmly against the chest with the other leg flat against the floor
Average		Able to hold one knee against the chest while the other knee is bent 2 to 4 inches off the floor
Fair		Able to hold the knee firmly against the chest while the other leg is 4 to 8 inches off the floor
Poor		Unable to pull one leg firmly against the chest without pain or discomfort and/or raising the other leg off the floor significantly (more than 8 inches)

Name _____ **Date** _____ **Section** _____

Assessment Activity 5-4

Trunk Extension

Directions: The purpose of this assessment is to measure the flexibility of the abdominal and hip flexor muscles. Begin the test by lying face down on the floor. Have a partner hold your legs as shown. Grasp your hands in the lower-back area, breathe in, lift your upper body as high off the floor as possible, and hold. A tester measures the distance between the floor and your chin. Repeat this two more times and record your best score. See the following chart for your classification.

Trial 1: _____ inches

Trial 2: _____ inches

Trial 3: _____ inches

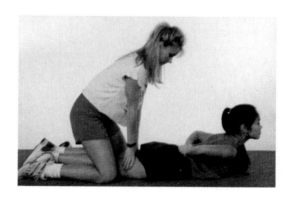

Trunk Extension Assessment Standards*

Classification	Men	Women
Poor	16	17
Average	17–18	18–19
Good	19–21	20–23
Excellent	22	24

*Scores are in inches.

nonnutrients - alcohol 7 cal/g
sweets

6-11 servings of carbohydrates

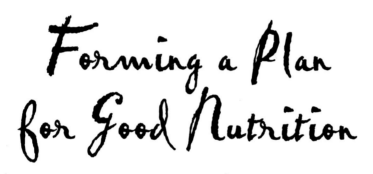

Forming a Plan for Good Nutrition

Key Terms

amino acids
antioxidants
botanicals
calorie
carotenoids
complex carbohydrates
Daily Values (DVs)
essential nutrients
fiber
folate
foodborne illness
Food Guide Pyramid (FGP)
food labels
free radicals
hydrogenation

legumes
minerals
monounsaturated fat
nutrient density
Olestra
phytochemicals
phytomedicinals
polyunsaturated fat
recommended dietary
 allowances (RDAs)
saturated fat
transfatty acids
vitamins
vitamin supplements

Goals for Behavior Change

- Decrease or increase your intake of the energy nutrients to meet dietary recommendations.
- Craft a nutrition profile that identifies your intake of essential nutrients and highlights your dietary strengths and shortcomings.
- Formulate a plan for implementing the *Dietary Guidelines for Americans* that addresses your dietary shortcomings.
- Identify and practice specific strategies for improving your diet.

Objectives

After completing this chapter, you will be able to do the following:

- Describe the functions and purposes of the essential nutrients.
- Discuss ways to apply the *Dietary Guidelines for Americans*.

- Explain the role of nutrients that are not classified as essential, such as fiber, phytochemicals, and botanicals, but that are thought to have unique health benefits.
- Determine your personal RDA for protein, carbohydrates, fat, and saturated fat.

utrition has captured the interest of Americans perhaps more than any other topic related to fitness and wellness. Whether concerning antioxidants or phytochemicals, homocysteine or cholesterol, omega-3 fatty acids or trans-fatty acids, HDLs or LDLs, nutrition issues make headlines in both scientific journals and popular magazines, and everybody seems to be an expert. So much is written by so many people that it is difficult to know what and whom to believe.

This chapter presents basic concepts of the science of *nutrition,* the study of nutrients and the way the body processes them, to guide you through the maze of nutrition information. The concepts presented here are within the framework of *Dietary Guidelines for Americans* and should provide you with a basis for sound nutritional planning.

Nutrition and Health

The relationship between nutrition and health has changed dramatically during the last fifty years. The deficiency diseases of the past, such as scurvy and rickets, have been replaced by diseases of dietary excess and imbalance. Chief among such excess is the disproportionate consumption of foods high in fat, often at the expense of foods high in complex carbohydrates, fiber, and other substances conducive to good health. Americans' dietary practices contribute substantially to the burden of preventable illness and premature death and are associated with four of the ten leading causes of death.[1] Coronary heart disease, stroke, and non–insulin-dependent diabetes mellitus have long been connected to nutrition. A growing body of research has also linked cancer to nutrition. It has been estimated, for example, that about 35 percent of all cancers are related to dietary factors, but a high intake of fruits and vegetables can cut cancer risk in half.[2]

Another important change in nutrition is the new attitude that previously established minimums for essential nutrients are insufficient to prevent today's major health problems. The **recommended dietary allowances (RDAs)** of essential nutrients were established to prevent acute deficiency diseases and to guide the consumption of the more than fifty nutrients necessary to meet the needs of nearly all healthy people in the population. Now the RDAs are being revised to prevent or delay the onset of chronic diseases. The RDA for vitamin C is a good example. An intake of 60 mg of vitamin C is considered adequate to prevent the deficiency disease scurvy. Studies today are investigating the potential additional benefits of 200 to 500 mg of vitamin C in preventing heart disease and cancer.

Also changing is the definition of *essential. Phytochemicals* (plant chemicals), *phytomedicinals* (plants

Eating a variety of foods is the best way to ensure that your diet is nutritionally balanced. Have you tried an unfamiliar food lately?

with medicinal benefits), and *antioxidants* (compounds that generally prevent the oxidation of substances in food or the body) are the nutrients of the twenty-first century. A countless number of studies exploring the benefits of these nutrients may have dramatic effects on future dietary guidelines.

While the hallmark of the American diet is excess, the low intake of some nutrients also causes concern. Here are a few examples:

- 55 percent of Americans don't get enough calcium
- 11 percent of nonpregnant women and 9 percent of children between the ages of 1 and 2 are deficient in iron[1]
- Only 24 percent of the population consume two servings of fruits a day (including apples in apple pie)
- Americans average only one-third of a serving of dark green and deep yellow vegetables a day (about two bites' worth)[3]
- The lack of sufficient water intake is a universal problem that the American Medical Association (AMA) believes is a significant contributor to poor health[4]

Fortunately, improving your diet is not difficult. You don't have to give up your favorite foods to achieve a healthy diet. For many people, cutting back on less healthful foods and making small dietary changes may profoundly affect health and wellness. It is never too late to benefit from dietary improvements. The easy availability of many healthy options makes dietary improvement a realistic goal for most Americans.

Essential Nutrients

Food is made up of six classes of nutrients: carbohydrates, fat, protein, vitamins, minerals, and water. These nutrients are called **essential nutrients** because they cannot be made by the body and, therefore, must be supplied through the diet. Some experts list fiber as a seventh nutrient, although technically some fibers are carbohydrates and are usually listed with the carbohydrates. Carbohydrates, fat, and protein are called *energy nutrients* because they provide energy (calories) to the body. Because they are needed in large amounts, they are also called *macronutrients*. Vitamins and minerals are called *micronutrients* because they are required in small amounts to regulate chemical processes. Water and fiber are nonnutrients and are also part of a healthy diet.

Calories

Food energy is expressed in kilocalories. A **calorie** is the amount of heat required to raise the temperature of a gram of water by 1° C. A kilocalorie equals 1000 calories of heat energy. Common reference to kilocalories usually excludes the prefix *kilo,* mainly for convenience. A gram of carbohydrates provides 4 calories (kilocalories) of energy, a gram of protein also provides 4 calories, a gram of fat provides 9 calories, and a gram of alcohol (which is not an essential nutrient) provides 7 calories.

The recommended diet for Americans emphasizes complex carbohydrates as the main source of energy.

About 55 percent of calories should come from carbohydrates, with at least 45 percent of these from complex carbohydrates and no more than 10 percent from sugar. No more than 30 percent of calories should come from fat; 15 percent of calories should come from protein. The typical American diet, however, excluding alcohol, consists of 34 percent fat, 50 percent carbohydrates, and 16 percent protein[4] (figure 6-1). While significant improvements have been made Americans' diets are still high in fat calories and low in carbohydrate calories. You can tell how your calorie sources compare with dietary recommendations by completing Assessment Activities 6-3 and 6-4.

Carbohydrates

Carbohydrates are sugars and starches obtained from plants. The simplest form of carbohydrates is sugar, also called *monosaccharide.* Monosaccharides include glucose and fructose (fruit sugar). Fructose is the sweetest of simple sugars. Disaccharides are double sugars, meaning that they are pairs of monosaccharides chemically linked. In this group of sugars are sucrose, or table sugar; lactose, or milk sugar; and maltose, or malt sugar.

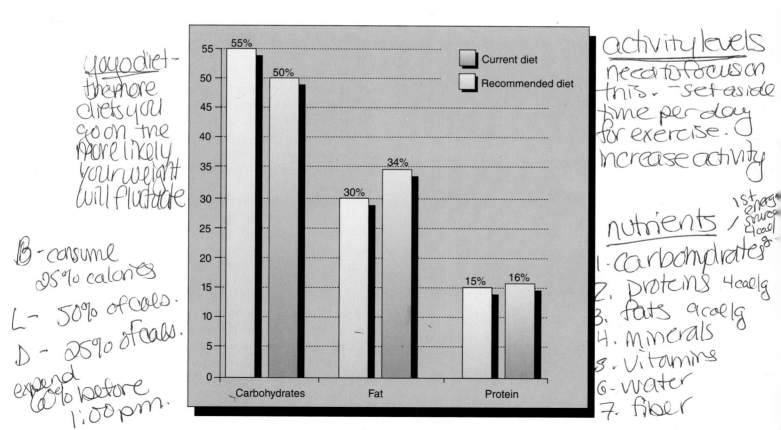

Figure 6-1 Comparison of Recommended and Actual Diets

Both diets are for Americans 20 years and older and exclude alcohol. Recommendations for carbohydrates and protein are minimums; the recommendation for fat is a maximum. Carbohydrates include sugars.

Starches, also called *polysaccharides,* are **complex carbohydrates.** Starches are the preferred source of carbohydrates because the foods that contain them also supply fiber, vitamins, and minerals. A diet high in starch is likely to be lower in fat, especially saturated fat and cholesterol, lower in calories, and higher in fiber. An added benefit of starch consumption over simple sugar consumption is that it helps the body maintain a normal blood-sugar level through a slower, more even rate of digestion and glucose absorption. It takes one to four hours for the body to digest starch. This is one reason athletes involved in endurance activities, such as marathons, load up on complex carbohydrates before competition.

All carbohydrates are broken down in the intestine and converted in the liver into glucose. Glucose is blood sugar that is carried to cells, where it is used for energy. Glucose in excess of the body's need for energy is stored in limited amounts as glycogen in the muscles and the liver for future use; when glycogen stores are satisfied, glucose is converted to fat.

Many weight-conscious people mistakenly avoid starches, thinking that they are high in calories. Starch foods are often made fattening when they are prepared. For example, a baked potato without additives yields a modest 90 calories. Adding fat in the form of butter, sour cream, margarine, or cheese adds substantially to the calories of a potato.

Recommended carbohydrate intake

At least 55 percent of the calories in your diet should come from carbohydrates. Many experts believe this percentage should be much higher. An estimate of your carbohydrate intake can be determined by completing Assessment Activity 6-1.

Vegetables, fruits, and grain products are high in carbohydrates, vitamins, and minerals and generally low in fat, depending on how they are prepared and what is added to them at the table. Most Americans of all ages eat fewer than the recommended servings of these foods, even though they are associated with a lower risk of many chronic conditions.

All starchy foods are plant foods. Grains, such as rice, wheat, corn, millet, rye, barley, and oats, are the richest food source of starch. Legumes, including peanuts and dried beans, are another good source of starch. They also contain a significant amount of fiber and protein, both of which are discussed separately in this chapter.

Protein

Protein is different from carbohydrates and fats in that it contains nitrogen as well as carbon, hydrogen, and oxygen. Because of their unique chemical structures,

proteins contain the basic materials that help the body form muscles, bones, cartilage, skin, antibodies, some hormones, and all enzymes.

The building blocks of protein are chemical structures called **amino acids.** There are approximately twenty amino acids: Eleven can be produced in the body, and nine must be supplied by the diet.[4] The latter are called *essential amino acid acids.* A *complete protein* is one that contains all the essential amino acids. A *high-quality protein* is a complete protein that contains the essential amino acids in amounts proportional to the body's need for them. Meat, fish, poultry, eggs, milk, and cheese are examples of high-quality, complete protein sources.

An *incomplete protein* does not contain all the essential amino acids in the proportions needed by the body. Generally, plant protein sources are incomplete. This fact has important implications for *vegans,* people who limit their diets to plant sources, because protein synthesis operates on the all-or-none principle. That is, the body cannot make partial proteins, only complete ones. If an amino acid is supplied by one source in a smaller amount than is needed, the total amount of protein made from the other amino acids will be limited. It is necessary to combine protein sources from cereal and grains with legumes to obtain all essential amino acids from plant sources. The practice of combining amino acids from various plant sources is called *protein complementing.*

One plant protein source unique among sources of amino acids is **legumes.** Legumes come from plants with seed pods that split on two sides when ripe, such as black-eyed peas, chickpeas (garbanzo beans), lentils, soybeans, and black, red, white, navy, and kidney beans. Legumes are low in calories, sodium, and fat and high in fiber and minerals. They are a nutritionally dense food (see table 6-1).

The most common legume crop in the world is the soybean.[6] The protein in soy is a complete protein—the most complete you can get from plant and vegetable sources—and just as good as animal protein.[7] Soybeans are high not only in protein but also in folate, omega-3 fatty acids, and minerals. In cultures in which soy is the main source of protein, rates of cardiovascular disease and some kinds of cancers are relatively low.[8] A possible reason for soy's benefits is that, by eating more soy, people consume fewer animal products. Another reason is that soy protein may change levels of certain hormones, which in turn may cause the liver to make less cholesterol. Soybeans also contain *phytoestrogens,* estrogenlike plant substances. Phytoestrogens unique to soybeans are called *isoflavones.* Isoflavones are thought to help prevent breast cancer by blocking natural estrogens.

Table 6-1 Comparison of Selected Legumes

	Calories	Protein (grams)	Fat (grams)	Iron (milligrams)	Calcium (milligrams)
Soybeans	86	14	8	4	88
Lentils	100	9	<1	3	19
Kidney beans	88	8	<1	3	25
Black beans	41	8	<1	2	25
Chickpeas	82	7	1	3	40

From American Dietetic Association. 1998. *Choosing Legumes: A Healthful and Versatile Food.* Available on-line at www.eatright.org/nfs45.html.

Soy is available in a variety of foods. Tofu, soy milk, soy nuts, and soy powder, which can be mixed into smoothies, scrambled into omelets, and baked into bread, are several examples.

Recommended protein intake

For most people, the recommended dietary allowance of protein is 0.36 grams per pound of body weight, or 54 grams for a 150-pound person and 72 grams for a 200-pound person. Growing children, pregnant or lactating women, and people recovering from illness require additional protein. Older adults may also need extra protein (see Wellness Across the Generations: Older Adults May Need More Protein). You can estimate your protein intake by completing Assessment Activity 6-1.

Exercise and other physical activities can change the body's need for protein (nutrition needs associated with physical activity are discussed separately in this chapter), but enough protein is usually already consumed. When more protein is consumed than is needed by the body, it is converted into energy or stored as fat. The body is less efficient at converting protein to energy than at converting carbohydrates to energy. High protein intake may cause the body to excrete calcium[10] and put excessive strain on the kidneys to excrete into the urine the excess nitrogen supplied by the protein. Although the kidneys of most healthy people can handle nitrogen excess easily, diseased kidneys have more difficulty. This is why people with kidney failure are placed on low-protein diets and why people who go on high-protein diets to lose weight (see Chapter 8) are encouraged to drink large quantities of water to flush the kidneys.

Fat

Fats are oils, sterols (such as cholesterol), waxes, and other substances that are not water soluble. Fat is an

Wellness Across the Generations

Older Adults May Need More Protein

The only three groups of people once thought to require extra protein were growing children, pregnant women, and lactating (breast-feeding) women. Now researchers think more protein may be needed by a fourth group: adults 55 years old and older. Recent studies suggest that older adults who consume the RDA of protein lose more protein than they take in. As a result, they lose muscle mass and have a reduced concentration of immunoglobulin, a substance that protects against illness. With weakened immunity, there is a greater risk of contracting a disease or of requiring more time to recover from illness or surgery. An estimated 25 percent of older adults consume less than the RDA of protein.

Based on the results of their own and other studies, researchers at highly respected Tufts University[9] advise older men and women to eat about 0.45 grams of protein per pound of body weight. That adds up to 68 grams of protein a day for someone who weighs 150 pounds and 90 grams for someone who weighs 200 pounds.

essential component of all cells. Fats help synthesize and repair vital cell transport and absorb fat-soluble vitamins. Fat stored as adipose tissue provides insulation and a ready source of energy.

Basic fat facts

Fat, also called *lipid,* is a compound made by chemically bonding fatty acids to glycerol to form glycerides. When three fatty acids are hooked to glycerol, the fat compound is a triglyceride. Almost 95 percent of fat stored in the body is a triglyceride, with the remaining 5 percent consisting of other glycerides and cholesterol. Scientific literature usually refers to triglycerides when it discusses fat. The fatty acids that make up triglycerides can be saturated, monounsaturated, or polyunsaturated.

Chemically, fats are chains of carbon atoms strung together with hydrogen atoms. If a fat is a **saturated fat,** the carbon chain carries all the hydrogen atoms it can. If it is an unsaturated fat, there is room in the carbon chain for more hydrogen. If the fat is a **monounsaturated fat,** there is room for two hydrogen atoms. If the fat is a **polyunsaturated fat,** there is room for four hydrogen atoms. If it is highly polyunsaturated, there is room for many more hydrogen atoms.

Many people mistakenly assume that the word *polyunsaturated* on a food label means that the fat in the food is not saturated, but because of food-processing techniques, this assumption may be incorrect. If the words *hydrogenated* or *partially hydrogenated* are on the food label, the food contains varying amounts of saturated fat. Because fats are less stable, they are prone to spoilage. Consequently, for many foods, manufacturers use a chemical process called **hydrogenation,** in which hydrogen atoms are added to the unsaturated or polyunsaturated fats to make them more saturated and more resistant to spoilage. This process of hydrogenating food yields a new type of fat not found in nature called **transfatty acids** (see Just the Facts: How Much Transfatty Acid Is in Food?). Transfatty acids are saturated fats commonly found in margarine, fried fast foods, cookies, cakes, and many other foods made with shortening. Some scientists believe that transfatty acids, even those originating from a polyunsaturated food source, are as detrimental to health as saturated animal fat. High levels of these fats are less effective in lowering total and LDL cholesterol than are the liquid oils from which they are made. Also they seem to depress HDL cholesterol.[11]

Saturated and unsaturated fats can be differentiated by their appearance. Saturated fat is typically solid at room temperature. Lard, fat marbled in meat, and hardened grease from a skillet are good examples. Polyunsaturated fats are usually liquid at room temperature. Examples are safflower and corn oils. Solid vegetable shortenings are partially hydrogenated and have a soft consistency. Coconut oil, palm kernel oil, and palm oil are exceptions. They are vegetable oils and are liquid at room temperature, but they are among the most saturated of fats.

Fish oils are among the most unsaturated fats available. They are roughly twice as unsaturated as vegetable oils. They do not harden, even at low temperatures. Their unsaturation has created special interest in relation to heart disease. Fatty acids in cold-water seafood, such as salmon, mackerel, sardines, herring, anchovies, whitefish, bluefish, swordfish, rainbow trout, striped bass, Pacific oysters, and squid, consist of omega-3 fatty acids, which are thought to be effective in lowering cholesterol and triglyceride levels and reducing clot-forming rates, thereby reducing the risk of heart disease. Canadian health experts believe omega-3s are important enough that Canada has specific recommendations for how much of these people should eat every day.[12]

Olestra

Olestra is a synthetic fat that has the flavor and taste of real fat but contains no calories. It cannot be digested or absorbed and, therefore, passes through the digestive system unaltered. It was approved by the Food and Drug Administration in 1998 for use in snack foods.

While consumption of Olestra in small amounts is unlikely to cause problems in healthy adults, several side effects have been reported. Olestra can cause abdominal cramps and loose stools. It also inhibits the absorption of the fat-soluble vitamins A, D, E, and K and the absorption of carotenoids, substances thought to aid the immune system in warding off some cancers, heart disease, and eye problems. To counter the effects of Olestra on the absorption of important nutrients, some snack foods are fortified with fat-soluble vitamins.

Relying on fat substitutes like Olestra can help reduce fat in your diet. It is important to remember, however, that just because a product has less fat does not mean it is also low in calories. Experts speculate that the reduction in calories associated with low-fat foods made with Olestra is unlikely to reduce obesity significantly because Olestra is not yet used in foods that contribute the most fat to our diets—high-fat meats.[4] It will be years before the true effects of fat substitutes on the American diet are known.

Cholesterol

Cholesterol, a waxy substance that is technically a steroid alcohol found only in animal foods, is probably the most researched blood lipid. High levels of cholesterol are usually included among the major risk factors for cardiovascular disease. (For information on cholesterol, see Chapter 2.)

Just the Facts

How Much Transfatty Acid Is in Food?

To determine how much transfatty acid is in food, it is necessary to have a complete breakdown of the food's fat content. For example, a popular low–saturated fat margarine contains 10 grams of total fat, including 2 grams of saturated fat, 1.5 grams of polyunsaturated fat, and 2 grams of monounsaturated fat. Adding the amounts of these three fats and subtracting them from the total leaves about 4.5 grams unaccounted for. These grams probably represent transfatty acids. Because food labels don't always provide a complete breakdown of fat content, it is difficult to assess the amount of transfatty acids contained in a particular food. Food composition tables such as shown in table 6-2 and nutrition software such as those available with this text provide sufficient information to help you estimate transfatty acid content.

Table 6-2 Fat Content of Selected Foods

Food	Fat/(g)	Percentage of Total Calories from Fat[†]			
		Total*	Saturated	Monounsaturated	Polyunsaturated
Egg, whole, raw	5.01	64	19	25	8
Butter (pat)	11.4	100	67	31	4
Margarine, regular, hard (stick)	91.0	100	20	45	32
Cheese, cream (1 ounce)	9.9	90	57	25	3
Cheese, cheddar (1 cup)	37.5	74	47	20	2
Cheese, cottage (1 cup)	10.1	39	25	11	1
Milk, whole (1 cup)	8.2	49	30	14	2
Milk, skim (1 cup)	1.0	6	4	1	Trace[‡]
Frankfurter (2 ounces)	16.6	82	33	40	3
Bologna, pork (slice)	4.6	72	26	36	8
Flounder, baked (0.8 ounce)	1.9	9	Trace	Trace	Trace
Fish sticks (1 ounce)	3.4	39	10	18	10
Tuna, canned, oil-packed (3 ounces)	6.9	38	8	10	17
Tuna, canned, water-packed (3 ounces)	2.1	7	Trace	Trace	Trace
Ground beef (3 ounces)	19.2	65	25	28	3
Steak, broiled, sirloin (2 ounces)	4.89	56	24	26	2
Pork chop, broiled (3 ounces)	22.3	62	23	29	7
Chicken breast, fried, flour-coated (7 ounces)	17.4	36	10	14	8
Beans, navy (1 cup)	2.1	4	Trace	Trace	3
Potato (baked)	0.06	1	Trace	Trace	4
Potato chips (1.5 ounces)	13.0	61	16	11	31
Ice cream, vanilla, regular (1 cup)	22.5	48	28	14	2
Apple (raw, unpeeled)	0.5	6	1	Trace	2
Danish pastry	13.6	50	14	29	4

*includes undifferentiated fats

[†]rounded off to the nearest whole number

[‡]*Trace,* less than 0.9% of fat.

Recommended fat intake

To many people, *fat* has negative connotations and is viewed almost as a toxin, but as stated earlier, fat is an essential nutrient. During the first twelve months of life, fat is critical to the development of the brain, spine, and central nervous system. At least 50 percent of an infant's calories must come from fat.[13] However, the body's need for fat drops dramatically after the first year. Experts recommend a diet that includes a total fat intake of no more than 30 percent of total calories. That percentage is considered a maximum; many experts believe it is too high.

Fat intake in excess of 30 percent of total calories is consistently associated with heart disease. Saturated fat is the major dietary contributor to total blood cholesterol levels, even more than cholesterol intake. Many associations have also been made between dietary fat and certain types of cancer, notably breast, prostate, and colon cancer. Another health problem related to high fat intake is obesity. Very little energy is used to transfer fat from foods to fat storage; the body requires only 3 calories to store 100 calories of dietary fat as fat tissue, compared with 23 to 27 calories to digest 100 calories of carbohydrates. Fat also yields more than twice as many calories as do protein and carbohydrates.

Just how low should your fat intake be? If 30 percent is good, it might stand to reason that 20, 15, or 10 percent would be even better. Surprisingly, the answer is controversial. Research conducted by Dean Ornish (see Chapter 2) has shown that a very low-fat diet (10 percent of calories from fat) combined with quitting smoking, exercising, and reducing stress can reverse atherosclerosis. On the other hand, some studies have found that cutting fat intake too much may actually increase health risks. Researchers from the University of Washington investigated selected health effects of year-long diets containing either 30 percent, 26 percent, 22 percent, or 18 percent of daily calories from fat. Subjects on the lowest-fat diet showed a reduction in HDL cholesterol and a slight increase in triglycerides. These people had an increase in risk factors associated with heart disease. The optimal level of fat intake for reducing cholesterol was 26 percent.[14] Another study compared a very low-fat diet (10 percent of calories from fat) to a low-fat diet (26 percent of calories from fat). On average, both diets lowered cholesterol by 13 percent. But the very low-fat diet produced a 31 percent drop in HDLs ("good" cholesterol), whereas the decline in HDLs on the low-fat diet was just 13 percent. Also, triglyceride levels increased by 33 percent on the very low-fat diet, compared with 13 percent on the low-fat diet. The study concluded that a very low-fat diet can actually boost the danger of heart disease for some people.[5]

Experts offer several explanations of why diets low in total fat may actually increase heart disease risk. First, low-fat diets may be associated with diets high in carbohydrates.[5] Diets high in carbohydrates and low in fat elevate triglyceride levels and lower HDL levels. Second, low-fat diets may have a higher-than-normal ratio of saturated fat to other types of fat. Studies indicate that as long as saturated fat intake is low, the total fat content of a diet has no effect on heart disease risk. When saturated fats are replaced with unsaturated fats, HDL cholesterol declines only moderately, and triglyceride levels remain stable. In a fourteen-year study of 80,000 women, Harvard University researchers documented the relationship between dietary fat intake and heart disease.[15] They learned that the replacement of 5 percent of energy from saturated fat with energy from unsaturated fats reduced the risk of coronary heart disease by 42 percent. In addition, the replacement of 2 percent of energy from transfatty acids with energy from unhydrogenated fats reduced the risk by 53 percent. Researchers concluded that replacing saturated and transfatty acids with unhydrogenated monounsaturated and polyunsaturated fats is more effective in preventing heart disease than is reducing overall fat intake. It is possible that the important issue is not one of total fat; rather, it may be the type of fat that counts (see figure 6-2 for a comparison of dietary fats). Until the issue of quantity versus type is settled, the best advice is to reduce total fat intake to less than 30 percent and to concentrate on lowering saturated fat intake. Moderation is an important principle for fat intake just as it is for nutrition in general.

Most Americans have an excessive fat intake and are challenged to make changes in both the amount and type of fat eaten. Table 6-3 presents a quick reference of maximum fat intake for selected caloric intakes. You can estimate your personal maximum fat intake by completing Assessment Activity 6-2. You can also learn how fatty your eating habits are by completing Assessment Activity 6-5.

Saturated Fat. Experts agree that saturated fats need to be reduced in the American diet. Diets rich in saturated fats unquestionably increase the risk of heart disease and some cancers. Assessment Activity 6-2 will help you estimate your maximum saturated fat intake. It is recommended that no more than 8 percent of total calories come from saturated fat. This amounts to 9 grams per 1000 calories. Americans currently get 12 percent of their calories from saturated fat.[16] People with heart disease, diabetes, or a high LDL cholesterol level should restrict saturated fat intake to no more than 7 percent of total calories.[5]

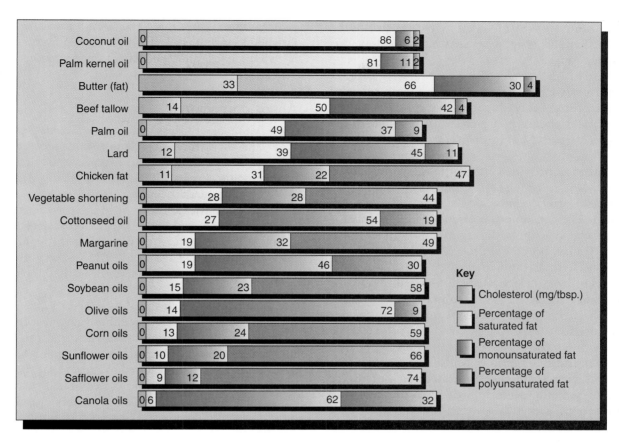

Figure 6-2 Comparison of Dietary Fats

Table 6-3 Maximum Fat and Saturated Fat Grams for Selected Caloric Intakes*

Daily Calorie Intake	Total Fat Grams per Day		Total Saturated Fat Grams per Day	
	30% Level	26% Level	10% Level	8% Level
1000	33	29	11	9
1500	50	43	17	13
2000	67	58	22	18
2500	83	72	28	22
3000	100	87	33	27

*If a person on a 1500-calorie diet wants to restrict fat intake to no more than 26% of calories, the limit is 43 grams (1500 × 0.26 − 390 total fat calories; 390 ÷ 9 = 43). Saturated fat intake at the 8% level is restricted to 13 grams (1500 × 0.08 = 120 saturated fat calories; 120 ÷ 9 = 13).

Monounsaturated Fat. Monounsaturated fats are liquid at room temperature and include olive oil, canola oil, and peanut oil. When monounsaturated fats are substituted for saturated fats, a person's blood fat profile usually improves and risk factors associated with heart disease and some forms of cancer are reduced. The recommendation for monounsaturated fats is 12 to 20 percent of total calories.[16] This amounts to 13 to 22 grams per 1000 calories.

Although the diet of people in Mediterranean countries is higher in fat than that of Americans, the incidence of heart disease and stroke in those countries is much lower. The main difference is that the Mediterranean diet is high in monounsaturated fat, usually from consumption of olive oil. This has prompted some scientists to suggest that Americans adopt this pattern of eating.

Polyunsaturated Fat. There are two main types of polyunsaturated (poly) fats: omega-6 and omega-3. The omega-6s make up 90 percent of poly fats in the American diet and come primarily from vegetable oils, such as soybean, corn, sunflower, and safflower oils. Omega-6 provides linoleic acid, an essential fatty acid. The omega-3s come primarily from seafood and provide linolenic acid, another essential fatty acid. The consumption of omega-6s and omega-3s is associated with cardiovascular benefits, including reduction of blood clotting, prevention of abnormal heart rhythms, and lowering of levels of total cholesterol and LDLs. Recommended intake of polyunsaturated fats is no more than 10 percent of total calories.[16] This amounts to 11 grams per 1000 calories.

Transfatty Acids. Transfatty acids start out as unsaturated fats but become like saturated fats because of the hydrogenation process. In high amounts, these fatty acids are associated with risk factors similar to those linked to saturated fats. Consumption of transfatty acids should be held to a minimum.

Vitamins

Vitamins are organic compounds (they contain carbon) that are necessary in small amounts for good health. The body can break vitamins down, but it cannot produce them, so vitamins have to be supplied in the diet. Unlike carbohydrates, fats, and proteins, vitamins yield no energy. Instead, some serve as catalysts that enable energy nutrients to be digested, absorbed, and metabolized. Some vitamins also interact with minerals. For example, vitamin C facilitates iron absorption, vitamin D improves calcium absorption, and thiamin requires the mineral magnesium to function efficiently.

Vitamins are either water soluble or fat soluble (see tables 6-4 and 6-5). Water-soluble vitamins include vitamin B complex and vitamin C. They are present in the watery components of food, distributed in the fluid components of the body, excreted in the urine, needed in frequent small doses, and unlikely to be toxic except when taken in megadoses (very large quantities).

Fat-soluble vitamins include vitamins A, D, E, and K and are found in the fat and oily parts of food. Because they cannot be dissolved and absorbed in the bloodstream, these vitamins must be absorbed into the lymph with fat and transported in lipoproteins. When consumed in excess of the body's need, fat-soluble vitamins are stored in the liver and fat cells. Their storage makes it possible for a person to survive for months or years without consuming them. At least three of the fat-soluble vitamins (A, D, and K) may even accumulate to toxic levels. Megadoses of these vitamins should be avoided.

Antioxidant vitamins

Three vitamins are classified as antioxidants—vitamins C, E, and the carotenoids. **Antioxidants** are protective substances because they help neutralize the activity of free radicals. **Free radicals** are naturally produced chemicals that arise from normal cell activity. Whenever the body uses oxygen or is exposed to a toxin, such as cigarette smoke, it forms free radicals. These unstable chemicals can damage cells throughout the body. They may damage a cell's DNA in ways that lead to cancer, interact with cholesterol in the bloodstream and form oxidized LDL (see Chapter 2), cause cataracts and rheumatoid arthritis, and be a factor in the physiological changes associated with the aging process. Anything that interferes with the destructive effects of free radicals offers a health advantage. Vitamins C and E and beta-carotene are believed to prevent the oxidation of cholesterol and other molecules linked to the diseases mentioned previously, most notably heart disease and cancer. A common cooking practice illustrates this antioxidant effect: Some foods like bananas, peaches, apples, and potatoes quickly turn brown when exposed to air. However, when such foods are dipped in lemon or orange juice, the vitamin C in the juice acts as an antioxidant and prevents browning.

Should Americans take supplements of antioxidant vitamins? Information from the research community is inconclusive. Until 1994 the evidence in support of vitamin supplements was so compelling that many scientists were beginning to believe that antioxidant vitamin supplements could be a highly effective, relatively inexpensive, and risk-free form of preventive medicine.

Interest in antioxidant supplements was dampened, however, with what is now referred to as the *Great Vitamin Scare of 1994*. That's when the six-year study on the effects of beta-carotene supplementation on more than 29,000 male smokers in Finland revealed that the incidence of cancer was 18 percent higher in the Finnish men who took the supplement than it was in those who didn't. Rather than lowering the incidence of cancer, beta-carotene supplementation appeared to increase the risk of cancer.

The results of the Finnish study are troubling and should not be dismissed. Clearly, more studies are needed. Despite all the promising leads, the value of antioxidant supplements in preventing disease is still unproven. It may be several years before large-scale studies provide more definitive conclusions. Even then it is unlikely that studies will ever establish a cause-and-effect relationship between antioxidants and

Table 6-4   Thirteen Essential Vitamins: Recommended Intake

Vitamins by Type	Recommended Intake		
	For Men	**For Women**	**When Used as a Supplement**
Fat-soluble vitamins			
1. Vitamin A	1000 RE (5000 IU)	800 RE (4000 IU)	*
2. Vitamin D	5 mcg (200 IU)	5 mcg: (200 IU)	400 IU
3. Vitamin E	10 mg (12–15 IU)	8 mg (12–15 IU)	200–400 IU
4. Vitamin K	70–80 mcg	60–65 mcg	Not recommended
Water-soluble vitamins			
5. Vitamin C (ascorbic acid)	60 mg	60 mg	100–200 mg
Vitamin B complex			
6. Thiamine (B-1)	1.2–1.5 mg	1.0–1.1 mg	Not recommended
7. Riboflavin (B-2)	1.4–1.7 mg	1.2–1.3 mg	Not recommended
8. Niacin	13–19 mg	13–19 mg	†
9. Pyridoxine (B-6)	2 mg	1.6 mg	‡
10. Pantothenic acid	4–7 mg	4–7 mg	Not recommended
11. Vitamin B-12	2 mcg	2 mcg	§
12. Biotin	30–100 mcg	30–100 mcg	Not recommended
13. Folate (folic acid)‖	400 mcg	400 mcg	#

*Vitamin A may be toxic in high doses. Beta-carotene supplements may increase lung cancer risk in smokers.

†Niacin may be prescribed in larger doses to lower cholesterol.

‡Pyridoxine megadoses may cause numbness.

§Strict vegetarians and adults over 60 years old may need vitamin B-12 supplements.

‖Folate comes from plants; folic acid is the human-made form used in vitamin pills and to fortify grains. Folic acid is twice as potent as folate (200 mcg of folic acid is roughly equivalent to 400 mcg of folate).

#Supplements of folate may be recommended before and during pregnancy.

From Margolis, S., and L. B. Wilder. 1998. *Nutrition and Longevity*. Baltimore, Md.: The Johns Hopkins Medical Institutions. Also from Tufts University. 1998. With age, calorie needs go down but nutrient needs go up. *Tufts University Health & Nutrition Letter* 16(10):4–5.

chronic diseases. There are too many factors to consider. For example, people who eat plenty of fruits and vegetables may also lead healthy lifestyles overall. Fruits and vegetables also contain thousands of plant chemicals (phytochemicals), many of which are just beginning to show promise against disease. Consequently, some scientists advocate patience until scientific consensus is reached, and they do not recommend taking supplements at this time. Other scientists believe that thousands of Americans may die prematurely of heart disease and cancer before a consensus develops and that the ground swell of evidence, despite some inconsistencies, supports taking antioxidants now, especially considering that only 36 percent of adults eat the recommended five to eight servings of fruits and vegetables each day.[1]

Presently there is only one strategy to combat disease that no scientist would dispute: Eat more produce. Fruits and vegetables are high in fiber and low in fat and contain hundreds of substances that have the potential to im-prove health—not just the few compounds that have been isolated and packaged as supplements. In all the research that has been done on diet, antioxidants, and disease, the strongest and most consistent pattern has been that eating a variety of fruits and vegetables produces benefits.

In preparing food for consumption it is important to remember that vitamin content is easily compromised. Improper storage, excessive cooking, and exposure to heat, light, and air may reduce the vitamin content in food.

Vitamin C

Vitamin C, also called *ascorbic acid,* is essential to the formation of collagen, a protein that is used to form all the connective tissues of your body. It is required in the breakdown and absorption of some amino acids and other minerals (such as iron) and in the formation of some hormones. It may also help the immune

Table 6-5 Vitamins: Food Sources and Wellness Benefits

Vitamins	Food Sources	Wellness Benefits
Fat-soluble vitamins		
1. Vitamin A	Liver, carrots, eggs, tomatoes, dark green and yellow-orange vegetables and some fruits	Healthy skin and mucous membranes, improved night vision, defense against infections; antioxidant benefits (from carotenoids)
2. Vitamin D	Fish oils and fortified milk; exposure to sunlight	Maintaining of blood levels of calcium and phosphorus; promotion of strong bones and teeth; possible reduction of risk of osteoporosis
3. Vitamin E	Plant oils (corn, soybean, safflower, etc.), nuts, seeds	Formation of red blood cells and utilization of vitamin K; antioxidant benefits
4. Vitamin K	Green vegetables, liver	Promotion of blood clotting; contribution to bone metabolism
Water-soluble vitamins		
5. Vitamin C (Ascorbic Acid)	Citrus fruits, green vegetables	Promotion of healthy gums and teeth; iron absorption; maintaining of normal connective tissues; help in wound healing; antioxidant benefits
Vitamin B complex		
6. Thiamine (B-1)	Whole grains, legumes, liver, nuts	Carbohydrate metabolism; nerve function
7. Riboflavin (B-2)	Dairy products, liver, enriched grains, spinach	Energy metabolism; production of red blood cells; improved health of skin and eyes
8. Niacin	Nuts, grains, meat, fish, tuna, mushrooms	Energy metabolism, fat synthesis, fat breakdown; lowering of cholesterol (when prescribed in large doses)
9. Pyridoxine (B-6)	Whole grains, meat, beans, nuts, fish, liver	Protein metabolism; possible immunity boost in the elderly; homocysteine metabolism
10. Pantothenic acid	Whole grains, dried beans, eggs, milk, liver	Energy metabolism; fat synthesis; production of essential body chemicals
11. Vitamin B-12	Animal foods, dairy products, seafood	Folate metabolism; nerve function; formation of red blood cells; homocysteine metabolism
12. Biotin	Cheese, egg yolks, mushrooms, grains	Glucose production; fat synthesis
13. Folate (folic acid)	Green leafy vegetables, liver, beans, grains, citrus fruits	DNA synthesis and protein metabolism; reduction of risk of certain birth defects; homocysteine metabolism

system prevent infections. As an antioxidant it may play a role in prevention of atherosclerosis and some forms of cancer.

Contrary to popular opinion, vitamin C does not prevent the common cold. Scientifically controlled studies reveal no difference in the incidence of colds among vitamin C users and nonusers. On a positive note, however, some studies suggest that large doses (about 2000 mg a day) can reduce the severity and duration of a cold's symptoms slightly. That much, however, might also cause diarrhea and kidney stones in susceptible people.[17]

The RDA of vitamin C is 60 mg, 70 mg during pregnancy, and 90 mg during lactation. For smokers the RDA is 100 mg because smoking appears to destroy some vitamin C. Advocates of increased vitamin C often recommend intakes of 200 mg or more.[4] Still, an intake of 200 mg/day can be achieved by food intake. Megadoses (2000 mg) of vitamin C offer little benefit to the body and may be harmful. As a water-soluble vitamin, doses in excess of the body's requirement are excreted through the kidneys. In other words, the body can only absorb so much. Side effects of large doses are diarrhea and abdominal discomfort. For those who absorb excess iron, supplements of vitamin C could be dangerous. Large intakes may also produce errors in the results of some diagnostic tests (such as the Hemoccult test which tests for glucose in urine).

Antioxidant vitamins from foods like citrus fruits may help protect young and old alike from heart disease and cancer.

Carotenoids

More than 600 **carotenoids** are found in nature. They give fruits and vegetables their yellow, orange, and red colors. They're also abundant in dark green vegetables. Three of the major carotenoids (alpha-carotene, beta-carotene, and beta-cryptoxanthin) can be converted by the body into vitamin A and are referred to as *provitamin A*. Until recently, beta-carotene was thought to offer the most health-protecting antioxidant effect. However, after studies showed that the incidence of lung cancer increased in smokers who took beta-carotene supplements, researchers concluded that beta-carotene was not the main protector.

One carotenoid currently being studied for its antioxidant potency is lycopene, the predominant carotenoid in the blood and in the prostate gland in males. It cannot be converted to vitamin A, but it has twice the antioxidant potency of beta-carotene. Benefits attributed to lycopene are a reduced risk of some cancers, especially those of the digestive tract and the prostate. The best source of lycopene is tomatoes.

Cooked tomatoes, such as those found in sauces, are a better source than raw tomatoes and tomato juice because heat ruptures plant cell walls, releasing the carotenoid. Also, lycopene is a fat-soluble substance, so some fat, like that found in pizza and most pasta sauces, is needed for it to be absorbed.[18]

Currently, carotenoid supplements, including beta-carotene and lycopene, are not recommended. Carotenoids interact with one another, and supplemental doses of one carotenoid may impair the absorption of others. Instead, eat a variety of vegetables and fruits to get a mix of carotenoids. Five servings a day of fruits and vegetables that are mostly yellow-orange, red, or dark green are recommended. It is likely that carotenoids are more beneficial to health when they are consumed together from food than when packaged separately, as in a supplement.

Vitamin E

Vitamin E is a fat-soluble vitamin and plays a role in the formation of red blood cells and maintenance of nervous tissues, and it aids in the absorption of vitamin A. Claims that vitamin E improves the skin, heals scars, prevents stretch marks, slows the aging process, and increases fertility are more folklore than fact.

The strongest evidence of the antioxidant benefits of vitamins exists for vitamin E.[7] Vitamin E is a potent antioxidant that attaches to LDL cholesterol and helps prevent damage from free radicals. Large-scale studies, involving tens of thousands of participants who were followed for an average of four to eight years, found that those who took vitamin E supplements were significantly less likely to develop coronary heart disease than were those who did not take supplements of vitamin E. Supplemental doses of 100 to 250 IU per day for at least two years resulted in a 37 and 44 percent decrease in heart disease risk for men and women, respectively.[5] The effect of consuming vitamin E from food versus obtaining comparable levels through supplements is difficult to determine because dietary vitamin E intake rarely reaches the 100 IU per day level, the minimum amount that appears to be protective. Vitamin E is found only in small amounts in a few foods. Low-fat diets are especially scarce in vitamin E.

Although these studies are impressive, there still is not enough evidence to recommend vitamin E supplements for the general population. Some experts warn of the dangers of tampering with the body's biochemistry; however, other experts recommend supplements of vitamin E because they believe it is not harmful and may be worthwhile. The people who stand to benefit the most from vitamin E supplements are those with coronary heart disease, diabetes, or high LDL cholesterol levels.[5] If you choose to take a supplement, select the natural form, rather than the synthetic, because it is absorbed more easily into the body. The label for natural vitamin E should read "d-alpha tocopherol."[19]

Folate, Vitamin B$_6$, Vitamin B$_{12}$

Folate is a part of the vitamin B complex and combines with vitamins B$_6$ and B$_{12}$ to form parts of DNA and RNA and to make heme, the iron-containing protein in red blood cells. These three also assist in the metabolism of amino acids. The terms *folate, folic acid,* and *folacin* are sometimes used incorrectly. Folate is the form that comes from plants; folic acid is the form found most often in your body and the form added to foods and supplements; *folacin* is a collective term for these and other forms of the vitamin. Folic acid is about twice as potent as folate. Vitamins B$_6$ and B$_{12}$ are plentiful in foods, and few people, with the possible exception of strict vegetarians, need to worry about deficiencies. With advancing age, some people have trouble producing stomach acids in sufficient quantities to separate vitamin B$_{12}$ from foods. They have no trouble absorbing B$_{12}$ from supplements because it is not attached to food, so older people may also need to supplement their diets with B$_{12}$. Good sources of these vitamins are meat products, dairy products, eggs, spinach, whole-wheat bread, and breakfast cereals.

Folate, as its name implies, is found in foliage— leafy vegetables, such as lettuce and spinach. It is also found in citrus fruits, whole-grain bread, and cereals. Of the three B vitamins mentioned here, folate is the one in which Americans are most likely to fall short.

Because folate has been associated with a reduction in the chances of neurological birth defects, such as spina bifida, a woman planning a pregnancy may be advised by her physician to eat foods rich in folate and possibly to take a supplement. In an effort to reduce the incidence of these birth defects, new food fortification guidelines were established in 1998 that require food manufacturers to fortify certain grain products, such as flour, bread, and cereal, with folic acid.

Current interest in folate was sparked by recent studies that demonstrated that people whose blood levels were low in folic acid had high homocysteine levels. *Homocysteine* is an amino acid that plays a role in the formation of two other amino acids, cysteine and methionine. To work properly, these amino acids require three B vitamins—folate, B$_6$, and B$_{12}$. If these vitamins are in short supply, homocysteine levels might rise.[4] High homocysteine levels are thought to increase the risk of heart disease (see Chapter 2). The compound has also been implicated in several other diseases, including cancer, diabetes mellitus, and neurological disorders.

The precise mechanism for the association between homocysteine levels and heart disease isn't clear. High concentrations of homocysteine are thought to make the artery walls sticky, promoting plaque formation. Whatever the reason, one thing appears clear: High homocysteine levels are associated with low folic acid levels. In the absence of folate, along with vitamins B$_6$ and B$_{12}$, homocysteine concentrations circulate unabated. There is speculation from the scientific community that during the next several years homocysteine levels might replace cholesterol as a major risk factor of heart disease.

The best way to lower homocysteine concentrations is to consume enough B vitamins. Emphasis should be on folate, which is more effective than B$_6$ and B$_{12}$.[5] Megadoses of folate should be avoided to prevent the possibility of a false negative for anemia (too few blood cells) caused by a vitamin B$_{12}$ deficiency. If you take folate supplements, tell your physician so that the appropriate tests can be ordered.

Vitamin supplements

Advertisements proclaim that vitamins provide energy, promote wellness, and prevent disease and that taking more results in more energy and better health. Consequently, 25 to 33 percent of all Americans take one or more **vitamin supplements** in multiple and single doses, in both natural and synthetic forms.[21] Vitamins do facilitate energy release from carbohydrates, fats, and proteins, but they do not provide energy. It is not possible to survive on water and vitamins.

The growing interest in vitamin supplements is primarily related to the antioxidant vitamins and folate. The relationship of these vitamins to health promotion and disease prevention, discussed previously, has sparked an unprecedented trend toward supplements. Despite this trend, however, strong definitive conclusions about supplements have not been advanced by the scientific community. The consensus among nutrition experts is that healthy adults who eat a variety of foods do not need them. These also advise that if you don't think you're getting enough vitamins in your food, taking a multivitamin pill with nutrients at RDA levels may offer some nutritional insurance, provided it is consumed in moderation and is not used as an excuse to eat a poor diet. According to the Center for Science in the Public Interest, if a supplement is needed, it is most likely to be folic acid, vitamin B$_{12}$, vitamin D, vitamin E, or calcium.[20] These supplements were identified because they are backed by years of supporting research and because Americans don't consume enough whole grains, fruits, and vegetables.

Although healthy people don't need vitamin supplements if they are eating a balanced diet, there are several situations[21] in which a vitamin or mineral supplement may be called for:

- **If you are age 65 or older,** you may need supplements of vitamins B$_6$, B$_{12}$, and D because of the difficulty in absorbing these vitamins with advancing age. Women, especially those not taking estrogen, may require more calcium and vitamin D to protect against osteoporosis.
- **If you are dieting,** consuming fewer than 1000 calories a day, you may benefit from a vitamin and mineral supplement.
- **If you have a disease** of the digestive tract, it may interfere with normal digestion and absorption of nutrients and justify your use of vitamin and mineral supplements.
- **If you smoke,** you may need vitamin C supplements.
- **If you drink excessive alcohol,** you may suffer from poor nutrition and the alcohol may interfere with the absorption and metabolism of vitamins.
- **If you are pregnant and lactating (breast-feeding),** supplements of folic acid, iron, and calcium may be recommended for you.
- **If you are a vegetarian** who eliminates most animal products from your diet, you may need additional vitamin B$_{12}$. Calcium and vitamin D supplements may also be warranted if your milk intake and sun exposure are limited.

Vitamin supplements are sometimes needed by people with irregular diets or unusual lifestyles or by people following certain weight-reduction regimens or strict vegetarian diets. In addition, infants and pregnant and lactating women may need supplements. When taken as supplements, vitamins should be viewed as medicine and, therefore, should be recommended by a physician.

When shopping for supplements, it is easy to be misled by advertising hype and inaccurate labels. Americans spend billions annually for vitamin, mineral, and herbal supplements. Much of this expenditure goes toward products with no scientifically proven health value. More than one-third of American investment in vitamins is wasted on pills and powders whose potency has expired or on items diluted by additives that do little more than boost prices. Consequently, it is important for consumers to be discriminating in their purchase of supplements (see Real-World Wellness: Consumer Tips for Vitamin Supplements).

Minerals

Minerals are simple but important nutrients. As inorganic compounds, they lack the complexity of vitamins, but they fulfill a variety of functions. For example, sodium and potassium affect shifts in body fluids, calcium and phosphorus contribute to the body's structure, iron is the core of hemoglobin (an oxygen-

Real-World Wellness

Consumer Tips for Vitamin Supplements

Vitamin and mineral supplements seem to be everywhere. Thousands of products are stocked in health food stores, and even my local grocery store has a special health food section. Given all of the hype about supplements, what are some shopping tips to help me be a discriminating consumer?

The following advice[22] will help you get the best value when you shop for supplements:

- Shop for supplements that comply with strict scientific standards set by the U.S. Pharmacopoeia. These products carry the letters *USP* on the label.
- If you take a multivitamin/mineral supplement, shop for the bargain price. Select one that provides 100 percent of the RDAs with the exception of calcium, which is too bulky to be included in a multiple-vitamin pill.
- Calcium, which can be dissolved only in the stomach, is most effective when taken with food. Split calcium intake by consuming one-half of the supplement with breakfast and the other half with dinner.
- If you take antioxidants for their possible health benefits, shop by price.
- Look for an expiration date that shows how long the supplement should retain its potency.
- Avoid supplements that advertise "sustained release" of nutrients. The delayed release may prevent the nutrients from being absorbed.
- Don't pay extra for herbal ingredients. They have not been proven to enhance the body's use of supplements. About the only thing enhanced are store profits. The more money you spend on supplements, the more you tend to waste.
- Don't waste money on most health store recommendations. If you need a supplement, it's most likely to be calcium, a multivitamin, or an antioxidant.

carrying compound in the blood), and iodine facilitates production of thyroxine (a hormone that influences metabolic rate).

There are twenty to thirty important nutritional minerals. Minerals should be consumed in smaller amounts than amounts of energy nutrients and water. Minerals that are present in the body and required in large amounts (more than 100 mg, or 0.02 teaspoon, per day) are called *major minerals* or *macrominerals*. They include, in descending order of prominence, calcium, phosphorus, potassium, sulfur, sodium, chloride, and magnesium. Major minerals contribute 60 to 80 percent of all inorganic material in the human body.

Minerals that are required in small amounts (less than 100 mg per day) are called *trace minerals* or *microminerals*. There are more than a dozen trace minerals, the best known being iron, zinc, and iodine (see Just the Facts: Minerals).

Some minerals are similar to water-soluble vitamins in that they are readily excreted by the kidneys, do not accumulate in the body, and rarely become toxic. Others are like fat-soluble vitamins in that they are stored and are toxic if taken in excess.

Minerals are different from vitamins; they are indestructible and require no special handling during food preparation. The only precautions that need to be taken are to avoid soaking minerals out of food and throwing them away in cooking water.

Major minerals are abundant in the diet; therefore, deficiencies are highly unlikely, especially if a variety of foods is included. If a deficiency in major minerals does occur, it is most likely to be a calcium deficiency, especially among women. Four out of five women ages 9 to 19, two out of three women ages 20 to 49, and three out of four women over 50 fall below the recommended allowance for calcium.[1] The RDA of calcium for adults 19 to 50 years old is 1000 mg, and 1200 mg is recommended for those 51 and older. Here are some tips for increasing your calcium intake:

- Try to consume as much calcium as possible from food. Skim milk and low-fat dairy products are excellent sources of calcium and are also fortified with vitamin D.
- Use calcium supplements to compensate for a calcium shortfall. Getting enough calcium from food requires consuming the equivalent of a quart of milk per day. As a result, many people benefit from an over-the-counter calcium supplement.
- Calcium is best absorbed in doses of 500 mg or less taken with meals.[23] The best type of calcium supplement is calcium carbonate, which is available in common antacids.
- Take calcium supplements with meals. Calcium is best dissolved and absorbed in stomach acids secreted during mealtime.
- Look for calcium-fortified foods. A cup of calcium-fortified orange juice, for example, contains about the same amount of calcium as a cup of milk and is absorbed more easily.
- Get the recommended intake of vitamin D. Vitamin D is necessary for the body to absorb calcium.
- If you're taking other supplements or medicines, check with your physician or pharmacist. Calcium

Just the Facts

Minerals

Here are some basic facts about minerals:

Major (Macro) Minerals
Types: calcium, phosphorus, potassium, sulfur, sodium chloride, and magnesium

Trace (Micro) Minerals
Types: iron, iodine, zinc, selenium, manganese, copper, molybdenum, cobalt, chromium, fluorine, silicon, vanadium, nickel, tin, cadmium

Minerals of Special Concern*

Calcium
Wellness benefits: contributes to bone and tooth formation, general body growth, maintenance of good muscle tone, nerve function, cell membrane function, and regulation of normal heart beat
Food sources: dairy products, dark-green vegetables, dried beans, shellfish
Deficiency signs and symptoms: bone pain and fractures, muscle cramps, osteoporosis

Iron
Wellness benefits: facilitates oxygen and carbon dioxide transport, formation of red blood cells, production of antibodies, synthesis of collagen, and use of energy
Food sources: red meat (lean), seafood, eggs, dried beans, nuts, grains, green leafy vegetables
Deficiency signs and symptoms: fatigue, weakness

Sodium†
Wellness benefits: essential for maintenance of proper acid-base balance and body fluid regulation; aids in formation of digestive secretions; assists in nerve transmission
Food sources: processed foods, meats, table salt
Deficiency signs and symptoms: rare

*Calcium and iron are of special concern because deficiencies are likely to exist, especially among women and children.

†Sodium is of concern because of potential for overconsumption.

can interfere with the absorption of iron, zinc, and certain medicines.

- If you have a history of kidney stones, exercise caution in taking large doses of calcium. High calcium intake might increase the risk of stone formation.

Starting your day with low-fat dairy products, such as milk and yogurt, is a good way to add calcium to your diet.

Of the various trace minerals, iron is the most abundant. It is also one of concern to nutritionists because certain groups are at risk of having low iron levels. These include young children and early teens, menstruating women, and people with conditions that cause internal bleeding, such as ulcers or intestinal diseases.[21]

Iron deficiency in the diet is responsible for the most prevalent form of anemia in the United States. Iron deficiency hampers the body's ability to produce *hemoglobin,* a substance needed to carry oxygen in the blood. A lack of hemoglobin can cause fatigue and weakness and can even affect behavior and intellectual function. Proper infant feeding through use of iron-fortified milk or breast-feeding is the best safeguard against iron deficiency in infants. Among adolescents and adults, iron intake can be improved by increasing consumption of iron-rich foods, such as lean red meats, fish, certain kinds of beans, dried fruits, iron-enriched cereals and whole-grain products, and foods cooked in a cast-iron skillet. For some people, especially premenopausal women with inconsistent diets, iron sup-

plements may be justified. In addition, consuming foods that contain vitamin C enhances the body's ability to absorb iron.

Iron deficiency is rare among healthy men and postmenopausal women. Even strict vegetarians can get iron in sufficient amounts by consuming legumes, dark-green leafy vegetables, and fortified breads and cereals. It is possible to get too much iron. Some studies report that high iron levels may be linked to heart disease, but the jury is still out on this issue. Also, some people have a rare genetic disorder called *hemochromatosis,* which permits an unhealthy buildup of iron. Iron overload may cause liver cancer, heart disease, diabetes, sterility, or other complications.

Zinc is another trace mineral that has received widespread publicity because of its link to the common cold. Early studies reported that zinc lozenges cured the cold within hours. More recent studies refute this claim and state that the one possible benefit is the shortening of the duration of a cold by about one day.

While zinc is essential for proper functioning of the immune system, too much can interfere with the body's use and absorption of other essential minerals, such as iron and copper. Also, excess zinc can lower HDL cholesterol.[24]

Water

Next to air, water is the substance most necessary for survival. Most everything in the body occurs in a water medium. Although people can live without vitamins and minerals for extended periods, death results within a few days without water.

Water makes up about 60 percent of the body's weight. Every cell in the body is bathed in water of the exact composition that is best for it. Even tissues that are not thought of as "watery" contain large amounts of water. For example, water makes up about 75 percent of brain and muscle tissues; bone tissue and fat tissue are about 20 percent water. As a rule, the bodies of men contain more water than do the bodies of women because men have more muscle tissue and muscle tissue holds more water than fat tissue, which is more prominent in the bodies of women.

Water performs many functions. It is vital to digestion and metabolism because it acts as a medium for chemical reactions in the body. It carries oxygen and nutrients to the cells through blood, regulates body temperature through perspiration, and lubricates the joints. It removes waste through sweat and urine, protects a fetus, and assists in respiration by moistening the lungs to facilitate intake of oxygen and excretion of carbon dioxide. It also assists with constipation relief and provides satiety, thus serving as a deterrent to the overconsumption of food.

Although most water intake comes from beverages, solid foods also make a significant contribution. Most fruits and vegetables are more than 80 percent water, meats are 50 percent water, bread is 33 percent water, and butter is approximately 15 percent water.

How much water should you drink? People are advised to drink 8 to 12 cups of fluids a day. Another general rule of thumb is to drink a quart of water for every 1000 calories expended.[25] More fluids are necessary before, during, and after physical activity (see Chapter 3). To determine when and how much fluid to drink, don't rely on thirst. If you're thirsty, the body has already lost too much fluid (see Real-World Wellness: How Can You Tell If You're Getting Enough Water?).

Plain tap water is the preferred source of fluid. Tap water has an advantage over bottled water in that it often contains fluoride, an additive that impedes tooth decay. Chlorine is another additive to municipal water supplies that provides a public health safeguard by destroying bacteria. Because it is added in such small quantities, fears about chlorine causing cancer are unsubstantiated. Another advantage of tap water over bottled water is that it is subjected to much more rigorous testing. Municipal water supplies, which are regulated by the Environmental Protection Agency, are tested every day for disease-causing microbes and chemical contaminants. Bottled water, which is regulated by the Food and Drug Administration, may or may not be tested.[26]

Under normal circumstances, too much water cannot be consumed because the body is efficient at getting rid of what it does not need. However, a sudden drinking binge in a short period early in the day will not satisfy the body's needs later; the excess will be excreted by the kidneys. Water consumption should occur throughout the day.

Real-World Wellness

How Can You Tell If You're Getting Enough Water?

Experts say that thirst is not a good indicator of when and how much water to drink. If that's the case, how can I tell if I'm drinking enough water?

The following guidelines[25] will help you determine whether to increase your fluid intake.

- Check your urine. It should be clear or pale yellow. Dark-colored urine in small amounts is a sure sign that the body's fluid needs are not being met. (Note, however, that some medicines and vitamin supplements can also cause dark urine.)

- Needing to urinate every two to four hours is a signal that your fluid intake is appropriate. Sometimes people limit fluid intake to avoid trips to the bathroom. This is a mistake. The bladder adjusts to extra fluid intake.

- If you're eating lots of protein, your kidneys need extra water to flush out the waste products of protein metabolism.

- Consume at least 8 to 12 cups of fluid each day. Water is preferred because it is absorbed faster than any other beverage. Juices, milk, and foods that are liquid at room temperature also count. Five servings of fruits and vegetables yield about 2 cups of water. Even solid foods, such as meats and bread, provide water. Alcohol and caffeinated beverages (coffee, tea, and colas) don't count because they act as diuretics and increase the need for water.

Other Nutrients with Unique Health Benefits

In addition to the six classes of essential nutrients, many other substances in food contribute to health. Three of the most notable ones are phytochemicals, botanicals, and fiber. Interest in these substances has given rise to two recent trends: the use of *nutraceuticals,* natural ingredients to promote and maintain health, and *chemoprevention,* the use of nutritional interventions to prevent diseases (such as cancer) by bolstering the immune system. New discoveries and recent developments in these areas have outpaced the scientific community's ability to monitor, test, and confirm various claims. Until these claims can be validated, the public should take a wait-and-see approach. While many of the chemical compounds in food promise to promote health or prevent disease, taken indiscriminately they may do more harm than good. The exception is fiber, for which most claims are backed by years of solid evidence. Some of the claims that have been studied and reported in the popular literature are highlighted here.

Phytochemicals

Phytochemicals are plant chemicals that exist naturally in all plant foods. Chemically they are not vitamins, minerals, fiber, or any of the energy nutrients. Rather they are the hundreds of thousands of active compounds found in small amounts in vegetables and fruits. Although phytochemicals have not been traditionally classified as essential nutrients, scientists believe that they might play an important role in preventing various diseases. For example, populations that consume higher amounts of fruits and vegetables have a lower risk of cancer.[27] Some phytochemicals have a structure similar to the body's natural forms of estrogen. These compounds are called *phytoestrogens* (or *plant estrogens*), and when ingested by way of the diet, they may reduce the potentially harmful effect of the more potent, naturally occurring estrogens often associated with breast and prostate cancer.[4] Although phytochemicals have largely been studied for their role in cancer prevention, current research is exploring their relationship to many other diseases, including cardiovascular disease, osteoporosis, diabetes, and hypertension.

There is a great deal of excitement in nutrition and food sciences about the potential of phytochemicals in health promotion. The reported health benefits of several phytochemicals are highlighted in table 6-6. As scientists continue to isolate, identify, and study specific plant chemicals, it is likely that the place of such chemicals in disease prevention will become more important. Some experts speculate that phytochemicals will be the "vitamins for the twenty-first century."

Botanicals (Phytomedicinals) (Herbs)

Plants used medically are technically called **botanicals** or **phytomedicinals.** The popular literature usually refers to them as *herbs*. Herbs number in the thousands; however, only twenty to thirty are backed by well-conducted research studies similar to those used to test over-the-counter drugs in the United States[28] Herbs, however, are not regulated as drugs; instead, they are classified as dietary supplements. Consequently, there is considerable debate about their effectiveness and safety. The names, food sources, and health claims of several popular herbs are presented in Just the Facts: Some Common Herbs Sold as Nutritional Supplements. Herbs are not to be confused with hormone supplements, such as melatonin, DHEA (dehydroepiandrosterone), and DMSO (dimethylsulfoxide). Unlike herbs, which are extracted from plants, these are synthetic compounds. The purported health benefits of these hormones have not yet been proved.

If you decide to take an herb, here are some tips:

- Check with your physician before taking herbs, especially for serious conditions. Inform your physician of herbs you are taking, just as you would for prescribed medicines. There are many potential interactions with other supplements and medicines.
- Avoid using herbs if you are pregnant or nursing.
- Check the label for the abbreviation *USP*. This means that the manufacturer has met the stringent guidelines of the United States Pharmacopoeia, ensuring the quality, strength, purity, and consistency

Table 6-6 Health Benefits of Selected Phytochemicals

Phytochemical	Food Source	Possible Benefit
Allyl sulfide	Garlic, onions, leeks, chives	Decreases reproduction of tumor cells; facilitates excretion of carcinogens; blocks nitrite formation in stomach
Caffeic acid	Fruits	Facilitates excretions of carcinogens
Capsaicin	Hot peppers	Acts as an antioxidant; inhibits carcinogenesis
Coumarin	Citrus fruit, tomatoes	Prevents blood clotting; stimulates anticancer enzymes
Dithiolthione	Cruciferous vegetables	Stimulates anticancer enzymes
Phytoestrogen (isoflavones)	Soybeans, dried beans	Help prevent breast cancer by stopping the estrogen produced by the body from entering cells
Flavonoids	Fruits, vegetables, red wine, grape juice, green tea	Acts as an antioxidant
Phenolic acids (ellagic acid, ferulic acid)	Fruits, grains, nuts	Prevents DNA damage in cells; binds to iron, which may inhibit the mineral from creating free radicals; binds to nitrites in the stomach, preventing them from being converted into nitrosamines
Indoles, isothiocynates, sulforaphane	Cruciferous vegetables	Stimulates anticancer enzymes
Limonene	Citrus fruits	Stimulates anticancer enzymes
Phytic acid	Grains	Binds to iron, which may inhibit the mineral from creating cancer-causing free radicals

Just the Facts

Some Common Herbs Sold as Nutritional Supplements

Here are usual dosages and possible benefits and problems[29] of various herbs:

- **Bilberry** (*Vaccinium myrtillus*)
  Usual dosage: 240–480 mg dried berry extract of bilberry shrub
  Possible benefits: useful for simple diarrhea, varicose veins, hemorrhoids, glaucoma, night blindness, cataracts

- **Echinacea** (*Echinacea purpurea*)
  Usual dosage: 15–30 drops of tincture from purple coneflower extracts, up to five times a day
  Possible benefits: immune booster for colds, flus, and respiratory infections
  Potential problem: some allergic reactions reported in people with autoimmune disorders like lupus or multiple sclerosis

- **Feverfew** (*Tanacetum parthenium*)
  Usual dosage: 125 mg. of dried leaf extract
  Possible benefits: prevention and treatment of migraines and associated nausea
  Potential problem: a potential allergen for people sensitive to ragweed

- **Garlic** (*Allium sativum*)
  Usual dosage: 3 cloves of dietary garlic daily or 1 tsp. dried garlic powder, or in oil or pill form
  Possible benefits: may promote antibacterial, antifungal, and antiviral activity including those associated with the common cold; may have cardiovascular benefits
  Potential problem: in excess, possible interactions with other herbs and/or medicines

- **Ginger** (*Zingiber officinale*)
  Usual dosage: 500 mg
  Possible benefits: treatment of motion sickness, nausea, indigestion
  Potential problem: may aggravate gallstones, heartburn; acts as a blood thinner

- **Ginkgo** (*Ginkgo biloba*)
  Usual dosage: 120–160 mg from leaf extract of ginkgo tree, in divided doses
  Possible benefits: may improve memory and mental functioning; acts as an antioxidant; aids blood flow to the brain and to the legs
  Potential problem: acts as a blood thinner; may cause gastrointestinal upset, headaches, allergic skin reactions

- **Ginseng** (*Panax ginsing*)
  Usual dosage: 300 mg or one-half ginseng root extract in hot water
  Possible benefits: may enhance immunity
  Potential problem: may increase blood pressure; may cause headaches and skin problems

- **Saw palmetto** (*Serenoa repens*)
  Usual dosage: 320 mg of dried fruit extract from sabal in one to two doses
  Possible benefits: may improve urinary flow in men with enlarged prostate
  Potential problem: may cause inaccurate readings on (PSA) tests

- **St. John's Wort** (*Hypericum perforatum*)
  Usual dosage: 300 mg dried leaf and flower extract
  Possible benefits: may alleviate mild to moderate depression
  Potential problem: not useful for severe depression; may cause complications with prescription antidepressants

- **Valerian** (*Valeriana officinalis*)
  Usual dosage: 400–450 mg of extract 30 minutes before bedtime
  Possible benefits: treatment for insomnia, mild anxiety, restlessness
  Potential problem: may cause complications with sedatives or antidepressants

of the product. The letters *NF,* which stands for *National Formulary,* also ensure that the product meets minimum standards. Presently, only a handful of herbs have been subjected to review using USP standards.

- Do your homework. Read about the herb; ask your pharmacist for information. There are several Web sites that provide helpful information:

United States Pharmacopoeia: www.usp.org/did/mgrphs/botanica

American Botanical Council: www.herbalgram.org

The Herb Research Foundation: www.herbs.org

- Monitor your body's response. Start with a dose that is lower than that recommended. Stop taking an herb if you have an adverse reaction.

- Don't expect miracles. Herbs take longer to work than prescribed and over-the-counter medicines.
- Take specific herbs for specific needs. Avoid taking herbs continuously.

Fiber

One advantage of a high-starch diet is that it will likely be high in fiber unless the foods are refined or highly processed.

Fiber (formerly called *roughage*) is a general term that refers to the substances in food that resist digestion. The amount of fiber in a food is determined by its plant source and the amount of processing it undergoes. In general, the more a food is processed, the more the fiber is broken down or removed and the lower its fiber content.

There are two kinds of fiber: *soluble fiber* dissolves or swells in hot water, and *insoluble fiber* does not dissolve in water. Every plant food usually contains a mixture of fiber types.

Soluble fiber

Soluble fiber appears to have several favorable effects. Because it forms gel in water, it adds bulk and thickness to the contents of the stomach and may slow emptying, thus prolonging a sense of fullness which may help dieters control their appetites. Studies have shown that soluble fiber also lowers blood-cholesterol levels. Soluble fiber binds with certain digestive acids made from cholesterol in the liver and then escorts the acids away in the stool. The liver responds by drawing cholesterol from the blood to make more acids, which lowers blood cholesterol. According to most studies, LDL cholesterol drops from 3 to 7 percent when a person changes from a low-fiber diet to a high-fiber diet.[30] Diets high in carbohydrates and fiber, especially soluble fiber, improve blood-glucose control, lower insulin requirements, and decrease blood cholesterol and blood pressure in people with diabetes. Soluble fiber also slows the absorption of sugars from the small intestine, another benefit for those with type II (non–insulin-dependent) diabetes.[31]

Good sources of soluble fiber are fruits, vegetables, and grains. Specific fiber-rich foods are prunes, pears, oranges, apples, legumes, dried beans, cauliflower, zucchini, sweet potatoes, and oat and corn bran (table 6-7).

Insoluble fiber

Insoluble fiber adds bulk to the contents of the intestine. This speeds the transit time (time of passage) of a meal's remnants through the small and large intestines. This in turn appears to offer the following important health benefits:

Table 6-7 Fiber Content of Selected Foods

Food	Fiber (g)
Fruits	
Apple, with peel	4.2
Banana	3.3
Blackberries (1 cup)	9.7
Dates, chopped (1 cup)	15.5
Grapes	1.0
Orange	2.9
Peach, peeled	2.0
Pear, with skin	4.9
Prunes, dried, pitted (10)	13.5
Raisins, seedless (1 cup)	9.6
Breads	
Oatmeal (1 cup)	0.86
Pumpernickel (1 slice)	1.33
Rye (1 slice)	1.65
Wheat (1 slice)	1.40
Whole wheat (1 slice)	3.17
White (1 slice)	0.68
Cereals	
Bran Chex (2/3 cup)	5
Bran flakes (2/3 cup)	5
Cheerios (1 1/4 cup)	2
Corn flakes (1 cup)	1
Grapenuts (1 1/4 cup)	2
Raisin Bran (1/2 cup)	4
Rice Krispies (1 cup)	Trace
Shredded Wheat (1 biscuit)	3
Life (2/3 cup)	3
Vegetables	
Lima beans (1 cup)	9.2
Green beans (1 cup)	3.1
Cauliflower (1/2 cup)	1.3
Corn, canned (1/2 cup)	6.3
Garbanzo beans (1 cup)	8.6
Greens (1 cup)	2.9
Navy beans (1 cup)	16.5
Baked potato, with skin	4.4
Tomato	2.2
Carrot	2.0

- It helps prevent constipation because insoluble fiber attracts water into the digestive tract, thus softening the stool. Softer stools reduce the pressure in the lower intestine, creating less likelihood that rectal veins will swell and cause hemorrhoids.
- It stimulates muscle tone in the intestinal wall, which helps to prevent *diverticulosis*, a condition that occurs when the intestine bulges out into

pockets, possibly leading to *diverticulitis,* a condition in which the pockets become infected and sometimes rupture.

- It may reduce the risk of colon cancer. A shorter transit time reduces the exposure of the intestines to cancer-causing agents in the food. Insoluble fiber also stimulates the secretion of mucus in the colon. Mucus coats the colon wall and may provide a barrier that keeps cancer-causing agents from reaching the colon's cells.

The best source of insoluble fiber is wheat bran. Other good sources are whole grains, dried beans and peas, and most fruits and vegetables, especially those eaten with the skin.

If you are not accustomed to eating fiber-rich foods, gradually add them to your diet over four to six weeks, following these suggestions:[30]

- Eat whole-wheat bread rather than white bread.
- Look for whole grains, such as whole wheat, on food labels. Whole grains contain the entire seed of a plant, including the bran, germ, and endosperm. Foods that are "made with whole wheat flour" are mostly refined. Wheat flour and unbleached wheat flour are not whole grain.
- Add 2 to 3 tablespoons of 100 percent bran to low-fiber foods, such as breakfast cereal, pudding, and applesauce.
- Substitute brown rice, millet, and bulgur wheat for white rice and potatoes.
- Snack on popcorn instead of potato chips.
- Eat whole fruit instead of drinking juice.
- Use raspberries as a topping for ice cream and yogurt.
- Snack on an unpeeled apple or pear.
- Choose bran flakes over cornflakes.
- Top your salads and casseroles with a whole-grain cereal, such as shredded wheat.
- Eat the skin on your potato.
- Include beans in soups and vegetable salads.
- Eat oats, legumes, and fruits for insoluble fiber.

How much fiber?

Most Americans consume 16 grams of fiber per day.[4] The daily recommendation is 25 grams for a 2000-calorie diet and 30 grams for a 3000-calorie diet. Most Americans have trouble meeting this recommendation because of their heavy intake of meat products. Meat provides little or no fiber; consequently, only vegetarians are likely to get enough fiber. Eating naturally high-fiber foods, such as whole grains, fruits, vegetables, and beans, is a good way to increase fiber intake. Starting or ending the day with a high-fiber cereal is another convenient way to increase your consumption not only of fiber but also of many vitamins and miner-als. Check the food labels which identify the amount of fiber per serving.

As with most other nutrients, fiber can be consumed in excess. Indiscriminate consumption of fiber may interfere with the body's ability to absorb other essential nutrients. A person who eats bulky foods but has only a small capacity may not be able to take in enough food energy or nutrients. A high intake of dietary fiber, such as 60 grams per day, also requires a high intake of water.[4]

Putting Nutrition to Work

Nutrition is a complex science and involves the study of thousands of nutrients and a countless number of possible interactions, all of which take place at the cellular level. Many of the results of nutritional practices, good or bad, take years or even decades to become apparent. Fortunately, it isn't necessary to be a biochemist to understand and follow nutritional practices that promote health and prevent the early onset of many health problems. The benchmark for developing a plan for good nutrition is the *Dietary Guidelines for Americans.* These guidelines, which were first published in 1980, are evaluated and revised every five years. The fourth and most recent version of these dietary guidelines[1] is listed here:

- Eat a variety of foods.
- Balance the food you eat with physical activity—maintain or improve your weight.
- Choose a diet with plenty of grain products, vegetables, and fruits.
- Choose a diet low in fat, saturated fat, and cholesterol.
- Choose a diet moderate in sugars.
- Choose a diet moderate in salt and sodium.
- If you drink alcoholic beverages, do so in moderation.

Eat a Variety of Foods

Variety is the first dietary guideline because it is the cornerstone of a healthy diet. Foods contain combinations of nutrients and other healthful substances, and no single food or food group can supply all of the RDAs of essential nutrients. For example, broccoli is loaded with vitamin C but contains no vitamin B_{12}; flounder provides vitamin B_{12} but no vitamin C. You should consume a variety of foods within each food group. Six flavors of gourmet ice cream are not what the experts have in mind when they recommend eating many different types of foods. It would be better to consume some low-fat milk, yogurt, cheese, and other dairy products over the course of several days than to focus on one dairy food. You can even have an occasional serving of gourmet ice cream. A diet that is

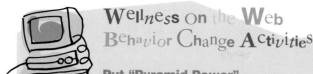

Wellness On the Web
Behavior Change Activities

Put "Pyramid Power" to Work for You

When you want to plan a nutritionally balanced diet, your best bet is to eat a variety of foods according to the federal government's Food Guide Pyramid. You can use the Pyramid to determine how many servings from each food group to include in your diet; it's also a great way to ensure that you consume the recommended dietary allowances (RDAs) of essential nutrients each day. To use an interactive Food Guide Pyramid, go to www.nal.usda.gov:8001/py/pmap.htm. Place your mouse on any portion of the Pyramid and click to obtain a list of foods and the appropriate portions for each food group.

Food Facts—or Fiction?

Can you lose weight on a grapefruit diet? Does gelatin make your nails hard? Are some vegetables and fruits negative-calorie foods? Nutrition has captured the interest of Americans more than perhaps any other aspect of fitness and wellness. Whether it's HDLs or LDLs, fat or fiber, phytochemicals or vitamins, nutritional issues make headlines in both scientific journals and popular magazines, and everyone seems to be an expert. Go to Thrive's on-line food quiz at www.thriveonline.com/eats/dyngames/gen/eats.mythquiz.html to take a Food Fact or Fiction Quiz. Decide whether each statement is true or false, then press the "vote!" button to see how you scored. How well did you do?

Match Wits with the Sphinx

Go ahead—take the Food Guide challenge! Go to Thrive's on-line "Match Wits with the Sphinx" at www.thriveonline.com/eats/pyramid/index.html to challenge yourself on the interactive Food Guide Pyramid. Tour its fabulous pyramids and discover the answers to the world's oldest nutrition questions. You'll view the Food Guide Pyramid and its many layers for a rich variety of foods. You'll be challenged to unlock the secret of a healthy diet by clicking on the numbered layers. You'll also find out what constitutes a serving size for easy weight management and optimum health. What's more, a number of challenging questions are posed at each level to test your comprehension of important nutritional principles. Good luck on your discovery tour!

diverse is more likely to provide an adequate distribution of essential nutrients. It also helps to minimize exposure to toxins, both natural and synthetic, that may be present in one type of food.

Food guide pyramid

The best way to ensure variety in your diet is to use the Food Guide Pyramid (figure 6-3) as the foundation for food selection (see Real World Wellness: How Varied Is Your Diet?). The **Food Guide Pyramid** (**FGP**) portrays dietary guidelines in picture form and provides a structure for dietary planning by recommending the number of servings for each food group. The largest area of the pyramid is the base, which calls for six to eleven servings of grain products. Foods from this group make up about 40 percent of the daily diet. The next largest areas of the FGP are the fruit and vegetable groups. Together, grain products, fruits, and vegetables make up nearly three-fourths of the recommended diet. The top of the pyramid allows for a smaller number of servings from meat or meat substitutes and dairy products. About 25 percent of the servings in your daily diet should come from foods in these groups. No recommendations are given for the number of servings of fats, oils, and sweets. The advice is to consume these sparingly.

As helpful as the FGP is for meal planning, it has received some criticism. One important omission is any reference to fluid intake. This is a serious oversight because most Americans do not get enough water each day (see Real World Wellness: How Can You Tell If You're Getting Enough Water?). The American Medical Association (AMA) believes strongly that inadequate or inappropriate fluid intake is a significant contributor to poor health.[32] Another criticism is of its lack of guidance for people who don't eat a typical American diet. For that reason, other food pyramids have been developed that meet the needs of alternative diets, such as those of vegetarians. One such version is presented later in this chapter (see p. 180).

The FGP identifies a range of servings for the food groups. The number of servings that fits your needs depends on your required number of calories. Your calorie requirements depend on many factors, including age, gender, height, weight, activity level, health status, and pregnancy (see Wellness Across the Generations: The Nutrient Gap). Three calorie levels along with the corresponding recommended number of servings are presented in table 6-8.

Serving size

What counts as a serving depends on the food and how it is prepared. Sorting through serving sizes can be confusing. One ounce of a ready-to-eat cereal, for example,

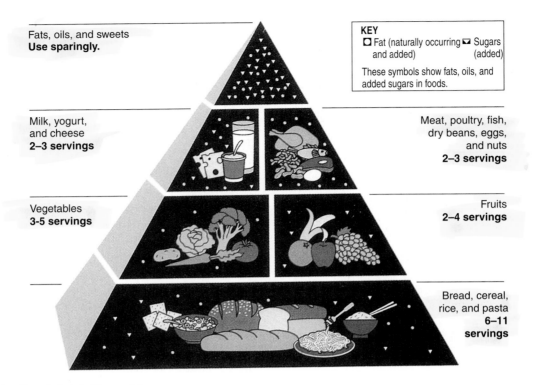

Figure 6-3 Food Guide Pyramid

Children, teenagers, and adults under 25 years of age should choose three servings from the milk, yogurt, and cheese group.

Real-World Wellness

How Varied Is Your Diet?

I seem to choose the same foods every week in the cafeteria and to prepare only a limited number of dishes for dinner. Does my diet have enough variety?

Dietary Guidelines for Americans emphasizes variety, but just what is variety? Ten foods a day? Twenty? According to researchers at Tufts University,[33] people who average seventy-one to eighty-three foods over the course of fifteen days have more nutritious diets than those who choose fewer than fifty-eight items. Fortunately, you don't have to track your food selections for fifteen days to assess variety. Three days will suffice. Circle the following foods that you eat during the next three days. If you can circle twenty-eight, you are probably doing well. If your number is closer to fourteen, improving the variety of your food selections should become a goal.

- cheese
- ice cream/milk-based desserts
- milk
- yogurt
- other dairy
- beans and legumes
- beef
- eggs
- fish
- lamb, veal, game
- liver/organ meats
- nuts and seeds
- pork
- poultry
- processed meats
- green leafy vegetables
- orange and yellow vegetables
- potatoes and other root crops
- tomatoes and tomato products
- other vegetables
- berries
- citrus fruits
- fruit juices
- melons
- other fruit
- cold breakfast cereals
- hot breakfast cereals
- pasta
- rice
- white bread
- whole-wheat bread
- other grains
- candy
- margarine, butter, and oils
- salty snacks
- soft drinks
- sweet baked goods and desserts

It has been estimated that as many as 25 percent of Americans 60 and older are malnourished. They do not suffer from nutritional diseases like scurvy or pellagra; rather, they consume insufficient amounts of key nutrients that have a direct effect on health and body function. Older adults usually expend less energy to meet the demands of their lifestyle than do their younger peers and therefore require fewer calories. This presents a dilemma because as their need for energy decreases, their need for nutrients increases or stays the same. Unfortunately, a decrease in caloric intake is usually associated with a decrease in key nutrients. There is a gap between what older adults need and what they get from food, as shown in the following chart:

Wellness Across the Generations

The Nutrient Gap

Nutrient	What They Need (Age 50+)	How They're Doing	Why Adults Age 50+ Need It
Calcium	1200 mg	The average intake is 400–600 mg	The capacity to absorb calcium declines with age
Folate	400 µg	Only one-fourth of older adults get 400 µg	Reducing homocysteine levels becomes more important as heart disease risks increase
Riboflavin	1.1 mg, women 1.3 mg, men	Only one-third get enough	The body's need is the same throughout adulthood
Vitamin B$_6$	1.5 mg, women 1.7 mg, men	50–90% don't get enough	The body's metabolism changes with age
Vitamin B$_{12}$	2.4 µg	20% of adults over 60 and 40% over 80 are deficient	Increased difficulty in absorbing vitamin B$_{12}$ comes with age
Vitamin D	_00 IU, ages 51–70; 600 IU, 71+	The average intake is 100–125 IU	Decreased ability of skin to synthesize vitamin D from sunlight comes with age
Protein	See Wellness Across the Generations: Older Adults May Need More Protein		

counts as a serving. This is equivalent to 1/2 cup of cooked cereal. One slice of bread is equivalent to one-half of a bagel. The fruit group is more confusing. One whole piece of fruit is the same as 1/2 cup of chopped fruit or 3/4 cup of fruit juice. The only sure way to determine serving size is to check food package labels. You can also refer to Just the Facts: What Counts as a Serving?

Moderation

Moderation is another important characteristic of the healthy diet. There is a place in the diet for almost any food if it is consumed prudently—the FGP doesn't label food "good" or "bad." Some foods do have a higher **nutrient density** than others, meaning they yield a higher ratio of nutrients to calories, but all foods contribute to nutrition (see Just the Facts: Nutrient Density). Moderation means exercising good judgment regarding quantity and frequency. It doesn't mean avoidance. The idea that a particular food is good or bad can be destructive to anyone trying to eat more healthfully. For example, a person with rigid attitudes who thinks that cheesecake is "bad" and then indulges in eating it might think, "I am bad, I have no willpower, and I am a weak person." The behavioral result might be a cheesecake binge, since the forbidden nature of the food makes it harder to resist. A more positive approach is to understand that cheesecake is not "bad" and that eating a slice does not make the eater a bad person.

Another reason for moderation is that even foods that are nutritionally dense can be consumed in excess. The interaction of the various substances in food can cause one nutrient to overpower or nullify the effects and benefits of another. The body's processes may be compromised or the nutrients in foods may interfere

Table 6-8 Nutrition Plan for Three Calorie Levels

	Calorie Level*		
	1600	2200	2800
Grain group servings	6	9	11
Vegetable group servings	3	4	5
Fruit group servings	2	3	4
Milk group servings[†]	2–3	2–3	2–3
Meat group servings[‡]	5	6	7
Total fat (g)	53	73	93
Percent fat calories	30	30	30
Total added sugars (tsp)[§]	6	12	18

*1600 calories is appropriate for many sedentary women and some older adults; 2200 calories is appropriate for most children, teenage girls, active women, and sedentary men (women who are pregnant or breast-feeding may need more). For teenage boys, many active men, and some very active women 2800 calories is appropriate.

[†]Women who are pregnant or breast-feeding, teenagers, and young adults to age 24 need 3 servings.

[‡]Meat group amounts are in total ounces.

[§]from candy, desserts, soft drinks, and other sweets

Just the Facts

What Counts as a Serving?

One way to estimate serving size when food labels aren't available is to use the parts of your hand. Here is how it's done:

1 thumb = 1 ounce of cheese

1 thumb tip = 1 teaspoon of foods such as mayonnaise, peanut butter, and sugar

3 thumb tips = 1 tablespoon

1 fist = 1 cup of pasta, rice, or vegetables

1 or 2 handfuls = 1 ounce of a snack food (1 handful of small foods, such as nuts, or 2 handfuls of larger foods, such as chips and pretzels)

1 palm (minus the fingers) = 3 ounces of meat, fish, or poultry

with the desired effects of medicines. Here are several examples of the negative effects of excessive consumption of various nutrients:

- Too much protein from animal sources may cause the body to lose extra calcium.[35]
- Botanicals such as garlic, ginger, and ginseng, when combined with vitamin E, fish oils, or blood thinning medicines (e.g., aspirin, Coumadin), may inhibit the blood-clotting mechanism of the body and cause internal bleeding.[36]
- Megadoses of vitamin A can cause birth defects.
- Megadoses of vitamin C can damage the cell's DNA, which can lead to cancer or heart problems. That is, large doses can negate vitamin C's normal antioxidant effect.[37] Large doses (2000 mg) can also cause diarrhea, nausea, abdominal cramps, and headache.[38]
- Excessive intake of vitamin D causes too much calcium to move from the bones to the blood and then to the urine through which it is excreted from the body.[39]
- High intake of folate may mask the symptoms of pernicious anemia, a condition associated with a vitamin B_{12} deficiency.
- Excess niacin may aggravate glucose intolerance associated with non–insulin-dependent diabetes.
- Foods high in vitamin K, such as broccoli, spinach, and turnip greens, may neutralize the effectiveness of blood-thinning medicines.

- Foods high in tyramine, such as cheese and sausage, can cause a sudden rise in blood pressure in people taking some antidepressant medicines.[40]

These examples are not meant to discourage your consumption of a particular food. Each food offers a unique contribution to health. Vitamin D, for instance, is required for calcium metabolism; however, too much of it may result in a depletion of calcium. Moderation is an important concept that applies to essential nutrients just as it applies to nutrients with bad reputations. Choosing foods from the FGP, with an emphasis on variety and moderation, not only satisfies the body's need for essential nutrients but also helps prevent problems associated with dietary excess.

Balance Food Intake with Physical Activity—Maintain or Improve Your Weight

The achievement and maintenance of a desirable body weight and composition are complex issues and are treated separately in this text. For a complete discussion of the principles of balancing food intake with physical activity for maintaining desirable body composition, refer to Chapters 7 and 8.

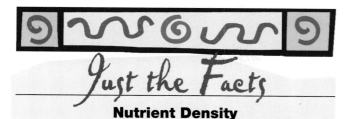

Just the Facts

Nutrient Density

A key strategy for eating well is to select foods that offer significant amounts of nutrients but small numbers of calories. If a particular food has a high ratio of nutrients to calories, it is a nutritionally dense food. You can determine the nutrient density of food by adding the percentages of the RDA for the essential nutrients and dividing by the number of calories per serving (see the following example). The higher the score, the higher the nutrient density. The concept of nutrient density can help the health-conscious and weight-conscious person make informed choices.

Calculating the Nutrient Density of Pizza (Cheese)

Calories	354
RDA %	
Protein	28%
Vitamin A	19%
Vitamin C	20%
Thiamin	25%
Riboflavin	29%
Niacin	19%
Calcium	33%
Iron	15%
Total	**188**

Nutrient density = 53% (188 ÷ 354 × 100)

Choose a Diet with Plenty of Grain Products, Vegetables, and Fruits

Grain products (bread, cereal, rice, and pasta) are emphasized in the FGP because they are rich in vitamins, minerals, complex carbohydrates, antioxidants, phytochemicals, and fiber. Most Americans of all ages eat fewer than the recommended number of servings from these three food sources.[1]

Clearly, the FGP emphasizes plant foods over animal products. This represents a dramatic change from the way many Americans eat. For example, in planning meals Americans often think first of the entrée, which is typically a meat dish. This is usually true whether we're eating at home or dining out. The FGP challenges us to reverse this approach by thinking of plant products first.

The vegetarian alternative

The importance of a plant-based approach to eating is evidenced by the fact that *Dietary Guidelines for Americans* now officially recognizes a vegetarian diet as a healthful and acceptable way of meeting all nutritional needs.[41] Some vegetarians avoid all animal products, including dairy products, poultry, eggs, and fish. Others include eggs and milk products but exclude fish, poultry, and red meat. There are many variations of vegetarian diet. The more common types are presented in table 6-9.

With the exception of vegans, most types of vegetarians have little trouble getting all of the essential nutrients, including protein. Milk products, eggs, fish, and poultry are sources of complete, high-quality protein. *Vegans,* who eat all-plant diets, need to be discriminating in their food selections because most plants are sources of incomplete protein. One notable exception, as mentioned earlier, is soy protein. Vegans who don't consume soy products need to combine complementary foods, such as grains and legumes, to obtain all of the essential amino acids.

The nutritional problem most likely to occur in a strict vegetarian diet is a deficiency in vitamin B_{12}, which occurs naturally only in animal products. Vegans can get vitamin B_{12} by taking a supplement or consuming food that has been fortified with B_{12}. Vitamin D is another potential problem to the vegan if he or she has limited exposure to the sun. Milk products, which are fortified with vitamin D, are about the only dietary source of vitamin D. However, the body can produce adequate amounts of this vitamin if the skin receives sufficient exposure to sunlight. During periods of limited sunlight exposure, vegans may need to take vitamin D supplements. Other essential nutrients richly supplied by animal products and thus of concern to vegans, such as riboflavin, iron, zinc, and calcium, can be easily derived from a variety of plant sources.

Figure 6-4, a food pyramid for ovolactovegetarians, presents a helpful plan for people trying to avoid meats. The recommended number of servings of grains, fruits, vegetables, and milk products is identical to the recommended amounts in the Food Guide Pyramid. The major difference is the exclusion of meat in favor of legumes, nuts, seeds, and eggs. Lactovegetarians can omit eggs from this pyramid.

Here are some practical tips for adding fruits, vegetables, and grains to the diet that should be helpful for people opting for a meatless meal, choosing to eat vegetarian for a day, or favoring vegetarianism as a lifestyle:

- Start off the day with fruit juice.
- Add fruit to a salad.
- Serve fruit for dessert.

Table 6-9 Types of Vegetarians

Type	What Is Excluded from Diet	What Is Included in Diet
Vegans	All animal products	Fruits, vegetables, grains, legumes, nuts, and seeds
Lactovegetarians	Eggs, fish, poultry, and meat	Milk products and fruits, vegetables, grains, legumes, nuts, and seeds
Ovolactovegetarians	Fish, poultry, and meat	Eggs (*ova*), milk products (*lacto*), plus fruits, vegetables, grains, legumes, nuts, and seeds
Pescovegetarians	Poultry and meat	Fish (*pesco*), eggs, milk products, fruits, vegetables, grains, legumes, nuts, and seeds
Pollovegetarians	Red meat	Poultry (*pollo*), fish, eggs, milk products, fruits, vegetables, grains, legumes, nuts, and seeds

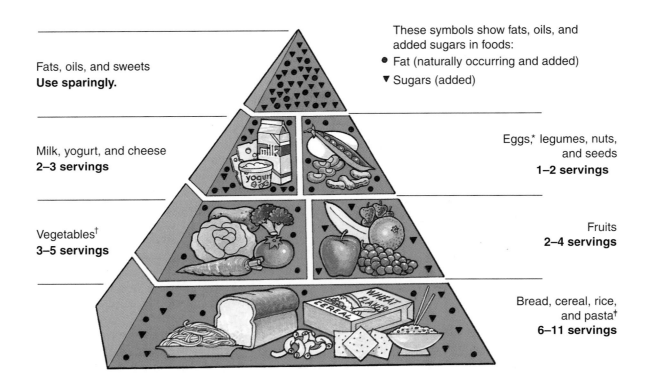

Fats, oils, and sweets
Use sparingly.

These symbols show fats, oils, and added sugars in foods:
● Fat (naturally occurring and added)
▼ Sugars (added)

Milk, yogurt, and cheese
2–3 servings

Eggs,* legumes, nuts, and seeds
1–2 servings

Vegetables†
3–5 servings

Fruits
2–4 servings

Bread, cereal, rice, and pasta‡
6–11 servings

* Lactovegetarians can omit eggs from this pyramid.
† Include one dark green or leafy variety daily.
‡ One serving of a vitamin- and mineral-enriched cereal is recommended.
¶ Contains about 75 g of protein and 1650 calories.
‖ Base serving sizes on those listed for the Food Guide Pyramid.

Figure 6-4 Food Pyramid for Ovolactovegetarians¶

- Have a smoothie (blend fruit juice, ice, and a banana).
- Add fruit to cereal.
- Eat cereal as a snack.
- Eat vegetable snacks.
- Aim for a colorful plate, with dark-green, yellow, and red vegetables.
- Increase the number of vegetables in a salad by adding tomatoes, carrots, cucumbers, peppers, spinach, or broccoli.
- Eat a vegetable pizza.
- Make a soup with leftover vegetables.
- Eat an all-vegetable meal.
- Mix legumes with a salad.
- Try a new fruit or vegetable.
- Top fat-free frozen yogurt with low-fat granola and berries.
- Top salad with whole-wheat cereal.

A properly selected vegetarian diet has many health benefits (see Just the Facts: Health Benefits of a Vegetarian Diet). People who have health conditions associated with diets high in fat and saturated fat and low in folate, carotenoids, phytochemicals, and antioxidants stand to benefit from a plant-based diet.

Another strategy for increasing your consumption of grain products, vegetables, and fruits is to cultivate a taste for ethnic food. The typical diets of many other countries favor grains, fruits, and vegetables and place less emphasis on animal fats. However, watch out for the Americanization of ethnic foods. For example, the traditional Italian pasta dish comes with a tomato-based sauce containing small amounts of meat or meatballs on the side, served with crusty Italian bread or pizza with an extra-thick crust and a mere sprinkle of tomato sauce, herbs, and cheese. Americanized, the same dish comes with less pasta, more creamy sauces, and more meat, served with buttery garlic toast or pizza with a thin crust, pepperoni, sausage, olives, and extra cheese. For additional comparisons, see Just the Facts: Do You Eat Real Ethnic Food?

A diet that emphasizes the first two of the seven *Dietary Guidelines for Americans* will go a long way in helping to meet the remaining guidelines. A diverse diet with plenty of grains, fruits, and vegetables is usually low in fat, saturated fat, and cholesterol and moderate in sodium and sugars, depending on how the food is prepared and what is added to it at the table.

Choose a Diet Low in Fat, Saturated Fat, and Cholesterol

Some dietary fat is needed for good health. Fats supply energy and essential fatty acids and promote absorption of the fat-soluble vitamins. Whether from plant or animal sources, fat contains more than twice the num-

---

Just the Facts

Health Benefits of a Vegetarian Diet

As a group, vegetarians have lower morbidity and mortality rates from several chronic degenerative diseases than do nonvegetarians.[42] Typically, vegetarian diets are lower in fat and saturated fat and have higher concentrations of nutrients (vitamins, minerals, and phytochemicals) associated with health benefits. Here are some of the benefits of a vegetarian diet over a nonvegetarian diet:

- Lower cholesterol level
- Lower level of low-density lipoproteins
- Lower incidence of hypertension
- Fewer complications and lower mortality from type II diabetes mellitus
- Reduced incidence of lung, colorectal, and breast cancer
- Improved kidney function
- Reduction of coronary artery disease

---

ber of calories as its carbohydrate or protein equivalents. Fats are represented in the apex of the FGP; *Dietary Guidelines for Americans* calls for no servings of fat because the body's need for essential fatty acids is easily satisfied by foods in the other food groups. Perhaps one of the greatest shortcomings of the American diet is the abundance of fat. Compounding this problem is the reality that fat is usually consumed at the expense of fruits, vegetables, and grains. For many people, reducing both the amount and type of dietary fat eaten is a formidable challenge. Table 6-3 presents a quick reference of maximum fat intake for selected caloric intakes. You can estimate your personal maximum fat intake by completing Assessment Activity 6-2. You can learn how fatty your eating habits are by completing Assessment Activity 6-5.

Tips for reducing dietary fat

Here are some suggestions for reducing total dietary fat consumption, lowering saturated fat intake, and replacing saturated fats with unsaturated fats:

- Assess your fat intake. Complete the assessments at the end of this chapter along with those in *Health-Quest* to determine your fat intake. Compare your fat intake with the recommendations in table 6-3.

Just the Facts

Do You Eat Real Ethnic Food?

The typical diets of many other countries tend to contain more high-carbohydrate foods and fewer foods high in animal fats than does the common American diet. However, when ethnic foods are prepared in the United States, especially in restaurants, they are often "Americanized" by inclusion of larger portions of meat and cheese and addition of sauces. What follows are descriptions of some traditional, high-carbohydrate ethnic foods and their higher-fat Americanized versions. Which versions of these ethnic foods do you tend to eat?

Chinese
- Traditional: large bowl of steamed rice with small amounts of stir-fried vegetables, meats, and sauces as condiments
- Americanized: several stir-fried or batter-fried entrees in sauces, with a small bowl of fried rice on the side

Japanese
- Traditional: large bowl of steamed rice with broth-based soups containing rice noodles, vegetables, and small amounts of meat
- Americanized: tempura (batter-fried vegetables and shrimp), teriyaki chicken, oriental chicken salad with oil-based dressing

Italian
- Traditional: large mound of pasta with tomato-based sauce containing small amounts of meat or meatballs on

the side, served with crusty Italian bread or pizza with an extra-thick crust and mere sprinkle of tomato sauce, herbs, and cheese
- Americanized: less pasta, more creamy sauces, and more meat, served with buttery garlic toast or pizza with a thin crust, pepperoni, sausage, olives, and extra cheese

Mexican
- Traditional: mostly rice, beans, warmed tortillas, and lots of hot salsa and chiles
- Americanized: crispy fried tortillas, extra ground beef, added cheese, sour cream, and guacamole (avocado dip)

German
- Traditional: large portions of potatoes, rye and whole-grain breads, stew with dumplings, and sauerkraut
- Americanized: fewer potatoes, less bread, more sausage and cheese

Middle Eastern
- Traditional: pita bread (round bread), pilaf (rice dish), hummus (chickpea dip), shaved slices of seasoned meat, diced vegetables, and yogurt-based sauces, all seasoned with garlic
- Americanized: meat kebabs, salads drenched in olive oil, less bread and pilaf

---

- Read labels and become familiar with the fat content of food. Try to identify foods that should be consumed in limited amounts; also identify foods that are low in fat (see table 6-2).
- Become familiar with sources of saturated, monounsaturated, and polyunsaturated fats (see figure 6-2).
- Check for the presence of transfatty acids by reading the fine print on food labels. Look for the words *hydrogenated* or *partially hydrogenated* to identify foods that should be consumed in limited amounts.
- Limit meat, seafood, and poultry to no more than 5 to 7 ounces per day.
- Eat chicken or turkey (without the skin) or fish instead of red meat in most meals.
- Substitute one or two meals of fish per week for red meats. Choose fish high in omega-3 fatty acids and

low in saturated fat, such as Atlantic cod, haddock, salmon, shrimp, scallops, sardines, tuna, red snapper, and trout.
- Choose lean cuts of meat, trim all the visible fat, and throw away the fat that cooks out of the meat.
- Substitute meatless or low-meat main dishes for regular entrees.
- Substitute legumes for meat one or two times per week.
- Eat a vegetarian diet at least one day a week.
- Use no more than 5 to 8 teaspoons of fats and oils per day for cooking, baking, and preparing salads.
- Choose foods that contain fewer than 3 grams of fat per 100-calorie serving.
- Choose foods that contain less than 1 gram of saturated fat per 100-calorie serving.
- Use low-fat dairy products (whole milk has more than eight times the fat calories as skim milk).

Even if your weight is healthy, too many high-fat take-out dinners may mean too few fruits and vegetables.

- Substitute pureed fruit, such as applesauce, when cooking from a recipe that calls for cooking oil (equal substitution).
- Use soft margarine in place of hard margarine.
- Use liquid or spray margarine when possible.
- Serve dressings and condiments (for salads, potatoes, etc.) on the side. Try to cut these servings in half.
- Avoid fried foods. Substitute another cooking method (baking, grilling, broiling, or roasting) for frying.
- Eat more vegetables and fruits.
- Eat low-fat foods that have a high satiety value, such as whole grains and high-fiber foods.
- Substitute olive oil or canola oil for margarine, butter, or lard.
- Try to add diversity to your diet. Cultivate a taste for low-fat ethnic foods.
- Avoid a "forbidden fruit" approach to food selection. Any food can be enjoyed in moderation. If you consume an unusually high-fat food or meal, try to compensate with more prudent choices during the week.

Choose a Diet Moderate in Sugars

Sugars are carbohydrates. During digestion, all carbohydrates except fiber break down into sugars. Americans eat sugars in many forms, and most people enjoy the taste of sugars. Some sugars are used as natural preservatives, thickeners, and baking aids in foods. Most of the simple sugar eaten by Americans has been added to foods and beverages during processing and manufacturing. A food is likely to be high in sugars if one of the following terms is listed first or second in the ingredients list on a food label: brown sugar, corn sweetener, corn syrup, fructose, fruit juice concentrate,

Carbonated soft drinks are a major contributor to high-sugar diets. How much soda do you drink?

glucose (dextrose), high-fructose corn syrup, honey, invert sugar, lactose, maltose, molasses, raw sugar, sucrose (table sugar), or syrup. Many foods contain a combination of sugars.

Nutritionists recommend that sugar consumption be limited to 10 to 15 percent of total calories. On average, Americans get 18 percent of their calories from sugar. Intake of sugar by children may exceed 50 percent of total calories.[4]

The major health problem associated with a high sugar intake is dental caries (cavities). The main offenders are foods that are sweet and gummy. They stick to the teeth and supply bacteria with a steady source of carbohydrate from which to make acids that can dissolve tooth enamel. Foods that promote caries are termed *cariogenic*.

Contrary to popular belief, there is little or no evidence that high sugar intake causes hyperactivity in children, heart disease, diabetes, or obesity. If that were the case, most Americans would have all of these conditions. The major nutritional problem of a high-sugar diet occurs when sugar is substituted for more nutritionally dense foods. When this happens, the result may be insufficient vitamin and mineral intake.

Choose a Diet Moderate in Salt and Sodium

Salt contains about 40 percent sodium by weight and is widely used in the preservation, processing, and preparation of foods. Sodium is an essential mineral, but it is one that Americans consume in excess. Average daily consumption of sodium is 4000 milligrams, which is eight times the minimum requirement of 500 milligrams (one-tenth of a teaspoon) and almost double the 2400 milligrams considered adequate.[43] The main health problems associated with consumption of too much sodium are hypertension, osteoporosis, and stomach cancer.[45] Of the three, hypertension, discussed in Chapter 2, is the most common problem. Sodium contributes to the development of osteoporosis because it pulls calcium from bones and causes the kidneys to excrete calcium. Sodium contributes to stomach cancer because it irritates the stomach lining, causing cells to replicate themselves, increasing the odds of cancer-cell initiation.

The majority of salt consumed is in the form of hidden salt added during the processing of food. Less than one third comes from the salt shaker.[44] Just how much salt is in a processed food can be determined by reading the package label.

Taste buds cannot always judge salt content. Some foods that taste salty may be lower in salt content than foods that do not. For example, peanuts taste salty because the salt is on the surface where the taste buds immediately detect it. However, cheese contains more salt than peanuts or potato chips, and chocolate pudding contains even more salt. To cut down on salt consumption, you should do the following:

- Avoid adding salt before tasting food.
- Add little or no salt to food at the table.
- Season food with sodium-free spices, such as pepper, allspice, onion powder, garlic, mustard powder, sage, thyme, and paprika.
- Avoid smoked meats and fish.
- Cut down on canned and instant soups.
- Read labels for sodium content, especially on frozen dinners or pizza, processed meat, processed cheese, canned or dried soup, and salad dressing. When shopping for canned and processed foods, select foods with no more than 200 mg of sodium per 100 calories.
- Eat plenty of fruits and vegetables high in potassium, calcium, and magnesium. These minerals may help keep blood pressure down.

Drink Alcoholic Beverages in Moderation

Dietary Guidelines for Americans recommends that alcoholic beverages be limited to one drink per day for women and two drinks per day for men.[5] (A drink is defined as 12 ounces of beer, 5 ounces of wine, or 1.5 ounces of 80-proof spirits.) The allowance for women is smaller because women, on average, are smaller than men, they have less muscle and, therefore, less water than men (so alcohol does not get diluted as well in their bodies), and they have less of an enzyme that breaks down alcohol before it reaches the bloodstream. A maximal level of alcohol consumption has not been set for women during pregnancy, so pregnant women and women who have a high chance of becoming pregnant should not use alcohol.

From a health perspective, alcohol has both advantages and serious risks. On the one hand, it is associated with drunk-driving injuries and deaths, cirrhosis of the liver, and a host of social ills caused by alcoholism. On the other hand, when consumed in moderate amounts as recommended by the *Dietary Guidelines*, it offers protection from heart disease and stroke in some people, even more so than does abstinence. Population studies show a 30 percent reduction in coronary risk among moderate drinkers, compared with abstainers. The data are similar in men and women and in various ethnic groups.[45]

Moderate consumption of alcohol is thought to be especially beneficial for people who are at risk for cardiovascular disease and stroke. Several theories have been advanced to explain this benefit: Alcohol may improve blood levels of high-density lipoproteins, and it may serve as a blood thinner by inhibiting the blood-clotting mechanism often associated with atherosclerosis. Contrary to popular belief, wine does not appear to offer any advantage over other forms of alcohol.

Regardless of alcohol's potential health benefits, experts don't recommend alcohol consumption for everyone. Some people have medical, religious, and personal reasons for abstaining. People with uncontrolled hypertension, liver disease, pancreatitis, or strong family histories of addiction should avoid alcohol. The same is true for women during pregnancy. Also, some medicines may have a potentiating effect when taken with alcohol. For women there is also some concern about the link between moderate consumption of alcohol and breast cancer. It is important to remember that the health benefits associated with alcohol come from a moderate level of consumption. Alcohol consumption in excess of that recommended in *Dietary Guidelines* can cause a variety of health problems that outweigh the potential benefits. As is the case with many health issues, moderation serves as the guiding principle for alcohol consumption.

Other Nutrition Issues of Concern

Nutrition and Pregnancy

Good nutrition is crucial to a successful pregnancy, and a healthy pregnancy starts before conception. Alcohol consumption, smoking, an inadequate diet, dietary excesses of some nutrients, drug abuse, and the interactions of a host of medicines are some of the factors that may threaten a pregnancy even before conception is known or confirmed. Poor health habits throughout pregnancy, especially during the first three months, can harm the mother and developing baby. Although genetic and environmental influences introduce some risk factors beyond the mother's control, there is a considerable amount of medical advice about weight gain and the nutritional needs unique to pregnant women.

Weight gain

Adequate weight gain for a mother is one of the best predictors of pregnancy outcome. A weight gain of 25 to 35 pounds yields optimal health for both mother and fetus if pregnancy lasts at least thirty-eight weeks. To accommodate the extra demands for energy, the expectant mother needs to increase her caloric intake by about 300 calories daily, particularly after the third month of pregnancy.[4] Inadequate weight gain can lead to many problems. It is important to monitor weight throughout the pregnancy. Large fluctuations in the recommended weight-gain pattern should be brought to the attention of the health care provider.

Nutrient needs

The RDAs for many nutrients increase during pregnancy:[4]

- The protein RDA increases by 10 to 15 grams daily.
- Extra vitamin D is needed to absorb and distribute extra calcium for developing fetal bones. Approximately 20 to 30 minutes of sun exposure several times a week, a quart of vitamin D–fortified milk, or a vitamin D supplement that contains 5 µg (200 IU) should suffice.
- Because of its role in DNA synthesis, folate is a crucial nutrient during pregnancy. The RDA for folate during pregnancy increases to 600 µg per day. Folate deficiencies have been linked to some neural tube birth defects, such as spina bifida. The increased need for folate can be achieved through the diet or a prenatal vitamin and mineral supplement.
- Iron intake should double during the final six months of pregnancy to achieve the RDA of 30 milligrams per day. The extra iron is needed to synthesize the additional hemoglobin required during pregnancy and to provide iron for the developing fetus. Women often need an iron supplement if their typical iron intake is marginal. Iron deficiencies during pregnancy may threaten the health of both the baby and the mother.
- Calcium is needed during pregnancy for skeletal and tooth development of the fetus, especially during the last three months, when growth of these tissues is most prolific. The RDA for calcium is 1300 mg. A prenatal supplement usually contains 200 mg of calcium.
- The zinc RDA increases 25 percent (to 15 milligrams) during pregnancy to satisfy the requirements for growth and development of the fetus. Foods rich in protein also supply zinc. Zinc deficiencies increase the chance of a low–birth-weight baby.
- Prenatal supplements may contribute to a successful pregnancy for some women and, with the possible exception of vitamin A, provide benefits that outweigh potential risks. Because of its role in cell differentiation, megadoses of vitamin A from both supplements and dietary sources are associated with birth defects, particularly when the vitamin A is consumed during the first three months of pregnancy. It is recommended that women set their limit of vitamin A according to the RDAs.

Slight modifications of the recommended servings in the Food Guide Pyramid should satisfy women's unique nutritional needs during pregnancy. The major differences involve adding a serving of food from two food groups: the milk group and the meat group. Women who practice either ovolactovegetarianism or lactovegetarianism generally do not have difficulty meeting their nutritional needs during pregnancy. Vegans, on the other hand, must plan their diets carefully to ensure adequate amounts of protein, vitamin D, vitamin B_6, iron, calcium, zinc, and vitamin B_{12}. Vegans need to increase their intake of grains, beans, nuts, and seeds to supply the required amounts of nutrients. Still, supplements of vitamin B_{12}, iron, and calcium along with a multipurpose prenatal supplement will probably also be necessary.[4]

Nutrition and Physical Activity

The relationship between physical activity and nutrition is obvious. The ability to engage in physical activity, whether it is low intensity and recreational or high intensity and competitive, is influenced by dietary intake. Conversely, nutritional needs change depending on the type, intensity, and duration of activity.

Nutrition and athletic performance are complex subjects involving not only the science of nutrition but also the sciences of biochemistry and physiology. While a presentation of the intricacies of sports nutrition is beyond the scope of this text, the following information should help you plan to meet your nutrient needs when you participate in regular physical activities.

Type of activity and energy source

The body's use of carbohydrates, fats, and protein for energy depends on the type of activity and the level of physical fitness. For high-intensity, anaerobic activities lasting for only a minute or less, such as a 100-yard sprint, carbohydrates are the major fuel source. For aerobic activities lasting from several minutes to four or five hours, a combination of carbohydrates, fats, and protein provides fuel for work. If the activity is intense, involving 75 percent or more of maximum oxygen consumption (such as of a runner trying to achieve a personal best in a 1-mile run), carbohydrates will be in greater demand. If the activity is moderately intense, using 40 to 60 percent of maximum (such as jogging or brisk walking), fats and carbohydrates are used evenly. If the activity lasts more than a few minutes and is less intense, using less than 30 percent of maximum (such as easy walking), fat becomes a major source of energy.[46] Energy from protein is minimal during most activities because protein functions as a fuel source primarily after carbohydrate fuel is depleted, such as might occur in activities of long duration (such as long-distance running), and then its contribution accounts for only about 10 percent of the energy. In general, carbohydrates are the main fuel source for both anaerobic and high-intensity aerobic activities; fat is the main fuel source for prolonged, low-intensity exercise; and protein is a minor fuel source, primarily for endurance activities.[4]

Recommended sources of energy

The diet of a physically active person should favor carbohydrates. The body is capable of converting carbohydrates to a usable form of energy more quickly and more efficiently than it can fats or protein. As a general rule, dietary intake of carbohydrates should account for 55 to 70 percent of the energy.[47] Tables 6-10 and 6-11 present some high-carbohydrate meal options that are appropriate as preactivity meals. An increase in carbohydrate intake should be accompanied by a decrease in fat intake. Fat should account for about 15 to 30 percent of energy, depending on the percentage of carbohydrate calories; protein should provide the remaining 15 percent.

Protein supplement

Many physically active people, especially athletes, have the mistaken notion that intense physical activities impose a greater than usual demand for protein. This idea

---

Table 6-10 Two High-Carbohydrate Preactivity* Meals

	Calories	Protein (grams)	Fat (grams)	Carbohydrate (grams)
Menu 1				
White bread, 2 slices	123	4	2	22
Peanut butter, 1 tbsp.	95	4	8	3
Grape jelly, 1 tbsp.	56	0	0	14
2% milk, 1 cup	125	8	5	12
Orange, 1 medium	60	1	0	15
Meal total:	459	17	15	66
Menu 2				
Vegetable lo mein (soft noodles with stir-fried vegetables), 2 cups	352	11	15	47
Fresh papaya, 1 cup	54	1	0	14
Herbal iced tea sweetened with honey, 12 oz.	56	0	0	13
Meal total:	462	12	15	74

*A preactivity meal should provide 1 to 4 grams of carbohydrate per kilogram of body weight, moderate amounts of protein, and small amounts of fat.

stems partly from the perception that, if a modest amount of a nutrient is good for you, large amounts must be even better and partly from the fact that protein is needed for the synthesis of new tissue. Both of these ideas can lead to mistaken conclusions. What athletes and others who are engaged in intense activities need is not extra protein but extra carbohydrates. The body's need for protein is biologically driven (see the previous discussion of recommended protein intake), and any excess in this amount if inefficiently converted to energy or stored as fat.

Two exceptions to this protein guideline occur for athletes engaged in endurance sports and athletes starting weight-training programs. The recommendations for protein range from 1.2 to 1.6 grams of protein per kilogram of body weight for the endurance athlete and 2.0 to 2.5 grams per kilogram of body weight for the weight-training athlete.[4] This represents a two- to threefold increase of the RDA for protein. Experts disagree about the importance of excessive protein intake for weight training.

Vitamins and minerals

Vitamin and mineral needs of the physically active person are about the same as those of the sedentary person. People who exercise usually eat more than sedentary

people do and therefore get more vitamins and minerals as a matter of course. Contrary to popular belief, especially among athletes, there is no need to take vitamin and mineral supplements if adequate servings of food from the FGP are consumed. The American Medical Association, the American Dietetic Association, the American Institute of Nutrition, the Food and Nutrition Board, and the National Council Against Health Fraud have published position statements affirming that, with rare exception, there are no benefits of supplements that exceed the RDAs.[47] Megadoses of vitamins and minerals may, in fact, be counterproductive.

If a mineral deficiency occurs, it is most likely to involve iron and calcium, especially for women athletes. A deficiency of either of these minerals not only impairs athletic performance but also may lead to serious medical conditions. Dietary intake of these two minerals should be monitored regularly.

Fatty acids and activity

Most of the body's energy reserve is in its fat stores. When fat stores are broken down, fatty acids move through the bloodstream and enter muscle cells, where they are converted to energy. Well-trained muscles have a greater capacity to execute this conversion process and the ability to burn more fat. Thus, improved physical fitness causes more fat to be used for energy.[4,47] Also, the body's use of fat stores is affected by the duration of the activity. Prolonged activities (lasting more than 20 minutes) cause fat storage to be tapped for energy, particularly when the activity remains at a low-intensity level. Unlike carbohydrate stores, which are limited, an unlimited amount of fatty acids is available to sustain energy needs of low-intensity activities. Weight-conscious people interested in physical activity as a strategy for using fat, therefore, are better served by low-intensity to moderately intense activities that can be endured for a long period of time.

Fluid intake and activity

Consuming the right amount of fluids before, during, and after physical activity, which is addressed in Chapter 3, is crucial for the regulation of body temperature and the dissipation of heat.

Food Safety

Today, Americans face a paradox: We are urged to eat more fruits, vegetables, fish, and poultry but we are warned about contamination and **foodborne illness.** Recently, 25 million pounds of ground beef were recalled because of possible *E. coli* bacteria contamination; 200 Michigan schoolchildren developed stomach pains and jaundice from contaminated strawberries

Table 6-11 Convenient Preactivity Meals

Breakfast (McDonald's)	Energy content
Hot cakes with syrup and margarine Orange juice, 2 servings English muffin (whole) with 2 tsp. margarine and 2 tsp. jam	900 cal 67% from carbohydrates (150 g)
Cheerios, 3/4 cup Low-fat milk, 1 cup Blueberry muffin Orange juice, 1 serving	450 cal 82% from carbohydrates (92 g)
Lunch or dinner (Wendy's)	
Chili, 8-oz. portion Baked potato with sour cream and chives Chocolate Frosty, 10 oz.	900 cal 65% from carbohydrates (150 g)
Grilled chicken sandwich Cola, 12 oz.	425 cal 65% from carbohydrates (70 g)

that had been grown in Mexico; an outbreak of infectious diarrhea was traced to raspberries imported from Guatemala; dozens of cases of bloody diarrhea and one death were caused by a batch of organic apple juice made from California apples; and four children died from contaminated hamburgers cooked at a fast-food restaurant. Current estimates suggest that up to 33 million cases of foodborne illness occur in the United States each year, causing about 9,000 deaths.[46] These illnesses are difficult to prevent because they involve different kinds of organisms infecting foods of all types that are grown in many parts of the world.

Here is a short list of organisms that are common culprits of foodborne illnesses, along with their food sources and symptoms:

- *Staphylococcus* toxins are usually present in meats, poultry, egg products, tuna, potato and macaroni salads, and cream-filled pastries. Symptoms occur two to six hours after exposure and include diarrhea, vomiting, nausea, and abdominal cramps. Recovery normally takes place in twenty-four to thirty-six hours.
- *Salmonella* infections are associated with eggs, poultry, meat, dairy products, seafood, and fresh produce. Symptoms usually occur within six to forty-eight hours and include nausea, vomiting, abdominal cramps, diarrhea, fever, headache, and sometimes a rash. *Salmonella* infections may be quite serious, even fatal, in infants, the elderly, and the sick.
- *Clostridium botulinum,* usually referred to as *botulism,* occurs in an anaerobic environment, such as in canned goods, and affects low-acid foods like green beans, mushrooms, spinach, olives, and beef. Symptoms occur twelve to thirty-six hours after exposure and affect the central nervous system. Paralysis and death may follow. Infected food usually has an odor. Avoid canned goods that show any signs of damage.
- *Campylobacter jejuni* contamination is linked to raw and undercooked poultry, unpasteurized milk, and untreated water. Symptoms usually occur in two to five days and include diarrhea, fever, abdominal pain, nausea, headache, and muscle pain. Infections may last seven to ten days.
- *E. coli* O157:H7 is typically present in undercooked and raw ground beef, raw milk, lettuce, untreated water, and unpasteurized fruit juices. Symptoms include severe abdominal pain and cramping and diarrhea (first watery, then bloody).
- *Listeria monocytogenes* is associated with soft cheeses, poultry, fish, and raw meats and vegetables. The illness causes flulike symptoms, including fever, and may progress to fatal infections of the blood and central nervous system.

- *Hepatitis A virus* comes from contaminated fecal material from people who harvest, process, or handle food, including workers on farms, in food-processing plants, and in restaurants. Symptoms, which may not occur for several weeks, include fever, nausea, abdominal discomfort, and sometimes jaundice. The infection is usually mild, though symptoms can be severe.

With the exception of hepatitis A, the organisms listed are bacterial. For most of them, treatment consists of hydration and the administration of antibiotics. Other types of organisms are involved in foodborne illnesses. Parasites such as *Trichinella spiralis* (found in pork and wild game) and tapeworms (found in beef, pork, and fish) also infect many people. The same is true of fungi, which produce mold spores that yield toxins such as aflatoxin.

Most foodborne illnesses can be prevented by observing some basic rules for storing, handling, and preparing food. Following these simple rules represents a surprisingly formidable challenge to most Americans: According to recent surveys, only 1 percent of households would pass the inspection required of restaurants.[48] In your own home, follow these safety rules:

- Avoid cross-contamination: Do not prepare foods in an unclean sink and do not allow utensils that have come into contact with an unclean surface to touch food.
- Wash hands when first starting to handle food and after handling garbage or dirty dishes.
- Use separate cloths, sponges, and towels for washing dishes, wiping counters and tabletops, wiping hands, and drying clean dishes.
- Measure the temperature of cooked or held foods to make sure they're hot enough to destroy bacteria (see Just the Facts: How Hot Is Hot Enough?). Studies reveal that 50 percent of the public eat raw or undercooked eggs, 23 percent eat undercooked hamburger, and 17 percent eat raw clams and oysters.[49]
- Do not consume foods whose "use-by" dates have expired.
- Transfer leftovers from deep pots and casseroles to shallow pans before refrigeration in order to speed cooling (and thereby slow bacterial growth).
- Quickly freeze or refrigerate all ground meat and other perishable foods after shopping.
- Wash hands, utensils, and work areas with hot soapy water after contact with raw meat to keep bacteria from spreading. Also wash your hands after using the bathroom, diapering a child, using the telephone, handling garbage, or touching your face, your hair, or other people.
- Keep the refrigerator temperature below 40° F (37° F is optimal). Keep the freezer at or below 0° F.

Just the Facts

How Hot Is Hot Enough?

The only way you can be certain that food has been cooked thoroughly is to use a kitchen thermometer.[50] Visual cues, such as color or texture, aren't reliable indicators of a food's safety. When checking a meat's temperature, insert the thermometer in the deepest, thickest part without touching a bone. A thermometer's accuracy can be checked by placing it in boiling water. If it shows 212° F, it is accurate.

What follows are the minimum internal temperatures that various meat cuts must reach to be considered safe:

- Ground beef, veal, lamb, pork   160° F
- Beef, veal, lamb (steaks, roasts, chops)   145° F
- Pork (roasts, chops)   160° F
- Ham
  - uncooked   160° F
  - precooked   140° F
- Poultry
  - ground chicken, turkey   165° F
  - whole chicken, turkey   180° F
  - breasts   170° F
  - thighs, wings   180° F
- Stuffing (cooked alone or in the bird)   165° F
- Egg dishes, casseroles   160° F
- Leftovers*   165° F

*Reheated soups and gravies should be brought to a rolling boil. All other leftovers should be hot and steaming.

- Wash whole produce. This includes melons and citrus fruits before cutting them open, to prevent the transfer of bacteria from the fruit's skin to the edible part.
- Wash or sanitize cutting boards between each use.
- Store meat products in separate containers from fruits and vegetables.
- Flip steaks with tongs or a spatula rather than with a fork during cooking. Unlike ground beef, in which bacteria are mixed throughout the meat during the grinding process, steak harbors bacteria only on the surface. Sticking a fork into meat before it is cooked injects the interior with bacteria from the outside.
- Cook fish until it flakes with a fork.

- Put your sponge or scouring pad in the dishwasher every time you run it. Or microwave your sponge on high for thirty to sixty seconds.
- Don't store raw foods on the refrigerator shelf above ready-to-eat foods.
- Don't thaw frozen food on the kitchen counter or at room temperature. Thaw frozen food in the refrigerator or microwave.
- Don't eat hamburgers or any form of ground beef until the juices run yellow, with no trace of pink left. (The color of the meat isn't a reliable indicator of doneness. Check the juice.)
- Don't let juice from raw meat, poultry, or fish drip on your hands or any fresh foods in your grocery cart.
- Don't consume unpasteurized milk and juice or consume foods made with raw eggs.
- Don't use tasting utensils that have touched food under preparation.
- Don't grill, barbecue, broil, or pan-fry meats, poultry, or fish at extremely high temperatures. (Grills can reach temperatures in excess of 640° F. Ovens roast at a temperature of 350° F.) Cooking meats at high temperatures promotes the formation of heterocyclic amines, HCAs. HCAs are thought to be carcinogenic. Boiling, steaming, poaching, stewing, and microwaving do not produce HCAs.[51]
- Don't serve or transport cooked food on the plate used for raw meat.
- Don't store raw fish in your refrigerator for more than twenty-four hours. Raw poultry or ground beef will keep for one to two days and raw red meat for three to five.

Nutrition Strategies and Disease Prevention

This chapter emphasizes dietary practices that promote health and wellness, but the connections between food and disease must not be overlooked. Many of these connections have been referred to in the presentation of various nutrients and dietary guidelines, starting with the introduction to the chapter and ending with the previous section on food safety. Still, it is important to highlight some of the major diet and disease connections, with an emphasis on prevention. Remember that the interaction between food and disease is complex, and twenty to forty years may be needed to determine a relationship between disease and diet. With this in mind, here are some strategies[5] that may prevent or reduce the risks associated with several chronic conditions:

Heart disease. Reduce saturated fat intake to no more than 8 percent of calories and total fat to no more than 30 percent and increase monounsaturated fat to 15 percent. Reducing fat consumption has the added advantage of lowering cholesterol levels. Cholesterol intake should be limited to 300 mg per day. Other strategies include reducing homocysteine levels by consuming plenty of folate, ingesting 25 grams of fiber, especially soluble fiber, and eating at least five servings of fruits and vegetables per day. Vitamin E supplements may also be helpful.

Hypertension. Dietary strategies thought to be effective in reducing or preventing high blood pressure include limiting sodium intake to no more than 2400 mg, consuming potassium-rich fruits and vegetables, and obtaining calcium by eating two to three servings of low-fat dairy products per day.

Diabetes mellitus. Strategies that apply to heart disease also apply to the management of blood sugar levels. Two additional tactics are to maintain a desirable weight, especially for people with non–insulin-dependent diabetes, and restrict intake of simple sugars and highly processed carbohydrates, such as white flour.

Osteoporosis. Consume at least 1200 mg of calcium and 400 IU of vitamin D daily.

Cancer. Many strategies that apply to heart disease also apply to cancer. In addition, consumption of cruciferous vegetables, such as cabbage, broccoli, brussels sprouts, and cauliflower, is thought to help prevent cancer of the gastrointestinal and respiratory tracts. Consumption of fruits and vegetables rich in carotenoids has been linked to a reduction in cancers of the ovaries, bladder, larynx, esophagus, and lung. Cancers of the stomach and esophagus are less common among people whose diets are rich in ascorbic acid, or vitamin C. To reduce the risks of breast cancer, limit alcohol consumption to fewer than seven drinks per week. The risks of colon cancer can be minimized by limiting the intake of red meat to two or three servings per week, consuming lean cuts of meat or no meat at all, and eating at least 25 grams of fiber, including insoluble fiber, per day. Prostate cancer risk can be reduced by following these guidelines and by eating several servings of cooked tomato products each week.

Food Labels

The FDA oversees the labeling of food products other than meat and poultry. With the passage of new label laws in 1992, virtually all processed and packaged foods are required to have uniform labels. These foods include processed meat and poultry, which are regulated by the USDA. Guidelines for voluntary labeling of raw vegetables and fruits and fish are also available and will likely be displayed in most supermarkets.

Food labels must indicate the manufacturer and the packer or distributor, declare the quantity of contents either by net weight or by volume, and list the common name of each ingredient in descending order of prominence. Information about those nutrients most closely associated with chronic disease risk factors—that is, the amount of total fat, saturated fat, cholesterol, sodium, sugar, dietary fiber, total carbohydrate, and protein—must also be included.

Labels are divided into two parts (figure 6-5) and present information according to generic standards called **Daily Values (DVs)**. Daily Values are benchmarks for evaluating the nutrient content of foods. They express this content as a percentage of a 2000-calorie diet (Recommended Dietary Allowances are not used as the standards because they are age and gender specific). Information in the top part of a label will vary according to the contribution one serving of that food makes to the Daily Values listed in the bottom part of the label.

The DV standards located on the bottom panel are the same on all food labels and are based on two calorie levels: 2000 and 2500 (table 6-12). This means that total fat intake should be fewer than 65 grams for a 2000-calorie diet and fewer than 80 grams for a 2500-calorie diet. Dividing the nutrient content listed in the top panel by the DVs listed in the bottom panel yields the percent Daily Value for one serving. For example, a serving of Mac' n' Cheese contains 15 grams of fat, or 23 percent of the Daily Value of 65 g for a person on a 2000-calorie diet. With the application of simple arithmetic, you can calculate the Daily Value percents for any food with a breakdown of nutrient content.

Standard food labels are useful if daily caloric intake is approximately 2000 or 2500 calories and if the goal is to conform to minimum dietary recommendations. If your diet calls for significantly more or less of a nutrient, your DVs will differ. If that is the case, simply keep track of the total amount of a nutrient. For example, if you are on a 1500-calorie diet and are trying to limit fat intake to 20 percent, keep a running total of fat grams to determine when 33 g have been reached.

In the past, manufacturers often used labeling ploys to deceive consumers. Currently, laws limit labels to the following health claims:

- High-calcium foods may reduce the risk of osteoporosis.
- A diet low in saturated fat and cholesterol may lower the risk for heart disease.
- A low-fat diet may reduce the risk of some cancers.
- A low-sodium diet has been linked with reduced incidence of hypertension.

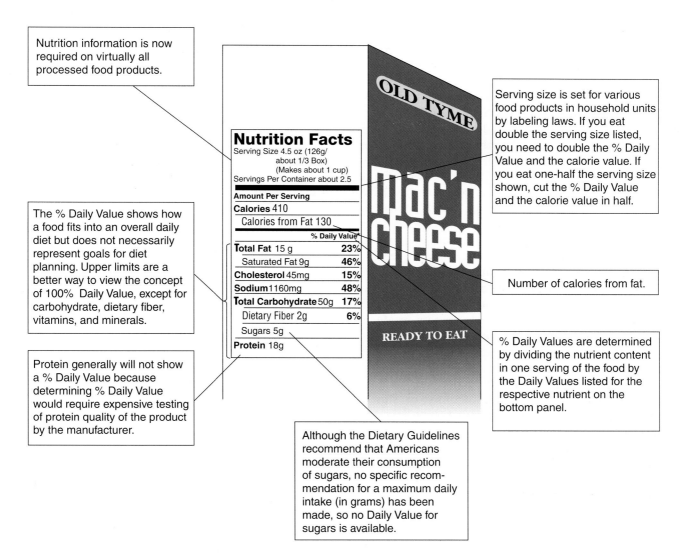

Nutrition information is now required on virtually all processed food products.

Nutrition Facts
Serving Size 4.5 oz (126g/ about 1/3 Box) (Makes about 1 cup) Servings Per Container about 2.5

Amount Per Serving

Calories 410

Calories from Fat 130

% Daily Value*

Total Fat 15 g 23%

Saturated Fat 9g 46%

Cholesterol 45mg 15%

Sodium 1160mg 48%

Total Carbohydrate 50g 17%

Dietary Fiber 2g 6%

Sugars 5g

Protein 18g

The % Daily Value shows how a food fits into an overall daily diet but does not necessarily represent goals for diet planning. Upper limits are a better way to view the concept of 100% Daily Value, except for carbohydrate, dietary fiber, vitamins, and minerals.

Protein generally will not show a % Daily Value because determining % Daily Value would require expensive testing of protein quality of the product by the manufacturer.

Serving size is set for various food products in household units by labeling laws. If you eat double the serving size listed, you need to double the % Daily Value and the calorie value. If you eat one-half the serving size shown, cut the % Daily Value and the calorie value in half.

Number of calories from fat.

% Daily Values are determined by dividing the nutrient content in one serving of the food by the Daily Values listed for the respective nutrient on the bottom panel.

Although the Dietary Guidelines recommend that Americans moderate their consumption of sugars, no specific recommendation for a maximum daily intake (in grams) has been made, so no Daily Value for sugars is available.

Figure 6-5 Food Label Showing Daily Values

Food labels provide information about those nutrients most associated with chronic disease risk factors.

Table 6-12 Standardized Daily Values on Food Labels

	Calorie Levels	
	2000	**2500**
Total fat	< 65 g	< 80 g
Saturated fat	< 20 g	< 25 g
Cholesterol	< 300 mg	< 300 mg
Sodium	< 2400 mg	< 2400 mg
Total carbohydrates	300 g	375 g
Fiber	25 g	30 g

- High-fiber foods may reduce the risk of heart disease and certain forms of cancer.
- Vitamins A and C in fruits and vegetables may reduce the risk of some types of cancer.
- Folate may reduce the risk of neural tube birth defects.
- Fruits, vegetables, and grain products that contain fiber, particularly soluble fiber, may reduce the risk of coronary heart disease.
- Sugar alcohols (e.g., sorbitol, xylitol, mannitol) may reduce the risk of dental caries.
- Soluble fiber from whole oats may reduce the risk of coronary heart disease.
- Soluble fiber from psyllium seed husks may reduce the risk of coronary heart disease.

The FDA has defined commonly used words describing calories, sodium, sugar, fiber, fat, and cholesterol in food. For example, when the word *free* is highlighted on a package in reference to calories, it means that the product yields fewer than 5 calories per serving; in reference to sodium, it means the product contains fewer than 5 milligrams; and in reference to fat, it means the product contains less than 0.5 grams. When *light* or *lite* is used on a package label, it means that the product has one-third fewer calories or 50 percent less fat than a similar product. *Low calorie* foods can have no more than 40 calories per serving; *low-fat* foods can have no more than 3 grams of fat per serving. *Healthy* means that a food meets the criteria for low fat and low saturated fat, does not exceed maximum levels for sodium and cholesterol, and contains at least 10 percent Daily Value for at least one of the following: vitamins A and C, calcium, iron, protein, or fiber. The word *organic* now can be used only on raw products that are grown without added hormones, pesticides, or synthetic fertilizers and on processed foods that contain 95 percent organic ingredients.

Freshness dates have also been defined. Phrases such as *Best Before, Better If Used Before,* or *Best If Used By* tell how long food will retain its best flavor or quality. The food is still safe to eat after the printed date, but it might become stale or change somewhat in taste or texture. The *Expiration, Use By,* or *Use Before* date, which appears on refrigerated foods, provides the deadline for consumption. A product past its expiration date is no longer of sufficient quality and should not be eaten. The *Sell By* date is usually found on highly perishable foods with a particularly short shelf life, such as meat, milk, or bread. It indicates the last day the product should appear on a supermarket shelf. If stored properly, most foods will remain safe to eat for about a week after the *Sell By* date.[52]

Serving sizes are not standardized. Nevertheless, the FDA has set serving sizes for 139 food and drink categories according to information obtained from surveys of what people actually eat. Consequently, serving sizes are more realistic than ever before, and they permit comparison shopping.

Even with the improvements in label laws, the unwitting consumer can still be misled. A brand of margarine changed its name from *Brand . . . Light* to *Brand . . . Light Taste*—manufacturers can still use light to describe taste, texture, or color. The makers of a brand of brownie mix claim that it is low fat. But the fine print says that the low-fat designation pertains only to each serving of the mix. Once an edible brownie is created by adding vegetable oil, its fat-gram content more than triples. Some foods promise fruit or other ingredients but deliver only flavor. One brand of strawberry frozen yogurt has no real strawberries despite pictures on the label of real strawberries; a brand of blueberry pancakes has no berries. Clearly, although labels have improved dramatically during the past several years, they still fall short in several areas. Deception in old labels was more obvious; today's labels challenge consumers to apply a higher level of discrimination to sort between fact and fantasy.

Changes in American Eating Patterns

Changes in the American family are mirrored in the trend toward convenience-food eating. For many families, time is a precious commodity that has a dramatic influence on how, where, when, and what people eat. Family meals at home are being replaced by a quick-stop, eat-on-the-go trend. Dining out has become a part of the quintessential American lifestyle, with one of every three people eating away from home at any one mealtime.[53] Not only do many people eat away from home, but they also skip meals. For example, college students typically eat two meals a day and make up the difference by eating many snacks. One-fourth of adults skip breakfast, which is the appropriate meal to replace the carbohydrate stores used during the night's sleep.[4] It should be of little surprise, therefore, that midmorning sluggishness is a common mental and physical disposition of students and workers alike.

Snacking

Snacking refers to consuming food between the three main meals of the day. Most Americans have at least one snack per day, and snack foods represent one of the fastest-growing markets in the food industry. From a nutrition point of view, snacking is neither good or bad. The three meals a day standard is based more on social custom than on physiology. The key issue is not the time or frequency of eating but what is eaten. Nutritionally dense foods eaten as snacks are just as good for health as they are when consumed as meals. The converse is also true; foods low in nutrient density eaten at mealtime are just as worthless as when they are eaten as snacks. With the exception of foods restricted for medical reasons, all foods can contribute to a healthful diet. Problems occur when a person's diet is dominated by foods low in nutrient density. Rather than rule out snacking, consume snack foods that enhance wellness. The most direct way to improve snacking behavior is the most obvious one: Purchase and make nutritionally dense foods available (see Real World Wellness: Snack Ideas).

From a nutritional viewpoint, the criticisms of fast-food eating are the same as those of the rest of the American diet: too much fat, too many calories, too

Real-World Wellness

Snack Ideas

After completing a thorough three-day dietary analysis, I was surprised to learn that the key to improving my overall nutritional profile is to make changes in my snack food choices. My meals are fairly well balanced, but my snacks are typically high in fat, high in sodium, high in sugar, and just basically low in nutrient density. What are some examples of nutritionally dense snacks?

The following snacks are surprisingly flavorful and satisfying and will help you improve your overall nutrition:

- Fresh raw vegetables served with a cottage cheese dip
- Fresh fruit, prewashed and cut into bite-size pieces
- Fruit dipped in yogurt
- Bagels topped with reduced-fat cream cheese
- Breadsticks
- Air-popped popcorn seasoned with herbs
- Frozen fruit-juice bars
- Low-fat frozen yogurt
- Pita chips with salsa
- Pretzels
- Rye crisps or rice cakes spread with a little peanut butter or low-fat cheese
- Broth-based soup
- Cereal (low sugar, low fat)
- Shelled sunflower seeds
- Gelatin with added fruit
- English muffins
- Flour tortillas with canned chili and grated low-fat cheese
- Pita bread topped with spaghetti sauce and grated low-fat cheese
- Fruit juice with added club soda
- Hot cocoa (low sugar, low fat)
- Milkshake made with low-fat milk and frozen fruit

much sodium, and not enough complex carbohydrates and fiber. The average meal of a cheeseburger, milk shake, and fries supplies about 1500 calories, 43 percent of which come from fat. Chicken and fish are just as fatty as other protein sources offered by fast-food restaurants because they are breaded and fried. Frying has the same effect on potatoes. Milk shakes get most of their calories from sugars. The Food Composition

Table located in the appendix of this text along with nutrition software like HealthQuest provide detailed information that can be used to compare many fast-food menu items.

Eating at fast-food restaurants does not have to be a nutritionally worthless activity. Many restaurants are now aware that Americans are becoming more knowledgeable about the nutrient content of food and are demanding wholesome, safe, and nutritious foods. Consequently, there has been a trend toward more nutritious menus, including salad, pasta, and potato bars. Guided by good judgment in the choice of foods, an occasional meal at a fast-food chain does not have to compromise a well-balanced diet.

Prepackaged Convenience Dinners

Prepackaged convenience dinners have also become part of the American diet. Consumers spend billions of dollars a year on them, and food manufacturers are constantly turning out new lines. The challenge for health-conscious consumers is to determine which ones fit easily into a nutritious diet.

Prepackaged convenience dinners can be evaluated by applying the following criteria:

- There should be no more than and preferably fewer than 30 percent of calories from fat.
- There should be no more than 200 milligrams of sodium per 100 calories.
- They should meet at least 40 percent of the RDA for vitamins A and/or C.

Just because a dinner meets these criteria does not necessarily mean that it provides every nutrient. Some meals are likely to be deficient in some nutrients, so foods that will compensate must be added.

Planning a Nutrition Strategy for Wellness

It is not necessary to be a nutritionist to form a nutrition strategy that works for you. A nutrition plan will work only if it is personalized. Several strategies should be helpful in personalizing your nutrition plan.

Assess Your Nutrition

You should take an honest look at your eating choices and analyze your nutrition profile through Assessment Activities 6-3, 6-4, and 6-6 to determine whether you are doing the following:

- Eating a variety of foods every day from the Food Guide Pyramid
- Avoiding high-fat foods (more than the equivalent of 3 grams of fat per 100 calories)

Nurturing Your Spirituality

Enjoy Your Food—the Missing Dietary Guideline

The fast-paced, eat-on-the-run trend among Americans comes with a high price: Fewer and fewer people spend time preparing good, home-cooked meals, and even fewer use mealtime as a time for relaxing and social bonding. Other cultures recognize that mealtime is a key social time of the day and reflect this value in the dietary recommendations health experts offer their citizens:[54]

- In Japan, immediately following the guideline to avoid too much sodium comes the advice "Happy eating makes for a happy family life; sit down and eat together and talk; treasure family taste and home cooking."
- In Great Britain, the first guideline is "Enjoy your food."
- Korea tells its citizens to "Enjoy meals and keep harmony between diet and daily life."
- In Norway, people are told, "Food and joy equal health."
- In Vietnam, the advice is to "Serve a healthy family meal that is delicious and served with affection."

The greatest nutrition challenge for Americans may not be to reduce fat intake or cut back on sodium. It may be to construct a positive view of food and of mealtime. One highly respected nutrition publication reminds us, "Healthful eating is about more than eating the right mix of nutrients. It's also about sustaining well-being in a way that can't be measured on a blood test but that is just as important to overall health as vitamins and minerals.[54]

- Including sufficient fiber in the form of whole grains, dried beans, and fresh fruits and vegetables
- Consuming 8 to 12 cups of water (8 ounces each) daily
- Consuming no more than three or four high-sugar desserts or sweets each week
- Restricting your intake of high-salt foods, such as processed meats
- Consuming no more than one or two alcoholic drinks a day and not letting drinking interfere with your appetite

Make Small Adjustments

The principle of changing health behavior is that the smaller the change, the longer it lasts (see Chapter 1). For example, rather than vowing to abstain from eating ice cream, reduce the amount or number of servings at first and substitute a low-fat brand. If your diet is heavy in salt, you can gradually substitute sodium-free seasonings. If you have a sweet tooth, you can try low-sugar snacks. If you eat for fullness, you can prepare less food or leave food on your plate. You should plan an approach that builds on the cumulative effect of many small successes.

Think of balancing your diet over a long period rather than in just a day or a meal. Try to meet the dietary guidelines over several days or a week. For example, every meal does not need to contain less than 30 percent fat. Keep portions of favorite high-fat foods small, and limit other sources of fat. Check labels to get an idea of what nutrients you are consuming, but don't keep a calculator by your plate. If you eat foods from the Food Guide Pyramid, you will get all the vitamins, minerals, and protein you need.

Choose Foods for Wellness

Choosing foods for wellness means following the *Dietary Guidelines for Americans.* Your diet should

- Be low in saturated fat (maximum of 8 percent)
- Emphasize complex carbohydrates, such as bread, potatoes, and pasta
- Provide eight to twelve glasses of water throughout the day
- Provide iron and calcium
- Emphasize fresh fruits and vegetables
- Be low in sugar, salt, alcohol, and caffeine

Finally, make sure when choosing foods for wellness to enjoy what you eat (see Nurturing Your Spirituality: Enjoy Your Food—the Missing Dietary Guideline).

Summary

- The six classes of nutrients are carbohydrates, fat, protein, vitamins, minerals, and water. The nutrients that provide energy in the form of calories are carbohydrates, fat, and protein.

- The recommended diet for Americans in *Dietary Guidelines for Americans* emphasizes complex carbohydrates as the major source of energy. A diet high in complex carbohydrates is likely to be lower in fat, lower in calories, and higher in fiber.

- A complete protein is one that provides all of the amino acids in amounts proportional to the body's need for them. Protein sources from animals are complete proteins. Plant sources of complete protein, such as soy protein, come from the legume family.
- One of the greatest shortcomings of the American diet is its excessive intake of fat, especially saturated fat.
- The amount of saturated, monounsaturated, and polyunsaturated fat in foods varies considerably. Most food contains a mixture of these fats.
- The process of hydrogenation increases the saturated fat content of polyunsaturated and monounsaturated fats and yields small amounts of fat not found in nature called *transfatty acids.*
- Dietary fat intake should favor foods high in monounsaturated fats, such as olive oil, canola oil, and peanut oil.
- The consumption of antioxidant vitamins, especially in fruits and vegetables, is associated with a reduced risk of heart disease and cancer.
- Adequate folate consumption is thought to lower the concentration of homocysteine, an amino acid associated with an increased risk of heart disease.
- Two minerals of special concern today are calcium and iron. Most women fall short of the RDA for calcium. People at risk for low iron levels include young children, early teens, menstruating women, and people with health conditions that cause internal bleeding.
- People are advised to drink eight to twelve cups of fluids a day. Plain tap water is the preferred fluid.
- Phytochemicals are plant chemicals found naturally in foods. They play an important role in preventing many diseases.
- Many botanicals are thought to have health benefits. Because they are considered nutritional supplements and are not regulated with the same rigor as drugs, there is debate about their effectiveness and safety. Twenty to thirty botanicals are backed by well-conducted research.
- Insoluble fiber benefits the body by adding bulk to the stool, thus speeding the transit of food through the body, which reduces the chance of developing colon cancer, and lowering blood-cholesterol levels. Soluble fiber also benefits the body by lowering blood cholesterol levels.
- A good nutritional plan is one that consists of a variety of foods from the Food Guide Pyramid.

- A food is nutrient dense when it has a high ratio of nutrients to calories.
- Variety and moderation are principles that should most influence eating habits. There is room in the diet for any food as long as it is consumed in moderation in terms of both quantity and frequency.
- *Dietary Guidelines for Americans* officially recognizes a vegetarian diet as a healthful and acceptable way of meeting all of our nutritional needs.
- The health benefits of a vegetarian diet include a lower cholesterol level; lower levels of LDLs; reduced incidence of hypertension, lung, colorectal, and breast cancer; and fewer complications from non–insulin-dependent diabetes mellitus.
- Americans consume sugar and sodium in excessive amounts. The major health issue associated with high sugar intake is dental caries; for sodium it's hypertension.
- Moderate consumption of alcohol may be beneficial for some people who are at risk for cardiovascular disease and stroke.
- Pregnancy imposes a greater demand for some nutrients, including protein, vitamin D, folate, iron, calcium, and zinc.
- Carbohydrates are the main source of energy for both anaerobic and high-intensity aerobic activities; fat is the main energy source for prolonged, low-intensity exercise; and protein is a minor fuel source, primarily for endurance activities.
- The risk of foodborne illnesses can be reduced by preventing cross-contamination of food; by washing hands, fruits, produce, and meats; and by exercising caution in the way food is prepared and stored.
- Food labels provide helpful information about nutrients associated with the common chronic health problems of Americans as well as about essential nutrients.
- The criticisms of snacking and fast-food eating are the same as those of the rest of the American diet: too much fat, sodium, and sugar; too many calories; and not enough complex carbohydrates and fiber.
- Americans are challenged not only to eat more healthfully but also to construct a positive attitude about food and mealtimes.

Review Questions

1. What is meant by "Nutritional diseases of the past have been replaced by diseases of dietary excess and imbalance"?
2. What was the rationale for revising the Recommended Dietary Allowances for essential nutrients?
3. Identify three nutrients that most Americans do not consume in sufficient amounts.
4. How many calories are supplied by carbohydrates, fat, and protein? What percent of total calories should come from each of these sources? How does Americans' intake of energy nutrients compare with dietary recommendations?
5. Why are carbohydrates the preferred source of energy?
6. What is the difference between a high-quality, complete protein and a low-quality, incomplete protein?
7. What plant sources of protein are unique in that they are considered complete proteins?
8. What are the differences between saturated, monounsaturated, and polyunsaturated fats? What are some food sources of each? What percent of fat calories should come from each type?
9. What are transfatty acids? Why should they be avoided?
10. List five dietary practices that will help lower consumption of fat, especially saturated fat.

11. What are the similarities and differences between water-soluble and fat-soluble vitamins?

12. Which vitamins are classified as antioxidants? What is the relationship between antioxidants and health?

13. What role does folate play in preventing disease?

14. Identify three situations or circumstances that would justify use of a vitamin or mineral supplement.

15. What are phytochemicals? How are they different from botanicals? How do they contribute to health?

16. What two minerals are Americans most likely to be consuming in insufficient amounts? Which segments of the population are most likely to be affected?

17. Explain why thirst is not a good indicator of how much water to drink.

18. What are the major health benefits associated with insoluble fiber? soluble fiber?

19. What is the rationale for the assertion that variety and moderation are the most important principles for a healthy diet?

20. List three negative health effects associated with the excessive intake of nutrients considered good for health when taken in recommended amounts.

21. Distinguish between the different types of vegetarianism. Which types are most likely to require some form of vitamin or mineral supplementation? What are the health benefits of a vegetarian diet?

22. Identify four nutrients that pregnant women require in larger amounts than those in the RDAs.

23. How do the intensity and duration of physical activities affect the way the body uses carbohydrates, fat, and protein for energy? What type of physical activity is most conducive to burning fat calories?

24. List six things a person can do to help prevent unnecessary exposure to foodborne illnesses.

25. Distinguish between Recommended Dietary Allowances and Daily Values.

26. What are the main criticisms of snacking and fast-food eating?

References

1. U.S. Department of Health and Human Services. 1998. *Healthy People 2010 Objectives: Draft for Public Comment.* Washington, D.C.: U.S. Department of Health and Human Services, Office of Disease Prevention.

2. Liebman, B. 1998. Diet and cancer—the big picture. *Nutrition Action Health Letter* 25(10):1–7.

3. Tufts University. 1997. Report card for Americans' eating habits. *Tufts University Health and Nutrition Letter* 15(4):1.

4. Wardlaw, G. 1999. *Perspectives in Nutrition* (4th ed.). St. Louis, Mo.: WCB/McGraw Hill.

5. Margolis, S., and L. B. Wilder. 1998. *Nutrition and Longevity.* Baltimore, Md.: The Johns Hopkins Medical Institutes.

6. American Dietetic Association. 1998. *Choosing Legumes: A Healthful and Versatile Food.* Available on-line at www.eatright.org/nfs45.html.

7. Mayo Foundation for Medical Education and Research. 1997. Soy—a healthful diet addition. *Mayo Clinic Health Letter* 15(5):7.

8. Liebman, B. 1998. The soy story. *Nutrition Action Health Letter* 25(7):1–8.

9. Tufts University. 1997. Older adults may not be getting enough protein. *Tufts University Diet and Nutrition Letter* 14(11):2.

10. Editors. 1998. Meat-eaters need to bone up on calcium. *Environmental Nutrition* 21(4):1.

11. Editors. 1996. The truth about trans-fatty acids: Scientists can't agree on risk. *Environmental Nutrition* 19(2):1–6.

12. Tufts University. 1997. A type of fat we may need more of. *Tufts University Health and Nutrition Letter* 15(1):4–5.

13. Thomas, B. November 1998. Healthful diet for baby boils down to 'what' and 'when,' experts say. *The Commercial Appeal* 1:F3.

14. Harvard Medical School Publications Group. 1998. Dietary fat: How low should you go? *Harvard Health Letter* 23(3):6.

15. Hu, F. B., M. J. Stampfer, J. E. Manson, E. Rimm, G. A. Golditz, B. A. Rosner, C. H. Hennekens, and W. C. Willett. 1997. Dietary fat intake and the risk of coronary heart disease in women. *The New England Journal of Medicine* 337(21):1491–1499.

16. Editors. 1998. Low fat, no fat, some fat . . . high fat? Type of fat may be key. *Environmental Nutrition* 21(4):1–6.

17. Gershoff, S. N. (ed.). 1998. Vitamin C earns an "A" for health benefits. Do you get enough? *Environmental Nutrition* 21(6):1–4.

18. Forman, A. (ed.). 1997. As beta-carotene promises fade, focus turns to other carotenoids. *Environmental Nutrition* 20(6):1, 4.

19. Cooper, K. 1998. Cells under attack? Fight back! Antioxidants. *Diabetes Wellness Letter* A(1):7–8.

20. Liebman, B. 1998. Vitamins and minerals—what to take. *Nutrition Action Health Letter* 25(4):1, 3–7.

21. Mayo Foundation for Medical Education and Research. 1997. Vitamin and mineral supplements—sorting out fact from fiction amid a storm of controversy. *Mayo Clinic Health Letter* Supplement 15(6):1–8.

22. Rock, A. 1995. Vitamin hype: Why we're wasting $1 of every $3 we spend. *Money* 24(9):83–90.

23. Antinoro, L. 1997. A confusion of calcium supplements and drinks. *Environmental Nutrition* 20(1):5.

24. Schardt, D., and S. Schmidt. 1996. That zincing feeling. *Nutrition Action Health Letter* 23(3):10–11.

25. Antinoro, L. 1998. Dodging dehydration: Are you getting enough fluids? *Environmental Nutrition* 21(5):2.

26. Gottlieb, B. 1998. Tall tales from the table. *Health* 12(5):82–85.

27. Joyal, A. 1995. Those mighty phytos: Beyond the benefits of broccoli. *Environmental Nutrition* 18(11):1, 4.

28. Klausner, A. 1998. The herbal renaissance of the 90's: What's old is new again. *Environmental Nutrition* 21(4):1, 4–5.

29. Klausner, A. 1998. *EN's* herbal medicine cabinet: Top 10 herbs you can trust. *Environmental Nutrition* 21(5):1, 4–5.

30. Mayo Foundation for Medical Education and Research. 1996. Fiber—why

Name _____ Date _____ Section _____

Assessment Activity 6-3

Nutrient Intake Assessment

One way to determine if you are getting sufficient quantities of the proper nutrients is to keep a record of your diet. Ideally, this record will cover a time span of at least one week. However, in this exercise you are asked to assess your dietary selections for only one day. Therefore, choose a day that is representative of your overall nutritional practices. (Your instructor may ask you to conduct a two- or three-day assessment. In this case photocopy additional copies of the assessment forms as needed.)

Directions There are two options for completing this assessment: (1) use the HealthQuest software that accompanies the textbook or (2) analyze your diet manually by following the instructions and completing the forms in Assessment Activities 6-3 and 6-4. Whichever option you choose, record all of the foods and beverages that you consume during one day with the exception of vitamin or mineral supplements. Be specific regarding the amount eaten, how it is cooked, and so on. List condiments and seasonings, such as mustard, ketchup, and butter, and dressings and trimmings, such as lettuce, onions, marshmallows, and sugar. The more detailed your record, the more accurate it will be and the more you will learn from it. Remember, the quality of the results is dependent on the quality of the information entered. A carefully and thoroughly prepared dietary recall will yield a quite accurate nutritional profile.

Instructions for Mosby's HealthQuest Once foods have been listed, you are ready to use the HealthQuest program to generate your personal nutrition assessment report. Follow the instructions for installing the program on your personal computer. Enter your new User Profile information. When you have completed data entry, print and arrange the results in the following order:

1. User profile with Instant Analysis information: recommended carbohydrate, fat, protein, total caloric intake, and BMI

2. Nutrient summary of macronutrients, vitamins, minerals (ABC button)
3. Nutrient spreadsheet (Spreadsheet button)
4. Food pyramid breakdown of servings for one day (Pyramid button)
5. Bar graph showing dietary intake analysis of nutrients and percent RDA (Bar graph button for RDA analysis)
6. Pie chart comparing breakdown of carbohydrates, fat, protein with recommendations (Left pie chart button)
7. Pie chart showing breakdown of fat (Right chart button)
8. Major source of nutrients for those vitamins and minerals that do not meet the RDAs in #2
9. Summary paragraph describing what you learned about your dietary strengths and deficiencies and what changes are needed to improve your nutrition profile

Instructions for Conducting a Manual Nutrition Assessment Complete Parts A, B, C, and D. Then proceed to Assessment Activity 6-4.

Part A: Recording Your Nutrient Intake

1. Use the following form to record your dietary selections for one day. Photocopy extra copies of the form as needed.
2. Refer to the Food Composition Table in the appendix and record appropriate values in the spaces provided. For foods not included in the appendix, refer to package labels, if available, to determine nutritive values.
3. Add the values for each nutrient and enter the result in the total column.

Foods for One Day: List in column headings. Photocopy extra copies as needed.

Nutrients							Total
Calories							
Protein (g)							
Carbohydrate (g)							
Fat (g)							
Cholesterol (mg)							
Saturated Fat (g)							
Sodium (mg)							
Potassium (mg)							
Iron (mg)							
Vitamin A (RE)							
Vitamin C (mg)							
Thiamin (mg)							
Riboflavin (mg)							
Niacin (mg)							
Calcium (mg)							
Fiber (g)							

Part B: Are You Meeting the RDA?

1. Transfer the values in the Total column in Part A to the Total column in Part B for the following nutrients.
2. Fill in the RDA column with your protein RDA results from Assessment Activity 6-1. For the remaining nutrients, look up your corresponding RDA in table 6-4.
3. Subtract the RDA from your totals and indicate your status in the appropriate column. A positive value means that you are meeting the RDA for that nutrient; a negative value means that you are deficient in that nutrient.
4. For nutrients with a negative value, identify several specific foods that will eliminate the deficiency. Refer to the Food Composition Table in the appendix.

Nutrient	Total	RDA	Status	Food Prescription
Protein				
Iron				
Vitamin A				
Vitamin C				
Thiamin				
Riboflavin				
Niacin				
Calcium		1000 mg (ages 19–50) 1200 mg (51+)		

Part C: Are You Meeting the DVs?

1. Transfer the values in the total column from part A to the total column in Part C for the following nutrients. (Refer to Assessment Activities 6-1 and 6-2 for your personal DV for fat, saturated fat, and carbohydrate.)

2. Compare the DV listed with your totals. Indicate your status by subtracting the DV value from your value. Note that some values are maximum and should not be exceeded; others are goals that serve as minimums.

Nutrient	Total	DV*	Status
Fat		(maximum)**	
Saturated fat		(maximum)**	
Cholesterol		300 mg (maximum)	
Sodium		2400 mg (maximum	
Carbohydrate		(goal)***	
Fiber		25 g (goal)	
Potassium		3500 mg (goal)	

*DV based on 2000-calorie diet.
**See Assessment Activity 6-2
***See Assessment Activity 6-1

Part D: What Did You Learn?

Write a summary paragraph describing what you learned about your dietary strengths and deficiencies and what changes are needed to improve your nutrition profile.

_____

_____

_____

_____

_____

_____

_____

_____

_____

_____

_____

_____

Name _____ Date _____ Section _____

Assessment Activity 6-4

How Does Your Diet Compare with the Recommended Diet?

Directions: The recommended guidelines suggest that carbohydrate calories should make up at least 55 percent of the diet (including complex carbohydrates and sugar), fat calories should be less than 30 percent, and protein calories should be 15 percent. The purpose of this assessment is to compare your diet with these recommendations. First convert your caloric intake to percentages as follows.

Percent Carbohydrate Calories Your carbohydrate intake (refer to total carbohydrate intake from Part I, Assessment Activity 6-3) multiplied by 4 equals your carbohydrate calories:

_____ g × 4 = _____ carbohydrate calories

Your carbohydrate calories divided by total calories (refer to Part I, Assessment Activity 6-3) multiplied by 100 equals percent carbohydrate calories:

_____ carbohydrate calories ÷ _____ total calories
× 100 = _____%

Draw a bar on the graph to indicate percentage of carbohydrate calories.

EXAMPLE: For a person on a 2000-calorie diet who consumed 175 grams of carbohydrate:

175 × 4   = 700 carbohydrate calories
700 ÷ 2000 = 0.35
0.35 × 100 = 35%

Percent Protein Calories Your protein intake (refer to total protein intake from Part I, Assessment Activity 6-3) multiplied by 4 equals protein calories:

_____ g × 4 = _____ protein calories

Your protein calories divided by total calories (refer to Part I, Assessment Activity 6-3) multiplied by 100 equals percent protein calories:

_____ protein calories ÷ _____ total calories
× 100 = _____%

Draw a bar on the graph to indicate percentage of protein calories.

EXAMPLE: For a person on a 2000-calorie diet who consumed 100 grams of protein:

100 × 4   = 400 protein calories
400 ÷ 2000 = 0.20
0.20 × 100 = 20%

Percent Fat Calories Your fat intake (refer to total fat intake from Part I, Assessment Activity 6-3) multiplied by 9 equals your fat calories:

_____ g × 9 = _____ fat calories

Your fat calories divided by total calories (refer to Part I, Assessment Activity 6-3) multiplied by 100 equals percent fat calories:

_____ fat calories ÷ _____ total calories × 100 = _____%

Draw a bar on the graph to indicate percentage of fat calories.

EXAMPLE: For a person on a 2000-calorie diet who consumed 100 grams of fat:

```
100 × 9      = 900 fat calories
900 ÷ 2000 = 0.45
0.45 × 100  = 45%
```

Example Profile The following graph shows the percentages for the example as the yellow bar below the recommended amount, which is shown as a red bar.

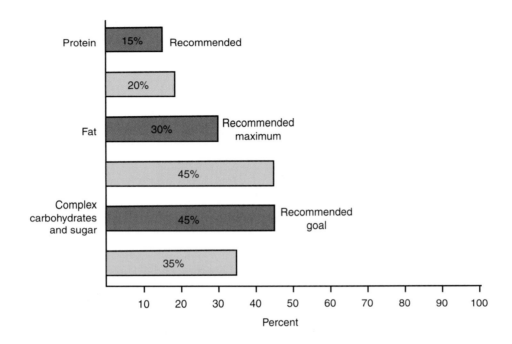

Your Profile Complete the bars with amounts calculated for your diet:

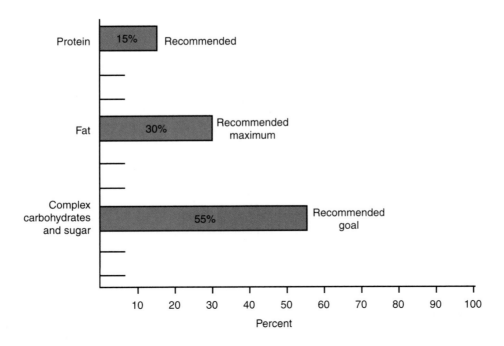

Assessment Activity 6-5

Do You Have Fatty Habits?

Fat has earned a bad reputation because of the health problems it contributes to in high-fat diets. The following questionnaire will help you think about the amounts and types of fat that you generally eat. For each general type of food or food habit, circle the category that is more typical for your diet. If you never or almost never eat any items of a particular food type, just skip it.

Food Type/Habit	High Fat	Medium Fat	Low Fat
Chicken	Fried with the skin	Baked, broiled, or barbecued with the skin	Baked, broiled, or barbecued without the skin
Fat present on meats	Usually	Sometimes	Never
Fat used in cooking	Butter, lard, bacon grease, chicken fat	Margarine, oil	Nonstick cooking spray or no fat used
Additions to rice, bread, potatoes, vegetables, etc.	Butter, lard, bacon grease, chicken fat, coconut oil	Margarine, oil, peanut butter	Butter-flavored granules or no fat used
Pizza toppings	Sausage, pepperoni, extra cheese, combination	Canadian bacon	Vegetables such as peppers, onions, and mushrooms
Sandwich spreads	Mayonnaise or mayonnaise-type dressing	Light mayonnaise, oil and vinegar	Mustard, fat-free mayonnaise
Milk and milk products (e.g., yogurt)	Whole-milk and whole-milk products	Low-fat milk products and milk products	Skim milk and milk products
Sandwich side orders	Chips, potato salad, macaroni salad with creamy dressing	Coleslaw, pasta salad with clear dressing	Vegetable sticks, pretzels, pickle
Salad dressings	Blue cheese, Ranch, Thousand Island, other creamy type	Oil and vinegar, clear-base dressing	Oil-free dressing, lemon juice, flavored vinegar
Typical meat portion	6–8 oz. or more	4–5 oz.	2–3 oz.
Sandwich fillings	Beef or pork hot dogs, salami, bologna, pepperoni, cheese, tuna or chicken salad	Turkey hot dogs, 85% fat-free lunch meats, corned beef, peanut butter, hummus (chickpea paste)	95% fat-free lunch meats, roast turkey, roast beef, lean ham
Ground meats	Regular ground beef, sausage meat, ground meat, ground pork (about 30% fat)	Lean ground beef, ground chuck, turkey sausage meat (20–25% fat)	Ground turkey, extra-lean ground beef, ground round (about 15% fat)
Deep-fried foods (e.g., french fries, onion rings, fish or chicken patties, egg rolls, tempura)	Eat every day	Eat once a week	Eat once a month or never
Bread for sandwiches	Croissant	Biscuit	Whole wheat, French, tortilla, pita or pocket bread, bagel, sourdough, or English muffin
Cheeses	Hard cheeses (such as cheddar, Swiss, provolone, Jack, American, processed)	Part-skim mozzarella, part-skim ricotta, low-fat cheeses	Nonfat cheese, nonfat cottage cheese, no cheese
Frozen desserts	Premium or regular ice cream	Ice milk or low-fat frozen yogurt	Sherbet, Italian water ice, nonfat frozen yogurt, frozen fruit whip

Food Type/Habit	High Fat	Medium Fat	Low Fat
Coffee lighteners	Cream, liquid or powdered creamer	Whole milk	Low-fat or skim milk
Snacks	Chips, pies, cheese and crackers, nuts, donuts, chocolate, granola bars	Muffins, toaster pastries, unbuttered commercial popcorn	Pretzels, vegetable sticks, fresh or dried fruit, air-popped popcorn, bread sticks, jelly beans, hard candy
Cookies	Chocolate coated, chocolate chip, peanut butter, filled sandwich type	Oatmeal	Ginger snaps, vanilla wafers, graham crackers, animal crackers, fruit bars
Scoring	(_____ × 2) +	(_____ × 1) +	(_____ × 0) =

Total score: _____

Once you have completed the questionnaire, count the number of circles in each column and calculate your score as follows: Multiply the number of choices in the left-hand (high-fat) column by 2 and multiply the number of choices in the middle (medium-fat) column by 1; then add these two values together. Based on your total score, rate yourself as follows:

Less than 10   =Excellent fat habits
10 to 20   =Good fat habits
20 to 30   = Fat habits needing improvement
Over 30   = Very high-fat diet

If your score is 20 or higher, try to substitute more foods from the middle (medium-fat) column or, better still, the right (low-fat) column for foods in the left-hand (high-fat) column.

Name _____ **Date** _____ **Section** _____

Assessment Activity 6-6

Eating Behaviors to Consider

Directions: Answer the following questions to reveal information about your eating habits, how you developed certain tastes, and your attitude about various foods:

1. When was the last time you tried a new food? What was the food? What were the circumstances? _____
   _____

2. What new foods have you learned to eat during the past year? _____
   _____

3. Name the foods that have been on your "will not try" list (that is, foods that you will not eat under any circumstances). _____

4. What special events do you celebrate in some way with food?_____

5. Where is your favorite place to eat? _____

6. If you were to go on an eating binge, what foods would you be most likely to eat? _____
   _____

7. Describe in detail your favorite meal._____
   _____

8. Do you consider yourself a slow eater, moderately fast eater, or gulper? What do you think is responsible for
   your eating pattern? _____
   _____

9. To what extent, if any, are your eating habits related to stress? Emotions?_____
   _____

10. What do you consider to be your good eating habits? Poor eating habits? _____
    _____

Improving Body Composition

Key Terms

amenorrheic
body composition
body mass index (BMI)

obesity
overfat
overweight

Objectives

After completing this chapter, you will be able to do the following:

- Define *body composition*.
- Define *essential fat* and *storage fat*.
- Define and differentiate between *obesity* and *overweight*.
- Discuss the health implications of regionally distributed fat.
- Discuss the limitations of height/weight tables for weight management.
- Calculate body mass index and interpret the results.
- Describe hydrostatic weighing, bioelectrical impedance, and skinfold measurements as methods for determining body composition.

Goals for Behavior Change

- Use table 7-3 to calculate your body mass index and interpret your results.
- Make a commitment to either maintain your existing weight or select a healthier weight for yourself.
- Formulate a long-range plan to achieve or maintain an ideal body weight and improve your body composition.

he body is composed of fat mass and fat-free mass. **Body composition** is the ratio between the two. Fat-free weight includes all tissues—muscle, bone, blood, organs, fluids—exclusive of fat. Fat is found in the organs (such as the brain, heart, liver, and lungs) and adipose cells. Adipose cells are fat cells that are located subcutaneously (beneath the skin) and surrounding various body organs. They are an insulator against heat loss and a protection for the internal organs against trauma. The majority of body fat is found in adipose cells, where it acts as a vast storage depot for energy.

A certain amount of fat is required for normal biological functions. This is referred to as *essential fat.* Essential fat is located in the bone marrow, organs, muscles, and intestines; it is a component of cell-membrane structure as well as of brain and heart tissue. The amount of essential fat in the male and female bodies differs. Essential fat constitutes 3 to 5 percent of the total weight of men and 8 to 12 percent of the total weight of women.[1]

The higher female requirement for essential fat is directly related to fertility and childbearing. Women whose body fat drops below essential requirements such as gymnasts, ballerinas, long-distance runners and anorexics, often become **amenorrheic**; that is, they stop having a menstrual cycle. The period of infertility continues until they gain weight and their essential fat is restored. In both genders, essential fat represents a minimal threshold or lower limit for the maintenance of health.

Obesity

Obesity, or overfatness, is gender specific. For men, **obesity** is defined as body fat equal to or greater than 25 percent of total body weight, and for women, it is equal to or greater than 32 percent of total body weight.[2] These values are arbitrary because the point at which fat storage actually increases health risks has not been determined. Contributing further to the confusion is the fact that methods of assessing the amount of body fat are indirect, and each contains a degree of measurement error.

Acceptable body fat percentages have been derived from young adult subjects, and these standards have been applied to all age groups—age-specific standards have yet to be determined, and it is very possible that such standards will vary somewhat with age. The results of studies of young adults demonstrate that fat typically ranges from 20 to 30 percent for young females and 10 to 20 percent for young males.[1] These data have led many authorities to suggest that body fat values of 25 percent for females and 15 percent for males are quite acceptable.

However, more recent body fat health standards that are based on age and gender allow for an increase in percent body fat with age. This allowance amounts to a trade-off in risks for chronic diseases, especially for women. Low body fat among middle-aged women is associated with losses of bone mineral content, which can lead to osteoporosis and bone fractures. However, leanness or low body fat helps protect these women against heart disease. It is best for women to be lean enough to prevent heart disease yet not so lean as to risk the development of osteoporosis. This is particularly problematic for small-framed women, whose bone mineral content is already low. See tables 7-1 and 7-2 for recommended body fat percentages for women and men of different ages. See also Nurturing Your Spirituality: Setting Realistic Fitness and Weight-Loss Goals.

Overweight

Overweight refers to excessive weight for height without consideration of body composition. Because the term *overweight* makes no allowances for body

Table 7-1	Recommended Body Fat Percentages for Women			
Age	Essential Fat %	Minimal Fat %	Recommended Fat %	Obese Fat %
Over 56	8–12	10–12	25–38	> 38
35–55	8–12	10–12	23–38	> 38
34 or younger	8–12	10–12	20–35	> 35

Adapted from Lohman, T. G., L. B. Houtkooper, and S. B. Going. 1997. Body composition assessment: Body fat standards and methods in the field of exercise and sports medicine. *ACSM Health Fitness Journal* 1:30.

Nurturing Your Spirituality

Setting Realistic Fitness and Weight-Loss Goals

Success in any endeavor requires the establishment of long-term goals. Goals that are challenging and worthwhile but not impossible to accomplish are the keys to success. For instance, it would be unrealistic to expect to run a marathon after a few months of sporadic training or to lose 30 pounds in one month and keep it off.

A more feasible approach is to set realistic short-term goals that can be accomplished relatively easily and quickly. The accomplishment of these will provide the feedback you need to stay on track and the reinforcement to continue the program.

Attainable, realistic goals for exercise should be consistent with the American College of Sports Medicine guidelines for exercise, and realistic weight loss should not exceed 1.5 to 2 pounds per week. People often throw themselves into exercise with a vengeance, as if to wipe out years of inactivity with a frenzied few weeks of activity. The same degree of impatience surfaces with weight-loss attempts.

The following guidelines increase the likelihood of succeeding with exercise and weight loss:

1. Genetics is responsible for 25 to 40 percent of all of the factors that determine how aerobically fit we may become.[3] We can all achieve our aerobic potential with regular exercise, but world-class endurance performances are beyond the reach of most of us. Exercise and enjoy it, be as good as you can, and be satisfied with a significant accomplishment. You should be encouraged to know that you are in the select 15 percent of the adult population who exercise regularly and vigorously.

2. Genetics is responsible for 30 to 50 percent of all of the factors that lead to overweight and obesity. Although this represents a substantial influence, authorities are convinced that overweight individuals inherit only the *tendency* to become overweight or obese.[4] Our physical activity patterns and eating habits determine whether genetic history becomes destiny.

3. For weight loss or physical fitness, participate in moderate physical activity (preferably low impact if you are a beginner) that builds exercise into your daily life, such as mowing the lawn, washing the car by hand, and climbing stairs instead of taking elevators, plus participate in a structured exercise program (walking, walking/jogging, cycling, swimming, aerobics, etc.). Thirty minutes or more of exercise per day, preferably five days per week, plus eating nutritious meals based on the Food Guide Pyramid will improve physical fitness and produce sensible weight loss that can be maintained for life.

4. Avoid the inflexible pursuit of artificial aesthetic ideals and aim for reasonable goals. Don't pressure yourself to achieve your goals too rapidly. Remember, healthy eating and sensible regular exercise are for a lifetime, not just a few weeks or months. Let the bodily changes that result from this lifestyle occur slowly, and you will be able to enjoy them for a lifetime.

Taking care of your body does not result in instant health. To make real changes in your lifestyle, you must change the way you think. You must do more than nurture your body; you must nurture your mind as well.

Table 7-2 Recommended Body Fat Percentages for Men

Age	Essential Fat %	Minimal Fat %	Recommended Fat %	Obese Fat %
More than 56	3–5	5	10–25	> 28
35–55	3–5	5	10–25	> 28
34 or younger	3–5	5	8–22	> 25

Adapted from Lohman, T. G., L. B. Houtkooper, and S. B. Going. 1997. Body composition assessment: Body fat standards and methods in the field of exercise and sports medicine. *ACSM Health Fitness Journal* 1:30.

Real-World Wellness

Practical Ways to Estimate Overweight and Obesity

What are some practical techniques I can use to determine whether I'm overweight or obese that don't require much time, a technician, or sophisticated measuring equipment?

Practical sources for measuring overweight and overfatness rely on subjective observations and other sensory information. These estimates do not quantify, in a real sense, the extent of the problem should one exist.

Our mirrors supply us with visual feedback. Stand naked in front of a full-length mirror and, as objectively as possible, observe the shape of your body, determine where fat has accumulated, and estimate the amount of muscle you have. Use a tape measure to measure the circumference of your waist and hips. Your hips should be larger than your waist. While you have the tape measure in your hands, measure the circumference of your ankle according to the directions in table 7-3. This will estimate your skeletal size or frame size. People with large frame sizes can carry more weight than can people of the same height with small frame sizes. Knowing your frame size may help you to more accurately interpret the results from the bathroom scale in conjunction with height/weight charts.

A few years ago the slogan "pinch an inch" became popular. If you can pinch an inch at various sites on the body, you are probably somewhat overweight.

The fit of your clothes will provide other clues. If your pants or dress size is increasing steadily, you are obviously gaining weight. Conversely, if the sizes are getting smaller, you are successfully losing weight, changing your body composition, or both. If you are not consciously trying to lose weight and don't need to lose but are doing so anyway, this could be a sign of emerging disease and should be evaluated by a physician.

There is always the feedback you receive from other people. They may tell you that you appear to have either gained or lost some weight. Their perceptions may or may not be correct, but your size has led them to their conclusions.

After all is said and done, remember this: About 40 percent of all men are dissatisfied with their appearance and two-thirds of young women between 13 and 19 years think they weigh too much. The fact is that millions of normal-weight Americans, particularly young women, are also attempting to lose weight.

We are preoccupied with thinness in the United States. Beauty is in the eye of the beholder, but the vision has been distorted by Madison Avenue's preoccupation with excessive leanness. We need to be realistic and understand that excessive leanness is not within the grasp of most people, nor should it be. Thinness does not always go hand in hand with robust health.

Table 7-3 Measurement of Ankles to Determine Body Frame Size

Measure the ankle at the smallest point above the two bones that protrude on each side of the ankle. The tape measure should be pulled very tightly. Read the tape measure in inches and see the table for an interpretation.

Gender	Small Frame	Medium Frame	Large Frame
Males	< 8 inches	8–9¼ inches	> 9¼ inches
Females	< 7½ inches	7½–8¾ inches	> 8¾ inches

composition, it is a poor criterion for determining the desirability of weight loss. For example, a well-muscled person may be overweight but lean in regard to body fat. By American social standards, such body mass is healthy, aesthetically pleasing, and desirable. It is also possible for a person to be well within the norms for total body weight but **overfat**; that is, such a person carries a large proportion of body weight in the form of fat rather than lean tissue. Overfat is unhealthy and unattractive according to American social standards.

See Real-World Wellness: Practical Ways to Estimate Overweight and Obesity.

Regional Fat Distribution

Deposition of fat varies among people. The amount of fat and the storage sites are influenced by heredity and gender (figure 7-1). After puberty, women generally deposit fat in the buttocks, hips, breasts, and thighs. These preferential sites are largely dictated by the female hormone estrogen.[4] This tendency is known as the *gynoid,* or feminine, pattern of fat deposition. Gynoid fat is not confined exclusively to women; a few men deposit fat in this configuration as well.

Because they produce very little estrogen, men usually deposit minimal amounts of fat in the female pattern. Instead, they primarily store fat in the abdomen,

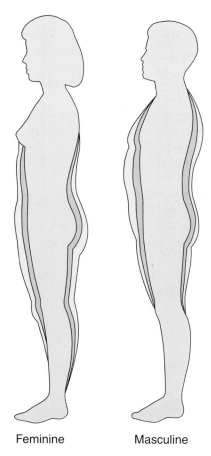

Feminine   Masculine

Figure 7-1 Feminine Versus Masculine Deposition of Fat

may be interpreted by comparing the WHR to the following standard:[6]

- Males: A WHR greater than 0.95 indicates an excessive amount of upper body fat. Acceptable levels are less than 0.95.

- Females: A WHR greater than 0.80 indicates an excessive amount of upper body fat. Acceptable levels are less than 0.80.

The WHR has been criticized for failing to recognize factors other than abdominal fat, such as skeletal size and muscle mass in the buttocks. An expert panel convened by the National Heart, Lung, and Blood Institute in 1998 concluded that a circumference measure of only the waist is more highly predictive of disease risk than is the WHR.[7] For males, a high waist circumference is greater than 40 inches, and for females it is greater than 35 inches. The power of waist circumference to predict heart disease is unaffected by height, and its predictive power is increased if combined with a body mass index greater than $25 kg/m^2$. Body mass index (BMI) is described in detail later in this chapter.

The masculine, or android, pattern of fat deposition is related to an increase in the risk for heart disease, stroke, type II diabetes, and some forms of cancer.[4] There are several reasons for this increased risk.

First, enzymes in abdominal adipose cells are very active, so fat moves in and out easily. In sedentary people, abdominal fat enters the bloodstream and is routed directly to the liver, where it becomes the raw material for the manufacture of very low-density lipoprotein (VLDL) triglycerides. Later these are converted to low-density lipoprotein cholesterol (LDL-C), and this increases the risk for cardiovascular disease. Conversely, active people direct abdominal fat to the muscles, where it is used as fuel for physical work.

Second, abdominal fat cells are larger than other fat cells. Large fat cells are associated with blood glucose (sugar) intolerance and excessive amounts of insulin in the blood. Such an environment is conducive to the development of type II diabetes because the cells' receptor sites become resistant to insulin. Higher than normal amounts of insulin must be secreted to transport sugar from the blood to the cells, but excessive insulin remains in the blood. The body's cells continue to resist insulin so blood sugar also remains high. This sequence of events is characteristic of glucose intolerance or poor regulation of sugar. Over the years these factors can lead to type II diabetes. A person does not have to be excessively overweight to be at risk for type II diabetes; it is enough that fat be concentrated in the abdominal region. This pattern of fat deposition increases the risk of developing type II diabetes 10 to 15 times.[8] Extra fat that accumulates in the hips (gynoid pattern) also increases the risk, but only 3 to 4 times.

lower back, chest, and nape of the neck. Some women store fat this way as well. After menopause, estrogen production decreases and the prevalence of android fat deposition increases.

Although the general claim is that android or upper body fat (sometimes called *central fat*) is harmful, newer evidence indicates that not all android fat is equal.[5] Intra-abdominal fat, which is stored deep within the abdominal cavity, carries a much higher risk than does subcutaneous abdominal fat, which is stored directly beneath the skin. Physical activity tends to reduce intra-abdominal fat as well as subcutaneous fat. Moderately intense physical activities, such as gardening and casual walking, may not improve one's cardiorespiratory endurance, but when coupled with modest caloric restriction, they can decrease abdominal fat.

The waist-to-hip ratio (WHR) is a simple method for determining the distribution of body fat. It requires an accurate measurement of the circumference of the waist at the narrowest point between the rib cage and the navel and of the hips at the largest circumference of the hip/buttocks region. The waist measurement is then divided by the hip measurement. The resulting value

$W_{ell}n_{ess}$ On the Web
$B_{eha}v_{ior}$ Change $A^{c}t_{iv}i_{tie}s$

What's Your BMI?

Body mass index (BMI) is definitely not everyone's favorite number. Why? Because it provides an acceptable estimate of the proportion of our body weight that's composed of fat. Although knowing your BMI is more fun if you're fit, don't be discouraged if you're not there yet—use this useful measure to help you achieve your desired level of fitness. Simply put, BMI is the ratio of body weight in kilograms to height in meters squared. There are several body mass index protocols, all of which represent attempts to adjust body weight to derive a height-free measure of body fat. Although BMI doesn't provide an estimate of percent body fat, it's far more useful than height/weight tables. Calculate your BMI easily and quickly by going to the "In Fitness and Health" website at www.phys.com/a_home/01home/home.htm and clicking on "Calculators." Select BMI, type in the information requested, then click on "calculate" to view your BMI.

Is There Really an "Ideal Weight"?

Your "ideal weight," if there is such a thing, depends on a host of factors: your gender, age, height, and frame size, to name the most prominent. Instead of agonizing over outdated height and weight tables published years ago by insurance companies, turn to the experts on the internet. You can calculate your ideal weight painlessly by going to the "In Fitness and Health" website mentioned above and clicking on "Calculators." Select "Ideal Weight," type in the information requested, then click on "calculate" and view your ideal weight.

Where's the "Beef"?

Do you have an android or a gynoid pattern of fat distribution? You can find out easily by determining your waist-to-hip ratio. Measure the circumference of your waist about ½ inch above the navel, and measure the circumference of your hips at the greatest protrusion of the buttocks. To find out what "shape" you're in, go to the "In Fitness and Health" website at www.phys.com/a_home/01home/home.htm and click on "Calculators." Select Health Risk and type in your age, gender, hip and waist measurements. Then click on "Calculate" and your fat distribution pattern will be calculated for you.

Third, excessive insulin in the blood interferes with the removal of sodium by the kidneys, possibly leading to hypertension. Concurrently, the high circulating level of insulin stimulates the overproduction of epinephrine and norepinephrine, both of which raise the blood pressure. This cluster of disorders—high blood pressure, high blood sugar (glucose intolerance), high blood lipids (cholesterol and triglycerides), and abdominal obesity—has deadly consequences. Researchers refer to this combination as *syndrome X* or *metabolic syndrome.*[9]

The good news about android fat is that it is more easily removed from the body than is fat stored in the gynoid pattern. People who store fat in the masculine pattern can usually lose it through exercise. Dietary restriction, although helpful, is often unnecessary. Fat stored in the feminine pattern, however, is highly resistant to removal from its storage depots. Losing gynoid fat usually requires calorie restriction and exercise. Even the best effort may not result in the removal of enough fat from the lower half of the body to satisfy the dieter. Lower-extremity fat is stubborn and much more difficult to lose than is upper-body fat.

Methods for Measuring Body-Weight Status

Height/Weight Tables

Optimal body weight is not necessarily reflective of optimal body composition. This fact was illustrated by a comparison of young and middle-aged men who were within 5 percent of their ideal weight as determined by height, weight, and frame-size charts. Although both groups were within the ideal range, the middle-aged subjects had twice the amount of fat as the young subjects.

Height/weight tables do not actually measure body composition. They simply act as a standard for total body weight based on height, body-frame size, and gender without regard to the composition of weight. These tables are therefore poor criteria for the establishment of weight-loss recommendations.

Body Mass Index

Another method for measuring body-weight status is to calculate **body mass index (BMI)**. Body mass index is the ratio of body weight in kilograms (kg) to height in meters (m) squared (BMI = wt [kg]/ht [m²]). There are several body mass index protocols, all of which originate from height/weight measurements. These protocols represent an attempt to adjust body weight to derive a height-free measure of obesity. Although BMI does not provide an estimate of percent body fat and although BMI uses height/weight data, it is more useful than the height/weight tables,[3] and it can be used to compare population groups. It also correlates fairly well (r = 0.70) with percent fat derived from underwater weighing.[4]

In June 1998, the American Heart Association added *obesity* to its list of major controllable risk factors for heart disease.[10] Obesity is now viewed as a chronic disease that represents a "dangerous epidemic" in this country. Later that same month, The National Heart, Lung, and Blood Institute (NHLBI) issued its initial clinical recommendations on obesity. A panel of twenty-four experts commissioned by the NHLBI conducted an extensive review of the research literature on obesity and concluded that people with BMIs of 25.0 to 29.9 kg/m² should be classified as overweight.[11] The panel recommended that people whose BMIs fall in this category should attempt to lose weight if they have two or more weight-related risk factors for illness. These include high blood pressure, diabetes, impaired glucose tolerance, and a waist circumference of greater than 40 inches for men and greater than 35 inches for women.

People whose BMIs are 30 kg/m² and higher are considered to be obese, and the panel advises these people to make serious attempts to lose weight.[11] According to the new BMI guidelines, approximately 55 percent of American adults (97 million people) are too fat.

There are two major limitations to using BMI measurements: (1) the technique is misleading for people with greater than average muscle mass because it measures overweight rather than overfat, and (2) the results are difficult for the general public to interpret, and the average person does not know how to apply BMI values to weight loss. The first limitation is easily surmounted. People with large amounts of muscle tissue should be directed to use a technique such as skinfold measurements or underwater weighing to measure their body composition.

The second limitation is more challenging. Follow these guidelines to establish and interpret BMI measurement. First, calculate BMI, taking care to accurately measure weight and height.

Weigh yourself in the morning after voiding and prior to breakfast. Wear light clothing and no shoes. For the height measurement, take off your shoes and stand with your back against a flat wall with your heels, buttocks, shoulders, and head against it. Have another person establish your height by using an object that has a right angle, such as a carpenter's square, a textbook, a clipboard on edge, or any other rigid item that is rectangular and has a 90-degree angle. The person doing the measuring should place the right angle against the wall and slide it down to the top of your head, mark the wall at the bottom of the right angle,

and use a tape measure to measure from the mark to the floor.

The simplest way to calculate BMI is to bypass the formula and to use table 7-4. Find your height in the left column and move across to your weight in the same row. The number at the top of this column is your BMI. For example, a man who is 71 inches tall and weighs 200 pounds has a BMI of 28 kg/m². This man is in the "overweight" category. How much weight would he need to lose if he wanted to achieve a BMI of 24 kg/m²? He can easily calculate this from the table. Find the column with the desired BMI of 24 kg/m² and drop down in the table to the row with his height (71 inches). He should weigh 172 pounds to achieve a BMI of 24 kg/m². Then subtract his desired weight (172 pounds) from his current weight (200 pounds). He needs to lose 28 pounds to reach his goal. Turn to Assessment Activity 7-1 to calculate your BMI and your desired body weight.

Measurement of Body Fat

The only direct means to measure the fat content of the human body is to perform chemical analysis on cadavers. The information obtained from cadaver studies has been used to develop indirect methods for estimating fat content. Because these estimates are indirect, they contain some degree of measurement error and should be interpreted accordingly. These indirect methods are commonly used in exercise physiology laboratories and fitness and wellness centers. See Wellness Across the Generations: Body Composition of Children and Adolescents.

Selected Methods for Measuring Body Composition

Underwater Weighing

Underwater weighing, one of the most accurate of the measurement techniques, involves weighing subjects both on land and while they are completely submerged in water (figure 7-2).

Whole-body density is calculated from body volume according to Archimedes' principle of displacement. Several thousand years ago, Archimedes discovered that a body immersed in water loses an amount of weight equal to the weight of the displaced water. The loss of weight in water is directly proportional to the volume of the water that is displaced or the volume of the body that displaces that water. The density of bone and muscle is higher than that of water and tends to sink. The density of fat is lighter than water and tends to float. Therefore, people with more muscle mass weigh more in water than do those who have less.

Table 7-4 Calculating Body Mass Index (BMI)

Each entry gives the body weight in pounds for a person of a given height and BMI. Pounds have been rounded off. To use the table, find the appropriate height in the far-left column. Move across the row to a given weight. The number at the top of the column is the BMI for that height and weight.

Height (Inches)	BMI (kg/m²)													
	19	20	21	22	23	24	25	26	27	28	29	30	35	40
	Body Weight (Pounds)													
58	91	96	100	105	110	115	119	124	129	134	138	143	167	191
59	94	99	104	109	114	119	124	128	133	138	143	148	173	198
60	97	102	107	112	118	123	128	133	138	143	148	153	179	204
61	100	106	111	116	122	127	132	137	143	148	153	158	185	211
62	104	109	115	120	126	131	136	142	147	153	158	164	191	218
63	107	113	118	124	130	135	141	146	152	158	163	169	197	225
64	110	116	122	128	134	140	145	151	157	163	169	174	204	232
65	114	120	126	132	138	144	150	156	162	168	174	180	210	240
66	118	124	130	136	142	148	155	161	167	173	179	186	216	247
67	121	127	134	140	146	153	159	166	172	178	185	191	223	255
68	125	131	138	144	151	158	164	171	177	184	190	197	230	262
69	128	135	142	149	155	162	169	176	182	189	196	203	236	270
70	132	139	146	153	160	167	174	181	188	195	202	207	243	278
71	136	143	150	157	165	172	179	186	193	200	208	215	230	286
72	140	147	154	162	169	177	184	191	199	206	213	221	258	294
73	144	151	159	166	174	182	189	197	204	212	219	227	265	302
74	148	155	163	171	179	186	194	202	210	218	225	233	272	311
75	152	160	168	176	184	192	200	208	216	224	232	240	279	319
76	156	164	172	180	189	197	205	213	221	230	238	246	287	328

Wellness Across the Generations
Body Composition of Children and Adolescents

The body composition of children changes during the growth process. It has been well established that obese children and adolescents have a higher probability of becoming obese adults than do normal-weight children and that dramatic changes in body fat and body composition can occur during the peripubertal years (the time before, during, and after puberty). The proportion of body fat in young children ranges from 10 to 15 percent, with boys toward the lower end and girls toward the upper.[12]

Body fat generally increases in adolescent boys and girls and continues to do so into young adulthood so that the percentage of fat in males increases to 15 to 20 percent, whereas that of females increases to 20 to 25 percent. As we age, the percentage of fat continues to increase while muscle mass decreases. By middle age, fat accumulation exceeds 25 percent of the total weight of many men and 30 percent of the total weight of many women. The reason is a growing disparity between energy intake (food consumption) and energy expenditure (level of physical activity). We become less active with age. Television, computers, automobiles, elevators, escalators, remote controls, golf carts, riding mowers, and a lack of quality physical education programs in the public schools have diminished the energy expended by American children and adults.

Skinfold measurements made on children and adolescents in the 1960s and 1970s have been compared with those made on similar subjects in the 1980s. A trend surfaced in this comparison, indicating that a systematic increase in body fat percentage had occurred during the interim.[13] For example, the incidence of obesity in the 6 to 11 age group increased from 17.6 to 27.1 percent. *The Surgeon General's Report on Physical Activity and Health* indicated that 15 to 25 percent of U.S. children are overweight.[14]

A study completed in 1992 examined the relationship between body fatness and health status among children and adolescents.[15] The risks for high blood pressure, high total and LDL cholesterol (the harmful form), and low HDL cholesterol (the protective form) were associated with body fat above 25 percent for men and 30 percent for women. These levels have subsequently been proposed as useful health standards for those who are between 6 and 18 years of age.

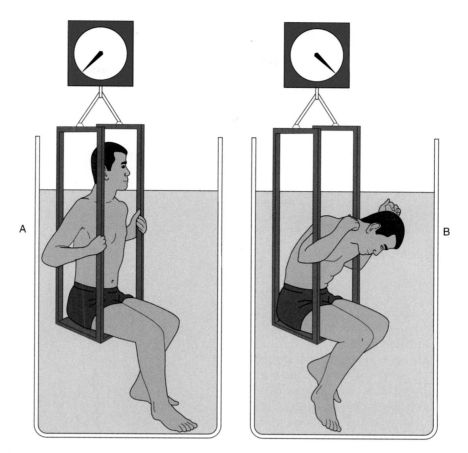

Figure 7-2 Underwater Weighing Apparatus

A, subject is in the ready position for underwater weighing. *B,* subject is being weighed.

Formulas have been developed that use weight on land and weight in water to determine the percent of the total weight that consists of fat.

Underwater weighing has an inherent error of measurement that can be minimized when the residual volume of air (the air left in the lungs after a maximal expiration) is accurately measured. If residual air is measured, the error is approximately 2.7 percent.[16] Accuracy also depends on the subject's ability to exhale maximally on each trial and to sit still while completely submerged for six to ten seconds.

The equipment required for underwater weighing includes an autopsy scale with a capacity of approximately 9 kg (about 20 lbs.). The scale is suspended over a tank of water that is at least 4 feet deep. The subject sits suspended chin-deep, exhales completely, and bends forward from the waist until entirely submerged. This position is maintained for 6 to 10 seconds to allow the scale to stabilize. Five to ten trials are required, and the underwater weight is attained by averaging the three heaviest readings. The subject's net underwater weight is calculated by subtracting the weight of the seat, its supporting structure, and a weight belt (if needed) from the gross underwater weight. Percent

body fat can be calculated from body density by using appropriate formulas.

Bioelectrical Impedance Analysis

Bioelectrical impedance analysis (BIA) is a relatively new and simple method of determining body composition. The equipment is portable and computerized but fairly expensive. It is safe, noninvasive, quick, and convenient to use (figure 7-3). Additionally, it does not require a high degree of technical skill, it intrudes less on the subject's privacy than other methods, and it is generally more comfortable.

The most common application of BIA employs a harmless, low-level, single-frequency electric current. This current is passed through the body of the person being measured via electrodes attached to specific sites on the right hand and foot, as shown in figure 7-3. Impedance represents resistance to the transmission of an electrical current. Impedance is least in lean body tissues because of their high water content (approximately 73 percent water). Water is an excellent conductor of electricity. Conversely, fat contains only 14 to 22 percent water and is resistant to electrical flow.[1]

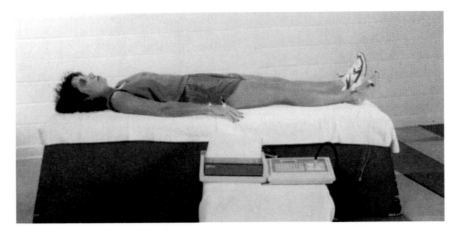

Figure 7-3 Bioelectrical Impedance Analysis

A major limitation of BIA is that it does not accurately estimate fat-free mass in very lean or very fat subjects. Body fatness is generally overestimated for lean subjects and underestimated in obese subjects.

Recent advances in BIA instrumentation have improved the technique.[1] The newer instruments use multiple electrical frequencies (MFBIA), which seem to be less susceptible to the hydration status of subjects. As a result, a better estimate of lean body mass can be achieved.

Bioelectrical impedance analysis is as accurate as skinfold measurements provided potential error sources are controlled.[1,16] The main sources of error are the hydration state of the subject and the prediction equation that is used. Hydration is affected by eating, drinking fluids, urination, and exercise, and it significantly influences the results. Technician error is relatively minor provided standard procedures for electrode placement and body position of the subject are followed. To reduce error, the temperature of the testing room should be comfortable, and the following guidelines should be given to subjects the day before they are scheduled for testing:

- No eating or drinking within four hours of the test
- No exercise within twelve hours of the test
- No urination within thirty minutes of the test
- No alcohol consumption within forty-eight hours of the test
- No diuretic medicines within seven days of the test

Skinfold Measurements

Skinfold measurements are one of the least expensive and most economical methods of measuring body composition. The cost of skinfold calipers can be as low as $10. Computerized models, however, can run as high as $600. The most accurate calipers maintain a constant jaw pressure of 10 g/mm² of jaw surface area.

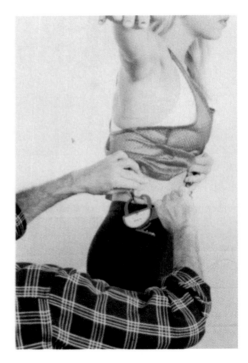

Figure 7-4 Suprailium Skinfold Measurement
Take a diagonal fold above the crest of the ilium directly below the midaxilla (armpit).

The thumb and index finger are used to pinch and lift the skin and the fat beneath it. The caliper is placed beneath the pinch (figure 7-4 through 7-8). Tables 7-5 and 7-6 show how to convert the sum of millimeters of skinfold thickness to percentage of body fat. When performed by skilled technicians, skinfold measurements correlate quite well (0.80 or greater) with body density calculated from underwater weighing.[2]

Table 7-5 Percentage of Fat Estimated for Men (Sum of Chest, Abdomen, and Thigh Skinfolds)

Sum of Skinfolds (mm)	Age to Last Year								
	Under 23	23–27	28–32	33–37	38–42	43–47	48–52	53–57	Over 57
8–10	1.3	1.8	2.3	2.9	3.4	3.9	4.5	5.0	5.5
11–13	2.2	2.8	3.3	3.9	4.4	4.9	5.5	6.0	6.5
14–16	3.2	3.8	4.3	4.8	5.4	5.9	6.4	7.0	7.5
17–19	4.2	4.7	5.3	5.8	6.3	6.9	7.4	8.0	8.5
20–22	5.1	5.7	6.2	6.8	7.3	7.9	8.4	8.9	9.5
23–25	6.1	6.6	7.2	7.7	8.3	8.8	9.4	9.9	10.5
26–28	7.0	7.6	8.1	8.7	9.2	9.8	10.3	10.9	11.4
29–31	8.0	8.5	9.1	9.6	10.2	10.7	11.3	11.8	12.4
32–34	8.9	9.4	10.0	10.5	11.1	11.6	12.2	12.8	13.3
35–37	9.8	10.4	10.9	11.5	12.0	12.6	13.1	13.7	14.3
38–40	10.7	11.3	11.8	12.4	12.9	13.5	14.1	14.6	15.2
41–43	11.6	12.2	12.7	13.3	13.8	14.4	15.0	15.5	16.1
44–46	12.5	13.1	13.6	14.2	14.7	15.3	15.9	16.4	17.0
47–49	13.4	13.9	14.5	15.1	15.6	16.2	16.8	17.3	17.9
50–52	14.3	14.8	15.4	15.9	16.5	17.1	17.6	18.2	18.8
53–55	15.1	15.7	16.2	16.8	17.4	17.9	18.5	19.1	19.7
56–58	16.0	16.5	17.1	17.7	18.2	18.8	19.4	20.0	20.5
59–61	16.9	17.4	17.9	18.5	19.1	19.7	20.2	20.8	21.4
62–64	17.6	18.2	18.8	19.4	19.9	20.5	21.1	21.7	22.2
65–67	18.5	19.0	19.6	20.2	20.8	21.3	21.9	22.5	23.1
68–70	19.3	19.9	20.4	21.0	21.6	22.2	22.7	23.3	23.9
71–73	20.1	20.7	21.2	21.8	22.4	23.0	23.6	24.1	24.7
74–76	20.9	21.5	22.0	22.6	23.2	23.8	24.4	25.0	25.5
77–79	21.7	22.2	22.8	23.4	24.0	24.6	25.2	25.8	26.3
80–82	22.4	23.0	23.6	24.2	24.8	25.4	25.9	26.5	27.1
83–85	23.2	23.8	24.4	25.0	25.5	26.1	26.7	27.3	27.9
86–88	24.0	24.5	25.1	25.7	26.3	26.9	27.5	28.1	28.7
89–91	24.7	25.3	25.9	26.5	27.1	27.6	28.2	28.8	29.4
92–94	25.4	26.0	26.6	27.2	27.8	28.4	29.0	29.6	30.2
95–97	26.1	26.7	27.3	27.9	28.5	29.1	29.7	30.3	30.9
98–100	26.9	27.4	28.0	28.6	29.2	29.8	30.4	31.0	31.6
101–103	27.5	28.1	28.7	29.3	29.9	30.5	31.1	31.7	32.3
104–106	28.2	28.8	29.4	30.0	30.6	31.2	31.8	32.4	33.0
107–109	28.9	29.5	30.1	30.7	31.3	31.9	32.5	33.1	33.7
110–112	29.6	30.2	30.8	31.4	32.0	32.6	33.2	33.8	34.4
113–115	30.2	30.8	31.4	32.0	32.6	33.2	33.8	34.5	35.1
116–118	30.9	31.5	32.1	32.7	33.3	33.9	34.5	35.1	35.7
119–121	31.5	32.1	32.7	33.3	33.9	34.5	35.1	35.7	36.4
122–124	32.1	32.7	33.3	33.9	34.5	35.1	35.8	36.4	37.0
125–127	32.7	33.3	33.9	34.5	35.1	35.8	36.4	37.0	37.6

Table 7-6 Percentage of Fat Estimated for Women (Sum of Triceps, Suprailium, and Thigh Skinfolds)

Sum of Skinfolds (mm)	Age to Last Year								
	Under 23	23–27	28–32	33–37	38–42	43–47	48–52	53–57	Over 57
23–25	9.7	9.9	10.2	10.4	10.7	10.9	11.2	11.4	11.7
26–28	11.0	11.2	11.5	11.7	12.0	12.3	12.5	12.7	13.0
29–31	12.3	12.5	12.8	13.0	13.3	13.5	13.8	14.0	14.3
32–34	13.6	13.8	14.0	14.3	14.5	14.8	15.0	15.3	15.5
35–37	14.8	15.0	15.3	15.5	15.8	16.0	16.3	16.5	16.8
38–40	16.0	16.3	16.5	16.7	17.0	17.2	17.5	17.7	18.0
41–43	17.2	17.4	17.7	17.9	18.2	18.4	18.7	18.9	19.2
44–46	18.3	18.6	18.8	19.1	19.3	19.6	19.8	20.1	20.3
47–49	19.5	19.7	20.0	20.2	20.5	20.7	21.0	21.2	21.5
50–52	20.6	20.8	21.1	21.3	21.6	21.8	22.1	22.3	22.6
53–55	21.7	21.9	22.1	22.4	22.6	22.9	23.1	23.4	23.6
56–58	22.7	23.0	23.2	23.4	23.7	23.9	24.2	24.4	24.7
59–61	23.7	24.0	24.2	24.5	24.7	25.0	25.2	25.5	25.7
62–64	24.7	25.0	25.2	25.5	25.7	26.0	26.7	26.4	26.7
65–67	25.7	25.9	26.2	26.4	26.7	26.9	27.2	27.4	27.7
68–70	26.6	26.9	27.1	27.4	27.6	27.9	28.1	28.4	28.6
71–73	27.5	27.8	28.0	28.3	28.5	28.8	29.0	29.3	29.5
74–76	28.4	28.7	28.9	29.2	29.4	29.7	29.9	30.2	30.4
77–79	29.3	29.5	29.8	30.0	30.3	30.5	30.8	31.0	31.3
80–82	30.1	30.4	30.6	30.9	31.1	31.4	31.6	31.9	32.1
83–85	30.9	31.2	31.4	31.7	31.9	32.2	32.4	32.7	32.9
86–88	31.7	32.0	32.2	32.5	32.7	32.9	33.2	33.4	33.7
89–91	32.5	32.7	33.0	33.2	33.5	33.7	33.9	34.2	34.4
92–94	33.2	33.4	33.7	33.9	34.2	34.4	34.7	34.9	35.2
95–97	33.9	34.1	34.4	34.6	34.9	35.1	35.4	35.6	35.9
98–100	34.6	34.8	35.1	35.3	35.5	35.8	36.0	36.3	36.5
101–103	35.3	35.4	35.7	35.9	36.2	36.4	36.7	36.9	37.2
104–106	35.8	36.1	36.3	36.6	36.8	37.1	37.3	37.5	37.8
107–109	36.4	36.7	36.9	37.1	37.4	37.6	37.9	38.1	38.4
110–112	37.0	37.2	37.5	37.7	38.0	38.2	38.5	38.7	38.9
113–115	37.5	37.8	38.0	38.2	38.5	38.7	39.0	39.2	39.5
116–118	38.0	38.3	38.5	38.8	39.0	39.3	39.5	39.7	40.0
119–121	38.5	38.7	39.0	39.2	39.5	39.7	40.0	40.2	40.5
122–124	39.0	39.2	39.4	39.7	39.9	40.2	40.4	40.7	40.9
125–127	39.4	39.6	39.9	40.1	40.4	40.6	40.9	41.1	41.4
128–130	39.8	40.0	40.3	40.5	40.8	41.0	41.3	41.5	41.8

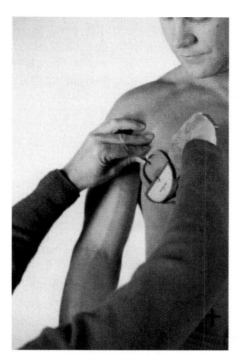

Figure 7-5 Chest Skinfold Measurement

Take a diagonal fold half the distance between the anterior axillary line and the nipple.

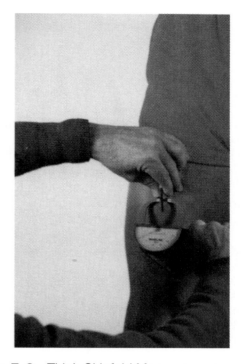

Figure 7-6 Thigh Skinfold Measurement

Take a vertical fold on the front of the thigh midway between the hip and the knee joint. The midpoint should be marked while the subject is seated.

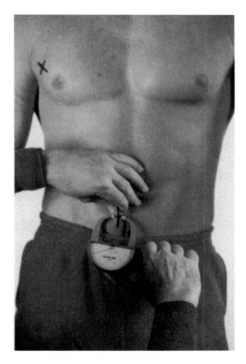

Figure 7-7 Abdominal Skinfold Measurement

Take a vertical fold about 1 inch from the navel.

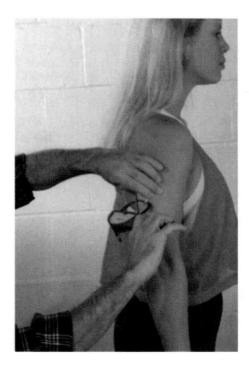

Figure 7-8 Triceps Skinfold Measurement

Take a vertical fold on the midline of the upper arm over the triceps, halfway between the acromion and olecranon processes (tip of the shoulder to the tip of the elbow). The arm should be extended and relaxed when the measurement is taken. All skinfold measurements should be taken on the right side. The calipers should be perpendicular to the fold. The photos do not reflect perpendicularity in order to show the site mark and the caliper face without the technician's hand in the way, obscuring both.

Determining Desired Body Weight from Body Fat

Calculating desirable body weight is a simple procedure when the percentage of body fat is known. The following example is for a 148-pound woman whose body fat is equal to 30 percent of her total body weight, based on her skinfold measurements. She wishes to reduce her body fat to 23 percent.

Find fat weight (FW) in pounds:

$$FW \text{ (lbs.)} = \frac{\text{Body weight (BW) (lbs.)} \times \% \text{ fat}}{100}$$
$$= \frac{148 \text{ lbs.} \times 30}{100}$$
$$= \frac{4440 \text{ lbs.}}{100}$$
$$= 44.4 \text{ lbs.}$$

Find lean weight (LW) in pounds:

$$LW \text{ (lbs.)} = BW - FW$$
$$= 148 \text{ lbs.} - 44.4 \text{ lbs.}$$
$$= 103.6 \text{ lbs.}$$

Find desirable body weight (DBW) in pounds:

$$DBW \text{ (lbs.)} = \frac{LW \text{ (lbs.)}}{1.0 - \% \text{ fat desired}}$$
$$= \frac{103.6 \text{ lbs.}}{1.0 - 0.23}$$
$$= \frac{103.6 \text{ lbs.}}{0.77}$$
$$= 134.5 \text{ lbs.}$$

The method for calculating desirable body weight based on percent body fat is relatively effective if the subject does the following:

· Exercises to maintain muscle tissue
· Loses no more than 1.5 pounds per week
· Is evaluated for body fatness two to three times during the weight-loss period
· Understands that indirect measurements of body fatness contain some error

Complete Assessment Activity 7-2 to determine your desirable body weight.

Summary

· Essential fat is necessary for normal biological function.
· Men carry 3 to 5 percent of their weight in the form of essential fat; women carry 11 to 14 percent of their weight as essential fat.
· *Obesity* is defined as overfatness.
· Men are obese when fat constitutes 25 percent or more of the body's weight, and women are obese when fat constitutes 32 percent or more of the body's weight.
· The majority of women store fat in the hips, buttocks, thighs, and breasts (gynoid fat).
· The majority of men store fat in the abdomen, lower back, chest, and nape of the neck (android fat).
· Height/weight tables are limited and poor instruments for weight-loss recommendations.

· Body mass index correlates fairly well with percent fat derived from hydrostatic weighing.
· A high body mass index correlates with hypertension, high total cholesterol, low HDL cholesterol, high serum triglycerides, and poor glucose tolerance.
· Bioelectrical impedance is a safe, quick, and relatively accurate method for assessing percent body fat.
· Skinfold measurements are one of the most economical methods of measuring body composition in terms of the cost of equipment and the time required to determine percent body fat.
· Underwater weighing is still considered the "gold standard" for measuring body composition.

Review Questions

1. What is essential fat and how is it distributed in men and women?
2. How would you define *obesity* and *overweight*?
3. At what level of fat deposition does obesity become a health hazard for men and women?
4. What are *gynoid obesity* and *android obesity*? Which is a greater health risk and why?
5. What are the limitations of height/weight tables for recommending weight loss?

6. What is body mass index and how is it classified for men and women?
7. How are underwater weighing, bioelectrical impedance, and skinfold measurements used to determine percent body fat?
8. How is healthy body weight determined when the percent body fat is known?

References

1. Going, S., and R. Davis. 1998. Body composition. In *ACSM's Resource Manual* (3d ed.), ed. J. L. Roitman. Baltimore, Md.: Williams & Wilkins.

2. ACSM. 1995. *ACSM's Guidelines for Exercise Testing and Prescription*. Baltimore, Md.: Williams & Wilkins.

3. Blair, S. N., et al. 1995. Changes in physical fitness and all-cause mortality. *JAMA* 273(14):1093.

4. Grilo, C. M., and K. D. Brownell. 1998. Interventions for weight management. In *ACSM's Resource Manual* (3d ed.), Baltimore, Md.: Williams & Wilkins.

5. Despres, J. P. 1997. Visceral obesity, insulin resistance, and dyslipidemia: Contribution of endurance exercise training to the treatment of plurimetabolic syndrome. *Exercise and Sport Sciences Reviews* 25: 271.

6. Bryant, C. X., and J. A. Peterson. 1998. Determining ideal body weight. *Fitness Management* 14(7):24.

7. NHLBI. 1998. *Obesity Education Initiative Expert Panel Clinical Guidelines on the Identification, Evaluation, and Treatment of Overweight and Obesity in Adults*. National Heart, Lung, and Blood Institute. Washington, D.C.

8. Bouchard, C., et al. 1993. Exercise, body fat, and the metabolic syndrome. *Medicine and Science in Sports and Exercise* 25:S1.

9. Gordon, N. F. 1998. Conceptual basis for coronary artery disease risk factor assessment. In *ACSM's Resource Manual* (3d ed.), ed. J. L. Roitman. Baltimore, Md.: Williams & Wilkins.

10. Harvard University. 1998. Guidelines call more Americans overweight. *Harvard Health Letter* 23(10):7.

11. Tufts University. 1998. Should fewer calories be in your future? *Tufts University Health and Nutrition Letter* 16(6):8.

12. Williams, M. A. 1998. Human development and aging. In *ACSM's Resource Manual* (3d ed.), ed. J. L. Roitman. Baltimore, Md.: Williams & Wilkins.

13. Robergs, R. A., and S. O. Roberts. 1997. *Exercise Physiology*, St. Louis, Mo.: Mosby.

14. U.S. Dept. of Health and Human Services. 1996. *Physical Activity and Health: A Report of the Surgeon General*. Atlanta: U.S. Dept. of Health and Human Services, Centers for Disease Control and Prevention, National Center for Chronic Disease Prevention and Health Promotion.

15. Williams, D. P., et al. 1992. Body fatness and risk for elevated blood pressure, total cholesterol, and serum lipoprotein ratios in children and adolescents. *American Journal of Public Health* 82:363.

16. Nieman, D. C. 1999. Exercise testing and prescription. Mountain View, Calif.: Mayfield Publishing.

Suggested Readings

Roche, A. F., S. B. Heymsfield, and T. G. Lohman, eds. 1996. *Human Body Composition*. Champaign, Ill.: Human Kinetics.

This book presents a full-scale treatment of the history and development of the techniques used to measure body composition. It describes the best and the most popular methods used.

Heyward, V. H., and L. M. Stolarczyk. 1996. *Applied Body Composition Assessment*. Champaign, Ill.: Human Kinetics.

This book, not for the casually interested reader, goes beyond the basics. It presents the scientific principles underlying some of the best and most popular techniques for measuring body composition.

Brown, J. E. 1999. *Nutrition Now*. Belmont, Calif.: West/Wadsworth.

A short chapter on body weight and body composition was written for those with little or no knowledge of these topics. The text covers in a very concise manner most popular techniques of measuring body composition.

Margolis, S., and L. J. Cheskin. 1998. *Weight Control*. Baltimore, Md.: The Johns Hopkins Medical Institutions.

Written for the layman, this book discusses methods for determining weight status and body composition and describes the advantages and disadvantages of using height/weight tables, body mass index, waist/hip ratio, underwater weighing, dual-energy X-ray absorptiometry (DEXA), and bioelectric impedance analysis. It is very informative, especially for beginners.

Howley, E. T., and B. D. Franks. 1997. *Health Fitness Instructor's Handbook*. Champaign, Ill.: Human Kinetics.

Chapter 9 covers body composition, discussing the impact of body weight and body composition on health status. It also describes in some detail many of the most effective and popular techniques for determining body composition.

Name _____ **Date** _____ **Section** _____

Assessment Activity 7-1

Using BMI to Estimate Body-Weight Status and Calculate Desirable Body Weight

Directions: Calculate your BMI:

1. Your body weight: _____ lbs.

2. Your height: _____ in.

3. Use the nomogram in table 7-4 to calculate your BMI.

    Your BMI: _____ kg/m²

4. Your desired BMI: _____ kg/m²

5. Once again, use the nomogram to calculate your desired body weight. Connect your desired BMI to your height and extend the line through the weight column.

    Your desired weight: _____ lbs.

6. Subtract your desired body weight from your current body weight to determine how much weight you need to lose or gain.

    Current weight – desired weight = weight to gain or lose

    _____ lbs. – _____ lbs. = _____ lbs.

Assessment Activity 7-2

Calculating Desirable Body Weight from Percent Body Fat

Directions: To find your desirable body weight, insert your current weight, percentage of body fat, and the desirable body fat that you wish to attain in the appropriate spaces. Then calculate fat weight, lean weight, and desirable body weight. Subtract desirable body weight from current weight. This figure tells you how much weight you must lose to achieve your desirable percentage of body fat.

Current weight = _____ lbs.

Current percentage of body fat = _____ %

Desirable body fat = _____ %

1. Fat weight

$$= \frac{\text{Body weight} \times \text{Percentage of fat}}{100}$$

= _____ lbs.

2. Lean weight
= Body weight − Fat weight

= _____ lbs.

3. Desirable body weight

$$= \frac{\text{Lean weight}}{1 - \text{Percentage of fat desired}}$$

= _____ lbs.

4. Amount of weight to lose = _____ lbs.

Achieving a Healthy Weight

Key Terms

anorexia nervosa
basal metabolic rate (BMR)
binge-eating disorder
body dysmorphic disorder
 (BDD)
bulimia
caloric deficit
caloric expenditure
caloric intake
diet resistance

fasting
hyperplasia
hypertrophy
overcompensatory eating
set point
thermogenic effect of food
 (TEF)
very-low–calorie diets
 (VLCDs)
weight cycling

Goals for Behavior Change

- Compare physical characteristics of your ideal body image with your actual body image.
- Estimate caloric expenditure for your basal metabolism and physical activity level.
- Adjust your caloric intake and physical activity as necessary to achieve a healthy weight.
- Formulate a plan for achieving a healthy weight.

Objectives

After completing this chapter, you will be able to do the following:

- Define *obesity* and *overweight*.
- Differentiate between hypertrophic and hyperplastic development of adipose cells.
- Identify and discuss the health aspects of obesity.
- Discuss biological and behavioral causes of obesity.
- Discuss the relationship of genetics, setpoint, overeating, and physical activity to body shape, fat distribution, and obesity.

- Define and identify *eating disorders* and their symptoms and treatment.
- Calculate the caloric cost of physical activities.
- Compare and contrast dieting and physical activity as strategies for weight management.
- Identify principles of weight management.

heoretically, achieving a healthy weight is a simple issue: A person balances **caloric intake**, calories supplied by food, with **caloric expenditure**, calories expended by physical activity and metabolism. In practice, however, people vary considerably in their responses to both caloric intake and caloric expenditure. No two people have identical experiences with dieting or physical activity regimens. Some people who chronically face weight problems eat no more and sometimes less than their normal-weight peers. Conversely, some normal-weight people have voracious appetites and do not expend any more calories than their overweight peers.

How can this be explained? Are the differences due to heredity, metabolism, or errors in reporting food intake and physical activity expenditures? Although on the surface body weight appears to be a function of the basic laws of nature (caloric intake vs. caloric expendi-

ture), in truth it is a complex issue that is still not fully understood by medical experts. For many people, self-improvement goals involving weight management are achievable and worthwhile. For others, formulating weight management goals means first constructing a realistic view of body image (see Nurturing Your Spirituality: Body Image Begins on the Inside). This chapter addresses some of the complexities of body weight issues and presents basic principles for achieving a healthy weight.

Americans' Obsession with Body Weight

Americans are preoccupied with their body weight. Books that offer creative but questionable advice for losing weight netted $141 million in sales in 1997.[2] The diet industry earns annual revenues of more than

Nurturing Your Spirituality

Body Image Begins on the Inside[1]

If you are unhappy with your body image, you are not alone. More than one-half of women and more than four of ten men are dissatisfied with their overall appearance; even more people are dissatisfied with their weight. Perceptions about body image are worse for young women. Almost two-thirds of girls and young women, ages 13 to 19, think they weigh too much. One-half of American women overestimate the sizes of their bodies.

Why are so many people unhappy with their body shapes or weights? Why do people tend to focus on their physical imperfections? Why does such a large discrepancy exist between the ways people see their own bodies and the ways others see them? Body image studies identify the following factors as being responsible for negative body images:

- Weight gain
- The media's preoccupation with thinness as the trademark for beauty
- Cultural pressures
- Disapproving messages from others
- Fluctuating moods
- Physical changes, such as pregnancy

- Chronic illness
- Childhood teasing
- Sexual abuse

What are the costs of an exaggerated negative body image? People who are deeply troubled about their appearance or preoccupied with selected physical "flaws" often limit their social activities; may not be assertive at work, school, or in personal relationships; may experience difficulty in forming a positive sexuality; may engage in high-risk behaviors; and often become victims of unrealistic fad diets. Extreme cases may involve a psychological disorder called *body dysmorphic disorder (BDD)*. People with this condition are so preoccupied with what they see as a disfiguring flaw that they shun social activities, including school and work.

Although self-improvement is a worthy goal for most people, when it comes to body image it is important to separate nature from nurture, heredity from environment. The challenge for many people with negative body images is to set realistic goals about what can be changed and to accept what can't be changed. Every one of us has a natural and unique size and shape. Our self-esteem depends on accepting the physical features that are unique to each of us. Changing what and how you think about your body can be healthier than constantly working to change your body weight and shape by diet and exercise. Having a positive body image is not just about losing weight or working with what is on the outside. It begins on the inside.

$33 billion by hawking far-out gadgets and gimmicks including lipo-slim briefs, which supposedly massage away cellulite; slimming insoles, shoe insoles that reportedly stimulate weight-loss acupressure points as you walk; and aroma pens, inhalants that come in banana, green apple, and peppermint claimed to squelch hunger pangs.[3,4,5] At any given time more than one-half of women and more than one–fourth of men are on a diet. Even children are getting the message that dieting is popular—50 percent of 9-year-old girls have dieted, although only 11 percent are overweight.[5,6] More than $30 billion a year are spent on gimmicks, gadgets, and strategies to trim, tuck, and tone waistlines.[2] Of adults, 50 million are dieting, and most of them are repeaters, averaging 2.3 diets per year.[3,4]

The evidence for this obsession can be found in advertisements and the news. Numerous television celebrities have engaged in special diet or weight-loss programs. Both the print and video media show countless numbers of advertisements that associate super svelte body images with almost every imaginable product. Consumers demand low-calorie versions of every consumable food, and much of this demand is motivated more by the desire to achieve an unobtainable physique than by health reasons. Consumers have been observed counting the number of calories even in a dose of laxatives. The phrase *calorie anxiety* applies to many Americans. Even health magazines and professional journals reinforce this preoccupation by featuring headlines of diet articles or diet studies on their covers. If some new diet finding is released by the scientific community, it will surely be headlined on national and local news shows and will quickly be followed by feature stories.

For some people the obsession with weight is so intense that it causes serious body-image problems, distorts their self-esteem, and eventually leads to eating disorders, such as anorexia nervosa, bulimia, and compulsive eating, three conditions that were almost unheard of twenty years ago. Extreme cases may involve a psychological disorder called **body dysmorphic disorder (BDD)**. BDD is an obsession with perceived flaws in physical appearance that is so extreme that it may disrupt a person's life and can lead to thoughts of suicide.[7]

The effects of weight obsession may be more subtle. Some people who are neither anorexic nor bulimic may develop aversive attitudes toward food, eating, and mealtime. Rather than serving as a source of pleasure and enjoyment, the eating experience becomes a constant test of willpower that rarely yields positive results. For too many people, attitudes about appearance, body weight, and food combined with the ubiquitous messages and body images promulgated by the media form a vicious cycle of guilt, denial, and unhappiness.

For example, the average height and weight of a contemporary fashion model is 5 foot 9 inches and 110 pounds. In contrast, the average height and weight of an American woman is 5 foot 4 inches and 142 pounds.[5] Only 10 percent of the population genetically fits models' height and weight zone.[8] The rest of the population is left with body images that are unobtainable and unrealistic. The challenge for many people is to break this cycle by constructing realistic views of their bodies, establishing positive attitudes toward food, and formulating realistic strategies to address the weight problem (see Assessment Activity 8-1).

Defining the Problem

For many Americans, weight loss is a healthy goal. Losing weight often means reducing the risk of developing common chronic health problems. However, many people who are not overweight and have good body composition try to lose weight. For them, losing weight offers no health benefits and may even be harmful.

The number of people who stand to benefit from weight loss is at an all-time high. New standards established by the National Institutes of Health define a healthy weight as a BMI equal to or more than 19 and less than 25. Being overweight is defined as having a BMI of 25 or higher; obesity is defined as having a BMI of 30 or higher. By these definitions, only 41 percent of U.S. adults 20 years or older are at a healthy weight—39 percent of males and 44 percent of females. Nearly one-fourth (22 percent) of U.S. adults are obese.[6] Both of these figures are significantly higher than comparison figures for each of the previous decades since data have been collected. Adults are not the only ones who are overweight. Eleven percent of all children and 10 percent of all adolescents are overweight or obese.[6] The dramatic increase in body weight has led some experts to proclaim that obesity is a chronic health condition of epidemic proportion. Obesity has been declared a disease by the National Institutes of Health (NIH); it has also been elevated to the status of a major risk factor for heart disease (see Chapter 2).

Americans are getting heavier for two obvious reasons: too much energy going in (as food) and too little energy going out (as exercise). The majority of Americans are sedentary; at the same time they are consuming more calories than they were fifteen years ago. Table 8-1 presents the calorie intakes for men and women between the ages of 16 and 39, based on the results of the *Third National Health and Nutrition Examination Survey (NHANES),* one of the major national surveys in the National Nutrition Monitoring and Related Research Program.[9]

Table 8-1	Average Calorie Intake* by Selected Age and Gender	
Age	Men	Women
16–19 years	3097	1958
20–29 years	3025	1957
30–39 years	2872	1883
Combined average	2998	1933

*Average calorie intake for all age groups and both genders from 2 months to over 80 years is 2200.

Although BMI provides a basis for classifying levels of overweight and obesity, it is not without its limitations (see Chapter 7). It is also important to remember that BMIs of 25 and 30 (for overweight and obesity, respectively) are not precise points on a scale that when exceeded magically increase a person's risk for health problems. For example, although a BMI of 29.9 does not technically fall into the category of obesity, it is a very small step away from the "magic number" of 30, the cutoff point for obesity. For all practical purposes, a BMI of 29.9 carries the same risk of obesity as a BMI of 30.

Health Aspects of Obesity

In declaring obesity a disease, the NIH signaled a new approach toward obesity. Medical experts no longer regard being obese as a simple failure of willpower. Instead, obesity is considered a chronic disease, such as hypertension or diabetes. In 1994 weight-loss experts advocated "a conceptual housecleaning" in the way medical doctors and the general public think about weight.[10] The result is new knowledge and a different attitude about the causes and treatments of obesity.

One aspect of obesity that has not changed is its medical consequences. Morbidity occurs more frequently and with greater severity and mortality occurs at an earlier age among obese people than among those of normal weight.[6] In an extensive review of the scientific literature on obesity and health, a panel of twenty-four experts summoned by the National Heart, Lung, and Blood Institute proclaimed that obesity is second only to smoking as the largest cause of preventable death in the United States.[11]

Obesity is highly correlated with coronary heart disease and stroke. LDL cholesterol, which contributes to the development of atherosclerosis, is associated with obesity. According to the Framingham Heart Study, a 20 percent weight loss may reduce the risk of coronary heart disease by 40 percent.[12] One-third of all cases of hypertension are considered a result of obesity. Many hypertensive people experience a decline in systolic and diastolic blood pressures within the first two to three weeks of a weight-loss program.[12]

Obesity is also a major risk factor for some forms of cancer; it predisposes men to cancers of the colon, rectum, and prostate and women to cancers of the ovaries, uterus, and breasts.

Fifty percent of people with impaired glucose tolerance are overweight.[6] For people with a predisposition to type II diabetes, losing 10 pounds can reduce the chances of contracting the condition by 30 percent. For those who already have diabetes, a 5 percent weight loss can significantly improve the body's use of insulin and lower blood sugar levels.[12]

Obesity increases the risk of osteoarthritis. It intensifies symptoms in those who already have the disease.

Obesity is a prime risk factor for gallbladder disease. Obese individuals have a 3 to 7 times greater risk of gallstones, stones usually composed of cholesterol, than do normal weight people. Weight loss can reduce the risk of gallbladder disease, even though rapid weight loss temporarily increases gallstone formation.[12]

Obesity is a leading cause of sleep apnea, a condition characterized by loud snoring and brief halts in breathing (for about ten to thirty seconds at a time) during sleep. This condition is thought to be caused, in part, by the accumulation of fat tissue in the upper airway, which obstructs breathing. Sleep apnea can lead to daytime sleepiness and may also adversely affect heart function. A 10 to 15 percent weight reduction may relieve or even cure this condition.[12]

For some people, the first symptom of strain placed on the body by excess fat is shortness of breath. As fat accumulates, it crowds the space occupied by organs. Some people cannot sit comfortably because of fat accumulation in their abdomens. In a sitting position a person's lungs have limited space in which to expand.

Postsurgery complications occur more often in overweight people than in those who are not overweight. Wounds don't heal as well or as fast. Infections are more common.

In addition to suffering from medical hazards, it is not uncommon for obese people to suffer psychological stress, depression, social discrimination, and reduced income. They pay higher premiums for health insurance or are denied coverage. Obese children are often ridiculed by their slim peers. Armed forces personnel are forced out of the military if they gain weight beyond an acceptable level.

The link between obesity and chronic disease is well established, but evidence has emerged indicating that the *distribution* of fat is equally important to the development of disease. Studies have confirmed that abdominal fat is associated with a higher rate of heart attack and stroke than is fat distributed around the hips and thighs (see Chapter 7). Guidelines for doctors now suggest that, in addition to calculating BMI, they should assess waist circumference. A waist measurement of more than 40 inches in men and over 35 inches in women is considered a marker for risk in people with BMIs of 25.0 to 34.9.[11]

In summary, the medical community clearly concurs that the health risks and complications of obesity are associated with premature death. This is not necessarily the case for overweight, however. A twelve-year study of 324,135 adults found that the risk of dying associated with being overweight was relatively modest and declined as people grew older. By age 65 the increased risk was slight, and by age 74 it had disappeared. People who were moderately overweight but not obese had no increased risk of premature death.[12]

The response of medical experts to these findings has been mixed. Any increased risk of premature death, however slight, is reason enough to view excess weight as a serious health hazard. However, the dangers of excess weight may have been exaggerated, and for some people, the cure may be worse than the condition. Although controversy exists about the health effects of being overweight, maintaining a healthy weight is associated with good health.

Weight Loss: A New Attitude Emerges

The term *weight loss* lacks specificity and it is often used in such a way as to imply that indiscriminate weight loss—of body fluids, protein, and fat—is desirable. A more appropriate weight-related goal is to measure success by the amount of fat lost, not by weight loss. The term *weight loss* should be replaced by the more specific term *fat-weight loss*.

Until recently, advice to overfat people was imprecise. For example, the suggestion to "cut back on calories" reinforces the misconception that diet alone can lead to fat-weight loss. Successful weight management is rarely the result of following a diet or counting calories for a specific time period. Successful weight management usually requires a lifelong lifestyle change. The loss or gain of body weight, the development of fat cells, and the causes of obesity are complex issues related to the interaction of three factors—heredity, diet, and exercise.

Development of Obesity

The body consists of 30 to 40 billion adipose cells (fat cells) that provide storage space for extra energy. Adipose cells may be viewed as collapsible, thin-walled con-

tainers with unlimited storage capacities (figure 8-1). In prehistoric humans large fat stores developed when food was available in spring and summer, and this proved biologically advantageous when winters were long and harsh and food was scarce. Energy stored in fat cells could be tapped for use later. This is not the case today. Food is available year-round for most Americans and surplus fat storage is not advantageous.

Obesity occurs when adipose cells increase excessively in size (**hypertrophy**) or number (**hyperplasia**) or both. Obesity that results from an increase in the size of fat cells is hypertrophic, obesity that results from an increase in the number of fat cells is hyperplastic, and obesity that results from an increase in both is hypertrophic/hyperplastic.

Adipose cells follow a normal pattern of growth and development. When obesity develops in infancy or childhood (juvenile-onset obesity), more adipose cells develop, and each cell grows greatly, resulting in hypertrophic/hyperplastic obesity. When obesity develops in adulthood (adult-onset obesity), a normal number of adipose cells usually develops, but each cell contains a large amount of fat (see Just the Facts: Classification of Obesity). In extreme cases, adult-onset obesity can be both hyperplastic and hypertrophic.[14] Once developed, fat cells do not disappear in the adult state.

Adipose cells have a long lifespan. If adult obesity is both hypertrophic and hyperplastic, is it more difficult to lose weight than if adult obesity is due to hypertrophy alone? Some evidence indicates that an increased number of fat cells increases the body's reluctance to reduce fat stores. The needs of adipose cells may require that they store at least nominal amounts of fat. More fat cells would then result in more fat storage, complicating efforts to lose weight. The longer a person remains obese, the more difficult it is to correct the problem.

Gender differences in depositing fat become noticeable during and after puberty. Men distribute fat primarily in the upper half of the body, and women tend to deposit it in the lower half. The percentage of fat in the body reaches peak values during early adolescence for boys and then declines during the remainder of adolescent growth. Girls experience a continuous increase in the percentage of fat from the onset of puberty to age 18.

From approximately 2 years of age, obese children develop a greater number of fat cells than do children of normal weight, often as many as three times more.[15] Although it is widely believed that obese children become obese adults, only about one-third of obese preschoolers in fact do. The risk of adult obesity is greater for children and young adults who are obese at older ages. Overweight and obese children and adolescents represent only 21 percent of all children and

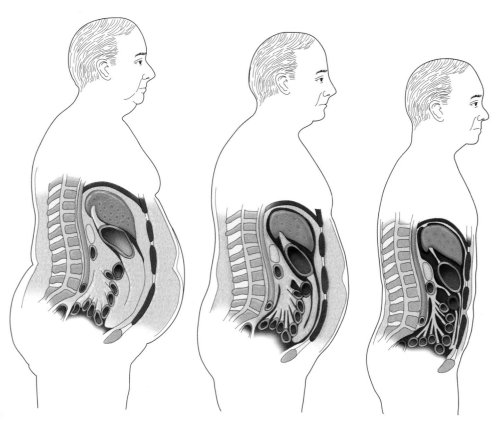

Figure 8-1 Adipose Cell Deposits

Adipose (fat) tissue can be deposited in many areas of the body. Losing fat and building lean muscle tissue boosts metabolism, reduces strain on the hips and knees, and may prevent lower-back pain.

Just the Facts

Classification of Obesity

There are several types of obesity, each resulting from different causes:

- Juvenile-onset obesity: Caused by an increase in both the number (hyperplastic) and size (hypertrophic) of fat cells

- Adult-onset obesity: Caused primarily by an increase in size of fat cells (hypertrophic)

- Other types of obesity: Caused by endocrine and/or genetic disorders, such as hypothyroidism, brain tumors, and Turner's syndrome

therefore do not account for the larger percent of obese adults. The large majority of obesity is thought to be adult-onset obesity.

Causes of Obesity

The laws of thermodynamics state that energy cannot be destroyed; it is used for work or converted into another form. Accordingly, the progressive accumulation of stored fat in the body is the result of consumption of more calories (energy) than are expended. Food energy in excess of the body's need results in storage of fat in adipose cells (figure 8-2). This relationship is demonstrated in almost all people. Excessive caloric intake and deficient energy expenditure are responsible for most obesity. What is more difficult to explain, however, is the difference among people's responses to the laws of energy conservation and expenditure. Two people may be overfed the same number of calories and yet differ in the amount of weight gained, even if their activity levels are held constant. What accounts for these differences? The answer suggests that obesity is a complex issue, involving both biological and behavioral theories.

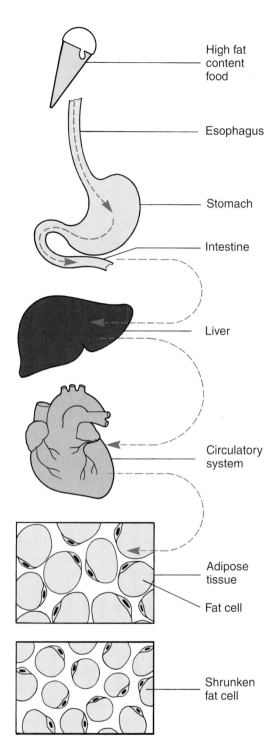

Figure 8-2 Fat Storage

Fat can be manufactured in the body from any food and stored when caloric intake exceeds expenditure. Fat droplets travel to the liver from the stomach and intestines and then enter the circulatory system, where they are delivered to the cells and organs. Excess fats are stored in adipose tissue. When more energy is needed, fats are released from adipose cells. If the energy needs continue, the cells shrink.

Biological Theories

Age, metabolism, gender, disease, heredity, and set point are biological factors that influence body weight and obesity. As people age, their amount of muscle tends to drop, and fat accounts for a greater percentage of their body weight. Metabolism also slows naturally with age. Together these changes reduce calorie needs, often adding an extra pound a year after age 35.[1] Women usually have higher fat-to-muscle ratios than men because of the influence of hormones that are unique to fertility and the female reproductive system. Also men typically have higher muscle-to-fat ratios than women, which increases metabolism and caloric expenditure. Diseases that affect the thyroid gland may have a dramatic impact on body weight. An overactive thyroid gland (hyperthyroidism) increases the resting metabolic rate (RMR) and may cause weight loss. Conversely, an underactive thyroid gland (hypothyroidism) lowers RMR and may lead to overweight or obesity.

The two major biological explanations of obesity are heredity and setpoint. Although they are interrelated, they are discussed separately here.

Heredity

Studies of adoptees, identical twins, and fraternal twins help to reveal the influence of the genetic component on obesity. In classic longitudinal studies, researchers at the University of Pennsylvania examined the relative obesity and the body type of adults who had been adopted during childhood.[16] They classified 540 adoptees in the following categories: thin, median weight, overweight, and obese. They found that the subjects resembled their biological parents rather than their adoptive parents even though they learned and practiced the lifestyles of their adoptive parents.

The same research team from the University of Pennsylvania studied identical and fraternal male twins for more than twenty-five years.[17] Height, weight, and BMI were measured when the subjects entered the military and again twenty-five years later. Identical twins are excellent subjects for these studies because they have identical genetic makeups. Any physical differences that occur in one of a pair of identical twins can be attributed to environmental and/or lifestyle factors. The identical twins in this study were very similar in height, weight, and BMI when they entered the military and again twenty-five years later. Each member of the pair gained the same amount of weight at approximately the same time in life. The similarity in the identical twins was twice that observed in fraternal twins (twins who emanate from separate eggs and do not have identical genes).

The connection between heredity and obesity is also confirmed in studies that correlate the prevalence of childhood obesity with the prevalence of obesity in parents. Eighty percent of children born to two obese parents will themselves become obese, compared to 40 percent of children born to one obese parent and 14 percent of children born to nonobese parents.[13]

Studies support the idea that obesity and fat deposition are significantly influenced by heredity. Approximately 33 percent of the reason a person weighs a certain amount is related to inherited factors.[12]

In addition to influencing body weight, heredity influences body shape. Body shape generally falls into one of three categories: ectomorph, endomorph, and mesomorph (see Chapter 7). Most people are a combination of all three with a tendency to be more like one or two of them. If a person's body shape strongly favors a particular classification, the person cannot realistically hope to attain another body type. It would be more appropriate for such a person to seek changes in body composition that reduce fat weight regardless of body-shape tendencies. Acceptance of one's natural shape along with its limitations is essential in constructing a realistic view of body weight. Rather than concentrating on weight or shape, the overweight or obese person would be better served by focusing on physical activity. According to Steven Blair, Director of the Cooper Aerobic Center in Dallas, physically fit obese people have a lower all-cause mortality (death from all causes) than do sedentary normal-weight persons.[18] In other words, it is possible to be obese and fit. Endomorphs with a BMI over 27 can negate the health risks associated with obesity through consistent participation in moderately intense physical activities.

Another factor that helps to explain the connection between heredity and obesity surfaced with the discovery of a protein that appears to control weight gain and loss. The protein is called *leptin* (from *leptos,* the Greek word for *thin*) and is made in fat cells by a gene called *ob* (for its connection with obesity), often referred to as the *fat gene.* Scientists hypothesize that obesity occurs for one of three reasons: (1) the gene fails to produce enough leptin, (2) the body's cells do not recognize leptin, or (3) the body develops a resistance to leptin. In experiments with mice, whose ob gene is nearly identical to human's, leptin injections caused the mice to lose weight, almost all of it fat. The mice also became more active and had higher metabolic rates during the treatment.[19] It is too early to know if the leptin connection is a true medical breakthrough or another false alarm, and experts warn against the idea that leptin is a magic bullet for weight loss. Even if human studies confirm the connection, leptin will still be a pharmaceutical adjunct to diet and exercise, not a replacement for them.

The set point theory

The set point theory of weight control also reflects the role of genetics. Proponents of this theory suggest that the body works to maintain a certain weight. More specifically, each person has an internal **set point** for fatness, sometimes called the *adipostat,* that seems to regulate the body by adjusting hunger, appetite, food intake, and energy expenditure. Researchers have demonstrated that human and animal subjects put on low-calorie or high-calorie diets lose and gain only to a certain level. When the diet ends, food consumption increases and they return to their approximate original weight.

How the body determines its set point is not known. One hypothesis is that the body is able to adjust its energy expenditure by varying how efficiently muscles burn calories. Researchers at New York's Rockefeller University discovered that a dieter's metabolism slows down after losing weight, so that doing the same amount of exercise at the new weight burns fewer calories.[20] The researchers found that, after losing 10 percent of their body weight, newly slimmer patients expended 15 percent less energy than expected for someone of similar size and body composition. The system also works in the other direction; when patients gained weight, their metabolisms increased 16 percent. After a quick weight gain, the metabolism speeds up to make muscle activity burn more calories, quickly bringing the body back to its normal weight—its set point. In other words, the body burns calories more slowly than normal when weight is lost and faster than normal when weight is gained. The body's metabolism adjusts in an effort to maintain the status quo. Whatever direction a person's weight goes, up or down, the body tends to resist that change.

Can a person change his or her set point? Proponents of the set point theory think that the set point does shift over time in response to behavioral factors: Eating a high-fat diet tends to raise the set point for fatness, and regular physical activity tends to lower it. This shift may be so slight and gradual as to go unnoticed for years.

Some proponents of the set point theory suggest that because some people are genetically programmed to have unwanted pounds, efforts to eliminate fat with diet, exercise, or both are doomed. The body can shut down its calorie-losing mechanism by lowering metabolism and can stimulate appetite to the point that a person must have food.

Other proponents of the set point theory argue that vigorous regular exercise brings about physiological changes in muscle that speed up metabolism and lower the set point, thereby lowering the level of fat the body will accept and defend. Exercise induces the body to stabilize at a lower body weight, which is precisely what dieters try to do. Unfortunately, there is no formula for calculating that a specific amount of exercise will result in the loss of a certain number of pounds.

Individual response to exercise varies in ways similar to the variations in response to dieting. Still, exercise seems to be the best way to overpower the body's set point.[23] This, tendency is a classic case of a genetic inclination being modified through appropriate lifestyle behavior. It supports the idea that heredity (that is, obesity) is not destiny. Living a healthy life—through regular exercise and sound nutritional habits—cannot negate heredity, but it can modify it.

Behavioral Theories

Behavioral explanations of obesity include excessive caloric intake (overeating) and lack of physical activity (hypokinesis).

Overeating

The basic laws of nature require that calories be consumed before energy can be stored as excess weight. The body cannot make energy on its own. For the obese and overweight, therefore, caloric intake is an important issue.

Do obese people eat more than normal-weight people? This has been a controversial question and researchers are divided in their answer. Some studies show that obese people eat no more and sometimes less than normal-weight people.[21] Researchers would suggest that blaming obesity on a lack of willpower is unfair and oversimplifies the facts. They maintain that the body of the obese person is simply more efficient at converting calories to adipose cells for reasons beyond his or her control, such as genetic predisposition or higher setpoint for fatness. Stated another way, obese people may not eat more than normal-weight people; they just consume more calories than are required by their bodies.

Other researchers claim that obese people do eat more than normal-weight people; the problem, they argue, is a discrepancy in reporting of food intake. In one study, obese subjects underestimated their intake by 47 percent and overestimated physical activity by 51 percent.[12] According to these researchers, the phenomenon referred to as **diet resistance**, the inability to lose weight by dieting, has little to do with innate biological factors.

Although researchers are divided on the issue of overeating, they tend to agree that the abundance of food high in fat and calories is a major factor in the prevalence of obesity in the United States. In his review of the literature on obesity—a review that included more than 300 citations from the scientific literature—Nieman wrote, "Of all the current theories attempting to explain the epidemic of obesity in most Western societies, the high dietary fat intake hypothesis is most widely accepted by experts."[13] Overweight people tend to eat a higher-fat diet than do people of normal weight. Ounce for ounce, fat yields more than double the number of calories than protein or carbohydrates do (9 calories versus 4). This energy difference partially explains the relationship between dietary fat intake and weight gain. It is not a complete explanation because, in studies that hold the total number of calories constant and in which more calories are consumed than needed, subjects eating high-fat diets tend to store more excess calories as body fat than subjects eating lower-fat diets.[22] Calories from fat appear to be more readily converted to body fat than are calories from carbohydrate and protein.

Excess carbohydrates are converted to glycogen in the liver and muscle. The body can only store a limited amount of glycogen. This is not true for fat. Fat cells are distributed throughout the body. Whereas carbohydrate storage is carefully regulated, fat storage is not, allowing a high degree of expansion. The body's capacity to make and store fat may have served a useful purpose in earlier times when humans faced the constant threat of famines and when an energy reserve meant greater likelihood of survival. But given the sedentary lifestyles of most Americans, glycogen stores are rarely exhausted. The reality for too many people is that they burn carbohydrates and store fat.

Dietary fat also has less of a thermogenic effect than does carbohydrate or protein and can thus be easily stored as adipose tissue. The **thermogenic effect of food (TEF)** represents the amount of energy required by the body to digest, absorb, metabolize, and store nutrients. The body expends only 3 calories of energy to process 100 calories from fat compared with 25 calories to process 100 calories from carbohydrates (see Just the Facts: Dietary Fat Versus Dietary Carbohydrate). Between 10 percent and 15 percent of total body energy goes to support the TEF.[12] For example, after a meal containing 1000 calories, the body uses 100 to 150 calories just to process the meal. The TEF helps explain why studies consistently show that, when adults and children overeat and consume high amounts of dietary fat, they tend to gain weight. Conversely, when the intake of dietary fat is low and the intake of carbohydrate and fiber is high from nutrient-dense foods, desirable body weight is more readily achieved.[13] Cross-cultural comparisons confirm the dietary fat-obesity relationship. For example, Americans eat more than twice as much fat as the Chinese, yet the Chinese consume 20 percent more calories and there is little obesity in China.[13]

The high-fat theory of obesity leads to an important question: Can a person lose weight by simply focusing on fat calories? The answer depends on whether or not a reduction in fat calories is also accompanied by a reduction in total calories. Studies of the eating habits of

Exercising with a friend is a fun way to stay active and keep your weight in check.

both men and women who consume low-fat products reveal that they often compensate by eating more snack and dessert foods high in sugar but low in fat so the use of low-fat foods becomes an excuse to eat more.[24] The idea that people can eat as much as they want as long as it is fat free appears to be more fantasy than fact. Although some researchers believe that fat is the main culprit associated with obesity; other experts emphasize calories. This helps to explain why Americans are getting heavier with each passing year, even though they are consuming a lower proportion of fat. Increased consumption of low-fat foods does not alone result in weight loss. Whereas eating low-fat foods is good for health and weight control, eating them in buffet-sized portions is not.

Lack of physical activity

Obesity is in large part caused by the sedentary lifestyle of most Americans. Scientific improvements have led to modern conveniences and labor saving devices that decrease the need for physical activity. Advancements in technology make it possible to bank, shop, and even complete college courses without leaving the desktop computer. Less than 1 percent of the energy for operating factories comes from muscle power. Devices such as mechanized golf carts have made leisure activities less strenuous. Each new invention fosters a receptive attitude toward a life of ease. The mechanized way is generally the most expedient way in the time-oriented American society. Exercise for fitness is now separate

from other parts of life. Even when people do exercise during their leisure time, their total daily energy expenditure still falls far short of what was typical several decades ago. The average sedentary person usually expends only 300 to 800 calories a day in physical activity, most of this through informal, unplanned types of movement.[13] Some experts believe that lack of physical activity is the distinguishing factor that separates the obese from those of normal weight.

The general decline in physical activity and fitness is correlated with the rise in obesity. More specifically, fitness is associated with increased BMR, improved body composition, preserved lean body mass during weight loss, lowered insulin levels, increased oxidative capacity of muscle tissues, larger amounts of glycogen stored in active muscles, and increased sensitivity to fat-mobilizing hormones that help to decrease body fat.[21] In the absence of exercise, the opposites of these factors work together to contribute to and exacerbate obesity.

Overweight people are usually less physically active than normal-weight people. Obese men informally walk an average of 3.7 miles per day, whereas normal-weight men walk 6 miles; obese women walk 2 miles per day, and normal-weight women walk 4.9 miles.[13]

To state that obese people are less physically active than normal-weight people is one thing; to claim that lack of physical activity causes obesity is quite different. Researchers are not clear which comes first: Does obesity lead to physical inactivity or does physical inactivity lead to obesity? The cause-and-effect nature of the relationship between these two factors has yet to be determined and is complicated by the fact that energy expenditure from exercise differs very little between the obese and the normal-weight. Because of their extra weight, the obese expend more energy when they participate in physical activity. In other words, even though they exercise less, they expend more energy in the course of activity. For this reason overeating is considered by most experts to be more important than inactivity as a determinant of obesity.[13] Still there is general agreement that exercise is vital to the success of weight maintenance. A statement included in a keynote speech delivered at the 1995 convention of the American College of Sports Medicine captures the essence of this dilemma: "The results of hundreds of studies reveal that while exercise in and of itself is not a major player in weight loss, it is the number one player in preventing weight gain."[25]

Dieting and Exercise: Strategies for Weight Maintenance or Weight Loss

To maintain weight, caloric intake must be balanced by caloric expenditure. To lose weight a person has to achieve a **caloric deficit** in which the number of calories burned exceeds the number of calories consumed. This is the basic principle of weight management. It is simple and straightforward, and it includes three obvious strategies: (1) restricting caloric intake by dieting, (2) increasing caloric expenditure through physical activity, and (3) a combination of dieting and physical activity. What is not so easy to explain is how two people can respond so differently to dieting and exercise weight-loss strategies. Complex forces, many of which are still not clearly understood, influence the success of weight-management/weight-loss efforts.

The loss of 1 pound of body fat requires a caloric deficit of 3500 calories. (The loss of 1 pound of adipose tissue yields more than 1 pound of body weight because fat storage includes some lean support tissue—muscle, connective tissues, blood supply, and other body components. A caloric deficit of 2700 calories results in a loss of 1 pound of body weight.)[14] A loss of 1 pound of body fat per week is a good goal and requires an average daily caloric deficit of 500 calories. A caloric deficit of more than 500 calories per day, unless medically supervised, borders on the extreme and is difficult to sustain over long periods of time. A loss of 2 pounds of body fat per week is considered a maximum goal.

Body fat loss in excess of 2 pounds per week is not practical for most people. For example, diets that promise a fat-weight loss of 10 pounds per week require a caloric deficit of 35,000 calories per week; that is an average of 7000 calories per day. For that kind of caloric deficit, a person would have to go to the extremes of fasting while running two marathons in one day. Weight loss in excess of a couple of pounds per week usually involves lean tissue weight, which should

be retained, and fluid weight, which needs to be replaced to prevent health consequences ranging from dehydration to electrolyte imbalance.

A desirable long-term goal for a person needing to lose weight is 1 to 2 pounds per week until about 10 percent of excess weight is lost. The emphasis should be on a slow, steady weight loss rather than on a rapid weight loss. Once this goal is reached, the dieter should go into maintenance for about six months before attempting more weight loss.[14] For example, a 250-pound person should go into a six-month maintenance program after losing 25 pounds. This is a conservative approach to weight loss that is likely to yield health improvements while promoting a more stable, consistent body weight.

Dieting

Statistics show that dieting is the method of choice for most Americans trying to lose weight. Although dieting usually works only temporarily, most people who fail to maintain weight loss are willing to try again. Many people seek the miraculous diet that will transform them from fat to thin, preferably with minimal effort and in the shortest time possible.

The success rate of diet-only strategies is dismal. Only 5 percent of all dieters are successful in reducing to a target weight and maintaining the weight for more than five years. Typically, one-third of the weight lost during dieting is regained within the first year, and almost all weight lost is regained within three to five years.[14] Maintaining postdiet weight is one of the major failures of weight loss through dieting because dieters do not learn the habits and behaviors needed to remain at the new weight. As a result, they lose and regain weight many times in their lives. This pattern of repeated weight loss and gain, known as **weight cycling,** *yo-yo dieting,* and *seesaw approaches* to weight loss, is potentially harmful and counterproductive.

The consequences of weight cycling are numerous. The most immediate negative effect is rebound weight gain. Typically, weight gained after dieting includes not only the weight that was lost but additional weight as well. After years of yo-yo dieting, many dieters experience a weight gain pattern that takes on a stair-step effect, increasing in small but noticeable increments with each successive effort. In addition, the weight regained is in the form of adipose tissue, whereas the weight that was lost consisted of a mixture of adipose and muscle tissue. The net result of weight cycling is not only extra weight but also extra fat weight.

Weight cycling also increases the risk of death, especially from cardiovascular conditions. Researchers at Harvard University[26] studied data on 11,703 subjects over thirty years to see whether weight cycling had any effect on longevity. As expected, those whose weight remained stable had a lower mortality rate. However, those who lost weight were more likely to die than were those who gained weight. Men who gained more than 11 pounds were 36 percent more likely to die than were those whose weight remained stable. The men who lost more than 11 pounds, however, had a 57 percent higher chance of dying. The explanation proposed was that those who had lost 11 pounds over the decade had actually gained and lost an average of 100 pounds over their lifetimes. The stress of yo-yo dieting contributed to the higher death rates. With the high recidivism rate of dieters, the researchers concluded that it is probably better to remain slightly overweight than to weight cycle. This is not true, however, for people whose excessive body weight increases their risk for diabetes, high blood pressure, and high cholesterol levels. In a 1994 report of forty-three studies on the effects of weight cycling, researchers concluded that the health gains from a weight loss of as little as 5 to 10 pounds, even if temporary, outweigh the hazards of weight cycling for people with histories of these chronic conditions.[27] Still, experts agree that it is better to lose weight and keep it off.

The high recidivism rate of diet-only programs coupled with the negative effects of weight cycling seems to negate dieting as a strategy for losing weight. The cold reality, however, is that weight loss requires a caloric deficit, and limiting food intake is the most direct and immediate way to get results. The mistake people tend to make with most diet-only strategies is to set unrealistic goals. They want to lose too much weight and they want to lose it immediately. An ideal approach is to lose weight at the same rate as weight is gained. For most people this would involve a plan of modest dietary restrictions implemented over a period of months or years, rather than days or weeks. Weight-loss goals structured according to the guidelines mentioned are more likely to be successful.

In diet-only strategies, the caloric intake should not drop below 1200 per day in women or 1500 per day in men.[12] Gender differences in caloric intake are due to differences in physical activity patterns, metabolism (from more or less muscle tissue), and size. Because fat is more than twice as energy dense as carbohydrates, many experts recommend concentrating on limiting fat intake rather than on counting calories. If an eating plan calls for a caloric intake below 1200 calories for women and 1500 calories for men per day, discuss it with your health care provider. You may need to take vitamin and/or mineral supplements. One last caveat to people who are frustrated because they can't lose weight on a 1200- or 1500-calorie diet: If you can't lose weight at this caloric level, you probably don't need to lose weight. You might be better served by reexamining your reasons for losing weight.

In structuring a diet, it is important to observe the dietary recommendations in Chapter 6. Follow the Food Guide Pyramid by adjusting the number of servings while still maintaining the proportion of servings that come from grains, fruits, and vegetables. The diet should include common foods that fit into any social situation. Further, the plan should make provisions for relearning eating habits that will make weight loss permanent.

Very low–calorie diets

Very-low–calorie diets (VLCDs) are diets containing fewer than 800 calories a day. They are considered extreme diets (food is usually replaced with a powdered supplement) and should be viewed as a medical intervention. Typically, VLCDs are undertaken under medical supervision and administered in hospital/clinic settings for a period of three to four months and include counseling, behavior management, nutrition and dieting classes, and support groups. Often, they include an exercise program. Once the diet is completed, dieters on a VLCD gradually return to food intake.

VLCDs are usually recommended for people whose obesity is threatening to their health and who are unable to lose weight through dieting and exercise. People who have insulin-dependent diabetes mellitus, liver disease, kidney disease, or a history of heart disease are warned against this method of losing weight.

For people who can stay on them, VLCDs produce dramatic reductions in weight. Still, they are not a panacea. About 25 percent of people who start a VLCD drop out of the program. Like most extreme dieting programs, VLCDs have a high recidivism rate. As a result, VLCD programs are worthless without careful attention paid to long-term maintenance that incorporates newly learned eating patterns.[12]

Low-fat diets

Low-fat diets are potentially effective techniques for losing weight. With its high-caloric yield, low thermic effect, and almost unlimited capacity for storage, fat is a major threat to weight maintenance. Consequently, Americans are currently fixated on fat-free or low-fat foods. The assumption is that, if a food is low in fat, it is also low in calories. Only 7 percent of Americans are concerned about calories, compared with 60 percent who cite fat as public enemy number one.[28] As a result, although Americans are consuming fewer fat calories percentagewise, they are consuming more total calories from all sources and are getting heavier. (Actual fat intake remains the same as it was during the past ten years. Percentagewise, it dropped from 36 to 34 percent because of an increase in total calories consumed.[29]

Low-fat foods and overcompensatory eating

Although diet experts advocate restricting fat calories, low-fat diets have not been effective for many dieters because of **overcompensatory eating**. This occurs when the consumption of low-fat foods is accompanied by an increase in total calories. Researchers at Pennsylvania State University demonstrated this point when, on separate occasions, they gave a group of women two kinds of yogurt: One was labeled *high fat,* and one was labeled *low fat.* The ingredients were manipulated so that both kinds of yogurt had the same number of calories. A comparison group of women was given the same, but unlabeled, yogurt. Thirty minutes after consuming the yogurt, the women ate lunch. After eating the yogurt labeled *low fat,* subjects compensated by taking in more calories during lunch than they did when they consumed the yogurt labeled *high fat.* This pattern of overcompensatory eating was not observed for the comparison group who ate the unlabeled yogurt. The researchers concluded that, when the women ate yogurt labeled *low fat,* they rationalized that they could indulge more at lunch. When they didn't know what kind of yogurt they had eaten, they were more tuned in to their bodies' physical cues and naturally adjusted the amount they ate.[30]

The attitude that people can eat what they want, in unlimited quantities as long as it is fat free is wrong. Calories do count. Fat-free foods can help people lose weight if they are used properly, if they don't result in overcompensatory consumption of food, and if total calories are kept in line.

Low-fat diets and Olestra

The recent approval of Olestra (Olean) as a fat substitute is partly responsible for the proliferation of low-fat and fat-free foods. Many people unwittingly consume foods in large quantities thinking that, if it is fat-free, it is also calorie free. A fat-free product made with Olestra may turn out to have more total calories (from carbohydrates) than a companion product made with typical ingredients, including fat. For that reason it is important to check labels. The bottom line to look for is total calories. Diets high in Olestra also carry the risk of compromising the body's use of essential nutrients, such as fat-soluble vitamins. For some people the consumption of Olestra causes various abdominal symptoms (see Chapter 6).

Portion sizes and volume eating

Managing caloric intake is made more difficult today than in years past because of not only the increased availability of food but also the way food is marketed,

Wellness On the We
Behavior Change Actio

Get Off the Merry-Go-Round

For many of us, weight control and diet have a strong emotional component that sometimes causes us to make choices that aren't in our best interest. In reality, the diet-weight equation is simple and straightforward: To maintain weight, your caloric intake must be balanced by your caloric expenditure. To lose weight, you must achieve a caloric deficit in which the number of calories you burn exceeds the number of calories you consume. This is the basic principle of weight management. What's your "EQ," or exercise quotient? To find out, go to the Weightloss 2000 website at **www.weightloss2000.com/exer/exer_OI_howfit.htm** and take the quiz to see how much exercise you get each day. If you become just a little more active, you can shed unwanted pounds painlessly.

Boost Your Metabolism—Naturally!

Looking for the "magic bullet" for successful weight management? Magic or not, compelling evidence points to the importance of regular exercise in weight control and weight-loss maintenance. People who lose weight and keep it off almost always exercise daily. Studies that attempt to identify predictors of successful weight maintenance point to physical activity as one of the best markers for long-term success. Walking is considered an excellent form of exercise for shedding pounds. To calculate how many calories you just burned walking, go to the Healthy Ideas website at **www.healthyideas.com/walking/burn** and enter your weight and the duration of your walk, then select your approximate speed and click on "walk it off" to calculate your calories burned.

Eating Disorder Alert

In today's appearance-focused culture, we're all familiar with the terms anorexia nervosa, bulimarexia nervosa, and binge eating. Although these eating disorders differ markedly from each other in many respects, people who have them share a common trait: an intense fear of becoming overweight. Does this describe you? Whether the answer is yes or no, go to the Eating Disorders Recovery Group at **www.mirror-mirror.org/sub7.htm** to complete a self-test that will help you determine whether you may have an eating disorder. The questions presented involve behaviors and feelings that are common to persons who have eating disorders. Whatever your results, remember that you and no one else are the final judge of whether or not you have an eating disorder. If you think you do, you'll find help and support from a wide array of reputable sources.

packaged, and delivered. In trying to get a better value for the dollar, people think *bigger* and *more* are better. Food producers know this and use this approach to gain an advantage over the competition. *Supersized, all-you-can-eat, buffet style eating,* and *a meal in a sandwich* are some of the catch phrases used to increase business. When it comes to calories, the phrases are not all hype. A medium-size baked potato served at a fast-food restaurant weighs 7 ounces compared with the typical potato which weighs 4 ounces; a medium bagel weighs 4 ounces, double the size listed in food composition tables; a medium muffin is 6 ounces, triple the size of regular muffins; a double hamburger at one popular fast-food restaurant has almost three times the number of calories as its single hamburger counterpart; one casual dining restaurant offers a no-frills entree that weighs as much as the Manhattan *Yellow Pages.*

Signs in supermarkets can also encourage people to buy more food. A consumer planning to purchase one carton of ice cream is likely to return home with two cartons if the product is priced at two for $8 instead of at $4 each. When grocers suggest purchase of a specific number of items, shoppers are more likely to buy more than the one or two they intended to buy. Finally, portion size does not equate to serving size. When a restaurant serves an entree, it is likely to be on a larger plate or in a deeper bowl than those used in years past. Pasta bowls, for example, are popular because they are big. Some hold 40 ounces or 2½ pounds.

Do people actually eat more when food is packaged in larger quantities? In trying to answer this question, researchers gave either a 1- or 2-pound bag of M&Ms plus either a "medium" or "jumbo" movie theater–sized tub of popcorn to participants. On average, participants ate 112 M&Ms from the 1-pound bag and 156 from the 2-pound bag. Likewise, the average person ate roughly half a tub of popcorn, whether it was medium or jumbo, which held twice as much as the medium tub. The researchers concluded that people often eat about 50 percent more of pleasure-foods such as candy, chips, and popcorn when they come in bigger packages. With other foods, the increase is usually about 25 percent.[31]

Some common-sense approaches help people avoid overeating in spite of the gluttony of supersized portions of food. See Real-World Wellness: Practical Tips for Coping with Supersize Foods.

Popular diets

Many diets on the market are nutritionally sound, and many are not. Some are potentially hazardous, and many are based on faulty nutritional and physiological concepts. Some require that food be eaten in a certain order and severely restrict foods. Diets such as Jenny

Real-World Wellness

Practical Tips for Coping with Supersize Foods

My friends and I enjoy eating out and prefer fast food or casual dining restaurants. The local restaurants provide some supersize bargains that fit a college budget. My problem is that I am a volume eater—I eat what is served, which is usually much more than I need and certainly more than is good for my waistline. But I live on a tight budget and refuse to throw away good food. What are some strategies that will help me manage my tendency for volume eating without being wasteful?

Here are some suggestions for volume purchasing without waste:

- Eat what you need, not necessarily what is served. Take the rest home.

- Share an entree, appetizer, or dessert. This saves calories and money. (Some restaurants add a surcharge for sharing meals.)

- Start each day with a plan. Think first in terms of your main meal and work around it. If you're planning a prime rib dinner, for example, favor vegetables and fruits for breakfast and lunch. One serving of prime rib is plenty of meat for one day.

- At a buffet, serve yourself small portions and eat slowly. Give your food time to digest. Emphasize vegetables and fruits in your food selections.

- Ask for a half order of an entree.

- Order only appetizers.

- When grocery shopping, plan ahead. Make a list of the amount or quantity of each item to buy. Stick to your list.

- If you're watching calories, learn what makes a serving. One small fistful of candy, french fries, or nuts is a serving. A portion of pasta, rice, or mashed potatoes is the size of your fist (see Chapter 6).

- Picture what you think is a reasonable serving before food is served. If more is served, take it home.

Craig come in premeasured servings. Some require medical supervision. Others impose unrealistic caloric restrictions, and still others make promises based more on fantasy than facts (table 8-2). The Food and Drug Administration (FDA) does not investigate every new fad diet, and many diet plans are published without the FDA's endorsement (see Just the Facts: Outlandish Weight-Loss Promises—What to Do). If a diet is published, it is usually because a publisher sees potential profits from its sales. Publishers know that the advice to "eat less fat and increase physical activity" will not sell books, but fad diets with secret ingredients or magic formulas will.

Because fad diets are unlikely to disappear, identifying some of the characteristics and marketing strategies used by diet promoters to appeal to unwitting consumers is helpful.[14] Fad diets

- Promote quick results
- Stress eating one type of food to the exclusion of others
- Emphasize gimmick approaches, such as eating food in a particular order
- Cite anecdotes and testimonials, usually involving well-known people
- Claim to be a panacea for everyone
- Often promote a secret ingredient
- Often recommend expensive supplements
- Rarely emphasize permanent changes in eating habits
- Usually show little concern for accepted principles of good nutrition (see Chapter 6)
- Are usually cynical about the evidence that comes from the scientific community

In general, dieting is an ineffective weight-management method. The expectation that temporary changes in eating habits will lead to permanent weight loss is unrealistic. Sensible and permanent dietary changes that depend on wise food choices are an excellent way to cut calories and a healthy way to eat. (Table 8-3 demonstrates how to reduce calories that come from fat and cholesterol by making appropriate substitutions.)

Diet Drugs

If recent history is a good predictor of the future, American dieters can anticipate a whole new arsenal of drug solutions for losing weight. Drugs that suppress appetite by stimulating the satiety center in the brain have helped many dieters lose weight temporarily. Drugs marketed under the names *fen-phen* (fenfluramine) and *redux* (dexfenfluramine) during the mid-1990s quickly sold in huge quantities. The popularity of these drugs did not last long, however, because of the plethora of side effects, including death, which eventually led to their withdrawal from the marketplace. Newer-appetite suppressant drugs such as Meridia (sibutramine) offer another pharmacologic solution for dieters. Although early studies of Meridia do not reveal the same side effects as those of its predecessors, the drug is not off the safety hook. Its short-term side effects are substantial and its long-term safety is a big unknown.[33]

Diet drugs are not intended for people who are overweight or marginally obese. Instead, they are intended for the management of severe obesity that does not respond to dieting and exercise regimens and for people whose obesity causes serious health risks that outweigh the possible risks of the medication. Unfortunately, many people are drawn to the quick-fix of a drug, and many physicians are willing to provide a prescription.

The reality, of course, is that drugs offer only a temporary solution. They do not correct the underlying cause of persistent weight gain. People who take weight-loss medications can anticipate the typical weight cycling effect of other dieting strategies with an added problem: Diet drugs are powerful medicines that tamper with the body's delicate balance of hormones and body chemicals. Except for the severely obese, long-term exposure to diet drugs creates harmful effects that may far outweigh the health benefits of fewer pounds of body weight.

Herbal Remedies

Herbal versions of prescription drugs used for losing weight are available in health food stores and many drugstores. Some herbs act as diuretics (chemicals that increase urine production), so they can help people lose water weight. Examples are buchu, celery seed, dandelion, juniper, parsley, and uva ursi. Diuretics are not effective for long-term weight loss because they trigger the body's thirst reflex to replace lost fluids. The body eventually adjusts to the continued use of diuretic herbs and retains water despite them.

Some herbs are stimulants that reportedly increase metabolism and suppress appetite. Examples are ephedra (in Chinese, *ma huang*) and caffeine. Ephedra (or ephedrine) is viewed as a natural form of fen-phen. To be effective, these herbs have to be taken in such large doses that they often cause unpleasant side effects such as insomnia, irritability, jitters, and elevated blood pressure. Ephedra has shown no weight-reduction benefits for mildly overweight people who simply want to lose 5 to 10 pounds.[34]

Another group of herbs produce a feeling of fullness. These are mucilaginous herbs: They absorb fluids, such as might occur in the stomach at mealtime, and expand substantially. The most notable herb in this group is psyllium. Psyllium seed is sold in bulk in herb shops and is also available in drugstores as the common bulk-forming laxative Metamucil. Studies of obese women taking psyllium before meals do not report any weight loss advantage.[34]

Hot, spicy herbs such as red pepper and mustard reportedly increase metabolism, which, in turn, causes more calories to be burned. Hot herbs also stimulate thirst. Researchers who observe weight-loss benefits from these herbs do not know if they are

Table 8-2 Popular Diets

Type	Description	Weight Loss	Health Drawbacks	Pros and Cons
Balanced (available in bookstores)				
Weight Watchers Quick Success Program (Weight Watchers International) *Jane fonda's New Workout & Weight Loss Program* *I Don't Eat (But I Can't Lose Weight)* *Complete University Medical Diet* *Jane Brody's Nutrition Book* *Fit or Fat Target Diet* *Popcorn Plus Diet* *Getting Thin* *Setpoint Diet* *Nautilus Diet* *Take Off Pounds Sensibly (TOPS)* *Overeaters Anonymous*	Recommend 1000 or more calories/day; provide at least 50% carbohydrate, less than 30% fat, 15–20% protein; include variety of foods from all food groups; require regular exercise and lifestyle changes	1–2 lbs./week; promotion of permanent loss of fat, especially if combined with regular exercise	None (no side effects in healthy people); include adequate amount of food in all major food groups; no specialized medical supervisions necessary for healthy people	Provide variety and good nutrition; combined with exercise, can be used as a basis of lifelong weight control; no vitamin supplementation necessary; weight lost is fat, not muscle
High Carbohydrate				
Bloomingdale's Eat Healthy Diet *Pritikin Permanent Weight Loss Manual*	Involve varying calorie levels; encourage increasing carbohydrate intake to more than 60% of diet; can severely restrict protein and fat intake; often advocate exercise and positive lifestyle changes	Gradual or rapid, depending on caloric intake	May be too low in protein and require vitamin and mineral supplements	Safe and effective if protein level and caloric intake are adequate; may be so restrictive as to be difficult to maintain
Formula/Rx*				
HMR (Health Management Resources) Medifast Optifast	Suggest only 800 calories or fewer/day; require dieters to forgo food for about 12 weeks and eat only a protein supplement; after initial fast, gradually reintroduce food; may encourage exercise and lifestyle changes	Very rapid, 3 to 4 lbs./week; protein supplements said to reduce loss of muscle tissue; unknown whether dieters keep weight off	Can produce severe metabolic disturbances, heart beat irregularities, hair loss, dehydration, kidney problems, and sense of feeling cold; vitamins and mineral supplements required	Expensive, with costs as high as $500 per month; only for obese people (20% or more overweight), for those with a weight-related health problem, or for those who have failed on other diets; require close medical supervision

248

Formula/OTC (over the counter)

Diet	Description	Weight loss		
Nutrament Slender Slim Fast	May advocate fewer than 1000 calories/day; replace one or more meals with a low-calorie shake or food bar that contains some combination of protein, carbohydrates, fats, vitamins, minerals	Can be rapid, 3 or more lbs./week if daily caloric level falls below 1000; possible promotion of water and muscle loss; weight often regained	May be low in protein, carbohydrates, vitamins, or minerals; can be dangerous if used as sole source of nutrition	Teach reliance on patented products, not on sound, lifelong eating habits

Low carbohydrate/high protein

Diet	Description	Weight loss		
Dr. Atkins' Diet Revolution *Complete Scarsdale Medical Diet* *Doctor's Quick Weight Loss Diet* (Stillman's "water diet") *The Zone/Protein Power/Healthy for Life*	Involve varying calorie levels; severely restrict carbohydrates such as bread, cereals, grains, starchy vegetables; maintains that carbohydrates cause an increase in insulin, which promotes fat accumulation	Rapid, 3 or more lbs./week; promotion of loss of water and muscle tissue; weight usually regained	Are usually unbalanced; may be very high in saturated fat and cholesterol; can cause fatigue, headaches, nausea, dehydration, and dizziness	Do not promote good eating habits; nutritional claims are unsound; not supported by scientific evidence

Very low calorie

Diet	Description	Weight loss		
Diet Principal Rotation Diet	Suggest fewer than 1000 calories/day for part of diet or for its entirety; based on low-fat, high-carbohydrate foods	Rapid, 3 or more lbs./week; initial loss of water and muscle, not fat; weight usually regained	May be unbalanced and require vitamin and mineral supplements	Usually do not teach long-term good eating habits

Novelty diets

Diet	Description	Weight loss		
Beverly Hills Diet Fit for Life Rice Diet Report Dr. Berger's Immune Power Diet Dr. Debetz Champagne Diet The Rotation Diet The Junk Food Diet Sun Sign Diet *The Diet Bible* The Love Diet	Usually involve fewer than 1000 calories/day; often make false claims that specific foods or combinations burn fat; suggest eating one type of food to exclusion of others	Can be rapid, depending on caloric intake; weight generally regained	Are unbalanced; may be dangerously low in protein; are often deficient in vitamins and minerals; can result in dizziness, diarrhea, gas, hair loss, brittle nails, and loss of vital muscle tissue	Are based on unsound nutritional guidelines; weight lost because of reduction in calories; can be dangerous; may be extremely restrictive and monotonous; may lead to bingeing

Company food programs

Diet	Description	Weight loss		
Diet Center Jenny Craig Nutri/System Physician's Weight Loss Center	Involve portion-control by providing awareness of how much food yields various calorie levels; involve the purchase of prepackaged food; may include vitamin supplements and stringent dieting	Gradual or rapid, depending on degree of participation and caloric intake	May require vitamin supplements; set unrealistic expectations	Include some individual and group counseling, prepackaged foods are expensive; foster preoccupation with clothing sizes and ultra-thinness

*available through a physician or hospital-run program

Just the Facts

Outlandish Weight-Loss Promises— What to Do

Quick and unrealistic weight-loss schemes that promise outlandish results are common, and the number of fad diets promoted in print and video media exceeds the FDA's capacity to check claims and promises.[32] One newspaper recently published an advertiser's claim: "Lose 40 pounds by Christmas." The date of the advertisement was November 3, about seven weeks before Christmas. This ad was an example of blatantly misleading advertising. The responsibility for demonstrating "proof" rests with authors and publishers, who are often motivated more by profits than by credible and reliable information. What can the average consumer do if he or she is exposed to some outrageous claims?

- First and foremost, adopt an attitude of skepticism. If it sounds too good to be true, it probably is. No one diet device or pill can work miracles. Even respectable diet programs require you to eat less and exercise more.

- Call your local chapter of the Better Business Bureau to check claims and reputation before you enlist in a program or buy a product or gadget.

- Register a complaint with the source (newspaper, magazine, television station) of the advertisement.

- If you see a suspect ad, send it to NAD, Consumer Inquiries, 845 Third Avenue, 17th floor, New York, NY 10022.

- And remember, if you don't lose weight with a particular product, don't automatically blame yourself. You may have not failed; the product may have failed you.

from the herbs' effect on metabolism or if they cause people to fill up on water and, therefore, ingest fewer calories.

The view that herbs are safe because they come from nature is misleading. When packaged in large, concentrated doses and taken as pills or supplements, they should be viewed as drugs with potential side effects. From a medicinal point of view, a major shortcoming of herbs is that they are classified as supplements and, therefore, are not subjected to the same scientific testing as are FDA-approved drugs. Medical groups usually recommend that herbal weight-loss

products be avoided, especially those containing ephedrine, until they are adequately tested.[35]

Fasting

Fasting, or complete starvation, has been practiced throughout history. Traditionally, people fasted for religious reasons. Although fasting is still used to achieve spiritual enlightenment by some people, a growing number of people fast for dubious physical reasons: to lose weight, to detoxify their bodies of impurities, and to cure everything from allergies to chronic diseases. The physical benefits of fasting have not been demonstrated in carefully planned studies. Most people who are in good health can tolerate a twenty-four–hour fast without a problem as long as they drink plenty of water. However, prolonged fasting can be harmful and even fatal.

Modified fasts that allow for fruit and vegetable juices in addition to water are generally safer. In terms of weight loss, however, fasting is not an effective strategy. Fasting, by its very nature, is an extreme action. Like any extreme diet plan, when this one is over, the weight returns. The one subjective benefit of fasting is that it may serve as a catalyst to help people create new health habits, gain a new appreciation for food, and learn how to distinguish hunger signals from cravings.[36] If you are healthy and still choose to fast, don't expect returns beyond a mental or spiritual lift. To be safe, don't fast for more than twenty-four hours and drink plenty of fluids. If you are taking medicines, consult your physician before fasting.[37]

Physical Activity

The optimal approach to weight loss combines mild caloric restriction with regular physical activity. Energy expenditure through physical activity should be increased at least 200 to 400 calories per day by increasing physical activity.[38] Together, physical activity and dieting should provide a caloric deficit of 300 to 1000 calories per day. This will lead to weight losses of ½ to 2 pounds per week and a 10 percent weight loss in six months.[13]

Use of calories

One of the obvious benefits of physical activity is that it burns calories. Calories are consumed according to body weight, so heavier people burn more calories per minute than do lighter people for the same activity. Table 8-4 presents the calorie consumption of some physical-fitness activities and a few common physical activities. To use it, multiply your body weight by the coefficient in the calories/min./lb. column and then

Table 8-3 Food Substitutions That Reduce Fat, Cholesterol, and Calories

Instead of eating . . .	Substitute . . .	To save*
1 croissant	1 plain bagel	35 calories, 10 g fat, 13 mg cholesterol
1 cup cooked egg noodles	1 cup cooked macaroni	50 mg cholesterol
1 whole egg	1 egg white	65 calories, 6 g fat, 220 mg cholesterol
1 oz. cheddar cheese	1 oz. part-skim mozzarella	35 calories, 4 g fat, 15 mg cholesterol
1 oz. cream cheese	1 oz. cottage cheese (1% fat)	74 calories, 9 g fat, 29 mg cholesterol
1 tsp. whipping cream	1 tbsp. evaporated skim milk, whipped	32 calories, 5 g fat
3.5 oz. skinless roast duck	3.5 oz. skinless roast chicken	46 calories, 7 g fat
3.5 oz. beef tenderloin, choice, untrimmed, broiled	3.5 oz. beef tenderloin, select, trimmed, broiled	75 calories, 10 g fat
3.5 oz. lamb chop, untrimmed, broiled	3.5 oz. lean leg of lamb, trimmed, broiled	219 calories, 28 g fat
3.5 oz. pork spare ribs, cooked	3.5 oz. lean pork loin, trimmed, broiled	157 calories, 17 g fat
1 oz. regular bacon, cooked	1 oz. Canadian bacon, cooked	111 calories, 12 g fat
1 oz. hard salami	1 oz. extra-lean roasted ham	75 calories, 8 g fat
1 beef frankfurter	1 chicken frankfurter	67 calories, 8 g fat
3 oz. oil-packed tuna, light	3 oz. water-packed tuna, light	60 calories, 6 g fat
1 regular-size serving french fries	1 medium-size baked potato	125 calories, 11 g fat
1 oz. oil-roasted peanuts	1 oz. roasted chestnuts	96 calories, 13 g fat
1 oz. potato chips	1 oz. thin pretzels	40 calories, 9 g fat
1 oz. corn chips	1 oz. plain air-popped popcorn	125 calories, 9 g fat
1 tbsp. sour-cream dip	1 tbsp. bottled salsa	20 calories, 3 g fat
1 glazed doughnut	1 slice angel-food cake	110 calories, 13 g fat, 21 mg cholesterol
3 chocolate sandwich cookies	3 fig bars	4 g fat
1 oz. unsweetened chocolate	3 tbsp. cocoa powder	73 calories, 13 g fat
1 cup ice cream (premium)	1 cup sorbet	320 calories, 34 g fat, 100 mg cholesterol

*The values listed are the most significant savings; smaller differences are not shown. Weights given for meats are edible portions.

multiply this value by the number of minutes spent participating in the activity. For example, to determine the calories expended by a 170-pound person who walks at 4.5 MPH for 30 minutes, do the following:

1. Multiply body weight by calories/min./lb.:

$$170 \text{ lbs.} \times 0.048 \text{ calories/min./lb.}$$
$$= 8.16 \text{ calories/min.}$$

2. Multiply calories/min. by the exercise time in minutes:

$$8.16 \text{ calories/min.} \times 30 \text{ min.} = 244.8 \text{ calories}$$

If this person performs this exercise daily, 1 pound will be lost in approximately fourteen days or 25 pounds will be lost in one year, provided caloric intake is unchanged. The annual weight loss is calculated as follows:

$$3500 \text{ calories/lb.} \div 245 \text{ calories/day} = 14.29 \text{ days/lb.}$$
$$365 \text{ days/year} \div 14.29 \text{ days/lb.} = 25.5 \text{ lbs./year}$$

Follow the example in Assessment Activity 8-2 and apply the directions to your situation or to a hypothetical situation.

Aerobic exercises, such as walking and cycling, contribute significantly to weight loss. Minimal guidelines for maintaining fitness and losing weight require 300 calories per exercise session performed at least three times per week or 200 calories per session performed at least four times per week.[38] Added weight loss can be accomplished by increasing the length of each exercise session and/or the number of sessions per week. High-intensity activities burn extra calories, but low-intensity exercises are recommended to prevent injury. Complete Assessment Activity 8-4 to determine the number of minutes that you should devote to your favorite activities to burn a minimum of 300 calories.

Deconditioned people should start slowly and gradually progress to using 200 to 400 calories per exercise session. For many people, low-intensity, long-duration physical activity, such as walking, is optimal.

Table 8-4 Estimated Caloric Cost of Selected Activities

Activity	Calories/Min./Lb.*
Aerobic dance (vigorous)	0.062
Basketball (vigorous, full-court)	0.097
Bathing, dressing, undressing	0.021
Bed making (and stripping)	0.031
Bicycling (13 MPH)	0.071
Canoeing (flat water, 4 MPH)	0.045
Chopping wood	0.049
Cleaning windows	0.024
Cross-country skiing (8 MPH)	0.104
Gardening	
Digging	0.062
Hedging	
Raking	0 034
Weeding	0.038
Golf (twosome, carrying clubs)	0.045
Handball (skilled, singles)	0.078
Horseback riding (trot)	0.052
Ironing	0.029
Jogging (5 MPH)	0.060
Laundry (taking out and hanging)	0.027
Mopping floors	0.024
Peeling potatoes	0.019
Piano playing	0.018
Rowing (vigorous)	0.097
Running (8 MPH)	0.104
Sawing wood (crosscut saw)	0.058
Shining shoes	0.017
Shoveling snow	0.052
Snowshoeing (2.5 MPH)	0 060
Soccer (vigorous)	0.097
Swimming (55 yds./min.)	0.088
Table tennis (skilled)	0.045
Tennis (beginner)	0.032
Walking (4.5 MPH)	0.048
Writing while seated	0.013

*Multiply calories/min./lb. by your body weight in pounds and then multiply that product by the number of minutes spent in the activity.

For weight loss, all calories do not have to be expended in one exercise session. Three 15-minute walks in a day result in a substantial expenditure of energy. Any physical activity above the amount normally done in a day is a bonus for weight control. The cumulative effect of activities such as walking upstairs, mowing the lawn, and mopping floors can be combined with a structured exercise program to produce steady, safe weight loss.

Exercise stimulates metabolism

Basal metabolic rate (BMR) is the energy required to sustain life when the body is in a rested and fasted state. BMR is measured in calories and represents the energy needed to keep the heart, lungs, liver, kidneys, and all other organs functioning. More calories are used to maintain BMR than to perform any other function.

Metabolism is affected by age, gender, nervous system activity, secretions from endocrine glands, nutritional status, sleep, fever, climate, body surface area, and amount of muscle tissue. Because men have more muscle tissue than do women, their BMRs average 5 to 10 percent higher. See Assessment Activity 8-3 to learn how to estimate your BMR.

Muscle tissue stimulates metabolism. Therefore, physical activity is a key strategy for weight management. This is especially true for people as they get older (see Wellness Across the Generations: Age and Weight Gain Do Not Have to Go Together).

The key to weight control

Although scientifically controlled studies have not yet proven that physical activity is instrumental in losing weight, they provide compelling evidence of its importance in weight control and weight-loss maintenance. People who lose weight and keep it off almost always exercise daily. Studies that attempt to identify predictors of successful weight maintenance point to physical activity as one of the best markers for long-term success.[13] Researchers at the University of California at Davis found that 90 percent of women who had lost 20 pounds and kept it off for at least two years were avid exercisers; of the women who had regained the weight, only 35 percent were physically active. At the Baylor College of Medicine in Houston, another group of researchers put 160 obese adults on one of three year-long weight-loss programs: diet-only, exercise-only, or exercise and diet. Everyone lost weight. (The exercise and diet group lost the most). But two years later, the exercise-only participants were the only ones to keep the weight off.[39] Other large-scale studies that follow men and women in weight-loss programs for ten years consistently show that major weight gain is much more likely to occur in people who are sedentary than in those who are physically active.[13] Thus, although physical activity as a singular strategy has modest effects on weight loss, it is the key strategy for lifelong weight control. More importantly, moderate exercise improves health and reduces risk factors associated with morbidity and mortality for the obese just as it does for normal-weight people.

Wellness Across the Generations

Age and Weight Gain Do Not Have to Go Together

Weight gain is one experience people ages 25 to 65 have in common. From the time people embark on their professional careers until the time they start thinking about retirement, they often experience creeping weight gain, sometimes obesity. Often they blame the aging process. But is creeping obesity a function of biological factors that are part of the aging process, or are other factors involved? Rather than aging, it is more likely to be a higher standard of living that is responsible for such weight gain. A higher standard of living usually results in an easier, less active life. Improvements in standard of living go hand-in-hand with labor-saving devices that add convenience and, of course, save energy. Many experts believe that weight gain associated with increased age is a function of the subtle changes in metabolism caused by less muscle tissue, which is caused by less physical activity.

Metabolism is an important issue for the weight-conscious person, because 70 percent of our energy is expended to support basic life processes. Muscle tissue burns more energy at rest than does fat tissue, so changes in body composition that favor muscle tissue over fat tissue provide a calorie-burning advantage throughout the day. Conversely, changes in body composition that favor fat over muscle lower the body's metabolism and promote weight gain. Metabolism declines with age, primarily because of the physical inactivity and muscle loss that often accompany aging. The annual decrease in BMR beginning at 25 years of age, though imperceptible, has serious ramifications for weight management and accounts for a significant amount of the weight gained with age. The loss of muscle tissue is equal to 3 to 5 percent every decade after age 25. The subsequent decline in BMR produces changes in body composition. Exercise and physical activities are the keys to weight management because they increase or sustain muscle tissue, thus accelerating metabolism and using calories.

Exercise intensity and fat loss

In Chapter 6 a distinction is made between the intensity and duration of exercise and the accompanying use by the body of energy nutrients. In general, carbohydrates are the main source of energy for high-intensity exercise, and fat is the main source of energy for low-intensity exercise sustained for a prolonged time. (The body instinctively spares its protein reserve except when needed for activities of exceptional duration.) The fat-burning benefit of low-intensity exercise should be a source of encouragement for people trying to shed extra fat, making exercise a viable option for most people. Walking, gardening, yard work, housework, and golfing (assuming you're walking) burn fat calories.

Does this mean that high-intensity exercises are of little value as a weight-management strategy? The answer is no, because the overall goal is to create a caloric deficit, and calories count regardless of exercise intensity. Physically demanding activities such as

Strenuous physical activities that develop muscle, such as rock climbing, can also increase your metabolism.

jogging, running, rock climbing, swimming, cycling, and aerobics burn more total calories than do low-intensity activities if participation time is held constant; they just require a higher proportion of fuel from glycogen stores than from fat. Still, both energy sources are tapped. As pointed out by one fitness expert, if you burn 240 calories exercising for a half hour at a low intensity, 41 percent of those calories come from fat, giving you a fat loss of 96 calories. If you exercise for the same amount of time at a high intensity, you burn 450 calories, including 108 fat calories, even though the percentage of energy supplied by fat is only 24 percent.[40] The point of this example is not to discourage participation in low-intensity activities but only to suggest that, if you're in good health and enjoy vigorous exercise, you do not need to limit yourself to low-intensity exercise. Exercising on a consistent basis is the best strategy for managing weight, regardless of intensity level.

Regular Exercise Is the Key to Weight Management: Make It Fun

Whatever kind of exercise you do on a regular basis, it is the best strategy for weight management. If your motivation for exercise is based solely on external factors, such as losing weight or preventing disease, it is unlikely that exercise will become a permanent fixture in your lifestyle. Many experts believe that physical activity is more likely to become a lifestyle pattern if it is motivated by intrinsic factors, such as fun, pleasure, and feeling good. Losing weight is a good reason to start exercising, but you probably won't sustain exercise unless you learn to enjoy it and to value the way it makes you feel. People who are consistently physically active shift their focus from the outcome (weight loss) to the process of exercise itself. Regular exercisers want to work out because they like it and it makes them feel better.[41] (For tips on making exercise fun, see Nurturing Your Spirituality: Fun Is the Key to Regular Exercise for Weight Maintenance.) With this approach to exercise, even if weight loss is modest, overall health is improved.

It is easy to lose perspective when exercising for weight management. Remember that the primary determinant of health benefits is the total quantity of physical activity performed, rather than the type, duration, and intensity of the activity itself, regardless of weight status.[42]

Combining Dietary Modification and Exercise

Because caloric consumption and expenditure are involved in weight management, both should be manipu-

Nurturing Your Spirituality

Fun Is the Key to Regular Exercise for Weight Maintenance

Experts have shifted the paradigm of weight management from counting calories burned in exercise to promoting movement that is social, playful, and pleasurable. If exercise is fun, if it makes you feel good about yourself, and if it provides that mini-vacation each day (a time and place where nothing else interferes), it is more likely to be incorporated permanently into daily living. As noted by one expert, "Inner joy is the key to dutiful exercise. The body fails to persist if the soul is in rebellion."[43]

Do you want to move from an occasional dreaded workout to one that you look forward to on a regular basis? Here are some tips passed on by others who once were couch potatoes:

- First, examine your likes and dislikes. Think in terms of activities that are fun for you. These may be taking a stroll in a park, working in the flower garden, skating to class, or joining a fitness club.

- Build relationships with people who share your interests and goals. Workout partners often provide incentive and encouragement for working out.

- Tell people if you notice improvements in their energy level and in appearance after exercising. Not only will they feel better but so will you, and the compliment will likely be returned at some point.

- Join a fitness club or participate in a structured fitness program that will increase your repertoire of skills and activities.

- Find a comfortable workout environment with a supportive staff.

- Vary your activities. Variety is the antidote for boredom; cross-training is the key for many longtime exercisers.

lated to be effective. Combining sensible exercise and sensible changes in eating habits that can be maintained for life is the most effective approach to permanent weight management. Dieting alone can promote significant weight loss, but a substantial component of the weight loss may be lean tissue. Physical activity alone results in modest fat loss and an increase in lean body mass. Combination strategies involving both food restriction and physical activity meet the goals of

Real-World Wellness

Behavioral Strategies for Reshaping Your Eating Habits

In Chapter 1, I learned about intervention strategies for changing behavior. In this chapter I've learned about the importance of gaining control over the tendency to overeat. How can I apply behavioral principles from Chapter 1 to my goal of curbing overeating?

Try the following strategies:

- Eat in a certain place—not in every room of your home.
- Eliminate from your immediate environment all food that can be eaten without careful preparation.
- Always eat at a carefully set place at the table and eat only one helping of planned foods.
- Prepare only enough food for one meal.
- Eat slowly.
- Chew each bite twenty-five to fifty times.
- Set down your utensils after every mouthful.
- Partway through the meal, stop and relax without eating for two to three minutes.
- Leave some food on your plate at each meal.
- Plan to eat some meals alone. (There is a tendency to overeat in social situations.)
- Eat a carefully balanced diet so that you are not deprived of a particular food element.

weight management most effectively: These strategies improve body composition by promoting weight loss, fat loss, and lean-tissue gain.

Behavioral Effects

Some evidence suggests that obese people are more likely than normal-weight people to eat in response to external cues. A clock that says it is suppertime; media messages advertising food and beverages; and the sight, sound, and aroma of food are more apt to elicit eating behavior in the obese. This tendency is the basis of the "externality" hypothesis: If people can learn to eat in response to external cues, they can also learn to recognize cues that stimulate eating behavior, substitute other behaviors for eating, and use techniques that decrease the amount of food eaten. As a result of this training the response to external cues should be reduced and replaced by attention to internal hunger signals. Many techniques have been developed over the past twenty years that may assist people in resisting the tendency to eat indiscrimi-

nately or to overeat. Generally, these techniques employ one or more of the following approaches:

1. *Self-monitoring:* A journal or daily log records food consumption, physical activities, and circumstances related to eating. In a recent study of dieters from two weeks before Thanksgiving until two weeks after New Year's, it was found that participants who were most consistent in monitoring food intake were also most successful in losing weight and keeping it off.[44]
2. *Control of precursors to eating:* The events and circumstances that elicit eating and overeating are identified.
3. *Control of eating:* Behavioral modification techniques are used to control, change, or modify specific eating behaviors. (See Real-World Wellness: Behavioral Strategies for Reshaping Eating Habits.)
4. *Reinforcement through the use of rewards:* Rewards tied to the achievement of behavioral goals are identified and used.

These techniques may be useful especially if they are combined with sensible food choices and exercise.

Eating Disorders

Anorexia nervosa (anorexia), bulimarexia nervosa (*bulimia*), and *binge-eating disorder* are eating disorders familiar to most Americans. Although they differ in key ways, they share a common factor: an intense fear of becoming overweight. Starvation is the primary strategy of the anoretic, but the bulimic gorges and then purges by vomiting or using diuretics and laxatives. Bulimics seldom starve to the point of emaciation; instead they are usually at or slightly above normal weight.[14] People may exhibit characteristics of anorexia and bulimia, severely limiting food intake and also purging. Such people are referred to as *anorexic-bulimic*. Most bulimics do not become anorexic, but many anorectics practice bulimic behavior.

Young females account for the majority of both disorders. Although the number of people who have full-blown bulimia or anorexia is small, symptoms of these disorders, such as induced vomiting and an extreme fear of gaining weight, are present in alarming numbers, especially among college students. Nearly one-fourth of college women and 14 percent of college men have been reported to engage in binge eating at least once a week.[13]

Anorexia Nervosa

The chief characteristic of **anorexia nervosa** is a refusal to maintain a minimally normal weight for age and height. Refusal to eat is the hallmark of the disease, regardless of whether other practices, such as binge-purge cycles, occur. Although specific causes of anorexia have not been identified, a combination of biological, social, and psychological factors contributes to the disorder. Support for an organic influence has centered on the hypothalamus (the portion of the brain reputed to house the appetite center) and the pituitary gland (the master gland of the body). Sociocultural theories focus on the compulsion of adolescent girls to become and remain lean. This exaggerated goal manifests itself at a time when girls are naturally depositing fat.

Anorexia is characterized by extreme weight loss, amenorrhea (absence of a menstrual period), and a variety of psychological disorders culminating in an obsessive preoccupation with the attainment of thinness. Fortunately, most anorectics recover fully after one experience with the disease. However, the longer a person practices anorexic behaviors, the slimmer the chance for recovery. Just the Facts: Criteria for Diagnosing

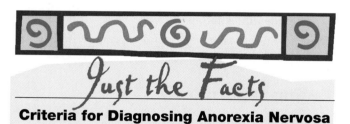

Just the Facts

Criteria for Diagnosing Anorexia Nervosa

The American Psychiatric Association [45] has identified the following criteria for a diagnosis of anorexia nervosa:

- Weight change
  - unwillingness to maintain minimal normal body weight for the person's age and height
  - weight loss that leads to the maintenance of a body weight that is 15 percent below normal
  - failure to gain the amount of weight expected during a period of growth, resulting in a body weight that is 15 percent below normal
- Inordinate fear of gaining weight or becoming fat despite being significantly underweight
- Disturbed and unrealistic perceptions of body weight, size, or shape; feeling of being "fat" although emaciated; possible perception of one specific part of the body as "too fat"
- Absence of at least three menstrual cycles for women when they would normally be expected to occur (amenorrheic women have a normal menstrual cycle only during administration of hormone therapy)
- Rigid dieting; maintenance of rigid control in lifestyle; security found in control and order
- Rituals involving food and excessive exercise

Anorexia Nervosa lists the criteria that have been developed by the American Psychiatric Association for diagnosing anorexia.[45]

When confronted, anorectics typically deny the existence of a problem and the weight-loss behaviors that have resulted in their emaciated physical appearance. They also avoid medical treatment, refuse the well-intended advice of family and friends regarding professional assistance, and submit to treatment only under protest. Anorexia is a subtle disease, and anorectics become secretive in their behaviors. They are evasive, and many hide their disease in deep denial even while undergoing treatment, making the diagnosis especially difficult.

The course of treatment for anorexia is complex, involving a coordinated effort by several health care specialists. Hospitalization is often required because anorectics may have to be fed intravenously or by some other method if they cannot or will not eat. Medications that stimulate the appetite and medications that calm the patient are usually necessary. Nutritional counseling and psychological counseling—individual, group, and family—are integral components of treatment (see Real-World Wellness: Helping a Friend Overcome an Eating Disorder). Finally, behavior modification techniques are used to help change the perceptions and lifestyle of the anorectic. At this point, no single treatment has proved to be unusually successful in the treatment of anorectic patients.

Bulimia (Bulimarexia Nervosa)

Bulimia is characterized by alternate cycles of binge eating and restrictive eating. Binge eating is distinguished from ordinary overeating in that it involves the consumption of a large amount of food in a relatively brief period of time (that is, within a one- to two-hour period) and is accompanied by lack of control. Bingeing is nearly always done in private; in public, the bulimic tends to eat normal or even less than normal amounts. Unlike the occasional splurge almost everyone has, the bulimic becomes compulsive and habitual and often resorts to secretive eating. The psychological aftermath is guilt, shame, and self-disgust. Binges are usually followed by purging, primarily by self-induced vomiting supplemented with laxatives and diuretics. The physical and psychological ramifications of such a struggle include esophageal inflammation, erosion of tooth enamel caused by repeated vomiting, the possibility of electrolyte imbalances, and altered mood states, particularly anxiety and depression.

The diagnostic criteria for bulimia are given in Just the Facts: Criteria For Diagnosing Bulimia.[45] These criteria specify that, to be diagnosed a bulimic, a person must vomit at least twice a week for three months. Binge-purge cycles may occur daily, weekly, or in other

Real-World Wellness

Helping a Friend Overcome an Eating Disorder

I suspect a friend of mine is struggling with an eating disorder. How can I help without making matters worse? Are there some internet resources available?

Try doing the following:

- Talk to the person alone.
- Tell the person why you are concerned.
- Be nonjudgmental; ask clarifying questions; listen carefully.
- Offer to go with the person to talk to someone.
- Encourage her or him to verbalize feelings.
- Show how much you care by asking frequently how the person is doing.
- Show an interest in the person's life outside of eating.
- Enlist the help of a counselor if you think the disorder is severe; however, eating disorders are usually not emergency situations.
- Anticipate and accept that denial and anger are part of the illness.

Avoid doing the following:

- Threaten or challenge the person.
- Give advice about weight loss.
- Get into an argument.
- Try to keep track of the person's food consumption.
- Try to force the person to eat.
- Be patronizing by being overly caring.
- Try to be a hero or rescuer; the person may resent such efforts.

Here are some internet sites that serve as good resources:

- Eating Disorders Awareness and Prevention, Inc., at www.hometown.aol.com/edapinc/home.html
- National Eating Disorders Information Centre at www.nedic.on.ca
- American Dietetics Association at www.eatright.org
- The Center for Eating Disorders at www.eatingdisorder.org
- Pale Reflections Weekly Newsletter for Those with Eating Disorders at www.members.aol.com/paleref/index.html

Just the Facts

Criteria for Diagnosing Bulimia

The American Psychiatric Association[45] has identified the following criteria for a diagnosis of bulimia:

- Episodic secretive binge eating characterized by rapid consumption of large quantities of food in a short time; never overeating in front of others
- At least two eating binges per week for at least three months
- Loss of control over eating behavior while eating binges are in progress
- Frequent purging after eating; using techniques such as self-induced vomiting, laxatives, or diuretics; engaging in fasting or strict dieting; or engaging in vigorous exercise
- Constant and continual concern with body shape, size, and weight
- Erosion of teeth; swollen glands
- Purchase of syrup of ipecac

intervals. Bulimic behaviors range from binge eating frequently or from time-to-time, binge eating with a feeling of being unable to control food intake, severely restricting the diet between binge periods, and binge eating followed by purging. Purging in the form of laxatives, vomiting, diuretics, fasting, and excessive exercise follows in the hope that weight gain will be blunted. Because many people with bulimia engage in binge-purge practices in isolation and because bulimics are often not excessively thin, they cannot be diagnosed easily or by their appearance.

Bulimics are treated similarly to anorectics except that hospitalization is usually not required. In addition to nutritional and psychological counseling, treatment often includes antidepressant medication because bulimia is associated with clinical depression. Treatment focuses on correcting typical bulimic behaviors, such as "all-or-none" thinking: "If I'm not perfect, I'm a failure, so one slipup—one cookie—justifies a binge." Generally, psychotherapy aims primarily to help a person with self-acceptance and to be less concerned with body weight.[14]

Binge-Eating Disorder

Binge-eating disorder is similar to bulimia in two ways: (1) it involves eating large amounts of food in a short period of time, and (2) it is accompanied by a sense of lack of control regarding eating. It is different from bulimia in that it is not associated with compensatory behaviors, such as purging, fasting, and excessive exercise. When binge eating occurs on average at least two days a week for six months, it becomes an eating disorder. The American Psychiatric Association has identified additional criteria for this disorder[45] (See Just the Facts: Criteria for Diagnosing Binge-Eating Disorder.)

Underweight

A small number of people who are not anorectic or bulimic are naturally thin, and some of them are dissatisfied with their appearance. Being underweight presents as much of a cosmetic problem for affected people as obesity does for the obese person. Many underweight people find it more difficult to gain a pound than it is for obese people to lose one.

In their attempts to gain weight, many very lean people consume large quantities of food, particularly those that are rich in calories. Unfortunately, these foods are also high in fat and sugar. This eating pattern is unhealthy for anyone, regardless of body

weight. The preferred approach is to combine muscle-building exercises with three well-balanced, nutritious meals supplemented by two nutritious snacks. The amount and type of weight gain should be closely monitored. Fat stores should not be increased unless the person is extremely thin and on the verge of dipping into stores of essential fat.

Principles of Weight Management: Putting It All Together

The best approach to weight management is the most obvious: maintaining a moderate lifestyle so that excess weight is not gained. In summary, the basic principles of weight maintenance and weight loss are the following:

1. Avoid the obsession with body weight. It is important to remember that body weight per se is not the most important issue; rather, body composition is. Modest weight gain distributed in the wrong places increases health risks. Conversely, significant weight gain in the form of muscle tissue enhances health and well-being. Women who had no weight problem when they were young can, with reasonable safety, add up to 15 pounds as they get older; most men who have had no weight problem can add up to 10 pounds.[46] Much greater weight gain, however, can lead to increased risk of early death and disability. You should consider losing weight if it becomes excessive or if you have a family history of disease that may be worsened by excess weight.

2. The most important factor in weight maintenance is physical activity. Americans weigh more now than ever before because of sedentary lifestyles. The challenge is either to sacrifice some labor-saving devices and their convenience or to consciously seek opportunities to impose extra physical demands on the body. This may mean choosing the stairs rather than the elevator or walking to class rather than driving. Participating in physical activities on a consistent basis is the best way to prevent excessive weight gain. It is also the best way to maintain weight loss over time. Almost all people who successfully lose weight and keep it off exercise daily. Exercise is the best way to overpower the body's set point for fatness.

Exercise is just as important to the chronically obese and overweight as it is to those who are trying to lose or maintain weight. Obese people who are fit enjoy the same health benefits as normal-weight people.

Just the Facts

Criteria for Diagnosing Binge-Eating Disorder

The American Psychiatric Association[45] has identified the following criteria for a diagnosis of binge-eating disorder:

- Recurrent episodes of eating an amount of food that is clearly larger than most people would eat in a similar circumstance

- Binge eating that occurs, on average, at least two days a week for six months

- A sense of lack of control over eating

- Binge eating associated with any three of the following:

  - eating large amounts of food when not feeling hungry

  - eating alone because of embarrassment over the amount of food eaten

  - eating much more rapidly than normal

  - eating far beyond comfort level

  - feeling guilty or depressed after eating

The ACSM recommends exercise that burns approximately 300 calories per session performed at least three times a week. This is equivalent to a 3-mile walk for most people. Remember, energy expenditure through exercise does not have to occur at one time. The effects of physical activity are cumulative and reinforce the value of activity spread throughout the day. The key issue in exercising is consistency and moderation. Plan an activity program that can be sustained one year and five years from now.

3. Follow the Food Guide Pyramid by eating nutrient-dense foods and stress consumption of complex carbohydrates. Calories from fat convert easily to fat, with only 3 percent being lost in the digestive process. By comparison, 25 percent of carbohydrate calories are lost in the process.

   Emphasize fiber in your diet. Because of fiber's high satiety value, people who eat a great deal of it usually consume fewer total calories at mealtime. An added benefit is that fiber may help block the digestion of some of the fat consumed with it. The less fat digested, the less absorbed in the bloodstream.[47]

4. Avoid volume eating. Calories count regardless of their source. The penchant to practice compensatory eating behavior may be especially common among people who choose low-fat and/or low-calorie products. People are eating food in larger quantities. Avoid buffet-style, all-you-can-eat restaurants. Practice behavioral strategies that make volume eating more difficult. And when eating low-fat or low-calorie foods, be aware of the tendency to overcompensate by eating more food. Remember, two servings of a low-fat food that contains 5 grams of fat yields 90 total fat calories and may actually exceed the number of fat calories in one serving of the regular, high-fat version.

5. Set realistic goals. Don't be misled by messages and advertisements that promise huge weight loss in a short period of time. Weight loss per week usually should not exceed 1 to 2 pounds. The ideal approach is to lose pounds at the same rate at which they were gained. In trying to set goals, ask yourself these questions: What is the least I have weighed as an adult, for at least a year? Based on past experiences what is the most weight I can expect to lose? Then, adjust your goals upward. Realize that people who succeed at maintaining a healthy weight almost never achieve their ideal. They become satisfied with a midpoint.[48]

6. Make a gradual lifestyle change. Such change represents a calm, deliberate approach rather than a frenetic "lose it now" attitude. A 200-pound person should exercise, reduce calories, and eat like a 180-pound person to become a 180-pound person. Once the weight is lost, the person cannot revert to the habits of a 200-pound person. A diet is only successful if the weight does not return.

7. Anticipate a plateau. During the first week of a diet, weight loss comes primarily from loss of protein, glycogen, and water but very little fat. As the body adjusts to a diet, fat loss increases. This adjustment takes about a week on a moderate diet and still longer when the diet is severe. Many dieters experience a plateau after about three to four weeks, not because they are suddenly cheating but because they have gained water weight while still losing body fat. If physically active, dieters may gain lean body mass and lose fat while maintaining weight. If weight loss is drastic during the early stages, it induces an adaptive response in the body that slows down metabolism. The body resists drastic change of any sort. Once its internal signals recognize a substantial reduction in caloric intake, it slows down to conserve fuel. After losing 20 to 30 pounds, expect to reach a stable plateau.

8. Avoid diet pills, special formula diets, all-you-can-eat diets, fat-burning concoctions, skin creams, and other fad diets. Some of these fads impose health risks, and others simply don't work or, if they do, their results are temporary and lead to weight cycling. The more extreme the diet, the less likely the weight loss will be permanent.

   The new generation of diet pills currently being investigated as a potential solution for the chronically obese should be viewed with caution. Even if such pills prove successful, they must be taken for life and they may have side effects as harmful to health as the extra weight. Many experts are reluctant to endorse a lifelong pharmaceutical solution to obesity.

9. Avoid very low-calorie diets. Such diets decrease BMR 10 to 20 percent, making weight loss success even harder. Results of four national surveys show that most people try to lose weight by eating 1000 to 1500 calories a day. Diets that cut calories to under 1200 (if you're a woman) or 1400 (if you're a man), however, do not allow enough food to be satisfying over the long haul.[15] A diet should minimize hunger and fatigue. Eating fewer than 1200 calories also makes it difficult to get minimal amounts of certain nutrients and promotes temporary loss of fluids rather than permanent loss of fat.

10. Develop an eating plan that includes easily obtained foods.

11. Develop a less rigid lifestyle, one that reduces the need to consciously control what is eaten. Maintaining weight loss is the antithesis of counting every calorie. In studies of children, researchers found that subjects who had the most body fat were those with the most controlling parents when it came to the amount of food eaten.[49] The studies found that children whose parents allowed them to be most spontaneous about food—eat when they were hungry and not necessarily finish all the food given to them—showed a natural instinct for regulating their own calories. Although parents are responsible for making sure children eat healthy food, children themselves are capable of figuring out how much to eat. The researchers concluded that these internal cues for food regulation, when interrupted by parents, may lead to overeating later in childhood and contribute to obesity later on. Parents are urged to relax control over the amount of food their children eat and to adopt a more flexible attitude toward their own dietary habits.

12. Avoid fasting and restrictive dieting. These practices often lead to a preoccupation with food, weight, and/or dieting. Dieting should allow people to attend parties, eat at restaurants, and participate in normal activities. People erroneously assume that if they have eaten just a little bit of a "forbidden" food, they have "crossed the line." Foods are neither "good" nor "bad." Labeling them as such often promotes a denial-guilt-preoccupation cycle in which one slight deviation from a diet or food choice is interpreted as a failure: A forbidden food is eaten (denial), a sense of relief from restraint leads to a binge, the binge leads to guilt and a feeling of failure, and both denial and guilt exacerbate the preoccupation. The preoccupation leads back to denial and the cycle continues. This cycle exerts considerable pressure on the dieter. To avoid the dissonance that comes with failure, the dieter often abandons attempts to lose weight. Given moderation and discretion, almost any food can be enjoyed. Food is one of life's pleasures, so you need not avoid any one food. If it is high in fat and calories, eat a small portion. If you do not deny yourself, you might not feel compelled to cheat.

13. Avoid meal skipping. One strategy that surprises some dieters with its effectiveness is eating frequent small meals and snacks. The more often a person eats, the less hungry that person feels and the less food that person will eat.[50] Eating five to six times a day—breakfast, a midmorning snack, lunch, an afternoon snack, dinner, and a before-bed snack—might require some retraining. Keep portions small and emphasize fruits and vegetables.

Resist the temptation to skip breakfast. People who eat a healthy breakfast generally feel less hungry throughout the day. Recent studies suggest that breakfast eaters take in significantly less fat, less cholesterol, and more fiber over the course of a day than do people who skip breakfast. Breakfast eaters also tend to be leaner.[51]

14. Form a buddy system or join a support group. The support and encouragement of a friend or relative are often the difference between success and failure.

15. If you stop smoking, don't be discouraged by subsequent weight gain. If you are a heavy smoker, you can expect on average an increase in weight of 10 pounds. That's not enough to make most smokers obese. From a health perspective, you would have to gain 100 to 150 pounds after quitting to make your health risks as high as when you smoked.[51]

16. Don't indulge yourself in self-blame for past failures. View past dieting attempts objectively as a psychologist would. Focus more on what you learned from past experiences. Most people who are successful at maintaining weight loss are not successful in their first attempt. In studies that track dieters listed in the Weight Control Registry, 90 percent of them are repeaters. In some studies, nearly 60 percent of dieters were found to have made five attempts before achieving success.[52] Rather than blaming yourself, reflect on what you learned about yourself and what worked and didn't work.

17. Finally, accept yourself. Before trying to lose weight, determine how great a risk your weight poses to your health. People at risk for chronic conditions, such as hypertension and type II diabetes, for example, often improve dramatically with a modest weight loss. Some people, however, are overweight despite their best efforts to reduce. For such people, striving to attain a certain weight may be futile and even damaging to health. If a person was overweight throughout childhood, chances are that person will never be thin. Be realistic and aim for a healthy weight for you, not for an actor or actress. Everyone cannot be skinny. Everyone can try to be healthy.

Summary

- Americans' obsession with body weight is evidenced by the large number of women, men, and even children who are trying to lose weight at any given time.
- A healthy weight is defined as a BMI of 19.0 to 24.9. Overweight occurs with a BMI of 25 or over. Obesity occurs with a BMI of 30 or over. Only 41 percent of U.S. adults meet current standards for healthy weight.
- Obesity is a risk factor for coronary heart disease, stroke, hypertension, LDL cholesterol, some forms of cancer, impaired glucose tolerance, osteoarthritis, gallbladder disease, and sleep apnea.
- Obesity occurs when fat cells increase excessively either in size (hypertrophy) or in number (hyperplasia). Most obesity is adult-onset and caused by hypertrophy.
- Heredity and set point are the major biological factors associated with obesity.
- The development and distribution of body fat is under substantial genetic control.
- Physical activity is the best way to alter the body's set point for fatness.
- Overeating and lack of physical activities are the major behavioral explanations of obesity.
- Dietary intake of too much fat and too many calories is the major cause of obesity.
- Dietary fat has less of a thermogenic effect than do carbohydrate and protein and therefore is more efficiently and easily stored as fat tissue.
- The general decline in physical activity is highly correlated with the rise in obesity.
- Engaging in a physically active lifestyle is the best way to prevent weight gain.
- Approximately 70 percent of the energy liberated from food is expended to support BMR.
- Physical activity improves body composition, increases BMR, improves insulin sensitivity, and increases oxygen capacity and glycogen storage in muscles.
- Weight loss requires a caloric deficit in which food intake and exercise are manipulated so that caloric expenditure exceeds caloric intake.
- Complex forces influence the success of weight-loss efforts and help to explain why people respond so differently to similar dieting strategies.
- Low-fat diets often result in overcompensatory eating behaviors as a result of which the dieter ends up consuming more total calories.
- A desirable long-term goal for losing weight is 1 to 2 pounds per week until about 10 percent of excess weight is lost. A six-month maintenance period is suggested before more weight loss is attempted.
- Diet-only strategies should provide a loss of at least 1200 calories per day for women and 1500 for men.
- The optimal approach to weight loss combines mild caloric restriction with regular physical activity. Together these two strategies should provide a caloric deficit that does not exceed 500 to 1000 calories per day.
- A good physical activity prescription for weight loss is to manipulate exercise intensity and duration to burn 200 to 400 calories per session.
- Diet drugs are not intended for people who are simply overweight or only marginally obese. The harmful effects of long-term exposure to diet drugs may outweigh the health benefits of losing weight.
- Low-intensity exercises sustained for a prolonged period of time are effective in burning fat calories. However, regardless of intensity level, exercising on a consistent basis is the best strategy for managing weight.
- Anorexia, bulimia, and binge eating are three potentially destructive eating disorders with complex causes.

Review Questions

1. What evidence exists to support the idea that Americans are obsessed with weight control?
2. In terms of BMIs, what are the definitions of *healthy weight*, *overweight*, and *obesity?*
3. What is the pattern of growth of adipose cells from birth through puberty?
4. What health problems and chronic conditions are associated with obesity?
5. What is the relationship between obesity and morbidity and mortality?
6. What are the major biological and behavioral factors that help to explain obesity?
7. What evidence can you use to support the existence of an influential role of heredity in the development of obesity?
8. What does *set point* mean in reference to body shape and body weight? What strategy is best for altering a person's set point for fatness?
9. What dieting strategies need to be emphasized in weight-loss programs?
10. Compare and contrast dieting and exercise as strategies for (a) losing weight and (b) maintaining or preventing weight gain.
11. What is weight cycling?
12. Why is the thermogenic effect of food an important issue in weight management?
13. What is the relationship between BMR, physical activity, and body composition?
14. What are the signs and symptoms of anorexia, bulimia, and binge-eating disorder?
15. What are ten principles that should be considered when structuring an approach to weight management and/or weight loss?

References

1. Mayo. Foundation for Medical Education and Research. 1998. Body Image: What Do You See in the Mirror? Available on-line at www.mayohealth.org/mayo/9704/htm/body_ima.htm.

2. Consumers Union. 1998. Top selling diets: Lots of gimmicks, little solid evidence. *Consumer Reports* 63(1):60.

3. Tufts University. 1998. Sniffing your way to weight loss? *Tufts University Health and Nutrition Letter* 16(2):6.

4. Environmental Nutrition, Inc. 1996. Advertisers get away with incredible weight-loss claims; how not to succumb. *Environmental Nutrition* 20(1):3.

5. Editors. 1996. Mission impossible. *People* 45(22):65.

6. U.S. Department of Health and Human Services. 1998. *Healthy People 2010 Objectives: Draft for Public Comment.* Washington, D.C.: U.S. Government Printing Office.

7. Lans, K. 1999. *When Minor Flaws Loom Large in the Mirror.* Available on-line at www.brown.edu/administration/george_street_Journal/v22/v22n5/dysmorph.html.

8. Womancomnetwork. 1998. *Imagetalk—Women's Wire on Body Image: Role Models?* Available on-line at www.womenswire.com/image/models2.html.

9. McDowell, M. A., et al. 1994. *Energy and Macro-Nutrient Intakes of Persons Ages 2 Months and Over in the United States: Third National Health and Nutrition Examination Survey, Phase I, 1988–91. Advanced Data from Vital and Health Statistics; No. 255.* Hyattsville, Md.: National Center for Health Statistics.

10. Harvard Medical School Publications Group, Inc. 1994. Losing weight, a new attitude emerges. *Harvard Health Letter* 4(7):1.

11. Harvard Medical School Publications Group, Inc. 1998. Guidelines call more Americans overweight. *Harvard Health Letter* 23(10):7.

12. Margolis, S., and L. Cheskin. 1998. *The Johns Hopkins White Papers: Weight Control.* Baltimore, Md.: The Johns Hopkins Medical Institutions.

13. Nieman, D. 1999. *Exercise Testing and Prescription—a Health Related Approach.* Mountain View, Calif.: Mayfield Publishing.

14. Wardlaw, G. M. 1999. *Perspectives in nutrition* (4th ed.). St Louis: WCB/McGraw-Hill.

15. Mayo Foundation for Medical Education and Research. 1994. Weight control—what works and why. *Mayo Clinic Health Letter* June (suppl.):1.

16. Stunkard, A., et al. 1986. An adoption study of human obesity. *New England Journal of Medicine* 314:193.

17. Stunkard, A., et al. 1986. A twin study of human obesity. *Journal of the American Medical Association* 256:51.

18. Blair, S. 1995. *The Health Hazards of a Sedentary Lifestyle.* Distinguished scholar presentation. Memphis: The University of Memphis.

19. Garnett, L. R. 1996. Is obesity all in the genes? *Harvard Health Letter* 21(6):1.

20. Leibel, R. L., M. Rosenbaum, and J. Hirsch. 1995. Changes in energy expenditure resulting from altered body weight. *New England Journal of Medicine* 332:621.

21. Hawks, S. R., and P. Richins. 1994. Toward a new paradigm for the management of obesity. *Journal of Health Education* 25(3):147.

22. Tufts University. 1997. On whether reduced-fat foods make reduced-fat bodies. *Tufts University Health and Nutrition Letter* 15(9):2.

23. Consumers Union. 1995. The facts about fats. *Consumer Reports* 60:389.

24. Massachusetts Medical Society. 1997. Low-fat, low sugar foods no guarantee of fewer calories. *HealthNews* 3(9):5.

25. Editors. 1995. Exercise won't usually help you lose weight, but . . . *Sports Medicine Digest* 17(10):1.

26. Editors. 1993. Do yo-yo dieters die young? *Health* 7(2):10.

27. Editors. 1995. Yo-yo diets aren't risky afterall. *Health* 9(1):18.

28. Flynn, M. E. 1995. Fat-free foods: A dieter's downfall? Studies show calories do count. *Environmental Nutrition* 18(4):1.

29. CSPI. 1994. Confusing fat. *Nutrition Action Health Letter* 21(4):4.

30. Liebman, B. 1997. Fooled by low-fat. *Nutrition Action Health Letter* 24(3):2.

31. Liebman, B. 1998. Supersize foods, supersize people. *Nutrition Action Health Letter* 25(6):6.

32. Goldblatt, B. I. 1997. Advertisers get away with incredible weight-loss claims; how not to succumb. *Environmental Nutrition* 20(1):3.

33. Environmental Nutrition, Inc. 1998. FDA clears diet drug, but safety an issue. *Environmental Nutrition* 21(1):3.

34. Nethealth, Inc. 1999. *Herbal Therapies.* Available on-line at www.weightloss2000.com/herbs/herbs_06_all.htm.

35. Mayo Foundation for Medical Education and Research. 1997. Weight-loss products: "Herbal" doesn't necessarily mean "safe." *Mayo Clinic Health Letter* 15(12):4.

36. Albertson, E. 1996. Fasting. *American Health* 15(6):65.

37. Environmental Nutrition, Inc. 1997. Fasting for health offers few benefits, questionable safety. *Environmental Nutrition* 20(5):7.

38. Roitman, J. L. 1998. *ACSM's Resource Manual for Guidelines for Exercise Testing and Prescription.* Baltimore, Md.: Lippincott, Williams & Wilkins.

39. Eller, D. 1997. The best way to lose weight. *Health* 11(4):34.

40. Brehm, B. 1996. Fat-burning: Getting down to the basics. *Fitness Management* 12(4):25.

41. White, D. 1999. Inner joy is key to dutiful exercise. *The Commercial Appeal* 160(4):C1.

42. Robison, J. 1997. Weight management: Shifting the paradigm. *Journal of Health Education* 28(1):28.

43. White, D. 1999. Inner joy is the key to dutiful exercise. *The Commercial Appeal* 160(4):C1–3.

44. Tufts University. 1998. Ever "forget" you're trying to eat less? Write it down. *Tufts University Health and Nutrition Letter* 16(8):8.

45. American Psychiatric Association. 1994. *Diagnostic and Statistical Manual of Mental Disorders* (4th ed.). Washington, D.C.: The Association.

46. Consumers Union. 1995. How much should you weigh? *Consumer Reports* 60:804.

47. Tufts University. 1998. Fiber cuts calories in more ways than one. *Tufts*

University Health and Nutrition Letter 16(2):3.

48. Manning, M. 1997. Imperfect beauty. *Health* 11(6):82.

49. Birch, L. L. 1995. Appetite and eating behavior in children. *Pediatric Clinicians of North America* 42:931.

50. Tufts University. 1998. Several small meals keep off body fat better than one or two large ones. *Tufts University Health and Nutrition Letter* 15(12):1.

51. Tufts University. 1996. If you want to quit smoking but fear the weight gain. *Tufts University Health and Nutrition Letter* 13(11):6.

52. Tufts University. 1998. What it takes to take off weight (and keep it off). *Tufts University Health and Nutrition Letter* 15(11):4.

53. Kolata, G. 1998. Study finds obesity doesn't hasten death to extent once thought. *The Commercial Appeal* 159(1):A4.

Suggested Readings

Abbas, M. A., and R. A. Abbas. 1998. *Beyond fen-phen: The secrets to modern, healthier, safer weight-loss.* Sytac Publishing.

This book explores the world of weight loss and obesity from diets, exercise, weight-loss medications, weight-reduction surgery, cosmetic surgery, and more. It is a comprehensive guide written for the overweight person struggling to lose weight.

Guay, M. 1998. *Don't Diet—Live It: Successful Weight Control for Real People who Enjoy Real Food.* Marietta, Ga.: White Papers Press.

This book maintains that the ultimate weight-control book only needs to contain four words: "Eat Less, Move More." Yet in our complicated society with its abundance of food, weight control is not that simple. Rather than offering a quick fix, the author provides a plan for those who are ready to make a permanent transition to a healthy lifestyle and lifelong weight control. There are no restrictive menus, no pills, no gimmicks but instead a sensible, flexible, achievable, and safe way to gain control of your lifestyle.

Hesse-Biber, S. 1997. *Am I Thin Enough Yet? The Cult of Thinness and the Commercialization of Identity.* Oxford: Oxford University Press.

This book discusses the preoccupation of American women with weight, analyzes the social, economic, and political pressures confronting women in a weight-obsessed society, and explains how women learn to equate thinness with beauty. It includes first-hand, intimate portraits of young women from a wide variety of backgrounds and draws on historical accounts from popular and scholarly sources to bring into focus the multitude of societal and psychological forces that compel American women to pursue the ideal of thinness at any cost.

Margolis, S., and L. Cheskin. 1998. *The Johns Hopkins White Papers: Weight Control.* Baltimore, Md.: The Johns Hopkins Medical Institutions.

Designed for the public, this monograph presents an overview of issues related to weight loss, compares popular weight-loss methods, describes medical conditions that may cause obesity, and outlines lifestyle treatments for weight loss. It is updated annually.

Nieman, D. 1999. *Exercise Testing and prescription—a Health Related Approach.* Mountain View, Calif.: Mayfield Publishing Co.

A chapter of this text is devoted to the relationship between physical activity and obesity. The author provides a comprehensive review of the literature on physical activity and obesity, citing more than 300 studies. Concepts, issues, and misconceptions are thoroughly discussed and researched.

Wardlaw, G. 1999. *Perspectives in Nutrition* (4th ed.). St. Louis: WCB/ McGraw-Hill.

This comprehensive reference text on nutrition features chapters on dieting, weight control, and eating disorders.

Name _____ Date _____ Section _____

Assessment Activity 8-1

Assessing Your Body Image

Accepting those physical characteristics that are unique to you is an important first step to constructing a positive body image. In this assessment you will assess your body image from two perspectives: ideal and actual.

Directions: The following sets of bipolar adjectives relate to physical characteristics and appearance. Indicate your rating of these characteristics as follows:

1. Ideal body image: Circle the number that best represents how you would like your body to be in terms of each characteristic.
2. Actual body image: Put an X through the number that represents how you believe your body actually is in terms of each characteristic.

Body Image Characteristics

Graceful	1	2	3	4	5	6	7	8	9	10	Clumsy
Tall	1	2	3	4	5	6	7	8	9	10	Short
Slim	1	2	3	4	5	6	7	8	9	10	Fat
Large	1	2	3	4	5	6	7	8	9	10	Small
Attractive	1	2	3	4	5	6	7	8	9	10	Unattractive
Rugged	1	2	3	4	5	6	7	8	9	10	Delicate
Flabby	1	2	3	4	5	6	7	8	9	10	Muscular
Soft	1	2	3	4	5	6	7	8	9	10	Hard
Shapely	1	2	3	4	5	6	7	8	9	10	Unshapely
Weak	1	2	3	4	5	6	7	8	9	10	Strong
Well-proportioned	1	2	3	4	5	6	7	8	9	10	Poorly proportioned

Now answer the following questions:

1. Which characteristics of the ideal body image, if any, do you think can be achieved by dieting alone? By exercise alone?
2. How many of the items had a gap between the circles and the Xs?
3. On those items with a large gap, which characteristics of your actual body image actually can be changed?

4. What difference would it make if your body conformed to your "ideal body image"? Would it have any real influence on your relationships and your happiness?

From *Your Body Image.* Available on-line at **www.hc-sc.gc.ca/ hppb/nutrition/pube/vtlk/vitlk13.htm.**

Name _____   Date _____   Section _____

Assessment Activity 8-2

Calculating Caloric Expenditure Through Exercise

Directions: This exercise illustrates the calculations used for determining weight loss through exercise. In the example in Part 1, a subject weighing 195 pounds wishes to lose 12 pounds by exercising 40 minutes per day five times per week. The form of exercise will be riding a bike at 13 MPH. Table 8-4 gives the appropriate coefficient (0.071) for this activity, and as previously mentioned there are 3500 calories in 1 pound of fat. Study this example and then apply it to the problem presented in Part II to answer the following questions:

- How many calories are expended per exercise session?
- How many pounds may be lost per week at this energy expenditure?
- How long will it take to lose 12 lbs.?

Part 1

1. Multiply body weight by the appropriate activity coefficient:
   195 lbs. × 0.071 = 13.8 calories/min.
   13.8 calories/min. × 40 min. = 552 calories

2. Multiply the number of calories expended per workout by the number of workouts per week:
   552 calories × 5 workouts/week = 2760 calories/week
   $$\frac{2760 \text{ calories/week}}{3500 \text{ calories/lb.}} = 0.79 \text{ lost/week}$$

3. Divide the total pounds you want to lose (12 lbs.) by the number of pounds lost per week:
   $$\frac{12 \text{ lbs.}}{0.79 \text{ lbs. lost/week}} = 15.2 \text{ weeks}$$

This subject would lose 12 pounds in fifteen weeks by riding a bike at 13 MPH for 40 minutes per day five times per week. Your weight-loss goals can be determined in the same way.

Part II

Now apply your knowledge of energy expenditure through exercise by solving the following problem. Jim weighs 220 pounds and wishes to lose 25 pounds by jogging at 5 MPH for 30 minutes per exercise session five days per week. Do the calculations to solve Jim's problem by following these steps:

1. Multiply body weight by the appropriate activity coefficient from table 8-4 for jogging 5 MPH.

   220 lbs. × _____ coefficient = _____ calories/min.

   _____ calories/min. × 30 min. = _____ calories

2. Multiply the number of calories expended per workout by the number of workouts per week:

   _____ calories × 5 workouts/week = _____

   _____ calories/week ÷ 3500 calories/lb. = _____ lbs. lost/week

3. Divide the total pounds to be lost by the number of pounds lost per week.

   25 lbs. ÷ _____ lbs. lost/week = _____ weeks

4. a. How many calories would Jim expend per exercise session? _____
   b. How many pounds will he lose per week at this energy expenditure? _____
   c. How many weeks will it take Jim to lose 25 pounds? _____

Assessment Activity 8-3

Estimating Your Basal Metabolic Rate

Directions: Study the example in Part 1 and then calculate your personal total energy expenditure in Part II.

Part 1

The calculations for estimating BMR use different constants for men and women. The constant for men is 1 calorie per kilogram (2.2 lbs.) per hour; for women is 0.9 calories per kilogram per hour. These constants are referred to as the *BMR factor*. An example for a 125-pound woman follows:

1. Convert body weight in pounds to kilograms:
   125 lbs. ÷ 2.2 lbs. = 56.8 kg
2. Multiply weight in kilograms by the BMR factor:
   56.8 kg × 0.9 calories/kg/hr. = 51.1 calories/hr.
3. Multiply calories per hour by 24 hours:
   51.1 calories/hr. × 24 hrs./day = 1226.4 calories/day
4. The BMR is 1226.4 calories per day.

To determine the total daily calories expended, you need to estimate the number of calories used in muscular movement during a typical day. This is a rough approximation at best, but you should be within your range if you follow these guidelines and select the category that fits you best.

1. Sedentary—student, desk job, sitting during most of your work and leisure time: add 40–50% of the BMR.
2. Light activity—teacher, assembly-line worker, walk 2 miles regularly: Add 55–65% of the BMR.
3. Moderate activity—waitress, waiter, aerobic exercise at about 75% of maximum heart rate: Add 65–70% of the BMR.
4. Heavy activity—construction worker, aerobic exercise above 75 percent of maximum heart rate: Add 75–100% of BMR.

   If our subject determines that her level of activity is in the light category, she will calculate the range of her daily total caloric expenditure as follows:

1. Multiply BMR by the level of activity:
   1226.4 calorie/day × 0.55 = 674.5 calories/day
   1226.4 calorie/day × 0.65 = 797.2 calories/day

2. Add BMR calories to level of activity calories to get total calories:
   a. 1226.4 + 674.5 = 1900.9 calories/day
   b. 1226.4 + 797.2 = 2023.6 calories/day

   This subject's total calorie expenditure in a day falls between 1900.9 and 2023.6 calories.

Part II

Calculate your BMR by doing the following:

1. Convert body weight (BW) in pounds in kilograms:

   _____ lbs. ÷ 2.2 = _____ kg
2. Multiply weight in kilograms by the BMR factor for your sex (male factor 1.0, female factor 0.9):

   _____ × _____ kg = _____ calories/hr.
3. Multiply calories per hour by 24 hours per day to get the number of calories burned per day:

   _____ calories/hr. × 24 = _____ calories/day
4. BMR: _____ calories/day

Determine your level of physical activity:

1. Multiply BMR by the level of activity factor:

   _____ × _____ = _____ calories/day

   _____ × _____ = _____ calories/day
2. Add the number of BMR calories to the level of activity calories to get the range of total calories expended in a day:

   _____ calories + _____ calories = _____ calories/day

   _____ calories + _____ calories = _____ calories/day
3. Total calories expended range from _____ to _____.

Name _____ **Date** _____ **Section** _____

Assessment Activity 8-4

Assessing Calorie Costs of Activities

According to the ACSM, optimal weight-loss benefits are derived from activities that burn 300 calories per activity session. The purpose of this assessment is to determine the amount of time required to expend 300 calories.

Directions: Following are listed the caloric costs for three activities (see table 8-4). Add seven activities of your choice from table 8-4 and complete the information required in each column to determine the amount of time required to burn 300 calories. An example is provided for a person weighing 180 pounds who walks at a rate of 4.5 MPH.

Activity	Caloric Cost/Min./Lb.	×	Weight	=	Calories/Min.	300 Calories/Min.	=	Recommended Workout Time
Example (180-lb. person):								
1. Walking	0.048	×	180	=	8.64	$\frac{300}{8.64}$	=	34.7 min.
Personal Assessment								
1. Walking	0.048	×	_____	=	_____	$\frac{300}{}$	=	_____
2. Aerobic dance	0.062	×	_____	=	_____	$\frac{300}{}$	=	_____
3. Raking	0.024	×	_____	=	_____	$\frac{300}{}$	=	_____
4. _____	_____	×	_____	=	_____	$\frac{300}{}$	=	_____
5. _____	_____	×	_____	=	_____	$\frac{300}{}$	=	_____
6. _____	_____	×	_____	=	_____	$\frac{300}{}$	=	_____
7. _____	_____	×	_____	=	_____	$\frac{300}{}$	=	_____
8. _____	_____	×	_____	=	_____	$\frac{300}{}$	=	_____
9. _____	_____	×	_____	=	_____	$\frac{300}{}$	=	_____
10. _____	_____	×	_____	=	_____	$\frac{300}{}$	=	_____

Coping with and Managing Stress

Key Terms

coping
distress
eustress
general adaptation
  syndrome (GAS)

psychoneuroimmunology
 (PNI)
relaxation techniques
stress
stressor

Goals for Behavior Change

- Identify your personal sources of stress.
- View stress as holding potential for personal growth.
- Develop a time-management plan.
- Select strategies for managing stress.
- Put into action a stress-management plan.

Objectives

After completing this chapter, you will be able to do the following:

- Define *stress.*
- Identify potential stressors.
- Describe the various types of stress.
- Describe the stages of the general adaptation syndrome (GAS).
- Explain the body's physiological response to stress.
- List the short- and long-term health effects of stress.
- Identify strategies that effectively deal with stress.

tress profoundly affects people's lives. Everyone—students, businesspeople, parents, athletes—lives with stress. Stress is frequently viewed as an enemy. This is a misconception. Stress is often neither positive nor negative. How people deal with or react to what they perceive as stress is what determines its effect on their lives. As has been stated, "It is often said that stress is one of the most destructive elements in people's daily lives, but that is only a half truth. The way we react to stress appears to be more important than the stress itself."[1] The effects of stress can be either positive or negative. Positively used, stress can be a motivator for an improved quality of life. Viewed negatively, it can be destructive.

What is Stress?

Dr. Hans Selye was the first to define the term **stress** as the "nonspecific response of the body to any demands made upon it." It can be characterized by diverse reactions, such as muscle tension, acute anxiety, increased heart rate, hypertension, shallow breathing, giddiness, and even joy. From a positive perspective, stress is a force that generates and initiates action. Using Selye's definition, stress can accompany pleasant or unpleasant events. Selye referred to stress judged as "good" as **eustress.** This form of stress is the force that serves to initiate emotional and psychological growth. Eustress provides the experience of pleasure, adds meaning to life, and fosters an attitude that tries to find positive solutions to even complex problems. Eustress can accompany a birth, graduation, the purchase of a new car, the development of a new friendship, the accomplish-

ment of a difficult task, and success in an area that previously produced anxiety. **Distress,** on the other hand, is stress that results in negative responses. Unchecked, negative stress can interfere with the physiological and psychological functioning of the body and may ultimately result in a disease or disability.[2]

Stress also provides humans with the ability to respond to challenges or dangers. It is vital to self-protection and also serves as a motivator that enhances human ability.

A **stressor** is any physical, psychological, or environmental event or condition that initiates the stress response (figure 9-1).

See Assessment Activity 9-2 to evaluate your own stress level in the different categories listed in figure 9-1.

What is considered a stressor for one person may not be a stressor for another. Speaking in front of a group may be stimulating for one person and terrifying for another. Some people experience extreme test anxiety and others feel very confident about written assessments. Fortunately, the stress response is not a genetic trait, and because it is a response to external conditions, it is subject to personal control. A person may not avoid taking a test, but he or she can apply techniques and take precautions that lessen the effects of the stress. For example, knowing the material thoroughly and engaging in deep breathing several minutes before a test helps dissipate anxiety. To maximize quality of life, people can find positive ways of coping with stress.

A stress response can enhance and actually increase the level of either mental or physical performance. This response is referred to as the *inverted-U theory.*[3] Not

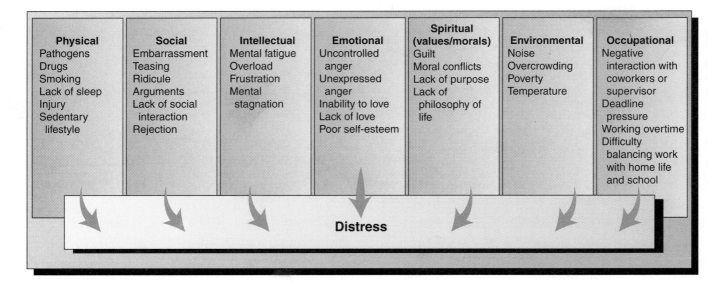

Figure 9-1 Stressors That Can Create Distress

enough stress (hypostress) may result in a poorer effort, but too much stress can inhibit effort. There appears to be an optimal level of stress that results in peak performance (figure 9-2). Achievement of an appropriate level of stress depends on the person and the type of task. Table 9-1 lists some of the potentially positive outcomes associated with stress. Your body is constantly attempting to maintain a physiological balance. This balance is referred to as *homeostasis*. Any event or circumstance that causes a disruption (a stressor) in your body's homeostasis requires some type of adaptive behavior. Physiologically, whether a stressor is perceived as positive or negative, the body responds with the same three-stage process. This series of changes is known as the **general adaptation syndrome (GAS)**.[4] The three phases are alarm, resistance, and exhaustion (figure 9-3).

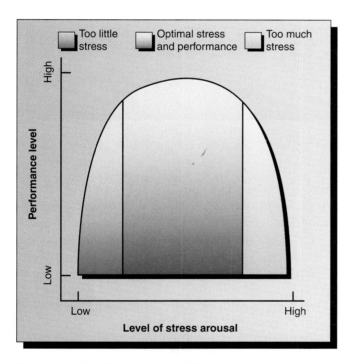

Figure 9-2 The Inverted-U Theory

The *alarm* phase occurs when homeostasis is initially disrupted. The brain perceives a stressor and prepares the body to deal with it, a response sometimes referred to as the *fight-or-flight syndrome*. The subconscious appraisal of the stressor results in an emotional reaction. The emotional response stimulates a physical reaction that is associated with stress, such as the muscles becoming tense, the stomach tightening, the heart rate increasing, the mouth becoming dry, and the palms of the hands sweating.

The second stage is *resistance*. In this phase the body meets the perceived challenge through increased strength, endurance, sensory capacities, and sensory acuity. Hormonal secretions regulate the body's response to a stressor. Only after meeting and satisfying the demands of a stressful situation can the internal activities of the body return to normal. Girdano and George[5] argue that people have different levels of energy to deal with stressors. For short-term stressors, only a superficial level of energy is required, allowing deeper energy levels to be protected. Superficial levels of energy are readily accessible and easily renewable. Unfortunately, all stress cannot be resolved with superficial energy levels. When long-term or deep levels of stress are experienced, the amount of energy available is limited. If sufficient stress is experienced for an extended period, loss of adaptation can result. Although some scientists believe that energy stores may be genetically programmed, all people can replenish their energy stores through exercise, good nutrition, adequate sleep, and other positive behaviors.

When stressors become chronic or pervasive, the third phase, *exhaustion,* is reached. In exhaustion, energy stores have been depleted and rest must occur. Although weeks to years may pass before the effects of long-term stressors occur, if a person does not learn how to adequately deal with stress, exhaustion will result. At this point, stress may affect the stomach, heart, blood pressure, muscles, and joints. Fortunately, the effects of stressors can be completely or partially reversed when adequate management techniques are initiated. The earlier these management techniques are learned and used, the fewer problems result.

Table 9-1 Positive Outcomes of Stress

Mental	Emotional	Physical
Enhanced creativity	Sense of control	High energy level
Enhanced thinking ability	Responsiveness to environment	Increased stamina
Greater goal orientation	Improved interpersonal relationships	Flexibility of muscles and joints
Enhanced motivation	Improved morale	Freedom from stress-related disease

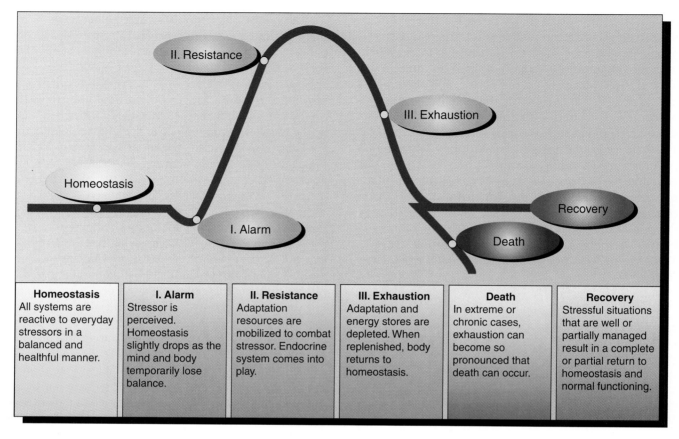

Homeostasis	I. Alarm	II. Resistance	III. Exhaustion	Death	Recovery
All systems are reactive to everyday stressors in a balanced and healthful manner.	Stressor is perceived. Homeostasis slightly drops as the mind and body temporarily lose balance.	Adaptation resources are mobilized to combat stressor. Endocrine system comes into play.	Adaptation and energy stores are depleted. When replenished, body returns to homeostasis.	In extreme or chronic cases, exhaustion can become so pronounced that death can occur.	Stressful situations that are well or partially managed result in a complete or partial return to homeostasis and normal functioning.

Figure 9-3 The General Adaptation Syndrome (GAS)

Sources of Stress and Warning Signs

Most stressful situations fall into one of three categories: (1) harm and loss, (2) threat, and (3) challenge.[6] Examples of *harm-and-loss situations* are the death of a loved one, loss of personal property, physical assault, physical injury, and severe loss of self-esteem. *Threat situations* may be real or perceived and can range from being caught in traffic to being unable to perceive an event. Threatening events tax a person's ability to deal with everyday life. Threat stressors are any stressors that result in anger, hostility, frustration, or depression. *Challenge situations* are catalysts for either growth or pain. These stressors often involve major life changes and include such events as taking a new job, leaving home, graduating from college, and getting married. Challenge events are usually perceived as being good but involve stress because they disrupt homeostasis and require considerable psychological and physical adjustment.

Being aware of the mental and physical signals associated with stress is the beginning step in learning how to manage it. Assessment Activity 9-1 will aid you in identifying some of the major stressors. By using self-assessments to monitor for signs of stress, you can avoid excessive stress. The negative results of distress are shown in table 9-2. Indicators of excessive distress include the following:

- Chronic fatigue, migraine headaches, sweating, lower-back pain, sleep disturbances, weakness, dizziness, diarrhea, and constipation
- Harder and/or longer work or study while accomplishing less, an inability to concentrate, general disorientation
- Denial that there is a problem or troubling event
- Increased incidence of illness, such as colds and flu or constant worry about illness or becoming ill; overuse of over-the-counter drugs for the purpose of self-medication
- Depression, irritability, anxiety, apathy, an overwhelming urge to cry or run and hide, and feelings of unreality
- Excessive behavior patterns, such as spending too much money, drinking, breaking the law, and developing addictions
- Accident proneness
- Signs of reclusiveness and avoidance of other people
- Emotional tension, "keyed up" feeling, easy startling, nervous laughter, anxiety, hyperkinesia, and nervous tics

Table 9-2 Negative Results of Distress

Mental	Physical	Emotional
Short-term effects		
Poor memory	Flushed face	Irritability
Inability to concentrate	Cold hands	Disorganization
Low creativity	Gas	Conflicts
Poor self-control	Rapid breathing	Mood swings
Low self-esteem	Shortness of breath	Chronic sleep problems
	Dry mouth	Acid stomach
		Overindulgence in alcohol, drugs, food
Long-term effects		
Bouts of depression	Hypertension	Overweight/underweight
Mild paranoia	Coronary disease	Drug abuse
Low tolerance for ambiguity	Ulcers	Excessive smoking
Forgetfulness	Migraine/tension headaches	Ineffective use of work/leisure time
Inability to make decisions/quick to	Strokes	Overreaction to mild work pressure
make decisions	Allergies	

HealthQuest Activities

- The *How Stressed Are You?* activity in Module 1 allows you to look at several areas of your life (including money, school, relationships, and health) and identify stress caused by events and daily hassles. You can also rate your perceived stress level for each area. Use this feature to find out which area or areas generate the highest levels of stress for you.

- The *CyberStress* activity in Module 1 simulates a stress-filled day and can be used to help you assess your reactions to daily stressors. Choose the scenario that most closely matches your own. For example, if you work and go to school, you should check both on the preferences screen. As you are presented with stressful situations, choose the reaction that is closest to how you would react. At the feedback screen, print the screen showing your score. Then evaluate your experience by answering the questions in the *What Do You Think?* section.

Factors Generating a Stress Response

As mentioned earlier, the criteria for a stressful event and the response to that event for any person are unique to the individual. Figure 9-4 provides an overview of the complexity of the stress experience and some of the many moderating effects. For instance, a dysfunctional homelife (characterized by an alcoholic parent, a difficult divorce, or extreme poverty) may contribute to a personality that is more susceptible to difficult events, such as poor grades or a failed relationship. This combination of inadequate preparation for life along with an event that is perceived as personal failure is likely to lead to depression, anxiety, or anger. Conversely, a person whose background has fostered a deep sense of self-worth and meaningfulness will be able to better handle a difficult event and not perceive the event as a personal failure. Poor grades may be the result of poor study habits, an undiagnosed learning behavior, or inadequate sleep, and a failed relationship may be simply the result of a poor match, bad timing, or immaturity.

Physiological Responses to Stress

Stress abounds in life and can be experienced as the result of happy and unhappy events. Regardless of the stressor, each time a stressful event occurs, a series of neurological and hormonal messages are sent throughout the body.

The nervous system serves as a reciprocal network that sends messages between the awareness centers of the brain and the organs and muscles of the body. Part of this system is referred to as the *limbic system*. The limbic system contains centers for

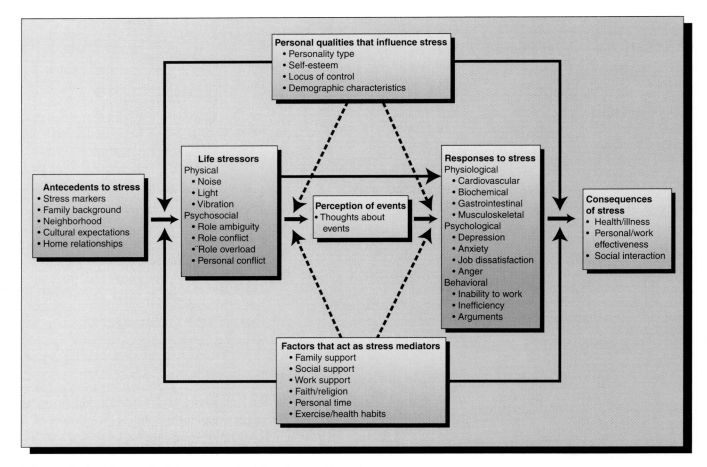

Figure 9-4 Theoretical Framework of the Stress Experience

emotions, memory, learning relay, and hormone production and includes the pituitary gland, thalamus, and hypothalamus.

When a stressor is encountered, the body sends a message to the brain via the nervous system. The brain then synthesizes the message and determines whether it is valid or not. If a message is not verified by the brain as being threatening, the limbic system overrides the initial response and the body continues to function normally. If the initial response is translated as accurate and a stressor is detected, the body responds with some emotion (fear, joy, terror), and the hypothalamus begins to act.

The hypothalamus sends a hormonal message to the pituitary gland, which then releases a hormone (ACTH) that helps signal other glands in the endocrine system to secrete additional hormones, providing fuel to respond with the fight-or-flight reaction. Systolic blood pressure may rise 15 to 20 mmHg while fluid is retained. The adrenal cortex increases blood pressure to facilitate transportation of food and oxygen to active parts of the body.[7] Blood volume is increased.

The hypothalamus also sends a message to release the hormones epinephrine and norepinephrine, which initiate a variety of physiological changes. These changes include increased heart rate, increased metabolic rate, increased oxygen consumption, and the release of hormones called *endorphins,* which decrease sensations of pain.

The autonomic nervous system is responsible for a second major set of physiological responses. In reaction to a threat, the autonomic nervous system increases heart rate, strength of the skeletal muscles, mental activity, and basal metabolic rate; dilates the coronary arteries, pupils, bronchial tubes, and arterioles; and constricts the abdominal arteries. This system also returns the body to a normal, relaxed state.

Stress and the Immune System

The mind and body act on each other in remarkable ways. Our immune system is a part of the body's defense against illness and disease originating from factors and conditions both outside and inside our bodies. The immune system consists of a variety of mechanical and chemical defenses that serve to protect against such outside invaders as microorganisms, allergens, and other substances as well as inside factors such as

Everyday problems can trigger the stress response. What are your biggest stressors?

mutating cells or improperly functioning tissue. The immune system is a functional system rather than an organ system and, as a result, seems to be prone to the effects of stress when fighting off the situations and conditions previously mentioned.[8]

The biological link between emotions and disease and even death is quite strong. Mortality is three times higher in people with few close relationships than in those with numerous such relationships, and people with strong support groups have additional protection against life stressors. Death rates are higher for cancer patients with pessimistic attitudes. Illness is more common among people who feel locked into strife-ridden marriages. AIDS patients with healthy psyches seem better able to withstand disease.[9]

The immune function seems to be affected by the relationship between the brain and nervous system. This relationship among brain, nervous system, and immune response has been the outgrowth from the field of study called **psychoneuroimmunology (PNI)**. This relatively new medical discipline seeks to explain the connection between the brain, the nervous system, and the body's response to infections and deviated cell division. Several studies have shown that chronic stress suppresses the body's ability to initiate an effec-

tive immune response. This suppression is attributed to an increase in corticosteroids, which are produced during chronic stress. This increase in corticosteroid levels delays and weakens the immune response.[10] O'Leary found that chronic stress suppresses the immune system, particularly when the stress is associated with social disruption (leaving home for the first time), psychological depression (feeling "down" for prolonged periods of time), or some negative personality attribute (lack of self-confidence).[11] It has also been found that immunosuppression is associated with loneliness and feelings of hopelessness.[12] Recently, stress has been demonstrated to be associated with infertility.[13,14] No known specific reason exists for this correlation. Whether the stress is the result of infertility problems or another source, stress reduction intervention results in significant improvement in conception rates.

Because stress affects the immune system, the body becomes more susceptible to a multitude of ailments, from colds to cancer. Respiratory conditions, such as asthma, may become worse. The cardiovascular system reacts by constricting the blood vessels while increasing blood volume. The net result is a rise in blood pressure throughout a stress-ridden day. Multiple increases in blood pressure can eventually contribute to chronic high blood pressure. More forceful contraction of the heart elevates levels of free fatty acids, enhancing the development of clogged arteries leading to and including the heart itself. In extreme cases, sudden death can occur, especially for a person who has been experiencing high levels of uncontrolled stress for an extended period.

Headaches, including migraines, have long been associated with stress. Tension headaches are caused by involuntary contractions of the scalp, head, and neck muscles. Typical muscular reaction to stress is contracting or tensing. When chronic stress occurs, the body reacts by being constantly ready to respond, and the muscles become braced, always in a state of tension. More stress magnifies the tension the muscles are already undergoing. Increased muscular tension manifests itself in headaches, backaches, neckaches, and other pains. The smooth muscles that control internal organs also experience pains. More intense contractions can lead to stomachache, diarrhea, hypertension, heartburn, gastritis, diarrhea, bloating, inflammation of the pancreas, and blockage of the bile ducts.

Stress decreases saliva in the mouth, often making speaking awkward. Swallowing may become difficult, and the increase in stomach acids contributes to ulcer pain. People tend to perspire more, and electrical currents are transmitted more quickly across the skin. Skin conditions such as acne, psoriasis, herpes, hives, and eczema are exacerbated.

Wellness Across the Generations
Women's Changing Roles

As many families now have two-career households and more women work outside the home, it is natural to wonder if the double demands of household and worksite pose a threat to women's physical and psychological health. A recent study done at Duke University Medical Center by Linda Luecken and her colleagues, suggests that they do.

The study focused on 109 women with full-time clerical and customer-service jobs. Some had children and some did not. The results indicated that working women with children at home had higher levels of cortisol (a stress hormone thought to reflect high levels of distress), a greater lack of personal control, and more risk for cardiovascular disease than working women with no children. Both groups of women reported similar levels of work strain, but the working mothers reported higher levels of home strain, including greater demands and less control. This increased strain seemed to be caused by the reality that these women performed most of the child-rearing and household duties. Such chores as laundry, cleaning, cooking, chauffeuring, and homework more often fell to the women in the study than to their male partners.

Luecken and her colleagues estimated that working women with children have up to twenty-one hours more work per week than men have. They also found that working mothers have little chance to "unwind," so they have increased sympathetic nervous system arousal both during and after work. Even if male partners help with household duties, they often finish their duties with enough time to relax. The presence of a spouse or significant other did not significantly reduce the physiological and psychological consequences of stress on the working mother. Interestingly, higher income, ethnicity, and the number of children at home did not influence the level of stress.[21]

Here are some ways working mothers might balance the demands of work and household duties:

- Set limits. Schedule and honor your own time to relax. Learn to say "no."
- Make lists of your priorities, from most important to least important. Get done what is really important and let the rest go.
- Remember that perfection is the enemy of happiness.
- Team up with other parents to share the load: child care, dinner clubs, or shuttling.
- Pay attention to the moments of joy that parenting and connecting with a partner and friends have to offer.[22]

Stress also seems to affect the body's nutritional status. Individual nutritional patterns can also influence stress management efforts. For example, eating too much or too little, eating the wrong kinds of food, and overusing products such as caffeine or alcohol upset homeostasis. Diets high in fat, sugar, and processed foods place a heavy burden on various body systems. Ingesting too few calories can lead to the breakdown of lean tissue. To meet the demands of stress, you should maintain adequate nutrition through a balanced and varied diet. (Chapter 6 provides guidelines for developing a beneficial nutritional plan.) Table 9-3 provides some insight into the interactive natures of stress, nutritional status, and immunity.

Ultimately, no body system escapes the effects of stress. Long-term presence of certain stress-associated hormones in the brain damages receptors and cells found in the hippocampus. (The hippocampus sends messages when stress is occurring.) Because brain cells do not regenerate, these cells are lost forever. The effects of this loss are unknown, but indications are that

eventually affected people become less able to respond to stress appropriately.[15] Assessment Activity 9-3 provides guidelines for identifying stress style and suggests relaxation activities.

Self-Esteem and Stress

How people feel about themselves and others and their perceptions of the stressors in their lives are part of the psychology of stress. Ability to cope with stress often hinges on impressions of how detrimental a stressor is and how adequately resources can deal with the situation. How much stress people feel themselves experiencing is closely associated with their own sense of self-esteem. Self-esteem includes beliefs and attitudes about changes, personal talent, skills, and one's ability to deal with the changes and challenges that inevitably occur in life. It is also the basis of self-efficacy and the locus of control (see Chapter 1). The most influential factor in determining response to stress may be people's own perceptions of themselves.

Table 9-3 Stress, Nutritional Status, and Immunity: An Interactive Effect

Although the mechanism is not completely understood, stress significantly affects nutritional status and therefore immunity. Several nutritional factors have implications for how your body responds to stress.

Energy

Stress can increase the body's basic caloric needs by as much as 200%. The stress hormones increase body heat production. When this heat is released, it is not available for cell metabolism. The caloric inefficiency induced by stress accounts for the increased need for energy intake.

Protein

Stress may increase the body's need for protein from 60% to as much as 500%. The integrity of the body's tissues, such as the skin and the tissue lining the mouth, lungs, and nose (called *mucosal tissue*), depends on adequate protein repair and maintenance of secretions of biochemicals that serve as protective agents. The formation of antibodies also requires protein.

Fats

Dietary fatty acids influence the synthesis of a group of fatty acid derivatives called *prostaglandins*. Prostaglandins stimulate or depress other cellular and immune functions in relation to stress.

Vitamins

Vitamin A functions to maintain healthy skin and mucous membranes. Individuals who are vitamin A–deficient have fewer mucous-secreting cells and those they do have produce less mucous—thus the protection provided by the mucous lining is diminished. Vitamin C has been shown to enhance the engulfing or "eating" actions of the immune cells called *macrophages.* If vitamin C is deficient, macrophages are less mobile and less able to consume disease-causing organisms. Deficiencies of vitamins A, B_{12}, and folate can impair production of the cells that enable antibody responses. Large doses of vitamin E have been associated with suppression of B cells, which are vital to the immune response. Finally, metabolic requirements for thiamin, riboflavin, and niacin are increased in response to a stressful situation.

Minerals

Deficiencies of zinc impair immune cell reproduction and responsiveness.

Wellness Across the Generations

The Time of Our Lives

Although middle age is often dreaded, the changes that inevitably occur as we grow older are not necessarily bad. In fact, more and more elderly adults report that the best time in their lives was not their youth, but rather their midlife years.

One recent study of this question involved more than 3000 people, each of whom answered more than 1100 questions. Researchers found that more than 70 percent of respondents viewed themselves as being in excellent health and felt their lives had purpose and meaning. In fact, nine of ten study participants said they had never experienced the proverbial midlife crisis. Most middle-aged people reported that they had been able to make the adjustment nesessary for life to remain rewarding. Most said that they did not have arthritis, backaches, skin problems, indigestion, constipation, depression, gum disease, high blood pressure, or migraines. And contrary to popular belief, most middle-aged women reported that menopause was a fairly benign experience.

One negative finding of the study is that middle-aged adults are not working very hard to maintain a high quality of life. In addition, respondents reported not having enough money and sex—probably two things lacking at any age, not just middle age. However, while sexual satisfaction was low, middle-aged adults seemed to be content overall with their marriages and relationships. Seventy-two percent said that their relationships were very good or excellent, and 90 percent felt that their relationships were unlikely to break up.

Finally, the survey found that by the time adults reached age 65, men felt an average of 12.6 years younger than their actual age and women felt 14.7 years younger than their actual age. As we grow older, our lives can become even more fulfilling, particularly if we can maintain a sense of control over our well-being by practicing healthful lifestyle habits. How can *you* ensure optimal health as you age?

Adapted from Johns Hopkins InteliHealth Online,
www.intelihealth.com/IH?ihtIH?d=dm

Wellness On the Web
Behavior Change Activities

What's Your Stress Index?

Over the last several years, the term "stress" has become a cultural cliché that's used to convey feelings of fatigue, burnout, tension, and discouragement, to name just a few. There's job stress, relationship stress, technological stress . . . and the list goes on. Cliché or not, though, we probably can all agree that, however we experience it, stress is real—and it can be extremely challenging to understand and manage. The destruction it causes can make our daily lives miserable. It can also affect every dimension of our health, sometimes severely. Strangely, we're not always aware that we're under stress. The signs and symptoms that can alert us to problems may be hard to recognize because we've become so accustomed to them. Want to quantify your stress level? The Canadian Mental Health Association has a 20-item checklist you can use to evaluate your stress index. Go to www.queendom.com/testjunkie.html and select "What is your stress index?" to complete the checklist, and then evaluate your results.

Are You Headed for Burnout?

When your stressors become chronic or pervasive, you've reached the third phase of the general adaptation syndrome: exhaustion. In the exhaustion phase, your energy stores have been depleted and rest is essential. This stage includes conditions like burnout, which occurs when highly committed people lose interest and motivation. Typically burnout affects hard-working, hard-driven people who become emotionally, psychologically, or physically exhausted. Cyberia Shrink has created a Burnout Inventory designed to evaluate your risk for burnout. Go to her website at www.queendom.com/burnout2.html and complete the 30 items. Read every statement carefully and indicate how often you feel that way or how often it applies to you. To obtain valid results, you need to answer all the questions. Click the "send" button. This inventory is scored on-line, so you'll receive your results on-screen. How did you fare?

What's Your Take on the World?

What's a severe stressor for one person may not be a stressor for another. Stress is often neither positive nor negative. How we deal with or react to what we perceive as stress is what determines its effect on our lives. Are you an optimist or a pessimist? Do you see the glass as half full or half empty? Your level of optimism can significantly affect how you respond to stressful situations. To determine your level of optimism or pessimism, go to www.psychtests.com/optimist.html and complete the "Optimism/Pessimism Inventory." How did you do?

Personality and Stress

Two physicians, Friedman and Roseman,[16] have written extensively about personality, cardiovascular disease, and stress. These researchers have described two stress-related personality types—type A and type B. Most people are neither type exclusively but fall somewhere between the two.

Type A personality is characterized by an urgent sense of time, impatience, competitiveness, aggressiveness, insecurity over status, and inability to relax. People with type A behavior characteristics are likely to be highly stressed. Type B people have a more unhurried approach to their lives. The type B personality does not become as upset at losing or not attaining a goal. Type B people also tend to set more realistic goals.[17] Researchers disagree on whether there is a possible relationship between the stress-prone type A personality and cardiovascular disease.[18]

In general, researchers believe that being a type A personality is not a problem if there is no underlying hostility. However, regardless of whether type A people are more susceptible to heart disease, they do experience more negative effects, such as tiredness and frustration, from short-term stress.

"Stress survivors"—people who have been found to handle stress successfully or have successful coping abilities—have several common characteristics. Psychologist Suzanna Kobasa[19] has isolated these attributes and characterized the type of person who exhibits them. A hardy personality tends to remain healthy even under extreme stress. Characteristics of a hardy personality or hardiness are challenge, commitment, and control (see Assessment Activity 9-5).

Challenge is the ability to see change for what it is—that is, not only inevitable but an opportunity for growth and development of unique individual abilities. *Commitment* is delineated by a strong sense of inner purpose. It is necessary to want to succeed in order to achieve success. Commitment is the ability to become really involved while maintaining the discernment to know when dedication and desire are harmful. *Control* is the recognition that one has power over one's own life and attitudes. People who have a sense of control act in situations rather than react to them.

Dealing with Stress

All events in life precipitate a reaction. How people react or respond to situations differs. **Coping** is the attempt to manage or deal with stress. Coping is independent of outcome—it does not necessarily result in success.

Dealing successfully with stress may require using a variety of techniques (see Real-World Wellness: Guidelines for Dealing with Stress). Because stress-related responses are based primarily on mental perceptions, coping strategies that achieve desirable results may need to originate in a change in attitude or outlook. If specific situations or people are perceived as disruptive, one solution is to avoid them, for example.

Although there are no easy answers, there is always some kind of answer or solution. When dealing with a stressor reaches a point where it seems there are no solutions, the tension from the situation becomes increasingly detrimental. It may then become necessary to consider changing attitudes, goals, and values.

Seeking the help of a professional counselor is frequently beneficial when attempting to resolve particularly stressful situations. Assessment Activity 9-4 identifies ways to recognize some of the positive and negative behaviors that can be used to deal with stress.

Learning about and using relaxation techniques can help alleviate or even prevent detrimental effects associated with stress. Engaging in positive self-talk and relabeling negative experiences (viewing difficulties as "challenges" rather than as problems, for example) are positive steps in reducing stress-related disorders. Eating well, taking time to enjoy life, laughing, exercising, and living in the present all reduce stress. People can handle stress effectively when they work on developing all of their abilities to the fullest, when they develop lifestyles that are compatible with personal values, and when they develop realistic expectations for themselves. Working toward these goals is the way to establish a wellness lifestyle (see Real-World Wellness: Marta's Day).

Successful coping includes being aware of incidents and situations that you might perceive as being stressful. Recognition of stressors means being aware of how your body responds to stress. Recognition requires continuous monitoring of your body and mind for evidence of excessive stress.

Successful coping takes real effort. One suggestion is to focus on the signals your body is sending when experiencing stress and then to think back to the event or situation that might have triggered those feelings. Another suggestion is to recreate a recent event that has been stressful. After visualizing the episode, write down six ways that the outcome could have been

Real-World Wellness

Guidelines for Dealing with Stress

Being in school can be so overwhelming. I have many classes, extracurricular activities, and a pile of homework each night. How can I balance it all?

Following are guidelines for effectively dealing with potential harmful stress:

- **Schedule time effectively.** Practice good time-management techniques by using time wisely. This means taking time out for yourself every day and scheduling work when you are usually at your peak ability (see Assessment Activity 9-5).

- **Set priorities.** Know what is important to you. Do not attempt to work on four or five projects simultaneously. Keep your efforts focused on one or two major items.

- **Establish realistic goals.** Goals must be achievable. Do not establish impossible expectations and then become frustrated when they are not accomplished as quickly as you would like. Write down long-range goals and then establish checks for keeping yourself on track and monitoring progress. Short-term goals help you see how you are moving toward your goal and provide rewards as you advance toward success.

- **See yourself as achieving the goals.** Visualize yourself as being successful. Go over in your mind what it will look and feel like to accomplish a goal.

- **Give yourself a break.** Take time every day to exercise and relax.

different—three ways it could have been worse and three ways it could have been better. The latter will increase awareness of how to better handle similar situations in the future. A last suggestion is to try something new. The idea is that you be challenged and meet that challenge successfully. Trying something new and meeting the challenge reinforces your sense of being able to deal with life successfully.[19]

Relaxation Techniques

The ultimate goal in stress coping and management is to reduce the negative effects of stress. Different **relaxation techniques** have proved successful. Brief descriptions of various techniques follow. If you are interested in pursuing the use of these techniques further, you can

Real-World Wellness

Marta's Day

This semester I've been getting up late for class, putting off studying, and eating poorly. I'm feeling very stressed out, and my grades have begun to suffer. What can I do to get out of this downward spiral?

Here is an analysis of Marta's day including her stress responses to events in her day and suggestions for other ways to react.

Event	Marta's Stress Response	A Better Approach
Morning: Is late rising for first class; stayed up late studying the night before	Skips first class to study for exam; misses notes from that class and cannot contact friend to see if she can use her notes; skips breakfast	Begin studying for a test a few days before the exam; do not attempt to cram everything into one night; get a good night's rest and get up early to review your notes; eat breakfast and attend first class.
Is late for test	Stays home too long and gets caught in traffic; arrives late for the test; does not have a full hour to complete the test	Leave early to allow for traffic and parking problems; be on time to concentrate on the test and have time to relax a few minutes.
Lunch	Skips lunch—has a soft drink and potato chips	Have a nutritionally balanced meal in a relaxing atmosphere; go with a friend just to chat.
Afternoon: Is late for work because had to return overdue library book	Rushes to library; has to pay fine; has to stand in line at the library for 15 minutes	Write down when books are due and return them on time; use a daily calendar to plan activities and allot time to take care of personal business.
Evening: Watches TV until midnight; neglects to study for test the day after tomorrow	Is too tired and "stressed out" to study so just watches TV all evening; has a hamburger and soda for dinner	Take a short nap after work and have a nutritious meal; plan the evening so that some time is spent watching TV and some is spent studying; go to bed early so you can get to school on time and rested.
Next morning: Gets up late for class again	Begins the same cycle of feeling tired and pressured and being late	Analyze current time constraints to determine where more time needs to be allotted and how to develop a more efficient plan (see Assessment Activities 9-5 and 9-6).

find more information about them in books or on tapes. These books and tapes can be purchased at bookstores or may be found at your library.

Deep Breathing

Deep breathing is the most basic technique used in relaxation and is often the foundation for other methods. The primary benefit of this technique is that it can be done anywhere and anytime. It is beneficial to practice deep breathing several times a day. The methodology consists of completely filling the lungs when breathing so that the abdomen expands outward. Begin by taking a deep breath and then exhaling slowly through the mouth. A hand can be placed on the stomach to ensure

that it is fully expanded. If the stomach does not rise, the breath is not deep enough or the abdomen is being held too tightly. Repeat this cycle several times and then rest quietly for 3 to 5 minutes.

Progressive Muscle Relaxation

Progressive muscle relaxation creates awareness of the difference between muscular tension and a relaxed state. This is a three-step process that begins with tensing of a muscle group and noticing how the tension feels. Next, make a conscious effort to relax the tension and notice that feeling. The third phase consists of concentrating on the differences between the two sensations. Beginning at either the head working down or at

Real-World Wellness

Progressive Muscle Relaxation

When I'm uptight, my muscles get so tense that I can't relax. What can I do to loosen them again?

There are numerous progressive muscle relaxation activities. The exercises are frequently structured by a facilitator. Some exercises begin with the feet, hands, or face, but because of space constraints, only the relaxing of the face will be described here. You can add the other parts of the body by recording the entire process on audiotape and listening to the tape as often as desired—usually once a day or two to three times a week. Take your time (3 to 4 minutes) for each area of the body.

- Assume a comfortable position and concentrate on the instructions. You may find it beneficial to lie down or sit in a comfortable chair.
- Close your eyes.
- Allow all your muscles to relax and feel loose and heavy. Take several deep breaths.
- Wrinkle your forehead and hold for 6 seconds.
- Notice the feelings.
  - Relax; allow the forehead to become smooth
  - Notice the feeling of relaxation.

- Frown with your eyes, forehead, and scalp and hold for 6 seconds.
  - Experience the sensation of tension.
  - Relax the muscles.
  - Notice the feelings of relaxation.
- Keeping your eyes closed, clench your jaw and push your teeth together.
  - Hold for 6 seconds.
  - Notice the tension.
  - Relax your jaw and allow your lips to part slightly.
- Now press your tongue against the roof of your mouth and feel the tension.
  - Hold for 6 seconds.
  - Allow your tongue to return to its normal position, experiencing the sensation of relaxation.
- Now press your lips together as tightly as possible.
  - Hold for 6 seconds.
  - Relax and notice the feelings of relaxation over your lips.
- Using the same principles, gradually move through the body from the shoulders to the arms, hands, fingers, back, chest, abdomen, hips, legs, ankles, feet, and toes.

the feet working up, tense and relax all major muscle groups (see Real-World Wellness: Progressive Muscle Relaxation).

Autogenics

Autogenics is the use of self-suggestion to produce a relaxation response. Autogenics begins with a deep breath and a conscious effort to relax. This technique may follow a progression from head to feet or feet to head. Repeat the phrase "My arm feels heavy and warm" several times before moving on to the next muscle group. You can repeat other phrases that carry a calming message such as "I am completely calm and relaxed." End the session by thinking, "I am refreshed and alert." Autogenics takes practice, time, and commitment and should be practiced twice a day for about 10 minutes. Commercial tapes may help guide people wanting to learn autogenics (see Real-World Wellness: Performing Autogenic Training).

Meditation

Meditation can be approached from a variety of perspectives. As a stress-reduction technique its purpose is to help the practitioner temporarily tune out the world

and to invoke relaxation. During a meditation session, the person meditating concentrates or focuses his or her attention on a *mantra*, or particular word or sound, while attempting to eliminate all outside distractions.

Begin by taking a comfortable position on a couch or in a chair. Take several deep breaths, slowly inhaling and exhaling. Shut your eyes or softly focus them on an object so that the details are blurred. Concentrate all your thoughts on a word or phrase that you have selected to use, such as *peace* or *relax,* while continuing to breathe slowly and deeply.[20] The relaxation response can also be initiated by counting breaths backward from 100 or by imagining a white light that slowly travels throughout your body, letting in light and energy while expelling tension and fear. Many commercial meditation tapes are available.

Visualization

Visualization (imagery) is a form of relaxation that uses the imagination. Begin by finding a comfortable position, shut your eyes, and take several deep breaths. Several variations of visualization can then be used. You can imagine a tranquil scene, such as a beach on a sunny day or a valley with a stream or forest, and then

Real-World Wellness

Performing Autogenic Training

I'm looking for a practical technique I can use to reduce my stress. I know it's important to relax, but I have a hard time relaxing sometimes. Merely telling myself to relax doesn't work. What can I do to help myself relax?

Autogenic training is a form of hypnosis that helps the practitioner develop images of warmth and relaxation. With practice, autogenic training can increase peripheral blood flow and reduce muscle tension. *Autogenic* means "self-generating." The technique is a type of self-hypnosis that utilizes deep breathing and conjures images through a series of phrases to evoke the relaxation response. Here are guidelines for practicing autogenics:

- Either sitting or lying down, begin by taking five to six deep breaths and contract any muscles that are tense.

- Repeat to yourself, "My breathing is slow and even, my breathing is smooth and rhythmic."

- Continue with the deep breathing and imagine you are on a warm, sunny beach with the waves moving in and over your body, generating a warm and relaxed feeling.

- Feel the waves move over your stomach, hips, back, legs, and feet.

- Repeat to yourself, "I am relaxed, I am calm, I am quiet. My breathing is smooth and rhythmic. My heartbeat is calm and regular."

- Starting with your right arm, repeat the following as the breathing continues slowly and regularly: "My right arm and hand are heavy and warm." Continue with your left arm.

- Focus on both arms and repeat the phrase, "My arms and hands are heavy and warm."

- Move the focus to your legs and feet and repeat, "My legs and feet are heavy and warm." Focus on the right side, the left side, and finally both legs at the same time.

- As you proceed through the session, visualize the waves of warmth and relaxation washing over your entire body. Continue to breath slowing and deeply.

- As you prepare to wrap up the session, continue to breath deeply and slowly and begin to get back in touch with where you are. Tell yourself you are warm, safe, secure, and relaxed.

- Count down from 5:
  4. Take a deep breath and visualize the room.
  3. Take a deep breath and begin to stretch.
  2. Take a deep breath and slowly open your eyes.
  1. You are mentally alert and ready to get back to your activity. You are fully awake.

place yourself in the scene. Imagine all of the scene's sights, sounds, smells, and feelings. People suffering from a terminal illness frequently imagine scenes in which their immune system attacks or destroys their disease, or they envision themselves as healthy and disease free. People who want to make major life changes, such as losing weight or stopping smoking, can envision themselves slim or not smoking or imagine themselves in trouble situations such as a situation in which you are tempted to overeat or smoke. Then people can envision themselves making wise choices or not engaging in undesirable behaviors. Visualization can also be used to improve athletic performance. Tapes are available that can assist people in learning how to develop this technique.

Biofeedback

Biofeedback, which is based on scientific principles, is designed to enhance awareness of body functions—it is an educational tool. Sensory equipment demonstrates subtle body changes, such as increases or decreases in skin temperature, muscle contraction, and brain wave variations. This biofeedback, or feedback on biological processes, enables people to become aware of what is happening in their bodies when stressed and learn how

to control tensions through awareness of sensations that are relaxing. After a few sessions, people should begin to recognize and thereby alter their typical bodily responses to situations that serve as stressors for them.

Massage Therapy

In recent years massage therapy has become an acceptable form of stress reduction and a healing alternative. Some people consider today's American society to be in the midst of a "touch famine." Appropriate touching is lacking even though we recognize the need for physical interaction. Babies who are not handled can actually die from this type of deprivation. Although adults are not likely to respond so extremely to lack of touch, the need to be touched does not disappear with age. Research findings indicate that massage can promote physical relaxation and well-being. Certified massage therapists are licensed by the American Massage Therapy Association.[24]

Music

The power of music is undisputed. A strong beat and rhythmic music instill in almost all people of any age the desire to respond by moving or dancing. Quiet music soothes by causing people to breathe more deeply, stilling turbulent emotions, reducing metabolic response, and calming the autonomic nervous system.

Humor

Laughter is a powerful stress-reducing agent. A deep laugh temporarily raises pulse rate and blood pressure and tenses the muscles. After a good laugh, however, pulse rate and blood pressure actually go down and the muscles become more relaxed. Laughter works in two ways. Being able to laugh at a situation reminds you that life is seldom perfect or predictable. Laughing helps keep events in perspective. Laughing also works to reinforce a positive attitude. Laughing or even smiling can actually improve mood.

Time Management

A major contributor to stress is the pressure associated with time constraints. By effectively using time, you can eliminate a great deal of stress. For the college student, effective use of time is crucial, especially when the student is working and attending school at the same time. Procrastination can add to stress and undermine academic work, personal relationships, and work efforts. Good time management including appropriate prioritizing, scheduling, and the completion of personal responsibilities can contribute to feelings of personal satisfaction.

Certain behaviors or habits can unnecessarily rob you of time:[25]

1. **Workaholism.** *Workaholism* is spending excessive amounts of time working, even though the activity may not be productive. Generally, people who engage in workaholic behavior like to work long hours and do not use time-saving techniques. They also may become overinvolved in unimportant tasks that eat away at their time, requiring them to use extra time to accomplish important tasks.

2. **Time juggling.** Time jugglers constantly overschedule themselves, often making promises to be in more than one place at a time. Because it is frequently impossible to do several things at once or be in two places at the same time, this behavior often results in the neglecting of important activities.

3. **Procrastination.** Procrastinators consistently put off until later things that could just as easily be done now. Some procrastinators choose the simplest of two tasks to do now to avoid the really important ones until the last possible minute, when the pressure is on.

4. **Perfectionism.** Perfectionists go beyond trying to do their best to achieve perfection. Because standards of perfection vary from one person to the next, this behavior rarely results in a sense of accomplishment, and the inability to achieve impossible goals contributes to feelings of dissatisfaction and failure.

5. **Yesism.** *Yesism* is the inability to tell anyone "no." Extremely nice people often suffer from this condition because they don't like to disappoint others or they fear being rejected, even if saying "yes" ends up only costing them.

Although difficult to overcome, many of the aforementioned characteristics can be moderated if you are determined to do so. Here are some suggestions for appropriate use of your time:

1. Write down realistic goals and priorities. Assess current activities to determine whether they are essential, important, or trivial. Ask yourself the question "When does the task have to be completed?" Write down the priorities for the next day before going to sleep each night and rank them in order. This strategy provides you with a night to "sleep on them." You can then approach them systematically, according to need, the next day.

2. Develop a time framework. To help alleviate stress, establish the amount of time to be spent on each activity. Some tasks cannot be completed in a day's time. If this is the case, estimate the days or weeks required to complete the task. This is especially important in accomplishing long-term commitments. Allotting blocks of time each day of each week helps to alleviate the extreme pressure of completing a difficult task in a short time. For example, if a term paper is due at the end of a semester, you can spend a certain number of hours each week working on the paper. You can establish goals for the completion of the paper and devise rewards for yourself each time you achieve a goal. Another strategy is to study for each course every day by allotting a specific time to read and review the subject material covered in each class.

3. Know where and when you can best complete a task. Know the circumstances under which you function best. Is it easier for you to concentrate if you work in the library or the dorm room? Where will you have the fewest interruptions? Do you concentrate best in the morning, afternoon, or evening?

4. Establish priorities. To find time for everything that must be done, you have to know your priorities. Divide tasks into those that must be done

immediately, those that can wait a brief time, and those that are not essential. Once you have established priorities, start with the highest priority item and work through the list.

5. Ask for help if responsibilities become overwhelming. Say "no" when there are too many tasks to handle. Do not feel guilty about saying "no"; this only adds more stress. For example, if sorority or fraternity demands are too great, either ask others to share the workload or refuse the responsibility.

6. Take a break. Every day should provide for fun, leisure, time alone, and relaxation. Make the most of every day. Schedule in time every day for yourself.

Assessment Activity 9-6 is a prioritization worksheet to help you organize your tasks. Assessment Activity 9-7 provides you with a log. Use it to record your daily activities for several days to a week. Then review it and see if you are spending your time as effectively as you thought or if you have overscheduled what you can do in a twenty-four–hour period. This can provide you with a basis for devising improved time-management plans.

Exercise

Because the fight-or-flight syndrome stimulates the body into action, exercise is a logical method of responding to that physiological command. Exercise has been found to directly affect the brain chemistry. Studies have shown an increase in endorphin levels after an easy or a strenuous run.[26] (Endorphins are natural pain killers that function to help alleviate sensations of pain and stimulate a positive response from the immune system.) Exercise is a positive stressor (eustressor) and, when properly used, seems to offset the adverse effects of distress.[24] Studies have demonstrated that exercise reduces the severity of the stress response, shortens the recovery time from the stressor, and diminishes vulnerability to stress-related disease. The higher the fitness level, the more beneficial the exercise in reducing stress. (The recommended types of exercise programs are discussed in Chapter 3.)

A correctly designed exercise program produces beneficial physiological responses and can induce psychological effects that serve to reduce anxiety, promote feelings of accomplishment, and evoke muscle relaxation.

Many people consider stretching a means of invoking feelings of relaxation, and stretching is also associated with reduced tension. Moderate levels of exertion are frequently considered most beneficial for most people. (A moderate-level activity is a walk at the rate of approximately 3 miles an hour.) Excessive or addictive exercise habits can have the reverse effect and actually contribute to feelings of tension and irritability. When

Exercise is a great way to reduce anxiety, increase positive feelings, and relieve stress.

engaging in exercise as a stress-reduction technique, strive to find the level that creates the greatest sense of well-being upon completion.

Selecting a Stress-Reducing Technique

No single stress-reduction technique automatically reduces stress for everyone. People are comfortable with and enjoy different activities, and personal preference is what determines long-term use. When dealing with stress, you must first become aware that a stress response is occurring. People are frequently unaware that the reason they are always tired or irritable or have body aches is they are experiencing stress's negative effects. Second, you find the stress-reduction techniques that work best for you. Usually, more than one approach is required, depending on the person and his or her type of stress response. Any technique that helps create a sense of relaxation, provides personal time,

Nurturing Your Spirituality

Enjoying Healthy Pleasures

Certain lifestyle patterns have detrimental effects upon our well-being and quality of life: not exercising, smoking, drinking to excess, not wearing a seat belt, and eating poorly. However, just as important as avoiding lifestyle patterns that can negatively affect quality of life is appreciating the joys, thrills, delights, and happiness that are part of our lives. The idea is to minimize the negative and maximize the positive in our lives. Pleasure has gotten a bad name and we have become almost phobic about enjoying ourselves and having fun. In their book *Healthy Pleasures*, Ornstein and Sobel[23] point out that, even though certain negative habits and addictions are unhealthy, we also must seek to feel good mentally and emotionally. We need to seek enjoyment to enhance our survival. Ornstein and Sobel emphasize that no better way exists to ensure healthy, life-saving behaviors than to make them pleasurable. From eating to reproduction to caring for others, pleasure can guide us to better health. Doing what feels good is often beneficial for health and survival.

A pleasurable experience can be as simple as taking time to enjoy a sunset, smell the air after a rain shower, napping for half an hour in the afternoon, making a kind comment to a stranger or friend, or letting go of anger toward another human being. Seeking out pleasure may involve giving ourselves positive self-talks, looking for humor, and hanging out with happy people. Enjoying our gifts of pleasure is powerful medicine and can be contagious. It is cheap and effective, and its only side effect is a happy life. The following website provides a storehouse of information on the importance of adding pleasure to your life: **www/arise.org.**

and allows you to gain control can lead to a happier, healthier, more enjoyable life. Third, the best form of stress management is the prevention of negative effects before they become unmanageable. Well-thought-out, prudent lifestyle decisions based on knowledge of health behaviors and understanding of your own needs and expectations may be the best contribution you can make to your own stress-management plan.

Summary

- Stress is the nonspecific response of the body to any demands on it.
- Anything that creates stress is a stressor.
- Stressors may generate eustress (good stress) or distress (bad stress).
- The general adaptation syndrome (GAS) explains how the body responds to a stressor. The three stages of GAS are alarm, resistance, and exhaustion.
- The stress response can enhance physical and mental performance. This is referred to as the *inverted-U theory*.
- Whether positive or negative, a stressful event always produces a series of neurological and hormonal messages that are sent through the body.
- The responses to stress can be physiological (cardiovascular, gastrointestinal, musculoskeletal), psychological (causing depression, anxiety, anger), or behavioral (generating an inability to work, arguments).

- The immune system can be compromised as the result of prolonged stress, resulting in increases of susceptibility to comunicable diseases and chronic conditions.
- High stress has been associated with infertility problems.
- People's perceptions of stress are associated with self-esteem, self-efficacy, and locus of control.
- People who deal effectively with stress seem to view stressful situations as opportunities for growth, have a sense of inner purpose, and view themselves as having power over their lives.
- Coping is the effort(s) made to manage or deal with stress.
- Many techinques—including autogenics, deep breathing, visualization, muscle relaxation, meditation, massage, biofeedback, exercise, yoga, music, and humor—can help reduce stress.
- Effective time management can be a key to stress reduction.

Review Questions

1. What is stress? What are stressors?
2. What are the stages the mind and body go through when exposed to a stressor?
3. What are some potential signals that a person is experiencing chronic stress and what are the possible effects?
4. What factors influence how a person perceives and copes with stress?
5. Define *hardiness* and how it may help a person effectively deal with stress.
6. What are some guidelines for handling stress positively?
7. Discuss various stress-reducing techniques.

References

1. Siegal, B. S. 1988. *Love, Medicine and Miracles.* New York: Perennial Library.
2. Selye, H. 1975. *Stress Without Disease.* New York: New American Library.
3. Hanson, P. G. 1986. *The Joy of Stress,* Kansas City, Kans.: Andrews, McMeel & Parker.
4. Selye, H. 1978. *The Stress of Life* (rev. ed.). New York: McGraw-Hill.
5. Girdano, D., and E. George Jr. 1989. *Controlling Stress and Tension.* Englewood Cliffs, N.J.: Prentice Hall.
6. Folkman, S. 1984. Personal control and stress and coping processes: A theoretical analysis. *Journal of Personal and Social Psychology* 46:839.
7. Seward, B. L. 1994. *Managing Stress.* Boston: Jones and Bartlett.
8. Blonna, R. 1996. *Coping with Stress in a Changing World.* St. Louis: Mosby.
9. Gelman, D., and M. Hager. November 7, 1988. *Body and soul. Newsweek* 88.
10. Glaser, R., et al. 1987. Stress-related immune suppression: Health implications. *Brain Behavior-Immunity* 1(1):7.
11. O'Leary, A. 1990. Stress, emotion, and human immune function. *Psychology Bulletin* 108(3):363.
12. Pellitier, K., and D. Herzing. 1988. Psychoneuroimmunology: Toward a mind-body model: A critical review. *Advances* 5(1):27.
13. Domar, A., and H. Dreher. 1996. *Healing Mind, Healthy Woman: Using the Mind-Body Connection to Manage Stress and Take Control of Your Life.* New York: Henry Holt.
14. Domar A., P. Zuttermeister, and R. Friedman. 1997. *The Relationship Between Distress and Conception in Infertile Women.* Paper presented at the Annual Meeting of the American Society of Reproductive Medicine, Cincinnati, Ohio.
15. Greenberg, J. 1990. *Stress Management.* Dubuque, Iowa: Wm. C. Brown.
16. Friedman, M., and R. Roseman. 1984. *Type A Behavior and Your Heart:* New York: Alfred A Knopf.
17. Flannery, R. B. 1987. Toward stress-resistant persons: A stress management approach to the treatment of anxiety. *American Journal of Preventive Medicine* 3(1):25.
18. Fischman, J. 1987. Type A on trial. *Psychology Today* 21(2):42.
19. Kobasa, S. 1984. How much stress can you survive? *American Health* 5(7):64.
20. Benson, H. 1985. *The Relaxation Response,* New York: Berkley.
21. Luecken, L. J., et al. 1997. Stress in employed women: Impact of marital status and children at home on neurohormonal output and home strain. *Psychosomatic Medicine* 59:352.
22. Light, K. C. 1997. Stress in employed women: A women's work is never done if she's a working mom. *Psychosomatic Medicine* 59:360.
23. Sobel, D. S., and R. Ornstein. 1989. *Healthy Pleasures.* Reading, Mass.: Addison Wesley.
24. Lamb, L. E. 1992. Understanding stress. *Health Letter* 39(suppl.):12.
25. Crews, D., and D. Landers. 1987. A meta-analytic review of aerobic fitness and reactivity to psychosocial stressors. *Medicine and Science of Sports Exercise* 19:5114.
26. Appenzeller, D., et al. 1980. Neurology of endurance training versus endorphins. *Neurology* 30:418.

Suggested Readings

Williams, V., and R. Williams. 1998. *Lifeskills.* New York: Times Books.

This review of the research on relationships and health goes on to describe a systematic self-help program to build better relationships to strengthen physical well-being. Eight basic life skills are described.

Schiraldi, G. R. 1997. *Conquer Anxiety, Worry and Nervous Fatigue: A Guide to Greater Peace.* Ellicott City, Md.: Chevron Publishing Corporation.

The purpose of this book is to help readers learn to recognize and understand the symptoms of worry and anxiety. It provides a guide to stress-management strategies, including relaxation, rational thinking, confiding past trauma, solution-focused problem solving, meditation, proper sleep, nutrition, exercise, time management, assertiveness training, building self-esteem, and strengthening spiritual commitment.

Maskach, C., and M. Leiter. 1997. *The Truth About Burnout: How Organizations Cause Personal Stress and What To Do About It.* San Francisco: Jossey-Bass Publishers.

The authors encourage employees and managers to view the problems of burnout as an opportunity to address the major contributing pressures, such as exhaustion, cynicism, and ineffectiveness at work. The book is based on the real-world experiences of the authors working with companies to prevent and deal with burnout.

Assessment Activity 9-1

Life Stressors

The following stress scale was developed by Miller and Rahe. It includes positive and negative events, since both require adaptation. Research has confirmed that stress can have a significant impact on physical and emotional health. The total score on this self-test offers you insight into your risk for illness as a result of recent life events. Stressful changes won't necessarily harm you; the potential for damage rests in how you handle stress.

Directions: To determine the possible impact of various recent changes in your life, circle the "stress points" listed that you experienced during the past year.

Health

An injury or illness that
- kept you in bed a week or more or sent you to the hospital ... 74
- did not require long bed rest or hospitalization ... 44

Major dental work ... 26
Major change in eating habits ... 27
Major change in sleeping habits ... 26
Major change in your usual type or amount of recreation ... 28

Work

Change to a new type of work ... 51
Change in your work hours or conditions ... 35
Change in your responsibilities at work
- to more responsibilities ... 29
- to fewer responsibilities ... 21

Home

Major change in living conditions ... 26
Change in residence
- within the same town/city ... 25
- to a different town/city/state ... 47

Change in family get-togethers ... 25
Major change in health or behavior of family member ... 55
Marriage ... 50
Pregnancy ... 67
Miscarriage or abortion ... 65
Addition of a new family member
- through birth of a child ... 66
- through adoption of a child ... 65
- through a relative moving in ... 59

Spouse beginning or ending work ... 46
Changes at work involving
- promotion ... 31
- demotion ... 42
- transfer ... 32

Troubles at work
- with your boss ... 29
- with coworkers ... 35
- with persons under your supervision ... 35
- involving other issues or people ... 28

Major business adjustment ... 60
Retirement ... 52
Loss of job
- due to being laid off from work ... 68
- due to being fired from work ... 79

Correspondence course to help you in your work ... 18

Personal and Social

Change in personal habits ... 26
Beginning or ending school or college ... 38
Change of school or college ... 35
Change in political beliefs ... 24
Change in religious beliefs ... 29
Change in social activities ... 27
Vacation trip ... 24
New close personal relationship ... 37
Engagement to marry ... 45
Girlfriend or boyfriend problems ... 39
Sexual difficulties ... 44
Child leaving home
- to attend college ... 41
- to marry ... 41
- for other reasons ... 45

Change in the marital status of your parents
- through divorce ... 59
- through remarriage ... 50

Change in arguments with spouse ... 50
In-law problems ... 38
Separation from spouse
- due to work ... 53
- due to marital problems ... 76

Divorce ... 96
Birth of grandchild ... 43
Death of spouse ... 119
Death of
- child ... 123
- brother or sister ... 102
- parent ... 100

Financial

Major change in finances
- through increased income ... 38
- through decreased income ... 60
- through investment or credit difficulties ... 56

Loss or damage of personal property ... 43

Moderate purchase	20
Major purchase	37
"Falling out" of a close personal relationship	47
Accident	48
Minor violation of the law	20
Being held in jail	75
Death of a close friend	70
Major decision about your immediate future	51
Major personal achievement	36
Foreclosure on a mortgage or loan	58

Total score: _____

Interpreting your score: Add up your points. A total score of 250 to 500 is considered a moderate amount of stress. If you score higher than that, you may face an increased risk of illness. If your scores is lower than 250, consider yourself fortunate.

From Miller and Rahe. 1997. Life changes scaling for the 1990s. *Journal of Psychosomatic Research* 43.

Name _____ Date _____ Section _____

Assessment Activity 9-2

How Stressed Are You?

Directions: The stress categories and stressors originally listed in figure 9-1 are also listed here. Underneath the stressors in each stress category is a blank. You can use this blank to rank yourself on each category and then to give yourself an overall stress rating. To rate yourself in each category, select a number from 1 to 10. A 1 indicates that you are currently experiencing no stress in that area of your life. A 10 indicates that the amount of stress you are experiencing in that area is overwhelming. This is a subjective rating and should be based on how you feel right now. After completing the assessment, note the areas that are currently creating difficulty for you and try to plan ways to reduce your overwhelming emotions in the next few days. Recheck your scores over the next few months to see how they change. If you chronically experience overwhelming stress in any area, you might want to seek the advice of a professional, such as a counselor or pastor.

Physical	Social	Intellectual	Emotional	Spiritual	Environmental
Bacteria	Embarrass-	Mental fatigue	Uncontrolled	Guilt	Noise
Drugs	ment	Overload	anger	Moral conflicts	Overcrowding
Smoking	Teasing	Frustration	Unexpressed	Lack of purpose	Poverty
Lack of sleep	Ridicule	Mental stagnation	anger	Lack of philosophy	Extreme
Injury	Arguments		Inability to love	of life	temperatures
Sedentary	Lack of social		Poor self-esteem		
lifestyle	interaction				
	Rejection				

_____ _____ _____ _____ _____ _____

Overall stress: _____

Questions to consider:
1. Is the stress created from personal pressure or outside factors?
2. What changes could you make to reduce or eliminate the identified stressor(s)?
3. With whom could you discuss your feelings concerning the identified stressor(s)?

Name _____ Date _____ Section _____

Assessment Activity 9-3

Stress Style: Body, Mind, Mixed?

Directions: Imagine yourself in a stressful situation. When you are feeling anxious, what sensations do you typically experience? Check all that apply.

_____ 1. My heart beats faster.

_____ 2. I find it difficult to concentrate because of distracting thoughts.

_____ 3. I worry too much about things that don't really matter.

_____ 4. I feel jittery.

_____ 5. I get diarrhea.

_____ 6. I imagine terrifying scenes.

_____ 7. I cannot keep anxiety-provoking pictures and images out of my mind.

_____ 8. My stomach gets tense.

_____ 9. I pace up and down nervously.

_____ 10. I am bothered by unimportant thoughts running through my mind.

_____ 11. I become immobilized.

_____ 12. I feel I am losing out on things because I cannot make decisions fast enough.

_____ 13. I perspire.

_____ 14. I cannot stop thinking worrisome thoughts.

There are three basic ways of reacting to stress—physically, mentally, or with a combination of the two. Physical stress type people feel tension in the body—jitters, butterflies, the sweats. Mental types experience stress mainly in the mind—worries and preoccupying thoughts. Mixed types react with both responses in about equal measure.

Give yourself a *Mind* point if you answered "yes" to each of the following questions: 2, 3, 6, 7, 10, 12, 14. Give yourself a *Body* point for each of these: 1, 4, 5, 8, 9, 11, 13. If you have more Mind than Body points, consider yourself a mental stress type. If you

have more Body than Mind points, your stress style is physical. Do you have about the same number of each? You are a mixed reactor.

Choosing a Relaxer
Body

If stress registers mainly in your body, you will need a remedy that will break up the physical tension pattern. This may be a vigorous body workout, but a slow-paced or even lazy muscle relaxer may be equally effective. Here are some suggestions to get you started:

Aerobics	Progressive relaxation
Swimming	Body scan
Biking	Rowing
Walking	Yoga
Massage	Soaking in a hot bath, sauna

Mind

If you experience stress as an invasion of worrisome thoughts, the most direct intervention is anything that will engage your mind completely and redirect it—meditation, for example. Some people find the sheer exertion of heavy physical exercise unhooks the mind wonderfully and is very fine therapy. Suggestions:

Meditation	Autogenic suggestion
Reading	Crossword puzzles
TV, movies	Games like chess or cards
Any absorbing hobby	Vigorous exercise
Knitting, sewing, carpentry, or other handicrafts	

Mind/body

If you are a mixed type, you may want to try a physical activity that also demands mental rigor:

Competitive sports, (racquetball, tennis, squash, volleyball, etc.)	Meditation
	Any combination from the Mind and Body lists

Name _____ Date _____ Section _____

Assessment Activity 9-4

Identification of Coping Styles

Directions: There are a variety of ways to deal with stress. Indicate whether you are using the following activities to deal with stress.

	Often	Rarely	Not at All
Listen to music			
Go shopping with a friend			
Watch television/go to a movie			
Read a newspaper, magazine, or book			
Sit alone in the peaceful outdoors			
Write prose or poetry			
Attend an athletic event, play, lecture, symphony, etc.			
Go for a walk or drive			
Exercise (swim, bike, jog)			
Get deeply involved in some other activity			
Play with a pet			
Take a nap			
Get outdoors, enjoy nature			
Write in a journal			
Practice deep breathing, meditation, autogenics, muscle relaxation			
Straighten up your desk or work area			
Take a bath or shower			
Do physical labor (garden, paint)			
Make home repairs, refinish furniture			
Buy something—records, books			
Play a game (chess, backgammon, video games)			
Pray, go to church			
Discuss situations with a spouse or close friend			
Other: _____ _____ _____			

Directions: Following is a list of negative coping behaviors. Indicate how much you currently use them to deal with stress.

	Often	Rarely	Not at All
Become aggressive			
Use negative self-talk			
Yell at spouse/kids/friends			
Drink a lot of coffee or tea			
Get drunk			
Swear			
Take a tranquilizing drug			
Avoid social contact with others			
Try to anticipate the worst possible outcome			
Think about suicide			
Smoke tobacco			
Chew your fingernails			
Overeat or undereat			
Become irritable or short-tempered			
Cry excessively			
Kick something or throw something			
Drive fast in your car			
Other: _____ _____ _____			

Scoring Instructions

Count the number of positive and negative coping techniques you use.

Number of negative techniques: _____

Number of positive techniques: _____

How often do you employ negative coping strategies?

_____

Do you use more positive than negative strategies or the reverse? _____

Do you recognize a need to change some of the techniques you are now using? If so, which ones? _____

_____

What are some ways in which you can maximize your positive coping behaviors? How can you minimize your negative ones? _____

Name _____ Date _____ Section _____

Assessment Activity 9-5

How Hardy Are You?

Directions: Following are twelve items similar to those that appear on a hardiness questionnaire. Evaluating an individual's hardiness requires more than one quick test, but this simple exercise can be a good indication of your own hardiness. Write down how much you agree or disagree with the following statements, using this scale.

0 = Strongly disagree
1 = Mildly disagree
2 = Mildly agree
3 = Strongly agree

_____ A. Trying my best at work makes a difference.
_____ B. Trusting to fate is sometimes all I can do in a relationship.
_____ C. I often wake up eager to start on the day's projects.
_____ D. Thinking of myself as a free person leads to great frustration and difficulty.
_____ E. I could sacrifice financial security in my work if something really challenging came along.
_____ F. It bothers me when I have to deviate from the routine or schedule I have set for myself.
_____ G. An average citizen can have an impact on politics.

_____ H. Without the right breaks, it is hard to be successful in my field.
_____ I. I know why I am doing what I'm doing at work.
_____ J. Getting close to people puts me at risk of being obligated to them.
_____ K. Encountering new situations is an important priority in my life.
_____ L. I really don't mind when I have nothing to do.

Scoring
These questions measure control, commitment, and challenge. For half of these questions, a high score (agreement) indicates hardiness; for the other half, a low score (disagreement) does.

To get your scores on control, commitment, and challenge, first write in the number of your answer—0, 1, 3, or 3—above the letter of each question on the score sheet. Then add and subtract as shown. (To get your score on control, for example, add your answers to questions A and G; add your answers to B and H; and then subtract the second number from the first.)

Add your scores on commitment, control, and challenge to get a score for total hardiness. A total score of **10–18 = hardy personality; 0–9 = moderate hardiness; below 0 = low hardiness.**

(_____ + _____) − (_____ + _____) = _____ = Control score
  (A)   (G)   (B)   (H)

(_____ + _____) − (_____ + _____) = _____ = Commitment score
  (C)   (I)   (D)   (J)

} = _____ = Total hardiness score

(_____ + _____) − (_____ + _____) = _____ = Challenge score
  (E)   (K)   (F)   (L)

Paths to Hardiness
Three techniques are suggested for becoming happier, healthier, and hardier:

- **Focusing:** Recognize signals from the body that something is wrong. Focusing increases the sense of control over plans and puts people in a psychologically better position to change.
- **Reconstructing stressful situations:** Think about a stress episode and then write down three ways the

situation could have turned out better and three ways it could have been worse. Doing this helps you feel better about the way situations turn out and appreciate other coping strategies.
- **Compensating through self-improvement:** It is important to distinguish between what can be controlled and what cannot. A way to regain control is by taking on a new challenge or task to master.

Assessment Activity 9-6

Time-Management Worksheet

Directions: What follows is a prioritizing worksheet. Copies can be made for the different days of the week, or you can develop your own format. First, make a list of all the things you absolutely, positively have to get done today, no matter what! There should be very few things on this list. If the list runs longer than two or three items, you need to rethink what is really essential to do and what it is you would really *like* to do. There is a difference.

Must Do List

1._____

2._____

3._____

Things That Are Important But Not Necessary

1._____

2._____

3._____

4._____

5._____

6._____

Other Things I Would Like to Get Done

1._____

2._____

3._____

4._____

5._____

6._____

Approximate how much time you think each activity will take. Some people like to spend an hour on one project and then switch to another; other people like to work continuously on one project until it is complete. Obviously your preference will affect your scheduling of work and the amount of time you allot. Your best friend may not work in the same way you do. That's okay. You need to prioritize your own list and set your own goals and timetable. Be sure to schedule time for yourself regularly. It is vital to your stress management.

Me time:_____

Activity: _____

Time allotment:_____

Assessment Activity 9-7

Analyzing Your Use of Time

Managing your time effectively can significantly contribute to your feeling of being in control of your life. A by-product of this sense of control is reduced stress and tension; with effective time management you will be able to meet daily demands with less effort. Since the basis of change is recognizing that there needs to be a change and then determining the areas in your life that require change, a good way to begin meeting your time management needs is to analyze how you are currently managing your time.

Directions: Make several copies of this log and keep track of your time for a week. Include all your activities—from classes to meals to driving time to conversations with friends. At the end of the day and week, rate each hour as to how important the activities that occurred during that time were. Taking time to relax, talk to friends, and be alone are considered important to total well-being and should not be discounted.

Daily Log

Time	Activities	Where	Essential, important, or trivial
6:00–7:00 AM			
7:00–8:00			
8:00–9:00			
9:00–10:00			
10:00–11:00			
11:00–12:00			
12:00–1:00 PM			
1:00–2:00			
2:00–3:00			
3:00–4:00			
4:00–5:00			
5:00–6:00			
6:00–7:00			
7:00–8:00			
8:00–9:00			
9:00–10:00			
10:00–11:00			
11:00 PM–6:00 AM			

Analyzing Your Log

1. What activities did you find to be the most productive for you? Which were the least productive? _____

_____

2. Where were your most productive activities performed? Your unproductive activities? _____

_____

3. What time of day did you find to be the most productive for you—morning, afternoon, or evening? _____

The analysis should be based on the full week's activities. You are looking for patterns of behavior that provide the best effects for you. You may find that you work best at home or in the dormitory in the afternoons or at the library in the evenings. Using this assessment, try to find the best patterns of achievement for you.

Taking Charge of Your Personal Safety

Key Terms

acquaintance rape
carbon monoxide
car jacking
date rape
elderly abuse
homicide

improper driving
intentional injury
partner abuse
rape trauma syndrome
road rage
unintentional injury

Objectives

After completing this chapter, you will be able to do the following:

- Identify potential dangers associated with unintentional and intentional injuries.
- List protective measures for maintaining a safe home environment.
- Discuss steps necessary to participate safely in recreational activities.
- Describe guidelines for the safe operation of a vehicle.
- Discuss measures for avoiding or dealing with road rage.

Goals for Behavior Change

- Identify and change three risky behaviors you now engage in.
- Make at least two alterations to your home environment to protect yourself and your family.
- Assess your safety precautions when participating in sports and recreational activities.
- Develop a personal safety plan for helping prevent unintentional injury.

- Identify measures to protect against rape.
- Discuss wellness in relationship to homicide, abuse, and hate crimes.
- List measures that help protect against crimes of violence, such as car jacking and ATM robberies.

his chapter follows the stress chapter for good reason. As we rush through our daily lives, one of the consequences of our high-stress, tension-filled lifestyles is accidents. Many of us experience close calls or minor mishaps during the periods when we are experiencing stress. Too often during these periods, we do not pay close attention, are careless in our behavior, or engage in behavior that puts us at greater risk for accidents or personal harm.

Statistics indicate that accidents are the leading cause of death for people between 1 and 45 years. Even if HIV does become the leading killer for certain subgroups within this age range, accidents will still be the number two killer. College students and other young adults tend to give too little thought to their personal safety. As they participate in their daily academic and recreational activities they encounter many potential dangers. No longer can the college campus be considered a safe haven from the violence and crime that are such significant parts of our society. Plenty of evidence indicates that people in a university environment are at significant risk for violence. Just because you feel safe does not necessarily mean you are. The chapter explores those areas where the decisions you make can greatly influence your safety.

The first section of this chapter examines **unintentional injury**, which can occur in the home, during recreational activities, or while driving. The second section deals with violence and **intentional injury**.

Home Safety

We all like to think that our homes are places where we can be safe. However, within the confines of the home, dormitory, or apartment many potential hazards exist. By conducting a personal survey and remaining alert to these dangers, you can minimize many risks. Here are some suggestions for safe living in one's home:

- Install smoke detectors and make sure they are in working order.
- If you are going to live above the fifth floor, make sure your fire department has the equipment necessary to reach above that level.
- Properly maintain all electrical and heating equipment.
- Plan and practice escape in case of an emergency.
- Plan alternative methods of escape in case your first-choice plan fails.
- Know how to get emergency help. Most areas of the country have 911 service, but many universities have special telephone numbers other than 911. Know your number.

- Never smoke in bed or leave lighted cigarettes unattended.
- Inspect living areas for surfaces, objects, or room design that can lead to slipping or tripping.
- Make sure all rugs have skid-proof backing.
- Never overload electrical outlets.
- Do not place extension cords under rugs or where people walk.
- Never use a portable heater in an unvented area or near flammable materials.
- Keep outside doors locked at all times. Install chain locks on all doors.
- Check carefully before allowing anyone to enter.
- Look through the peephole or ask who is there before opening the door.
- Require people who claim to be maintenance workers to show identification before you allow them to enter.
- Place metal poles in the tracks of sliding doors so that they cannot be opened unless you remove the poles.
- Be especially careful in parking garages, laundry rooms, and hallways and when entering and leaving living quarters.
- Always tell someone where you are going, and whenever possible have a friend accompany you.
- See Just the Facts: Firearms in the Home for firearm safety guidelines.

This list is not all-inclusive, but it includes items for which you need to take responsibility. Discuss the rules for safe living with your housemates to help ensure each person's safety (see Assessment Activity 10-1).

Fire Detection Devices

There are two types of devices that warn of fire: (1) heat detectors, which activate when the temperature reaches a certain point, and (2) smoke detectors, which sense the first traces of smoke and set off an alarm before toxic levels of smoke and gas are reached. Heat detectors are not recommended for the home. Smoke detectors are either photoelectric or ionization chamber detectors. Both types are effective and reliable. Both types come in battery-operated models and models that depend on household electrical current. It is advisable to have a smoke detector for each level of an apartment or home. In placing the detector, be aware that (1) it should be on the ceiling or a sidewall 6 to 12 inches from the ceiling, (2) it should not be placed in the corner of a room because air does not circulate well in the corners, and (3) it should be at least 3 feet from registers and air vents so that drafts will not affect proper functioning.[1]

It is estimated that between 40 and 55 percent of fire deaths could be prevented by properly installed and well-functioning smoke detectors. In 1994, this estimated percentage would have represented more than 3000 saved lives in the United States.

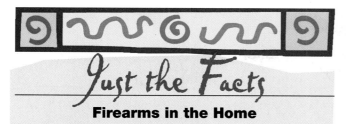

Just the Facts

Firearms in the Home

Many homes in the United States have firearms. If you choose to have a rifle, shotgun, or handgun, follow these guidelines for safely maintaining it:

* Keep all firearms unloaded within the home.
* Make sure firearms are locked and secured in a rack or case and have a trigger lock.
* Check to be sure a firearm is not loaded before storing it.
* Keep firearms in good working order.
* Keep your finger off the trigger when handling any firearm.
* Always point the muzzle in a safe direction (never point it at anything you do not intend to shoot).
* Store ammunition in a place separate from firearms.
* Lock the ammunition in a secure place.
* Educate all members of the household about gun safety.
* Enroll in a gun safety course if your are a new owner of a firearm.

Carbon Monoxide Detection

A relatively new detector alerts you to carbon monoxide dangers. **Carbon monoxide** is a colorless, odorless, tasteless gas that results from incomplete combustion of carbon-containing fuels. Anywhere fuels that contain carbon are burned there is the potential danger of death from carbon monoxide (CO) poisoning. A report by the National Center for Health Statistics (NCHS) illustrates the magnitude of this problem. According to the NCHS, of 900 deaths reported for inhaled poisoning, 75 percent were the result of CO poisoning.[2] Motor vehicle exhausts are the leading cause of CO deaths, but deaths also result from poorly vented cooking stoves, furnaces, and ventilating systems. Death occurs when the oxygen normally found in the red blood cells is replaced by CO. Thus, to prevent CO accidents, several precautions ought to be observed: (1) never operate a motor vehicle in an enclosed area; (2) never use charcoal in an enclosed area, such as an apartment, garage, or bed of a pickup with a camper top; and (3) make sure furnaces and all ductwork are inspected annually. Very small amounts of CO are potentially harmful, and anyone renting an apartment or living in a house should

be aware of this danger. There are several clues you can look for to detect CO in your home. Consistently stuffy, stale, or smelly air; high humidity; moisture on the windows; no draft in the chimney; soot gathering around the outside of a furnace or fireplace; and the smell of exhaust fumes all point to the presence of CO.

Battery-operated and wired CO detectors are available. Although these detectors are usually more expensive than smoke detectors, it is recommended that all homes and apartments have at least one. Placement should be in approximately the same location as fire detectors. If a second CO detector is used, it should be placed near the heating source.

Ten percent blood level is considered the vital cut off for exposure to carbon monoxide. CO affects children and people with smaller bodies more quickly. A healthy person can withstand a 60 to 80 percent CO blood level. Someone with heart disease may die at CO levels as low as 35 percent.[1]

Recreational and Outdoor Safety

One of the joys of life is participating in recreational or sporting activities. To reduce stress, improve cardiovascular conditioning, and promote personal spirituality, some people find that there is nothing more satisfying than being outdoors. Regardless of the season there are risks if personal alertness is not maintained (see Assessment Activity 10-2). Heat- or cold-related emergencies are always a potential problem. Chapter 3 discusses prevention of these types of emergencies.

In addition to the emergencies created by extreme heat or cold, many other injuries can result from involvement in recreational activities. Some of the more common injuries are blisters, bruises, sprains, muscle cramps, nosebleeds, wounds, and sunburns. Table 10-1 provides information on how to deal with these injuries.

The list of outdoor recreational activities is almost inexhaustible, as is the potential for the unexpected to happen. As you prepare to engage in outdoor or recreational activities, it is important to be familiar with the safety rules of your endeavor, have safe and appropriate equipment for the activity, and maintain an attitude of alertness to potentially dangerous situations. Although not all-inclusive, the following rules will help keep you safe in a variety of recreational settings:

* Seek training and instruction from certified or respected instructors.
* Purchase appropriate safety equipment for the activity. Make sure your eyes and head are properly protected.
* Make sure all equipment is in proper operating order.

Table 10-1 Recreational Injuries and Conditions

Injury	Signs and Symptoms	Prevention	Treatment
Blisters	Fluid under skin	Wear shoes that fit and gloves on your hands.	Avoid breaking them; if painful, clean area, puncture, squeeze, leave skin, cover with sterile dressing.
Contusions (bruises)	Swelling, pain, discoloration	Wear protective equipment.	Rest; apply cold compression; bandage.
Sprains	Pain, tearing sensation, tenderness, loss of function, swelling	Warm up before activity; strengthen your muscles.	Apply RICE—Rest, Ice, Compression, Elevation.
Muscle cramps	Painful muscle contractions (legs most often affected)	Condition for the activity; warm up before the activity; strengthen your muscles.	Stretch affected muscles.
Nosebleeds	Bleeding from nostrils	Protect your face; moisten your nose linings in dry air or high altitude.	Pinch your nose with your fingers for 5 minutes; apply ice.
Wounds (skin)	Cut, bleeding skin	Wear protective equipment and clothing; inspect equipment before use.	Apply direct pressure, elevate, clean with soap and water, and apply a sterile dressing.
Sunburns	Redness, pain, chills, blisters	Use sunscreen with a protection factor of at least 15; avoid sun exposure during peak hours.	Apply cool compresses; after pain has stopped, use a cream to keep skin moist; don't treat with oil-based products.

- Obey the laws related to your recreational pursuit.
- Begin any activity slowly and do not attempt advanced skills or actions until you are experienced enough to meet the necessary skill level.
- Stay aware of weather conditions. Always prepare for the worst possible weather.
- Never use alcohol when engaged in a dangerous recreational endeavor or during extremely hot or cold conditions. Alcohol increases the likelihood of emergency situations.
- Take a first-aid course that will prepare you to deal with a variety of unexpected situations.[3]

See Real-World Wellness: Trampoline, Mini-Tramp, and Double Mini-Tramp Safety.

Bicycling

The National Safety Council estimates that 57 million Americans ride bikes. Biking can be a highly enjoyable and, with proper precautions and common sense, safe activity. Safe biking begins with the rider. Defensive riding is the key to protecting against injury or even death. The National Safety council reported that, in 1995, 900 bicyclists were killed and more than 600,000 cyclists suffered disabling injuries. To ensure safe bik-

ing, taking precautions in traffic and wearing protective equipment are essential. Follow these guidelines for safe riding:[5]

- Always wear a helmet with a stiff outer shell designed to distribute impact and protect against sharp objects.
- Obey traffic rules. Cyclists must follow the same rules as motorists.
- Ride in single file with traffic, not against it. Watch for opening car doors, sewer gratings, soft shoulders, broken glass, and other debris.
- Use hand signals so that drivers will know your intention to make a turn, change lanes, or stop.
- When riding at night, wear reflective clothing. During the day, wear bright clothing that is very visible.
- Make sure your bicycle has the proper safety equipment: a red rear reflector; a white front reflector; a red or colorless spoke reflector on the rear wheel; an amber or colorless reflector on the front wheel; pedal reflectors; a horn or bell; and a rearview mirror. A bright headlight is recommended for night riding.
- Keep a safe distance from others and never hitch a ride on another vehicle.
- Be especially careful on wet surfaces, because stopping is much more difficult when brake pads and rims are wet. Be very careful when applying the

front brakes in wet conditions, because it is very easy to be thrown over the front handlebars.

Skateboarding

More than 80,000 people require hospital emergency room treatment each year from injuries associated with skateboarding. Common skateboarding injuries range from fractures to death as a result of falls or collision with motor vehicles. Wrist injuries (fractures or sprain) are the primary injuries associated with skateboarding. Irregular surfaces account for more than half of the skateboarding injuries involving falls. To make skateboarding as safe as possible, observe the following guidelines:[6]

- Wear protective equipment, including slip-resistant shoes, a helmet, and specially designed padding. This may not protect from fractures, but it will protect against the number and severity of cuts and scrapes.
- Use a helmet that fits properly and has a chin strap. The helmet should have a hard outer shell with ample padding to help absorb any blows to the head. Because there are no government standards, all equipment should be selected carefully.
- Wear wrist braces, knee and elbow protectors, and skateboarding gloves. You might also consider padded shorts and shirts.
- Learn how to fall. Although it is difficult to do, try to relax your body as you are falling. Attempt to roll rather than absorb the force with your arms.
- Check your skateboard each time before beginning to ride. Check the wheels and the board for cracks, loose screws, and nuts.
- Never ride in the street.
- Obey the city laws. Pay attention to traffic and avoid areas where skating is prohibited.

In-Line Skating

One of the most popular forms of recreational activity is now in-line skating. The concept of in-line skating originated with hockey players who wanted to extend their off-season training options. In-line skating is now utilized by everyone from hockey players to skiers to fitness and recreation enthusiasts. In-line skating burns as many calories as cycling or running. In addition, it is low impact, causing less stress to the lower body joints than caused by other sports. In-line skates protect ankles well because they are heavy, are made of thick plastic, and rise above the ankle.[5] Be sure to follow these safety tips:[7]

- Select good skates. If the plastic of the boot can be squeezed, the material is not strong enough to support your ankle.
- When buying skates, try them on with thick socks to ensure proper fit and comfort.
- Wear safety equipment, including a helmet, knee and elbow pads, and wrist braces.
- Know how to fall. See skateboarding guidelines for recommendations for falling.
- Learn how to skate on a smooth surface while learning how to stop and slow down. Achieve a basic skating proficiency before tackling more challenging surfaces.
- Be conscious of other skaters, joggers, walkers, and bicyclists.
- Watch for changes in skating surfaces and conditions such as potholes, sewer grates, gravel, broken pavement, or obstacles. Do not skate on wet or oily surfaces.

- Check your skates regularly to make sure they are in good condition. Replace worn wheels and brake rubbers.
- Warm up before beginning to skate.

Boating and Using Personal Watercraft

Everyone who plans to operate a boat should take a course on boat or personal watercraft (PWC) safety. Most boating deaths are caused by drowning preventable through the use of a personal flotation device (PFD), according to spokespeople for the U.S. Coast Guard. Most major accidents and deaths while boating are caused by "operator error." The four major factors associated with operator error are the following:

1. Inattention: looking away from the direction in which the boat is moving
2. Carelessness: boating in bad weather or rough water conditions
3. Intoxication
4. Speeding[4]

Operator safety awareness is key to saving lives and preventing injuring. It is the responsibility of the operator to know and practice Coast Guard safety recommendations and to ensure that every passenger has and, preferably, is wearing a PFD. The National Safety Council, the Coast Guard, and most boat dealers have information about the various types of PFDs.

The number of people using PWCs is also growing. This growth in use has resulted in an increase in injuries and fatalities. From 1987 to 1996 there were 349 fatalities and almost 8500 PWC-related injuries.[8] These small boats (sometimes referred to as *jet skis* or *wave riders*) range in size from one-person to three-person machines. They tend to be very quick and maneuverable. The key to the safe operation of PWCs is understanding their nature and practicing safe operation through proper adherence to the safety rules. The Underwriters Laboratories and the National Safety Council make the following recommendations to PWC operators:[9]

- Remember that a PWC is jet propelled. This means that, when the throttle is released, the ability to steer the craft is lost. Operators must know the characteristics of their boats and the space and time needed to safely slow their boats.
- Never get on a PWC without first putting on a vest-type PFD. This vest should be worn even when launching the PWC from a trailer.

Outdoor recreation is safer when you use proper safety equipment, observe appropriate safety rules, and learn as much as you can about each activity you engage in.

- Take a safe boating class.
- Use extra precautions when operating a PWC. Know the state laws regarding age limits for operation, other regulations, and PFD requirements.
- Never loan your PWC to an inexperienced operator.
- Never rent a PWC without learning and practicing, with supervision, the operation of the craft.
- Don't jump the wakes of other boats. Maintain a safe distance from other boats and PWCs.
- Don't operate a PWC after drinking alcoholic beverages or while intoxicated.

Snowmobiling

A highly enjoyable cold weather recreational activity is snowmobiling. The Snowmobile Safety and Certification Committee (SSCC) is a nonprofit organization sponsored by the manufacturers of various types of snowmobiles. Through the efforts of this group, standards have been developed for brakes, controls, seats, lights, shields, guards, handgrips, fuel systems, and sound levels. Anyone considering buying or renting a snowmobile should look for Certification 1 of the SSCC on the right side of the machine.

The second goal of the SSCC is to promote safe operation. Here are some of their guidelines for safe operation of a snowmobile:[10]

- Always perform an inspection of the machine before attempting to start it (check the brakes, throttle, steering controls, loose fittings, screws, and nuts).
- Make sure no one is standing in front of the machine when you turn on the ignition.
- Before operating a snowmobile, receive basic instruction in how to start it, steer it, turn it, and stop it and in how to shift you weight when on the machine.
- Ride only on easy trails at first. Don't attempt difficult trails or off-trail riding until your experience level permits it.
- Ride with an experienced operator until you are accomplished at riding safely.

- Wear protective clothing that provides protection from the cold and safety equipment, such as a helmet with a full face shield. A full face shield helps provide warmth as well as protection from branches or other debris.
- Never drink alcohol and operate a snowmobile at the same time. A study in Wisconsin found that more than 60 percent of those fatally injured in snowmobile accidents had elevated blood alcohol concentrations.[11]

Vehicle Safety

Human error accounts for nearly 85 percent of all vehicle accidents.[9] Experts use the term **improper driving** for speeding, failure to yield right-of-way, driving left of center, incorrect passing, and following too closely. Figure 10-1 provides information on the types of accidents and ages of victims.

One major cause of accidents is speed. In 17 percent of all fatal motor vehicle accidents, speed is the major factor. Another persistent hazard is the use of alcohol and other drugs. Estimates are that two of five Americans will be involved in an alcohol-related crash at some point in their lives. In 1997, alcohol was involved in 39 percent of all fatal crashes.[13] The role that other drugs play in accidents is not totally clear, but a study by the National Highway Traffic Safety Administration reported that drugs other than alcohol were found in the blood samples of 18 percent of people killed in vehicle accidents.[14] In most cases these other drugs were used in combination with alcohol.

Alcohol and high speeds are not the only factors that affect driving. Drowsiness is another important factor. See Real-World Wellness: Driving Drowsy for ways to minimize your risk of injury while driving your vehicle. The type of vehicle you or others drive is another factor in accidents. See Real-World Wellness: Kings of the Road for a discussion of sport utility vehicle safety.

Type of accident	Collision with railroad train	Collision with pedalcycle	Pedestrian accidents	Collision between motor vehicles	All motor-vehicle accidents
Death total	400	700	5700	21,300	43,200
Change from 1996	0%	0%	-2%	+9%	.05%
Death rate	0.1	0.3	2.1	8.0	16.1

Figure 10-1 Accident Types, 1997

SOURCE: From National Safety Council, *Accident Facts, 1998.*

Real-World Wellness

Driving Drowsy

Sometimes when I'm driving, I seem to get really tired. What can I do to help myself remain awake and alert when driving?

A number of conditions lead to driver drowsiness. First, today's cars and trucks have interiors with comfortable seats, are quiet and carpeted, and have temperature-regulated environments. Many vehicles also have cruise control, which can allow a driver's concentration to drift. Second, highways are constructed to eliminate sharp curves, hills, and bumps, which contributes to drowsiness while driving. Third, the repetitive patterns of oncoming light and of white and yellow lines during night driving can cause a trancelike state known as *highway hypnosis*. To prevent drowsiness and falling asleep behind the wheel of a vehicle, the National Safety Council offers the following tips:[17]

- Before starting a trip, get enough sleep—at least seven to eight hours—the night before.

- Don't start a trip late in the day. Driving long distances is hard work and you need to be fresh and alert.

- If possible, don't drive alone. Passengers can take turns driving and help keep each driver awake. Never allow all passengers to sleep in the vehicle at the same time.

- Avoid long drives at night because night driving increases the risk of "highway hypnosis."

- Make sure the vehicle environment is cool in both the summer and winter. Turn the radio volume up and switch stations frequently; avoid soft, sleep-inducing music.

- Stay involved in the driving process—don't use cruise control. Don't allow yourself to become too comfortable. Drive with your shoulders back, your buttocks against the seat back, and your legs flexed at about a 45-degree angle.

- Never use alcohol when driving.

- Take frequent breaks—stop for light meals, stop at a gas station, walk in a safe area for a few minutes.

- If you feel yourself drifting off and no one else can share the driving, stop at a safe place such as a truck stop, well-lit gas station or rest area and sleep for a short time; even twenty minutes will help. Always keep the doors locked.

- If you feel yourself getting drowsy, getting off the road may determine not only whether you stay awake but also whether you stay alive!!!

Real-World Wellness

Kings of the Road

I'm considering buying a new vehicle. Should I buy a sports utility vehicle since I've heard they are safer than other types of vehicles?

The answer to the question is "yes and no." When involved in an accident you are probably safer in a sports utility vehicle, or SUV, particularly if the accident involves a collision with a regular automobile. Here are some thoughts to ponder about cars and SUVs:[18,19,20]

- When a car is involved in a head-on collision with an SUV, the occupants of the car are four times more likely to be killed than are the occupants of the SUV.

- If there is a side crash, occupants of a car are nearly three times more likely to be killed than are the occupants of the SUV.

- In general, occupants of small cars are nearly fifty times more likely to be killed than are occupants of SUVs.

- Large SUVs can weight more than 5,000 pounds, which is more than 2.5 times the weight of some automobiles.

- A Chevy Metro is 12 feet 8 inches long, 5 feet 2 inches wide, and 4 feet 7 inches tall. Compare this size to that of a Ford Expedition, 17 feet long, 6 feet 6 inches wide, and 6 feet 2 inches tall. Designed for off-road use, the Expedition weighs 5497 pounds and still meets all government safety requirements.

- Because of an SUV's height, its bumpers tend to be much higher than those of a normal car. An SUV bumper may be at windshield height on some cars.

- Because of their higher centers of gravity, SUVs have a greater tendency to tip over than do cars.

Here are some ways our society might reduce the high risks involved in collisions between SUVs and other types of automobiles:

- Base the SUV on a car frame rather than a truck frame. This would make the SUV smaller, cheaper, and more fuel efficient. SUVs would, however, be less safe for their occupants.

- Raise insurance premiums of drivers of SUVs to discourage people from buying them.

- Give cars and SUVs equal chances in accidents: Make SUVs lighter and closer to the ground. Mercedes did this with its SUV (M-class) by making it with crumple zones and lower bumpers. However, this has made the SUV less safe.

- Improve the safety of automobiles to more closely resemble that of SUVs.

One of the most important factors in vehicle safety is the use of restraint systems (seat belts and air bags). The National Highway Traffic Safety Administration now requires all 1998 passenger cars and all 1999 multipurpose vehicles (jeeps, SUVs) to have dual airbags. It is estimated that at least 5000 deaths and 70,000 critical injuries could be prevented if people would just wear their seat belts.[1]

However, in order for restraint systems to improve safety, they must be used properly. Children and infants should be placed in the back seat in car seats designed for their age and size. Deaths of young children have been caused by deployed air bags. Some companies have reduced the force of air bags' deployment and/or have provided drivers with the ability to disengage the passenger side air bag. Many states have passed laws requiring that all children riding in cars be in a restraint system. All drivers transporting children should become familiar with the related state laws and be sure to use the type of car seat and restraint system recommended, according to age and size, for their child passengers. The use of restraint systems in not a luxury for adults, either. Proper restraint use is imperative to significantly improve the chances of surviving an automobile accident.

In the last few years, two other factors in vehicle safety have received a great deal of public attention. The first is the use of car phones while driving. While car phones are convenient and can add a measure of safety for people traveling on highways and in areas of high risk, too often car phones are a distraction that can cause accidents. The National Safety Council recommends that drivers who do use cellular phones when driving should be sure to use a phone that allows the driver to keep both hands on the steering wheel, a phone that features a microphone that can be installed on the sun visor, out of the driver's line of vision. Here are some guidelines for car phone users:

- Safe driving should be the priority, not talking on the phone.
- Do not attempt to use the phone in heavy traffic conditions that require complete concentration.
- Program frequently called telephone numbers into speed dial to minimize the loss of concentration on driving required by dialing a bunch of numbers.
- Do not attempt to dial a number when the vehicle is moving. Wait for a stoplight or pull into a safe area.
- Do not attempt to take written notes while the vehicle is moving. If you need to write something down, pull off the road to a safe location.
- When using the phone, drive in the slow traffic lane in case you have to pull over.

The second factor of concern is overaggressive driving. The United States seems to have become a nation of rude, unthinking, aggressive drivers, manifested in what has become known as **road rage** (see Assessment Activity 10-3). According to a recent report, over the last ten years aggressive driving has killed an average of 1500 people each year, injured another 800,000, and cost the country roughly $24 billion in medical costs, property damage, and lost time from work.[15] This study, conducted by the National Highway Traffic Safety Administration, used information from 400 police departments nationwide at which some 500,000 accidents were analyzed from 1988 through 1997. The investigators believe the actual numbers were underreported since many aggressive driving crashes do not cause injuries, and in many such crashes there is not enough evidence to justify a citation. Also, aggressive driving does not always result in an accident.[15]

Men have typically been considered more aggressive drivers than have women. The profile of an aggressive driver is of a poorly educated man, with some record of criminal activity or a history of violence and substance abuse. Such a profile makes many people feel better about themselves, but it is important to remember that there are hundreds of examples of successful men and women of all ages and with no violent histories committing acts of belligerence, hostility, and physical violence against fellow drivers.[15] Women are now viewed as being as aggressive as their male counterparts and are increasingly displaying the aggressive driving characteristics once associated primarily with men. As a nation of road ragers, we have come to use our cars as weapons, along with tire irons, golf clubs, guns, pepper spray, and even crossbows.[15]

What we must remember, in our overaggressive commutes to our daily destinations, is to give our fellow drivers a break. It is not our responsibility to teach others how to drive. To respond with less anger to our fellow drivers, we may have to leave a few minutes early to reach our destinations; listen to quiet, relaxing music while driving; and even pretend that the person in the next car (the one possibly driving dangerously or carelessly or too slowly or stupidly) is a loved one. Each of us must assume the personal responsibility to drive in a courteous manner. Be willing to give up the right-of-way and don't take another's foolish, inconsiderate behavior personally. Some guidelines that may help to prevent road rage are provided in the Just the Facts: Reducing the Incidence of Road Rage.

Motorcycle Safety

Motorcycles and mopeds offer several advantages over other modes of transportation. Their cost of operation is low, they consume less fuel, they take up less room on already overcrowded roads, and they provide their drivers with an often exhilarating feeling of freedom. Unfortunately, they are also two of the most dangerous transportation modes. The only protection most riders have is a helmet, and some states do not require that riders wear one. Of fatal motorcycle crashes, 60 percent involve collisions with other vehicles. It has been reported that 65 percent of all motorcycle-vehicle collisions are caused by the actions of vehicle operators and not motorcyclists.[21] The weather, malfunctioning equipment, and the surface of the road play a role in 10 percent of accidents. In addition, most cyclists do not receive formal training in safe riding. This becomes evident in analysis of the evasive actions of motorcycle riders. When avoidance actions are taken, 77 percent of those actions are improper.[21] Skidding from over-braking is the most common problem, and failure to use both brakes when attempting to avoid a collision is the second. A constant problem is the use of alcohol. Approximately 55 percent of motorcycle accidents involve use of alcohol by the cyclist.[11] Finally, motorcycles present a visibility problem: Even with their head-

Just the Facts

Preventing Road Rage

Here are some guidelines for reducing the incidence of road rage:[16]

- Give the other person a break.
- Do not tailgate.
- Do not let the car phone distract you.
- Do not switch lanes without signaling.
- If you are moving more slowly than most of the traffic, use the right lane.
- Do not drive in the passing lane when not attempting to pass another vehicle.
- Do not park in handicap parking if you are not disabled.
- Do not let your doors hit another person's car in a parking lot.
- Do not make obscene gestures to another motorist.
- Do not make faces at other drivers.
- Do not roll down the window and scream at other drivers.
- When confronted with an aggressive driver, slow down and back off.

Wellness On the Web
Behavior Change Activities

Home Sweet (Safe) Home
We all like to believe our home is a safe haven—but to a large degree, safety is something we must create for ourselves. Whether you live in a dormitory or an off-campus apartment, your personal safety depends on being alert to potential hazards and knowing what you can do to prevent or minimize them. Go to the CollegeEdge website at www.collegeedge.com/COLLEGE/Articles/ready/safety.stm to learn more about the dangers related to living on or near campus and what you can do to lower your risk. Select areas where you may be most vulnerable and write down things you can do now that will reduce your risk.

What's Your Domestic Violence "IQ"?
Domestic violence shouldn't happen to anybody, ever. But it does—and when it does, help is available. Maybe you've lived with abuse, maybe experienced it just once; maybe you work or live next to someone who is being abused right now. Today, family patterns are much more complex than years ago. Sociologists indicate that families, and the individuals in those families, are under more stress than ever. To test your knowledge of this problem, go to the Domestic Violence Handbook Homepage at www.domesticviolence.org/content.html and select "True or False." Answer the questions related to domestic violence. How much did you know?

Sleeping and Driving Don't Mix
You know how dangerous drinking and driving is, but you may not know that driving drowsy can be just as hazardous as driving drunk. In fact, when you're behind the wheel of a car, being sleepy can be a death warrant. Drowsiness slows reaction time, decreases awareness, and impairs judgment, just like drugs or alcohol. And, just like drugs and alcohol, drowsiness can contribute to a collision. Pennsylvania Turnpike and New York Thruway studies estimate that about 50 percent of their fatal crashes are caused by drowsy drivers. Go to the AAA Foundation for Traffic website at www.aaafts.org/Text/wakeup.html and complete the sleep quiz. How did you do?

lights on, many cyclists are not seen or are simply overlooked by vehicle drivers.

Here are some "rules of the road" that make motorcycle and moped riding safer:

- Always wear a helmet. Even though some states do not require you to, you significantly improve your chances of surviving an accident on a motorcycle or moped if you wear an approved helmet.

- Helmets should meet the federal safety standards set by the Department of Transportation, indicated by the word *DOT* appearing on the helmet. Some helmets will read, "Approved by the Snell Memorial Foundation," which means they have passed tests even more stringent than the federal standards.
- Wear gloves, boots, and heavy clothing to protect your body if you slide on the pavement, sidewalk, or gravel.
- Seek proper training in how to ride your vehicle; take a course in safe riding.
- Do not ride after drinking alcohol or taking medications that can diminish alertness or performance.
- Ride defensively. Motorcycles are harder to see and some motorists take advantage of their superior vehicle size and weight.
- Avoid riding in the rain or other wet conditions.

Pedestrian Safety

In their haste to get from one class to another, college students are notorious jaywalkers. The majority of the time nothing of consequence happens. However, nearly 60 percent of pedestrian accidents involve attempts to cross a street at either an intersection or between intersections. Usually, such accidents are the pedestrians' fault. Pedestrians make poor choices on when and where to cross streets, or they do not adequately observe traffic before attempting to cross. The student who darts suddenly from between two parked cars puts the motorist at a distinct disadvantage for seeing him or her and for stopping the vehicle. An invention of modern society, the stereo headset, causes users to be unaware of traffic noise and other sounds that would alert them to possible hazards or dangers.

The obvious implication of statistics about accidents involving pedestrians is to be extremely careful when crossing a street. Remaining alert at all times, not wearing stereo headsets, crossing only at designated crosswalks, and not entering the street from between parked vehicles are important safety precautions. When walking or jogging at night, wear light-colored clothing. Even better, wear a jacket or other apparel with reflective strips to make you visible to oncoming motorists. Statistics indicate that alcohol was a factor in 36 percent of fatal pedestrian accidents involving adults. These adults had blood alcohol content (BAC) levels at or above 0.10 (the legal level of intoxication in most states).[22]

Violence and Intentional Injury

As we go about our daily activities, we are constantly conscious of violence. Acts of violence include assault, homicide (murder), sexual assault, domestic violence,

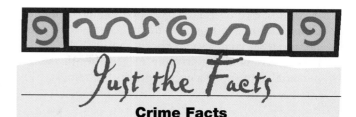

Just the Facts

Crime Facts

What follows are data[23] that represent the annual ratio of crime to fixed time intervals in the United States.

- One violent crime occurs every 22 seconds.
- One property crime occurs every 3 seconds.
- One burglary occurs every 11 seconds.
- One motor vehicle theft occurs every 20 seconds.
- One murder occurs every 22 minutes.
- One forcible rape occurs every 5 minutes.
- One robbery occurs every 47 seconds.
- One aggravated assault occurs every 28 seconds.

(Federal Bureau of Investigation: Uniform Crime Reports, 1996)

suicide, and various forms of abuse (see Just the Facts: Crime Facts). Each year in the United States, intentional violence accounts for 50,000 deaths and more than 2 million nonfatal injuries.[1] Violence has the potential to touch the lives of the college student regardless of school, gender, or ethnicity (see Assessment Activity 10-4). This section deals with one aspect of violence—assault.

Safety at the Automated Teller Machine

Many people use automated teller machines (ATMs) to carry out various banking transactions. These machines provide a convenient way to make deposits or withdrawals in a variety of locations and at almost anytime, when banks are closed, during holidays, evenings, and weekends. Over the last few years many violent crimes have been committed at ATM sites. If you must make an ATM transaction, keep the following rules in mind at all times:

- Use the ATM during daylight hours if possible. If you must use an ATM at night, take someone with you and only use a machine in a well-lighted area.
- Before using the machine, check to make sure no one is acting suspiciously or hanging around the area. Trust your instincts if you feel uneasy. Seek a machine in another area if you sense something is not right where you are.
- Make sure no one attempts to crowd you while you are using the ATM. Take all receipts with you—do not discard your receipt nearby.
- Do not write down your personal identification number (PIN) or carry it in your billfold or purse.

- If you drive to an ATM, park in a highly visible location and under a light at night. Always lock your car and hold your keys in your hand.
- Do not assume that a drive-up ATM is free of assault potential. Always be alert to your surroundings.

Car Jacking

One of the crimes of the 1990s that seems to be becoming more prevalent is **car jacking,** a crime in which someone attempts to steal a car while the driver or owner is present. Of car jackings, 45 percent occur on the street and another 30 percent occur in parking lots or garages. A gun is used in 70 percent of car jackings, which makes this crime potentially violent.[9] To protect yourself against such crime and to help reduce the risk of potential assault, do the following:

- Keep the doors of your car locked at all times, even when you are in it.
- Always park in a well-lighted, busy area. Avoid parking in underground or enclosed parking because the security may be poor.
- Always check the backseat before entering your car.
- When walking to your car at night, have a friend or a security guard accompany you. Take your friend to his or her car.
- If you become lost, go to a police station or well-lighted service station for directions. Do not ask bystanders or other motorists for directions.
- If you break down on the road, raise the hood, put a white cloth on the antenna, turn on your flashers, and stay in the car. If approached, lower the window slightly and ask the person to call the police. Do not get out of the car or accept a ride.
- If you are bumped from behind and the circumstances seem to be suspicious, stay in the car and drive to a police station or well-lighted service station and ask for help.
- Never pick up a hitchhiker.

Date or Acquaintance Rape

The terms *acquaintance* and *date rape* have been brought to the national consciousness over the last decade. **Acquaintance rape** is forced sexual intercourse between people who know one another well. **Date rape** is a form of acquaintance rape that involves forced sexual intercourse between people who are in a dating situation. Statistics indicate that 50 percent of rapes are committed by people the victims know or are dating.[24,25] Researchers reported that 24 percent of college women claimed to be victims of attempted rape, and 17 percent claimed to have been forced to have sex against their will.[26]

In the college setting, poor communication is associated with behavior that results in attempts at seduction. One survey of 600 college men and women found there was substantial agreement among both genders that aggression and coercion usually occurred when one partner felt "led on" and the other did not make it clear how far she or he was willing to go.[27] Obviously, one solution is for couples to learn that "no" really means "no" regardless of the tone or hesitancy with which it is stated. See Just the Facts: Guidelines for Avoiding Acquaintance and Date Rape.

Car jacking is an increasingly frequent crime.

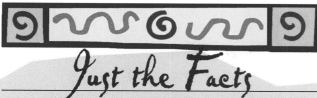

Guidelines for Avoiding Acquaintance and Date Rape

Men should observe these guidelines:

- *Know your sexual desires and limits.* Be aware of the effects of social pressure. It's okay not to "score."

- *Being turned down when you ask for sex is not a rejection of you personally.* If someone says "no" to sex with you it does not mean you are being rejected personally; what is being expressed is the desire not to engage in a single sex act. Personal actions are within your control.

- *Accept the woman's decision.* Don't read other meanings into the situation; "no" means exactly that!

- *Don't assume that the way a woman dresses or flirts indicates she wants to have sexual intercourse.*

- *Don't assume that previous permission for sexual contact applies to the current situation.*

- *Avoid excessive use of alcohol and drugs.* Alcohol and drugs interfere with clear thinking, perception, and effective communication.

Women should observe these guidelines:

- *Know your sexual desires and limits.* Believe in your right to set limits.

- *Communicate your limits clearly.* If you are offended, say so in a firm manner and do so immediately. Say "no" when you mean no.

- *Be assertive.* Men sometimes interpret passivity as permission. Be direct and firm with anyone who is pressuring you sexually.

- *Be aware that your nonverbal actions send a message.* If you dress in a sexy manner and flirt, men sometimes assume you want to have sex. You should be able to dress as you please and flirt without it meaning anything. However, be aware of the possibility for someone to misunderstand and misinterpret your actions.

- *Pay attention to your surroundings.* Do not put yourself in vulnerable situations.

- *Trust your intuitions.* If you feel you are being pressured, you are!

- *Avoid excessive use of alcohol and drugs.* Drugs and alcohol interfere with clear thinking, perception, and effective communication.

Researchers also point to a special problem on some college campuses on which there are strong fraternity or sorority organizations. Just because some athletic and other campus groups have condoned inappropriate actions on the part of their group members does not mean that all student social organizations are suspect. However, given the drinking, potential for intimacy, sexual teasing, and competitiveness characteristic of the house party, such gatherings sponsored by social organizations may provide social settings that encourage aggressive sexual behavior.[4] Today many sorority and fraternity organizations have classes that educate members in an effort to improve mutual understanding and avoid date coercion or rape.

An important strategy in avoiding date and acquaintance rape is to not use alcohol or drugs. Statistics indicate that 75 percent of male students and 55 percent of female students involved in rape had been drinking or using drugs when rape occurred.[18] For a discussion of Rohypnol, the so-called date-rape drug, see Just the Facts: Rohypnol—Set-up for Rape.

When a traumatic, often violent experience occurs, such as acquaintance or date rape, the victim usually experiences a great amount of enduring and substantial psychological damage. Date rape victims are particularly vulnerable because they are the victims of misplaced trust. Once the trust in a relationship is broken because of forced sex, developing new relationships becomes much more difficult for the victim.[6]

Regardless of how psychologically strong they are, most rape victims are likely to experience shock, anxiety, depression, shame, and a host of other psychosomatic symptoms. The psychological reactions following a rape are referred to as **rape trauma syndrome.** The syndrome is characterized by fear, nightmares, fatigue, crying spells, and digestive upset. Sexual function and desire may be impaired. The victim of violent sex may want her partner to be warm, tender, affectionate, and understanding, but she may not desire sexual intercourse for a long time after the rape. Sometimes lengthy counseling is necessary to help the rape victim reestablish a trusting attitude toward her relationships and sexuality.[24]

Another common psychological effect of rape is self-blame (the victim blames herself for what occurred). The victim tends to review every single aspect of the attack to understand what she could have done differently to have prevented the rape. Although most victims are blameless, self-accusation is quite common.[28] Self-blame is particularly prevalent in the cases of acquaintance or date rape because victims believe such rapes occurred because they created situations that permitted sexual coercion. Victims also tend to view their friends as being successful in the dating situation; it is common for victims to believe they are

Just the Facts

Rohypnol—Setup for Rape

The drug Rohypnol is a type of sleeping pill (flunitrazepam) which is illegal in the United States and Canada. Here is some key information about the drug:[30]

- It is produced legally in Mexico by Hoffmann-LaRoche.
- It is the most widely prescribed sedative or hypnotic in Europe.
- Manufactured illegal versions are available—the branded product seems to be preferred by illicit users.
- In the United States, it appears to be most frequently used in conjunction with alcohol, creating an enhancing (synergistic) effect.
- It is odorless and tasteless when mixed with alcohol.
- The drug seems to produce amnesia and a loss of inhibition.
- Several arrests have been made in conjunction with alleged date rape involving the use of Rohypnol. Allegations are that the drug was added to women's drinks without their knowledge.
- Adverse effects can include loss of memory, impaired judgment, dizziness, and prolonged periods of blackout. Although a sedative, Rohypnol can produce aggressive behavior.
- Use appears to be spreading among high school and college age groups.
- Street names include *rophies, roofies, ruffies, R2, roofenol, Roche, roachies, larocha, rope,* and *rib.*

Just the Facts

What to Do If You Are Raped

If you are raped, you should do the following:

- Call the police and tell them you were raped. Provide your location.
- Don't wash or douche before the medical exam. Take a change of clothes, but do not change until you have been examined.
- At the medical facility you will have a complete examination. Point out any bruises, cuts, scratches, and so on.
- Tell the authorities exactly what happened. Be honest and thorough.
- Be sure you are checked for pregnancy and STDs.
- Contact the campus agency that can help with rape counseling or contact the nearest Rape Crisis Center for counseling.

assertively may prevent or terminate many potentially devastating situations.

Homicide

Murder, or **homicide,** is a crime that has been on the decline for the last several years. FBI statistics indicate that the number of murders per 100,000 people was 6.8 in 1997. This represents an 8.1 percent drop from 1996 and is the lowest murder rate per 100,000 since 1967.[30] Even though the latest statistics are encouraging, two trends seem to emerge from the data. First, young African-American males (ages 14–25) are still at high risk for being murdered—they face a one in twenty-one lifetime chance of becoming murder victims.[31] Second, a great many murders involve illegal drug activity. Some research has indicated 25 to 50 percent of all homicides are drug related—these murders often result from disputed drug transactions. Many of the buyers involved in these transaction are college-age people. Even if making a one-time buy for fun or experimentation, a person engaging in a drug transaction is at high risk for losing his or her life. The obvious message here is to stay out of harm's way.

Domestic Violence

Today's families take many shapes, including single parents, blended families, and two-career families. More and more children are being left unattended

the only ones who have so "failed." Rape victims tend to perceive themselves as having permitted a social occasion to turn into a painful event. Victims need the understanding of friends, family, significant others, and possibly professional counselors to help them work through these feelings.[29] Just the Facts: What to Do If You Are Raped describes the steps a rape victim should follow or be encouraged to follow as soon as possible after the assault.

The best protection against date or acquaintance rape is preparation and remaining aware that the potential always exists for unwanted sexual advances and potentially traumatic sexual experiences. Planning what to do if faced with unwanted advances and acting

Nurturing Your Spirituality

Learning to Communicate

Much of what occurs in relationships can be traced to how couples learn to communicate. As couples fall in love, it is important that, as they experience the wonderful, sometimes overwhelming emotions of being in love with another person, they become aware of how their communication patterns are developing.

Each person brings to a relationship a different history and different perceptions and expectations. Dating couples who find that their methods of communication (or lack thereof) lead to periods of intense angry or physical confrontation, such as pushing or hitting one another, should seek to find more effective ways to communicate or, perhaps better yet, end the relationship completely.

Growing relationships should involve a maturing of love, care, trust, and concern. Such growth can occur only if people learn to communicate effectively and in a nonthreatening manner. Even though everyone wants to avoid physically and emotionally abusive situations, learning how to understand and communicate with a person whom you care deeply about is not just something that happens. Couples must work at developing communication. The starting point is how each person views the other: No one "belongs" to someone else, no one is anybody else's property. People make choices to be with and share their lives with others and actively attempt to do so by behaving with kindness and thoughtfulness and by exhibiting a desire to grow with their partners along the journey of life. For continued personal growth, we must find ways to communicate effectively with our partners.

The starting point for good communication is mutual *trust* between partners. Honest communication requires some vulnerability. A partner who is untrustworthy may misuse personal, private information by mocking it, revealing it to others, or using it to justify behavior. When both partners respect and treasure verbal intimacy, trust is created.

Partners should agree on the ground rules for approaching conversations in which there is potential for disagreement. Each partner should listen carefully to what the other is saying—not to try to win the conversation, but in order to understand. Each person should be allowed to speak about his or her perceptions and feelings without interruption or fear of verbal or physical abuse. Each person should ask clarifying questions and attempt to repeat what the other expressed. Anger does not lead to effective communication, and people should know when to take a time out and move away from each other for a few minutes to allow their anger to subside.

When communicating, it is important to use *I* messages whenever possible. *I* messages convey what the speaker is feeling, not what the speaker thinks his or her partner is feeling or doing. For example, "You make me feel angry" is not an *I* message, but "When you mention my family, *I* feel angry" is an *I* message. Through *I* messages, the speaker takes responsibility for his or her feelings and does not attribute them to a partner.

When communicating, it is also important to demonstrate an interest in listening and understanding. This entails maintaining eye contact and nodding or saying yes.

Finding ways to resolve conflict can improve the quality and extend the longevity of relationships. Remaining silent only serves to foster anger and indifference. Failing to discuss issues in a relationship merely builds walls, one brick at a time. The feelings of frustration and anger may eventually manifest themselves in extreme verbal or physical abuse or they may lead to indifference and loss of love.

---

while parents are either working or commuting home. Parents frequently feel overworked and children may feel neglected. The mix of related and unrelated people living in the same home can create new problems.

What can emerge from such situations and many others in our volatile society are various forms of domestic violence, including partner abuse, child abuse, or abuse of an elderly family member. (It is beyond the scope of this text to comprehensively discuss the particulars of these three areas of abuse.)

It is estimated that more than 2.5 million women are the victims of some form of violence each year.[14] **Partner abuse** cuts across all social and economic groups, but reported cases tend most often to involve young, unmarried, African-American and Hispanic women living in

large cities and lacking economic power.[32] Authorities estimate that only about half of all crimes of violence against a partner are ever reported. It is easy to be critical of people who do not report these crimes, but there are compelling reasons for their silence: Many women do not report abuse for fear of being killed or further injured and concern for the lives of any children that are part of the household. Since many abused women may have little or no financial support other than the abuser, they feel trapped. See Nurturing Your Spirituality: Learning to Communicate for some insight into the basis for some domestic violence.

Perhaps no form of abuse is more discussed than child abuse. The most frequent form of child abuse is neglect, followed by physical abuse, and then sexual abuse.[32] Any form of child abuse has both short- and long-term and frequently devastating consequences. Research has shown that abused children are more likely than other children to become abusers themselves, perform poorly in school, and become involved in adult crime and violence.[32]

More than 1.5 million elderly are estimated to be abused in the United States. Most often the abuser is the adult child of the victim. **Elderly abuse** can take the form of denial of food and medical care or of hitting, kicking, or robbing the victim. Suggested causes for such abuse range from the stress involved in caring for the victim to the abuser's having also been abused. For some elderly abusers, chemical dependence may be involved.

Regardless of the causes for any of the three types of abuse mentioned, there is no reason any person should have to suffer the indignity of abuse. Every person has the right to the highest quality life possible and no one has a right to inflict physical or psychological pain on anyone else. Anyone aware of an abusive situation has the moral and ethical responsibility to report the suspected abuse to authorities so that action can be taken to protect the innocent victim and to help ensure either the punishment or rehabilitation of the abuser.

Hate Crimes

Hate crimes are crimes directed at people or groups because of perpetrators' hatred of their race, nationality, ethnicity, religion, or sexual orientation. In 1996, 8759 hate-motivated criminal incidents were reported to the FBI. Of these offenses, 5396 were motivated by racial bias; 1401 by religious bias; 1016 by sexual-orientation bias; 940 by ethnicity or national origin bias; and 6 by multiple biases.[33] In 1996 the majority of hate crime incidents (31 percent) occurred in or on residential properties. Twenty-one percent of incidents were perpetrated on highways, on roads, in alleys, and in streets. Nine percent of hate crimes occurred at schools or colleges.[34] Perhaps the 9 percent occurring at schools or colleges is one of the most alarming statistics, because colleges are institutions in our society that we might expect to celebrate diversity. Hate crimes can occur anywhere, but educated college students and faculty should understand the importance of tolerance and acceptance of individual differences. No person should have to suffer a diminished quality of life because of another's hatred of his or her race, religion, sexual orientation, ethnic background, nationality, or political beliefs.

Summary

- Accidents are the leading cause of death for people 1 to 25 years of age.
- Awareness of potentially hazardous situations is imperative for accident prevention.
- A personal survey should be conducted to determine potential hazards, dangers, and risks in the home.
- Heat detectors and smoke detectors are the two types of devices for warning of fire. Heat detectors are *not* recommended for the home.
- Carbon monoxide is a colorless, odorless, tasteless gas that results from incomplete combustion of carbon-containing fuels. It can be potentially deadly in very small amounts.
- Knowing and obeying the rules for safe participation in recreational activities is the first step to fully enjoying a wide variety of activities.
- Common recreational injuries include blisters, bruises, sprains, muscles cramps, nosebleeds, wounds, and sunburns. A first-aid course that teaches how to manage emergencies is most helpful for safe participation in recreational activities.
- Over 57 million Americans ride bikes. Defensive riding is the key to protecting against injury and death.
- More than 80,000 people require hospital emergency room treatment each year for skateboarding accidents. Protective gear is essential. Wrist fractures and sprains are the number-one injury to skateboarders.
- In-line skating is a very popular recreational activity. Protective gear and knowing how to fall are imperative.

- Anyone planning to operate a powerboat or personal water-craft (PWC) should be familiar with safe boating practices and the rules of boating.
- Being familiar with how to operate water craft and wearing a personal flotation device (PFD) are essential to boating safety. Alcohol should be avoided when operating watercraft.
- Snowmobiling is an enjoyable activity in cold climates. Knowing how to safely operate the machines and wearing proper protective clothing are essential. Alcohol and operation of a snowmobile should not be mixed.
- All firearms in a household should be stored in a locked area and have trigger locks. Ammunition should be stored in a separate location from firearms.
- Trampolines are not good equipment to have for backyard recreation.
- Most vehicle accidents are caused by human error.
- Alcohol is involved in 39 percent of all fatal crashes.
- All occupants of a vehicle must use a restraint system (seat belts).
- Car phones can contribute to inattention and accidents during driving.
- Aggressive driving contributes to many accidents and other verbal and physical assaults.
- The United States is a nation of road ragers who commit acts of belligerence, hostility, and physical violence.
- Helmets are essential for riders of motorcycles and mopeds.
- Sixty percent of fatal motorcycle crashes are caused by collisions with other vehicles.

- Fifty-five percent of motorcycle accidents involve the use of alcohol.
- Nearly 60 percent of pedestrians accidents involve jaywalking.
- A pedestrian should always remain alert, never wear stereo headsets, and cross only at designated crosswalks.
- Acts of violence can occur anywhere and anytime. Acts of violence include assault, homicide, sexual assault, domestic violence, suicide and various forms of abuse.
- Try limiting use of ATM machines to daylight hours. Never use an ATM machine at night alone.
- To help protect against car jacking, always lock the doors, park in a well-lighted area, and check the backseat before entering the vehicle.
- Acquaintance rape is forced sexual intercourse between people who know one another well. Date rape is a form of acquaintance rape.

- Most rape victims suffer psychological effects, such as shock, anxiety, depression, and shame.
- Rape trauma syndrome is characterized by fear, nightmares, fatigue, crying spells, and digestive disturbances.
- Rohypnol is a drug associated with rape. It induces loss of inhibition and amnesia.
- Homicide has been declining for the last several years.
- Domestic violence can take the form of partner abuse, child abuse (physical and sexual), and elderly abuse.
- Hate crimes are crimes directed at people or groups solely because of the perpetrators' hatred of victims' sexual orientation, race, ethnicity, nationality, or religion. Nine percent of all hate crimes occur on college campuses.

Review Questions

1. What is the difference between intentional and unintentional injury?
2. Discuss some of the guidelines to follow to maintain a safe home environment.
3. What precautions should be taken to prevent fires and to protect oneself if one occurs?
4. What are the guidelines for safely participating in any recreational activity?
5. How should a firearm in a household be stored?
6. What does the term *improper driving* connote and what are some guidelines for safer driving?

7. What guidelines should men and women consider following to prevent rape?
8. How can rape trauma syndrome affect a victim?
9. Why does alcohol seem to be associated with intentional and unintentional injury and violence?
10. What needs to be done to prevent crimes such as abuse, murder, car jacking, and robbery?
11. What steps need to be taken to prevent hate crimes on college campuses?

References

1. Bever, D. L. 1996. *Safety: A Personal Focus* (4th ed.). St. Louis: Mosby.
2. National Safety Council. 1994. *Accident facts: 1994 Edition*. Chicago: The National Safety Council.
3. Payne W. A., and D. B. Hahn. 1996. *Understanding Your Health* (4th ed.). St. Louis: Mosby.
4. Consumer Reports. 1998. Consumer reports on health—special report on health guide to medication. *Consumer Reports* 10(4):1.
5. The National Safety Council. 1998. *Safe Bicycling Fact Sheet*. Itasca, Ill.: The National Safety Council.
6. The National Safety Council. 1998. *Skateboarding Fact Sheet*. Itasca, Ill.: The National Safety Council.
7. The National Safety Council. 1998. *In-Line Skating Fact Sheet*. Itasca, Ill.: The National Safety Council.
8. Acerrano, A. 1997. Danger afloat. *Sports Afield* 49.

9. The National Safety Council. 1998. *PWC Popularity Continues—Underwriters Laboratories Inc. and the National Safety Council Offer Recommendations for Riders*. Itasca, Ill.: The National Safety Council.
10. International Snowmobile Industry Association. 1982. *Snowmobile Fact Book*. Annandale, Va.: ISIA. Available on-line at **www.snowmobile.org/t_safety.htm.**
11. Peter, R., and F. Wenzel. 1986. A ten-year survey of snowmobile injuries and fatalities in Wisconsin. *The Physician and Sports Medicine* 14(1):140.
12. USA Gymnastics. Available on-line at **www.USA-gymnastics.org/publications/technique/1995/4/trampoline.html**
13. The National Safety Council. 1998. *Accident Facts: 1998 Edition*. Itasca, Ill.: The National Safety Council.

14. The National Highway Traffic Safety Administration. 1994. *Traffic Safety Facts 1993: State Alcohol Estimates*. Washington, D.C.: NHTSA.
15. Bowles, S., and P. Overberg. November 23, 1998. Aggressive driving: A road well-traveled. *USA Today* 17A.
16. AAA Foundation. 1997. *Road Rage on the Rise*. Available on-line at **www.webfirst.com/aaa.**
17. The National Safety Council. 1998. *Driver Fatigue Fact Sheet*. Itasca, Ill.: The National Safety Council.
18. Fix, J. L. February 10, 1998. Cars lose in crashes with sport-utilities—weight, height of impact lethal study shows. *Detroit Free Press*.
19. **www.auto.com/autonews**
20. King of the Road, **www.hypatia.wright.edu/dept/eng/kings.htm.**
21. National Highway Traffic Safety Administration. 1994. *Traffic Safety Facts*

1993: Motorcycles. Washington, D.C.: NHTSA.

22. National Highway Traffic Safety Administration. 1994. *Traffic Safety Facts 1993: Pedestrians.* Washington, D.C.: NHTSA.

23. FBI. 1996. *Uniform Crime Reports, 1996.*

24. Bureau of Justice Statistics. 1989. *Injuries from Crime: Special Report.* Washington, D.C.: U.S. Department of Justice, U.S. Government Printing Office.

25. Rynd, N. 1988. Incidence of psychometric symptoms in rape victims. *The Journal of Sex Research* 24:155.

26. Ledserman, D. 1995. College report rise in violent crime. *The Chronicle of Higher Education* A32. vol. 45.

27. Copenhaver, S., and E. Grauerhola. 1991. Sexual victimization among sorority women: Exploring the link between sexual violence and institutional practices. *Sex Roles* 24:3142.

28. Muelhlenhard, C. L., and M. A. Linton. 1987. Date rape and sexual aggression in dating situations: Incidence and risk patterns. *Journal of Counseling Psychology* 34(2):186.

29. Hass, K., and A. Hass. 1993. *Understanding Sexuality.* St. Louis: Mosby.

30. National Institute of Drug Abuse. 1995. *Epidemiologic Trends in Drug Abuse—Advanced Report by the Community Epidemiology Work Group.* NIDA. Washington, DC.

31. U.S. Department of Justice. 1998. *Federal Bureau of Investigation Crime Statistics for 1997.* Uniform Crime Reporting Program Press Release. Available on-line at **www.fbi.gov/ucr/urr97prs.htn.** Washington, DC.

32. Department of Justice. 1992. *Drugs, Crime, and the Justice System: A National Report.* Washington, D.C.: U.S. Department of Justice, U.S. Government Printing Office.

33. Bachman, R. 1994. *Violence Against Women: A National Crime Victimization Survey Report.* Washington, D.C.: U.S. Department of Justice. U.S. Government Printing Office.

34. Federal Bureau of Investigation. 1997. *Uniform Crime Reports—Hate Crimes Statistics, 1996.* U.S. Department of Justice, U.S. Government Printing Office.

Suggested Readings

Dreissman, B. and Kreissman. 1997. *The Complete Winter Sports Safety Manual: Staying Safe and Warm Snowshoeing, Skiing, Snowboarding, Snowmobiling and Camping.* Helena, Mt.: Falcon Publishing Company.

This book provides the information needed to stay safe while participating in winter sports, including information about emergency equipment and emergency field procedures.

Gillis, J., A. B. Cheng, K. Fierst, and A. B. Curran. 1998. *The Car Book 1998: The Definitive Buyer's Guide to Car Safety, Fuel Economy, Maintenance, and Much More.* New York: Harper-Perennial Library. Easy-to-read ratings concerning crash tests, fuel economy, preventive maintenance, insurance costs, and consumer satisfaction are provided for all vehicles.

Gutman, B. 1996. *Be Aware of Danger (Focus on Safety).* Breckenridge, Colo.: TwentyFirst Century Books.

This book focuses on helping children deal safely with strangers and dangerous situations in school and on the streets. It is an excellent resource for parents who have children ages 9 through 12.

Marques, L., L. Carter, and M. Nelson. 1998. *Child Safety Made Easy.* Concord, Calif.: Screamin' Mimi Publications.

This humorous, easy-to-read publication explores poignant issues about safety for children and families. Excellent safety tips for people caring for newborns and children up to 5 years of age.

Tilton, B. 1995. *Camping Healthy Hygiene for the Outdoors.* Merrillville, Ind.: Ics Books.

This publication provides tips on how to camp safely and protect yourself from disease and illness at the campsite.

Assessment Activity 10-1

How Safe Is Your Home?

Directions: This activity is designed to help you assess the safety of your living environment—apartment, dormitory, or house. Indicate whether each statement is or is not true for you or if you are unsure about it. A scale is provided at the end of the assessment.

General Concerns	Yes	No	Not Sure
I have homeowners or renters insurance.			
I have personal liability insurance.			
There is at least one smoke detector per floor (including the basement).			
There is a carbon monoxide detector on each floor.			
All detectors are in working order.			
There is at least one fire extinguisher in the house.			
I know (and my housemates know) the location and operation of the fire extinguisher.			
Electrical outlets are never overloaded.			
There is a rehearsed plan of escape from the house.			
Everyone in the household knows how to protect herself/himself in a fire emergency.			
Emergency phone numbers are posted near every phone.			
All guns are safely stored with trigger locks engaged.			

Entryways and windows

	Yes	No	Not Sure
Doors and windows are locked at all times.			
There are deadbolts on all the doors.			
I use the peephole before allowing anyone to enter.			
Strangers are not allowed to enter without first showing identification.			
There are safety bar locks on all the sliding doors.			

Surfaces, hallways and stairs	Yes	No	Not Sure
There are slip-proof floor coverings on all floors.			
There is sufficient lighting in halls, stairs, and entryways.			
Electrical outlets are childproofed.			
Halls, stairs, and entryways are clear of obstacles.			

Kitchen

	Yes	No	Not Sure
Surfaces are clean and free of dangerous objects and substances.			
Sharp objects are properly stored.			
There are slip-proof floors and throw rugs.			
I position panhandles safely while cooking.			
All food preparation surfaces are clean.			
Household cleaning agents and other dangerous products are kept in a safe location.			

Bathroom

	Yes	No	Not Sure
Electrical appliances are not near sinks or tubs.			
There is a bath mat or nonskid strips in each tub.			
Toilets are clean, free of mildew, and bacteria.			
Drugs and other dangerous products are kept out of reach of children			
Drugs and other products are stored in their original containers.			

Living room and den

	Yes	No	Not Sure
Electrical cords are placed in safe locations and do not trail across the floor.			
Unused outlets are covered.			
Rugs are secured with slip-proof backing.			

Bedroom and Nursery

Smoke and carbon monoxide detectors are installed and working.

There are night-lights in the room or adjoining hallway.

There is no high threshold to trip over.

Unused electrical outlets are covered.

Scoring Although this assessment is designed only to be a thought-provoking activity, the following scale may help increase awareness of the potential dangers within your house. Give yourself one point for each "yes" answer. Give yourself zero points for each "no" or "not sure" answer:

39–34:   Good score, but stay alert
33–28:   Check carefully for potential hazards
27 and below: Significant risks; changes are necessary

Name _____ Date _____ Section _____

Assessment Activity 10-2

Recreational Safety—How Safe Are You?

Directions: This activity is designed to assess your susceptibility to accidents and events when participating in recreational activities. Indicate whether each statement is always, sometimes, or never true for you. Skip over the activities in which you never participate.

General Considerations	Always	Sometimes	Never
I seek proper instruction before participating in a recreational activity.	_____	_____	_____
I take a safety class for each new recreational activity.	_____	_____	_____
I use appropriate safety equipment.	_____	_____	_____
All my equipment is in excellent working order.	_____	_____	_____
I do not use alcohol or drugs when engaging in a recreational activity.	_____	_____	_____
I can swim well enough to save myself in a given situation.	_____	_____	_____
I know the basic first aid and CPR for a given situation.	_____	_____	_____
I can effectively deal with heat and cold emergencies.	_____	_____	_____
I use sunscreen when in the sunlight.	_____	_____	_____
I obey rules, laws, and regulations related to my activity.	_____	_____	_____
I am aware of weather conditions when engaging in my activity.	_____	_____	_____

Bicycling

	Always	Sometimes	Never
I obey traffic rules and follow the same rules as motorists.	_____	_____	_____
I use hand signals to inform others of my intentions.	_____	_____	_____
I wear a helmet.	_____	_____	_____

General Considerations	Always	Sometimes	Never
I wear a helmet with the following features:			
—a stiff outer shell designed to distribute impact and protect against sharp objects	_____	_____	_____
—an energy-absorbing liner 1/2 inch thick	_____	_____	_____
—a chin strap and fastener	_____	_____	_____
—lightweight, cool, and comfortable clothing	_____	_____	_____
At night I wear brightly colored, reflective clothing.	_____	_____	_____
I ride in single file with traffic, not against it.	_____	_____	_____
I remain alert to holes, sewer gratings, soft shoulders, broken glass and other debris, and people opening car doors.	_____	_____	_____

Motorcycling

	Always	Sometimes	Never
I wear a helmet (regardless of state laws).	_____	_____	_____
I wear boots, gloves, and heavy clothing to protect my skin when riding.	_____	_____	_____
I keep abreast of safety techniques and regulations through proper training.	_____	_____	_____
I avoid riding in wet or icy weather.	_____	_____	_____
I do not take drugs or drink alcohol when riding.	_____	_____	_____
I ride defensively, giving up the right-of-way.	_____	_____	_____

Boating & Personal Water Craft (PWC)

	Always	Sometimes	Never
I know the latest rules of operation for a power boat.	_____	_____	_____
I do not operate boat while drinking alcohol or intoxicated; I do not ride in a boat operated by someone who is or has been drinking alcohol.	_____	_____	_____

General Considerations	Always	Sometimes	Never
I wear a personal flotation device (PFD) when in a boat.	_____	_____	_____
I make sure I have an observer when water skiing or operating a watercraft pulling a skier.	_____	_____	_____
I am alert to changing weather conditions.	_____	_____	_____
I do not ride or operate PWC without wearing a securely fastened PFD.	_____	_____	_____
I do not drink alcohol when operating a PWC.	_____	_____	_____
I look in all directions when operating a PWC.	_____	_____	_____
I do not jump the wakes of boats.	_____	_____	_____
I remember that, when I release the throttle, the PWC cannot be steered or controlled.	_____	_____	_____
I cruise an area to check for hazards before skiing, operating a PWC, or operating a boat at increased speed.	_____	_____	_____

In-line skating

	Always	Sometimes	Never
I wear protective equipment (helmet, elbow & knee pads, light gloves, wrist guards).	_____	_____	_____
I practice stopping, turning, and making general movements on the skates before skating on streets.	_____	_____	_____
I am skilled at skating backwards.	_____	_____	_____
I can safely stop by using the heel stop, T-stop, or power stop.	_____	_____	_____
My skates fit me properly.	_____	_____	_____
I obey all traffic laws.	_____	_____	_____
I am watchful of pedestrians, cyclists, and autos when skating.	_____	_____	_____
I do not pass other skaters or pedestrians without alerting them.	_____	_____	_____
I inspect my equipment before skating.	_____	_____	_____

Skateboarding

	Always	Sometimes	Never
I wear protective equipment (helmet, elbow and knee pads, light gloves, wrist guards).	_____	_____	_____

General Considerations	Always	Sometimes	Never
I wear slip resistant shoes.	_____	_____	_____
My skateboard has a slip resistant surface.	_____	_____	_____
I inspect my board prior to riding.	_____	_____	_____
I do not ride in the street.	_____	_____	_____
I do not skate in crowds of nonskateboarders.	_____	_____	_____
I obey the laws about where and where not to skate.	_____	_____	_____
I know and practice how to fall.	_____	_____	_____
I do not hitch a ride from a car, bicycle, or other vehicle.	_____	_____	_____

Firearms

	Always	Sometimes	Never
Gun safety is a high priority.	_____	_____	_____
I obey the gun possession laws in my state.	_____	_____	_____
My guns are in proper operating condition.	_____	_____	_____
I consider every gun to be loaded.	_____	_____	_____
I keep the safety on until ready to shoot.	_____	_____	_____
I keep the gun barrel pointed down.	_____	_____	_____
When stored, my gun has a trigger lock on it.	_____	_____	_____
I do not store a loaded gun.	_____	_____	_____
I do not handle a firearm when drinking or intoxicated.	_____	_____	_____
I target practice only at approved ranges.	_____	_____	_____

Assessment

This activity is designed to help you assess your behavior when participating in a variety of activities. Evaluate your participation in any of your activities. Any check in the "never" or "sometimes" column means that precautions should be taken to correct the situation. Safe participation in any activity requires careful planning—not doing so can place you at serious personal risk. Here are some questions to consider:

1. What needs to be done to correct each of the "sometimes" or "never" items?
2. What are the potential consequences of not taking corrective action(s)?
3. Are you endangering others through your present actions?

Assessment Activity 10-4

Encounters of the Dangerous Kind

Unfortunately, our everyday lives seem to be associated with many aspects of violence. This activity is designed to help you determine how at risk you are for such violence as car jacking, ATM robbery, gang violence, domestic violence, rape, and even homicide. This survey will ask you to think about some issues and situations that can have dangerous, life-threatening consequences.

Directions: Indicate whether each statement is always, sometimes, or never true for you.

General Safety Considerations	Always	Sometimes	Never
I am aware of my surroundings.	_____	_____	_____
I tell someone where I am going when leaving my home.	_____	_____	_____
I am careful about providing personal information and daily schedule information to people I do not know.	_____	_____	_____
I vary my daily routine and walking patterns.	_____	_____	_____
If I walk at night, I walk with others.	_____	_____	_____

Car jacking

	Always	Sometimes	Never
I look in the backseat before entering my car.	_____	_____	_____
I survey the location before parking, stopping, or getting into or out of my car.	_____	_____	_____
I keep my car doors locked.	_____	_____	_____
I have a plan of action if my car should break down.	_____	_____	_____
I check my mirrors & scan ahead for potential dangers.	_____	_____	_____
I avoid driving alone at night.	_____	_____	_____

General Considerations	Always	Sometimes	Never
I avoid dangerous areas that have a reputation for being high-risk areas.	_____	_____	_____
If hit from behind, I travel to the nearest police station, motioning to the person who hit me to follow.	_____	_____	_____
If I notice anyone loitering near my car, I do not go near it but go to a safe place and call the police.	_____	_____	_____

ATM Safety

	Always	Sometimes	Never
I avoid using an ATM at night.	_____	_____	_____
I attempt to take someone with me when going to use an ATM.	_____	_____	_____
I look for suspicious people or activity before entering an ATM area.	_____	_____	_____
If I drive to an ATM, I park under a light in a highly visible area.	_____	_____	_____
I remember my PIN number.	_____	_____	_____
I take all receipts with me.	_____	_____	_____
Even if using a drive-up ATM, I survey the area carefully.	_____	_____	_____

Violence, rape, and homicide

	Always	Sometimes	Never
I avoid dangerous areas of my city or campus.	_____	_____	_____
I watch my alcohol intake carefully when at parties.	_____	_____	_____
I do not drink alcohol on a first date.	_____	_____	_____
I avoid arguments or potentially violent situations after drinking alcohol.	_____	_____	_____
I refuse to be with anyone who seems to be violent.	_____	_____	_____

I do not strike or allow
myself to be struck by
another person.   _____   _____   _____

I do not allow myself to
be around anyone who
has a gun and is drinking
alcohol or using other
drugs.   _____   _____   _____

I break off a relationship
that is verbally or physically
abusive.   _____   _____   _____

Scoring In each section of the survey give yourself 3 points for each time you checked the "always" column and 2 points for each check in the "sometimes" column. Give yourself 0 points for any checks in the "never" column. Although not scientific, the following point scheme may help you assess your total risks. Even though your score may reflect a high level of safety, make sure to examine each section for too many "sometimes" or "never" answers, which could indicate you are at serious risk.

87–81: You are probably safe if you continue to observe current precautions.

80–70: You may have some areas to reexamine and change.

69 and below: You may engage in some behaviors that require significant change.

Taking Responsibility for Drug Use

Key Terms

alcohol
addictive behavior
addictive disorder
binge drinking
caffeine
cocaine
depressants
designer drugs
drug
inhalants

mainstream smoke
marijuana
narcotics
nicotine
passive smoking
psychoactives
reward deficiency
 syndrome
sidestream smoke
stimulants

Goals for Behavior Change

- Make more informed decisions about alcohol, tobacco products, and other drugs.
- Assess your personal attitudes about drugs and drug use behavior.
- Discontinue any risky behaviors related to drug use.
- Develop a personal plan for your use of alcohol.

Objectives

After completing this chapter, you should be able to do the following:

- Identify reasons people use drugs.
- Define specific terms associated with drugs and drug use.
- Explain how drugs are classified.
- Describe the dangers associated with the use of various drugs.

uality of life is a frequently used term that refers to the "how" of life—how well you live, how healthy you are, how much you are able to accomplish your goals, and how happy you are. The primary determinants of quality of life are the decisions you make that affect your life either positively or negatively. As suggested by this book, a high quality of life balances the physical, mental, emotional, social, and spiritual needs of a person for optimal health, satisfaction, and enjoyment. Achieving this goal means making intelligent choices—ones that contribute to your well-being—both for the moment and for your future. To make informed choices, you must have accurate information and you must understand that your actions have consequences. The decisions you make are cumulative. As time goes on and as you age, the consequences of previous decisions, actions, habits, and modes of behavior increasingly affect the way your body and your mind function. The emphasis of much of this book is on personal behaviors, such as exercise, weight maintenance, proper nutrition, and the prevention of disease through lifestyle. Other factors and decisions also influence your quality of life.

This chapter deals with drugs. Drug use or nonuse can strongly affect your health and quality of life. Drugs used for treatment, cure, prevention, or relief of pain or disease are categorized as medicines. Many people are alive because of the therapeutic effect of drugs used to prevent or manage disease and maintain health. However, not all drugs are used as medicines. When usage involves reasons other than medicinal, even if usage is considered recreational, the potential exists for tragic consequences. Understanding potential problems can help you make wiser decisions about drug use.

Reasons for Drug Use

A **drug** is any substance that kills organisms (such as bacteria and fungi) in the body or that affects body function or structure.[1] (Other terms that may be important for understanding drugs are listed in Just the Facts: Understanding Drug Terminology.) People use drugs for many reasons. Some need drugs for health reasons—to maintain a normal life or to alleviate symptoms or complications of diseases or other conditions. Others indulge in drugs to alter their moods. Researchers have identified several reasons people use drugs:[1]

- *Medicinal purposes:* Medicines are used for a wide range of purposes—from reducing symptoms of the cold and flu or treating headaches to lowering blood pressure or cholesterol to extend life and maintain quality of life. People who suffer from chemical imbalances such as with bipolar disorder or depression would be unable to live normal lives without the availability of certain drugs. Methylphenidate (Ritalin), commonly used illegally as a stimulant, is also used to treat adults and children who have attention-deficit disorder. When used in this capacity, Ritalin frequently helps such people focus on and complete tasks—something difficult for these people to do without medical intervention. Medicines, although dangerous even under a physician's supervision if misused or prescribed incorrectly, are invaluable to many for maintenance of an active, positive lifestyle.

- *Recreational/social facilitation:* People frequently use drugs with the belief that they will lessen the tension associated with social encounters. Marijuana and alcohol are particularly popular in social situations. Potential dangers of using drugs for this purpose include mental dependency on the drug and an inability to cope with social events without using the drug.

- *Sensation seeking:* Some people enjoy taking risks. For them, drugs fulfill the need for excitement and adventure. Others turn to drugs out of boredom or a feeling of inadequacy in their lives. Unfortunately, when they become tolerant to the drug or they do not find the type of "high" they were looking for, users frequently turn to increasingly dangerous drugs or to increased doses to provide equivalent or more exciting thrills.

- *Religious or spiritual factors:* Throughout history people have used drugs to enhance their spirituality or to achieve spiritual states or awarenesses. Too often in these situations, the drug itself becomes the object of worship. Though many people have tried, the spiritual realm has not been achieved through use of mind-altering drugs.

- *Altered states:* Drugs are sometimes used to increase the intensity of a mood or create a state of euphoria. Some people attempt to enhance physical performance or stimulate artistic creativity. Evidence indicates that perceptions of improved abilities induced by drugs are false.

- *Rebellion and alienation:* The use of drugs can be a deliberate act of rebellion against social values, especially the values of parents or society. Many people who experience extreme pressures and have difficulty coping turn to drugs as an escape. These people include college-age students facing academic pressure and increased personal freedom.

- *Peer pressure and group entry:* People who have a great desire to feel accepted socially often use drugs to demonstrate their sameness with other members

Just the Facts

Understanding Drug Terminology

Here are possibly unfamiliar terms that are useful for understanding the effects of substances:

- **Addiction:** Compulsive, uncontrollable, chronic dependence on a drug or drugs to the degree that severe emotional, mental, or physiological reactions occur; a desire to use drug(s) contrary to legal and/or social prohibitions.
- **Antagonistic:** Opposing or counteracting.
- **Designer drugs:** Illegally manufactured psychoactive drugs that are similar to controlled drugs on the FDA's schedule.
- **Drug abuse:** The excessive and pathological use of a drug that has dangerous side effects.
- **Drug misuse:** The use of a drug for purposes other than intended.
- **Effective dose:** The amount that produces the desired effect.
- **Habit:** As pertains to drug use, a patterned, regular, and possibly involuntary involvement with a particular drug.
- **Lethal dose:** The amount capable of causing death.
- **Medicines:** Drugs used to prevent illness or to treat symptoms of an illness.

- **Over-the-counter (OTC) drugs:** Nonprescription drugs.
- **Physical dependence:** A physiological need for a drug.
- **Polyabuse:** The use of multiple drugs.
- **Potentiating:** Describes an exaggerated drug response obtained when two drugs are taken together; a much greater effect is obtained than when either drug is taken separately.
- **Prescription drugs:** Drugs obtained only by order of a physician or dentist.
- **Psychoactive:** Affecting mood and/or behavior.
- **Psychological dependence:** An emotional or mental need to use a drug.
- **Synergistic:** Describes a combined effect that is greater than the sum of the individual effects when two or more drugs are used at the same time; the combination produces an exaggerated effect or a prolonged drug action.
- **Therapeutic index:** The difference between the minimum amount of a drug needed for a therapeutic effect and the minimum amount that has a toxic concentration or effect.
- **Toxic dose:** The amount that produces a poisonous effect.

---

of their group. People claim to use drugs to feel accepted, to imitate people they admire, and to attempt to create an identity or project a specific image. Self-esteem seems to be a vital component. People with high self-esteem see themselves as competent, successful, self-sufficient, accepting, outgoing, and well rounded. People with low self-esteem tend to feel isolated and unloved and have a reduced capacity for joy or self-fulfillment. To overcome these sensations and perceptions, many people turn to drugs.

Curiosity: Many people first experiment with drugs out of curiosity—the desire to see what using the drug feels like or what the attraction is for chronic users. Although curiosity is normal and healthy in may circumstances, the primary problem associated with experimentation with drugs out of curiosity is the inability to know how a drug will affect any one person. Whereas one person may consider the effects of a drug pleasurable, someone else may have a different, occasionally fatal, reaction. Most

people try alcohol during their lives. For most people this creates no problem; they can choose to use it or not use it. For some people, however, one act of curiosity can result in the disease of alcoholism.

The reasons any person uses drugs are usually not easily categorized. (List yours in Assessment Activity 11-2.) Most drug-use situations depend on personality, experience, perceptions of the environment, and expectations (see Just the Facts: What's the Cause of Addictions?).

Drug Classification

Drugs can be classified in a number of ways. For example, they can be classified according to legality (legal or illegal), whether their effects are primarily physiological or psychological, or whether their use has more medicinal benefits or a greater potential for abuse. This latter system is based on the Controlled Substance Act of 1970, which classifies narcotics and other dangerous drugs. The system contains five classifications called

Just the Facts

What's the Cause of Addiction?

Addiction has been defined as "a condition characterized by the compulsive abuse of a drug or drugs."[1] In other words, addiction is a pathological relationship with a substance that has life-damaging potential. Here are some recent theories about addiction:

- The spectrum of addictions ranges from alcohol and tobacco to behavior such as eating and working.

- The causes of addiction are complex and interrelated. A number of interacting variables may contribute to the development of addiction.

- Variables that may contribute to addiction include genetics, family influences, friends, life events, social and cultural values, availability, and personality.

- Studies indicate that some inherited traits may lead to alcoholism.[8,9] For instance, alcoholics may have an inherited inability to determine their levels of intoxication when drinking alcoholic beverages.

- Studies have found that addictive, impulsive, and compulsive disorders may have a common genetic origin.[10] These disorders may result from the failure of cells to signal molecules in the brain's reward system, so that the brain is unaware of certain sensations of pleasure or success. This failure is viewed as a type of sensory deprivation of the brain's pleasure mechanisms. The manifestation of this disorder is referred to as **reward deficiency syndrome.**

- Personality type, temperament, and attitudes may also contribute to drug use and addiction. **Addictive behavior** is any behavior that is excessive, compulsive, and psychologically or physically destructive.

- Personality traits associated with drug abuse include rebelliousness, resistance to authority, independence, and low self-esteem. In addition, people who abuse drugs seem to have a high tolerance for deviance in others, place a low value on education and religion, display low levels of competence in task performance, have low degrees of obedience, and have an underdeveloped sense of diligence.[11]

- Because innumerable circumstances, factors, and conditions influence personality and predisposition to addiction, it has not yet been determined whether predetermination of addiction is chemical, genetic, or psychological.

schedules. Schedule I drugs have no medical use and a high potential for abuse (such as heroin and LSD); schedule II through V drugs have approved medicinal uses with varying potentials for abuse and significant psychological and physical dependence. Excluded from this classification system are two of the most deadly drugs found in modern society: alcohol and tobacco products.

Drugs are also classified according to the physiological effect they have. Categories include stimulants, depressants, hallucinogens, narcotics, and inhalants. Two other types are also important. Designer drugs are manufactured to mimic the effects of drugs found in the previously mentioned categories, and marijuana, or cannabis, is difficult to classify but is usually included as a hallucinogen. Depending on the dose, marijuana can mimic a variety of substances found in other categories. The following is a list of drug categories and the effects they have on the body:

- *Stimulants:* **Stimulants** speed up the central nervous system, producing an increase in alertness and excitability. Examples are amphetamines, cocaine, crack cocaine, methamphetamines, and drugs such as Ritalin and phentermine (Ionamin).

- *Depressants:* Also known as *sedatives* and *tranquilizers,* **depressants** slow down the central nervous system, causing a feeling of relaxation. Examples of the depressant drugs are barbiturates, methaqualone (Quaaludes or "quad"), and tranquilizers such as diazepam (Valium), chlordiazepoxide HCl (Librium), and meprobamate (Miltown).

- *Psychoactives:* **Psychoactives** can alter feelings, moods, and/or perceptions. Marijuana is classified as a psychoactive drug but can exhibit effects similar to those of stimulants, depressants, and narcotics. Some examples of psychoactive drugs are lysergic acid diethylamide (LSD), mescaline, peyote, phencyclidine (PCP), and psilocybin.

- *Narcotics:* **Narcotics** are powerful painkillers. They also produce pleasurable feelings and induce sleep. The narcotic drugs include codeine, heroin, methadone, morphine, opium, and substances such as oxycodone (Percodan), propoxyphene (Darvon), pentazocine (Talwin), and difenoxin (Lomotil).

- *Inhalants:* **Inhalants** are volatile nondrugs that cause druglike effects if inhaled. Examples are glue and gasoline. Some, such as nitrous oxide and amyl nitrate, have medical uses.

- *Designer drugs:* **Designer drugs** are drug analogs of amphetamines, methamphetamines, narcotics, and hallucinogens that are manufactured in illegal laboratories to mimic controlled substances. They are often more powerful and less predictable than the drugs they imitate. The number and variations of designer drugs available are increasing rapidly.

Currently, three main types of illegal synthetic analog drugs are available: (1) analogs of phencyclidine (PCP); (2) analogs of synthetic narcotic analgesics, such as Demerol; and (3) analogs of amphetamines and methamphetamines. Perhaps one of the best known analogs in the third category is MDMA, known as *ecstasy* or *Adam*. It is widely used in the college setting as a euphoriant.[3]

Commonly Abused Substances

Kari

This section briefly examines some of the most well-known and frequently used drugs—caffeine, alcohol, nicotine, cocaine, marijuana, and designer drugs. This section is not intended to be all-inclusive. There is a wide range of other substances that are potentially dangerous if misused or abused. Because these drugs are so frequently used, it is important for you to understand their positive and negative effects so that you may make decisions based on information rather than myth.

Caffeine

Caffeine is probably the most commonly used drug in American society. Each day millions of Americans drink, chew, or ingest approximately 4 mg of caffeine for every 2.2 pounds of body weight. Approximately 3 percent of the population consumes 600 mg or more of caffeine daily.[3] Caffeine is a stimulant that speeds heart rate, temporarily increases blood pressure, and disrupts sleep. It also relieves drowsiness, helps in the performance of repetitive tasks, and improves work ability.[4] Negative effects include insomnia, anxiety, heart dysrhythmias, gastrointestinal complaints, dizziness, and headaches.

The active ingredient in caffeine belongs to a group of drugs with similar structures known as *xanthines.*

Most adults consume only moderate amounts of caffeine, and an afternoon with friends at the local coffeehouse can be considered a healthy pleasure.

Xanthines include a substance found in cocoa beans, which are used to make chocolate, and in tea leaves. In the past, caffeine consumption was thought to cause birth defects, breast-feeding problems, cardiovascular disease, cancer, and fibrocystic breast disease. Current research has found no substantial association with these conditions.[5,6] However, pregnant and nursing women should consume no more than two cups of coffee a day and should consume tea and caffeinated soft drinks only in moderation (fewer than 300 mg per day).[6] Furthermore, women who suffer from premenstrual tension (PMS) should eliminate caffeine. Research has indicated that women who drink one-half to four cups (25 to 200 mg) of caffeinated tea a day are twice as likely to suffer PMS symptoms as are women who drink none at all.[6]

The majority of adults can consume relatively low doses of caffeine (the equivalent of two to three cups of coffee per day) safely. Approximately 10 percent of the adult population experiences *caffeinism,* a condition in which frequent high-dose use causes psychological and physical problems. Doses as low as 250 mg per day can produce restlessness, nervousness, excitement, insomnia, flushed face, diuresis, muscle twitching, rambling thoughts and speech, and stomach complaints. Doses greater than 1 gram per day can cause muscle twitching, rambling thoughts and speech, heart dysrhythmias, and motor agitation. Higher doses can cause ringing in the ears and flashes of light.[3]

It is easy to consume a great deal of caffeine. By becoming familiar with the amount of caffeine in a product and restricting your consumption to fewer than 400 mg of caffeine per day, you can benefit from the effects of the drug without suffering any negative effects.[4]

Alcohol

Alcohol use is pervasive. **Alcohol** is a drug that is generally deemed socially acceptable. Nevertheless, no other drug causes so much physical, social, and emotional damage to people and their families. People drink alcoholic beverages in many situations and for many reasons. They drink when they are among friends and when they are upset or depressed. People drink to spark romantic feelings, to put themselves at ease in social situations, and to celebrate special occasions. In addition, people drink because their role models drink and because the advertising industry has convinced them that alcohol contributes to self-enhancement. Unfortunately, the devastation associated with alcohol is often not mentioned. Table 11-1 summarizes the short- and long-term effects of the drug. Because society has labeled alcohol appropriate and even necessary for some occasions, abstinence may seem unrealistic for many people.

Table 11-1 Effects of Alcohol Use

	Short-Term or Immediate		Long-Term	
Number of Drinks*	Blood Alcohol Concentration (BAC)	Effect(s)	System/Organ	Health Risks
1–2	0.00–0.05	Usually relaxation and euphoria; decrease in alertness	Breast	50% higher risk for cancer in women who drink any alcohol; 100% increase for women having three or more drinks per day
2–3	0.05–0.10	Exaggerated feelings and behavior, emotional instability, increased reaction time and diminished motor coordination, impaired driving; a legally drunk designation in most states	Cardiovascular	High blood pressure; irregular heartbeat; chest pain/angina; myocardial infarctions; damage to coronary arteries
4–5	0.10–0.15	Loss of peripheral vision; highly impaired driving ability; unsteady walking/standing	General gastrointestinal	Risk of mouth, tongue, throat, esophageal, stomach, and liver cancer; pancreatitis; malnutrition; digestive impairment
5–10	0.15–0.30	Significant impairment of sensory perceptions; slurred speech; decreased sensitivity to pain; difficult and staggering walk	Immune system Liver Pancreas	Lower resistance to infectious diseases Hepatitis; cirrhosis Interference with insulin production
10+	>0.30	Stupor or unconsciousness; anesthetization; possible death at levels greater than 0.35	Small intestine Stomach Muscular system Nervous system Reproductive system	Interference with or prevention of absorption of proteins, iron, calcium, thiamine, and vitamin B_{12} Bleeding from irritation, ulcers Destruction of muscle fibers Destruction of brain cells; interference with neurotransmitters; slowing of reaction time Impotence; decreased testosterone production; fetal alcohol syndrome; miscarriage

*1 drink = 12 oz. beer, 6 oz. wine, 1 oz. whiskey

As with many drugs, there are times and places where medicinal and health reasons are cited for alcohol use. Current research suggests that moderate amounts of alcohol may help reduce the risk of heart disease. The possible benefits and pleasures of the use of alcoholic beverages do not eradicate the dangers that result from misuse or abuse, however (see Assessment Activity 11-1). Nearly half of all annual traffic deaths are caused by accidents involving alcohol consumption. This figure does not include permanent physical injuries and emotional damages caused by alcohol-induced traffic accidents and deaths nor does it include the increased number of violent acts associated with alcohol intoxication. Drinking of alcohol, if it occurs, ought to be approached responsibly, with recognition of the potential for harm to self and others. Real-World Wellness: Responsible Drinking provides suggestions for responsible drinking.

Although there are several types of alcohol, the intoxicating agent in all alcohol drinks is ethyl alcohol, a colorless liquid with a sharp, burning taste (see Just the Facts: How Much Alcohol Is in Beer, Wine, and Other Drinks?). The percentage of alcohol in a beverage is measured by its proof, which is twice the percentage of alcohol. A beverage that is 40 percent alcohol has a proof of 80. The blood alcohol concentration (BAC) is

Jason Alan Bitter was killed on November 19, 1994, by a drunk driver who crossed the center line. The offender's BAC was .36, more than three times the legal limit in Missouri. Dina Khoury-Hager was also killed in the crash. Both were 17 years old and would have graduated from college in 1999.

the percentage of alcohol content in the blood. This percentage determines the alcohol's effect on a person (table 11-1). The more quickly the alcohol is absorbed, the quicker the BAC increases.

Alcohol enters the bloodstream quickly from the stomach and even more quickly from the small intestine. In the stomach, food inhibits absorption of alcohol. Food does not affect absorption in the small intestine.[7]

Here are some other factors that affect the rate of absorption and effect of alcohol:

- *Rate of consumption:* How quickly is the beverage consumed? Large amounts of alcohol quickly consumed expose the brain to higher peak concentrations, altering perceptions and response times.
- *Type of beverage:* Beer and wine contain substances that slow the rate of absorption; thus, the effects are experienced more slowly than are the effects of drinking distilled spirits, even when the same amount of alcohol is consumed. Carbonated beverages added to liquor speed absorption, but diluting them with water slows the process.

Real-World Wellness

Responsible Drinking

I enjoy an occasional drink, and I often invite friends to my home to celebrate holidays and special events. How can I make sure I'm drinking and hosting parties responsibly?

Following are suggestions to help each person be a responsible drinker and host:

- Drink slowly; never consume more than one drink per hour.
- Eat while drinking, but do not eat salty food.
- When mixing drinks, measure the amount of alcohol; never just pour.
- Serve and choose nonalcoholic drinks as an alternative.
- As host, always serve the guests or hire a bartender. Do not have an open bar or serve someone who is intoxicated.
- Stop using or serving alcohol one hour before a party is over.
- Don't drink and drive. Have a nondrinker drive or call a cab.

Just the Facts

How Much Alcohol Is in Beer, Wine, and Other Drinks?

Did you know that all of the following contain the same amount of alcohol? Each contains the equivalent of 3 ounces of pure alcohol. A 160-pound person who consumed these amounts within a two-hour period would be considered legally intoxicated in most states:

- Six 12-oz. glasses of beer
- 15 ounces of fortified wine (about 2 glasses)
- 24 ounces of table wine (about 4 glasses)
- Six servings of liquor (1.3 oz. of 80 proof)
- One measure of vermouth
- One jigger (1 1/2 oz.) of whiskey

Body weights: Body weight and body composition do not influence the rate of absorption, but they do influence the effects of alcohol. More weight and/or more muscle mass (muscle with more fluid volume

HealthQuest Activities

- The alcohol self-assessment activity in Module 8 will help you understand your current drinking behavior and determine how that behavior may affect your health. You can assess your beliefs about alcohol and take a critical look at your ideas about whether alcohol use harms various aspects of your life, such as your friendships, family relationships, and appearance. *HealthQuest* will help you estimate your risk of becoming a problem drinker or alcoholic. After completing the assessment activity, briefly record your answers to the following questions: Do your beliefs about alcohol reflect your own drinking behavior? What factors might cause a person's beliefs and behaviors to be incompatible? What life experiences or influences, such as family, religion, and advertising, have helped form your beliefs about alcohol? Do you think your beliefs and behavior patterns are fixed, or will they change over time?

- The *Alcohol Decision Maze*, found in Module 8, simulates an evening out with a friend. The activity prompts you to make a variety of choices throughout the evening that may influence whether or how much you drink. First you will choose among several companions for the evening. Then you must decide where to go. At each location, such as a restaurant or sporting event, you can choose from a list of activities in which to participate. The choice to buy or drink alcohol surfaces often. *HealthQuest* will then provide feedback on the outcome of the evening and estimate your blood alcohol content. Complete this activity several times, making different decisions each time. Does the outcome of the evening reflect the drinking behavior resulting from your decisions?

than fat) results in a greater distribution of the alcohol, lowering its concentration in the body and weakening its effects.

Tolerance to alcohol: Some people seem to remain sober while others react very quickly to the same amount of alcohol. One drink for a novice may have the same effect as three drinks for a more experienced drinker. This indicates that the experienced drinker's body has adapted to the alcohol at the cellular level and is encouraging increased consumption. Tolerance consists of an increase in the rate of alcohol absorption metabolism as well as a reduced response to the drug. It is the reduced response that is frequently associated with physical and psychological dependence. Increased tolerance to alcohol can also result in a decreased response to other drugs, specifically other central nervous system depressants.

Alcoholism is a disease in which a person loses control over drinking. According to a definition approved by the National Council on Alcoholism and Drug Dependence and the American Society of Addiction Medicine, alcoholism is a "primary, chronic disease with genetic, psychosocial, and environmental factors influencing its development and manifestations. The disease is often progressive and fatal."[8] An alcoholic is a person who suffers from the disease of alcoholism. For alcoholics, alcohol increasingly becomes the focus of life, and family, social, work, or school responsibilities become less important and are eventually disrupted by the desire and need for alcohol. Some alcoholics make this transition very rapidly, whereas others maintain the appearance of being social drinkers for many years. Unfortunately, predetermining who will have trouble with alcohol is impossible. Alcoholism crosses all social and economic barriers and can affect everyone from clergy, medical doctors, high school students, and college students, to professors.

Women who are alcoholics face certain unique problems, and women who use alcohol or tobacco during pregnancy put their children at risk of developing certain health problems. The rate of alcoholism is increasing among younger women (see Wellness Across the Generations: Alcohol and Tobacco Use Among Young Women).

There is no single accepted reason why any person becomes an alcoholic. Most researchers think that a variety of events, genetic tendencies, and situations working together result in alcoholism for some people. The medical model of alcoholism includes biological or genetic explanations of abuse. It views alcohol abuse as uncontrollable because of physiological differences between alcoholics and nonalcoholics. Each year, more research seems to link alcoholism to an inherited susceptibility or predisposition for the disease:[6] Children of alcoholic parents are four times more likely to become alcoholics even when raised by nonalcoholics.

Treatment for alcoholism is often long-term. The course of treatment usually occurs in three stages: (1) detoxification (eliminating the alcohol from the body), (2) medical care (attending to any health-related problems), and (3) changing long-term behavior (helping the recovering alcoholic overcome long-established drinking patterns and destructive behaviors). Several sources provide long-term medical and psychological support to people with drug or alcohol problems. See Just the Facts: Finding Help.

Alcoholics remain alcoholics for life, regardless of whether they drink. Recovering alcoholics must therefore be careful about any products they consume, in-

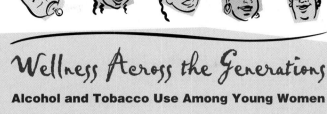

Wellness Across the Generations

Alcohol and Tobacco Use Among Young Women

At one time it was thought that alcohol-related problems occurred more often in men than women. Now mounting evidence indicates that women—especially young women—are drinking more. This fact is reflected in the increased number of admissions of younger women to treatment centers.[15] Women who are alcoholics often drink for reasons different from those that prompt men to abuse alcohol, and some of the consequences of drinking are different between the genders. Smoking, too, poses special risks for women, especially those who are pregnant. Here are some of these gender differences:

- More women than men who abuse alcohol can identify a specific triggering event that prompted them to start drinking, such as a death, a divorce, a job change, or the departure of a child from home.

- Women tend to begin abusing alcohol later in life than men do and to progress more quickly in their abuse pattern.

- Women are prescribed more mood-altering drugs than men are and are thus at greater risk for drug interactions and cross-tolerance.

- Alcoholic women are less likely than men are to have a family support system to aid them in their recovery attempts.

- Women alcoholics tend not to receive as much social support as men do during their treatment for and recovery from alcoholism.

- Women tend to have more financial problems than men do, which makes entry into a treatment program more difficult.[16]

Here are some alcohol- and tobacco-related effects of concern to parents and couples considering pregnancy:

- The children of pregnant women who drink are at a high risk for fetal alcohol syndrome (FAS), which causes a variety of birth defects ranging in severity from abnormal eye alignment to nose and jaw irregularities, cleft palate, joint defects, heart defects, and inadequate brain development. FAS has been reported in children of women who drank as little as 30 milliliters of alcohol per day (about two mixed drinks, three bottles of beer, or two glasses of wine). Thus it is recommended that women abstain from drinking any alcohol during pregnancy.

- Babies born to mothers who smoke have a lower average birth weight and length and have a smaller head circumference.[17]

- Infants born to mothers who smoke are more likely than children born to nonsmokers to die from sudden infant death syndrome (SIDS).[17]

- Smoking during pregnancy may cause hyperactivity in children.

Finally, men and women who smoke should know the following:

- Smoking by both men and women is associated with premature facial wrinkling.

- Osteoporosis (loss of calcium from the bone) is associated with smoking.

---

cluding medicines and mouthwashes, which sometimes contain alcohol. Currently, an estimated 10 million adults and 3 million adolescents under the age of 18 are alcoholics.[8]

Alcohol use has been demonstrated to have a strong association with crime and violence. Data clearly indicate that homicide is more likely to occur in a situation in which drinking has occurred.[12] In this same study all incidents of spousal and child abuse were correlated with drinking. A Canadian study found that at least 42 percent of violent crimes involved alcohol.[2] In addition, 75 percent of suicide attempts involved alcohol use.[1]

As explained in the safety chapter, alcohol and driving can be a lethal combination. Alcohol is linked to at least half of all highway fatalities, and this figure includes only crashes involving drivers classified as legally intoxicated. Finally, in single-vehicle fatal wrecks occurring on weekend nights, the driver is legally intoxicated almost 70 percent of the time.

Binge drinking among college students

Almost 60 percent of the U.S. population 18 years and older consumes alcohol. Within the drinking population, the average drinker consumes 2.43 gallons of pure

Just the Facts

Finding Help

Alcoholics Anonymous (AA)

AA uses a group approach to help people who have decided to stop drinking and who want the support of others who have made the same decision and understand the emotions and thoughts associated with it. AA members view their condition as a disease that they must manage daily. A group support system and buddy system help each person through difficult times. AA also helps people with other types of drug problems or makes referrals to groups such as Narcotics Anonymous and Cocaine Anonymous. Groups such as Alateen, Alatot, and Al-Anon help the families of alcoholics.

Drug Therapy

Usually part of an aftercare program, the drug disulfiram (Antabuse) is used to create a severe reaction if alcohol is consumed. Reactions produced include headache, neck aches, nausea, vomiting, and other unpleasant symptoms. Disulfiram works by blocking the enzymes that metabolize alcohol.

Group Therapies

AA provides a model for many different group therapies. Another widely used approach is a behavioral model that teaches coping skills. Special attention is paid to developing self-esteem and to conducting intense self-analysis to modify attitudes, emotional states, and behavior.

Other Sources of Help

The telephone numbers listed here can be used to find information and help. In addition, local agencies can usually provide information and help:

- **National Alcohol Hotline 24-Hour Helpline**
  1-800-ALCOHOL
- **Alcoholics Anonymous** (New York, NY)
  Contact the local chapter (listed in the phone book) or call for information throughout the United States.
  (212) 870-3400
  www.alcoholics-anonymous.org
- **Al-Anon** (New York, NY)
  Provides help for families of alcoholics. Contact the local chapter or call for information throughout the United States.
  (212) 254-7230
  www.al-anon-alateen.org
- **BACCHUS and GAMMA Peer Education Network**
  (303) 871-3068
  www.bacchusgamma.org
- **National Cocaine Hotline**
  1-800-COCAINE
- **National Clearinghouse for Alcohol and Drug Information** (Rockville, MD)
  (301) 468-2600
- **MADD (Mothers Against Drunk Driving)** (Irving, TX)
  (214) 744-6233
  www.madd.org
- **SADD (Students Against Destructive Decisions)**
  P.O. Box 800
  Marlboro, MA 01752
  (508) 481-3568
  www.saddonline.com

alcohol annually.[13] Obviously, some drinkers consume much less than this amount and others consume a great deal more. One group that has a high drinking rate is college students. Many college students can be classified as heavy drinkers. According to a recent report, the average college student consumes 5.11 drinks per week, with 7.8 percent drinking an average of 16 or more drinks per week. In the same study, 28 percent reported having binged more than once in the two weeks before the study.[14] **Binge drinking** is defined as consuming five or more drinks in a single session at least once during the previous two weeks. (For a discussion of how much alcohol is contained in various types of alcoholic drinks, see Just the Facts: How Much Alcohol Is in Beer, Wine, and Other Drinks? on p. 337.)

This information is alarming in light of the number of deaths in the last few years caused by binge drinking during fraternity or campus rituals. Problems associated with student binge drinking include residence hall damage, fights, sexual assault, and drunk driving. The greater a student's alcohol use, the poorer his or her academic performance.[14] The most distressing fact is that binge drinking too often causes unnecessary deaths of drinkers, their friends, and other innocent victims.

Fortunately, most college students moderate their drinking after their college years. However, about 12 percent are unable to control their drinking and continue to abuse alcohol. You should weigh carefully the potential harmful consequences of alcohol use and abuse before partaking in binge or heavy drinking. Is it worth the price?

Just the Facts

Risks of Smoking

Here is some information about the risks of smoking:

Conditions and Diseases That Can Be Caused by Cancer	

Risks	Results
Coronary heart disease	An estimated 169,000 to 226,000 deaths from coronary heart disease can be attributed to cigarette smoking.
Peripheral arterial disease	Smokers are two to three times more likely to suffer from abdominal aortic aneurysm than are nonsmokers. Smokers have more atherosclerotic occlusions.
Lung cancer	Smoking cigarettes is the major cause of lung cancers in men and women. Rates are currently increasing faster among women than men.
Cancer of the larynx	Laryngeal cancer is 2.0 to 27.4 times more likely in smokers than in nonsmokers.
Oral cancers	Use of smokeless tobacco and snuff is associated with an increased risk of oral cancer. Pipes and cigars are also major risk factors. Use of alcohol seems to enhance the possibility of developing oral cancer.
Cancer of the esophagus	Smoking cigarettes, pipes, and cigars increases by as much as 9 times the risk of dying from esophageal cancer. Alcohol use in combination with smoking adds to that risk.
Bladder cancer	The percentage of bladder cancer attributed to smoking is estimated at 40 to 60 percent in men and 25 to 35 percent in women.
Cancer of the pancreas	Smokers have twice the risk of nonsmokers for cancer of the pancreas.
Chronic obstructive pulmonary (lung) disease (COPD)	Between 80 and 90 percent of more than 60,000 deaths per year from COPD are caused by smoking.
Peptic ulcers	Cigarette smokers develop peptic ulcers much more frequently than do nonsmokers. Ulcers are also more difficult to cure in smokers.
Complications in pregnancy, illnesses in children	Smoking mothers have more stillbirths and babies with low birth weight. The hospital admission rate for pneumonia and bronchitis is 28 percent higher for children of smoking mothers than for children of nonsmoking mothers. Asthma is more common among children of smoking mothers. Parental smoking is a risk factor associated with persistent middle-ear effusion in young children.

Tobacco Products

All tobacco products, including cigarettes, cigars, pipes, and smokeless tobacco (snuff and chewing tobacco), contain the drug **nicotine**. Nicotine is an addictive substance and an alkaloid poison. It affects the body by increasing heart and respiratory rates, elevating blood pressure, increasing cardiac output and oxygen consumption, and constricting the bronchi (the two main branches of the trachea that lead to the lungs). A person inhales nicotine when smoking a tobacco product. Nicotine in smokeless tobacco is absorbed through membranes of the mouth and cheek.

Smoking is directly or indirectly responsible for the conditions and diseases listed in Just the Facts: Risks of Smoking. Some components of cigarette smoke are known as *carcinogens* (substances that cause cancer or foster the growth of cancer cells). Nicotine, tars, and carbon monoxide are all found in cigarette smoke. The tar in tobacco is a black, sticky, dark fluid composed of thousands of chemicals. Many of the chemicals found in tar are cancer causing. Carbon monoxide is a deadly gas emitted in the exhaust of cars and in burning tobacco. The carbon monoxide level in cigarette smoke is 400 times greater than what is considered safe in industrial settings. Carbon monoxide binds to hemoglobin more readily than oxygen, interfering with the ability of blood to transport oxygen to the body. Carbon monoxide impairs the nervous system and increases the risk of heart attacks and strokes.

The addictive nature of nicotine has recently come under substantial public scrutiny. Some experts consider nicotine to be as addictive as cocaine and other

drugs. Tobacco is considered the leading preventable contributor to disease and early death in the United States (from heart disease and cancer specifically) and is listed as a primary risk factor for heart disease by the American Heart Association. Cigarettes are responsible for 435,000 deaths annually.[18] Because of the health risks and because of what is seen by many as an effort on the part of tobacco companies to intentionally increase nicotine addiction to increase sales of cigarettes, some people suggest that tobacco should be made an illegal drug.

Secondhand and sidestream smoke

Passive smoking is the inhalation of what is known as *secondhand cigarette smoke* from the environment by a nonsmoker. Smokers inhale what is known as **mainstream smoke;** passive smokers most frequently inhale **sidestream smoke** which results from burning tobacco products (the end of the lighted tip of a cigarette, cigar, or pipe).[19] Because it is not filtered by either a cigarette filter or the smoker's lungs, sidestream smoke contains higher concentrations of carbon dioxide and carbon monoxide. For each pack of cigarettes smoked indoors by a smoker, a nonsmoker in the vicinity passively smokes the equivalent of three to five cigarettes.[1] Research shows that nonsmokers living with smokers have a 20 percent higher mortality rate than do the nonsmoking partners of nonsmokers. Nonsmoking wives of smokers have been found to be at greater risk of lung cancer than the wives of nonsmoking husbands. Other studies have reported that nonsmokers living with smokers have a greater risk of developing respiratory problems and that nonsmoking women living with smokers have a greater risk of cervical cancer.[20] The bottom line about passive smoking is that there is no safe level of exposure to tobacco smoke.

Cigars and pipes

In the hope of avoiding the dangers associated with cigarette smoking, some smokers have turned from cigarettes to cigars or pipes. Since pipe and cigar smokers don't inhale, they do seem less likely to develop lung and heart disease. However, pipe and cigar smokers have a much higher risk of developing mouth, larynx, and esophageal cancers because they hold the nicotine and tars from their tobacco products in their mouths

Real-World Wellness

Charting a Plan to Quit Smoking

I've tried several times to quit smoking, but I'm still lighting up. This time I want to be prepared. Is there a plan I can follow that will help me quit for good?

The *Mayo Clinic Health Letter* offers the following suggestions:[13]

- *Set a date:* Make the date reasonably soon. Make a list of reasons you want to quit.

- *Start stopping before you reach the date:* Taper off the number of cigarettes you are currently smoking. Choose a milder brand.

- *Make your plans known:* Tell a friend, your family, and colleagues of your plans. Ask for their support.

- *Take it one day at a time:* Get up every morning and decide not to smoke that day. Focus your attention on that day only.

- *Change your routine:* Avoid or change situations in which you have previously smoked.

- *Alter your surroundings:* Start new activities, such as exercising or needlepoint.

- *Time the urge:* Identify when your urge to smoke is the strongest. Being prepared will help you resist.

- *Use substitutes:* Substitutes can include gum, celery, carrots, and pickles.

- *Prepare a daydream:* Have a pleasant daydream ready to help fight off the desire to smoke. This can be an image of yourself without a cigarette in a situation you find highly desirable.

- *Use relaxation techniques:* Deep breathing or progressive muscle relaxation can help.

- *Stay busy:* Find ways to keep yourself and your mind occupied so you do not miss smoking or having a cigarette in your hand.

- *Practice positive thinking:* Tell yourself, "I can make it." Remember that you *can* do it.

---

instead of inhale them. Furthermore, when a cigarette smoker switches to cigars or a pipe, he or she tends to continue to inhale and, thus, to remain at the same risk for lung and heart disease while the risk of other cancers increases.

Smokeless tobacco products

Smokeless tobacco products consist of snuff and chewing tobacco. Snuff is a finely shredded or powdered tobacco that is sniffed by the user, allowing nicotine to be absorbed through the mucous membranes of the nose and mouth. Chewing tobacco consists of loose-leaf tobacco mixed with molasses or other flavors and pressed into what are called *plugs* or twisted into rope-like strands. This material is then placed between the gums and cheek or lower lip, where the nicotine is absorbed. In 1994 it was estimated that more than 6 million men and 730,000 women used smokeless tobacco products.

Smokeless tobacco is not a safe alternative to cigarettes. It contributes to the development of periodontal (gum) disease, which can result in bleeding gums, loss of teeth, staining of teeth, and tooth decay. Periodontal disease is less significant than the oral cancers that may be caused by frequent contact of the cells of the gums and cheek with the carcinogenic agents in the tobacco. Two early danger signs of such cancers are the formation of leukoplakia (white spots) or erythro-plakia (red spots), which indicate precancerous conditions and should be evaluated by a physician immediately. If treatment is delayed, cancer can quickly spread to the jaw, neck, brain, and digestive and urinary systems.[1]

Clove cigarettes

Some people smoke clove cigarettes as an alternative to regular cigarettes. Clove cigarettes usually consist of 60 percent tobacco and 40 percent clove buds. Clove cigarettes generate even more nicotine, tar, and carbon monoxide than do regular cigarettes, so the dangers are even greater. Some users have developed serious lung and respiratory illnesses.[21]

Advantages of quitting

Smoking is an extremely strong addiction. To quit completely, many people require the help of trained professionals (see Real-World Wellness: Charting a Plan to Quit Smoking and Real-World Wellness: Choosing a Smoking Cessation Aid). Although quitting is difficult, the health benefits gained far outweigh the problems. When people stop smoking, their risk of developing heart disease and some kinds of cancer (if not already present in the body) eventually decreases to that of nonsmokers; in other words, some of the effects of smoking are reversible (see figure 11-1).

Real-World Wellness

Choosing a Smoking Cessation Aid

I've been smoking since my freshman year in high school, and I'm about to graduate from college and enter the workforce. I'd like to quit, but I'm confused about all the smoking cessation products available. How do I choose the one that's best for me?

Several tools are available to help smokers wean themselves off cigarettes. These smoking cessation aids can be purchased over the counter (OTC) or with a doctor's prescription. The dosages for prescription and OTC versions can vary widely. For this reason, it is probably better to seek a prescription version, which will more specifically be targeted to your needs. Read the following information about three commonly used methods, and then talk to your doctor to choose the one best suited to your own needs.

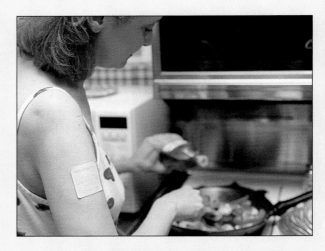

Many people have used nicotine patches to help them quit smoking. If you're a smoker, have you considered giving the patch a try?

- *Nicotine-containing gum:* Nicotine gum requires immediate smoking cessation. The dosage is 2 to 4 mg of nicotine per piece of gum. When used under a physician's guidance, the success rate is about 40 percent. Chewing the gum may cause mouth ulcers and nausea in some people, and the product should not be used by pregnant or nursing women. Initial doses of the chewing gum cost about $50, with weekly refills costing about $30.

- *Transdermal patches:* The patch is designed to aid smoking cessation by relieving nicotine withdrawal cravings. Two types are available: a step-down version and a single-dose version. The single-dose version provides the same milligrams of nicotine in each dose (15 mg). The step-down version provides different levels of nicotine for various periods of time after cessation, theoretically reducing the amount of nicotine available as the person is weaned away from the drug. The step-down method is designed to ease withdrawal by making the symptoms less severe and withdrawal more gradual. The patches contain 15 to 21 mg of nicotine a day for the first weeks. After four to twelve weeks, the dosage is reduced

to 10 to 14 mg a day. A final set of patches used for two to four weeks contains 5 to 7 mg of nicotine. Single-dose patches eliminate the step-down effect. Used alone, both versions of the patch seem to be less than 25 percent effective. When used with the prescription medication mecamylamine, however, the effectiveness rate rises to 40 percent. The patch can cause skin irritation, redness, and irregular heart rate in some users. The cost is about the same as for nicotine-containing gum.

- *Nicotrol™ inhaler.* A federal advisory panel to the FDA recently endorsed a prescription inhalation device that is an alternative to transdermal patches and chewing gum. The Nicotrol inhaler is meant to simulate cigarette smoking. The device has a mouthpiece with a nicotine plug attached to it. Seventy to eighty puffs on the inhaler provide the amount of nicotine in ten puffs on a regular cigarette. Having the inhaler to handle may help smokers who miss having something to do with their hands while simultaneously providing a low level of nicotine to ease cravings.

HealthQuest Activities

- Module 7 of HealthQuest allows you to assess your risk of disease caused by exposure to tobacco smoke. If you're a smoker, you can evaluate the reasons you may be ready to quit or cut back. If you have loved ones or friends who smoke, you will also benefit from this exercise—the feedback you'll receive in the personal risk section will take into account both direct and indirect exposure to tobacco smoke. Feedback about reasons for quitting is based on the relative importance of each reason to the smoker. For example,

you might want to quit for health reasons, while a friend of yours might want to quit because smoking is inconvenient at work.

- The *Tobacco Ads and You* activity in Module 7 introduces you to the messages that tobacco advertisements send to consumers and the ways in which young people are manipulated to become smokers. This exploration activity helps you examine your beliefs and feelings about cigarette advertising by rating how each ad appeals to you. You can also participate in a survey about the messages the ads are trying to convey and your own use of tobacco products and promotional items.

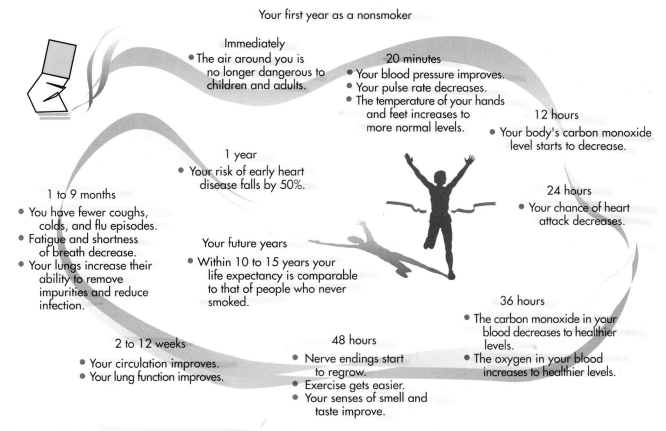

Your first year as a nonsmoker

Immediately
• The air around you is no longer dangerous to children and adults.

20 minutes
• Your blood pressure improves.
• Your pulse rate decreases.
• The temperature of your hands and feet increases to more normal levels.

12 hours
• Your body's carbon monoxide level starts to decrease.

1 year
• Your risk of early heart disease falls by 50%.

24 hours
• Your chance of heart attack decreases.

1 to 9 months
• You have fewer coughs, colds, and flu episodes.
• Fatigue and shortness of breath decrease.
• Your lungs increase their ability to remove impurities and reduce infection.

Your future years
• Within 10 to 15 years your life expectancy is comparable to that of people who never smoked.

36 hours
• The carbon monoxide in your blood decreases to healthier levels.
• The oxygen in your blood increases to healthier levels.

2 to 12 weeks
• Your circulation improves.
• Your lung function improves.

48 hours
• Nerve endings start to regrow.
• Exercise gets easier.
• Your senses of smell and taste improve.

Figure 11-1 Health Benefits of Quitting Smoking
Quitting smoking results in benefits that begin immediately and become more significant the longer a person stays smoke-free.

Illegal Drugs

Cocaine

At one time **cocaine** was considered the drug of upper-class America. Unfortunately, the use of cocaine and its derivative, crack, is now epidemic. It is estimated that 25 to 30 million people have experimented with cocaine in the United States. Approximately 5 million people use the drug regularly. Among young adults, 6.7 percent have tried crack and 40 percent have tried cocaine.[22] From 1987 to 1991, cocaine use reportedly decreased. However, since 1991, the use of cocaine appears to have rebounded, especially among young people.[23]

A powerful stimulant, cocaine is derived from the leaves of the South American coca shrub and ground into a crystalline powder. The most common methods of using the drug are either snorting it, liquefying it and then injecting it, or freebasing (smoking). When snorted, the white powder is sniffed up through the nose. The most potent and expensive method of cocaine use is freebasing. The drug is usually smoked in a water pipe because this provides faster absorption into the bloodstream.

Crack is relatively easy to make and fairly inexpensive to buy. At $10 to $15 a dose, crack is the form of cocaine that is most prevalent on the streets. When snorted, crack reaches the brain in about 5 minutes. When injected or smoked, it takes only a few seconds for the drug to take effect.

Use of cocaine produces feelings of well-being, euphoria, and extreme exhilaration. Mental alertness seems to increase. Blood vessels constrict, causing heart rate and blood pressure to rise. Cocaine is rapidly metabolized by the liver. Snorting cocaine results in a 5- to 15-minute "high," and the effects of crack last 20 to 30 minutes. Psychological and physical dependency on crack develop rapidly because of the brief period of stimulation. The feelings of exhilaration experienced while under the influence of the drug are quickly followed by depression.

The physical consequences of cocaine use are extreme and highly dangerous. Cocaine use can cause headaches, exhaustion, shaking, blurred vision, nausea, impaired judgment, hyperactivity, loss of appetite, loss of sexual desire, and paranoia that can lead to violence. Snorting cocaine can destroy the septum in the nose. Freebasing may damage the liver and the lungs; fluid buildup in the lungs caused by freebasing has resulted in death. Cocaine can initiate strokes, bleeding in the brain, heart attacks, irregular heartbeat, and sudden death.[22]

Cocaine addiction is extremely difficult to overcome. Addiction researchers currently believe a broad-based treatment program, including medical, psychiatric, pharmacological, and psychosocial elements, is the most successful.

Marijuana

Approximately twenty-five years ago, **marijuana** became a cultural phenomenon, the symbol of one generation's disregard for or anger with another. The marijuana found on the streets at that time, however, lacked the potency of current crops. Crossbreeding of more potent varieties, improved cultivation, and use of different parts of the plant all contribute to increased levels of delta-9-tetrahydrocannabinol (THC), the major psychoactive drug found in marijuana. Some marijuana currently grown in the United States rivals the previously stronger varieties of Mexico, Jamaica, and other areas. The THC percentage of *Cannabis sativa* (the Indian hemp plant from which marijuana is derived) in plants grown in the United States can range from 2 percent to as high as 7 percent. A variety of marijuana know as *sinsemilla*, which is made from the buds of flowering tops of female plants, can have a potency as high as 24 percent.[3] The higher the percentage of THC, the more potent the drug. Marijuana is composed of the dried leaves and flowering tops of the cannabis plant. Hashish, which has stronger effects, is processed from the resin of the plant. The resin is either dried and pressed into cakes or sold in liquid form called *hash oil*. marijuana is used more extensively than hashish in the United States.

H_{ea}l_{th}Q_{ue}s_t Acti_{viti}es

• Drug abuse can occur with illegal drugs or with over-the-counter or prescription drugs. Complete the assessment activity *Drugs: Are You at Risk?* in Module 9 to raise your awareness of the many decisions you make about drugs. What is your overall risk score? Do you think the score is accurate? Do you think your score reflects campuswide drug use? What are the causes of drug abuse and what can be done to prevent it?

More than 400 known chemicals constitute marijuana. More than sixty of these are *cannabinoids*, chemicals found only in cannabis. THC is the cannabinoid that appears most responsible for the sensations experienced by marijuana users. Cannabinoids are different from other drugs in that they are fat soluble rather than water soluble; they have a decided affinity for binding to fat in the human body. Although other drugs enter and then leave the body within relatively short periods, marijuana tends to attach to fatty organs, such as the gonads and brain, and remain.[24] A single ingestion of THC may require up to thirty days to be eliminated from the body.

Marijuana can be eaten in baked goods, such as brownies, but the effects tend to be less predictable. Because it better controls amount ingested, smoking is generally a more efficient and powerful technique for achieving the desired effect. When inhaled, THC reaches the brain in as few as fourteen seconds. Hashish is so concentrated that a single drop can equal the effects of an entire marijuana joint (cigarette). Cannabis products are difficult to classify but are considered hallucinogens.

Small doses or short-term use of marijuana creates sensations of euphoria and relaxation often accompanied by hunger or sleepiness. Time seems to slow, and the senses appear heightened. Memory of recent events, physical coordination, and perceptions may be impaired. Students, for example, may have difficulty remembering events that occurred when they were high. Even with small amounts of marijuana, driving ability can be affected. Physiologically, heart rate speeds up and certain blood vessels become dilated, which may create problems for people with any types of heart problems. Some users experience anxiety, panic, and paranoia. In rare cases or with stronger doses, people may suffer from a sense of depersonalization, image distortion, and hallucinations. Chronic use seems to lead to behavioral changes in some people that may be permanent. Lack of motivation or interest in activities unrelated to drug use is one result. Use by teenagers leads to impaired thinking, poor reading comprehension, and reduced verbal and mathematical skills.

All the long-term effects of marijuana use have not been determined. This is partly because of the lesser potency of marijuana used previously. In addition, people vary greatly in their responses to the drug. Chronic users may experience psychological dependence and need increased doses as tolerance develops. Very heavy users experience withdrawal symptoms of restlessness, irritability, tremors, nausea, vomiting, diarrhea, and sleep disturbances.[24]

Physically, marijuana appears to be more carcinogenic than tobacco. Known carcinogens occur in larger amounts in marijuana, and when marijuana is smoked, the smoke is held in the lungs. Cannabis smoke contains more tars than does tobacco smoke. Marijuana use quickly affects pulmonary function adversely, and long-term use causes cellular changes in the lungs. People who have angina pectoris (chest pains associated with heart disease) may be significantly at risk because more oxygen is required during marijuana use. Marijuana binds readily to hemoglobin, reducing the amount of oxygen carried to the heart and other tissues.

Many people consider cannabis an aphrodisiac. Over time it actually has the opposite effect, depressing the sex drive and causing impotence. Regular male users show a decrease in sperm count and reduced motility of sperm. Proportionately, more sperm appear abnormally shaped, a phenomenon associated with lessened fertility. In women, THC blocks ovulation. Pregnant women who smoke marijuana frequently use other drugs, all of which have a detrimental effect on the fetus. Marijuana also depresses the immune system.[24]

Therapeutic use is still being explored. At this time the most promising application seems to be as an antinausea drug for chemotherapy patients. Glaucoma patients may have access to and may use marijuana to reduce intraocular pressure (pressure within the eye).

Marijuana is an illegal drug. Many people who use marijuana eventually experiment with or use other harder drugs. Some researchers consider marijuana thus to be a *gateway drug*. As with alcohol and all other drugs, the way a person reacts to marijuana or is most adversely affected by it cannot be predicted. People do not begin use with the intention of having a drug become the focus of their lives, but some ultimately allow the drug to control them. Marijuana is a drug that has that potential.

Other Drugs of Concern

Drugs discussed in the following sections have been abused for many years. Unfortunately, some that had become less popular seem to be reappearing, along with a dangerous new generation of illicit drugs. All illegal drugs have quality control problems: Because there is no federal regulation of these drugs and because people involved in the transportation and distribution of illegal drugs are not always concerned about purity or quality, dangerous and even poisonous substances may be added to drugs. Also, it is frequently impossible to determine the potency of a drug. A very pure form of a drug can easily be lethal for a person who has been using a less potent form.

Heroin

Heroin is a narcotic that is synthesized from morphine. This drug induces a strong sensation of euphoria but quickly leads to physical and psychological dependency. The physical tolerance for heroin develops rapidly. Because heroin is usually injected, addicts often share needles, which increases the risk of contracting diseases, such as AIDS and hepatitis. Experts fear the younger generation may become addicted to heroin through a substance called *moonrock*—a mixture of heroin and cocaine that can be injected, smoked, or snorted. Heroin is used in this way to reduce the paranoia and depression that follow a cocaine high. Heroin use is considered to be on the rise.

In recent years heroin use has increased significantly, especially among well-educated people, often women, employed in white-collar and other professional jobs.[25] Heroin use has also reportedly increased among junior high and high school age groups. One reason for this trend may be the availability of more potent forms of heroin, which allow the user to experience a more pronounced effect by snorting it instead of injecting it, which people may be reluctant to do in part because of fear of HIV transmission. In addition, many users believe that smoking or snorting heroin, unlike injecting it, is nonaddicting.[25] Heroin may appeal to children because it is cheap and can be purchased fairly easily on the street. Users may not realize they are becoming addicted because they may function normally for some time after starting to use the drug before their behavior changes significantly enough for friends and family to become aware of their use. Heroin is undeniably rearing its ugly head once again in the form of increased use, and it has reached the country's youth regardless of educational attainment, social class, or ethnic and racial background.

Methamphetamine (Crank)

Methamphetamine is a potent stimulant that can cause uncontrollable manic behavior or paranoid thinking. The most current use of this drug is as crystal methamphetamine, or *ice*. Although crystal methamphetamine has been touted as a safe alternative to cocaine, evidence indicates otherwise. Recent headlines told about a father who, under the influence of methamphetamine, decapitated his son. Overdoses are often fatal, and the drug is extremely addictive. In many areas of the United States, use of ice is a widespread problem.

Lysergic Acid Diethylamide (LSD)

LSD is a hallucinogenic drug that has become more popular in recent years, especially among the upper class. The substance induces altered perceptions of shapes, images, time, self, and sound. Tolerance to the drug develops quickly with daily use.[12] Flashbacks can occur in some people.

Phencyclidine (PCP)

PCP was originally intended for use as a surgical anesthetic for humans. However, the drug was determined unsuitable for this purpose because of its unusual and undesirable effects on patients.[9] Also called *angel dust*, PCP provokes a variety of unpredictable responses in users. These reactions include feelings of unreality, depersonalization, confusion, depression, anxiety, aggressive and violent behavior, acute or permanent psychosis, and coma. Users often fail to experience sensations of pain and report feeling uncoordinated in their movements. Classified as a hallucinogen, PCP has been used as an additive to cocaine, a combination that multiplies the toxic effects of both drugs.

Designer Drugs

Designer drugs resemble those that are controlled by the Federal Drug Administration (FDA); that is, they act like known drugs but have a different chemical composition. Probably the two best-known designer drugs currently being used are *China white*, an analog of heroin, and *ecstasy*. Ecstasy is an analog of the amphetamines and hallucinogens under FDA control since 1985. Designer drugs appear so rapidly that it is difficult or impossible to restrict sales. Poor quality control and combinations with other, often poisonous, substances can result in neurological damage or death. Brain damage is often caused by a single dose.[26]

Nurturing Your Spirituality

Finding Alternatives to Drug Use

The best treatment for any alcohol or drug abuse problem is to prevent it. Adolescents and college-age students need attractive alternatives to drugs, such as participation in organizations or groups that fulfill in safe, constructive ways their need for camaraderie, acceptance, and group involvement. These organization or groups can be developed around athletics, recreational activities, career development, or service opportunities. Involvement in enjoyable and meaningful activities tends to discourage drug use by providing a strong reinforcement system that helps people feel good about themselves and their abilities. All people, young and older, need a positive group atmosphere that fosters self-esteem, develops participants' ability to help others, and provides role models who pursue selfless, achievement-oriented goals.

At the college and university level, students aged 25 and younger may be faced with an autonomy never before experienced when they leave home to go to school. They are faced with the fact that no one is standing over them to ensure their attendance at and productivity in school, at work, or in other areas. Their decision-making power is increased as well as is the pressure to conform to peer standards, many of which they are encountering for the first time. This newfound freedom sometimes requires a continuation of prevention education and activities that direct them toward positive activities and behaviors. University administrators should seek to make such programs highly visible within the institutions they serve.

In fact, it is helpful for everyone connected with a college or university to demonstrate positive behaviors concerning the prevention of drug and alcohol abuse on campus. This may require that the president not serve alcoholic beverages at receptions and that faculty actively discourage binge drinking and other dangerous forms of drinking and be willing to engage in activities outside the classroom that involve positive alternatives to alcohol and other drug use. Another important component of any alternative program is a strong peer education network, in which student leaders promote a healthy campus life by discouraging alcohol and drug abuse and related problems, such as property destruction, violence, and sexual assault.

Other prevention-oriented programs are recreational activities, such as hiking, camping, and canoeing, and leadership challenge courses, such as rope courses and outward-bound experiences. The programs should offer diverse opportunities that appeal to a wide variety of student interests. Art exhibits, musical events, movie or book clubs, and community service programs, such as Humanity for Mankind, can all offer further opportunities for students to engage in activities that are both personally and socially beneficial. Having mentors assigned to incoming first-year students and holding group discussions of various problems associated with collegiate life, perhaps with mandatory attendance by first-year students, may also be helpful. In addition, the college or university should emphasize to students that the purpose of higher education is to gain the experience and expertise to better serve one's family, community, and country. To truly accept responsibility for their lives, all people need to understand and accept responsibility for their own behavior and recognize that alcohol and drug use never offers a long-term solution to personal, emotional, or spiritual difficulties.

Over-the-Counter Drugs

An area of drug use that is sometimes overlooked and assumed to be safe is the use of over-the-counter drugs (OTCs). The power of OTCs is often underestimated. As with all drugs, the ultimate responsibility for correct use of OTC drugs rests with each person. Because OTCs are readily available, abuse is a real possibility. OTCs may potentiate the effects of prescription drugs, other OTCs, herbs, vitamins, or alcohol, especially when not taken according to directions. OTCs can cause physiological damage to various body structures, with symptoms ranging from disorientation to kidney or liver damage. Here are some guidelines for safe use of OTCs:[3]

- Always know what you are taking and what the product's active ingredients are.
- Know the drug's effects (including its undesired ones) and possible side effects. Be sure you understand how the drug is supposed to work.
- Read and heed warnings and cautions concerning use of the product.

- Don't use any OTC product continuously for more than two weeks. If the problem for which you took the drug persists, consult your physician.
- Be particularly cautious if you are also taking any prescription drugs, since serious interactions can occur.
- If you have any questions about an OTC product, consult a pharmacist.
- If you don't need a drug, don't use it.

A Final Thought

To develop a high level of wellness, you must address the issue of drug use. Drugs prescribed as medicine can promote quality of life, but unwise use severely diminishes quality of life. Alcohol continues to be the most abused drug among college students. Perhaps as people become more aware of the dangers associated with alcohol and drug use, a smaller percentage of college students will use them (see Nurturing Your Spirituality: Finding Alternatives to Drug Use).

Summary

- People use drugs for a variety of reasons, including for recreational or social enjoyment, to seek novel sensations, to enhance religious or spiritual experiences, to alter consciousness, to rebel or alienate oneself from society, and to submit to peer pressure.
- Drugs are commonly classified in a variety of ways, including according to their physiological effects.
- Caffeine is probably the most commonly used drug in the United States. It is a stimulant that speeds heart rate, increases blood pressure, and can cause insomnia.
- Alcohol is a socially acceptable drug that is a major source of physical and emotional damage and death.
- The blood alcohol concentration (BAC) of ethyl alcohol is affected by the rate of consumption, the type of alcoholic beverage being consumed, and the drinker's body weight and tolerance to alcohol.
- Binge drinking often occurs on college campuses and can lead to property destruction, sexual assault, and even death.
- Alcoholism is a disease in which a person loses control over drinking.
- Determining who will become an alcoholic is impossible because alcoholism crosses all social, economic, gender, educational, and racial lines.
- Nicotine is an addictive drug contained in tobacco. The tars found in tobacco are carcinogenic agents.
- No tobacco product is safe. Cigarettes, cigars, pipes, and smokeless products all pose threats to health.
- Carbon monoxide, which is formed when tobacco is smoked, interferes with the body's ability to transport oxygen and increases the risk of heart attack and stroke.

- Sidestream smoke has a higher concentration of tar and nicotine than the smoke inhaled by the smoker.
- Clove cigarettes contain even more nicotine and carbon monoxide than do regular cigarettes.
- Cocaine use has become epidemic in the United States. Cocaine can be snorted, injected, or freebased (smoked).
- The primary psychoactive ingredient in marijuana is delta-9-tetrahydrocannabinol.
- Carcinogens can be found in more potent levels in marijuana than in tobacco.
- Hashish is more potent than regular marijuana. Sinsemilla is a form of marijuana that can have a potency as high as 24 percent.
- Short-term effects of marijuana use include euphoria and perceptual impairment. Some people experience anxiety, a sense of depersonalization, and hallucinations.
- Some drugs, such as heroin, methamphetamine (crank), and LSD, have been abused in our society for many years.
- The newest form of methamphetamine is ice, which is smokable and more addictive, potent, and destructive than crack cocaine.
- Heroin use has been increasing among college and high school students.
- Designer drugs are analogs of controlled substances and are more powerful and less pure and have less predictable effects than do controlled substances.
- OTC drugs must be used carefully to avoid psychological and physiological problems.

Review Questions

1. What are some reasons people choose to use drugs?
2. Discuss the ways in which drugs can be classified.
3. What are the positive and negative effects of caffeine use?
4. What factors affect a drinker's blood alcohol concentration (BAC)?
5. How can a person practice responsible drinking?
6. What are some potential effects of long-term alcohol use?
7. Discuss the risks of using any tobacco product.
8. Discuss the specific benefits of quitting smoking.
9. Why is heroin use increasing among high school and college students?
10. What makes cocaine such a dangerous drug?
11. What factors should you consider before using any OTC product?

References

1. Pinger, R., W. Payne, D. Hahn, and E. Hahn. 1998. *Drugs: Issues for Today.* Dubuque, Iowa: WCB/McGraw-Hill.
2. Schlaadt, R. G., and P. T. Shannon. 1994. *Drugs: Use, Misuse, and Abuse.* Needham Heights, Mass.: Allyn and Bacon.
3. Hanson, G. and P. J. Venturelli. 1998. *Drugs and Society.* Boston: Jones and Bartlett.
4. Consumer Reports. September 1997. What caffeine can do for you—and to you. *Consumer Reports on Health.* 97–101. Vol 9:9.
5. Mayo Clinic. February 1992. Second opinion. *Mayo Clinic Health Letter.* 8. Vol 10:2.
6. Tufts University. February 1990. Grounds for breaking the coffee habit. *Tufts University Diet and Nutrition Letter.* 3–6. Vol 7:2.
7. Carroll, C. R. 1993. *Drugs in Modern Society (3d ed.).* Dubuque, Iowa: Wm. C. Brown.
8. Morse, R. M., and D. K. Flavin. 1992. The definition of alcoholism. *JAMA* 268:1012–1014.
9. National Institute on Drug Abuse. 1996. Genetic factors in drug abuse and dependence. In *The Biobehavioral Etiology of Drug Abuse,* eds. H. W. Gordon and M. D. Glantz. Research Monograph. 159.
10. Blum, K., G. Cull, E. Braverman, and D. Comings. 1996. Reward deficiency syndrome. *American Scientist* 84:132–145.
11. Hawkins, J. D., D. M. Lishner, and R. F. Catalano. 1985. Childhood predictors and the prevention of adolescent substance abuse. *National Institute on Drug Abuse Research Monograph* 56:87–1335.
12. Pernanen, K. 1991. *Alcohol in Human Violence.* New York: Gullfor Press.
13. U.S. Department of Health and Human Services. 1996. *National Household Survey on Drug Abuse: Population Estimates.* Washington D.C.: U.S. Government Printing Office.
14. Presley, C. A., and P. W. Meilman. 1992. *Alcohol and Drugs on American College Campuses: A Report to College Presidents.* Southern Illinois University Student Health Program Wellness Center, Carbondale, Ill.: U.S. Department of Education.
15. U.S Department of Health and Human Services. 1995. *Alcohol and Health: Seventh Special Report to the U.S. Congress.* Washington, D.C.: U.S. Government Printing Office.
16. Kinney, J., and G. Leaton. 1999. *Loosening the Grip: A Handbook of Alcohol Information* (6th ed.). Dubuque, Iowa: WCB/McGraw-Hill.
17. Bartecchi, C. E., T. D. MacKenzie, and R. W. Shrier. 1995. The global tobacco epidemic. *Scientific American.* 49.
18. Aldrich, L. 1995. Tobacco tax increase would reduce smoking. In *Smoking,* ed. by K. L. Swisher. San Diego, Calif.: Greenhaven Press, 28–29.
19. Ray, O., and C. Ksir.1999. *Drugs, Society, and Human Behavior* 8th edition. Dubuque, Iowa: WCB/McGraw-Hill.
20. Environmental Protection Agency. 1993. *Respiratory Health Effects of Passive Smoking.* Fact sheet. Washington, D.C.: EPA.
21. Clark, G. C. 1990. Comparison of the inhalation toxicity of kretek (clove cigarette) smoke with that of American cigarette smoke. *Archives of Toxicology* 64(7):515–521.
22. Editors. November 1988. Hour by hour crack. *Newsweek.* 64–75.
23. Johnson, L. 1996. *University of Michigan Annual National Surveys of Secondary Students.* Lansing, Mich.: University of Michigan. Available from author at 412 Maynard, Ann Arbor, MI.
24. Nahas, G. G. 1994. *Marijuana in Science and Medicine.* New York: Raven Press.
25. Fields, R. 1998. *Drugs in Perspective* (3rd ed.). Dubuque, Iowa: WCB/McGraw-Hill.
26. Akers, R. L. *Drugs, Alcohol, and Society—Social Structure, Process and Policy.* Belmont, Calif.: Wadsworth Publishing.

Suggested Readings

Nakken, C. 1996. *The Addictive Personality: Understanding the Addictive Process and Compulsive Behavior.* Center City, Minn.: Hazelden.
This book examines genetic factors tied to addiction, cultural influences on addictive behavior, the progressive nature of the disease, and the steps necessary for a successful recovery.

Whelan, E. M. 1997. *Cigarettes: What the Warning Label Doesn't Tell You: The First Comprehensive Guide to the Health Consequences of Smoking.* Amherst, N.Y.: Prometheus Books.
Noted experts detail all the known health risks of smoking, explaining clearly how cigarette smoking can damage the body.

Zimmer, L, and J. P. Morgan. 1997. *Marijuana Myths, Marijuana Facts: A Review of the Scientific Evidence.* The Lindesmith Center. New York: NY.

This book offers an accurate, up-to-date review of the scientific evidence and the benefits and risks of marijuana.

Fisher, E. B., and T. L. Goldfarb. 1998. *American Lung Association 7 Steps to a Smoke-Free Life.* John Wiley & Sons. Somerset: NJ.

This program is based on the American Lung Association's Freedom from Smoking Program. It succeeds by adjusting for individual differences among smokers and outlining a multi-step process that includes getting motivated, designing a plan to quit, preparing for quit day, quitting, resisting the temptation to start again, and maintaining a smoke-free life.

Schuckit, M. A. 1998. *Educating Yourself about Alcohol and Drugs: A People's Primer.* Plenum Press. New York: NY.

This practical guide explains what drugs are and how they can harm the body, discusses the physical, emotional, and interpersonal problems drug use can cause, shows how to tell whether someone you know has an alcohol or other drug problem, and tells you where to go for help.

Name _____ **Date** _____ **Section** _____

Assessment Activity 11-1

Do You Have a Drinking Problem?

Many self-tests have been published for people to use to determine whether they are alcoholics or have drinking problems. None can provide a definite diagnosis; deciding whether someone should seek help is usually a complex, subjective matter. One of the most popular printed self-tests appeared in a "Dear Abby" Column, and it is offered here as a guide. If these questions seem to indicate that you or a friend needs to seek help, you should visit a counselor, psychologist, or physician who is experienced in the assessment of chemical dependency.

Directions: Check all that apply.

_____ 1. Have you ever decided to stop drinking for a week or so but only lasted for a couple of days?

_____ 2. Do you wish people would stop nagging you about your drinking?

_____ 3. Have you ever switched from one kind of drink to another in the hope that this would keep you from getting drunk?

_____ 4. Have you had a drink in the morning in the past year?

_____ 5. Do you envy people who can drink without getting into trouble?

_____ 6. Have you had problems connected with drinking during the past year?

_____ 7. Has your drinking caused problems at home?

_____ 8. Do you ever try to get "extra" drinks at a party because you did not get enough to drink?

_____ 9. Do you tell yourself you can stop drinking anytime you want, even though you keep getting drunk when you don't mean to?

_____ 10. Have you missed days at work (or school) because of drinking?

_____ 11. Do you have blackouts?

_____ 12. Have you ever felt that your life would be better if you did not drink?

If you checked four or more of these items, you should seek the guidance of a specialist in chemical dependency or seek help directly through Alcoholics Anonymous (AA) or a similar organization. It is perfectly acceptable to go to an open AA meeting, listen to what is being said, and decide for yourself if their program would be useful to you.

Name _____   Date _____   Section _____

Assessment Activity 11-2

What Are Your Reasons for Drug Use?

Directions: In the following table are listed various drugs and products that can affect your life either positively or negatively. Think about how you view each product and what the long-term and short-term consequences of use might be. You might wish to consult other sources to help you determine possible effects. In the last column, explain briefly why you choose to use or to refrain from using the drug or product.

Drug	Possible Negative Effects	Possible Positive Effects	Reasons for Using or Not Using
Caffeinated drinks (tea, coffee, cola)			
Alcohol			
Cigarettes			
Pipe or cigar			
Cocaine (any form)			
Marijuana (any form)			
Designer drugs (any form)			
Heroin			
Over-the-counter medications			

Points to Ponder
1. Which drugs do you view positively?
2. Are you unsure of your feelings about any substance? If so, why?
3. What potential is there for abuse or misuse of any of the drugs (even those you have positive feelings about)? If so, what is the potential source of problems?

12

Preventing Sexually Transmitted Diseases

Key Terms

acquired immunodeficiency
 syndrome (AIDS)
chlamydia
cunnilingus
fellatio
genital warts
gonorrhea
hepatitis B
herpes

human immunodeficiency
 virus (HIV)
nucleoside analogs
protease inhibitor
safer sex
sexually transmitted
 diseases (STDs)
syphilis
viral hepatitis

Goals for Behavior Change

- Make choices regarding your personal sexual behavior.
- Practice safer sex if you have chosen to be sexually active.
- Take responsibility for the potential consequences of your sexual behavior.
- Learn how to talk with your partner about your sexual history.

Objectives

After completing this chapter, you will be able to do the following:

- Discuss the difference between being HIV positive and having AIDS.
- Identify the signs and symptoms of various STDs.
- Evaluate the risks of having multiple sex partners.
- Discuss the meaning of having a monogamous relationship.
- Identify safer sex practices.

exuality is a lifelong part of a person's life, affecting and being affected by relationships, anatomy, behaviors, thoughts, and values. Sexual behavior is only one aspect of sexuality.

Decisions concerning sexual behavior have many far-reaching consequences. These choices can enhance or severely diminish feelings of well-being. Sex can be wonderful and fulfilling but may also cause serious problems. This chapter examines some of the **sexually transmitted diseases (STDs)** that can result when people engage in behavior that puts them at risk. The chapter also identifies how to avoid contracting and spreading STDs. The chapter examines viral, bacterial, and other common STDs and infections.

Safer Sex

This book discusses the various components of optimal wellness. Sexual behavior can have a strong positive or negative impact on physical and emotional health (see Assessment Activity 12-2). Making decisions concerning sexual behavior is not easy (see Nurturing Your Spirituality: Making Decisions About Sex). If people (whether heterosexual or homosexual) choose to have multiple sexual partners, they must realize that each time a sexual act occurs, the potential sexual histories of two people are brought together. Even though it may be the first experience for one, the other partner may have had sex with three other people. In this case, the person for whom it is the first experience is essentially exposed to the sexual histories of four others. The diseases or infections of any of those four people may be brought to the present relationship (see Assessment Activity 12-1).

Unfortunately, people are not always honest about their past relationships. For many reasons, they may not tell the truth about the number of past partners or about the frequency of condom use. The potential for dishonesty in others makes prevention of STDs a personal responsibility for everyone.

Some people choose abstinence. Abstinence means voluntarily refraining from all sexual acts—which includes practicing sexual activities that involve vaginal, anal, or oral stimulation or penetration. People choose abstinence for a number of reasons, most frequently moral or religious.

A second frequent choice is to have sexual contact within a monogamous (involving only one long-term partner) relationship. Monogamy obviously is dependent upon both partners' willingness to maintain a monogamous relationship. Monogamy may be a choice for two people who have never had sexual intercourse with anyone else or for two people who have had sex partners in the past but have decided to limit their future sexual practices to those they share with each other. Having sex with only one uninfected and faithful partner is as equally effective in preventing STDs (not pregnancy) as abstinence—if it is practiced consistently by both partners. However, even with monogamy, precautions are necessary to prevent unwanted pregnancies.

People embarking on a monogamous relationship who have had partners in the past need to discuss their sexual histories as well as their commitment to the present relationship. This commitment may involve a willingness to be tested for possible STDs (see Real-World Wellness: Communicating with Your Partner About STDs). Some STDs take time to manifest themselves and so testing for them may have to be done several times over a period of years. Assuming that the people involved are committed to monogamy and are honest about their sexual histories, monogamy can serve to protect against the spread of STDs.

In modern society, many relationships are not of long duration, and the practice of *serial monogamy* is common. *Serial monogamy* is monogamy for as long as a relationship is intact; for the duration of their relationship, two partners only have sex with each other. Because relationships may be of relatively brief duration (ranging from weeks to years) and each partner may then seek new partners, the risk with serial monogamy for contracting and spreading an STD is significant.

A third choice is to have sex with more than one partner but to practice **safer sex**. There is no such thing as *safe* sex with multiple partners, but steps can be taken to help ensure *safer* sex. Regardless if you are heterosexual or homosexual, or male or female, you can follow certain practices to limit your exposure to STDs. The starting point for safer sex is utilizing some of the guidelines outlined in Real-World Wellness: Communicating with Your Partner About STDs on page 360. Anyone who is sexually active with multiple partners should be checked every three to six months for possible STDs. It is often the case that people, especially women, who are not disease free are asymptomatic (have no symptoms);[1] no persons should let their lack of symptoms lull them into assuming they are disease-free.

Here are some practices for people who are straight or gay that represent safer sex:

Safer practices
- Hugging
- Kissing (not deep or French kissing)
- Petting
- Watching erotic videos, reading erotic books, and so on
- Masturbation (solo or mutual unless there are sores, lesions, and/or abrasions on the genitalia or hands)

Nurturing Your Spirituality

Making Decisions About Sex

Everyone must decide at some point whether to engage in sexual activity. For some people the decision is ongoing. Even after having a sexual experience, a person must decide whether to have sex with the first partner again, to have sex with another person, or not to have sex. Having sex *is* always a choice, unless rape or abuse is involved.

People sometimes change their minds about wanting to have sex. A person may have sex with someone once or many times and then decide to refrain from having sex with that person again. Some people decide to wait to have sex until they are married or until their financial, social, or emotional circumstances change. Some decide to change their sexual behavior to be more closely aligned with moral, ethical, or religious beliefs.

Why do people change their minds about sex? The decision to refrain from further sexual intercourse is sometimes referred to as *secondary virginity*. Couples choosing to engage in sex must make sure that their choice fits with their value systems and understand that they are emotionally, socially, and financially responsible for the results of their decisions. Before initiating sexual intercourse, couples should discuss the following:

- Their thoughts and feelings about sexual activity

- Whether sexual intercourse fits their moral and ethical codes

- Willingness to practice safer sex to protect themselves as well as to deal with the potential pregnancy created as the result of their decision

What considerations are important when deciding whether to have sex? Reasons for having or not having sex are varied. Some couples may believe their feelings are strong enough for one another that sex would seal their commitment to the relationship. Others may decide that if two people love one another it is okay to have sex. Some

people engage in sexual activity because they see it as a way to be popular or as evidence that they are attractive. Some people have sex simply because they think everyone else is and that not to have sex would make them outsiders. (Not everyone is having sex! Many people, young and old, choose to abstain until marriage or some other long-term commitment.)

Some people choose to refrain from having sex until marriage because they view sex outside marriage as morally wrong. Another reason for abstinence may be a desire to get to know one's partner well (which takes time) before sex. Having sex may alter expectations and the nature of a relationship; some people do not have sex because they don't want their relationship to change. If the physical component of a relationship is emphasized over other aspects, partners may find it difficult to get to know each other well. Many people choose to abstain because they do not want to risk unwanted pregnancy, STDs, or the financial, emotional, and social responsibility of having sex. Some say that not having sex allows them to know themselves better and to figure out what they are looking for in a potential mate. Still others say that not having sex reduces the stress in their lives, freeing them from worries about problem pregnancies or STDs.

How do you decide whether to have sex? It is vitally important to know what your values are and to do only what furthers your total wellness. If you are choosing to have sex because of peer pressure or fear of being alone, then you are not acting out of a wellness perspective. If you are having sex for what you consider to be valid reasons and you are truly comfortable with your decision, then having sex may be an overall positive experience for you. Young adults often fail to realize that, during the next few years, they will be going through many changes as they move from home and from school out into the work world. These changes will alter their self-perceptions and their values. Making the wrong decision now may put that future in jeopardy. Taking time to consider behaviors carefully is crucial, because the regret of an unwanted pregnancy or a lifelong STD can be life altering or even fatal.

What factors will affect your decision to have or not have sex?

Possibly safer practices:

- Deep, French kissing, unless there are sores in the mouth
- Vaginal intercourse with a latex condom with nonoxynol-9
- **Fellatio** with a latex or polyurethane condom
- **Cunnilingus** with a latex dental dam, unless a female partner is menstruating or has a vaginal infection
- Anal intercourse with a latex condom with nonoxynol-9, but there is a great amount of dis-

agreement concerning the safety of this practice even with a condom—this is the most risky sexual behavior

Unsafe practices:

- Vaginal or anal intercourse without a latex condom with nonoxynol-9
- Fellatio or cunnilingus without a condom or latex dental dam
- Oral-anal contact
- Contact with blood, including menstrual blood

Real-World Wellness

Communicating with Your Partner About STDs

My partner and I have been very close to having sex on several occasions. I am very worried about contracting an STD. I really don't know much about my partner's past sexual history. How do I open the discussion or ask the questions concerning safe sex practices? How do I find out if there is anything I should be aware of in this person's past?

The decision about whether to have sex is extremely important. Considerations include the possibility of contracting an STD, the potential for an unwanted pregnancy, and the psychological and emotional ramifications of intimate contact should the relationship end. Sex represents a psychological, physical, emotional, and financial commitment to another person. Don't be reluctant to bring up the topic of safer sex. The ability to discuss important issues is a sign of personal and social maturity. Here are some suggestions on ways to introduce the topic. What others can you suggest?

- "I feel that we both are thinking about sex, but before I make a final decision, I have some concerns I'd like to discuss with you."

- "I've always practiced safer sex in the past and, if we're going to have sex, I think it's important for us to use condoms."

- "What type of protection do *you* have if we decide to have sex? This is the type of protection *I* have.

- "I know if you really care about me you'll be willing to use a condom."

- "Before this relationship goes any further, I want to ask you about your past sexual history and our plans for practicing safer sex."

- "I really like you and I hope we can have a more intimate relationship at some point. But I think there are some important things we should talk about first."

- You're so sexy sometimes I just get carried away when I'm close to you. Why don't we have a quiet dinner together to discuss our sexual past and what we want from this relationship?"

You can probably think of even better ways to approach a conversation concerning sex. What is important to remember is that sex can be a wonderful emotional and physical experience, but it's not worth dying for.

Just the Facts

Effective Condom Use

Condoms can be effective in protecting against STDs if used properly. Here are some guidelines for proper use:

- Use one every time you have sexual intercourse or oral sex involving a penis.

- Use only latex or polyurethane condoms.

- When having vaginal or anal intercourse, make sure the condom has nonoxynol-9.

- Put the condom on before any contact with the vagina.

- When the condom is on the penis, there should be about a half-inch of space left at the condom tip to hold the ejaculate.

- Withdraw the penis soon after ejaculation. Hold the base of the condom firmly against the penis as it is withdrawn so the condom does not come off.

- Use foam, spermicide, or a female condom in combination with a condom.

- Check for possible breaks immediately after use of any condom.

- Always use a water-based lubricant such as K-Y jelly. Vaseline or other oil-based lubricants can cause the condom to break down and become ineffective.

- Never reuse a condom.

- Taking semen in the mouth
- Sharing a vibrator or other sex toys without washing them between uses

See Just the Facts: Effective Condom Use.

Sexually Transmitted Diseases (STDs)

Each year in the United States it is estimated that more than 12 million people contract an STD.[2,3] Approximately 25 percent of all new cases occur among teenagers. Two-thirds of STD cases occur in people under the age of 25.[4] Another particularly disturbing fact is that young women under 24 years of age may be at more risk of STDs than are older women because the cells of the cervix in young women are immature and more easily infected.[5] An important component of these statistics is that a large number of STD cases go unreported because many are asymptomatic (particu-

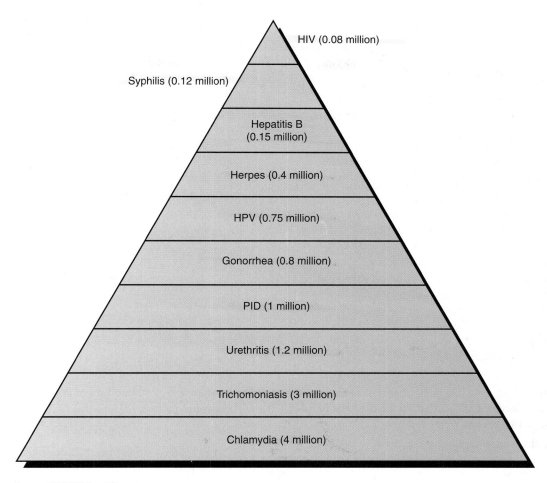

Figure 12-1 Annual STD Incidence

larly in women) or because they are treated by a private physician and never reported. Consequently, the estimated 12 million may reflect a vast underreporting of the number of cases. The estimates for annual STD incidence are shown in figure 12-1.[5]

Viral Diseases

Human Immunodeficiency Virus and Acquired Immunodeficiency Syndrome

Damage to the immune system as a result of infection with **human immunodeficiency virus (HIV)** leads to a complex of rare diseases called **acquired immunodeficiency syndrome (AIDS).** The Centers for Disease Control (CDC) lists two conditions to be used in diagnosing AIDS. These are an HIV seroconversion and a T-cell count below 200 cells per millimeter regardless of other specific symptoms that may or may not be present.[6] A normal range of T-cells is 800 to 1000. In the presence of these two conditions, some other condi-

tions may be used to diagnose AIDS. These conditions fall into several categories and are presented in Just the Facts: Conditions Used to Diagnose AIDS.

People infected with HIV may experience a variety of symptoms or may appear to be quite healthy. A small percentage of HIV-positive people seem to have been able to suppress and survive HIV infection for more than twenty years without ever developing AIDS. The reason for this is not understood by experts. It has been suggested that suppressor compounds formed by the immune system cells may be responsible. However, even people with no obvious symptoms can transmit HIV to others. The indicators of possible HIV infection include persistent diarrhea, dry cough, and shortness of breath; fatigue; skin rash; swollen lymph nodes (neck, armpits, groin); candidiasis; unexplained fever or chills; night sweats (over several weeks); and unexplained weight loss of 10 pounds or 10 percent of body weight in fewer than two months. Women may experience these symptoms as well as abnormal Pap smears, persistent vaginal candidiasis, and abdominal cramping as a result of pelvic inflammatory disease (PID). These infections are a result of HIV infection and are caused by

Just the Facts

Conditions Used to Diagnose AIDS

Here are some conditions besides HIV seroconversion and low T-cell counts used to diagnose AIDS:

Opportunistic infections (infections that take advantage of a weakened immune system)

- Pneumocystis carinii pneumonia (PCP)—A type of lung disease caused by a protozoan or fungus, which is usually not harmful to humans

- Tuberculosis—either *Mycobacterium avium-intracellulare* (MAI) or *Mycobacterium tuberculosis* (TB), with MAI being most common among AIDS patients

- Bacterial pneumonia—caused by several common bacteria

- Toxoplasmosis—a disease of the brain and central nervous system

Cancers

- Kaposi's sarcoma, a cancer that causes red or purple blotches on the skin

- Lymphomas, cancers of the lymphatic system

- Invasive cervical cancer—more common in women who are HIV positive

Other conditions

- Wasting syndrome, which involves persistent diarrhea, severe weight loss, and weakness

- AIDS dementia, impairment of mental function, mood changes, and impaired movement as a result of HIV infection of the brain

Other infections

- Candidiasis (also called *thrush*), a fungal infection that affects the vagina, mouth, throat, and lungs

- Herpes, a common viral STD described later in this chapter

- Cytomegalovirus, a virus that, in AIDS patients, can lead to brain infection, infection of the retina, pneumonia, or hepatitis

Wellness On the Web
Behavior Change Activities

What Do You Know About STDs?

More than twenty sexually transmitted diseases (STDs) have been identified, and all are preventable. But STDs are thriving, and it's largely because of ignorance and inaction. People who have multiple sex partners are at highest risk of contracting STDs. The only sure ways of preventing STDs are to abstain from sex or for two uninfected people to participate in a mutually monogamous relationship. Another effective but not foolproof way to reduce the risk of infection is the proper use of condoms. The Mayo Clinic has put together a quiz to test your knowledge about sexual safety. Go to www.mayohealth.org/mayo/9708/htm/sex_pgl.htm and complete the quiz. How much did you know about STDs?

Safer Sex: It's a Matter of Choice

It's much easier to prevent sexually transmitted diseases than it is to cure them. The prevention of STDs clearly is a personal responsibility. If one chooses to have sex with someone, it's essential to ask questions about that person's sexual history. The honesty of one's partner is of vital importance. To learn more about the risks involved in STDs, go to the Unspeakable website at www.unspeakable.com/profiler/profiler-frame.html and complete the Risk Profiler. You can create your profile by clicking on the button next to your answer for each question. After you answer, watch this space and the meter to the right to see the relative risk associated with your answer. The "Generate Report" button makes a report of your answers that you can use for future reference.

Breaking the Silence: Talking About Sex

Safer sex sounds like a great idea, but it can be difficult to achieve because few people want to discuss it. In this case, silence definitely is *not* golden. Having sex should be viewed as a major decision that may have lifelong consequences. The choice to engage in safer sexual behavior rests with each individual. One of the best ways to protect yourself is to know as much as possible. To find out the answers to a number of questions about sex frequently asked by adults, go to the Unspeakable website mentioned above and select from the categories of questions listed. You're sure to find some questions whose answers you'll find helpful.

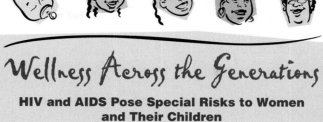

In 1997 women represented 22 percent of all AIDS cases reported.[7] AIDS is the third leading cause of death among women aged 25 to 44 years. The number of AIDS cases involving teenage girls is almost three times higher than it is for women over 30.[8]

Wellness Across the Generations

HIV and AIDS Pose Special Risks to Women and Their Children

Most women are infected through use of injected drugs or through sex with infected partners. Activities that put women at high risk include being a partner of an injected-drug user or of a gay or bisexual man or having multiple sex partners. Although lesbians with HIV are in a very small minority, they can and do contract HIV in the same ways as heterosexual women. Lesbians who share sex toys without first washing and cleaning them are at greater risk for HIV than are those who practice safer sex.

Heterosexual women are at greater risk for contracting HIV from an infected man than are non–HIV-positive men from HIV-positive women. Women are more susceptible to HIV infection because they have more surface area of contact in the vagina and the tissue there is softer and more easily scratched or torn. Further, semen is often ejaculated directly into the uterine and cervical canal. Semen normally contains 10 to 100 times more migratory lymphocytes than does cervical mucus, thus placing more virus in the area for potential infection.[8]

Women tend to be diagnosed at a later stage in the HIV process than are men and they have almost a 30 percent greater chance than men do of dying before they have an AIDS-defining condition.[1] Further, women tend to be excluded from many clinical trials. Because female physiology is different from male physiology, women need to participate in clinical trials to ensure that new experimental drugs and therapies work for them as effectively as they do for men.

A pregnant woman has about a 25 to 35 percent chance of passing the virus to her newborn. The Centers for Disease Control and Prevention has recommended HIV testing for all pregnant women. HIV transmission from mother to infant can be reduced from almost 26 percent to slightly more than 8 percent when both the HIV-positive mother (predelivery) and infant (postdelivery) are given doses of a drug called *AZT*. An HIV-positive mother can infect her newborn by breast-feeding. The exact risk for this form of transmission is not known, but the risk can be completely avoided through the use of formula as opposed to breast milk.

immunodeficiency, but they are not AIDS (see Wellness Across the Generations: HIV and AIDS Pose Special Risks to Women and Their Children).

The reason some people develop AIDS rapidly and others do not is not known. Factors that may contribute to the advancement of the condition are weakening of the immune system through other infections, alcohol or drug abuse, poor nutrition, and stress.[2] The longer the virus is in the system, the greater the chances of developing AIDS. In one study spanning six years, 30 percent of the participants with the virus developed AIDS, 49 percent displayed symptomatic HIV infections, and 21 percent remained free of symptoms. All these people could continue to spread the disease.[7] Another problem is the rapid development and emergence of new drug-resistant strains of HIV.[11]

Two types of HIV have been identified.[8] Almost all cases of HIV in the United States are a virus known as HIV-1. Another type of virus, HIV-2, is found mainly in West Africa and appears to take longer than HIV-1 to damage the immune system. The virus replicates inside human cells and is transmitted by blood, blood products, semen, vaginal secretions, and breast milk.

HIV is an extremely fragile virus in that it does not survive in air and can be destroyed readily by soap and water, household bleach, and chlorine used in swimming pools. Just the Facts: How HIV Is and Is Not Transmitted explores transmission in greater detail.

The HIV virus attacks the helper T-lymphocytes, specifically the T-4 cells, which are possibly the most critical element in the body's immune system. HIV attaches to the part of the T-cell that recognizes viral infections and blocks its ability to react to them. Over time, HIV may even multiply and destroy T-cells, leaving the body more defenseless against invasion by opportunistic organisms that can lead to illness and eventually death.[9] Among adults ages 25 to 44, AIDS is the leading cause of death for men and it is the fourth for women.[7,12]

In the United States, whether through homosexual or heterosexual contact, anal intercourse is still the most prevalent means of spreading HIV infection. This may be because this activity increases the likelihood of making small tears that facilitate the spread of the virus from semen to blood. Vaginal and oral sex are also considered highly dangerous.[10] Sharing of needles among drug users and having sex with an IV

How HIV Is and Is Not Transmitted

Here are possible means of transmission of HIV and some activities that, contrary to misinformed opinion, do not transmit HIV:

How HIV is transmitted
Sexual activity
- Homosexual, between men
- Heterosexual, from men to women and women to men

Blood
- Through needle sharing among intravenous drug users
- Through transfusion of blood and blood products
- To health care workers through a needle stick, an open wound, or mucous membrane exposure
- Through injection with an unsterilized needle (including needles used in acupuncture, medical injections, ear piercing, and tattooing)

Childbirth
- Intrauterine (within the uterus)
- Peripartum (during labor and delivery)

How HIV is Not transmitted
- Through food and water
- Through sharing of eating and drinking utensils
- Through shaking or holding hands
- Through use of the telephone
- Via a toilet seat
- Via insects
- In whirlpools or saunas
- Through coughing or sneezing
- Via domestic pets
- Through an exchange of clothing
- From swimming in a pool
- Through bed linens

drug user are high-risk activities. Sex with a prostitute is a significant risk factor. Anyone who has had multiple sexual partners during the last five to ten years is at risk because there is no way of knowing the sexual histories of all the sex partners of one's multiple sex

partners. People who are not sexually active are not at risk. People in monogamous relationships in which neither partner has an STD or has used IV drugs are considered safe. Based on present trends, it is estimated that HIV infections among non–drug-using heterosexuals in the United States will double during the 1990s.[16]

AIDS is a preventable disease, and education is still the best defense. People who have sex outside a monogamous relationship and those who share needles from intravenous drugs are still at extremely high risk for infection.

HIV is spread through intimate sexual contact; through transfusion of blood from an infected individual; and from an infected mother to her fetus during the prenatal period, the birth process, or breast feeding (see Just the Facts: Preventing the Spread of AIDS). In no case has HIV been spread through casual contact—this includes close contact between family members or friends and infected adults or children. Very few health care professionals working with AIDS patients have contracted the disease, and their infection was caused by rare mishandling of blood. The AIDS virus is not transmitted from toilet seats, foods, beverages or social kissing. The virus is found in small amounts in tears and saliva, although transmission through these mediums is undocumented.

Of great concern in the AIDS epidemic is the loss of life's most productive years; because 25 to 44 year olds made up more than half the work force in 1992, loss of life in that age group has been disruptive to society. It is projected that more than 80,000 American children will lose their mothers to AIDS by the year 2000.[13]

Probably no other infectious disease has taken or is taking such a devastating toll on Americans. By the end of December 1996, more than 500,000 Americans had been diagnosed with AIDS and more than 300,000 people had died (62.3 percent) since the disease was first reported in 1991.[14] It is estimated that the cost of treating one AIDS patient is $119,000—$50,000 before the development of AIDS and $69,000 after its development.[15]

Testing for HIV

Two tests are currently being used to detect HIV. The ELISA is the antibody test initially used. If the ELISA result indicates that the patient has HIV, another test—the Western blot technique—is administered for confirmation. A person may not have abnormal results on the ELISA if the virus has not been present long enough for antibodies to develop. Antibodies may develop within two months or may take up to thirty-six months to develop.[11] Usually, Western blot results are clearly either HIV positive or negative. If there is an inconclusive Western blot test, the person should be retested in six months. A third test, the single-use diagnostic system (SUDS), is currently being readied for determining if HIV infection has occurred. A home test is now available for over-the-counter use. However any positive HIV home test should be followed up with one of the aforementioned tests for HIV. Remember: Anyone who tests positive is infected with HIV and can transmit the infection.

Treatment for HIV and AIDS

At present no cure exists for HIV and AIDS, which results in a multitude of infections leading to death. The type of treatment that seems most effective in the treatment of AIDS is the use of a triple-drug therapy, consisting of a **protease inhibitor,** which blocks an enzyme (protease) that helps the virus develop at a later stage in the viral life cycle, and two drugs from another group of antiviral drugs called **nucleoside analogs** (AZT, ddI, and ZVD), which work by blocking reverse transcriptase, the enzyme used by HIV to copy itself in a host cell.

Early, aggressive treatment with a combination of a protease inhibitor and two nucleoside analogs (AZT and ddI), sometimes called a *cocktail,* has cut the death rate by 70 percent and inhibited opportunistic infections by 73 percent.[16] However, dangerous side effects seem to accompany this type of therapy, including diabetes, abnormally high cholesterol and triglyceride levels, shrinking limbs, and the bizarre appearance of disfiguring deposits of fat on parts of the body.[16]

Even with this dramatic improvement, the AIDS crisis is far from over. Although some patients appear virus free, no one knows that the virus is not "hiding" in other locations of the body or if the HIV virus will find a way to mutate so that the current cocktail is no longer useful. Further, no one knows, if the current therapy is discontinued, whether HIV will return. The cost for this type of treatment is very high, and only a few people can access the treatment. Even with all the advancements, the best protection for those choosing to be sexually active is education and the practice of safer sex.

AIDS is the most deadly of all STDs, but it is preventable. With education, wisdom, and reduction in high-risk behaviors, AIDS can be prevented (see Just the Facts: Preventing the Spread of AIDS). Information on AIDS can be obtained through various sources (see Just the Facts: AIDS and HIV Sources of Information).

Just the Facts

Preventing the Spread of AIDS[7]

The spread of AIDS can be stopped by preventing the transmission of the AIDS virus from one person to another. This means eliminating direct sexual contact with infected people and not using contaminated needles. Recommendations to reduce the possibility of becoming infected include the following:

- Practice abstinence or mutual monogamy.

- Always use protection (that is, latex condoms and spermicide, such as nonoxynol-9) if having sex with multiple partners or with people who have multiple partners.

- Do not have unprotected sex with people with AIDS, those who engage in high-risk behavior, or those who have had a positive test for the AIDS virus.

- Avoid sexual activities that might cut or tear the rectum, vagina, or penis, such as anal intercourse.

- Do not have sex with prostitutes.

- Do not use IV drugs or share needles. Refrain from having sex with IV drug users.

Herpes

Herpes is caused by the herpes simplex virus (HSV). Five different strains of the herpes virus infect human beings. The most common strains are herpes simplex-1 (HSV-1) and herpes simplex-2 (HSV-2). Type 1 is usually confined to congenital areas in the form of cold sores or fever blisters. It is a very common form of herpes but is not categorized as an STD. Type 2 generally causes lesions on and around the genital areas and is an STD. However, through either direct or indirect contact, type 1 can affect the genital area and type 2 can produce sores in the mouth. The common sites for type 1 and type 2 can thus be reversed. Estimates indicate that 30 million people in the United States are infected with genital herpes.[17]

Type 2 herpes usually appears as a single blister or a series of very painful blisters on the penis or inside the vagina or cervix. The blisters may also be present on the buttocks and thighs and in the groin area. Following a short prodromal (time interval between the

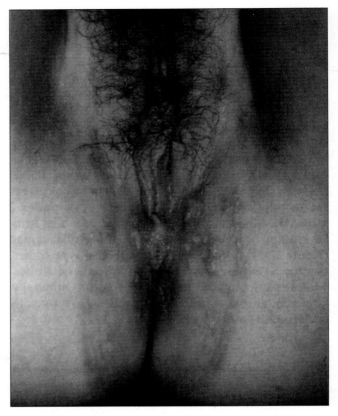

A severe herpes infection.

earliest symptoms and appearance of actual disease) of tingling, discomfort, or itching, small red lesions appear. This phase is followed by the formation of a small blister filled with clear fluid. This fluid is highly contagious. The infection usually lasts one to three weeks and then abates, but it does not leave the body. The virus retreats to the nerve endings where it remains dormant. Herpes can become active again without any warning; that is, the disease may be recurrent. Menstruation, stress, trauma to the skin (such as too much sunlight), lack of sleep, and poor nutrition seem to trigger recurrences. Recurrences are generally less severe and of shorter duration than the initial episode.[18]

Men do not seem to experience any major long-term complications from herpes. Women, however, may be faced with the possibility of cancer of the cervix and infection of their newborns during the birth process. Any woman with a history of herpes should have an annual Pap smear test. Physicians attending the pregnancy of a woman with a history of herpes should

be informed so that the course of the pregnancy can be monitored. If herpes becomes active or the physician feels the baby would be at risk through a vaginal birth, caesarean section delivery (surgical removal of the fetus through the abdominal wall) is often used. Additional hazards of herpes infection are herpes encephalitis, in which the virus invades the brain, and herpes keratitis, or eye infection. These two conditions are rare and can be effectively treated with antiviral drugs.

Three antiviral prescriptions drugs are now available for treating herpes. Acyclovir (brand name Zovirax, now available as a generic) promotes healing and helps suppress future outbreaks. Two newer drugs, valacyclovir and famciclovir, are similar to Zovirax but are designed to make higher levels of the drug's active ingredient available to the body. Some physicians prescribe a course of suppressive therapy with one of these drugs, which keeps herpes from recurring in up to 90 percent of patients. Patients must start taking the drugs at the first hint of symptoms. This therapy works only as long as the drug is taken, and if the drug is stopped there may be recurrences.[17] Warm compresses, sitz baths, and aspirin may help relieve discomfort.

Hepatitis B

Hepatitis is an inflammation of the liver caused by one or more viruses. There are five distinct types of **viral hepatitis** known: Hepatitis A (formerly *infectious hepatitis*), hepatitis B (formerly *serum hepatitis*), hepatitis C (non–A, non–B hepatitis), hepatitis E (another form of non–A, non–B), and hepatitis D, or *delta hepatitis*.

Hepatitis B is considered the most serious of the five types of hepatitis. It has an incubation period of between 45 and 160 days. The symptoms of hepatitis B include vomiting, abdominal pain, loss of appetite, and jaundice (an excess of a bile pigment in the blood that causes the skin to look yellow). Some infected people do not develop the worst symptoms of the disease but experience mild flulike illness without jaundice. However, the CDC estimates that approximately 25 percent of carriers suffer chronic symptoms, and these people are at the greatest risk for one of the most serious consequences of infection, cirrhosis of the liver. Cirrhosis is a degenerative disease in which liver cells are damaged and scarred with the eventual outcome of death or the necessity of liver transplantation. All carriers of hepatitis B are at greater risk of developing primary liver cancer than are noncarriers. At one time, hepatitis B was spread primarily through tattoo needles, the sharing of needles by drug users, and transfusions of contaminated blood. Today, it is more commonly spread through body secretions, including sweat, breast milk, and semen. A vaccine has been developed to immunize against the disease.

Symptoms of all forms of viral hepatitis are similar. They include fatigue, loss of appetite, mild fever, nausea, vomiting, diarrhea, aching muscles and joints, and tenderness in the upper right abdomen. A few people may have jaundiced (yellowed) skin and eyes, itching skin, darkened urine, and light-colored feces. Still others may exhibit no symptoms except those usually associated with the flu. This group does not usually seek treatment but still can transmit the infection to others.

Viral hepatitis is a type of liver injury. Most patients with hepatitis recover without serious problems. However, serious scarring of the liver or even death may occur. In some cases of hepatitis B the person with the disease becomes a chronic carrier or can develop chronic progressive hepatitis that eventually leads to liver failure.

Genital Warts

Warts on the genitalia, around the anus, in the vagina, and on the cervix are called **genital warts,** or *condyloma.* These warts are caused by the human papilloma virus (HPV). There are more than fifty forms of HPV. Experts postulate that this condition is the third most

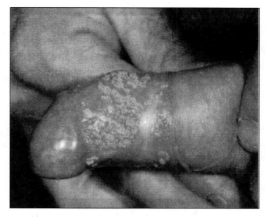

Genital warts are the result of human papilloma virus.

prevalent STD after chlamydia and gonorrhea. It is also estimated that 1.2 million people are infected annually. Approximately one in ten Americans may be carrying the virus.[18] Genital warts most commonly involve people between the ages of 15 and 24.

Genital warts are cauliflowerlike. In moist areas, they are soft and either pink or red. On dry skin, they are usually yellow-gray and hard. The warts are transmitted sexually and generally appear one to six months after exposure. There are fifty-six distinct varieties of HPV, some of which have been specifically linked to cervical cancer and cancers of the rectum, vulva, skin, and penis. The warts appear most often on the shaft of the penis, the vulva, the vaginal wall, the cervix, and the perineum. They may also be found in the anal area of both sexes and are associated with anal intercourse with an infected partner. Cryosurgery (freezing) is the treatment of choice, although electrocautery (burning) and use of the topical agent podophyllin also are successful methods of treatment. Podophyllin should not be used during pregnancy or on warts in the cervical area. If the infected person has had a variety of partners, the genitalia of all partners should be examined so that treatment can be initiated if appropriate.

Bacterial Diseases

Chlamydia

Chlamydia is thought to be the most common STD in the United States, with an estimated 4 million new cases each year.[19] The causative agent is the bacterium *Chlamydia trachomatis.* Chlamydia is frequently found with other STDs, such as gonorrhea, herpes, and syphilis, and it may be contracted through oral, anal, and vaginal intercourse.

In men the infection is usually manifested by inflammation of the urethra (urethritis). Infected men generally experience a burning sensation during urination and possibly a mild discharge. One-third of all men with chronic chlamydia infection develop no symptoms.

Symptoms in women include vaginal discharge, intermittent vaginal bleeding, and ill-defined discomfort or pain on urination. Infected mothers may pass the infection to their babies during the birth process. This may result in conjunctivitis in the baby or a more serious condition known as *chlamydial pneumonia.* More than 30,000 newborns are affected by this condition each year.[19]

When left untreated, chlamydia can lead to arthritis and can damage the heart valves, blood vessels, and heart muscle itself. In men the condition can also lead to sterility. In women the disease can infect the uterus, fallopian tubes, and upper reproductive areas, producing the chronic condition pelvic inflammatory disease, or PID. This scarring of the fallopian tubes by PID causes sterility and an increased risk of ectopic pregnancy (a condition in which the embryo is implanted outside the uterus).

Tetracycline, erythromycin, and doxycycline are the drugs used for treatment. They are taken orally for one to three weeks. Taking the full course of medication is extremely important because relapse can occur. All sexual partners should be treated or the disease can be passed among them.

Gonorrhea

Nearly 2 million cases of **gonorrhea** are reported each year, making it the second most prevalent STD. Gonorrhea is caused by the bacterium *Neisseria gonorrhoeae,* which attacks the mucous membranes of the penis, vagina, rectum, throat, and eyes. The disease is spread by vaginal, oral, and rectal contact.

Gonorrhea produces symptoms in 80 percent of men. The symptoms appear two to ten days (an average three to five days) after contact with the bacteria and include a thick, milky discharge from the penis and a painful, burning sensation on urination. These signs should cause men to seek medical treatment immediately. Untreated gonorrhea can result in sterility.

The symptoms in women are discharge and burning on urination, but they may be so mild that they are unnoticed. The bacteria can survive in the vagina and other areas of the female reproductive system for years. During this time, women can infect any sex partners and their fetuses if they become pregnant. Contact by the baby with the bacteria during childbirth can lead to an eye infection resulting in blindness. Untreated gonorrhea can lead to PID, the leading cause of sterility in women. In both men and women, rectal and oral gonorrhea may go unnoticed. The disease can develop into a serious infection, resulting in arthritis; meningitis; skin lesions; and liver, heart, brain, and spinal cord problems.

Gonorrhea is diagnosed by obtaining a smear from the penis or cervix. Penicillin is the drug of choice for treatment. If a person is allergic to penicillin, tetracycline is usually used. Physicians commonly treat for chlamydia as well when gonorrhea has been diagnosed. Gonorrhea can be completely cured, although there is no immunity to the disease. If a person has multiple sexual partners, medical help and advice must be sought regularly.

Syphilis

Syphilis is caused by a corkscrew-shaped bacterial spirochete called *Treponema pallidum.* Kissing, oral-genital contact, and intercourse are the most common forms of transmission. The spirochete dies quickly when exposed to air, so primary entry to the body is through a break in the skin. Once in the bloodstream, it exists in a variety of organs and mimics the symptoms of many major chronic diseases. Because of this ability to mimic other diseases, it is referred to as *the great imitator.*

One interesting fact concerning syphilis is that some HIV infections seem to be exacerbated by it. The lesions caused by syphilis seem to help the HIV virus seep into or out of the body. Not everyone who has sex with a person who is HIV positive becomes infected, but if either partner also has primary or secondary syphilis, the risk of transmission increases sixfold.[20] There are four stages of syphilis.

Primary syphilis

The initial sign of primary syphilis is a lesion called a *chancre* located at the site of entry of the pathogen. The incubation period can range from ten to ninety days (an average of twenty-one days) before symptoms appear. The chancre can vary from the size of a pinhead to the size of a dime. Even though the chancre may look painful, it is not and may go unnoticed. If the lesion occurs on the labia, vagina, or rectum, it can very easily remain undetected. The chancre disappears within three to six weeks. In 90 percent of women and 50 percent of men the chancre is difficult to identify.

Secondary syphilis

From four to twelve weeks after the chancre disappears, the symptoms of secondary syphilis may appear. Symptoms include headaches, swollen glands, low-grade fevers, skin rash, white patches on the mucous membranes of the mouth and throat, hair loss, arthritis pain, and large sores around the mouth and genitals. These sores contain the bacteria responsible for syphilis, and contact with them can spread the disease. Symptoms may be mild or severe, and in rare instances no symptoms appear. If left untreated, symptoms usually run their course, lasting anywhere from a few days to several weeks. The pathogen remains active in the body even with the absence of symptoms and will reappear later—perhaps as long as twenty years after the initial infection.

Latent syphilis

During latent syphilis there are few or no clinical signs that the disease exists, although the spirochetes are invading the various organs and systems of the body, including the brain, heart, and central nervous system. The spirochetes multiply relentlessly and begin to destroy the tissues, bones, and organs. At this stage a person is not contagious.

Late syphilis

From fifteen to twenty years after the onset of latent syphilis, the disease progresses to its most devastating stage. Late syphilis can cause heart damage, central nervous system damage, blindness, deafness, paralysis, and psychosis. Death from the effects of this stage of syphilis is probable.

Penicillin is the preferred drug for treating syphilis. People who are penicillin sensitive are placed on other antibiotics, such as tetracycline or erythromycin. Antibiotics can kill the pathogen at any stage, but any damage incurred cannot be reversed. People with syphilis commonly have other STDs, such as gonorrhea and chlamydia, thereby requiring greater doses of antibiotics.

Other Common STDs

In addition to the STDs mentioned, there are several others that have potential for harm. Table 12-1 lists several other common STDs.

Table 12-1 Other Common STDs

STD	Causative agent	Symptoms	Treatment
Candidiasis (yeast infection)	A fungus (*Candida albicans*) that can be transmitted through sexual coitus or an imbalance of the acidity of the vagina	White "cheesy" discharge, irritation of vaginal and vulva tissue	Vaginal cream or suppositories, such as miconazole (Monistat)
Chancroid	A bacteria (*Haemophilus ducreyi*) that can be contracted through a lesion or its discharge	Cluster of small bumps or blisters on the genitals or around the anus that rupture and ulcerate	Antibiotics, such as erythromycin
Granuloma inguinale	A bacteria (*Calymmatobacterium granulomatis*) that can be contracted through contact with a lesion or its discharge	Painless red bumps or sores in the groin that ulcerate and spread	Antibiotics, such as tetracycline or doxycycline
Nongonococcal urethritis (NGU)	A bacteria (mostly *Chlamydia trachomatis*) that can be transmitted during coitus	Inflammation of the urethra; for men, discharge and irritation during urination; for women, possible mild discharge of pus from the vagina or no symptoms	Antibiotics, such as tetracycline, doxycycline, or erythromycin
Pediculosis (Crabs)	*Phthirus pubis* (pubic lice)	Intense itching in the genital area	Shampoos, such as those with lindane solution (Kwell)
Trichomoniasis (trich)	Protozoan parasite (*Trichomonas vaginalis*) contracted through sexual intercourse; can be spread by towels, toilet seats, or bathtubs used by an infected person	White to yellow discharge with a most unpleasant odor	Antiinfectives, such as metronidazole (Flagyl)
Pelvic inflammatory disease (women only)	Caused by untreated chlamydia or gonorrhea; may lead to infertility or arthritis	Low abdominal pain, bleeding between menstrual periods, persistent low fever	Penicillin or other antibiotics

Summary

- The only way to completely avoid acquiring an STD is to abstain from sex or to have sex in a purely monogamous relationship.
- Practicing safer sex helps reduce the possibility of contracting an STD. The use of condoms is associated with decreased risk.
- The human immunodeficiency virus (HIV) attacking the immune system causes a complex of rare diseases called *acquired immunodeficiency syndrome* (AIDS).
- Although no cure exists for AIDS, some of the latest combinations of drugs seem to be prolonging life and reducing the HIV content in the body.
- Genital herpes is a viral disease characterized by lesions around the genital area. The disease can recur at any time and represents a serious threat to women by increasing their risk of cancer of the cervix. Three drugs are used to treat the disease (acyclovir, valacyclovir, and famciclovir).

- Viral hepatitis is an injury to the liver. There are several types of hepatitis. Hepatitis B is perhaps the most serious.
- Genital warts, or condyloma, are caused by the human papilloma virus (HPV) and have been linked to some cancers.
- Chlamydia is a bacterium that produces the most common STD in the United States. Untreated, it can cause arthritis, sterility, damage to the heart and blood vessels, and ectopic pregnancies.
- Gonorrhea is probably the second leading STD. It can lead to sterility in both men and women. The symptoms are often unnoticed by women.
- Syphilis is a bacterial disease that has four stages. The stages are primary, secondary, latent, and late.
- Several other STDs that have damaging potential are candidiasis, chancroid, pelvic inflammatory disease (PID), granuloma inguinale, nongonococcal urethritis (NGU), pediculosis, and trichomoniasis.

Review Questions

1. How can people accept responsibility for their sexual behavior?
2. What makes HIV an extremely dangerous infection?
3. What precautions can you take to protect against the spread of AIDS?
4. What are the various kinds of viral hepatitis and how are they spread?
5. Discuss why HPV is more dangerous for women than for men.

6. Why does chlamydia represent a serious problem?
7. Why is gonorrhea a more serious problem today than it was just a few years ago?
8. List and explain the four stages of syphilis.
9. Discuss some other common STDs.
10. If one STD is present, why may it be necessary to get treatment for more than one?

References

1. Strong, B., C. DeVault, and S. B. Werner. 1999. *Human Sexuality—Diversity in Contemporary America* (3d ed.). Mountain View, Calif.: Mayfield Publishing Company.
2. Center for Disease Control and Prevention. 1997. *1996 Report* available on-line at www.wonder.cdc.gov/wonder/STDSTDD007.PCW.html.
3. National Women's Health Resource Center. 1998. *Women and Sexually Transmitted Diseases (STDs)*. Available on-line at www.healthywomen.org/qa/std.html#1.
4. U.S. Department of Health and Human Services. 1996. *HIV/AIDS Surveillance Report* 8(20):18.
5. American Social Health Association. Jan. 1999. STD statistics available on-line at www.ashastd.org/std/stats/html.
6. Centers for Disease Control and Prevention. 1997. *HIV/AIDS Surveillance Report* 9(2):1.
7. Cox, F. D. 1999. *The AIDS Booklet* (5th ed.). Boston: WCB/McGraw-Hill.

8. Stine, G. J. 1993. *Acquired Immune Deficiency Syndrome—Biological, Medical, Social, and Legal Issues*. Englewood Cliffs, N.J.: Prentice-Hall.
9. Nevid, J. S. 1995. *Choices: Sex in the Age of STDs*. Boston: Allyn and Bacon.
10. Notes from the Twelfth World AIDS Conference, Geneva, Switzerland. June 26–July 12, 1998. www.mhhe.com/hper/health/personal health/aidsnotes.mhtml
11. Nowak, M. A., and A. J. McMichael. 1995. How HIV defeats the immune system. *Scientific American* 273(2):58.
12. Center for Disease Control and Prevention. 1996. *HIV Surveillance Report* 7(2):10.
13. Editors. 1994. Heterosexual AIDS is no myth. *Newsweek* 52(3):70.
14. Mayo Clinic. 1994. HIV and AIDS: A current look. *Mayo Clinic Health Letter* 12(2):5.
15. Hellinger, F. J. 1993. The lifetime cost of treating a person with HIV. *Journal*

of the American Medical Association 270(4):474.
16. Palella, F. L., et al. 1998. HIV outpatient study investigators. Declining morbidity and mortality among patients with advanced human immunodeficiency virus infections. *New England Journal of Medicine* 338(13):853.
17. University of California at Berkeley. 1999. Herpes: new strategies. *University of California, Berkeley, Wellness Letter* 15(4):4.
18. Nuovo, G. J., et. al. 1990. Human papillomavirus types and recurrent cervical warts. *Journal of the American Medical Association* 263:1223.
19. Centers for Disease Control. 1993. Evaluation of surveillance for Chlamydia trachomatis genital infection. *Morbidity and Mortality Weekly Report* 42(3):21.
20. Editors. December 22, 1998. Syphilis eradication: So near, so elusive. *USA Today* 6D.

Suggested Readings

Nevsid, J. S., and F. Gotfried. 1993. *201 Things You Should Know About AIDS and Other Sexually Transmitted Diseases.* Boston: Allyn and Bacon.
This book provides information on all the common STDs, offers guidelines for prevention, and lists available treatments.

Centers for Disease Control. 1998. *1998 Guidelines for Treatment of Sexually Transmitted Diseases.* New York: International Medical Publications.
This replaces the *1993 Guidelines for Treatment.* It was developed by CDC staff members after consultation with a group of experts on the treatment of STDs.

Shilts, R. 1987. *And the Band Played On: Politics, People, and the AIDS Epidemic.* New York: St. Martin's Press.
This classic book written by a gay man with AIDS expresses his views about the political aspects of AIDS and the difficulties in receiving treatment.

Assessment Activity 12-1

Are You at Risk for a Sexually Transmitted Disease?

Directions: Review each of the following sexual behaviors listed. If you engage in any of the listed activities, assess your personal risk for contracting a sexually transmitted disease through that activity by checking the appropriate line.

There is no risk for activity 1. The risk is low for activity 2. The risk is high for activities 3, 4, 5, and 6.

After reviewing the different categories of activities, are there areas of concern for you?

Activity	Risk	Precautions
1. _____ No sex	No risk: There is virtually no chance of getting an STD.	No precautions are necessary.
2. _____ Sex with only one partner	Low risk: If both partners have no other sexual partners and no disease, there is almost no risk of getting an STD.	Remain monogamous.
3. _____ Sex with a variety of partners	High risk: Each time there is another partner, the risk increases.	Choose partners carefully, use condoms and spermicides, wash after sex, do not douche, and urinate after sex.
4. _____ Sex with a partner who has sex with a variety of partners	High risk: The more partners, the greater the risk an STD will be transmitted.	Be aware of symptoms.
5. _____ Sex with someone who is or has been an IV drug user	High risk: If needles are shared, the risk is great, particularly of getting AIDS and hepatitis B.	Know the social and sexual history of your partner.
6. _____ Oral sex	High risk.	Know your partner; do not engage in oral sex if you do not know the history of your partner.

Assessment Activity 12-2

Making a Decision

The decision to have sexual intercourse is a major one. Many factors affect this decision, and many factors will be affected by it. People engage in sexual activity for a variety of reasons that are often unrelated to love and often without regard to the consequences of that behavior.

Directions: Listed here are factors that may influence your decision to engage in sexual activity. Rank each of these factors as to how they affect your behavior now and when you are in a situation in which you have to make a decision. Answer as truthfully as possible—you do not need to submit this activity to your instructor.

Factor	Not Important	Slightly Important	Important	Very Important	Extremely Important
Risk of AIDS					
Risk of other STD					
Risk of pregnancy					
Sexual history of partner					
History of partner with regard to IV drug use					
Biological gratification (physical sensations)					
Need for money					
Desire to be accepted by partner or social or cultural group					
Chance to reduce stress or to get mind off other problems					
Intense need to feel loved or cared for					
Desire to show commitment to a relationship					
Desire to express love for partner					
Monogamous nature of relationship					
Desire for a variety of partners					
Chance to feel desirable					
Chance to prove sexual prowess					

Consider asking your potential partner to also take this assessment as a basis for discussion. As you assess your responses, note the factors that are important to you in making this decision.

What are the most important factors? _____

_____

_____

Does the person you are considering having sex with have any history, behaviors, or other qualities that you consider to be negative in terms of your decision to have sex? What are they? _____

_____

_____

How important are these histories, behaviors, and other qualities to you? _____

_____

_____

How severe are the potential consequences of your or your partner's ideas and/or actions? _____

_____

_____

Reducing Your Risk of Cancer

Key Terms

basal cell carcinoma
benign
cancer
carcinoma
carcinogens
leukemia

lymphoma
malignant melanoma
metastasis
oncogene
sarcoma
squamous cell carcinoma

Objectives

After completing this chapter, you will be able to do the following:

- Define *cancer*.
- Identify the various types of cancer.
- List the signs and symptoms of the various types of cancer.
- Identify ways of protecting against various cancers.
- Discuss treatments for cancer.

Goals for Behavior Change

- Identify and change two behaviors that put you at risk for cancer.
- Begin an exercise program for preventing cancer as well as promoting overall wellness.
- Regularly perform the self-examinations for cancer described in this chapter.
- Consult your physician to arrange any appropriate medical screening tests, such as a mammogram or a PSA test.

ith the possible exception of AIDS, there is probably no disease that strikes more fear in people than cancer. The term **cancer** refers to a group of diseases characterized by uncontrolled disorderly cell growth. It is the second leading cause of death, accounting for 20 percent of all deaths.[1] It is the leading cause of death among adults ages 25 through 64.[2]

Between 1991 and 1995, the national cancer death rate fell 2.6 percent. Most of the decline was attributed to decreased mortality from cancers of the lung, colon-rectum, and prostate in men and breast, colon-rectum, and gynecologic sites in women.[1] In 1998 almost 564,800 Americans were expected to die of cancer, almost 1500 people a day.[1] (Heart disease deaths, the number-one cause of deaths, fell 50 percent during the same time period.)

Death rates for many major cancers have leveled off or declined over the past fifty years. Still, one of four Americans will eventually develop one or more of the 100 different forms of cancer; 40 percent of people who get cancer will be alive five years after diagnosis and considered cured. Others, however, who survive for five years may still show evidence of cancer.[1] *Cured* means that a patient has no evidence of disease and has the same life expectancy of a person who never had cancer. Although it strikes more frequently with advancing age, cancer causes the deaths of more children than any other disease (see Wellness Across the Generations: Children and Cancer). The chances of developing cancer can be reduced by assuming control of your daily behaviors and activities (see Just the Facts: Tips for Cancer Prevention; see Assessment Activity 13-2: Are You Practicing Cancer Prevention?).

Cell growth is controlled by deoxyribonucleic acid (DNA) and ribonucleic acid (RNA) in the nucleus of each cell in the body. If the nuclei lose the ability to regulate and control this growth, cellular metabolism and reproduction are disrupted and a mutant cell is

Wellness Across the Generations
Children and Cancer

Despite its rarity, cancer is the chief cause of death by disease in children under the age of 15. Cancer is usually a devastating event, particularly when the diagnosis occurs in children. The overwhelming emotional and psychological trauma associated with cancer affects not only the child but also brothers, sisters, parents, and relatives. If there is any good news to report, it is that mortality rates have declined 57 percent since the 1970s. St. Jude Children's Research Hospital, the only cancer research center in the world devoted solely to children, reports that, since 1962, the survival rates for various childhood cancers have risen significantly. For example, children with acute lymphocytic leukemia (cancer of the blood) now have a survival rate of 80 percent compared with the 1962 rate of 4 percent. Children now have the following survival rates (see list below):

Even though the survival rates are significantly better today than they were in 1962, the families of children diagnosed with cancer still need support. St. Jude provides not only medical treatment for the child, but also social support, psychological counseling, and education about the cancer for all the members of the family. Its mission is to serve as an advocate for the family as well as for the child affected, regardless of the prognosis.

As researchers move slowly toward providing cures and increasing life expectancy of children affected by cancer, we can all hope that, one day, we will only know of children dying from cancer through reading about them in textbooks. For more information about childhood cancers, visit the following website: **www.stjude.org**

	Now	1962
Hodgkin's lymphoma (cancer of the lymph nodes):	90%	50%
Non–Hodgkin's lymphoma (malignant tumor):	80%	7%
Retinoblastoma (cancer affecting the eyes):	90%	75%
Neuroblastoma (cancer of the nervous system):	56%	10%
Wilms' tumor (cancer of the kidney):	90%	50%
Osteosarcoma (bone cancer):	70%	20%
Rhabdomyosarcoma (cancer affecting the muscles):	75%	30%

Just the Facts

Tips for Cancer Prevention

To improve your chances of avoiding cancer, observe the following guidelines:

What to Do

- Eat more broccoli, cauliflower, and brussels sprouts. Eat more cabbage-type vegetables, such as cabbages and kale. These vegetables protect against cancers of the colon, rectum, stomach, and lung.

- Add more high-fiber foods to your diet. Eat more peaches, strawberries, potatoes, spinach, tomatoes, wheat and bran cereals, rice, popcorn, and whole-wheat bread. Fiber protects against cancer of the colon.

- Choose foods containing vitamin A. Eat more carrots, peaches, apricots, squash, and broccoli. Fresh foods are the best sources and are far better than vitamin pills. Vitamin A protects against cancers of the esophagus, larynx, and lung.

- Choose foods containing vitamin C. Eat more grapefruit, cantaloupe, oranges, strawberries, red peppers, green peppers, broccoli, and tomatoes. These help fight cancers of the esophagus and stomach.

- Practice weight control. Exercise and eat foods low in calories. A good exercise for most people is walking. Obese people have a high chance of getting cancers of the uterus, gallbladder, breast, and colon. Check with your doctor before you start an exercise program or a special diet.

What to Avoid

- Avoid fat. Eat lean meat, fish, and low-fat dairy products. Cut extra fat off meats and skin poultry before cooking. Avoid pastries and candies. A high-fat diet increases the chance of getting cancer of the breast, colon, and prostate. Calories loaded with fat cause weight gain.

- Avoid salty foods. Stay away from nitrite-cured and smoked foods. Bacon, ham, hot dogs, and salt-cured fish are examples. People who eat these foods have a greater chance of cancer of the esophagus and stomach.

- Avoid smoking. Smoking is the main cause of lung cancer. Pregnant women who smoke harm their babies. Parents who smoke at home cause breathing and allergy problems for their children. Chewing tobacco can cause cancers of the mouth and throat. Pick a day to quit and call the American Cancer Society for help.

- Avoid alcohol in excess. If you drink a great deal, you may get cancer of the liver. It is worse to smoke and drink. This increases the chances of getting cancers of the mouth, throat, larynx, and esophagus.

- Avoid too much sun. The sun causes skin cancer and other damage to skin. Use a sunscreen. Wear long sleeves and a hat between 11 A.M. and 3 P.M. Do not use indoor sunlamps, visit tanning parlors, or take tanning pills. Be alert for changes in a mole or sore that does not heal. If changes occur, go to a doctor.

produced that varies in form, quality, and function from the original. When a mass of these cells develops, it is considered a neoplasm, or tumor. It may be malignant (cancerous) or **benign** (noncancerous). A benign tumor will not spread throughout the body. It is enclosed by a membrane that prevents it from invading other tissues. A benign tumor is not life threatening unless it is in an area that interferes with normal functioning. A malignant tumor is the most dangerous tumor because it has a tendency to spread from its original location to other parts of the body, which can make it life threatening. Cancer cells can crowd out normal cells, invade surrounding tissue, and move through the lymphatic or circulatory system to infiltrate other areas of the body. (The lymphatic system is a network of nodes and vessels that serves to drain fluid from tissues and return it to the bloodstream. It is also part of the body's immune system.) The process by which cancer-

ous cells spread from their original site (primary site) to another location (secondary site) is called **metastasis.** The ability of cancerous cells to metastasize makes early detection critical. Table 13-1 describes the types of cancer and where they are most often found.

Causes and Prevention

Cancer is caused by both external (chemicals, diet, radiation, viruses, pollutants, etc.) and internal (hormones, immune conditioning, and inherited mutations) factors. Any combination of these factors may initiate or promote carcinogenesis—the development of cancer cells. Ten or more years often pass between exposures or mutations and the actual detection of cancer.[3]

Although the causes of cancer are not clearly understood, correlations have been found between cancer and everything from genetic factors to exposure to the

Table 13-1 Types of Cancer and Most Common Sites

Type	Most Common Site	Method of Spread
Carcinoma	Tissues covering body surfaces and lining the body cavities are the most common locations. Sites include the breast, lungs, intestines, skin, stomach, uterus, and testes.	Lymphatic and circulatory system
Sarcoma	The connective system is most commonly affected. Sites include bones, muscle, and other connective tissue.	Circulatory system
Lymphoma	The condition develops in the lymphatic system, infectious regions of the neck, armpits, groin, and chest. Hodgkin's disease is an example.	Lymphatic system
Leukemia	The blood-forming tissues, bone marrow, and spleen, are particularly affected.	Circulatory system

Table 13-2 Factors That Can Cause Cancer[1]

Carcinogen	Site of Cancer	Comments
Alcohol	Liver, larynx, pharynx, breast, esophagus	Heavy drinking increases the risk of cancer, especially when accompanied by cigarette smoking or use of chewing tobacco.
Smoking	Lungs, mouth, pharynx, larynx, bladder, esophagus	Smoking accounts for about 30 percent of all cancer deaths. It is considered the number-one carcinogen in the United States and the most preventable cause of death. It is responsible for 87 percent of lung cancer deaths.
Ultraviolet radiation	Skin	Almost all skin cancers are sun related.
Ionizing radiation	Blood-forming tissues, lungs	Excessive exposure to radiation increases cancer risk. Excessive radon exposure increases the risk of lung cancer.
Smokeless tobacco	Mouth, larynx, pharynx, esophagus	Oral cancer increases with the use of chewing tobacco and snuff.
Estrogen	Endometrium (uterus), liver, breast	Oral contraceptives increase the risk of liver cancer. Estrogen treatment to control menopausal symptoms increases the risk of cancer. The risk is reduced with simultaneous progesterone treatment.
Industrial agents		Industrial chemicals and agents, such as nickel, chromate, asbestos, and vinyl chloride, increase the risk of various cancers.
Dietary fat		High consumption of dietary fat is related to cancers of the colon, prostate, and pancreas; replacing fat with complex carbohydrates provides protection against several cancers (see Chapter 6).

sun's radiation. Many **carcinogens** (cancer-causing agents) trigger the development of cancer. (Table 13-2 contains a list of substances known to be carcinogenic.)

An inherited tendency for cancer has been theorized for years. Everyone seems to have genes that may cause cancer, but not everyone gets cancer. In most cases environmental factors actually activate the cancer. A good example of the interplay between genetic and en-vironmental factors is found in cigarette smoking. Approximately 87 percent of lung cancers occur in ciga-rette smokers,[1] but only 15 percent of smokers develop lung cancer. Why not the other 85 percent? The 15 percent who develop cancer are thought to be suscepti-ble to the disease on the basis of their genes. If they had not activated the cancer genes by smoking, they proba-bly would not have contracted the disease.

A gene that causes cancer is called an **oncogene**. Within a tiny segment of DNA is an area that can be activated to form an oncogene. All cells have normal regulatory genes called *proto-oncogenes*. A variety of genetic mutations, viral infections, or other carcinogens cause these normal genes to somehow lose their ability to replicate themselves in a normal genetic fashion. If the gene that is miscopied is one that controls specialization, replication, repair, or tumor suppression, the result is a cancer-producing gene. Unless it is activated, however, it will never cause cancer. If an oncogene is formed, it acts with other oncogenes to produce abnormal cells that can replicate and spread.

Suppressor genes also play a role in cancer. Suppressor genes, which exist in normal cells, control cell growth. If suppressor genes mutate, cells are permitted to grow unrestrained.

Another explanation of cancer is an error in cell duplication on the basis of chance alone. Several trillion new cells are formed each year, and perfect duplication does not occur with each new cell formation. When an abnormal cell develops, the immune system recognizes it as a rogue cell and attacks it. Every cancer cell needs to be killed because almost all cancers arise from a single cancer cell. Cancer develops as a result of the immune system's failure to clear the body of cancer cells. This is one reason the immune system is receiving considerable attention from cancer researchers.

Much research appears to link psychological states with the prevalence of disease in certain people. People with positive, involved attitudes who view life's challenges as opportunities for personal growth seem to have fewer diseases and recover from them more often. People who feel lonely and depressed and lack appropriate social support are more cancer prone than are their mentally healthy counterparts.

Emotional factors, such as stress, lack of social support, and the inability to express and cope with the range of emotions brought on by a frightening diagnosis of cancer, have been linked to the progression of cancer. Several studies have reported that patients who participate in support groups while receiving standard medical care live significantly longer than do those receiving medical care alone. Conversely, cancer patients who are socially isolated have poorer survival rates than do those with more social connections.[5] This doesn't suggest that stress and social isolation cause cancer. It does suggest a significant correlation between emotion and the progression of cancer once the disease is established. Many experts believe that a person's emotional state may somehow bolster the body's natural cancer-fighting power.

Although some of these concepts are controversial, it is generally accepted that substances such as tobacco, tobacco smoke, alcohol, asbestos, herbicides and pesti-

HealthQuest Activities

- The self-assessment activity *Cancer: What's Your Risk?* found in Module 6 allows you to examine how your family history, personal health history, occupation, environment, and behavior affect your risk of developing cancer. *HealthQuest* will estimate whether you are at decreased, average, or above average risk of developing several kinds of cancer. Complete the self-assessment and then gather more information about the cancers for which you are at increased risk. Use the Cancer Info feature in the Connections section to help you.

- Like other chronic diseases that occur more frequently as people age, cancer may appear to young adults to be an unlikely possibility. Review the *Cancer Info* feature to learn how cancer affects quality of life. Then read the Connections article on social support for people with cancer. Finally, increase your awareness of skin cancer prevention by using the *Skin Cancer Exploration*. List the factors that put a person at highest and at lowest risk for skin cancer. Then determine which factors are modifiable and which are not.

cides are carcinogens. Scientists believe that more than 80 percent of all cancers are associated with lifestyle factors that are easily controlled—diet, smoking, and exposure to the sun.[6] Almost two-thirds of cancer deaths are attributed to diet and tobacco (figure 13-1). According to a twenty-year study of 115,195 healthy women ages 30 to 55, one-third of cancer deaths are caused by excessive weight.[7] (Chapter 6 provides guidelines for cancer prevention as related to diet; Chapter 8 provides guidelines for weight maintenance.)

One of the major carcinogens may be sun radiation—more specifically, excessive exposure to the ultraviolet (UV) rays of the sun. People who spend hours in the sun without protection have an increased risk for skin cancers. UV light peaks from 10 A.M. to 2 P.M. (11 A.M. to 3 P.M. during daylight savings time). Avoiding sun exposure during these hours can cut UV-light exposure by up to 60 percent. Most major newspapers now include the UV index as a routine part of the weather report. Using tanning beds also increases the risk for skin cancer.

Finally, the herpes viruses have been connected with cancer of the cervix. Viruses may be involved in the development of some forms of leukemia, Hodgkin's disease, and Burkett's lymphoma. The exact role of viruses in causing cancer is not known, but they may

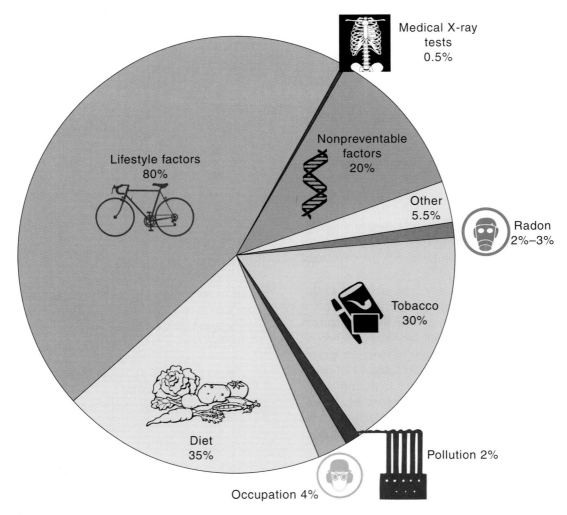

Figure 13-1 Percent of Cancer Deaths Caused by Preventable Factors[5]

provide an opportunistic environment for cancer development. Other researchers have suggested that it is a combination of factors, in which the virus may play a part, rather than the virus itself that causes cancer.

Cancer Site

The American Cancer Society reports each year on the incidence and number of deaths from cancer for a variety of sites (figure 13-2). Skin cancer is the most common cancer. More than 1 million people are diagnosed annually with basal and squamous cell skin cancer. Almost all of these are considered sun-related cases.[1] Fortunately, the majority of skin cancers are highly curable. For both genders the cancer that kills most often is lung cancer. Excluding basal cell and squamous cell carcinomas, the breasts are the most prevalent cancer site for women, and the prostate is the leading cancer site for men. In 1995 an estimated 184,500 new cases of prostate cancer and 178,700 new cases of breast

cancer were reported. For any cancer, early detection is imperative (see Assessment Activity 13-1). If cancer is diagnosed while it is still localized, the cure or survival rate may be 90 percent or higher for some cancers such as skin, colon, and rectum cancers.[2]

Exercise and Cancer Prevention

Researchers are continuing to investigate the role of exercise in the prevention of some types of cancer, including of the colon, breast, and reproductive system. In 1996 regular physical activity was added to the list of cancer-prevention measures developed by the American Cancer Society. Mounting research indicates that lack of exercise is a contributing factor to the development of cancer. In fact, a panel of cancer experts concluded that as many as 30 to 40 percent of all cancers worldwide could be prevented if people exercised, maintained proper weight, and followed a proper diet.[4]

Cancer cases by site and sex

Male	Female
Prostate 184,500	Breast 178,700
Lung 91,400	Lung 80,100
Colon & rectum 64,600	Colon & rectum 67,000
Urinary bladder 39,500	Endometrium (uterus) 36,100
Non-Hodgkin's lymphoma 31,100	Ovary 25,400
Melanoma of the skin 24,300	Non-Hodgkin's lymphoma 24,300
Oral cavity 20,600	Melanoma of the skin 17,300
Kidney 17,600	Urinary bladder 14,900
Leukemia 16,100	Pancreas 14,900
Stomach 14,300	Cervix (uterus) 13,700
All Sites 627,900	All Sites 600,700

Cancer deaths by site and sex

Male	Female
Lung 93,100	Lung 67,000
Prostate 39,200	Breast 43,500
Colon & rectum 27,900	Colon & rectum 28,600
Pancreas 14,000	Pancreas 14,900
Non-Hodgkin's lymphoma 13,000	Ovary 14,500
Leukemia 12,000	Non-Hodgkin's lymphoma 11,900
Esophagus 9,100	Leukemia 9,600
Urinary bladder 8,400	Endometrium (uterus) 6,300
Stomach 8,100	Brain 6,000
Liver 7,900	Stomach 5,600
All Sites 294,200	All Sites 270,600

Figure 13-2 Cancer Incidence and Death by Site and Sex—1995 Estimates*

*Excluding basal and squamous cell skin cancer and in situ carcinomas except urinary bladder.

American Cancer Society, Surveillance Research, 1998.

Another study found that, over an eight-year period, physically unfit men had four times the overall cancer death rate of the most fit men. For women, an even greater difference exists in the death rate between the fit and unfit.[5] Many researchers have followed various groups for long periods to determine whether those who exercise seem to have some measure of protection against cancer. The most impressive results have shown exercise providing protection against colon, breast, and prostate cancers.

Exercise and Colon Cancer

In a review of many studies, it was found that people who tend to sit the majority of the workday or remain inactive in their leisure time have a 30 to 100 percent greater chance of contracting colon cancer.[6] One study of 17,607 college graduates, ages 30 to 79 years, confirmed a lower risk of colon and lung cancer among men who were physically active.[8] A study done at Harvard University reported that, among 48,000 men, colon cancer risk decreased 50 percent in the most physically active group. This protective effect seemed to occur when the men exercised on average about one to two hours a day.[8] Another study of nearly 90,000 nurses also confirmed the protective effect of physical activity for women against colon cancer.

There are several possible explanations of why exercise is beneficial in protecting against colon cancer. One theory is that exercise increases peristalsis of the large intestine, thus decreasing transit time and the time during which potential carcinogens can be in contact with the cell lining of the colon. Another theory is that exercisers tend to be of more normal weight and are less likely to be obese than nonexercisers. Both obesity and lack of exercise increase levels of insulin, which in turn increase the growth rate of cells lining the colon, thereby increasing the likelihood of developing cancer.[9]

Another interesting aspect of the Harvard study was the discovery that exercisers ate an average of 29 grams of fiber daily, whereas nonexercisers ate only 12 grams.[8] The increased fiber serves to increase peristalsis.

Exercise and Breast Cancer

In a study of 545 premenopausal women, it was found that women exercising 3.7 hours per week reduced their risk for breast cancer by more than 50 percent.[10] A study of Norwegian women who engaged in regular exercise demonstrated a 37 percent reduction in breast cancer risk.[11] If the women were both lean and exercisers, their risk was reduced by 72 percent.

Some researchers feel that exercise helps reduce the amount of body fat and protects against obesity. As mentioned in the case of colon cancer, obesity is associated with higher blood insulin levels, which promote the growth of breast cancer cells. Thus, exercising women may be protected from breast cancer because of the indirect effects of exercising on exposure to their own hormones.[12]

Exercise and Prostate Cancer

In a study on over 17,000 college alumni, prostate cancer was found to be reduced by 47 percent in highly active men compared to sedentary men 70 years old and older.[13] At the Cooper Clinic in Dallas it was found that men in the highest fitness group had a 74 percent smaller risk than those in the lowest fitness group of developing prostate cancer.[14] This same study found that men expending more than 1000 calories a week in exercise had less than half the risk of prostate cancer of their sedentary counterparts.

The protective nature of exercise against the development of prostate cancer seems to be the result of repeated bouts of exercise that lower blood levels of testosterone. Men who exercise a great deal tend to expose their prostate to less testosterone, thus reducing their risk for cancer.[15]

Cancers of Concern to Everyone

Lung Cancer

Although breast cancer and prostate cancer (see the next sections) receive the majority of attention in the United States, lung cancer is the leading cause of cancer death in the United States[3] and throughout the world.[16] This is largely because lung cancer is more difficult to detect and thereby more deadly than other, even more frequently occurring types of cancer. Lung cancer is one of the most preventable forms of cancer, because the vast majority of cases are directly associated with lifestyle—smoking cigarettes. All cancers caused by cigarette smoking are 100 percent preventable.

The incidence of lung cancer is highest among people who started smoking cigarettes at an early age and who smoke the most cigarettes daily. The single best prevention of lung cancer is never to smoke. Passive, or involuntary, smoke also contributes significantly to lung cancer. A person who lives or works with smokers significantly increases his or her risk of developing lung cancer even if choosing to not smoke. Symptoms of lung cancer typically include a persistent cough, blood in the sputum, chest pain, recurring pneumonia, or bronchitis.

The good news about lung cancer (and nearly all cancer deaths) is that, for the first time, all cancer deaths declined between 1990 and 1995 (by 3 percent).[3] Part of this decrease is due to the reduction in the total number of smokers. The bad news about lung cancer is that early diagnosis tends to be rare. Regular X rays of the lungs and checking for blood in the sputum seem to be ineffective means of early detection, perhaps because of the altered appearance and function of lung cells from smoking. By the time most lung cancers are detected, the cancer is either not treatable because of widespread metastasis or the treatment is limited to ensuring a short-term extension of life. Five-year survival rates following diagnosis of lung cancer are between 7 and 12 percent, which is quite low.

The colorless, odorless gas radon has been somewhat inconsistently associated with increased risk of lung cancer.[3] People living in areas designated high in radon should have their homes measured. Asbestos inhalation has also been associated with lung cancer.

Although the absolute best ways to prevent lung cancer are to not smoke, not living with a smoker, not working in a smoking environment, ensuring that radon levels in the home are safe, and avoiding asbestos, substantial evidence exists for the role of diet in lung cancer prevention.[3,16,17,18] A diet high in whole fruits and vegetables seems to protect against lung cancer. Smokers who regularly consume much produce (fruits and vegetables) seem to have reduced incidence. While regular consumption of whole fruits and vegetables does not ensure that a smoker (or anyone else) will not get cancer, especially lung cancer, there is convincing evidence that a healthy diet provides some protection.

Colorectal Cancer

Colon cancer and cancer of the rectum rank as the second leading causes of cancer deaths in the United States (they are the third leading causes for women, behind lung and breast cancers, and the third leading causes for men, behind lung and prostate cancers).[16] When detected early, 90 percent of localized colorectal cancers can be cured. Once the cancer has spread, however, this chance drops to only 10 percent.[19]

A family history of colon cancer doubles the risk, but family history only accounts for 10 to 15 percent of all colon cancers.[16] People with a family history need to be extra vigilant, participating in regular screenings, but so do people with family histories of benign polyps in the colon. Frequent constipation has been implicated as a risk factor; experiencing constipation even once a month may double one's risk.[20] Any change or increases in constipation or chronic constipation suggest the need for follow-up screening for abnormal growths. Consuming large numbers of calories may increase colon cancer risk.[3] Symptoms of colorectal cancer include a change in bowel habits, chronic abdominal discomfort, sudden weight loss, lack of appetite, or rectal bleeding. Long-term survival rates are much higher when potential cancers are detected before symptoms develop. Detection of colorectal cancer can frequently be accomplished via screenings, although many people avoid the screenings because they find them somewhat distasteful.

Identification of polyps (growths) is a primary screening method. The occurrence of polyps in the colon and rectum does not mean a person will develop cancer. In cases in which the polyps do become cancerous, the length of time from initiation to cancer may be five to ten years.[19] The type of screening test used depends on the age of the person as well as family and personal history. Anyone over age 50, even without a family history of the disease, should be tested.

Anyone can undertake prevention of colorectal cancer. Diet is believed to be the primary cause for its development. The National Cancer Institute, the American Cancer Society, and the American Institute for Cancer Research recommend, a diet high in vegetables (especially cruciferous vegetables) and fiber and low in fat is recommended.[3,16,18] Regular physical activity and maintaining recommended body weight are also probably preventive. Long-term (fifteen years or more) ingestion of the B-vitamin folate may reduce the risk of colon cancer.[21] Recent studies suggest that 81 mg of aspirin (the lowest observable amount that produced desirable results) may also have a protective effect against colon cancer.[3,22] Although aspirin is a drug with side effects, some potentially life threatening, it may also be beneficial for people at elevated risk who can tolerate it. However, aspirin as a preventive should never be taken without prior consultation with a physician.

Stomach, Liver, and Pancreatic Cancer

Stomach cancer

Stomach cancer except for cancer of the upper part of the stomach (which may be associated with obesity) has steadily declined in the United States and other developed countries. This decrease seems to be strongly linked to the availability of refrigeration, eliminating the need for salt as a preservative. Refrigeration also provides year-round availability of fresh fruits and vegetables, which is linked to decreased risk. The recent popular interest in green tea consumption may prove beneficial in reducing the risk for stomach cancer. Diets high in salt probably increase the risk for stomach cancer. The major non-lifestyle cause of stomach cancer is infection with the *Helicobacter pylori* bacteria.[16]

Most types of stomach cancer can be prevented by diet. Even though the numbers of cases are declining, stomach cancer still ranks among the top ten cancer killers in the United States. Symptoms are nonspecific and diagnosis at early stages is not usual.

Liver cancer

Liver cancer is relatively uncommon in the United States and other developed countries. No effective treatment exists for it; the five-year survival rate is only 6 percent. Many liver cancers are lifestyle-related. The primary risk factor for liver cancer is infection with hepatitis B or hepatitis C viruses. The major method of transmission for these viruses is the sharing of needles or sexual contact.[16] Recent findings suggest that hepatitis B can also be transmitted by sharing a rolled paper used for snorting cocaine or other drugs.[23] Regular, heavy (more than moderate) consumption of alcohol, leading to cirrhosis and a condition known as *alcoholic hepatitis*, is closely associated with the development of liver cancer.[16] Ingestion of aflatoxins (a type of food mold) from contaminated food has been demonstrated to produce liver cancer, particularly among people in developing countries,[24] but tends to be rare in the United States.

Pancreatic cancer

Pancreatic cancer, lesser known than the cancers mentioned previously, ranks among the leading five causes of cancer death in the United States. Pancreatic cancer does not seem to get the publicity of many other types of cancer, yet it is extremely deadly and almost impossible to diagnose. In 1998, 29,000 new cases were diagnosed, and 28,900 people died from it.[1] At the time of publication, no effective method existed to screen or

Wellness On the Web
Behavior Change Activities

Cancer: An Ounce of Detection Is Worth a Pound of Cure

Time after time, we hear the same tragic story from cancer patients: "I knew I had a lump, but I was afraid it would be cancer, so I didn't go to the doctor," or "By the time I realized something was wrong, the cancer had metastasized." The very word "cancer" strikes fear into the hearts of the bravest—yet reliable studies show that the earlier cancer is diagnosed, the better the chances of survival. Both health care providers and the public look to the American Cancer Society (ACS) for guidelines to help detect cancer at the earliest possible stage. The ACS publicizes its recommendations (and most doctors follow them) about Pap smears and mammograms for women, prostate examinations for men, and colorectal examinations for anyone over age 50. These procedures offer hope of detecting cancer early, when it's most treatable. Go to the ACS website www.cancer.org and select "Cancer Information." Then select "Prevention Guidelines" and read through the list of recommended early detection tests.

What Causes Cancer?

What is cancer, and how does it originate? Thanks to sophisticated research, medical science is coming closer than ever to solving these riddles and opening the door to possible cures. In the meantime, we're learning a great deal about the risk factors that increase a person's chance of developing cancer. Different cancers have different risk factors. According to the American Cancer Society, existing scientific evidence suggests that about one-third of the cancer deaths that occur in the United States each year are caused by cigarette smoking, and another third are the result of dietary factors. This means that for the majority of Americans who don't use tobacco, dietary choices and physical activity become the most important modifiable determinants of cancer risk. To learn more about individual risk factors, go to the ACS website www.cancer.org and select "Cancer Information." Then select "Risk Factors" and read through the list of risks for different types of cancers. Were you surprised by anything you learned?

Skin Cancer: Shun the Sun

The dangers of prolonged exposure to the sun's ultraviolet rays are well known, but many people still choose to risk skin cancer rather than give up their golden tan. Mainly because sun worshiping is still associated with the glow of health, skin cancer is the most common cancer. More than 800,000 people are diagnosed annually with basal cell and squamous cell skin cancer. Go to the Maui website www.maui.net/~southsky/introto.html# now to learn more about what causes skin cancer and to assess your personal risk of developing this potentially life-threatening disease.

---

diagnose this cancer. Occasionally, depending upon where the tumor originates, jaundice may occur while the tumor is in an early stage. Even so, the five-year survival rate is only 4 percent. Very little is known about pancreatic cancer except that smoking increases the risk. Because the pancreas is related to digestion and absorption, speculation is that diet affects the development and course of this cancer, but no specifics are known at this time.

Leukemia and Lymphoma

Leukemia and lymphoma (Hodgkin's disease and non–Hodgkin's lymphoma) are two of the most frequent childhood cancers, but they strike more adults than children every year. **Leukemia** occurs in adults nearly 12 times more often than in children. The causes of leukemia are largely unidentified, although people with genetic abnormalities, such as Down's syndrome, experience it more frequently. Excessive exposure to certain chemicals, such as benzene, or infection with the retrovirus HTLV-I also place people at elevated risk. Symptoms resemble those of many other condi-

tions, so they are frequently overlooked initially. They include fatigue, paleness, weight loss, repeated infections, easy bruising, and nosebleeds or other hemorrhages. Children usually experience the onset of these symptoms abruptly, but adults with chronic leukemia will progress slowly and exhibit few symptoms.

Early, appropriate diagnosis is the key to long-term survival for leukemia. Depending on the type of leukemia and stage of diagnosis, five-year survival rates may be as high as 57 percent for adults and 80 percent for children.[1]

Lymphoma is a condition in which a tumor composed of lymphoid tissue occurs. The two most general categories of lymphoma are Hodgkin's disease and non–Hodgkin's lymphoma, which includes all types of lymphoma other than Hodgkin's. Hodgkin's disease rates have declined, especially in the elderly, but cases of non–Hodgkin's lymphoma have nearly doubled since the 1970s. The causes are unidentified but involve reduced immune function and exposure to infectious agents via organ transplants or viruses like HIV (human immunodeficiency virus) or Epstein-Barr. Herbicides and other chemicals may influence the development of the disease.

Symptoms include enlarged lymph nodes, itching, fever, night sweats, anemia, and weight loss. The fever may come and go over periods of weeks or months. Survival rates vary greatly, according to the type of disease and stage at diagnosis but can be as high as 51 to 81 percent after five years.[1]

Skin Cancer

The most frequently occurring types of cancer are skin cancers. Skin cancers fall into three main categories: basal cell carcinoma, squamous cell carcinoma, and melanoma. Of the three categories, melanoma is by far the most deadly.

Basal cell carcinoma

Basal cell carcinoma is the most common skin cancer and, along with squamous cell, is responsible for approximately 1 million cases of skin cancer a year. Basal cell carcinoma occurs in the outermost skin layers and tends to spread by widening rather than by growing deeper into the skin. The cancer develops into a central sore that crusts over and bleeds but does not go away.[24] Basal cell carcinoma grows slowly and rarely spreads to other parts of the body.

Squamous cell carcinoma

The second most common type of skin cancer is squamous cell. **Squamous cell carcinoma** grows faster than basal cell cancer but still grows fairly slowly and can metastasize to other parts of the body. Typically, a squamous cell skin lesion is a firm, red, painless nodule.[24] Both basal cell and squamous cell carcinomas are usually the result of overexposure to sunlight. They occur on a part of the body that has been exposed to the sun.

Malignant melanoma

Although it is the least common type of skin cancer, about 75 percent of all skin cancer deaths are due to **malignant melanoma.** All skin cancers, but especially malignant melanoma, have increased in number in recent years so that the current lifetime risk of developing malignant melanoma is about one in eighty-two. Although the use of sunscreens with an SPF of 15 or higher seems to reduce the number of basal and squamous cell skin cancers, it does not appear to decrease the risk for melanoma. Genetics is a strong factor in getting malignant melanoma, but it does not explain the explosive increase in the disease that has occurred in the last few decades. Melanoma often grows on parts of the body that are rarely exposed to the sun (such as the buttocks or feet) and does not increase in

incidence among people whose occupations require them to spend long hours in the sun (such as farmers).[25] Melanoma appears to be more highly associated with intermittent sun exposure and blistering sunburns occurring early in life (before age 15).

All adults are susceptible, but particularly those with the following risk factors:

- A family history of melanoma
- A personal history of one or more severe sunburns as a child
- Fair skin and many freckles, blonde or red hair, and light eyes
- Occupational exposure to industrial radiation or certain chemicals
- Consumption of medications that increase sensitivity to ultraviolet light

People with these factors should check their entire bodies regularly for any change in the size or color of a mole or other spot; any scaling, oozing, or bleeding from a bump or nodule; pigmentation spreading beyond its border; and a change in sensation, itchiness, tenderness, or pain. Any skin growth that bleeds or crusts should be seen by a physician.[26] See figure 13-3.

Knowing the ABCDs of skin cancer can help people identify melanoma during the early stages when it is still highly treatable (with a 95 percent five-year survival rate):

- Asymmetry: If you drew an imaginary line through the center of the mole or pigmented area, the two halves would be shaped differently.
- Border: Most normal moles are regularly shaped and their outside borders are regularly shaped. If a border appears to have scalloped edges or to be poorly defined in areas or uneven, it is not normal.

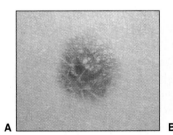 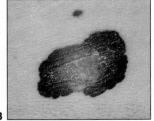

A   B

Figure 13-3 Comparison of Nonmalignant and Malignant Skin Growths

A: Normal mole. Note its symmetrical shape, regular borders, even color, and relatively small size (about a half centimeter). *B:* Malignant melanoma. Note its asymmetrical shape, irregular borders, uneven color, and relatively large size (about 2 centimeters).

- Color: A mole should be one color. Variation in color—differing shades of black or brown or tan or red or some combination or colors—or an intensely black color indicates a problem and need for further investigation.
- Diameter: A mole or pigmented area greater than 6 mm (the size of a pencil eraser) should be looked at by a specialist.

As with all cancers, the first line of defense is prevention. Because most skin cancers are directly related to overexposure to the sun's ultraviolet rays, take caution to limit this exposure. Although the use of sunscreen (with an SPF of 15 or higher) may not prevent malignant melanoma, it does decrease the incidence of basal and squamous cell skin cancers. Newer sunscreens block a wider range of ultraviolet rays and may prove to reduce even melanoma over time. Children particularly should always wear sunscreen when playing outside to prevent the blistering sunburn associated with melanoma later in life. The sun's rays are the strongest between 10 A.M. and 2 P.M. (even on cloudy days) and direct exposure at that time should be avoided, even with a sunscreen. Protective clothing such as hats, long-sleeve shirts, long pants, and ultraviolet-protecting sunglasses (too much sun can lead to cataracts or melanoma in the eyes) should be worn. Avoid tanning booths and sunlamps (see Real-World Wellness: Are Tanning Devices Hazardous to Your Health?). No matter how dark a person's skin is, he or she becomes darker when exposed to the sun. Although the risk is greatly reduced for darker-skinned people, anyone can get skin cancer.

Oral Cancer

Oral cancers are cancers of any part of the oral cavity, including the lip, tongue, mouth, and throat. Oral cancer occurs more than twice as often in males than in

Real-World Wellness

Are Tanning Devices Hazardous to Your Health?

I want to be tan this summer and thought I would get a head start by using a tanning bed. Is it safe for me to do so?

Sunlight produces two types of ultraviolet radiation: ultraviolet A (UVA) and ultraviolet B (UVB). UVB is 1000 times more likely to cause burns than is UVA. Because it penetrates the skin more deeply, UVA radiation causes the skin to tan or burn more slowly. A small amount of UVB radiation, however, can cause skin damage.

Most tanning devices (for example, sunlamps) give off either mostly UVA or UVB radiation. Newer UVA sunlamps give off as much as 10 times more UVA than is received from the sun or given by older UVB sunlamps. Although exposure to UVA sunlamps is less likely to cause burns of the skin and eyes, UVA radiation in high doses may increase the risks of skin cancer and premature skin aging. Studies also suggest that skin cancer is exacerbated when people combine tanning in the sun with tanning by sunlamps. Here are some facts concerning tans and tanning devices:

- *Skin cancer* risks increase each time the skin is exposed to UV radiation.
- *Burns* of the skin and eyes may occur.
- *Photosensitivity* means being extra sensitive to UV radiation as a result of using or consuming various substances that may cause allergic reactions, severe skin burns, itchy and scaly skin, and rash. Examples of photosensitizing products are soaps, shampoos, makeup, birth control pills, antibiotics, antihistamines, diuretics, and tranquilizers.
- *Cataracts,* an eye condition in which the lens becomes cloudy, may develop as a result of unprotected exposure to UVA and UVB radiation. For this reason, it is required that tanning devices have labels warning users to wear protective eyewear.
- *Premature skin aging,* in which the skin becomes dry, wrinkled, and leathery, is one of the most noticeable signs of repeated UV exposure.
- *Blood vessel damage and reduced immunity* may result from exposure to UV radiation.
- People who have red or blond hair and blue eyes, are fair-skinned, have freckles, and sunburn easily are at highest risk for skin damage. If you burn and do not tan in sunlight, you will probably burn and will not tan using sunlamps.
- A UVA tan offers some protection against further UV damage—about the same as an SPF of 2 or 3. Even with a dark tan, UV damage continues to accumulate.
- Sunscreens are not recommended for tanning indoors except to protect parts of your body you do not want to tan (for example, the lips). Sunscreens do not prevent UVA allergic-type reactions of people who are photosensitive.
- Always wear special goggles that block UV radiation, avoid using photosensitizing products, avoid tanning if your skin never tans, and follow the manufacturer's recommended time of exposure for your skin type.

females. This is because the risk factors of cigar and pipe smoking and the use of smokeless tobacco are practiced much more frequently by men than by women. Cigarette smoking and excessive consumption of alcohol (both on the rise among women) are also considered risk factors. Wiser lifestyle choices (choosing not to use tobacco products and reducing the consumption of alcohol) could practically eliminate oral cancers.

Cancers That Can Affect Women

Breast cancer

Some women are at increased risk for breast cancer. Breast cancer is often fatal (in approximately 25 percent of cases). On the brighter side, advances in breast cancer research have escalated in recent years (see Just the Facts: Drugs and Breast Cancer Treatment). Women's groups have done a good job of getting the word out about early detection and have supported efforts for improved treatment. These efforts have led to a decline in cancer deaths, although the surgeries and other treatments associated with breast cancer can still be devastating. Although breast cancer is relatively rare in men about 1600 men were diagnosed with it in 1998.

One in nine women who live to age 85 will develop breast cancer. Being over the age of 60 automatically places a woman in a high-risk category. Having an in-

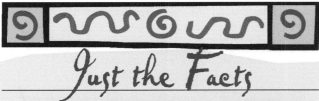

Just the Facts

Drugs and Breast Cancer Treatment

The drug tamoxifen has received a great deal of coverage in the press about its use as an anticancer drug. As with all drugs, tamoxifen has side effects. These particular side effects can be deadly, and usage of the drug should be carefully considered. Tamoxifen has also been used as a cancer preventive among women at high risk (which can include any woman over 60 years of age as well as younger women with several factors, including breast cancer in first-degree relatives). Other drugs that seem to reduce the rate of invasive breast cancer are raloxifene (a drug used to prevent bone loss); taxol, as a treatment in even late-stage cancer; and herceptin, which seems to delay progression of late-stage cancer.[29,30] Good news emerges almost daily about treatment for breast cancer. Early detection can result in a complete recovery.

herited mutation in the genes known as *BRCA1* and *BRCA2* accounts for about 10 percent of all cancers. This means 90 percent of cases are due to causes other than recognized inherited genetic factors. A woman with a mother or sister who has had breast cancer has double the risk of getting breast cancer herself. This risk is particularly high if the cancer occurred in the relative before menopause or involved both breasts or if it affected more than one first-degree relative (for example, a mother and sister or two sisters) or other close relatives in several generations.

Still, most cases of breast cancer cannot be explained because most women have at least one risk factor. Other risk factors include early menarche (before age 12), late menopause (after age 55), recent use of oral contraceptives or postmenopausal estrogens; never having had children or having given birth to a first child late in life.[1,27] Understanding the role of lifestyle factors remains somewhat nebulous at this point. Although breast cancer is worldwide, a strong cultural relationship exists between diet, especially high fat intake, and cancer. The reasons for this relationship have not been established.[1] Other factors that appear related to the incidence of breast cancer but that are unexplained at this time are alcohol intake (perhaps as few as three to five drinks a week), weight gain, particularly following menopause, and physical inactivity.[28]

Early detection is the best means of reducing mortality (see Just the Facts: Cancer-Related Checkup Guidelines). The five-year survival rate for localized cancers is 97 percent. Localized spread of the cancer lowers that survival rate to 76 percent, and distant metastasis yields only a 21 percent five-year survival rate.[1] Eighty percent of breast cancers are found by the affected women themselves through self-examination. Monthly self-examination remains the primary way to find small, localized cancers, especially in young women (see Just the Facts: Breast Self Examination). Mammograms are useful tools but are more useful for detection in older women whose breast tissue is less dense. Even the best mammogram misses 10 percent of all tumors, because breast tissue extends beyond the area X-rayed in a mammogram. Examinations by qualified physicians are helpful in detecting breast cancer, but most examinations occur only on an annual or biannual basis. The time lapse between such exams provides aggressive, fast-growing tumors with time to spread to surrounding tissue or lymph nodes.

Symptoms include a tumor that may feel like a piece of gravel or hard nodule. The tumor will not enlarge and shrink in size from month to month. Other symptoms include thickening, swelling, dimpling, scaling, pain, and tenderness of the nipple or discharge from the nipple. Breast cancer can occur at any age,

Just the Facts

Cancer-Related Checkup Guidelines

Listed here are checkup guidelines to help healthy people with early cancer detection. These are guidelines and not rules. They apply only if none of the following seven warning signs is present:

C hange in bowel or bladder habits

A sore that does not heal

U nusual bleeding or discharge

T hickening or lump in breast or elsewhere

I ndigestion or difficulty swallowing

O bvious change in wart or moles

N agging cough or hoarseness

Summary of American Cancer Society Recommendations for the Early Detection of Cancer in Asymptomatic People

Site	Recommendation
Cancer-related checkup	A cancer-related checkup is recommended every three years for people ages 20 to 40 and every year for people age 40 and older. This exam should include health counseling and, depending on a person's age, possibly examinations for cancers of the thyroid, oral cavity, skin, lymph nodes, testes, and ovaries as well as for some nonmalignment diseases.
Breast	Women 40 and older should have an annual mammogram and annual clinical breast exam (CBE) performed by a health care professional and should perform monthly breast self-examinations. The CBE should be conducted close to the scheduled mammogram. Women ages 20 to 39 should have a clinical breast exam performed by a health care professional every three years and should perform monthly breast self-examinations.
Colon and rectum	Men and women 50 or older should follow *one* of the following examination schedules: • A fecal occult blood test every year and a flexible sigmoidoscopy every five years • A colonoscopy every 10 years • A double-contrast barium enema every five to ten years • A digital rectal exam at the same time as the sigmoidoscopy, colonoscopy, or double-contrast barium enema (people at moderate or high risk for colorectal cancer should talk with a doctor about a different testing schedule)
Prostate	The ACS recommends that both the prostate-specific antigen (PSA) blood test and the digital rectal examination be offered annually, beginning at age 50, to men who have a life expectancy of at least ten years and to younger men who are at high risk. Men in high-risk groups, such as those with strong familial predispositions (i.e., two or more affected first-degree relatives) or African-Americans, may begin at a younger age (i.e., 45 years).
Uterus	**Cervix:** All women who are or have been sexually active or who are 18 and older should have an annual Pap test and pelvic examination. After three or more consecutive satisfactory examinations with normal findings, the Pap test may be performed less frequently. Discuss the matter with your physician. **Endometrium:** Women at high risk for cancer of the uterus should have a sample of endometrial tissue examined when menopause begins.

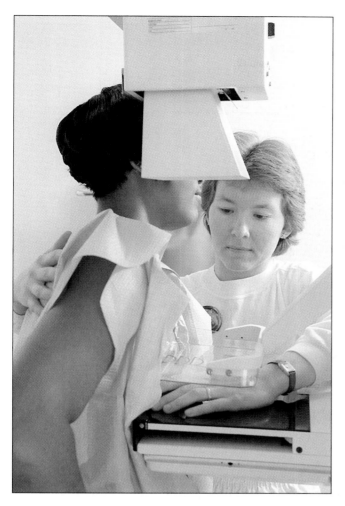

Mammography is important in the early detection of breast cancer.

even in very young women. Anyone (male or female) detecting these symptoms should consult a physician without delay.

Uterine cancer

Uterine cancers can occur either in the cervix (cervical cancer or cancer in the neck of the uterus) or in the endometrium (endometrial cancer or cancer of the lining of the uterus). Cervical cancer is closely linked to sexual behavior, especially through transmission of the human papillomavirus. Because of its close association with sexual activity (sex at an early age, multiple partners, a partner who has had multiple partners, multiple pregnancies, and a history of sexually transmitted diseases such as herpes and genital warts), many experts considered it a sexually transmitted disease. However, this is not the only reason people develop this cancer. As women have participated more fre-

quently in annual Pap smears and preventive reproductive health, the number of deaths from cervical cancer has declined significantly (70 percent decrease).[3] Smoking seems to increase the risk of the disease. Prevention involves following safer sex practices (see Chapter 12), not smoking, and having regular Pap smears.

Symptoms include abnormal vaginal bleeding or spotting or discharge. Late symptoms include pain. When diagnosed early, invasive cervical cancer is one of the most treatable cancers, with a five-year survival rate of 91 percent. Regular Pap smears after either age 18 or after sexual activity is initiated (no matter how young) can detect early, abnormal cells or localized cancers. Women should have regular Pap smears for the rest of their lives.

The lining of the uterus is the endometrium. Endometrial cancers occur in the upper, more broad portion of the uterus, as opposed to in the more narrow opening (the cervix). Endometrial cancer is more common among women over the age of 50, following menopause. Increasing evidence points to high levels of the hormone estrogen as contributing to the course of the disease. This is because estrogen causes the lining of the uterus to grow, which can lead to a premalignant condition that can lead to invasive cancer.

Risk factors include being overweight (extreme obesity), diabetes, high blood pressure, early menarche (before age 12), late menopause (after age 52), never giving birth, and receiving unopposed estrogen replacement therapy. The Pap smear detects endometrial cancer less than half the time. Those with risk factors should check with their gynecologists.[31]

Ovarian cancer

Ovarian cancer is difficult to diagnose, having few symptoms until reaching an advanced stage. Five to 10 percent of ovarian cancers are inherited, meaning that family history and mutations in the same genes that are related to breast cancer (*BRCA1* and *BRCA2*) serve as potential markers. Symptoms are frequently vague and may include cramping, discomfort, distention of the abdomen resulting from fluid buildup, diarrhea or constipation, gas, or a feeling of incomplete emptying of the bladder. Full-term pregnancies and breast feeding as well as the use of oral contraceptives seem to reduce the risk. A high-fat diet seems to increase the risk. Fertility drugs that stimulate ovulation may be associated with increased risk.

Although considered a relatively rare cancer, late diagnosis can be deadly. If found in stage I, the cure rate is about 90 percent. The average age of women whom ovarian cancer is diagnosed is 61.[1,32]

Just the Facts

Breast Self-Examination

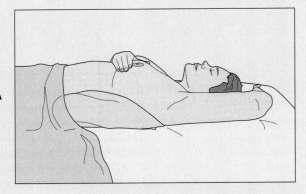

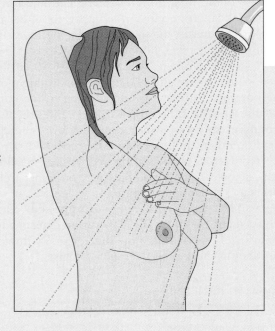

A

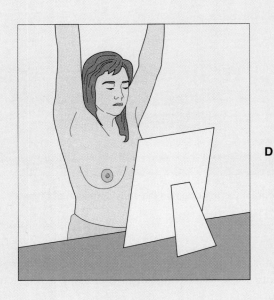

B

C

D

E

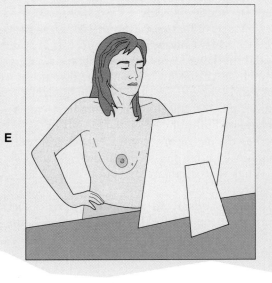

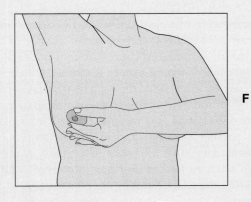

F

continued

Just the Facts

continued

Here are the proper techniques for examining the breasts.

1. Lying in bed, place a pillow under one shoulder to elevate and flatten the breast. Examine each breast using the opposite hand, first with your arm under your head and again with your arm at your side (**A**).
2. Make small circular motions with the flat pads (not the tips) of your fingers (**B**).
3. Examine your breasts in concentric circles from the rims inward toward the nipples. Feel for knots, lumps, thickenings, indentations, and swellings. Be sure to include the armpit (**B**).
4. Wet, soapy skin makes it easier to feel lumps. Keep one hand overhead and examine each breast with the opposite hand while you are in the shower(**C**).
5. In front of a large mirror, stand with your arms relaxed at your sides. Examine your breasts for swelling, dimpling, bulges, retractions, irritations, and sores or changes in mole or nipple color, texture, or orientation. Repeat with the arms extended and again with your arms clasped behind your head (**D**).
6. Repeat the inspection in step 5 while contracting your chest muscles: first clasp your hands in front of your forehead, squeezing your palms together, then place your palms flat on the sides of your hips, pressing downward. This highlights the bulges and indentations, which may signal the growth of tumors (**E**).
7. Bend forward from the hips, resting your hands on your knees or two chair backs. Use a mirror to examine your breasts for normal irregularities and abnormal variances; both are pronounced in this position.
8. Squeeze your nipples to inspect for secretions and discharge (**F**).
9. Report any suspicious findings to your doctor without delay.
10. Supplement your self-examination with a breast examination by your doctor as part of a regular physical examination and cancer checkup.

Just the Facts

Testicular Self-Examination

Cancer of the testes (the male reproductive glands) is one of the most common cancers in men 15 to 34 years of age. It accounts for 12 percent of cancer deaths in this group. The best hope for early detection of testicular cancer is a simple, 3-minute monthly self-examination. The best time is after a warm bath or shower when the scrotal skin is most relaxed.

Roll each testicle gently between the thumb and fingers of both hands. If you find any hard lumps or nodules, see your doctor promptly. The lumps or nodules may not be malignant, but only a doctor can make the diagnosis.

After a thorough physical examination, your doctor may perform X-ray studies for the most accurate diagnosis.

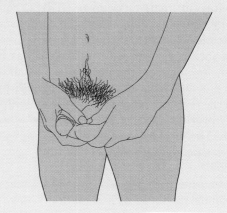

Cancers Than Can Affect Men

Testicular cancer

About 5000 men and boys, usually ages 15 to 34, are diagnosed with testicle cancer per year. These are usually treatable. Testicular cancer is painless and asymptomatic, but it is detectable by self-examination. Every boy old enough to be in high school and every man should do a monthly self-exam until reaching the age of 40 (see Just the Facts: Testicular Self-Examination). Signs of possible testicular cancer include any lump, enlargement, or hardening of either testis. Any changes should be followed up with an examination by a physician. Undetected, the disease can spread to the lymph nodes and beyond. Early detection results in a high cure rate.[33]

Men should be checked regularly for testicular cancer or prostate cancer, depending on their age and risk factors.

Prostate cancer

Most men who live long enough will have some evidence of prostate cancer. The second leading cause of cancer death among men, prostate cancer has a 100 percent cure rate when diagnosed while localized (58 percent of all prostate cancers). Improvement in diagnosis has resulted from a blood test for prostate-specific antigen (PSA test). The PSA test, in combination with a digital (manual) rectal exam (DRE), has made prostate cancer much easier to detect at earlier stages.

Men at elevated risk include African Americans (who have incidence and death rates twice as high as those of white men), increasing age (PSAs and DREs should be annual events in men over age 50; prostate cancer is very rare in young men), and men with family histories of prostate cancer. Dietary fat intake may also be a factor. African-American men and those with family histories should begin annual checkups before they reach age 50.

Symptoms for prostate cancer tend to be nonspecific and similar to those of a condition known as *benign prostate hypertrophy*. They include weak or interrupted urine flow; inability to urinate; difficulty starting or stopping urine flow; a frequent need to urinate, especially at night; pain or burning on urination; and continuing pain in the lower back, pelvis, or upper thighs.

Treatment

Cancer is treated in several ways. Traditionally, treatment has involved the use of surgery, radiation, chemotherapy, or some combination of the three

modalities. Today, these more traditional approaches are being combined with new, experimental approaches. At the same time, traditional methods are being continuously refined, and every year, more experimental methods are being used. For example, a mutated cold virus is being used to invade and render harmless certain types of oncogenes, and an altered type of white blood cell is being used to secrete a toxin to a certain protein that is secreted by malignant breast cells.[34,35]

Surgery

Cancers are often treated surgically. A surgeon removes the malignant tissue and some additional normal tissue. Current surgical techniques focus on removing less surrounding normal tissue than before and combining surgery with chemotherapy and/or radiotherapy. Surgery is used most often with breast, skin, gastrointestinal tract, female reproductive organ, prostate, and testicular cancers.

Chemotherapy

Chemotherapy is the use of drugs and hormones to treat cancers. Some of the most important advances in the treatment of cancer have been in the area of chemotherapy. These advances include new drugs and more effective combinations of new drugs and familiar chemotherapy. Most chemotherapeutic agents work by destroying the cancer cells' ability to carry out cell division and replication. Unfortunately, chemotherapy influences all cell division, even in healthy cells that need to divide in order to function normally. As a result, people having chemotherapy often have side effects, some of which can be dangerous. These side effects include suppression of the immune system, diarrhea, and hair loss.

Radiotherapy

Radiotherapy is the use of radiation to destroy cancer cells or their reproductive mechanisms so that they cannot replicate. As a result of radiation, side effects such as diarrhea, itching, and difficulty swallowing can occur. However, as the ability to more carefully plan the preciseness of focus, length of exposure, and time of treatment has improved, the damage to noncancerous cells and the potential side effects have decreased.

Immunotherapy

Immunotherapy is the use of a variety of substances to trigger a person's own immune response, which then attacks malignant cells or keeps them from becoming active. The substances being used in this therapy are manufactured through genetic engineering techniques.

Nurturing Your Spirituality

Living Well with Cancer

Chemotherapy and other drug treatments offer potentially life-saving solutions for cancer patients. But does the cure lie solely in the doctor's office? Perhaps not. Research indicates that spiritual practices may increase a cancer patient's chance of survival and enhance his or her quality of life.

Scientists have recently begun studying how the mind affects the neurological and immune systems. This new discipline, known as *psychoneuroimmunology,* is of great interest to cancer researchers. For example, participation in support groups has been shown to increase the life expectancy of people with cancer. The results of a study reported by Johns Hopkins University are striking: "Women with breast cancer who took part in a support group lived an average of eighteen months longer (a doubling of the survival time following diagnosis) than those who did not participate. In addition, all the long-term survivors belonged to the therapy group."[36]

Although support groups do not improve physical health, they seem to provide a camaraderie that contributes to overall wellness. Belonging to groups such as prayer circles also plays a beneficial role in recovery. Support groups offer patients a sense of connectedness that promotes wellness. Conversely, social isolation—lack of a support network of friends and family—seems to increase the likelihood of death.[37] Although the extent of its influence is unknown, the nurturing of cancer patients' spiritual side as well as care for their physical health seems to help in the effort to maintain wellness.

Among these technologies are interferon, interleukin-2 (proteins produced by the body to protect against viral invasions of healthy cells), tumor necrosis factor (TNF), and bone marrow growth regulators. Interferon is used for treatment of a rare blood cancer called *hairy cell leukemia.* Interleukin-2 is under study in the treatment of kidney cancer and melanoma. Vaccines against several types of cancer are also being developed.

Complementary Therapies

New technologies enhance the diagnosis and treatment of cancer. Magnetic resonance imaging (MRI) and computerized tomography (CT scanning) help to detect and map hidden tumors. Bone marrow transplantation is now a treatment option for select patients with leukemia and lymphoma.

Other approaches that have been used or are under investigation as alternatives to conventional treatment or as methods to use in conjunction with traditional therapies are acupressure, acupuncture, herbs, vitamins (for prevention and free radical removal), biofeedback (monitoring body functions to control bodily functions), homeopathy (use of extremely small doses of toxic substances), reflexology (massaging of certain areas of the feet), therapeutic touch (redirecting the "life forces" of the body), and visualization (envisioning a cure happening). Some of these alternative methods have been proven to help in the treatment process. Others are still being investigated (see Nurturing Your Spirituality: Living Well with Cancer). Some may become part of more traditional treatments.

Summary

- *Cancer* refers to a group of disorders characterized by uncontrolled disorderly cell growth.
- Cancer is the second leading cause of death, and one in four Americans will eventually develop one or more of the 100 different forms.
- There are two types of tumors or neoplasms. A malignant (cancerous) tumor can spread or metastasize (move from one location to another), while the second type of tumor, called *benign,* cannot.
- Cancer is caused by either external (chemicals, diet, radiation, viruses, pollutants), or internal (hormones, immune, inherited) factors.
- A carcinogen is anything that triggers the development of cancer.

- A gene that enables cancer to develop is called an *oncogene.*
- Exercise has been found to help prevent colon, breast, and prostate cancers.
- Lung cancer is the leading cause of cancer death in the United States and throughout the world.
- Lung cancer is almost 100 percent preventable if people never smoke.
- Passive smoke (smoke from other people's tobacco products) is dangerous to the nonsmoker by increasing risk of developing cancer.
- Colon and rectum cancer, when detected early, are very curable. Colon cancer is associated with family history, constipation, and high calorie consumption. Diet is believed to be the primary cause.

- Stomach cancer is relatively uncommon in the United States, although it is still ranked among the top ten cancer killers. It is best prevented by a healthy diet.
- Liver and pancreatic cancers are relatively uncommon. Both are difficult to treat. The five-year survival rate for pancreatic cancer is only 4 percent.
- Leukemia is cancer of the blood-forming mechanisms, involving the white blood cells. It strikes both children and adults.
- Lymphoma is cancer of the lymphoid tissue. The two types of lymphoma are Hodgkin's disease and non–Hodgkin's lymphoma. Non–Hodgkin's includes all lymphomas except Hodgkin's.
- The three types of skin cancer are basal cell, squamous cell, and melanoma. Basal and squamous cell cancers are most treatable. Melanoma, although most deadly, is very treatable if detected early. Exposure to the sun's ultraviolet light is most responsible for causing the three types of skin cancer.
- The ABCDs of skin cancer are helpful in identifying melanoma: A = Asymmetry; B = Borders uneven; C = Color (different shades of brown or black); D = Diameter greater than 5 mm.
- Oral cancer affects the lip, tongue, mouth, and throat. Risk factors are cigar and pipe smoking and the use of smokeless tobacco.
- Statistics show that one in nine women who live to age 85 will develop breast cancer.
- A woman with a mother or sister with breast cancer has double the risk for breast cancer. Early detection is the best means of reducing mortality.
- Breast self-examination and mammograms are useful tools for preventing breast cancer.

- Uterine cancers can occur either in the cervix or in the endometrium. Cervical cancer is closely associated with sexual behavior, especially through transmission of the human papillomavirus. Smoking seems to increase the risk.
- Risk factors for uterine cancers include obesity, diabetes, high blood pressure, early menarche, late menopause, never giving birth, and unopposed estrogen replacement therapy.
- Ovarian cancer is difficult to detect. Its symptoms are frequently vague and may include cramping, discomfort, distention of the abdomen, diarrhea or constipation, gas and the feeling of incomplete emptying of the bladder.
- Testicular cancer is painless and asymptomatic but is detectable by self-examination. Early detection results in a high cure rate.
- Prostate cancer is the second leading cause of cancer death among men. The PSA and a digital rectal exam have made prostate cancer much easier to detect at earlier stages. These should be done annually after age 50. Symptoms include weak urine flow, inability to urinate, frequent need to urinate, painful or burning urination, and continuing pain in the lower back or upper thighs.
- Cancer is treated through the use of surgery, chemotherapy, radiotherapy, and immunotherapy.
- Bone marrow transplantation is now a treatment option for select patients with leukemia and lymphoma.
- Several complementary therapies are under investigation as treatment alternatives to conventional approaches or to be used in conjunction with conventional approaches. These include acupressure, acupuncture, vitamins, biofeedback, homeopathy, reflexology, therapeutic touch, and visualization.

Review Questions

1. Describe the process by which cancer cells develop.
2. What characteristics differentiate cancer cells from other cells?
3. Discuss lifestyle factors that may contribute to the development of cancer.
4. What factors other than lifestyle factors contribute to the development of cancer?
5. Explain the concept of oncogenes.

6. What role does exercise play in the prevention of colon, breast, and prostate cancers? What mechanisms seem to be aiding in the prevention of these cancers?
7. Differentiate between the three types of skin cancer.
8. What are the leading sites of cancer in females? Males?
9. Describe the conventional methods of treating cancer.
10. What are some unconventional approaches to cancer treatment and adjunct therapies?

References

1. American Cancer Society. 1998. *Cancer Facts and Figures—1998*. Atlanta, Ga.: The American Cancer Society.
2. Fravenkneckt, M. 1995. Cancer prevalence and prevention: Demonstrating the role of personal responsibility. *Journal of Health Education* 26:240.
3. Margolis, S., and J. M. Samet. 1998. *The Johns Hopkins White Papers: Early Detection and Prevention of*

Cancer. Baltimore, Md.: The John Hopkins Medical Institutions.
4. Hellmich, N. October 1, 1997. Fighting cancer: Diet and exercise. *USA Today* D-1,2.
5. Blair, S., et al. 1989. Physical fitness and all-cause mortality: A prospective study of men and women. *Journal of American Medical Association* 262:2395.

6. Slattery, M., et al. 1997. Energy balance and colon cancer—beyond physical activity. *Cancer Research* 57:75.
7. Lee, I., and R. Paffenbarger. 1994. Physical activity and its relation to cancer risk: A prospective study of college alumni. *Medicine and Science in Sport and Exercise* 26:831.
8. Giovannucci, E., et al. 1995. Physical activity, obesity, and risk for colon

cancer and adenoma in men. *Annals of Internal Medicine* 122:327.

9. Nieman, D. 1999. *Exercise Testing and Prescription—a Health-Related Approach* (4th ed.). Mountain View, Calif.: Mayfield Publishing.

10. Bernstein, L., et al. 1994. Physical activity and the risk of breast cancer in young women. *Journal of the National Cancer Institute* 86:11403.

11. Thune, I., T. Brenn, E. Lund, and M. Gaard. 1997. Physical activity and the risk of breast cancer. *New England Journal of Medicine* 336:1269.

12. McTiernan, A. 1997. Exercise and breast cancer—time to get moving? *New England Journal of Medicine* 336:1311.

13. Lee, I., R. Paffenbarge, and C. Hsieh. 1992. Physical activity and risk of prostatic cancer among college alumni. *Journal of Epidemiology* 135:169.

14. Oliveria, S., H. Kohl, D. Trichopoulos, and S. Blair. 1996. The association between cardiorespiratory fitness and prostate cancer. *Medicine and Science in Sports and Exercise* 28:97.

15. Hackney, A. 1996. The male reproductive system and endurance exercise. *Medicine and Science in Sports and Exercise* 28:180.

16. World Cancer Research Fund/American Institute for Cancer Research. 1997. *Food, Nutrition and the Prevention of Cancer: A Global Perspective.* Washington, D.C.: American Institute for Cancer Research.

17. Consumer Reports on Health. 1998. Fruits and vegetables: Nature's best protection. *Consumer Reports* 10(6):1.

18. Potter, J. D. 1998. Diet and cancer: The big picture. *Nutrition Action Health Letter* 1. Vol 25:10.

19. University of California at Berkeley. 1998. Six tests for colon cancer. *University of California at Berkeley Wellness Letter* 15(2):2.

20. Editors. July 25, 1998. Risks for colon cancer. *Health News* 7.

21. Leibman, B. 1998. Vitamins and colon cancer, *Nutrition Action Health Letter* 25(10):8.

22. Mayo Clinic. 1995. Update—aspirin's effect on colon cancer boosts image as wonder drug. *Mayo Clinic Health Letter* 13(12):4.

23. Editors. November 10, 1998. Hidden cases of hepatitis C damaging livers in millions. *USA Today* A-1.

24. Anderson, K. N., and L. E. Anderson. 1990. *Mosby's Pocket Dictionary of Medicine, Nursing, and Allied Health* St. Louis: Mosby.

25. University of California at Berkeley. 1998. Casting a shadow on sunscreens. *University of California at Berkeley Wellness Letter* 14(9):2.

26. Editors. 1997. Health news: Evaluating melanoma risk. *The New England Journal of Medicine* 3(8):1–2.

27. Harvard University. 1997. Advances in breast cancer research. *Harvard Women's Health Watch* 5(11):2–3.

28. University of California at Berkeley. 1997. The best advice about breast cancer and exercise. *University of California at Berkeley Wellness Letter* 13(11):1.

29. Harvard University. 1998. Tamoxifen and beyond. *Harvard Women's Health Watch* 5(10):1.

30. Harvard University. 1998. Advances in breast cancer research. *Harvard Women's Health Watch* 5(11):1.

31. Mayo Clinic. 1985. When found and treated early, this form of uterus cancer usually can be cured. *Mayo Clinic Health Letter* 3(11):1.

32. Harvard University. 1998. Ovarian cancer. *Harvard Women's Health Watch* 6(2):4-5.

33. Mayo Clinic. 1985. This painless self-exam can help reveal testis cancer early, when treatment is most effective. *Mayo Clinic Health Letter* 3(11):8.

34. Pennsi, E. 1996. Will a twist of viral fate lead to a new cancer treatment? *Science* 274:342.

35. Chen, S. Y., et al. 1997. Potent antitumour activity of a new class of tumour-specific killer cells. *Nature* 385:78.

36. John Hopkins University. 1999. *Overview of NIH Office of Alternative Medicine Fields of Practice: Mind/Body Control.* Available on-line at **www.intelihealth.com.**

37. Mayo Health Clinic. 1999. *Mind Over Malignancy? Altitude and Cancer Survival.* Available on-line at **www.mayo health.org/mayo9703/htm/ mindover.htm.**

Suggested Readings

Anderson, G. 1990. *The Cancer Conqueror: An Incredible Journey to Wellness.* Kansas City, Mo.: Andrews & McMeel.

This book, which describes how a positive attitude affects cancer and may even help contribute to its cure, provides an encouraging message for people with cancer and their families.

Anderson, G. 1993. *50 Essential Things to Do When the Doctor Says It's Cancer.* Bergenfield, N.J.: Plume.

A cancer survivor offers readers fifty proactive steps to take when faced with a diagnosis of cancer.

Sinclair, G. 1997. *All Things Work for Good: A Book of Encouragement for People with Cancer, Their Family and Friends.* Sharon, Mass.: The Positive Press.

A survivor writes about the many spiritual, mental, and physical questions a diagnosis of cancer can elicit. The author writes candidly, humorously, and with clarity about his personal struggle.

Name _____ Date _____ Section _____

Assessment Activity 13-1

Cancer Early Detection Inventory

This inventory was developed to help in the early detection and treatment of cancer. It presents common symptoms for various cancer sites. If you have symptoms, check with your physician. The chances are that you will not have cancer, but any symptoms suggest a potential problem with your health—it is wise to be safe and consult your physician.
Directions: For each cancer site, check any of the symptoms you experience.

Bladder
1. Blood in urine? _____
2. Unusual change in bladder habits? _____
3. Discomfort during urination? _____
4. Change in flow during urination? _____
5. Urge to urinate more frequently? _____

Bone
1. Pain in the bone or joint? _____
2. Swelling in the bone or joint? _____
3. Unusual warmth in the bone or joint? _____
4. Protruding veins along the bone or joint? _____

Breast
1. Thickening or lump in the breast? _____
2. Lump under the arm? _____
3. Thickening or reddening of the skin of the breast? _____
4. Puckering or dimpling of the skin of the breast? _____
5. Nipple discharge? _____
6. Inverted nipple, if nipple was previously erect? _____
7. Persistent pain and tenderness of the breast? _____
8. Unusual changes in the nipple and surrounding skin? _____
9. Benign breast lumps? _____

Colon and Rectum
1. Continuous constipation or diarrhea? _____
2. Rectal bleeding? _____
3. Change in bowel habits? _____
4. Increase in intestinal gas? _____
5. Abdominal discomfort? _____

Lung
1. Unusual cough? _____
2. Shortness of breath? _____
3. Sputum streaked with blood? _____
4. Chest pain? _____
5. Recurring attacks of pneumonia or bronchitis? _____

Lymphatic System
1. Painless enlargement of a lymph node or cluster of lymph nodes? _____
2. Profuse sweating and fever? _____
3. Weight loss? _____
4. Unexplained weakness? _____
5. Unusual itching? _____

Oral
1. Sore in the mouth that does not heal? _____
2. Lump or thickening that bleeds easily? _____
3. Difficulty in chewing or swallowing food? _____
4. Sensation of something in the throat? _____
5. Restricted movement of the tongue or jaw? _____
6. Poor oral hygiene? _____

Prostate
1. Weak or interrupted flow of urine? _____
2. Inability to urinate or difficulty in starting urination? _____
3. Need to urinate frequently, especially at night? _____

4. Blood in urine? _____

5. Urine flow that is not easily stopped? _____

6. Painful or burning urination? _____

7. Continuing pain in lower back, pelvis, or upper thighs? _____

Skin

1. Obvious change in wart or mole? _____

2. Unusual skin condition? _____

3. Chronic swelling, redness, or warmth of the skin? _____

4. Unexplained itching? _____

5. Overexposure to the ultraviolet rays of the sun? _____

Testes

1. Enlargement and change in the consistency of the testes? _____

2. Dull ache in the lower abdomen and groin? _____

3. Sensation of dragging and heaviness? _____

4. Difficulty with ejaculation? _____

Thyroid

1. Lump or mass in the neck? _____

2. Persistent hoarseness? _____

3. Difficulty in swallowing? _____

4. Overexposure to head and neck X-ray treatments? _____

Uterus and Cervix

1. Irregular bleeding? _____

2. Unusual vaginal discharge? _____

3. Positive Pap smear, class 2 to 5, some signs of abnormality? _____

4. Recurring herpes simplex virus? _____

5. Fibroid tumors of the uterus? _____

Application Carefully evaluate any statement you have checked. If the symptom appears severe (such as blood in the stool), see a physician immediately. However, nonsevere symptoms (such as pain in a joint) may be observed for a short period to see if there is improvement. Never wait longer than two weeks to see a physician if the symptom persists.

1. How many symptoms have you checked? _____

2. How serious do these symptoms seem? _____

_____

3. Should you see a physician now or wait? _____

_____

Name _____ **Date** _____ **Section** _____

Assessment Activity 13-2

Are You Practicing Cancer Prevention?

Listed here are several common cancers and the significant risk factors for each. As you look at each risk factor, determine whether you should increase or decrease that factor. If the factor does not apply to you or your lifestyle, leave the I/D column blank.

Cancer	Smoking		Fruits and Vegetable Consumption		Exercise		High Fat Percentage		Smokeless Tobacco Use		Meat Consumption		Obesity		High Alcohol Consumption	
	RF*	I/D	RF	I/D	RF	I/D	RF	I/D	RF	I/D	RF	I/D	RF	I/D	RF	I/D
Lung	+		+													
Colon and rectum			+		✓		✓				?		?			
Breast			?		✓		?						✓		✓	
Prostate			?								?		✓			
Stomach	✓		✓													
Kidney	+												✓			
Esophagus	+		✓						+						✓	
Oral	+		✓						+						✓	
Larynx	+		✓						+						✓	

RF = Risk factor

I/D = Increase or decrease?

+ = Solid body of evidence suggests a link between this lifestyle factor and cancer.

✓ = Many studies suggest a plausible link between this lifestyle factor and cancer.

? = Some research suggests a connection; the jury is still out.

Follow-up Questions

1. Are you following a more positive lifestyle for the prevention of cancer?
2. How many lifestyle factors do you need to increase? decrease?
3. What would you say are your main strengths in the effort to prevent cancer?
4. What are your greatest risk factors for cancer?

Managing Common Conditions

Key Terms

allergens
arthritis
asthma
Crohn's disease
diabetes mellitus
extrinsic asthma
headaches
inflammatory bowel
  disease (IBD)

influenza
intrinsic asthma
osteoarthritis
osteoporosis
rheumatoid arthritis
ulcerative colitis

Goals for Behavior Change

- Identify your personal risk factors for the conditions discussed in this chapter.
- Select strategies for prevention of these conditions.
- Initiate a prevention plan for any of the conditions identified as a potential personal risk.

Objectives

After completing this chapter, you will be able to do the following:

- Differentiate between type I and type II diabetes mellitus.
- Identify the common forms of arthritis.
- Describe the effects of calcium hormone therapy and exercise on osteoporosis.

- Discuss preventive measures and treatments that help reduce the severity and length of asthma attacks.
- Differentiate between the common cold and influenza.
- Distinguish between the different types of headache.
- Identify environmental factors that may trigger headaches.

his chapter focuses on conditions that are detrimentally affected by lifestyle. If precautions are taken against the onset of these diseases, their impact on the body may be lessened or even avoided. Although every condition affected by lifestyle cannot be described, those that frequently occur and those on which lifestyle has the greatest impact are discussed, including diabetes, the common cold, headaches, influenza, arthritis, asthma, and osteoporosis.

Diabetes Mellitus

Diabetes mellitus is actually a group of diseases resulting from one of the following situations: The body does not make insulin, the body doesn't make enough insulin, or the body doesn't use insulin properly.[1] Diabetes is a metabolic disorder involving the pancreas. People with diabetes experience an abnormality in the way their bodies use glucose (blood sugar); this results from the deficient production of insulin by the pancreas or from resistance of the body's tissues to the action of insulin.[2] The blood may contain ample glucose (blood sugar), but without enough insulin available for use, the glucose cannot move from the bloodstream into the cells, where it is needed for fuel. As a result, people with diabetes cannot use the energy they consume, and high glucose levels build up in the blood and urine, leading to a condition known as *hyperglycemia* (high blood sugar). Large amounts of sugar in urine require additional water so that the sugar can be diluted for elimination. The increased need by the body for water leads to a depletion of the body's water stores, causing excessive thirst and frequent urination. When the body becomes unable to completely break down glucose as a source of energy, fat must be used. Fat is metabolized differently than glucose, and its breakdown is incomplete when glucose is not available. Incomplete metabolism causes an excess amount of chemicals called *ketone bodies* to build up in the body. The buildup of ketones is used to perform the functions that glucose would perform under normal conditions (supplying energy), but the excess amounts of ketone bodies disrupt the body's chemical balance, altering the blood's chemistry and making it more acidic. Acidic conditions in the body are extremely hazardous.

Diabetes can be a serious disorder. Symptoms include excessive thirst, increased urination, hunger, a tendency to tire easily, wounds that heal slowly, blurred vision, and frequent skin, vaginal, and urinary tract infections. Dehydration and buildup of ketones can cause ketoacidosis (the accumulation of ketones) and nausea, vomiting, abdominal pain, lethargy, and drowsiness. Ketoacidosis often leads to severe sickness,

coma, and even death. Of equal significance is that prolonged periods of elevated glucose levels disrupt normal enzyme and membrane functions. Chronic complications that may result are eye disease, kidney disorders, painful nerve and muscle symptoms, and decreased circulation. Diabetes is a leading cause of foot and leg amputations. Diabetes can also produce impotence in men and increased risk of heart disease and heart attacks in both genders. Of the 16 million people with diabetes in the United States, nearly one-half are unaware they have it (see Assessment Activity 14-1). By the time people realize they have this condition, they may have already suffered severe consequences.[1]

Type I Diabetes

Diabetes consists of two diagnostic categories. *Type I diabetes* occurs most commonly in children and young adults, although it may develop at any age. Type I is an autoimmune disease in which the body produces antibodies that attack and damage its own cells, in this case the insulin-producing cells of the pancreas.[2] Symptoms may be quite sudden and sometimes progress rapidly, requiring quick intervention to prevent death. People with type I diabetes produce little or no insulin and require insulin injections to function. Before insulin was discovered, the average life span for a person with type I diabetes was two years after diagnosis. Properly treated, these people now live almost as long as the general population.

Type II Diabetes

Type II diabetes is the most common type and is found primarily in people over the age of 40. Scientists believe that it is strongly linked to genetic factors. If an identical twin develops type II diabetes, the other most likely will as well. People with type II either develop a resistance to insulin activity or experience insufficient insulin action. Their bodies are usually capable of producing adequate amounts of insulin—something a person with type I diabetes cannot do. The difficulty in type II diabetes is that body cells become resistant to insulin at the receptor sites (the place where insulin attaches to the cell). Type II is linked strongly to obesity. Almost 80 percent of all diabetics with type II are overweight at the time of diagnosis.[2] Often the only treatment necessary for type II is weight loss, although some people still require medication or injections of insulin to help control the condition.

Causes

Type I diabetes is an autoimmune disease. This means the body's own immune system attacks a part of the body that is well. In type I diabetes, the body produces antibodies that attack and damage the area of the pancreas that produces insulin. Initially, the ability to produce insulin is impaired, but eventually, usually in less than a year, little or no insulin is produced. The onset is usually before age 35 and often in childhood. Type I diabetes is sometimes associated with a viral infection within the insulin-producing cells, resulting in the inability to produce insulin.[1]

Heredity plays a role in type II diabetes. In a study of 218 people with type II diabetes, 66 percent reported at least one relative with diabetes, and 46 percent reported at least two relatives with diabetes. Patients whose mothers had diabetes were twice as likely to develop the disease than were those whose fathers had diabetes.[1]

Obesity also is an important factor (see Just the Facts: Preventing and Controlling the Effects of Diabetes). Not all people who are obese develop diabetes, but 90 percent of people with (diabetes) are overweight. Tumors of certain endocrine organs such as the pituitary gland, adrenal glands, and pancreas can all interfere with or destroy insulin production. Taking corticosteroids, which are used to treat asthma or arthritis, may result in latent diabetes.[1]

Treatment

Although there is no cure for diabetes, the disease can be controlled by diet, exercise, and/or insulin. People with type I have to have insulin injections, usually several a day, and they must manipulate dosage levels according to dietary and activity levels (see Just the Facts: American Diabetes Association Guidelines for Diabetes Screening). Self-administered blood glucose tests help them monitor blood sugar levels and determine the appropriate insulin dose. Good blood sugar control reduces the risk of the complications associated with type I diabetes.

People with type II diabetes can often control the disease through weight loss, exercise, and adequate nutrition. Losing weight helps to lower insulin resistance, enabling the body to make more efficient use of the insulin available. New nutrition guidelines developed by the American Diabetes Association (ADA) dispel the notion of a diabetic diet that is good for everyone with the disease. For example, the previous emphasis on sugar consumption has given way to an emphasis on

---

Just the Facts

Preventing and Controlling the Effects of Diabetes

Several lifestyle behaviors can significantly reduce the likelihood of developing type II diabetes:

- Maintaining normal weight
- Exercising regularly
- Not smoking
- Maintaining blood pressure levels or treating high blood pressure
- Maintaining normal blood lipid levels
- Eating a low-fat, high-fiber diet

Just the Facts

American Diabetes Association Guidelines for Diabetes Screening

Here are the cutoff points for diagnosis. They are based on fasting glucose levels:

- Blood glucose levels of 126 mg/dl or higher, in at least two tests done on separate days, indicate diabetes.
- Blood glucose levels between 110 mg/dl and 125 mg/dl indicate impaired fasting glucose.
- Normal blood glucose levels should be less than 110 mg/dl.

The ADA offers the following guidelines for testing frequency:

- People 45 years and older should be tested every three years if their results fall within the normal range.
- More frequent testing, beginning at a younger age, should be considered for people with the following factors:

  Obesity
  First-degree relative with diabetes
  Membership in a high-risk ethnic group, including African Americans, Hispanics, and Native Americans
  Having delivered a baby weighing more than 9 pounds or having developed diabetes when pregnant (gestational diabetes)
  Hypertension
  Low level of HDL cholesterol (35 mg/dl or lower) or triglyceride level more than 250 mg/dl
  Impaired glucose tolerance detected by a previous test

- Testing should be done immediately if the classic symptoms of diabetes are observed: abnormal thirst, frequent urination, and unexplained weight loss.

To successfully manage their condition, people with type I diabetes must periodically test their blood glucose level.

Wellness Across the Generations

Are Illness and Chronic Disease Inevitable as We Age?

As the population of the United States continues to age, chronic conditions are becoming increasingly common. The largest group of maturing adults, known as *baby boomers,* were born after World War II between 1946 and 1964. Are they doomed to develop age-related conditions? Will you or someone close to you inevitably have to face a chronic condition or disease associated with aging?

The answer for all age groups is a resounding "NO." We may have genetic predispositions of which we should be aware; however, we can embrace the concepts of wellness, including maintaining an active lifestyle, eating properly, not smoking, and controlling stress. By doing so, we may be able to delay the onset of many chronic conditions, diminish their severity, or prevent the factors that cause them. The earlier we begin to practice positive behaviors, the greater the likelihood of healthy outcomes.

All people can make health-related choices that enhance their well-being and that of their families and communities. It is imperative that we accept responsibility for improving our own lives. Regardless of age, we are empowered through our attitudes and actions to create a high quality of life. Wellness is a journey, not a destination, filled with opportunities for joy, happiness, learning, and making the most of each day.

carbohydrate consumption.[3] The total amount of carbohydrate, regardless of its source, is what affects blood sugar levels.[4] Another example is that diabetics are now encouraged to consume monounsaturated fats. Type II studies at four different medical centers showed better control of blood glucose levels when 45 percent of the calories came from fat, with highly monounsaturated olive oil as the predominant fat, and 40 percent from carbohydrate than when 55 percent came from carbohydrate and 30 percent came from fat.[5]

Evidence that links exercise to a decreased incidence of type II diabetes is increasing. A recent study of 5990 men showed that incidence rates declined as energy expenditure increased. For each 500-calorie increment in physical activity, the risk of type II diabetes decreased by 6 percent. Men who increased their energy expenditure by 2000 calories decreased their risk by 24 percent.[4,6] In a study of more than 21,000 male physicians, men who exercised just once a week had

23 percent less chance of developing type II diabetes than did men who did not exercise.

Exercise lowers blood sugar levels by reducing the body's resistance to insulin. Cells become more sensitive to insulin and more capable of absorbing glucose. The net effect is lower levels of circulating blood sugar. This benefit of exercise, however, lasts for only twenty-four hours, which means exercise must be done every day. Regular activity doesn't seem to have the same dramatic effect on type I diabetes, but it does lower the amount of insulin needed and the risk of cardiovascular disease.[1]

Many of the complications associated with diabetes are preventable or treatable, but diagnosis and proper treatment are necessary (see Wellness Across the

Just the Facts

Major Complications of Diabetes

Several serious complications can result from diabetes. Most of the following complications are caused by blood vessel damage:

- *Coronary heart disease (CHD):* People with diabetes have two to four times more risk of dying from CHD than do people without diabetes.

- *Nerve damage:* Between 60 and 70 percent of people with diabetes have some form of nerve damage.

- *Foot problems:* Because of peripheral nerve damage, foot problems can go unnoticed. Proper treatment for conditions such as athlete's foot, blisters, and calluses is extremely important. Any sign of infection should be treated immediately to avert the need for amputation.

- *Kidney damage:* 30 to 40 percent of people with type I diabetes and 20 percent of those with type II diabetes eventually develop kidney disease, which can lead to kidney failure.

- *Peripheral vascular disease (PVD):* Diabetes and smoking can double or triple the risk of PVD (atherosclerosis) in the arteries of the legs, which increases the risk of foot and leg problems, including the possibility of amputation.

- *Skin problems:* People with diabetes are at increased risk for skin infections.

- *Stroke:* People with diabetes have a two to four times greater risk of stroke.

- *Vision loss:* Diabetic retinopathy (retina disease) is the leading cause of blindness. People with diabetes are also at increased risk for glaucoma and cataracts.

Generations: Are Illness and Chronic Disease Inevitable as We Age?). Neglect of diabetes and its complications may result in early death (see Just the Facts: Major Complications of Diabetes).

Arthritis

Arthritis is an inflammatory disease of the joints. The more than 100 varieties of arthritis include gout, ankylosing spondylitis, systemic lupus erythematosis, osteoarthritis, and rheumatoid arthritis. Osteoarthritis and rheumatoid arthritis are found most often. Both result in pain and deformed joints.

Osteoarthritis, also known as *degenerative joint disease,* is the most common form of arthritis, affecting more than 20 million Americans. By age 40, about 90 percent of all people have X-ray evidence of osteoarthritis in the weight-bearing joints, such as the hips and knees, although actual symptoms generally do not appear until later in life.[7] Men typically develop symptoms before age 45, whereas women usually have them after age 55. Men more often have osteoarthritis in the hips, knees, and spine, and women are more likely to have it in the hands and knees.[7] It is the most limiting chronic condition affecting women in the United States.[7]

Osteoarthritis is characterized by the gradual breakdown of cartilage, which comes with age. The first signs are microscopic pits and fissures on the cartilage surface that cause the cartilage to crack and lose its resilience.[8] Tiny pieces of cartilage may break off into the joint cavity. The result is a change in the contours of the articular surfaces. Finally, patches of exposed bone appear, causing mechanical-type friction and irritation. The bone responds by trying to repair itself, but the repair is disorderly. As a result, joint surfaces thicken and bone spurs (osteophytes) form.

The deterioration associated with osteoarthritis seems related to the wear and tear of daily living, age, and injury. Other factors may include heredity, diet, abnormal use of joints (for example, throwing a curve ball every day year after year), excessive weight, stress, and impaired blood supply to affected joints.

Treatment for osteoarthritis includes aspirin and cortisone drugs to relieve pain. Mild exercise, heat, cold, or a combination of heat and cold application accompanied by massage can be used. Exercise is used for therapeutic purposes to help maintain range of motion and to strengthen the muscles that can help alleviate joint problems. Exercise is usually prescribed by a physical therapist. Occasionally, surgery is performed to replace joints or repair tendons and ligaments.

Should a person with osteoarthritis exercise to avoid deconditioning, or will the exercise cause further damage to the arthritic joints? The answer seems to be "yes" and "no" to both questions, depending on the person. An eight-week walking study[9] involving patients with osteoarthritis of the knee (one of the most common arthritic problems) provides a reason for optimism regarding exercise. Patients who walked thirty minutes three times a week reported a 27 percent decrease in pain and an improved ability to walk longer distances compared with a nonwalking control group. The researchers concluded that supervised walking can be helpful for people with significant arthritis of the knee. Stretching exercises also help to relieve arthritis pain by lengthening tendons, which reduces muscle spasms, the source of much of the pain in osteoarthritis.

However, the results of other studies have shown that exercise may not contribute to relief of pain. In addition, exercise of an arthritic joint may cause pain that can be relieved only by rest.

Rheumatoid arthritis is one of the most crippling forms of arthritis. It affects about 1 percent of the adult population worldwide. More than 2.5 million Americans have this condition, and more than 60 percent of those affected are women.[10] Onset of rheumatoid arthritis is usually between the ages of 20 and 45. Although the exact causes are unknown, this form of arthritis may be an autoimmune disease. The most obvious damage occurs in joints, but the disease affects the whole body. Symptoms of rheumatoid arthritis include joint swelling, redness, stiffness, pain, muscle atrophy, joint deformity, and limited mobility. The condition is unpredictable because it can suddenly flare up and just as suddenly go into remission. Emotional stress is often associated with an attack. The disease frequently results in disability.

Treatment includes a mixture of rest periods, gentle exercise, physical therapy, and medication. Emphasis is on relieving pain, reducing inflammation, maintaining function of the joints, and preventing deformities (see Nurturing your Spirituality: Living Well with a Chronic Condition).

Osteoporosis

Osteoporosis is a chronic disease in which the mineral content of the bones progressively decreases so that the bones become brittle and are easily broken. It is linked to more than 1 million fractures of the hip, spine, and other bones each year. Vertebral bones in the spine shrink and fracture, causing a deformed spine. Bones in the wrist are also common fracture sites. Some 25 million Americans, 80 percent of whom are postmenopausal women,[11] are affected by osteoporosis. Although postmenopausal white and Asian women are at highest risk, men and women of all ages and ethnicities can be affected.[12]

Though bones may seem hard, they are made of living cells that require calcium and vitamin D (necessary for optimum absorption of calcium) to grow and stay

Nurturing Your Spirituality

Living Well with a Chronic Condition

Many people have potentially debilitating or even life-threatening conditions, such as asthma, diabetes, and high blood pressure. Proper management of these conditions makes it possible for these people to live long lives. A person with a chronic condition may even have a quality of life as high as that of someone who does not have a chronic condition. If you have a chronic disease, you can learn to manage it effectively.

First, of course, you need to know as much as you can about your condition. Knowledge is power. The more you know, the better you will be able to understand the condition and its treatment. More important, great strides are being made every day in the treatment of many diseases, and a cure may be possible in your lifetime. A trusted physician who takes the time to listen to you and to explain your options can be very helpful. You should explore your alternatives and participate in making decisions. Taking an active role helps physically, because no one knows your body like you do, and it empowers you to avoid feeling like a victim.

Second, having a support system, such as your family or a group of people who have the same condition you do, can foster your emotional well-being in many ways. Having someone to whom you can express your frustrations or fears and from whom you can receive unconditional support provides security. Knowing others who share your feelings can make you feel less alone. Often, those who have the same condition as you can offer solutions you hadn't considered. You can also find ways to laugh together about those moments of utter distress when you feel different from everyone else. The bonds people create when they share their problems can be lifelong, making the difficult times easier to bear.

Life lessons can be learned in many situations. Everyone has his or her share of problems. Sometimes having a chronic condition may seem unfair, but we are all less lucky than some and better off than others. All people struggle to find ways to be grateful for life every day and to jump life's hurdles. Take care of yourself, make friends, find inner peace, and share with others. Then your life will be full no matter what challenges life hands you.

strong. Almost all of the body's calcium stores are located in bone.[12] During growth and development, bones typically receive more calcium than they give up. By age 25, when bone density peaks, calcium absorption levels off; at age 30, the bone-building process is over. This is when bone-mass maintenance and calcium are especially important.[13] If blood levels of calcium drop, the body withdraws what it needs from its bones. With adequate dietary intake of calcium, bones are spared the effects of calcium depletion that may accelerate osteoporosis.

Calcium is not the only factor associated with bone loss. Estrogen depletion during menopause triggers bone loss of up to 1 percent a year. By the time a woman is 80, she may have lost 30 to 40 percent of her bone mass. When bone-mass loss becomes excessive, a fall may not be needed to fracture bones. Simply bending over and lifting 25 pounds—a heavy bag of groceries—could cause injury. During menopause, hormone-replacement therapy in the form of estrogen supplementation is recommended for many women as protection against osteoporosis.[11]

Because nicotine is thought to decrease blood levels of estrogen, smoking also contributes to bone loss. Smokers go through menopause on average at least two years earlier than nonsmokers.[12] Genetics may also play a role in osteoporosis. Researchers have identified an osteoporosis gene that determines how well vitamin D facilitates the absorption of calcium. People who have the gene are more resistant to absorbing available calcium. Caffeine and alcohol have also been implicated in bone loss. A recent study found that women who drank two or more cups of caffeinated coffee a day and drank no milk experienced significant loss of bone density after menopause. The effects of caffeine can be negated with consumption of milk. In the same study, coffee drinkers who drank at least one glass of milk per day had 6.5 percent higher bone density than the coffee-only group.[12]

The National Osteoporosis Foundation recommends several simple steps to reduce the risk of contracting this disease. First, consume adequate amounts of calcium, preferably from food. If this doesn't work, calcium supplements are recommended. The Foundation suggests 1500 mg, which is almost double the amount given in the RDA.[14] Second, consume enough vitamin D (400 IU) to permit absorption of the calcium. Third, consider hormone-replacement therapy (estrogen) and discuss its use with your medical doctor, especially if you have a family history of osteoporosis. And fourth, participate in weight-bearing activities, such as walking, running, and weight training, to prevent bone loss. In one study, women who participated in a year-long exercise program and received daily doses of estrogen experienced a 7 percent increase in bone density and fared better than women on estrogen alone.[11] Physical exercise forces bones to adapt to the stresses imposed on them, and they hypertrophy in response. Bones atrophy when they are unstressed.

People with osteoporosis can and should exercise, but the type of physical activity and the intensity of exercise must be carefully selected. Forceful contractions of muscles and high-impact activities should be avoided because they may stress the bones beyond their breaking point. Swimming, water aerobics, stationary cycling, walking, and light weight training are good starting activities for those with osteoporosis.

Asthma

Asthma is a chronic respiratory condition characterized by attacks of wheezing and difficulty in breathing. The cause of asthma attacks is partial obstruction of bronchi and bronchioles resulting from the contraction or spasm of the muscles in the bronchial walls. Attacks may be mild or severe and may last anywhere from a few minutes to a few days. Asthma may develop at any age, although many children with asthma outgrow the condition as they get older and the bronchial passages widen. Asthma may be hereditary.

The two major types of asthma are extrinsic and intrinsic. **Extrinsic asthma** is the most common type and is typically triggered by a hypersensitivity to irritants or **allergens,** such as dust, pollen, feathers, animal dander, molds, smoke, extremely cold or dry air, and air pollutants. (Allergens are substances that cause allergic reactions, such as asthma, in some people.) For some asthmatics, drugs, food allergies, and exercise may induce an attack.

Intrinsic asthma is caused by factors such as stress or frequent respiratory tract infections. This form of asthma is less common than extrinsic asthma, but its symptoms are similar.

There is no cure for asthma, but there are preventive measures and treatments that help reduce the severity and length of an attack. One form of prevention is immunotherapy in which the asthmatic is desensitized through injections of weakened allergens. Medications, such as corticosteroid drugs, reduce inflammation and serve as a primary intervention for many asthmatics.

Bronchodilator drugs (medicines that open the bronchioles) are used routinely by asthmatics when an asthma attack occurs. These drugs are breathed in through an inhaler and usually restore normal breathing in several minutes.

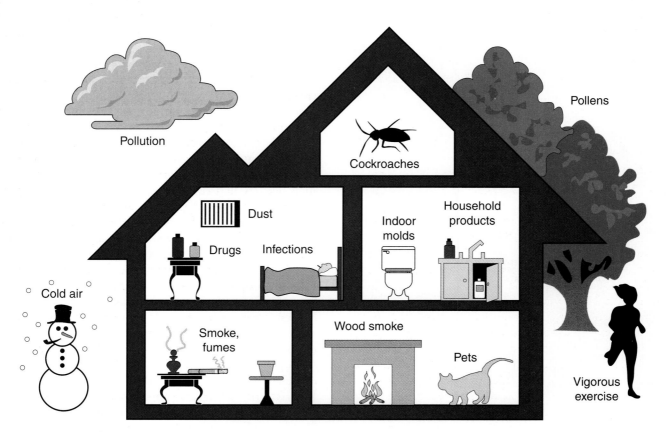

Pollution

Pollens

Cockroaches

Dust

Drugs   Infections

Indoor molds

Household products

Cold air

Smoke, fumes

Wood smoke

Pets

Vigorous exercise

Figure 14-1   Common Asthma Triggers

If you have asthma, do you know which triggers are troublesome for you?

One way to anticipate an impending attack or to determine the severity of an actual attack is to use a peak-flow meter, a small hand-held device (available at drugstores) that measures airflow. Peak airflow will go down hours and sometimes even a day or two before an attack, so the meter can serve as an early warning system. During an attack, it provides an objective way to determine how much the air passages in the lungs narrow.

Exercise-induced asthma is common among asthmatics. Symptoms include a coughing attack and tightness in the chest during or shortly after exercise. It appears to be most common when the asthmatic exercises in cold, dry air. Still, physical activity remains an integral part of wellness for people with exercise-induced asthma. Improvements in fitness and health status occur in asthmatics who exercise. An added benefit is that for many asthmatics exercise is accompanied by a decrease in the frequency and severity of exercise-induced attacks (figure 14-1). See Assessment Activity 14-2, Managing Your Asthma.

The Common Cold

More than 200 viruses, known as *rhinoviruses,* can cause the common cold.[15] A person may develop a temporary immunity to one or two viruses and still be infected by another. Any time people are together, viruses that cause the common cold are present. Adults average two to three colds each year, and children experience six to ten. Colds can be spread by shaking hands, sneezing, and breathing. Evidence indicates that hand-to-hand contact is the most common way a cold is spread. When infected people blow or touch their noses, the virus is transferred to their hands. When an uninfected person touches the infected person's hands, the virus is again transferred. Touching the face with hands that carry the virus leads directly to developing a cold. Frequent hand washing may prevent the spread of the virus.

The signs and symptoms of a cold are easily recognized. They include a feeling of listlessness, general aches and pains, watery eyes, and runny nasal passages. As the cold progresses, the nasal membranes swell, resulting in a stuffy nose. Infections affecting the throat can lead to sore throats and coughing. These symptoms tend to last seven to ten days. As an old axiom points out, if a cold is treated, it will go away in seven days and if left alone, it will last a week. A cold may occasionally persist for several weeks, but complications are infrequent in adults and older children. When they do occur, they most often are middle ear or sinus infections.

Antibiotics do not cure the common cold because they fight only bacterial infections. Over-the-counter decongestants—in spray or pill form—constrict blood

Washing your hands often is the best way to prevent the common cold.

vessels to shrink nasal swelling and open air passages, providing temporary relief of cold symptoms. Nasal sprays are more effective because they deliver a greater concentration of medicine to the nasal passages and give immediate relief.[16] But their overuse can cause a rebound effect, making congestion even worse. Nasal sprays should not be used for more three consecutive days. Antihistamines are not very effective for cold symptoms and may lead to drowsiness. Cough suppressants, which may offer relief from nagging coughing episodes, should be used with caution. On the positive side, the cough reflex is nature's way of clearing the lungs; on the negative side, persistent coughing may irritate the airway. A pharmacist or medical doctor should be consulted for help matching the appropriate cough medicine with the type of cough (dry or loose mucus).

The best advice for treating a cold is to take aspirin, ibuprofen, or acetaminophen (young children shouldn't take aspirin with cold symptoms because it may cause Reye's syndrome); drink plenty of fluids; eat a nutritious diet; and get plenty of rest.

Influenza

Influenza, or flu, is also caused by a virus. There are three primary strains of the influenza virus: A, B, and C. Most influenza develops from the A and B strains. These strains can change genetically, reappearing in an altered form every few years. Symptoms of all types of flu include chills, fever, weakness, headache, sore throat, dry cough, nausea, vomiting, and muscular aches and pains. All symptoms may not be present, and the severity varies greatly among people. Treatment for flu is the same as for the common cold. Aspirin should not be taken by children or teenagers because the potentially fatal Reye's syndrome can develop.

Vaccines can prevent particular types of influenza. Current recommendations are that priority in vaccination should be given to children and adults with chronic cardiovascular and lung disorders, residents of nursing homes, medical personnel who may transmit the virus to high-risk patients, everyone over 65, and anyone with conditions such as diabetes, kidney disease, hereditary anemias, and impaired natural immunity.

Headaches

One of the conditions that causes great discomfort is the headache. Some **headaches** may be the result of injury or brain disease, but most are caused by distress, tension, anxiety, and environmental factors. Tension headaches are the most common. Caused by involuntary contractions of the scalp, head, and neck muscles, tension headaches may be precipitated by anxiety, stress, and allergic reactions. Tension headaches can often be relieved by massaging the scalp and muscles in the neck. Aspirin or other pain relievers usually alleviate tension headaches.

Migraine headaches are characterized by throbbing pain that can last for hours or even days. Nausea and vomiting occasionally occur. Migraines, which seem to be initiated by stress, range from mild to severe. Migraines are now considered a neurological disease with a hereditary link.[17] An abnormal drop in serotonin (a brain chemical that regulates blood vessel changes and controls pain) causes blood vessels near the surface of the brain to dilate, prompting nerve sensations that are perceived as pain. People who experience migraines may have advance warning symptoms, such as dizziness, sensitivity to flashing lights, the appearance of a blind spot, and an indescribable feeling that a headache is coming.

Migraine sufferers have been able to get relief with the drug sumatriptan (Imitrex) since it was approved by the FDA in 1993. Recently, an easier-to-use nasal spray version of this drug became available. The nasal spray provides relief much more quickly than the pill, within fifteen minutes to two hours.[18] The drug is thought to work by mimicking the neurotransmitter serotonin.

Cluster headaches usually cause a knifelike pain behind the eye that quickly spreads to the forehead. The pain can spread to the neck, to the back of the head, and even into the teeth. The nose often runs, and the involved eye tears. The pain is often described as one of the worst pains a person can endure.

Cluster headaches get their name because they occur in clusters, at least one each day and sometimes several times a day. The attacks begin suddenly and may last from several minutes to several hours. In extreme cases they may last a few weeks or several months. Affected people may be symptom free for weeks or months. The cause of cluster headaches is unknown, but these headaches also appear to be related to arterial constriction and dilation.

A wide range of environmental factors may trigger headache pain. Exposure to smoke (including secondhand smoke), carbon monoxide (automobile exhaust, defective furnaces), alcohol, caffeine, and certain foods cause headaches in many people. Alcohol causes blood vessels to dilate, adding blood flow to irritated nerve endings. Caffeine in small amounts may help relieve headache pain by constricting blood vessels; in larger quantities (more than 2 cups), blood vessels dilate, which may lead to rebound headaches. Heavy coffee drinkers may experience withdrawal headaches if they try to cut out caffeine cold turkey. A progressive reduction in caffeine over the course of a week or two should provide an appropriate acclimatization. Food triggers are most likely to be those containing amines. Amines cause blood vessels to constrict and dilate. Common dietary sources are aged cheeses, red wine, citrus fruits, and chocolates. Food additives, such as nitrates in hot dogs, smoked foods, and cold cuts, and flavor enhancers, such as monosodium glutamate (MSG), are often accused of provoking headaches.[20]

Many illnesses can cause a headache. Sinusitis, teeth and gum problems, high blood pressure, hypothyroidism, acute anemia, Cushing's disease, and Addison's disease are common offenders.[20] A complete physical exam can help identify specific medical causes. A headache should be evaluated by a physician if it is chronic, associated with a fever, accompanied by numbness or paralysis, associated with a stiff neck, interfering with thinking or memory, and/or continuing to get worse.

Treatment of headache pain includes a full gamut of interventions. Techniques such as deep breathing, progressive relaxation, biofeedback, meditation, and visualization seem to help relieve the pain in some sufferers. New drugs that block headache pain without negatively affecting other parts of the body are in the final stages of testing and could become available in the near future (see Real-World Wellness: Dealing with Headaches).

Inflammatory Bowel Disease

Inflammatory bowel disease (IBD) is a term that represents a variety of diseases that cause inflammation in the intestines. The two main types of IBD are Crohn's disease, which causes inflammation in the digestive tract, and ulcerative colitis, which creates severe ulcers in the inner lining of the colon and rectum. Both condi-

Real-World Wellness

Dealing with Headaches

I've heard about many remedies for headaches. What are the best ways to deal with the various types of headaches?

Here are some methods[19] for managing headaches:

• Migraines	Sumatriptan: an injectable, oral, or nasal application constrict the arteries of head. Can be used alone or in combination with the drugs ergotamine, tartrate, cafergot, or belladonna
• Tension	Over-the-counter analgesics; if chronic, antidepressants
• Cluster headaches	For acute attacks, sumatriptan or inhaled oxygen; preventive drugs such as methysergide, steroids, or lithium
• Sinus	Decongestants; antibiotics if needed

tions can result in frequent and intense diarrhea, abdominal pain, gas, fever, and rectal bleeding.[21]

Crohn's disease affects men and women equally and seems to predominate in some families. About 20 percent of people with Crohn's disease have a blood relative with some form of IBD.[21] The cause of the disease is not fully understood, but in addition to a genetic predisposition, an autoimmune response may be responsible.[22] Currently, researchers speculate that a viral or bacterial agent interacting with the body's immune system may be at fault. No evidence supports the theory that Crohn's disease is caused by tension, anxiety, or other psychological factors.[21] The success of treatment depends on the location, the severity, the complications, and the response to previous treatments. The goal of any treatment is to control inflammation, correct nutritional deficiencies, and relieve symptoms. Treatment may include drugs, nutritional supplements, surgery, or some combination of these options. Treatment can help control the condition, but no cure exists.

Ulcerative colitis is a chronic inflammation of the colon lining. It is different from Crohn's disease in that the inflammation affects only the colon.[23] The condition develops in fewer than one person in every 10,000 people. It typically appears in people between the ages of 15 and 35. The cause is unknown, but it is most common among Caucasians and seems to be familial. Controlling stress and avoiding any foods that cause discomfort may help relieve symptoms. To prevent flare-ups, anti-inflammatory drugs may be used. Researchers are testing nicotine patches after finding that they improve colitis symptoms.[23] Between 20 and 30 percent of people with ulcerative colitis need surgery. These are patients in whom complications have become severe and medication has not worked.

Summary

- Diabetes mellitus is a group of diseases with one of the following symptoms: The body does not make insulin, it doesn't make enough insulin, or it doesn't use insulin properly.
- The two major categories of diabetes are type I and type II.
- Type I diabetes usually occurs early in life and requires insulin injections because the pancreas loses its ability to produce insulin.
- Type II diabetes occurs most often in people over 40 years of age who do not exercise and are obese.
- Arthritis is an inflammatory disease of the joints. The most common form of arthritis is osteoarthritis, which is characterized by deterioration of the cartilage covering the surfaces of the bones in certain joints.
- It is believed that rheumatoid arthritis is a disease of the immune system that results in joint swelling, pain, deformity, and decreased mobility.
- Asthma may be caused by extrinsic factors, such as pollen or dust, or intrinsic factors, such as stress.
- The common cold is caused by rhinoviruses, of which there are more than 200 varieties. Antibiotics do not cure colds.
- Influenza is caused by only three strains of virus, but these agents have the ability to change and reappear in different forms. Because influenza can range widely in severity, certain high-risk groups are encouraged to have an annual flu vaccine.
- Osteoporosis is a chronic disease characterized by a loss of mineral content of the bones, which makes them brittle and vulnerable to breakage.
- Mild to moderate exercises are effective in promoting bone strength in the elderly.
- Headaches are divided into three categories—tension, cluster, and migraine. People who experience migraines can use techniques such as deep breathing and meditation to alleviate pain or prevent the onset of a headache.
- Inflammatory bowel disease (IBD) is a group of diseases involving the gastrointestinal system.
- Crohn's disease is a type of IBD that results from erosion of the inner and middle layers of the intestinal tract wall.
- Ulcerative colitis is a type of IBD characterized by inflammation of the colon.
- Both conditions can trigger frequent and intense diarrhea, abdominal pain, gas, fever, and rectal bleeding.

Review Questions

1. Explain the difference between type I and type II diabetes.
2. Describe the main symptoms of diabetes.
3. What are the most serious potential complications of uncontrolled diabetes?
4. What steps can be taken to prevent the development of type II diabetes?
5. Explain the differences between the two most common forms of arthritis, their causes, and possible treatments.
6. Discuss the relationship between calcium, estrogen, exercise, and osteoporosis.
7. What are some measures and treatments that help reduce the severity and length of an asthma attack or prevent it altogether?
8. What behaviors may help prevent and treat the common cold?
9. Explain how the influenza viruses differ from the common cold viruses.
10. Explain the differences between tension headaches and migraine headaches. How do the causes, symptoms, and treatments differ?
11. What environmental factors can trigger headache pain?
12. What role does physical activity play in the various conditions discussed in this chapter?

References

1. Mayo Clinic. 1998. Diabetes—weight control and exercise may keep you off the road to high blood sugar. *Mayo Clinic Health Letter* 16(2).
2. Margolis, S., and C. D. Saudek. 1998. *The Johns Hopkins White Papers: Diabetes Mellitus—1998.* Baltimore, Md.: The Johns Hopkins Medical Institution.
3. Dinsmoor, R. S. 1994. Lifting the sugar embargo. *Harvard Health Letter* 19(12):7.
4. Editors. 1997. Dealing with diabetes: Diet and exercise hold key to control. *Environmental Nutrition—the Newsletter of Food, Nutrition and Health* 20(12).
5. Editors. 1994. Diabetic diet shifts emphasis from carbs toward "mono" fats. *Environmental Nutrition—The Newsletter of Food, Nutrition and Health* 17(10).
6. Helmrich, S. P., D. R. Ragland, and R. S. Paffenbarger. 1994. Prevention of noninsulin-dependent diabetes mellitus with physical activity. *Medicine and Science in Sports and Exercise* 26:824.
7. Margolis, S., and J. A. Flynn. 1998. *The Johns Hopkins White Papers:* *Arthritis.* Baltimore, Md.: The Johns Hopkins Medical Institution.
8. Harvard Medical School Publications Group. 1995. *Arthritis: A Harvard Letter Special Report.* Boston: Harvard Medical School.
9. Lamb, L. 1992. Exercise helps osteoarthritis. *Health Letter* 39(11):4.
10. Mayo Clinic. 1997. Rheumatoid arthritis. *Mayo Clinic Health Letter* 15(6):1.
11. Farrow, C. 1996. Estrogen, exercise aid bone density, study claims. *Commercial Appeal* 157(2):C4.
12. Alberts, N. 1995. Osteoporosis. *American Health* 14(9):70.
13. Willensky, D. 1995. Bone: How it works. *American Health* 14(9):87.
14. Liebman, B. 1994. Calcium: After the craze. *Nutrition Action Health Letter* 21(5):1.
15. Winker, M., and A. Flanagin. 1996. Infectious diseases—a global approach to a global problem. *Journal of American Medical Associates* 275(3):245.
16. Consumers Union. 1996. Finding the right cold medicine. *Consumer Reports* 61:62.
17. Editors. 1998. Managing migraines and other headaches: Diet's controversial role. *Environmental Nutrition— the Newsletter of Food, Nutrition, and Health* 21(6):1.
18. Editors. 1997. Healthnews—straight talk on the medical headlines: New options for migraines. *The New England Journal of Medicine Health News.* 3(13):1.
19. Harvard University. 1998. Migraine— more than a headache. *Harvard Health Letter* 23(3):4.
20. Halpern, G. M. 1994. Headache can be a pain in the neck. *Healthline* 13(7):9.
21. National Digestive Diseases Information Clearinghouse. 1999. *Crohn's Disease.* Available on-line at **www.niddk.nih.gov/health/digest/ pubs/crohns/crohns.htl.**
22. Doughty, D. B., and D. Jackson. 1993. *Gastrointestinal Disorders.* St. Louis: Mosby.
23. Mayo Clinic. 1995. Ulcerative colitis. *Mayo Clinic Health Letter* 13(12):1.

Suggested Readings

American Diabetes Association. 1997. *American Diabetes Association Complete Guide to Diabetes: The Ultimate Home Diabetes Reference.* ADA. Alexandria, VA.

This book is a comprehensive resource of information about diabetes self-care, covering nutrition, blood sugar, exercise, and potential complications.

Kandel J., and D. B. Sudderth. 1998. The Anti-arthritis Diet: Increase Mobility and Reduce Pain with This 28-Day Life-Changing Program. Rocklin, Calif.: Prima Publishing.

Robbins, L. D., and S. S. Lang. 1995. *Headache Help:* A Complete Guide to Understanding Headaches and the Medicines That Relieve Them. St. Charles, Ill.: Houghton Mifflin.

The authors seek to narrow the doctor-patient communication gap by equip-ping headache sufferers with essential information to help stop pain. The book provides a guide to prescription and nonprescription headache drugs.

Brody, J. 1995. *Jane Brody's Cold and Flu Fighter*. Scranton, Penn.: W. W. Norton.

This is an informative guide to preventing and treating colds and flu. The book dispels many age-old myths and contains a special section on treating children's colds and flu.

Name _____ **Date** _____ **Section** _____

Assessment Activity 14-1

Are You at Risk for Diabetes?

Directions: Check the appropriate column in response to the following questions to assess your probability of having diabetes. The more questions that you answer with a "yes," the higher the probability you have of becoming diabetic.

Taken alone, any "yes" answer does not necessarily indicate you are diabetic. However, if you have answered "yes" more than five times, consult your physician for a urine test.

	Yes	**No**
1. Is there a history of diabetes in your family?	_____	_____
2. Do you tire quickly or seem always to be fatigued?	_____	_____
3. Do you urinate frequently?	_____	_____
4. Are you constantly thirsty?	_____	_____
5. Is your vision blurry?	_____	_____
6. Have you suddenly lost weight?	_____	_____
7. Are you overweight?	_____	_____
8. Do you eat excessively?	_____	_____
9. Do wounds heal slowly?	_____	_____
10. Is your skin frequently itchy?	_____	_____

Name _____ **Date** _____ **Section** _____

Assessment Activity 14-2

Managing Your Asthma

Directions: If you have asthma, there are many things you can do to help manage your condition effectively. To assess your personal health management, place a check mark next to each statement that applies to you.

Reducing or Avoiding Asthma Triggers

_____ I have identified my asthma triggers.

_____ I do not smoke and I avoid environmental tobacco smoke.

_____ I use and properly maintain an air filter and an air conditioner to keep my home cleaner and more comfortable.

_____ I avoid vacuuming or I use a dust mask when vacuuming.

_____ I avoid mowing the lawn or I use a dust mask when mowing.

_____ I avoid woodstoves and fireplaces.

_____ I use dust-proof encasings on my pillows, mattress, and box spring.

_____ I use a dehumidifier as necessary in my home to reduce indoor mold.

_____ I use window shades or curtains made of plastic or other washable material for easy cleaning.

_____ My closets contain only needed clothing. Anything I do not currently wear is stored in plastic garment bags.

_____ I do not sleep or lie down on upholstered furniture.

_____ If I have a pet, it does not sleep in or go into my bedroom.

_____ I avoid perfume and cologne, cleaning chemicals, paint, and talcum powder as much as possible.

Preventing and Managing Asthma Attacks

_____ I have learned everything I can about asthma.

_____ I take my medications as prescribed by my physician.

_____ I carry my inhaler with me at all times.

_____ I have a crisis plan for managing a severe asthma attack.

_____ I keep emergency numbers by the phone and with me at all times.

_____ I know how quickly my asthma medications should work.

_____ I use a peak-flow meter to anticipate and respond quickly to asthma attacks.

Interpretation

17 or more items checked: You are doing a great job avoiding asthma triggers and preventing and managing asthma attacks.

14–16 items checked: In many ways you are doing a good job of managing your asthma. However, you may be unnecessarily exposing yourself to common asthma triggers, or your plan for preventing and managing attacks may need some work.

13 or fewer items checked: You need to manage your asthma much more effectively. Remember that an asthma attack can be fatal.

Discuss this assessment with other members of your family or your roommates. Ask them to help you with your asthma prevention and management program.

15

Becoming a Responsible Health Care Consumer

Key Terms

alternative medicine
contraindications
defensive medicine
diagnostic laboratory tests
double-blind study
epidemiologic studies
false negative
false positive
health fatalism
health insurance
health maintenance
  organization (HMO)
immunizations
implied consent
informed consent
periodic examinations

placebo
point of service (POS)
preferred provider
  organization (PPO)
primary-care physician
reliability
risk factor
scientifically controlled
  studies
selective health
  examinations
self-care
statistical relationship
statistical significance
validity

Goals for Behavior Change

- Apply criteria for determining whether health information is valid, reliable, and based on scientifically controlled studies.
- Identify specific strategies for enhancing communication with your physician.
- Determine the diagnostic tests and immunizations that are appropriate for your age, gender, and health status.
- Find a specific on-line newsgroup or patient support group that might be helpful to you.

Objectives

After completing this chapter, you will be able to do the following:

- Explain how to evaluate the accuracy, validity, and reliability of health information.

- Discuss criteria for determining when, where, and how to choose health care.
- Describe the functions and purposes of the major components of a physical examination.

raditionally, Americans have had a rather passive attitude toward health care. Whether taking medicine, purchasing health care products, undergoing surgery, or having a diagnostic test administered, people have operated as if following orders. Fortunately, this attitude is changing. People are viewing themselves as active participants in their health care. They are asking questions, placing demands on *health care providers* (people and/or facilities that provide health care services), getting second opinions, and sometimes even refusing treatments. People now realize that they must assume more responsibility for safeguarding their health. With this responsibility, however, comes the challenge of knowing what one can and should do for oneself. The purpose of this chapter is to lay the groundwork to enable you to become an informed, active participant in the health care marketplace.

Understanding Health Information

The first and perhaps most difficult challenge for consumers is to make sense of the health-information explosion. Many popular magazines regularly print health articles, newspapers often devote entire sections to medicine, the publications of health newsletters abound, television programs feature numerous health stories, and a plethora of scientific health-related studies are published daily. There are more than 5000 reports and articles written every day in 3500 medical journals worldwide, and this does not include the larger number of nontechnical articles.[1] Interest in health information appears to have reached an all-time high.

The availability of so much health information has drawbacks; the major drawback is that so much of the information is confusing, sometimes even contradictory. Even medical experts have trouble separating fact from fiction. It is not unusual for a new finding to be headlined one day and completely refuted the next. It has been speculated that as much as 50 percent of the medical advice we follow today will be considered obsolete or at least will undergo major modification during the next five years.[2] For some people the ubiquity of refutations and contradictions leads to an attitude sometimes referred to as **health fatalism,** the attitude that nothing can be believed. People with a fatalistic view disregard health information because they believe that future findings will inevitably contradict facts accepted as true.

An example involving the consumption of hot dogs illustrates the point. Researchers found that children who ate more than a dozen hot dogs a month had nine times the normal risk of childhood leukemia.[3] This was the featured headline in a nationwide television news show broadcast during prime time. Public reaction bordered on the hysterical. Scared parents overreacted, failing to demand and consider all the facts. They believed the story was completely true simply because it was reported in the news. It should be of little surprise, therefore, that countless numbers of people felt deceived and misled. The resulting fatalistic attitude toward health care and medical advice was understandable. In the big picture of leukemia research, this was just one very preliminary study that had some serious shortcomings. For instance, the results were based on crude dietary histories. Also, researchers could not determine whether it was the hot dogs or something else that hot dog eaters do or eat that might increase the risk of leukemia. If there is a cause-and-effect relationship between hot dogs and leukemia, it will take larger, more sophisticated studies to prove it.

The point of this example is that an appropriate approach to health information is to adopt a skeptical and suspicious attitude, especially toward extreme and sensational health claims. The First Amendment to the U.S. Constitution, which guarantees freedom of the press, also guarantees Americans the right to publish health-related hogwash. The more you read, generally the more conflicts and contradictions you will uncover. This should not make you feel uncomfortable but, to the contrary, make you realize that medicine is still as much art as science.

Guidelines for Evaluating Health Information

Adhering to the guidelines that follow should help your search for correct health information.

Avoid Jumping to Conclusions

Most health misinformation is actually based on facts, not lies. The problem is that facts get exaggerated and sometimes lead people to wrong conclusions.

A good example involves tea, the second most widely consumed beverage in the world (water is first). Researchers are interested in tea because an increase in tea consumption has been associated with a decrease in cancer and heart disease. Supposedly something in tea interferes with the ability of cancer-causing substances to bind to DNA, which is where cancer cell initiation takes place. Also, tea contains antioxidants. The Japanese, who smoke nearly twice as many cigarettes as Americans but far surpass Americans in tea consumption, have only about one-half as much lung cancer.[4] The question is this: Does tea consumption actually cause a change in cell physiology that prevents cancer?

So far, cause and effect have not been demonstrated. The 100 studies that show an association between tea consumption and lower cancer rates use observational techniques, which have inherent limitations. Unknown factors can influence findings of observation. For example, people might not be able to remember or report accurately their tea consumption over decades. Even if they are able, their high tea consumption still doesn't prove that tea is what affected their risk of cancer. Because epidemiologic studies don't establish cause and effect, researchers turn to experimental studies with animals or humans to build stronger cases.

Another example involves potato chips, which have long been considered a junk food. Actually, the quick cooking process of potato chips preserves nutrients better than mashing, boiling, or baking potatoes. Ounce per ounce, potato chips provide more nutrients than do other forms of potatoes. This information alone might convince people to begin consuming large quantities of potato chips. However, because potato chips are cooked in oil, they are high in fat and calories and are not recommended for people trying to lose weight. This extra bit of information gives a completely different angle to the perspective on potato chips. By being aware that the truth of most health issues is not simple, the tendency to oversimplify and overgeneralize health information can be thwarted.

Remember That Health Discoveries Take Time

Health discoveries often make their way into media headlines, but a cardinal rule of science is that findings must be replicable. Health information based on a dramatic discovery is not usually considered valid unless it is confirmed in several follow-up studies or experiments.

Beware of Headline Reading

Newspaper, magazine, and television headlines are intended to arouse your curiosity primarily for one purpose: to make you buy or watch. A headline might cleverly capture the essence of a story or it might present a partial truth that leads to wrong conclusions. A common media strategy is to sensationalize a story by crafting a headline that contradicts conventional wisdom. Consider some recent examples: "New Study Weighs In: More Fat, Fewer Strokes." "'Dirty Drug' Nicotine Has Positives, Research Shows." "Low Sodium Diets Increase Blood Pressure." "A Drink a Day Can Help You Live Longer." These headlines are fraught with possible deceptions. They may represent the results of isolated studies that run against mainstream medical thought. They may serve as punchlines for stories that are based on studies with many shortcomings. Or they may actually represent new trends in

thinking supported by a medical consensus. The only way to know for sure is to become a well-informed, discriminating consumer of information the way you are a consumer of products, goods, and services. The challenge is to avoid the tendency toward headline reading and to apply the criteria for determining if health information is both valid and reliable.

Apply the Criteria for Determining Validity and Reliability of Health Information

Health information that can be trusted is based on studies that are valid, reliable, and reported in a way that includes research and statistics in their proper context. When assessing validity and reliability it is important to know the type of study that serves as the basis for new information. Knowing the meanings of the following terms will help to put new information in a proper context.

Validity

In health research, **validity** means *truthfulness*. If a study is designed and conducted properly, its findings are likely to be valid. For example, it was found that adding vitamin E to human cells in the laboratory stimulated cell division and growth. This was used to support the erroneous conclusion that vitamin E would delay the aging process. This was not a proper generalization because a simple laboratory experiment is not a valid procedure for demonstrating something as complex as aging.

Reliability

Reliability is another key criterion for evaluating health information. It refers to the extent that health claims can be consistently verified. If a claim is reliable, it can be demonstrated to occur consistently in study after study. The test of time is perhaps the ultimate criterion for evaluating the trustworthiness of new information.

Statistical significance

Researchers and reporters alike often use the phrase **statistical significance** to give meaning and credibility to findings. For example, in a study a group of college students who ate breakfast every morning before going to class did better in school than a comparison group who skipped breakfast. The differences were reported to be "statistically significant." Does this mean that the differences between the two groups were large, maybe equivalent to a full letter grade? Does this mean that breakfast is the key to academic success? Statistical significance does not necessarily imply largeness, but it does imply probability. *Statistical significance* means that the probability that a study's findings are due to chance alone is less than 5 percent. That is, 95 of 100 times similarly designed studies would yield similar results. If the differences between two groups are not statistically significant, they may be due to chance findings and might not show up again if a study were repeated. Because so many studies are performed, some studies that yield statistically significant results eventually prove to be wrong. Consequently, it takes hundreds of studies, many of them conflicting, to create a consensus on a particular health issue. Any health claim worth considering should be based on numerous studies or experiments conducted over many years.

Statistical relationship

Statistical relationship refers to the extent that two or more variables or events are associated with each other. Much health literature is based on research involving statistical relationships or associations. For example, it is well known that a statistical relationship exists between the consumption of salt and high blood pressure for some people. In other words, an increase in salt intake is accompanied by an increase in blood pressure. Conversely, a drop in salt intake is associated with a decrease in blood pressure. This is helpful information, but does it mean that high salt intake actually causes high blood pressure? No. If this were true, then all Americans who eat too much salt would have high blood pressure. The mistake many people make is to conclude that one event in a statistical relationship causes the other. Relationships are important and helpful clues to health and they provide a basis for better understanding health risks. However, they cannot and do not establish cause and effect.

Risk factor

The term **risk factor** refers to health habits and/or practices that increase the risk of getting certain diseases. The emphasis in Chapter 2, for example, is on those risk factors related to heart disease. In the popular press, risk factors are often presented out of context. For example, consider the following headline: "Bicycle Deaths Quadruple Auto Deaths on College Campus." The basis for the headline was a study that reported that the risk of death from bicycling to school increased 100 percent over the previous year, whereas deaths caused by driving to school increased by only 25 percent. The reporter incorrectly concluded that bicycling is four times more risky than driving. What is missing is information about actual baseline risk. If the baseline risk of deaths from bicycling is 1 in 1000, a 100 percent increase would raise it to 2 in 1000. If the baseline risk for driving to school is 400 in 1000, then

a 25 percent increase would increase the risk of death by 100 to 500 in 1000. Driving to school would then turn out to be 250 times more risky than bicycling to school, a complete reversal of the meaning of the headline. Although this example is hypothetical, it serves as a reminder of the importance of inquiring about the chances of getting a disease in the first place before drawing conclusions regarding risk factors, diseases, and death.

Ask the Following Questions About Information

Answers to four questions about the nature and type of study will help you sort through the contradictory findings and claims reported in the popular press.

What type of study was used?

There are several types of studies and each has certain advantages and limitations.

Epidemiologic studies are population studies (rather than scientifically controlled experimental studies) that observe the health habits and lifestyles of thousands of people for a period of time. The Framingham Study in Framingham, Massachusetts is perhaps the longest running and most famous epidemiologic study in the United States. It has yielded information that has been invaluable to our understanding of the risk factors associated with many diseases, especially heart disease. Epidemiologic studies may be *prospective* or *retrospective*. In a *prospective* study researchers follow a group of people at a specific point in time and identify relationships between lifestyle and diseases. In a *retrospective study* researchers look back in time to identify possible disease relationships. Retrospective studies are generally considered less reliable than prospective studies. Many of the tea studies mentioned previously are retrospective studies.

An advantage of epidemiologic studies is that they tend to be more generalizable to the population at large. A disadvantage is that they do not prove cause and effect.

Scientifically controlled studies are experiments conducted in controlled settings. The classic study is a **double-blind** study that includes at least two groups, one that is an experimental group and receives some form of experimental treatment and another that is a control group and receives no treatment. The double-blind feature of a study ensures that neither the researcher nor the subjects knows who is receiving an experimental treatment, and, therefore, will not influence the outcome with that knowledge. If a researcher wanted to prove, for example, that a particular brand of soap prevents athlete's foot, one group of subjects would use the experimental soap, and the other would use a **placebo** or soap substitute. Researchers administering the soap treatment would not know which soap each subject was using, nor would the subjects in the experimental and control groups know. If the experimental group has significantly fewer cases of athlete's foot, the results could then be attributed to the treatment.

The experimental-control, double-blind requirement of scientific research is a difficult standard to meet. Such studies are costly and require considerable resources and manpower. Typically, they are referred to in the press as *clinical trials* or *population intervention studies*. The advantage of scientifically controlled studies is that they control the variables so that it is often possible to establish cause-and-effect relationships. The disadvantage is that results usually apply to a narrowly defined population group and lack generalizability to the general population.

What were the characteristics of the people included in the study?

Scientific studies require random sampling of subjects to represent the diverse racial, religious, gender, and cultural characteristics of the population at large. Medical breakthroughs should not be based on a small number of homogeneous, or similar, subjects. Broadly designed human clinical trials that are randomized, placebo controlled, and include a double blind offer the strongest proof of reliable information.[5] If a study is limited to one gender or racial or ethnic group, its findings will not apply to anyone of a different gender, race, or ethnicity. If the study involves animals, avoid drawing conclusions until subsequent human studies are conducted.

If you are at low risk for a particular condition being studied, the results probably do not apply to you. The consumption of alcohol illustrates the point. A number of studies report that one drink per day for a woman and up to two drinks a day for a man may reduce the risks associated with heart disease. These studies affect only people who have heart disease and consume alcoholic beverages. If you do not have heart disease and if you do not drink beverages that contain alcohol, the study findings are not relevant to you.

Remember, true breakthroughs in medical research are the exception rather than the rule.

How many people were in the study?

In general, the more people included in a study, the better. Studies that report results based on a small number of subjects are seriously limited in their generalizability, regardless of how tightly controlled they are. Unfortunately, small research projects with intriguing results can make headlines that are just as big as those given to larger, more comprehensive studies.[6]

Who funded the study?

Businesses stand to gain or lose substantial sums of money (and reputation) from headline stories featuring their products. Consider the huge upswing in profits experienced by businesses in the pharmaceutical industry when several studies reported the weight loss benefits of new diet drugs. Profits were staggering; so were the losses when the drugs were later pulled off the market. Before jumping to conclusions, inquire about the funding source. The advice of the editor of the *New England Journal of Medicine* is appropriate: "You have to look at the motivations of everyone involved in telling you that there is some breakthrough that is going to change your life."[6]

Consider the Sources of Information

Valid and reliable health information comes from respected journals, magazines, and newsletters. Such publications have experienced health or medical editors who subject their articles to peer review and criticism by other scientists. Because little or no space is devoted to advertising, they are less inclined to be influenced by the need to protect the reputation or promote the product of a sponsor or advertiser. Several of these newsletters are available free on-line (see Just the Facts: Health Help You Can Trust on the Internet).

Health information and the internet

A 1998 report on the use of the internet revealed that health is the fastest growing sector on the World Wide Web, with more than 10,000 health-related sites available. Seventeen percent of American adults use the internet, and 37 percent of them have sought health information on-line.[7] People who have access to a computer and an internet service provider can obtain health and medical information that once was available only to those in the medical profession who had user privileges at major medical libraries and research centers. Websites provide information regarding most diseases and health conditions. Some sites provide access to news groups, chat rooms, bulletin boards, support groups, and even to medical specialists (see Nurturing Your Spirituality: Support Is Just a Click Away). Perhaps more than any other development of recent times, the internet has been the single best means of empowerment for people who want and need information so that they can be actively involved in their health care. Armed with the latest information,

425

Just the Facts

Health Help You Can Trust on the Internet

The internet has grown so rapidly that it would take volumes to list all of the available websites that offer health information. Even if that were feasible, there would be little assurance that the information could be trusted. Fortunately, several respected health organizations have reviewed selected websites and identified the ones that are useful and reliable. A few of these sites are listed here. Remember that many more excellent sites are available. (A $$ sign indicates that the website may charge a fee for use.)

Newsletters
- Harvard Medical School Publications at www.harvardhealthpubs.org/Harvard_Search HealthNews at www.onhealth.com
- Johns Hopkins InteliHealth Newsletter at www.intelihealth.com
- Mayo Health Oasis at www.mayohealth.org
- Nutrition Action Health Letter at www.cspiorg.com
- Tufts University Health and Nutrition Newsletter at www.phys.com

Medical Database, Links, and/or Search Engines
- Achoo at www.achoo.com
- Hardin Meta Directory of Internet Health Sources at www.arcade.uiowa.edu/hardin-www/md.html
- Health-Resource at www.thehealthresource.com ($$)
- HealthAtoZ at www.Healthatoz.com
- Healthtouch at www.healthtouch.com

- Medical Matrix at www.slackinc.com/matrix
- MedicineNet at www.medicinenet.com
- MEDLINE (also National Library of Medicine) at www.nim.nih.gov
- Medscape at www.medscape.com
- MedSearch at www.medsearchinc.com ($$)

Other Health Sites
- Aging information at bcm.tmc.edu/hcoa/ll.html
- Complementary medicine information at www.halcyon.com/libastyr/netbib.html
- American Cancer Society at www.cancer.org
- American Dental Association at www.ada.org/topics/top-menu.html
- American Heart Association at www.amhrt.org
- American Medical Association at www.ama-assn.org
- American Psychiatric Association at www.apa.org
- Hospital Information at neuro-www.mgh.harvard.edu/hospital/web.nclk
- Institute for Safe Medication Practices at www.ismp.org
- Nutrition information at www.navigator.tufts.edu
- Prescription drugs at www.pharminfo.com
- U.S. Food and Drug Administration at www.fda.gov
- U.S. Pharmacopeia (pharmaceutical information) at www.usp.org

people can be better prepared to ask questions and become partners with their physicians when serious health issues occur.

According to a recent study in which medical consultants reviewed selected web pages, much of the information available on-line is "as good as any you'll find in a good medical library—and in some cases more complete than the information your own physician could provide."[8] But the same study called the internet a "wild frontier" mixed with all sorts of information—good and bad, true and false, complete and dangerously incomplete. Some information may be outdated and some may be presented in websites that are not managed by knowledgeable sources or have not been subjected to peer review. Asking the following questions[9] should help determine if the information found at a particular website can be trusted:

- *Where does the information come from?* Information that comes from established medical institutions like hospitals, universities, or government organizations can generally be trusted. Reputation counts on the internet just as it does elsewhere. But be cautious of soundalike names. One website hosted by an organization whose name sounds very much like *American College of Sports Medicine* posted information about a questionable treatment for atherosclerosis that has never been proved effective.[8]
- *Does the site reflect more than one opinion?* Quality sites often feature more than one perspective.

Nurturing Your Spirituality

Support Is Just a Click Away

On-line patient support groups can be very useful, especially for people with chronic illness. With just the click of a mouse it is possible to interact with others who share health problems. One of the most direct methods of communicating with others on the internet is through newsgroups. Newsgroups are locations where electronic messages (e-mail) related to a medical topic are posted. These are usually plain text messages rather than sophisticated, color-graphic presentations. Newsgroups are not a collection of news items. Essentially, they are virtual bulletin boards open to anyone who wants to participate. Newsgroups make it possible to locate other people who are experiencing the same health concerns you are and to hear about their experiences as well as tell about yours.

There are more than 15,000 newsgroups available on the internet.[8] To locate the name of a specific newsgroup that might be helpful to you, visit one of the following websites:

- Deja News at www.dejanews.com
- Reference.com at www.reference.com
- The National Health Information Center at nhic-nt.health.org
- Self-Help Sourcebook at www.cmhc.com/selfhelp
- Healthfinder at www.healthfinder.gov/selfhelp.htm

Following are some popular newsgroups devoted to specific health issues (some of these websites are managed by Princeton University at www.princeton.edu/newsgroups/newslist/misc.health.html):

- AIDS at misc.health.aids
- Alternative health at misc.health.alternativehealth
- Arthritis at misc.health.arthritis
- Asthma at alt.support.asthma
- Cancer at sci.med.diseases.cancer
- Depression at alt.support.depression
- Diabetes mellitus at misc.health.diabetes
- Eating disorders at alt.support.eating-disord
- Headaches at alt.support.headaches.migraine
- Infertility at misc.health.infertility
- Stop smoking at alt.support.stop-smoking

A newsgroup may receive dozens and even hundreds of new postings each day. You can read all of them or select just those that seem to be most relevant. Messages on a related topic often are grouped together in a *thread,* making it easier to follow a conversation. Often, participants share practical tips for daily living. Sometimes, experts offer medical advice. Some groups are managed by administrators who screen submissions. However, most groups are uncontrolled, which means that they may contain inaccurate information.

Participating in a health-related newsgroup allows you to exchange information with people who share your concerns.

- *How often is the information updated?* Check to see if the information you are reading has been updated since its original posting. Ideally, a website will update its information on a monthly if not weekly basis.
- *Does the site promote products or procedures?* Exercise caution if a site uses anecdotal records and testimonials to promote specific products or procedures. Also be suspicious of sites that dwell on the shortcomings of mainstream medical science.

Health information and the telephone

Several telephone service businesses are now available that offer live interaction with health care professionals (see Just the Facts: Medical Telephone Services). These services, which are available through toll-free 800 and moderately expensive 900 numbers, provide consumers with a private and convenient option for getting answers to questions on topics ranging from the side effects of a particular medicine to the need for a second opinion regarding a particular diagnosis.

Just the Facts

Medical Telephone Services

Name: Ask-a-Nurse
Telephone Number: 1-800-535-1111 (available in 38 states; call to find out whether this service operates in your calling area)
Hours: 24 hours a day, 7 days a week
Type of Service: Calls on health problems, medical procedures, diagnostic tests, and treatments are answered by registered nurses with an average of ten years of experience in emergency room, critical care, or occupational health settings.
Cost: None

Name: Doctors by Phone
Telephone Number: 1-900-77-DOCTOR
Hours: 8 AM to midnight EST, 7 days a week
Type of Service: Most physicians on duty are board certified, and many have newly established practices in internal medicine or are completing specialized fellowships. They can answer a wide range of general and/or specific medical questions.
Cost: $3 per minute; the average call lasts 5 to 6 minutes

Name: Pharmacy Question? Ask the Pharmacist
Telephone Number: 1-900-420-0275
Hours: 24 hours a day, 7 days a week
Type of Service: Questions about medicines are answered by pharmacists licensed in North Carolina who on average have been in practice for more than seven years.
Cost: $1.95 per minute; the average call lasts 5 minutes

Name: Mental Help Line
Telephone Number: 1-800-226-6565 or 1-900-420-2525 (pay via your telephone bill)
Hours: 24 hours a day, 7 days a week
Type of Service: Licensed therapists, psychologists, and psychiatrists provide therapy and counseling on a wide range of emotional, psychological, and interpersonal problems and issues.
Cost: Initial consultation is free; subsequent charges are $3.99 per minute or $60 per hour.

There are obvious limitations to what medical and pharmaceutical advice telephone services can provide because telephone practitioners do not know callers' medical histories and cannot perform physical examinations. These calls do not substitute for visits to physicians. Instead, the calls are informational, advisory, and possibly helpful to people deciding whether a medical procedure, test, or treatment is warranted.

Pharmacists are an excellent yet often overlooked source of information when a health product or medicine is called for. They can advise you on the value and benefit of over-the-counter and prescription medicines. And they can help assure that you get the right treatment and that you avoid treatments that could worsen your condition.

Managing Health Care

A major theme throughout this text is that you can control many factors that influence your health. An outgrowth of this attitude is the **self-care** movement, which is the trend toward becoming an active partner in the management of one's health rather than a passive recipient of medical treatment. Armed with correct information, you can manage many aspects of your health care that were once thought to be solely within the realm of a physician. An added bonus of becoming actively involved in self-care is a shift from feelings of helplessness and despair to feelings of control, responsibility, and involvement (see Assessment Activity 15-3).

Answers to the following questions guide the use of health care services, providers, and products and facilitate the self-care approach to wellness:

- When should you seek health care?
- What can you expect from a stay in the hospital?
- How can you select a health care professional?

When to Seek Health Care

Many people tend to fall into two extreme groups regarding health care: those who seek health care for every ache and pain and those who avoid health care unless experiencing extreme pain. Both groups unwisely use the health care establishment. Those in the first group fail to understand that too much health care can be ineffective or even harmful. They also fail to recognize the powerful recuperative powers of the body. An estimated 80 percent of people who seek medical care are unaffected by treatment, 10 percent get better, and 9 percent experience an iatrogenic condition in which they get worse because of the medical treatment. Those who avoid health care fail to recognize the value of early diagnosis and detection of disease. This is especially true for men; 30 percent of men have not been to a doctor in a year or more, one-third have never had their cholesterol checked, and three-fourths have not been checked for prostate cancer during the previous year.[10]

Perhaps the best way to find a balance between too much and too little health care is to establish a physician-patient relationship with a general practitioner. The general practitioner may be a family practice physician or an internist who specializes in internal medicine.

It is important to visit your doctor while you are in good health. This permits your doctor to serve as a facilitator of wellness and provides him or her with a benchmark for interpreting symptoms when they occur.

A second important way to balance health care is to trust your instincts. Nobody knows when something is wrong with your body better than you do. Health and illness are subject to a wide variation in interpretation. If you are attuned to your body, you are your own best expert for recognizing signs and symptoms of illness.

Several signs and symptoms warrant medical attention without question. Internal bleeding, as shown by blood in the urine, bowel movement, sputum, or vomit, or blood from any of the body's openings require immediate attention. Abdominal pain, especially when it is associated with nausea, may indicate a wide range of problems from appendicitis to pelvic inflammatory disease and requires the diagnostic expertise of a physician. A stiff neck when accompanied by a fever may suggest meningitis and justifies immediate medical intervention. Injuries, many first aid emergencies, and severe disabling symptoms require prompt medical care.

There is debate about when medical care is needed in the case of fever. An elevated temperature may be a sign that the body's immune system is responding to an infection and working to destroy pathogens or disease-producing organisms. If left untreated for an extended time, a fever may cause harm to sensitive tissues in the body, such as connective tissue found in joints and tissues in the valves of the heart. Body temperature is generally about 98.6° F. Body temperature varies with exercise, at rest, by climate, and by gender. *Fever* means a reading over 99° F. It is not usually necessary for an adult to seek medical care for a fever. Home treatment in the form of aspirin, acetaminophen, and sponge baths usually lowers fever. You should consult your physician if fever remains above 102° F despite your actions or, in the case of a low-grade fever (99° F to 100° F), if there is no improvement in seventy-two hours. You should consult a physician if fever lasts more than five days, regardless of improvement. Some ailments such as sore throat, ear pain, diarrhea, urinary problems, and skin rash may be the cause of a fever and should be treated. Fever in young children should be discussed with a physician.

Entering a Hospital

A hospital is driven by the goal of saving lives. It may range in size and service from small units that provide general care and low-risk treatments to large, specialized centers offering dramatic and experimental therapies. You may be limited in your choice of a hospital by factors beyond your control, including insurance coverage, your physician's hospital affiliation, and the type of care accessible in your location.

The large majority of Americans benefit from the care and services provided by hospitals. People usually check in, receive treatment, and leave better off than they were when they were admitted. Still, you should be aware of possible dangers. Well-known hospital hazards are unnecessary operations, unexpected drug reactions, harmful or even fatal blunders, and hospital-borne infections. The Institute for Health Care Improvement reported that errors or accidents may harm up to 20 percent of all hospitalized patients.[11] The greatest single danger that a hospital presents is infection, which is largely preventable. Every year from 80,000 to 150,000 people die from infections they did not have before they entered the hospital. That is more than the number who die from homicides and auto accidents combined. A full one-third of hospital-acquired infections could be prevented by the most basic of infection-control health practices: hand washing.[12]

What can laypeople do to ensure proper and safe care while in the hospital? The following guidelines should be considered:

- If you have a choice of hospitals, inquire about their accreditation status. Hospitals are subject to inspection to make sure they are in compliance with federal standards.
- Before checking into a hospital, you need to decide on your accommodations. Do you want to pay extra for a single room? Do you want a nonsmoker for a roommate? Do you need a special diet? Do you need a place to store refrigerated medicine? If someone will be staying with you, will he or she need a cot? You should try to avoid going in on a weekend when few procedures are done. When you get to your room, speak up immediately if it is unacceptable.
- You need to be familiar with your rights as a patient (see Just the Facts: Do You Know Your Medical Rights?). Hospitals should provide an information booklet that includes a Patient's Bill of Rights. The booklet will inform you that you have the right to considerate and respectful care; information about tests, drugs, and procedures; dignity; courtesy; respect; and the opportunity to make decisions, including about when to leave the hospital.
- You should make informed decisions. Before authorizing any procedure, you must be informed about your medical condition, treatment options, expected risks, prognosis, and the name of the person in charge of treatment. Your agreement to a procedure based on your having been informed of

Just the Facts

Do You Know Your Medical Rights?

The following is a short list of some of your rights as a patient in the health care system:

- You have the right as a parent to stay with your children during tests and treatments, provided you don't interfere with medical treatment or are not suspected of child abuse.

- You have the right to request that a relative or friend accompany you during a test or treatment or hospitalization unless you're in a semiprivate room.

- You have the right to see your medical records if your state law permits it. Some states allow you to copy parts of your record under certain conditions (see Just the Facts: Are Your Medical Records Yours?).

- You have the right to emergency care whether you have insurance or not.

- You have the right to refuse to sign any form. The health care provider can also refuse to provide treatment in the absence of your signed authorization.

- You have the right to a second opinion, but your doctor can also stop treating you for challenging him or her.

- You have the right to leave the hospital at any time, even against medical advice or without paying the bill.

- You have the right to refuse or stop any treatment, whether or not it is experimental.

- You have the right to an itemized, detailed bill for all medical services.

- You have the right to know the results of all tests unless the doctor has reason to believe that the information will be harmful (for example, cause you to commit suicide).

Just the Facts

Are Your Medical Records Yours?[13]

A patient's right to gain access to medical records varies according to state law. If your state has no law, it may be possible for you to get copies of your medical records.

- States with laws permitting patients access to medical records in general are AZ, CA, CO, CT, FL, GA, HI, IL, MA, MN, NE, NY, OK, RI, UT, WI. Oregon encourages providers to give access but does not require it.

- States granting access to hospital records only are IN, OH, TN, VA. Louisiana law applies only to state hospitals.

- States that have declared that medical records are confidential (regardless of whether they give patients access to them) are AZ, CA, CO, FL, IL, MA, MN, RI, WI.

- Authorization of a medical procedure may be given nonverbally, such as through your appearance at a doctor's office for treatment, your cooperation during the administration of tests, or your failure to object when you could easily refuse consent. Your agreement to a procedure in such situations is called **implied consent.**

- You need to weigh the risks of drug therapy, X-ray examinations, and laboratory tests against their expected beneficial results. When tests or treatments are ordered, you should ask about their purpose, possible risks, and possible actions if a test finds that something is wrong. Finally, you should inquire about prescribed drugs. Avoid taking drugs, including pain and sleeping medication, unless you feel confident of their benefits and are aware of their hazards. This is particularly true for antibiotics, which in general have been overprescribed to the point that some bacteria no longer respond to their use. Your chances of harboring drug-resistant bacteria are greater if you have taken many antibiotics or have not taken them as prescribed. Even if you have never had an antibiotic, you can still acquire drug-resistant bacteria from others.[14,15]

- When scheduled for surgery, prepare for anesthesia. In rare cases, general anesthesia can cause brain damage and death. One cause of such catastrophes

these matters, is called **informed consent.** The only instances in which hospitals are not required to obtain informed consent are life-threatening emergencies, cases involving unconscious patients when no relatives are present, and compliance with the law or a court order such as those regulating sexually transmitted diseases. If you are asked to sign a consent form, you should read it first. If you want more information, you should ask before signing. If you are skeptical, you have the right to postpone a procedure and discuss it with your doctor.

Wellness On the Web Behavior Change Activities

How Can You Choose Quality Health Care?

If you're like most people, you want the very best health care available—but you may not know how to evaluate the quality of care you're receiving. The Agency for Health Care Policy and Research (AHCPR), a part of the U.S. Department of Health and Human Services, is the lead agency charged with supporting research designed to improve the quality of health care, reduce its cost, and broaden access to essential services. AHCPR's research programs bring practical, science-based information to medical practitioners as well as consumers and other health care purchasers. The agency has published "Your Guide to Choosing Quality Health Care," which shows how you can rate the quality of health care services you and your family receive. It describes quality measures, including consumer ratings, clinical performance measures, and accreditation— what they are, where to find them, and how to use them. The Guide has checklists, questions, charts, and other tools to help you make the health care decisions that are right for you. Take a moment to read about this information, which you'll find on-line at www.ahcpr.gov/consumer/qntool.htm.

Choosing a Physician Who's Right for You

The most important factor in the quality of health care you receive is your personal physician, or primary care provider. At certain times in your life, you may need to choose a physician. You may have moved recently or perhaps have a new health care plan that doesn't work with your provider. You may have become dissatisfied with your current physician and want to make a switch. Whatever the reason, selecting a new physician can be a daunting task if you're unsure where to begin. How do you know who's right for you or your family if all you have to go on is a list of names? You could just call a doctor's office at random and make an appointment, but chances are you'll make a better choice if you do a little homework up front. The Mayo Clinic website has a section dedicated to helping you select a primary care physician. Go to www.mayohealth.org/mayo/9712/htm/findtips.htm to learn more about choosing a physician who's right for you.

What Insurance Coverage Meets Your Needs?

The search for quality medical care can be challenging—and so can the search for comprehensive yet affordable health insurance. The cost of health care in the United States is high and continues to escalate. Few Americans can afford the cost of medicines, physicians' fees, or hospitalization without some form of health insurance. Health insurance is a contract between an insurance company and an individual or group for the payment of medical care costs. Choosing health coverage can be a complex and confusing task, because health plans differ greatly in services performed, choice of providers, and out-of-pocket costs. The more you know, the easier it will be for you to decide what insurance plan best fits your personal needs and budget. The Mayo Clinic website has a special section that offers tips on choosing a health care plan. Go to www.mayohealth.org/mayo/9712/htm/findplan.htm to learn more about choosing a plan that meets your needs.

---

is vomiting while unconscious. To reduce the risk, refuse any food or drink that may be offered by mistake during the eight hours before surgery.[16]

- You need to know who is in charge of your care and record his or her office number and note when you can expect a visit. If your doctor is transferring your care to someone else, you need to know who it is. If your doctor is not available and you do not know what is happening, you can ask for the nurse in charge of your case.
- You should keep a daily log of procedures, medicines, and doctor visits. When you get your bill, compare each item with your written record. Insist on an itemized bill.
- You should stay active within the limits of your medical problem. Many body functions begin to suffer from just a few days' inactivity. Moving about, walking, bending, and contracting muscles help to clear body fluids, reduce the risk of infec-

tions (especially in the lungs), and minimize the stress of hospital procedures which can add to the depression and malaise of hospitalization.

- Ask questions until you know all you need to know. Know the three Ps: Be polite, be pleasant, and most of all be persistent. According to some experts, the best way to avert hospital errors can be summarized in two words: "Speak up!"[11] The more you assert yourself and the more questions you ask, the fewer mistakes that will result.
- Insist that hospital workers who enter your room wash their hands for at least 15 seconds with soap in your presence. Infectious disease control experts suggest that this is one of the most important things a patient can do to prevent the spread of infection. Concern for this basic hygiene measure takes on added importance when patients are subjected to invasive diagnostic procedures and/or surgery.

Selecting a Health-Care Professional

Choosing a physician for your general health care is an important and necessary duty. Only physicians are discussed here, but this information applies to the selection of all health care practitioners. You must select one who will listen carefully to your problems and diagnose them accurately. At the same time, you need a physician who can move you through the modern medical maze of technology and specialists (see Just the Facts: Selected Health Care Specialists [Allopathic]).

For most people, good health care means having a **primary-care physician,** a professional who assists you as you assume responsibility for your overall health and directs you when specialized care is necessary. Your primary-care physician should be familiar with your complete medical history as well as your home, work, and other environments. You will be better understood in periods of sickness if your physician has also seen you during periods of wellness.

For adults, primary-care physicians are usually family practitioners, once called "general practitioners," and internists, specialists in internal medicine. Pediatricians often serve as primary-care physicians for children. Obstetricians and gynecologists, who specialize in pregnancy, childbirth, and diseases of the female reproductive system, often serve as primary-care physicians to women. General surgeons may offer primary care in addition to the surgery they perform. In some states, osteopathic physicians also practice family medicine.

There are several sources of information about physicians in your area:

- Local and state medical societies can identify doctors by specialty and tell you a doctor's basic credentials. You should check on the doctor's hospital affiliation and make sure the hospital is accredited. Another sign of standing is the type of societies in which the doctor has membership. The qualifications of a surgeon, for example, are enhanced by a fellowship in the American College of Surgeons (abbreviated as FACS after the surgeon's name). An internist fellowship in the American College of Physicians is abbreviated FACP. Membership in academies indicates physicians' special interests.
- All physicians board certified in the United States are listed in the *American Medical Directory* published by the American Medical Association and available in larger libraries.
- The American Board of Medical Specialists (ABMS) publishes the *Compendium of Certified Medical Specialties,* which lists physicians by name, specialty, and location.
- Pharmacists can be asked to recommend names.
- Hospitals can give you names of staff physicians who also practice in the community.
- Local medical schools can identify faculty members who also practice privately.
- Many colleges and universities have health centers that keep lists of physicians for student referral.
- Friends may have recommendations, but you should allow for the possibility that your opinion of a doctor may differ from theirs.
- Check your state Department of Health website for information on licensure for all health professionals. Disciplinary information may also be available.

Once you have identified a leading candidate, you can make an appointment. You need to check with the office staff about office hours, availability of emergency care at night or on weekends, backup doctors, procedures when you call for advice, hospital affiliation, and payment and insurance procedures. You should schedule your first visit while in good health. Once you have seen your doctor, reflect on the following: Did the doctor seem to be listening to you? Were your questions answered? Was a medical history taken? Were you informed of possible side effects of drugs or tests? Was respect shown for your need of privacy? Was the doctor open to the suggestion of a second opinion?

Patient-physician communication

Most doctors are not disinterested in you, but they are busy—so busy that many patients complain that their doctors cannot or will not listen to them. This is a problem because, according to the American Society of Internal Medicine, correct diagnoses depend largely on what you tell your doctor. Patients who do not speak up and who do not insist on being heard may get plenty of medical advice and prescription drugs, but they do not necessarily get the best results. According to a leading health publication, "Patients who really understand their illness and are aggressive in finding out about it—not only from their doctor, but from reading and talking it over with friends and partners—do better in managing their illness. There is growing evidence that people who take charge of their medical care, who communicate honestly with their clinicians, and who are decisive actually receive better care and end up healthier."[17] (See Assessment Activity 15-1.)

Patients can do much to facilitate the development of a physician-patient partnership. Understanding the meaning of commonly used medical words, abbreviations, suffixes, and prefixes can enhance this

Just the Facts

Selected Health Care Specialists (Allopathic)

The following lists show the fields of specialty of selected health care specialists:

Name of specialist	Field of specialty
Medical specialists	
Allergist	Allergic conditions
Anesthesiologist	Administration of anesthesia (such as during surgery)
Cardiologist	Coronary artery disease, heart disease
Dermatologist	Skin conditions
Endocrinologist	Diseases of the endocrine system
Epidemiologist	Study of the causes and sources of disease
Family practice physician	General care physician
Gastroenterologist	Stomach, intestines, digestive system
Geriatrician	Diseases and conditions of the aged
Gynecologist	Female reproductive system
Hematologist	Study of blood
Immunologist	Diseases of the immune system
Internist	Treatment of diseases in adults
Neonatologist	Newborns
Nephrologist	Kidney disease
Neurologist	Nervous system
Neurosurgeon	Surgery of the brain and nervous system
Obstetrician	Pregnancy, labor, childbirth
Oncologist	Cancer, tumors
Ophthalmologist	Eyes
Orthopedist	Skeletal system
Otolaryngologist	Head, neck, ears, nose, throat
Otologist	Ears
Pathologist	Study of tissues and the essential nature of disease
Pediatrician	Childhood diseases and conditions
Plastic surgeon	Use of material to alter or rebuild tissues
Primary-care physician	General health and medical care
Proctologist	Disorders of the rectum and anus
Psychiatrist	Mental illnesses
Radiologist	Use of X-rays
Rheumatologist	Diseases of connective tissues, joints, muscles, tendons
Rhinologist	Nose
Surgeon	Surgery
Urologist	Urinary tracts of men and women and reproductive organs of men
Dental Specialists	
Dentist	General care of teeth and oral cavity
Endodontist	Diseases of teeth below the gum line (root canal therapy)
Orthodontist	Teeth alignment, malocclusion
Pedodontist	Dental care of children
Periodontist	Diseases of supporting structures
Prosthodontist	Construction of artificial appliances for the mouth

communication (see Just the Facts: Communicating with Health Care Professionals). The following are some tips to ensure good communication:

- When you see your physician about a problem, you should state the most important problem first. Doctors tend to believe that the first thing a patient says is most important.
- You should be specific. If you have a headache, where does it hurt? How long does it last? How often does it occur?
- You should know your family history. Because many illnesses run in families, you may be at higher risk for certain diseases. Before your first visit, you should contact your parents and close relatives to learn of their health problems, especially heart disease, cancer, stroke, arthritis, diabetes, alcoholism, and tuberculosis.
- You need to list medications and treatments you are receiving, including over-the-counter drugs. The possibility of overdosing on either prescription or over-the-counter drugs is a growing problem, especially for older people—those over 65 years of age (see Wellness Across the Generations: Older Adults Can Go Too Far with Self-Care).[18] You will also need to identify any allergies and drug reactions.
- You should ask questions. You can bring a written list of questions but try to make them brief and specific. You should ask about anything that is unclear and repeat the answers in your own words.
- Before leaving the doctor's office, you need to make certain you know the diagnosis or how to follow the recommended treatment. If drugs are prescribed, you should inquire about the possible **contraindications** (reasons for not using a drug), side effects, and generic substitutions.
- When appropriate, ask your physician to write down instructions or recommend reading material for more information on a particular subject. Finally, inquire about the next steps in the treatment, if and when a return visit is required, and danger signs to look for and report back to your physician.

Second opinions

Chronic pain, recurring illnesses, and conditions involving elective surgery often benefit from a second opinion. A second opinion is often appropriate and peace of mind is a sufficient reason for seeking it.

In some cases, such as elective surgery, your health insurer may require a second or third opinion before authorizing payment for certain treatments. (See Real-World Wellness: How to Get a Second Opinion for advice on getting a second opinion.)

If you decide to ask for a second opinion, common courtesy dictates that you discuss it with your physi-

cian. Your physician may suggest bringing in a consultant to assess your situation and discuss it with you and your physician. You can also ask your physician for the name of someone to see separately.

A physician may feel that a second opinion is a waste of time or money. Regardless, your wish for more information should be respected. Reputable physicians do not feel threatened by another opinion; to the contrary, they may welcome another perspective on a difficult case. If your physician expresses displeasure for or resists your wish to have a second opinion, you may want to consider looking for another doctor.

Alternative Medicine

Alternative medicine, also called *complementary medicine,* is the body of therapies that are not taught in U.S. medical schools and that are generally unavailable from doctors or hospitals.[31] More than one-third of Americans use some form of alternative medical therapy despite the skepticism of many providers of traditional medical care (also called *allopathic* medicine, which refers to the treatment of diseases using scientifically proven and established measures).[32] These therapies vary considerably in their approach and include herbal medicine, biofeedback, magnetic therapy, light therapy, sound therapy, reflexology, and prayer therapy, among others (see Just the Facts: Alternative Medicine—Selected Approaches and Therapies).

Proponents of alternative medicine acknowledge that allopathic medicine is superb when it comes to surgery, emergency, and trauma. But they claim that alternative approaches work better for almost everything else, especially chronic degenerative diseases, because they focus on prevention and target causes rather than symptoms. Many alternative methods are thought to work by helping the body heal itself instead of by introducing strong drugs often to compensate for the side effects of other drugs.[33]

Skeptics of alternative medicine claim that its effectiveness has not been proven and worry about the indiscriminate use of some therapies. They offer numerous reasons for their concerns:[31]

- Patients often delay starting conventional medical treatment that has a proven track record to try an alternative approach touted as a miracle cure.
- There is the false perception that "natural" remedies are risk free. Many herbal medicines when taken in large amounts may have serious and even fatal side effects. For example, ephedra, or Ma huang, is an herb that has a stimulant effect claimed to boost energy and help people lose weight. It can also cause a dangerous rise in blood pressure and speed up the heart rate. A 1997 health newsletter

Just the Facts

Communicating with Health Care Professionals

Here are some words, abbreviations, suffixes, and prefixes that are often used in health and medical care.

Term	Meaning
A (prefix)	Without
Aberration	Different from normal action
Acute	A condition that occurs suddenly
Adult	Developed fully
Affinity	Attraction
-algia (suffix)	Pain in
Angio- (prefix)	Vessels (veins or arteries)
Arrest	Stopping, restraining
Arthr- (prefix)	Joint related
Asymptomatic	Without symptoms
Bowel	Intestine
BP	Blood pressure
Cardiac (cardio-)	Relating to the heart
CAT	Computerized assisted X-ray
CCU	Coronary care unit
Chronic	A condition that occurs for a long time
Coma	Complete loss of consciousness
Congenital	Existing at or before birth
Contraindication	A reason for not prescribing a drug, procedure, or treatment
Coronary	Relating to the heart
CVA	Cerebrovascular accident (stroke)
Degenerative	Deterioration of a part of the body
Diagnosis	Determining of a disease
Dilation	Stretching, increase in size
Distention	Widening or enlargement
DO	Doctor of osteopathy
Dose	Amount of medication to be given at one time
Dysfunction	Impairment of function
Edema	Swelling from accumulation of fluid
EEG	Electroencephalogram
EKG, ECG	Electrocardiogram
Embolus	Blood clot floating free in the bloodstream
Emia- (prefix)	In the blood
Endemic	Disease prevalent in a particular area
Entero- (prefix)	Intestine
Epidemic	Disease prevalence that is higher than normal
ER/ED	Emergency room/emergency department
Etiology	Reference to the cause of a disease
Extra- (prefix)	Outside of
Gastr- (prefix)	Stomach
GP	General practitioner
Hem- (prefix)	Blood
Hemorrhage	Bleeding

continued

Just the Facts

continued

Term	Meaning
Hyper- (prefix)	Excessive
Hypo- (prefix)	Insufficient
Indication	Condition that leads to a prescribed drug, procedure, or treatment
ICU	Intensive care unit
Innate	Hereditary, congenital
Innocuous	Harmless
Insidious	Refers to a disease that does not show early symptoms of its advent
-ism (suffix)	Condition, theory, method
-itis (suffix)	Inflammation
IV	Intravenous (within a vein)
Jaundiced	Yellow
Malady	Illness
Malaise	Uneasiness
MD	Medical doctor
Ml	Myocardial infarction
MRI	Magnetic resonance imaging
Myo- (prefix)	Muscle
Nephro- (prefix)	Kidney
-opothy (suffix)	Cause unknown
Pandemic	Disease that is prevalent over a large region
Pernicious	Severe, fatal
Phag- (prefix)	To eat
Primary	Principal, most important
Prognosis	Medical outlook of a disease
Pulmo- (prefix)	Lung
Renal	Kidney
Sepsis	Infection
Sign	Something tangible that can be observed
Stenosis	Constricted, decreasing in size
Symptom	Intangible evidence of a disease
Symptomatic	Relating to symptoms
Syndrome	Set of symptoms that occur together for unknown causes
Systemic	Affecting all systems of the body
Thrombus	Solid blood clot
TIA	Transient ischemic attack
TPR	Temperature, pulse, respiration
Trauma	Injury from external force
Tumor	Growth

reported that the herb caused more than 800 injuries and seventeen deaths.[32]

- There is a lack of evidence from scientifically controlled studies that demonstrate a therapy's effectiveness to make good on its promise.
- Proponents tend to rely on anecdotal records (isolated incidents) and testimonials to promote therapies.
- Because herbs and vitamins are processed and excreted primarily by the liver and kidneys, as are most drugs, they can cause serious drug interactions with prescription and over-the-counter medications.

Many health problems, such as chronic pain, lower-back problems, and stress-related problems such as anxiety and insomnia, don't respond well to conventional medical approaches. If at first conventional treatments aren't effective, alternative therapies may offer some benefit. If you consider using a form of alternative medicine, experts recommend you do the following:[32]

In an effort to assume responsibility for their own health care, people sometimes go too far. This is especially true for older people—those over 65 years of age—who are taking medications, both over-the-counter and prescription drugs. Common mistakes include the following: (1) taking larger doses of over-the-counter medicines than called for on the label; (2) mixing different types of medicines, both over-the-counter and prescription, without understanding the potential impact of taking two different drugs at the same time (such as analgesics and alcohol); and (3) taking someone else's medicine.

The risks and potential dangers for self-medication mistakes increase for the elderly. Drug companies typically set dosages for new drugs high enough to be effective for 90 percent of the intended population. Many times this dosage is too high even for people under age 65, and for those over 65, the risk of harmful side effects increases significantly.[18] Three characteristics are used to determine dosages by drug companies: (1) how much of the drug is actually absorbed into the bloodstream from the intestine; (2) how much of the drug is broken down in the body; and (3) how quickly the drug is eliminated from the body. The tests used to determine these characteristics are usually completed on

Wellness Across the Generations
Older Adults Can Go Too Far with Self-Care

healthy, young volunteers with healthy, young intestines, livers, and kidneys.

Unfortunately, as humans age, their organs tend to decline in function and the processes responsible for eliminating drugs decrease, thus allowing an "overloading" effect on the user. This problem is made worse when an elderly person is taking more than one type of drug, as many elderly people do. The more drugs ingested, the greater the possibility of drug interactions. Drug interactions can increase the potency of a drug, render it ineffective, or cause other side effects that might be life threatening. Older people in particular seem to be highly sensitive to drugs that affect the central nervous system, such as tranquilizers, antidepressants, and sleeping pills. Generally, older people are at increased risk for side effects if they are taking antidepressants, arthritis medications, blood thinners, dementia drugs, diabetes drugs, muscle relaxants, pain relievers, or sedatives or tranquilizers.[18]

To avoid potential overdoses, elderly patients should make both the physician and the pharmacist aware of all medications being taken so that more appropriate dosages can be prescribed and closer monitoring of effects can occur.

Real-World Wellness

How to Get a Second Opinion

I am considering elective surgery and want a second opinion. What are some good sources for referral?

Here are some options for finding second opinions:

- Ask your primary-care physician for the names of two or three experts in the field.
- Call a medical center or hospital and ask to talk to the chief of surgery for a surgical opinion or to the chief of medicine for a nonsurgical question.

- Call the county medical society.
- Call the Second Surgical Opinion Hotline (800-638-6833) for medical organizations, which provides referrals on surgical questions.
- Call Health Benefits Research Corporation, which offers a Second Opinion Hotline (800-522-0036, 800-631-1220 in New York) and referral service. Consultation with a board-certified specialist is available for a fee.
- Call the American Board of Medical Specialists to determine if the opinion you're getting is from a board-certified physician. The number is 800-776-CERT.

- Keep a diary to track symptoms. Writing down when symptoms begin and when they abate is a good way to determine if there is an association between treatment and relief.

- Add one therapy at a time. It is hard to know which therapy may be helping and which may be causing side effects when multiple therapies are used. Use the diary to track one treatment at a time.

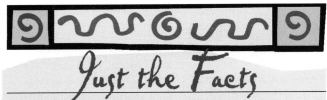

Just the Facts

Alternative Medicine—Selected Approaches and Therapies

Alternative medicine offers a wide variety of treatment options ranging from acupuncture to yoga. While treatment options may vary, they are linked by four common emphases: structural balance, biochemical balance, mental and emotional balance, and energetic levels.[32] Some of the therapies that address these emphases are listed here.[33] To learn more about how these therapies are thought to contribute to health and/or prevent disease, see the Suggested Readings at the end of this chapter.

- **Structural balance:** bodywork, chiropractic, craniosacral therapy
- **Biochemical balance:** diet, nutritional supplements, herbal medicine, enzyme therapy
- **Mental and emotional balance:** mind/body medicine, biofeedback, meditation, hypnotherapy, guided imagery, neurolinguistic programming
- **Energetic levels of the body:** acupuncture, homeopathy, energy medicine, magnetic field therapy, neural therapy
- **Multiple approach:** Ayurvedic medicine, naturopathic medicine, traditional Chinese medicine

- Discuss alternative therapies with your conventional physician. Potential interactions between conventional and alternative therapies can cause serious health problems.
- Discuss conventional therapies with your alternative physician. If an alternative physician suggests discontinuing a drug, check with your conventional physician first.

Assessing Your Health

Many tests, procedures, gadgets, and machines assess various aspects of health and wellness. They range from the hands-on physical examination to the use of sophisticated diagnostic tests.

The Physical Examination

Until recently the annual physical examination was viewed as a normal and necessary part of health care. Now, considerable debate exists among medical ex-

perts as to who needs a physical examination, how often it is needed, and what it should include. The emphasis today is on the use of selective health examinations and periodic examinations. **Selective health examinations** are specific tests used for specific problems. The assumption of this approach is that tests are more useful if they are matched to specific complaints. **Periodic examinations** are assessments that are given according to age, health habits, predisposition for certain conditions, and/or risk factors.

The periodic exam includes only those tests that are warranted by the information coming from a thorough medical history and discussion of those lifestyle factors related to diseases. The assumption is that behavior and habits are the best criteria for predicting disease risk.

Criticisms of the comprehensive annual physical examination for a healthy adult are not meant to undermine the doctor-patient relationship. They simply cast doubt about the efficacy of the physical examination. However, this does not nullify the value of regular visits to the doctor. To the contrary, seeing a physician for a limited examination at regular intervals can be good preventive medicine.

How often?

The need for a complete physical exam depends on a person's age, health, and lifestyle. People over the age of 45 benefit from a checkup every year. People in good health and under the age of 45 should see their physicians for routine tests at least every two years.[19]

Regardless of their age, people with family histories of heart disease, stroke, high blood pressure, cancer, and diabetes can benefit from periodic checkups, even if they are in good health. The same is true for people whose health habits or occupations put them at higher than normal risk for chronic diseases and disabling conditions. Even in these cases, good judgment and discretion should rule the choice of tests to be included in the physical examination.

Components

The three basic tools for completing a physical examination are medical history, hands-on examination, and diagnostic/laboratory tests.

A medical history is the most important part of the physical examination, especially during the first visit with your physician.[20] According to some experts, a good medical history gives 90 percent of the information needed to make a diagnosis.[21] This includes information about health habits, lifestyle, family history, and symptoms. Many physicians use health-risk appraisals, detailed questionnaires that provide information about health habits. This is one area of the physical examination for which a patient can prepare. By following the guidelines for communicating with your physician presented earlier in this chapter, you can help your physician obtain an accurate health profile.

¿ The hands-on examination is the second part of the physical examination. It consists of touching, looking, and listening. Physicians can feel or palpate for enlarged glands, growths, and tumors with procedures such as the breast examination, pelvic examination, rectal examination, and hernia examination. Thumping the back and chest lets the physician know whether any fluid has built up in or around the lungs. Tapping a knee for reflexes may reveal nervous system damage. A stethoscope is used to listen to the heart, lungs, abdomen, and glands located near the surface of the skin. Possible problems that can be detected with the stethoscope range from a heart murmur to poor circulation, lung infection, intestinal blockage, and an overactive thyroid gland.

Physicians have access to a number of instruments to visually inspect for problems. An ophthalmoscope is used to view the brain through the eye. The first sign of some brain diseases is an unhealthy-looking optic nerve. Leakage in the blood vessels of the eye may be a sign of diabetes or hypertension. An otoscope is used to inspect the ear, particularly the tympanic membrane. The proctoscope and sigmoidoscope are used to examine the rectum and colon. The laryngoscope and bronchoscope provide a look at the larynx and bronchial tubes.

The last part of the physical examination includes **diagnostic laboratory tests,** which may vary from a simple urinalysis to invasive dye tests. The effectiveness of these tests is being debated. Tests conducted for specific symptoms may be invaluable in pinpointing disabling conditions. They may be just as valuable for what they do not reveal as they are for what they do reveal. This can be reassuring to the patient and physician. On the negative side, many physicians rely too heavily on laboratory tests. Patients often demand or acquiesce to more tests than are necessary and sometimes than are good for them.

Many times tests are recommended more for the purpose of protecting the doctor against medical malpractice suits than for their diagnostic value. This practice, which is called **defensive medicine,** paints a sobering picture of the difficulty in making medical decisions for doctors and patients alike. A doctor may know with 99 percent certainty a particular diagnosis but order a test or procedure anyway as protection against liability should he or she be sued later. Malpractice suits are a reality; they have increased 300 percent in the past thirty years.[22] Almost two-thirds of physicians say that the threat of liability influences them to order

extra tests.[23] Of course, patients always have the right to decline prescribed tests. The decision must be made by patient and doctor and should be based on the test's potential for contributing to an effective medical intervention.

Thus, when you go for a physical examination, you can determine which tests you are willing to be subjected to by asking the right questions:

- *What do you expect to find?* You should start by asking why you need the test. How will it help facilitate a diagnosis? You need to ask about alternatives and the disadvantage of waiting and not testing. Sometimes the best test is the test of time. Agreeing to a test because it is routine procedure is not a satisfactory explanation.
- *What risks are associated with the test?* No test is risk free; you should compare potential benefits and risks.

One problem with tests is that they are not 100 percent accurate. An inaccurate result can lead to a wrong diagnosis. A **false positive,** in which a test incorrectly reveals an abnormality, may occur. False positives provoke needless anxiety, causing some people to feel and even act sick. Conversely, normal results do not necessarily indicate good health. A **false negative** in which a test indicates normality even though a person is sick, may occur. These results may lead to a false sense of health and may delay much needed treatment at critical stages of a disease.

Statistically, test results are accurate for about 95 percent of the population. Thus, 5 percent of patients can be expected to have false positives or false negatives on any laboratory tests. Other factors that may cause test errors are the taking of certain medications, exercise, stress, diet, time of day, and mistakes in handling or processing specimens.

Another problem with tests is that they may involve physical risks. Some of the more common risks are infection, bleeding, damage to vital structures, and reactions to anesthetics, drugs, and dye-contrast materials. Again, it is important to ask questions.

- *What are the options after the test?* If a test is positive, then what? If none of the options is plausible to you, why have the test administered? If it is impossible to treat a disease that a test reveals, the test is not justified. The diagnosis of a treatable disease, on the other hand, usually justifies the test.
- *What is the value of the test?* This question need not be perceived as confrontational. If approached with sincerity and courtesy, discussions about the physical examination in general and laboratory tests in particular can serve as a basis for forming an active partnership with your physician in making decisions about your health care.

Common Diagnostic Laboratory Tests

Americans are having many diagnostic tests performed. Home medical tests, available from most pharmacies, allow you to monitor a growing list of medical conditions including high blood pressure, high body temperature, asthma, allergies, urinary tract infections, pregnancy, diabetes mellitus, colon cancer, cholesterol, and HIV infection. The tests should not be viewed as substitutes for your doctor. The accuracy rates and reliability of over-the-counter medical kits vary considerably, and their instructions do not always explain how to interpret the results. These tests procedures are also subject to human error, but they provide a useful way to get involved in your own health care.

Some other inexpensive items should be included in your medicine cabinet (see Just the Facts: Essentials for Your Medicine Cabinet and table 15-2: Which Pain Reliever Is Right for You?). These items should help you cope with most common minor aches and pains.

Depending on your health status, gender, age, symptoms, and risk for a disease, some of the more common tests may be recommended when you go to your physician for a checkup.

Multiple blood screening tests check for high blood sugar, which indicates diabetes; blood urea nitrogen, an indicator of kidney function; an overactive parathyroid gland; blood count, a screen for anemia; and much more (see Assessment Activity 15-2).

Blood cholesterol screening is recommended every five years for women 45 to 65 and men 35 to 65.[19] The test should measure total cholesterol, lipoprotein, and triglyceride levels.[20] (See Chapter 2 for a thorough discussion of cholesterol and lipoprotein.)

Fecal occult-blood tests, also called *hemoccult tests*, are used to detect hidden blood in bowel movements. If a test is positive, it may indicate signs of an early cancer of the colon. People over 50 should either test themselves (home screening kits are available in most pharmacies) or have their stools tested for blood every year.[19]

Self-care medical kits, such as home pregnancy tests, allow you to become more involved with your own health care.

Just the Facts

Essentials for Your Medicine Cabinet

With the exception of personal items and prescription medicines, what should you keep in your medicine chest? The following are the essentials according to experts:

1. A *thermometer* to assess body temperature (oral, rectal, ear, and electronic models available).
2. *Ipecac* to induce vomiting in case of poisoning.
3. *Acetaminophen* to reduce fever and pain (in liquid form for children; aspirin should not be given to children under 15 years of age because of its link to Reye's syndrome). See table 15-2 for information on types of pain relievers available over the counter.
4. An *antiseptic*, such as hydrogen peroxide, for cleaning open wounds.
5. *Gauze and tape* to treat minor wounds.
6. An *ice bag* to reduce swelling.
7. *Ace bandages* to wrap pulled muscles or twisted ankles or to bind a splint.
8. *Benadryl* or a similar antihistamine to reduce allergic reactions.
9. An *antibiotic ointment* or *cream* to prevent infections from cuts.
10. *Pepto-Bismol* or another antidiarrheal medication to treat diarrhea.

Pulse rate may be an indicator of a health problem. The normal resting heart rate is between 60 and 80 beats a minute. Resting heart rates above 80 beats per minute put a person in a higher risk category for heart attacks and sudden death. The high heart rate does not increase the risk but is an indicator of basic problems, such as cigarette smoking, too much caffeine, stress, anxiety, hyperthyroidism, and most commonly a poor level of physical fitness.

Slow heart rates are normally found in physically fit people; in them slow heart rates are a sign of good health. Very slow rates below 50 beats per minute can occur in people who are not fit and who have heart problems. These people should seek medical advice.

Blood pressure measurements should be monitored regularly, especially for people who have had previously high readings or have family histories of hypertension (high blood pressure). Inexpensive, accurate home blood pressure kits can be purchased at most drugstores. Because all kits are not equally reliable, you should ask your pharmacist for a recommendation. People who have measurements higher than 140 over 90 mmHg or lower than 100 over 60 mmHg should keep records of their blood pressure and present them to their physicians during periodic checkups.

Mammography, an X-ray examination of the breast, detects early signs of breast cancer. Women 50 and older should get mammograms yearly; for women between 40 to 49, a mammogram every one to two years is recommended.[19] High-risk women may be advised to have mammograms more often and at an earlier age.

Pelvic examination and *Pap smears* detect abnormalities of the ovaries, uterus, and cervix. Pap smears should be performed annually for three years beginning at age 18 or the age of first intercourse, if they are

---

Table 15-2 Which Pain Reliever Is Right for You?

There are five types of pain relievers: aspirin, acetaminophen, ibuprofen, naproxen sodium, and ketoprofen. These medicines, also referred to as NSAIDS, short for *nonsteroidal anti-inflammatory drugs,* help to reduce swelling and inflammation and relieve pain and fever. (Technically, acetaminophen is not an NSAID, but it does have some of the same effects and appears to be more closely related to NSAIDs than to other classes of pain-relief medications.[24]) Each of these is available over-the-counter and gives you some control over the treatment of your own aches and pains. Although they are safe when taken as directed, they are not risk free. About 25 percent of people who regularly take NSAIDs develop ulcers.[25] Some benefits and shortcomings of each group are listed here. If in doubt about the use and/or interaction of any of these medicines, be sure to read the package insert for side effects and contraindications and/or consult your pharmacist or doctor.

Drug	Benefit	Shortcoming
Acetaminophen (Tylenol)	Relieves aches and pain without irritating the stomach; ideal for people allergic to aspirin; doesn't interfere with blood clotting; doesn't cause Reye's syndrome in children with the flu or chicken pox.	Doesn't reduce inflammation associated with arthritis or muscle soreness; overdoses can be toxic to the liver; alcohol enhances toxic effects.
Aspirin (Anacin, Bayer)	Is the least expensive pain reliever; provides mild relief of inflammation; a long-term low dose is associated with reduced risks of heart attacks and some forms of cancer.	Irritates stomach; can cause allergic reactions; is less effective than the following drugs for pain relief; avoid if you have asthma or are taking a blood thinner.
Ibuprofen (Advil, Nuprin)	Is more effective than aspirin and acetaminophen as a pain reliever; effective against menstrual cramps and dental pain; useful against inflammation.	May irritate the stomach and intestines; may cause kidney damage; avoid if you're allergic to aspirin or have asthma, heart failure, kidney problems, or ulcers.
Naproxen Sodium (Aleve)	Is comparable to ibuprofen in effectiveness but provides longer-lasting pain relief per dose (8–12 hrs.); effective for arthritis and chronic pain.	Its longer duration of action increases the chance for complications (stomach irritation or kidney damage); avoid if you're allergic to aspirin or have asthma, heart failure, kidney problems, or ulcers.
Ketoprofen (Orudis)	Is comparable to ibuprofen in effectiveness but may produce faster relief than other drugs listed.	May irritate the stomach and intestines and may cause kidney damage; avoid if you're allergic to aspirin or have asthma, heart failure, kidney problems, or ulcers.

normal, they may be performed every two to three years thereafter.[19] Pap smears should not be done during the menstrual period. The test is more accurate during the first half of the cycle if oral contraceptives are taken. Midcycle is preferred in most other menstruating women.

A complete *eye examination* includes a test for visual acuity; *tonometry,* a painless test for glaucoma; and a cataract check. The American Academy of Ophthalmology recommends a complete eye examination from puberty to age 40 only if eye discomfort or vision problems occur. After age 40 a glaucoma test and cataract (a clouding over the lens) check should be done every two to three years.

Electrocardiograms (ECGs) are used to detect irregularities of the heart. Although there is some debate about the use of ECGs as routine screening procedures for *asymptomatic* (without symptoms) low-risk people, periodic ECG readings starting at age 40 are recommended.[26] Chest pain, hypertension, and symptoms of cardiovascular disease justify earlier ECGs. *Stress tests* use ECGs to assess how the heart functions under the stress of exercise. They are routine when symptoms are present.

Chest X-ray examinations are valuable diagnostic tools for people with chest symptoms, respiratory diseases, and heart problems. For people without symptoms, their routine use is questionable. Several groups of experts, including those associated with the Food and Drug Administration, recommend discontinuation of chest X-ray examinations in most cases. However, if you go to a hospital or often visit a doctor's office, you can anticipate a chest X-ray study more out of the need to comply with business policy than for diagnostic potential. Avoid a chest X-ray test if you may be pregnant.

Prostate cancer tests detect prostate cancer, a leading cause of cancer among men. Men 40 years and older should have an annual digital rectal examination. Combined with a blood test that looks for prostate-specific antigens (PSA), the digital examination significantly improves the chances of detecting early signs of cancer. The blood test for PSA should be performed annually on men starting at age 50 (45 for African Americans).[19] Because not all experts endorse this procedure, discuss the advantages and disadvantages of annual PSAs with your physician.

An *HIV test* is recommended for people who think they may have been infected with the HIV virus. This includes people who have had unprotected sex or a blood transfusion, have used IV drugs, or have participated in high-risk behaviors. After the blood test, these people should avoid high-risk behavior for six months to a year and then retest.

A *sigmoidoscopy* involves the insertion of a flexible viewing scope into the lower bowel to check for col-

orectal cancer. It should be performed every three to five years, starting at age 50.[19]

A visual *skin test* for skin cancer is recommended every three years for people 20 to 39 and annually for people over 40. An annual skin examination performed by a dermatologist is important for anyone with a history of many moles, pale skin, a family history of melanoma, and two or more blistering sunburns in childhood or adolescence.[27]

A fasting *blood glucose test* is recommended to detect diabetes mellitus. The test requires a small blood sample following a twelve-hour fast. It is recommended for people with symptoms of diabetes, including excessive thirst and frequent urination, people who are overweight, and those who have strong family histories of the disease.

A *bone density* test is recommended for women after menopause when hormone replacement therapy or bone-building drugs are being considered. Bone density is measured with an X-ray absorptiometry, or DXA, at two sites: spine and hip. It is sensitive enough to detect bone loss down to 1 percent. [27]

Immunizations for Adults

Many people believe that **immunizations** (administrations of preparations or vaccines, usually in the form of injections, for providing immunity or preventing a disease) are only for children. Consequently, many thousands of adults die every year of diseases they would not have acquired if they had received standard vaccines. For example, 40,000 people die prematurely each year because they fail to get pneumonia vaccines.[28] Adult immunization is recommended to prevent or ameliorate influenza, pneumonia, some forms of hepatitis, measles, rubella (German measles), tetanus, diphtheria, and chicken pox.

People born between 1957 and 1970 may need to be reimmunized for measles, mumps, and rubella (MMR) because the earlier vaccine may not have provided complete coverage.[29] A booster is not suggested for those born before 1957 because of the likelihood that they have natural immunity.

Booster shots should be given for tetanus and diphtheria every ten years (tetanus and diphtheria vaccines are usually combined). A booster shot is required annually for protection against common strains of influenza, whereas a pneumonia vaccine is usually good for life if administered after age 65.

Vaccines against hepatitis A, hepatitis B, and chicken pox are recommended for adults who are at risk because of their jobs, travel, or exposure to susceptible children or infected people. Hepatitis A vaccine lasts for several years. No booster shots are required for hepatitis B or chicken pox. If you are not sure whether you've had the disease, a blood test can check for antibodies.

Paying for Health Care

The cost of health care in the United States is expensive and is escalating. A majority of Americans cannot afford the cost of medicines, physicians' fees, or the cost of hospitalization without some form of health insurance. **Health insurance** is a contract between an insurance company and person or group for the payment of medical care costs. After the person or group pays a premium to an insurance company, the insurance company pays for part or all of the medical costs depending on the type of insurance and benefits provided. The type of insurance policy purchased greatly influences where a person goes for health care, who provides the health care, and what medical procedures can be performed.

Preferred Provider Organization (PPO)

A **preferred provider organization** (PPO) is a network of independent physicians, hospitals, and other health care providers who contract with an insurance company to provide medical care at discount rates. Subscribers are given incentives (reduced costs) if they use PPO-approved providers. This plan usually includes a *deductible,* an amount paid by the patient before being eligible for benefits from the insurance company. For example, if your expenses are $1000, you may have to pay $200 before the insurance company will pay the other $800. After the deductible is met, the insurance provider pays a percentage of the remaining balance. PPO subscribers can use out-of-network providers, but they then usually pay more because the care is not discounted. The advantages of this plan are that a patient usually has more options in choosing health care providers and is not required to obtain a referral from a primary care physician to seek the services of a specialist. Several disadvantages of this insurance option are that substantial costs may be incurred if unexpected illnesses or injuries occur and patients may not routinely receive comprehensive, preventive health care.

Point of Service (POS)

A **point of service** (POS) is an insurance plan in which subscribers use approved providers who have agreed to accept fixed copayments. The delivery of health care starts with and is coordinated by the primary-care physician. Before going to a specialist, a patient must first be referred by the primary-care physician. Out-of-plan providers can be seen but at a higher cost. Medical charges above the maximum allowed by the insurance company are the responsibility of the patient. Advantages of this insurance option are comprehensive health care coordinated by the primary-care physician,

lower costs in the case of unexpected illnesses or accidents, and no deductibles. A disadvantage is the loss of accessibility to specialists without first obtaining referral approval.

Health Maintenance Organization (HMO)

A **health maintenance organization** (HMO) is a managed health care plan that provides a full range of medical services for a prepaid amount of money. For a fixed monthly fee, usually paid through pay-roll deductions by an employer, and often a small copayment, subscribers receive care from physicians, specialists, allied health professionals, and educators who are hired or contractually retained by the HMO.

HMOs provide an advantage in that they provide comprehensive care including preventive care at a lower cost than private insurance over a long period of coverage. One drawback is that patients are limited in their choice of providers to those who belong to the HMO.

Indemnity Plan

An indemnity plan is one in which a person pays a premium, which ensures health care on a fee-for-service basis. In addition to the premium, subscribers pay part of the cost for medical care. Typically, the insurance company pays 80 percent after the deductible has been met, and the subscriber pays 20 percent. Usually, there are fixed indemnity benefits, specified amounts that are paid for particular procedures. If your policy pays $500 for a tonsillectomy and the actual cost is $1000, you owe the health care provider $500. There are often exclusions, certain services that are not covered by the policy. Common examples of exclusions are elective surgery, dental care, vision care, and preexisting illnesses and injuries. An advantage of an indemnity plan is that there are no limits on the providers you can use or on how often you see them. A disadvantage is that this type of insurance usually costs more than PPOs, POSs, and HMOs.

Government Insurance

In a government insurance plan the government at the federal, state, or local level pays for health care costs of eligible participants. Two prominent examples of this plan are Medicare and Medicaid. Medicare is financed by Social Security taxes and is designed to provide health care for people 65 years of age and older, the blind, the severely disabled, and those requiring certain treatments such as kidney dialysis. Medicare Part A covers hospital, skilled nursing, and home health care costs. People who qualify for Social Security also qualify for Part A. Medicare Part B is optional for an extra premium and covers physician fees and costs of outpatient care and physical therapy.[30] Medicaid is subsidized by federal and state taxes. It provides limited health care, generally for people who are eligible for benefits and assistance from two programs: Aid to Families with Dependent Children and Supplementary Security Income.

Summary

- Health information that can be trusted is based on scientifically controlled studies that yield consistent results over time.
- Health fatalism occurs when people disregard health information because they believe that new findings will be contradictory.
- A study is considered reliable if its findings can be confirmed in repeated studies conducted over the course of many years.
- Scientifically controlled studies involve experimental and control groups, use randomly selected participants, and feature double-blind procedures.
- *Statistical significance* is a phrase health journalists and researchers use to indicate probability. If a finding is statistically significant, 95 of 100 times similar studies would yield similar findings.
- *Statistical relationship* is a phrase used to indicate the degree of association between two or more variables (e.g., dietary fat and heart disease). Statistical relationships do not demonstrate cause and effect.
- Epidemiologic studies are population studies that observe the health habits and lifestyles of many people over time. They may be prospective or retrospective.
- Health information is the fastest growing sector on the World Wide Web. The discriminating use of the internet can yield helpful information for most health conditions.
- Signs and symptoms that warrant immediate medical attention are signs of internal bleeding, abdominal pain associated with nausea, a stiff neck accompanied by fever, and serious first aid emergencies and injuries.
- People can help to ensure proper and safe care while in a hospital by checking on the hospital's accreditation status, deciding on accommodations before admission, knowing their patient rights, discussing treatments and procedures with their physicians, asking questions, and staying active.

- Good health care means establishing a doctor-patient relationship while in good health.
- The doctor who manages the general care of patients and directs patients to specialized services is the primary-care physician.
- *Alternative medicine* is the use of therapies that are not taught in U.S. medical schools and are generally unavailable from doctors or hospitals. More than one-third of Americans use some form of alternative medical therapy.
- When telling a physician about a problem, you can enhance good communication by presenting the most important problem first, being as specific as possible, being familiar with your family medical history, knowing the names of medicines you are taking, and asking questions.
- The three major components of a physical examination are the medical history, hands-on examination, and diagnostic laboratory tests.
- A medical history is the most important part of the physical examination, especially during the initial visit to a doctor.
- A selective health examination involves the use of specific tests for specific problems. A periodic exam involves the use of tests and procedures after a complete medical history and a discussion of personal lifestyle factors and risk factors.
- Defensive medicine is the practice of prescribing tests and procedures for the purpose of protecting doctors from medical-malpractice lawsuits.
- The eight diseases for which adults need to maintain immunization are influenza, pneumonia, hepatitis, measles, rubella, tetanus, diphtheria, and chicken pox.
- Health insurance options include the Preferred Provider Organization (PPO), the Point of Service (POS), the Health Maintenance Organization (HMO), the indemnity plan, and government insurance.

Review Questions

1. How does health fatalism negatively influence understanding of health information?
2. What are some examples of health information contradictions?
3. What criteria must a research study satisfy before its claims can be trusted?
4. What are some techniques and strategies that manufacturers and producers of health products use to mislead and deceive the public?
5. Explain the meaning and significance of *scientifically controlled, double-blind studies*. Cite an example.
6. What do the phrases *statistical significance* and *statistical relationship* mean in reference to health studies?
7. How do epidemiologic studies differ from scientifically controlled studies?
8. Why is it important to see a physician while in good health?
9. What can laypeople do while in a hospital to ensure that they receive safe and proper care?
10. What is the major role and function of a primary-care physician?

11. Define *alternative medicine*. What reasons do conventional medical doctors give for being concerned about the indiscriminate use of alternative medicine?
12. List four sources of information for researching physicians and specialists in your geographical area.
13. Identify four techniques that facilitate communication between patient and physician.
14. Identify six rights patients have when in a hospital.

15. Differentiate between *selective health exam. periodic exam*, and *comprehensive physical examination*.
16. Define *defensive medicine*. Discuss its impact on both the quantity and quality of health care provided to patients.
17. Explain the meaning of *placebo effect*.
18. Identify immunizations for adults.
19. Compare and contrast the basic plans of health insurance.

References

1. Medical Information Service. 1998. *Consumer Guide to Medical Information*. Menlo Park, Calif.: Medical Information Systems, Inc.
2. Lamm, S. 1995. Making sense of medical news, *American Health* 14(8):32.
3. Tufts University. 1998. Yet another study—should you pay attention? *Tufts University Health and Nutrition Letter* 16(7):4.
4. Tufts University. 1995. Reading tea leaves for health benefits. *Tufts University Health and Nutrition Letter* 13(8):4.
5. Crowley, S. L. 1998. What's good for you? Don't go by headlines. *AARP Bulletin* 39(2):1, 10.
6. Consumer's Union. 1997. Medical news: How to assess the latest breakthrough. *Consumer Reports* 62(6):62.
7. Atkinson, H. 1998. Be a savvy surfer on the internet. *HealthNews* 4(1):4.
8. Consumer's Union. 1997. Finding medical help online. *Consumer Reports* 62(2):27.
9. Mayo Foundation for Medical Education and Research. 1997. Health info. on the internet. *Mayo Clinic Health Letter* 15(4):6.
10. Center for Science in the Public Interest. 1995. For men only. *Nutrition Action Healthletter* 22(5):4.
11. Zuger, A. 1998. Having a safe hospital stay. *HealthNews* 4(2):4.
12. Griffin, K. 1996. They should have washed their hands. *Health* 10(7):82.

13. Sandroff, R. 1997. AHAdvocate. *American Health* 16(6):41.
14. Mayo Foundation for Medical Education and Research. 1997. Antibiotics: 'Miracle drugs' are losing ground to infections. *Mayo Clinic Health Letter* 15(9):4.
15. Poirot, C. 1999. Overuse is reducing effectiveness of antibiotics. *The Commercial Appeal* 160(18):C1, C3.
16. Consumers Union. 1995. How to survive a hospital stay. *Consumer Reports* 60:740.
17. Frishman, R. 1996. Don't be a wimp in the doctor's office. *Harvard Health Letter* 21(10):1.
18. Consumer's Union. 1998. Special report on health guide to medication. *Consumer Reports* 63(4):1.
19. Consumer's Union. 1998. Checkups: Are you getting what you need? *Consumer Reports* 63(8):17.
20. Harvard Medical Information Publications Group. 1995. What is a good checkup? *Harvard Health Letter* 20(3):6.
21. Tankoos, A. 1996. Please tell me all about it. *American Health* 15(4):22.
22. Devita, E. 1995. The decline of the doctor-patient relationship. *American Health* 14(5):63, 105.
23. McIntosh, D. M., and D. C. Murray. 1994. Medical malpractice liability: An agenda for reform. *Medical Benefits* 11(11):1.

24. Mayo Foundation for Medical Education and Research. 1997. NSAIDs—helpful medications with serious side effects. *Mayo Clinic Health Letter* 15(12):4.
25. Tufts University. 1998. Common pain relievers can cause ulcers. *Tufts University Health and Nutrition Letter* 16(3):2.
26. Tufts University. 1997. Special report of mammograms, rectal exams, electrocardiograms. *Tufts University Health and Nutrition Letter* 15(6):4.
27. Griffin, K. 1996. 8 medical tests you shouldn't ignore. *Health* 10(3):107.
28. Mayo Foundation for Medical Education and Research. 1998. Second opinion. *Mayo Clinic Health Letter* 16(10):8.
29. Editors. 1996. Are your immunizations current? *Healthline* 15(7):2.
30. Mayo Foundation for Medical Education and Research. 1996. Health-care debate terms. *Mayo Clinic Health Letter* 14(9):4.
31. Atkinson, H. 1997. Discussing alternative medicine. *HealthNews* 3(10):4.
32. Harvard Medical Information Publications Group. 1997. Alternative medicine, time for a second opinion. *Harvard Health Letter* 23(1):1.
33. The Burton Goldberg Group. 1998. *Alternative Medicine, the Definitive Guide*. Puyallup, Wash.: Future Medicine Publishing, Inc.

Suggested Readings

The Burton Goldberg Group. 1998. *Alternative Medicine, the Definitive Guide*. Puyallup, Wash.: Future Medicine Publishing, Inc.

This comprehensive resource describes forty-three alternative therapies. Included in each description is the rationale for the therapy and an explanation of how the therapy works, its physiological effects, instructions on how to use the therapy, health conditions improved by the therapy, warnings and cautions, consumer tips, and additional resources.

U.S. Pharmacopeia. 1999. *Complete Drug Reference: 1999*. Griffin Trade Paperback.

This objective guide to virtually every medicine used in the United States is compiled independently of any manufacturer influence. It is based on thorough reviews and the consensus of hundreds of medical authorities. It provides valuable information in direct language written for the layperson taking or administering a drug.

U.S. News & World Report. 1996. *America's Best Hospitals*. John Wiley & Sons. New York, NY.

This guide examines each of the nation's hospitals and offers national, state, and urban rankings. It provides detailed information on seventeen different specialties of hospitals from AIDS to urology, including information on mortality rate, doctor and nurse–to–patient ratios, and number of beds. It features advice about when a top hospital can make a difference, how to get admitted to a top hospital, and when local alternatives are just as good.

Name _____ **Date** _____ **Section** _____

Assessment Activity 15-1

Are You Communicating with Your Physician?

Directions: Using the following scale, circle the appropriate number for each question. Total your responses and find your score at the end of the activity.

When I go to my physician for a health problem,	Almost Always	Very Frequently	Frequently	Occasionally	Never
I plan ahead of time how I am going to describe my problem.	5	4	3	2	1
I describe my most important problem first.	5	4	3	2	1
I check with my immediate family to determine if my problem runs in the family.	5	4	3	2	1
I take a list of medications, over-the-counter drugs, and treatments I am receiving.	5	4	3	2	1
Before the visit, I prepare a written list of questions to ask.	5	4	3	2	1
I ask about anything that is unclear to me.	5	4	3	2	1
I repeat in my own words the physician's answers to my questions.	5	4	3	2	1
I understand the doctor's diagnosis of my problem.	5	4	3	2	1
I make sure I know the benefits and risks of prescribed treatments.	5	4	3	2	1
I know if and when to return for a follow-up visit.	5	4	3	2	1

Scoring
46–50 = Excellent communication
41–45 = Good
36–40 = Average
31–35 = Fair
Less than 30 = Poor

Name _____ **Date** _____ **Section** _____

Assessment Activity 15-2

Assessing the Results of Diagnostic Tests

Directions: Use this assessment to record the dates and results of commonly administered diagnostic med- ical tests. Refer to information in this chapter to review the purposes of these tests.

Test Name	Typical Reference Range	What's Being Tested	Your Results	Date
1. Alanine aminotransferase (ALT)	1–75 U/l	Heart, liver, muscle damage		
2. Albumin	4–5 g/dl	Kidneys		
3. Alkaline phosphate	35–128 mg/dl	Liver, parathyroid glands, bone disease		
4. Aspartate aminotransferase (AST)	1–50 U/l	Liver, heart, muscle damage		
5. Bilirubin	0.3–1.5 mg/dl	Liver, kidneys		
6. Blood urea nitrogen (BUN)	8–22 mg/dl	Kidneys		
7. Calcium	8.9–10.2 mg/dl	Parathyroid glands, cancer, bone disease		
8. Carbon dioxide	20–34 mEq/l	Lungs and heart		
9. Chloride	96–106 mEq/l	Dehydration		
10. Cholesterol (total)	125–210 mg/dl	Heart and artery disease		
11. Creatinine	0.8–1.4 mg/dl	Kidneys		
12. Free T4 hormone	1.0–4.3 mg/dl	Thyroid gland		
13. Globulin	1.5–3.8 g/dl	Infections		
14. Glucose	65–115 mg/dl	Diabetes mellitus		
15. Hematocrit	42–52%	Anemia		
16. High-density lipoprotein (HDL)	32–96 mg/dl	Heart and artery disease		
17. Iron (total)	50–180 mg/dl	Anemia		
18. Lactic dehydrogenase	90–250 U/l	Liver		
19. Low-density lipoprotein (LDL)	<130 mg/dl	Heart and artery disease		
20. Lymphocyte	20–40%	Immune deficiency disorder		
21. Phosphorous	2.3–4.6 mg/dl	Kidneys		
22. Potassium	3.8–5.3 mEq/l	Kidneys		
23. Protein	6.6–8.1 g/dl	Kidneys, nutrition		
24. Red blood cells (RBC)	4.2–6.1 m/ml	Anemia		
25. Sedimentation rate	(<50) 15–20 mm/h	Infections		

Test Name	Typical Reference Range	What's Being Tested	Your Results	Date
26. Sodium	135–143 mEq/l	Kidneys, water retention		
27. Thyroid-stimulating hormone (TSH)	0.1–5.0 mU/l	Pituitary gland, thyroid gland		
28. Total iron-binding capacity (TIBC)	250–390 mg/dl	Excessive iron		
29. Triglycerides	30–200 mg/dl	Heart disease		
30. Uric acid	3.6–8.1 mg/dl	Gout		
31. White blood cell (WBC) count	4.8–10.8 thou/cumm	Infections		

Name _____ Date _____ Section _____

Assessment Activity 15-3

Self-Care Inventory

Directions: Using the following scale, circle the appropriate number for each statement. Total your responses and find your score at the end of the activity.

Statement	Never	Occasionally	Most of the Time	Almost All of the Time
1. I read health-related advertisements in a critical and careful manner.	1	2	3	4
2. I maintain a suspicious attitude about health claims.	1	2	3	4
3. I have a primary-care physician.	1	2	3	4
4. I know which hospitals my physician recommends.	1	2	3	4
5. I ask about fees before using health care services.	1	2	3	4
6. I ask about the risks and benefits of a medical test before its use.	1	2	3	4
7. I seek second opinions when I feel uncertain or uncomfortable with a recommended treatment.	1	2	3	4
8. I maintain adequate health insurance coverage.	1	2	3	4
9. I ask about the contraindications and side effects of prescription drugs before taking them.	1	2	3	4
10. I thoroughly read labels before taking nonprescription drugs.	1	2	3	4
11. I look for evidence of scientifically controlled studies when reading sensational health claims.	1	2	3	4
12. I am familiar with the medical history of close relatives.	1	2	3	4
13. I follow directions when taking medicines, including continuing their use for the prescribed duration.	1	2	3	4
14. I keep a supply of essential items in my medicine cabinet.	1	2	3	4
15. I keep records of the times, dates, and results of medical tests.	1	2	3	4
16. I keep a record of my immunizations.	1	2	3	4
17. I engage in appropriate medical self-care screening procedures.	1	2	3	4
18. I understand which health conditions are covered in my health insurance policy and which are not.	1	2	3	4
19. I know the deductible amount of my health insurance policy.	1	2	3	4
20. I go for selective health examinations according to the recommended schedule.	1	2	3	4

Scoring
70–80 = A highly skilled, discriminating, and assertive health consumer
60–69 = An adequately skilled health consumer
50–59 = A health consumer who tends to be passive
0–49 = A passive consumer

Food Composition Table

Modified from Wardlaw GM, Insel PM: *Perspectives in nutrition,* ed 3,
New York, 1996, The McGraw-Hill Companies.

Code	Name	Amount	Unit	Grams	Kilocalories	Carbohydrates (g)	Protein (g)	Fat (g)
11001	ALFALFA SEEDS, SPROUTED, FRESH	½	CUP	16.5	5	1	1	0
12067	ALMONDS, TOASTED, UNBLANCHED	½	CUP	71.0	418	16	14	36
19294	APPLE BUTTER	1	TBSP.	18.0	33	9	0	0
9400	APPLE JUICE, UNSWEETENED	¾	CUP	185.8	87	22	0	0
9003	APPLES, FRESH, W/ SKIN	1	MEDIUM	138.0	81	21	0	0
9020	APPLESAUCE, SWEETENED	½	CUP	127.5	97	25	0	0
9019	APPLESAUCE, UNSWEETENED	½	CUP	122.0	52	14	0	0
9024	APRICOTS, CND, JUICE PACK	½	CUP	124.0	60	15	1	0
9022	APRICOTS, CND, WATER PACK	½	CUP	121.5	33	8	1	0
9032	APRICOTS, DRIED, SULFURED	¼	CUP	32.5	77	20	1	0
9021	APRICOTS, FRESH	3	MEDIUM	106.0	51	12	1	0
11015	ASPARAGUS, CND	½	CUP	121.0	23	3	3	1
11011	ASPARAGUS, FRESH	½	CUP	67.0	15	3	2	0
11019	ASPARAGUS, FRZ, CKD	½	CUP	100.0	28	5	3	0
9037	AVOCADOS, FRESH	1	MEDIUM	201.0	324	15	4	31
10124	BACON	1	SLICE	6.0	35	0	2	3
10131	BACON, CANADIAN-STYLE, GRILLED	1	SLICE	21.0	39	0	5	2
62528	BACON, TURKEY	1	SLICE	14.0	25	0	3	2
18001	BAGELS, PLAIN	1	3½ IN.	71.0	195	38	7	1
19400	BANANA CHIPS	1	OUNCE	28.4	147	17	1	10
9040	BANANAS, FRESH	1	MEDIUM	114.0	105	27	1	1
6150	BARBECUE SAUCE	½	CUP	125.0	94	16	2	2
15187	BASS, FRESHWATER, CKD, DRY HEAT	3	OUNCE	85.1	124	0	21	4
16006	BEANS, BAKED, CND. VEGETARIAN	½	CUP	127.0	118	26	6	1
16007	BEANS, BAKED, CND. W/BEEF	½	CUP	133.0	161	22	8	5
16008	BEANS, BAKED, CND. W/ FRANKS	½	CUP	128.5	182	20	9	8
16009	BEANS, BAKED, CND. W/ PORK	½	CUP	126.5	134	25	7	2
16315	BEANS, BLACK, CKD	½	CUP	86.0	114	20	8	0
11056	BEANS, GREEN, CND	½	CUP	68.0	14	3	1	0
11052	BEANS, GREEN, FRESH	½	CUP	55.0	17	4	1	0
11061	BEANS, GREEN, FZN	½	CUP	67.5	18	4	1	0
16029	BEANS, KIDNEYS, CND	½	CUP	128.0	104	19	7	0
16073	BEANS, LIMA, CND	½	CUP	120.5	95	18	6	0
11040	BEANS, LIMA, FZN	½	CUP	90.0	95	18	6	0
16039	BEANS, NAVY CND	½	CUP	131.0	148	27	10	1
16044	BEANS, PINTO, CND	½	CUP	120.0	94	17	5	0
16103	BEANS, REFRIED, CND	½	CUP	126.5	135	23	8	1
13347	BEEF, CORNED, BRISKET, CKD	3	OUNCE	85.1	213	0	15	16
13355	BEEF, CURED, PASTRAMI	3	OUNCE	85.1	297	3	15	25
13357	BEEF, CURED, SAUSAGE, SMOKED	3	OUNCE	85.1	265	2	12	23
13358	BEEF, CURED, SMOKED, CHOPPED	3	OUNCE	85.1	105	2	17	4
13360	BEEF, CURED, THIN-SLICED	3	OUNCE	85.1	151	5	24	3
13300	BEEF, GROUND, EXTRA LEAN, PAN-FRIED	3	OUNCE	85.1	217	0	21	14
13307	BEEF, GROUND, LEAN, PAN-FRIED	3	OUNCE	85.1	234	0	21	16
13312	BEEF, GROUND, REGULAR, BROILED	3	OUNCE	85.1	246	0	20	18
13314	BEEF, GROUND, REGULAR, PAN-FRIED	3	OUNCE	85.1	260	0	020	19
13327	BEEF, LIVER, CKD, PAN-FRIED	3	OUNCE	85.1	185	7	23	7
13004	BEEF, STEAKS AND ROASTS, CKD, 1/4 IN. FAT	3	OUNCE	85.1	259	0	22	18
7043	BEEF, THIN SLICED	1	SLICE	4.2	7	0	1	0
11081	BEETS, CKD	½	CUP	85.0	37	8	1	0
18009	BISCUITS, PLAIN OR BUTTERMILK	1	EACH	35.0	127	17	2	6
9050	BLUEBERRIES, FRESH	½	CUP	72.5	41	10	0	0
9055	BLUEBERRIES, FROZEN, SWEETENED	½	CUP	115.0	93	25	0	0
10126	BOLOGNA	1	SLICE	23.0	57	0	4	5
12078	BRAZILNUTS, DRIED, UNBLANCHED	½	CUP	70.0	459	9	10	46
19167	BREAD PUDDING	1	CUP	252.0	423	62	13	15
18080	BREAD STICKS, PLAIN	1	STICK	10.0	41	7	1	1
18020	BREAD, BANANA	1	SLICE	60.0	203	33	3	7
18024	BREAD, CORNBREAD	1	PIECE	65.0	173	28	4	5
18025	BREAD, CRACKED-WHEAT	1	SLICE	25.0	65	12	2	1

Saturated Fat (g)	Monounsaturated Fat (g)	Polyunsaturated Fat (g)	Fiber (g)	Cholesterol (g)	Folate (g)	Vitamin A (RE)	Vitamin B6 (mg)	Vitamin B12 (μg)	Vitamin C (mg)	Vitamin E (mg)	Riboflavin (mg)	Thiamin (mg)	Calcium (mg)	Iron (mg)	Magnesium (mg)	Niacin (mg)	Phosphorus (mg)	Potassium (mg)	Sodium (mg)	Zinc (mg)
0	0	0	0	0	6	3	0	0	1	-	0	0	5	.2	4	.1	12	13	1	.2
3	23	8	8	0	45	0	.1	0	0	-	.4	.1	201	3.5	216	2	390	549	8	3.5
-	-	-	0	0	0	0	0	0	0	-	0	0	1	0	1	0	1	16	0	0
0	0	0	-	0	0	0	.1	0	77	0	0	0	13	.7	6	-	13	221	6	.1
0	0	0	4	0	4	7	.1	0	8	.8	0	0	10	.2	7	.1	10	159	0	.1
0	0	0	2	0	1	1	0	0	2	-	0	0	5	.4	4	.2	9	78	4	.1
0	0	0	1	0	1	4	0	0	1	-	0	0	4	.1	4	.2	9	92	2	0
0	0	0	2	0	2	210	.1	0	6	-	0	0	15	.4	12	.4	25	205	5	.1
0	0	0	2	0	2	157	.1	0	4	-	0	0	10	.4	9	.5	16	233	4	.1
0	0	0	3	0	3	235	.1	0	1	-	0	0	15	1.5	15	1	38	448	3	.2
0	0	0	3	0	9	277	.1	0	11	-	0	0	15	.6	8	.6	20	314	1	.3
0	0	0	2	0	116	64	.1	0	22	-	.1	.1	19	2.2	12	1.2	52	208	472	.5
0	0	1	0	86	39	.1	0	9	-	26	.1	.1	14	.6	12	.8	38	183	1	3
0	0	0	-	0	135	82	0	0	24	-	.1	.1	23	.6	13	1	55	218	4	.6
5	19	4	12	0	124	123	.6	0	16	-	.2	.2	22	2.1	78	3.9	82	1204	20	.8
1	1	0	0	5	0	0	0	.1	0	-	0	0	1	.1	1	.4	20	29	96	.2
1	1	0	0	12	1	0	.1	.2	5	-	0	.2	2	.2	4	1.5	62	82	325	.4
1	-	-	-	10	-	0	-	-	0	-	-	-	0	0	-	-	-	-	170	.4
0	0	0	1	0	16	0	0	0	0	-	.2	.4	53	2.5	21	3.2	68	72	379	.6
8	1	0	2	0	4	2	.1	0	2	-	0	0	5	.4	22	.2	16	152	2	.2
0	0	0	3	0	22	9	.7	0	10	.3	.1	.1	7	.4	33	.6	23	451	1	.2
0	1	1	1	0	5	109	.1	0	9	-	0	0	24	1.1	22	1.1	25	217	1019	.2
1	2	1	0	74	14	30	.1	2	2	-	.1	.1	88	1.6	32	1.3	218	388	77	.7
0	0	0	6	0	30	22	.2	0	4	-	.1	.2	64	.4	41	.5	132	376	504	1.8
2	2	0	-	29	58	28	.1	0	2	-	.1	.1	60	2.1	33	1.3	108	426	632	1.6
3	4	1	9	8	39	19	.1	0	3	-	.1	.1	62	2.2	36	1.2	134	302	553	2.4
1	1	0	7	9	46	23	.1	0	3	-	0	.1	67	2.2	43	.6	137	391	524	1.8
0	0	0	-	0	128	1	.1	0	0	-	.1	.2	23	1.8	60	.4	120	305	204	1
0	0	0	1	0	22	24	0	0	3	-	0	0	18	.6	9	.1	13	74	171	.2
0	0	0	2	0	20	37	0	0	9	-	.1	0	20	.8	14	.4	21	115	3	.1
0	0	0	2	0	6	36	0	0	6	-	0	0	30	.6	14	.3	16	76	9	.4
0	0	0	-	0	63	0	.1	0	2	-	.1	.1	35	1.6	40	.6	134	329	444	.7
0	0	0	6	0	61	0	.1	0	0	-	0	.1	25	2.2	47	.3	89	265	405	.8
0	0	0	-	0	14	15	.1	0	5	-	0	.1	25	1.8	50	.7	101	370	26	.5
0	0	0	7	0	82	0	.1	0	1	-	.1	.1	62	2.4	62	.6	176	377	587	1
0	0	0	4	0	72	0	.1	0	6	-	.1	.1	44	1.9	32	.4	110	361	499	.8
1	1	0	7	0	106	0	.1	0	8	-	.1	.1	58	2.2	49	.6	106	497	536	1.7
5	8	1	0	83	5	0	.2	1.4	14	-	.1	0	7	1.6	10	2.6	106	123	964	3.9
9	12	1	0	79	6	0	.2	1.5	3	-	.1	.1	8	1.6	15	4.3	128	194	1044	3.6
10	11	1	0	57	3	0	.1	1.6	10	-	.1	0	6	1.5	11	2.7	89	150	962	2.4
2	2	0	0	39	7	0	.3	1.5	18	-	.1	.1	7	2.4	18	3.9	154	321	1070	3.3
1	1	0	0	35	9	0	.3	2.2	12	-	.2	.1	9	2.3	16	4.5	143	365	1224	3.4
5	6	1	0	69	8	0	.2	1.7	0	-	.2	.1	6	2	18	4	136	265	60	4.6
6	7	1	0	71	8	0	.2	1.9	0	-	.02	.1	9	1.9	17	4.1	135	254	65	4.4
7	8	1	0	77	8	0	.2	2.5	0	-	.2	0	9	2.1	17	4.9	145	248	71	4.4
8	8	1	0	76	8	0	.2	2.3	0	-	.2	0	9	2.1	17	5	145	255	71	43
2	1	1	0	410	187	9125	1.2	95.1	20	-	3.5	.2	9	5.3	20	12.3	392	310	90	4.6
7	8	1	0	75	6	0	.3	2.1	0	-	.2	.1	9	2.2	19	3.1	173	266	53	5
0	0	0	0	2	0	0	0	.1	1	-	0	0	0	.1	1	.2	7	18	60	.2
0	0	0	1	0	68	3	.1	0	3	-	0	0	14	.7	20	.3	32	259	65	.3
1	2	2	-	0	2	0	0	0	0	-	.1	.1	17	1.2	6	1.2	151	78	368	.2
-	-	-	2	0	5	7	0	0	9	-	.1	0	4	.1	4	.3	7	65	4	.1
-	-	-	2	0	8	5	.1	0	1	-	.1	0	7	.4	2	.3	8	69	1	.1
2	2	0	0	14	1	0	.1	.2	8	-	0	.1	3	.2	3	.9	32	65	272	.5
11	16	17	4	0	3	0	.2	0	0	-	.1	.7	123	2.4	158	1.1	420	420	1	3.2
6	5	2	-	166	33	164	.2	-	2	-	.6	.2	287	2.8	48	1.6	275	564	582	1.3
0	0	0	-	0	3	0	0	0	0	-	.1	.1	2	.4	3	.5	12	12	66	.1
2	3	2	-	26	7	14	.1	.1	1	-	.1	.1	11	.8	8	.9	34	79	119	.2
1	1	2	-	26	12	35	.1	.1	0	-	.2	.2	162	1.6	16	1.5	110	96	428	.4
0	0	0	1	0	10	0	.1	0	0	-	.1	.1	11	.7	13	.9	38	44	135	.3

Code	Name	Amount	Unit	Grams	Kilocalories	Carbohydrates (g)	Protein (g)	Fat (g)
18342	BREAD, DINNER ROLL, PLAIN	1	EACH	35.0	105	18	3	3
18347	BREAD, DINNER ROLL, WHEAT	1	EACH	33.0	90	15	3	2
18029	BREAD, FRENCH OR VIENNA	1	SLICE	25.0	69	13	2	1
18033	BREAD, ITALIAN	1	SLICE	30.0	81	15	3	1
18035	BREAD, MIXED-GRAIN	1	SLICE	26.0	65	12	3	1
18037	BREAD, OAT BRAN	1	SLICE	30.0	71	12	3	1
18041	BREAD, PITA, WHITE, ENRICHED	1	PITA	60.0	165	33	5	1
18042	BREAD, PITA, WHOLE-WHEAT	1	PITA	64.0	170	35	6	2
18044	BREAD, PUMPERNICKEL	1	SLICE	32.0	80	15	3	1
18046	BREAD, PUMPKIN	1	SLICE	60.0	199	31	2	8
18047	BREAD, RAISIN	1	SLICE	26.0	71	14	2	1
18060	BREAD, RYE	1	SLICE	32.0	83	15	3	1
18064	BREAD, WHEAT (INCLUDES WHEAT BERRY)	1	SLICE	25.0	65	12	2	1
18069	BREAD, WHITE	1	SLICE	25.0	67	12	2	1
11091	BROCCOLI, CKD	½	CUP	78.0	22	4	2	0
11093	BROCCOLI, FRZ, CHOPPED, CKD	½	CUP	92.0	26	5	3	0
18151	BROWNIES	1	EACH	56.0	227	36	3	9
11099	BRUSSELS SPROUTS, CKD	½	CUP	78.0	30	7	2	0
62601	BUFFALO (CHICKEN) WINGS	4	EACH	91.0	190	2	18	12
18351	BUNS, HAMBURGER OR HOT DOG, MIXED-GRAIN	1	EACH	43	113	19	4	3
18350	BUNS, HAMBURGER OR HOT DOG, PLAIN	1	EACH	43.0	123	22	4	2
4146	BUTTER, W/ SALT	1	PAT	5.0	36	0	0	4
1145	BUTTE,R W/O SALT	1	PAT	5.0	36	0	0	4
1002	BUTTER, WHIPPED	1	TBSP.	11.0	79	0	0	9
11110	CABBAGE, CKD	½	CUP	75.0	17	3	1	0
11749	CABBAGE, FRESH	1	CUP	70.0	17	4	1	0
18096	CAKE, CHOCOLATE, W/ CHOCOLATE FROSTING	1	SLICE	64.0	235	35	3	10
18110	CAKE, FRUITCAKE	1	PIECE	43.0	139	26	1	4
18113	CAKE, GERMAN CHOCOLATE, W/ FROSTING	1	SLICE	111.0	404	55	4	21
18119	CAKE, PINEAPPLE UPSIDE-DOWN	1	SLICE	115.0	367	58	4	14
18120	CAKE, POUND	1	SLICE	28.4	110	14	2	6
18133	CAKE, SPONGE	1	SLICE	3.0	110	23	2	1
18139	CAKE, WHITE, W/ FROSTING	1	SLICE	74.0	264	42	4	9
18140	CAKE, YELLOW, W/ CHOCOLATE FROSTING	1	SLICE	64.0	243	35	2	11
18141	CAKE, YELLOW, W/ VANILLA FROSTING	1	SLICE	64.0	239	38	2	9
11655	CARROT JUICE, CND	¾	CUP	184.5	74	17	2	0
11125	CARROTS, CKD	½	CUP	78.0	35	8	1	0
11124	CARROTS, FRESH	1	MEDIUM	60.0	26	6	1	0
11131	CARROTS, FRZ, CKD	½	CUP	73.0	26	6	1	0
12585	CASHEWS, DRY ROASTED	½	CUP	68.5	393	22	10	32
15235	CATFISH, CHANNEL, FARMED, CKD, DRY HEAT	3	OUNCE	85.1	129	0	16	7
15011	CATFISH, FRIED	3	OUNCE	85.1	195	7	15	11
11935	CATSUP	1	TBSP.	15.0	16	4	0	0
11135	CAULIFLOWER, FRESH	½	CUP	50.0	13	3	1	0
11138	CAULIFLOWER, FRZ, CKD	½	CUP	90.0	17	3	1	0
11144	CELERY, CKD	½	CUP	75.0	14	3	1	0
11143	CELERY, FRESH	½	CUP	60.0	10	2	0	0
8183	CEREALS, WHOLE WHEAT HOT NATURAL CEREAL	1	CUP	242.0	150	33	5	1
1150	CHEESE SPREAD, PAST. PROCESSED, AMERICAN	2	OUNCE	56.7	165	5	9	12
1147	CHEESE, AMERICAN, PASTEURIZED PROCESSED	2	OUNCE	56.7	213	1	13	18
1004	CHEESE, BLUE	1½	OUNCE	42.5	150	1	9	12
1005	CHEESE, BRICK	1½	OUNCE	42.5	158	1	10	13
1006	CHEESE, BRIE	1½	OUNCE	42.5	142	0	9	12
1008	CHEESE, CARAWAY	1½	OUNCE	42.5	160	1	11	12
1009	CHEESE, CHEDDAR, AMERICAN DOMESTIC	1½	OUNCE	42.5	171	1	11	14
1011	CHEESE, COLBY	1½	OUNCE	42.5	167	1	10	14
1015	CHEESE, COTTAGE, LOWFAT, 2% FAT	1½	OUNCE	42.5	38	2	6	1
1017	CHEESE, CREAM	1½	OUNCE	42.5	148	1	1	15
62554	CHEESE, CREAM, FAT FREE	2	TBSP.	35.0	35	2	5	0
62553	CHEESE, CREAM LIGHT	2	TBSP.	32.0	70	2	3	5

Saturated Fat (g)	Monounsaturated Fat (g)	Polyunsaturated Fat (g)	Fiber (g)	Cholesterol (g)	Folate (g)	Vitamin A (RE)	Vitamin B6 (mg)	Vitamin B12 (µg)	Vitamin C (mg)	Vitamin E (mg)	Riboflavin (mg)	Thiamin (mg)	Calcium (mg)	Iron (mg)	Magnesium (mg)	Niacin (mg)	Phosphorus (mg)	Potassium (mg)	Sodium (mg)	Zinc (mg)
1	1	0	1	0	11	0	0	0	0	-	.1	.2	42	1.1	8	1.4	41	47	182	.3
1	1	0	-	0	5	0	0	0	0	-	.1	.1	58	1.2	14	1.3	39	44	112	.3
0	0	0	1	0	8	0	0	0	0	-	.1	.1	19	.6	7	1.2	26	28	152	.2
0	0	0	1	0	9	0	0	0	0	-	.1	.1	23	.9	8	1.3	31	33	175	.3
0	0	0	2	0	12	0	.1	0	0	-	.1	.1	24	.9	14	1.1	46	53	127	.3
0	0	1	1	0	8	0	0	0	0	-	.1	.2	20	.9	9	1.4	32	34	122	.3
0	0	0	1	0	14	0	0	0	0	-	.2	.4	52	1.6	16	2.8	58	72	322	.5
0	0	1	5	0	22	0	.1	0	0	-	.1	.2	10	1.8	44	1.8	115	109	340	1
0	0	0	2	0	11	0	0	0	0	-	.1	.1	22	.9	17	1	57	67	215	.5
1	2	4	-	26	7	334	0	0	1	-	.1	.1	11	1	8	.8	32	55	188	.2
0	1	0	1	0	9	0	0	0	0	-	.1	.1	17	.8	7	.9	28	59	101	.2
0	0	0	2	0	16	0	0	0	-	-	.1	.1	12	.9	13	1.2	40	53	211	.4
0	0	0	1	0	10	0	0	0	0	-	.1	.1	26	.8	12	1	38	50	133	.3
0	0	0	1	0	9	0	0	-	0	-	.1	.1	27	.8	6	1	24	20	135	.2
	0	0	2	0	39	108	.1	0	58	-	.1	0	36	.7	19	.4	46	228	20	.3
0	0	0	3	0	52	174	.1	0	37	-	.1	.1	47	.6	18	.4	51	166	22	.3
2	5	1	1	10	7	11	0	.1	0	-	.1	.1	16	1.3	17	1	57	83	175	.4
0	0	0	3	0	47	56	.1	0	48	-	.1	.1	28	.9	16	.5	44	247	16	.3
-	-	-	100	-	60	-	-	-	1	-	-	-	24	.4	-	-	-	-	900	-
	1	0	2	0	12	0	0	0	0	-	.1	.2	41	1.7	21	1.9	52	65	197	.5
	1	0	-	0	12	0	0	0	0	-	.1	.2	60	1.4	9	1.7	38	61	241	.3
3	1	0	0	11	0	38	0	0	0	.1	0		1	0	0	0	1	1	1	0
3	1	0	0	11	0	38	0	0	0	.1	0	0	1	0	0	0	1	1	41	0
6	3	0	0	24	0	83	0	0	0	-	0	0	3	0	0	0	3	3	91	0
0	0	0	2	0	15	10	.1	0	15	-	0	0	23	1	6	.2	11	73	6	.1
0	0	0	-	0	40	9	.1	0	36	-	0	0	33	.4	11	.2	16	172	13	.1
3	6	1	2	29	5	18	-	.1	0	-	.1	0	28	1.4	22	.4	78	128	214	.4
0	2	1	2	2	1	8	0	0	0	-	0	0	14	.9	7	.3	22	66	116	.1
5	9	5	-	53	4	23	0	.1	0	-	.1	.1	53	1.2	19	1.1	173	151	369	.5
3	6	4	-	25	8	75	0	.1	1	-	.2	.2	138	1.7	15	1.4	94	129	367	.4
3	2	0	-	63	3	44	0	.1	0	-	.1	0	10	.4	3	.4	39	34	113	.1
0	0	0	-	39	5	17	0	.1	0	-	.1	1	27	1	4	.7	52	38	93	.2
2	4	2	-	1	5	12	0	.1	0	-	.2	.1	96	1.1	9	1.1	69	70	242	.2
3	6	1	1	35	5	17	0	.1	0	-	.1	.1	24	1.3	19	.8	103	114	216	.4
2	4	3	-	36	6	12	0	.1	0	-	.1	0	40	.7	4	.3	92	34	220	.2
0	0	0	1	0	7	4751	.4	0	16	-	.1	.2	44	.8	26	.7	77	539	54	.3
0	0	0	3	0	11	1915	.2	0	2	-	0	0	24	.5	10	.4	23	177	51	.2
0	0	0	2	0	8	1688	.1	0	6	-	0	.1	16	.3	9	.6	26	194	21	.1
0	0	0	3	0	8	1292	.1	0	2	-	0	0	20	.3	7	.3	19	115	43	.2
6	19	5	2	0	47	0	.2	0	0	-	.1	.1	31	4.1	178	1	336	387	438	3.8
2	4	1	0	54	6	13	.1	2.4	1	-	.1	.4	8	.7	22	2.1	208	273	68	.9
3	5	3	-	69	14	7	.2	1.6	0	-	.1	.1	37	1.2	23	1.9	184	289	238	.7
0	0	0	0	0	2	15	0	0	2	-	0	0	3	.1	3	.2	6	72	178	0
0	0	0	1	0	29	1	.1	0	23	-	0	0	11	.2	8	.3	22	152	15	.1
0	0	0	2	0	37	2	.1	0	28	-	0	0	15	.4	8	.3	22	125	16	.1
0	0	0	1	0	17	10	.1	0	5	-	0	0	32	.3	9	.2	19	213	68	.1
0	0	0	1	0	17	8	.1	0	4	-	0	0	24	.2	7	.2	15	172	52	.1
-	-	-	-	0	27	0	.2	0	0	-	.1	.2	17	1.5	53	2.2	167	172	564	1.2
8	4	0	0	31	4	107	.1	.2	0	-	.2	0	319	.2	16	.1	496	137	921	1.5
11	5	1	0	54	4	164	0	.4	0	-	.2	0	349	.2	13	0	252	92	369	1.7
8	3	0	0	32	15	97	.1	.5	0	-	.2	0	224	.1	10	.4	165	109	592	1.1
8	4	0	0	40	9	128	0	.5	0	-	.1	0	286	.2	10	.1	192	58	238	1.1
7	3	0	0	43	28	77	.1	.7	0	-	.2	0	78	.2	9	.2	80	65	268	1
8	4	0	0	40	8	123	0	.1	0	-	.2	0	286	.3	9	.1	208	40	293	1.3
9	4	0	0	45	8	129	0	.4	0	-	.2	0	307	.3	12	0	218	42	264	1.3
9	4	0	0	40	8	117	0	.4	0	-	.2	0	291	.3	11	0	194	54	257	1.3
1	0	0	0	4	6	9	0	.3	0	-	.1	0	29	.1	3	.1	64	41	173	.2
9	4	1	0	47	6	186	0	.2	0	-	.1	0	34	.5	3	0	44	51	126	.2
0	-	-	-	5	-	100	-	-	0	-	-	-	120	0	-	-	-	-	180	-
4	-	-	-	15	-	80	-	-	0	-	-	-	48	8	-	-	-	-	150	-

Code	Name	Amount	Unit	Grams	Kilocalories	Carbohydrates (g)	Protein (g)	Fat (g)
62579	CHEESE, FAT FREE SLICES, WHITE	1	SLICE	21.3	30	2	5	0
62578	CHEESE, FAT FREE SLICES, YELLOW	1	SLICE	21.3	30	2	5	0
1019	CHEESE, FETA	1½	OUNCE	42.5	112	2	6	9
1156	CHEESE, GOAT, HARD TYPE	1½	OUNCE	42.5	192	1	13	15
1159	CHEESE, GOAT, SOFT TYPE	1½	OUNCE	42.5	114	0	8	9
1022	CHEESE, GOUDA	1½	OUNCE	42.5	152	1	11	12
1025	CHEESE, MONTEREY	1½	OUNCE	42.5	159	0	10	13
1028	CHEESE, MOZZARELLA, PART SKIM MILK	1½	OUNCE	42.5	108	1	10	7
1026	CHEESE, MOZZARELLA, WHOLE MILK	1½	OUNCE	42.5	120	1	8	9
1161	CHEESE, MOZZARELLA, SUBSTITUTE	1½	OUNCE	42.5	105	10	5	5
1032	CHEESE, PARMESAN, GRATED	1	TBSP.	5.0	23	0	2	2
1035	CHEESE, PROVOLONE	1½	OUNCE	42.5	149	1	11	11
1037	CHEESE, RICOTTA, PART SKIM MILK	1½	OUNCE	42.5	59	2	5	3
1036	CHEESE, RICOTTA, WHOLE MILK	1½	OUNCE	42.5	74	1	5	6
1038	CHEESE, ROMANO	1½	OUNCE	42.5	164	2	14	11
1040	CHEESE, SWISS, DOMESTIC	1½	OUNCE	42.5	160	1	12	12
1044	CHEESE, SWISS, PASTEURIZED PROCESSED	2	OUNCE	56.7	189	1	14	14
18148	CHEESECAKE, NO-BAKE TYPE	1	SLICE	80.0	219	28	4	10
9072	CHERRIES, SWEET, CND, JUICE PACK	½	CUP	125.0	67	17	1	0
9070	CHERRIES, SWEET, FRESH	½	CUP	72.5	52	12	1	1
9076	CHERRIES, SWEET, FROZEN, SWEETENED	½	CUP	129.5	115	29	1	0
18308	CHERRY PIE	1	SLICE	125.0	325	50	3	14
19033	CHEX MIX	1	CUP	42.5	181	28	5	7
5283	CHICKEN SALAD SANDWICH SPREAD	3	OUNCE	85.1	170	6	10	11
5054	CHICKEN, BACK, MEAT ONLY, CKD, FRIED	3	OUNCE	85.1	245	5	26	13
5055	CHICKEN, BACK, MEAT ONLY, CKD, ROASTED	3	OUNCE	85.1	203	0	24	11
5050	CHICKEN, BACK, MEAT & SKIN, CKD, FRIED, FLR	3	OUNCE	85.1	282	6	24	18
5051	CHICKEN, BACK, MEAT & SKIN, CKD, ROASTED	3	OUNCE	85.1	255	0	22	18
5063	CHICKEN, BREAST, MEAT ONLY, CKD, FRIED	3	OUNCE	85.1	159	0	28	4
5064	CHICKEN, BREAST, MEAT ONLY, CKD, ROASTED	3	OUNCE	85.1	140	0	26	3
5059	CHICKEN, BREAST, MEAT & SKIN, CKD, FRIED, FLR	3	OUNCE	85.1	189	1	27	8
5060	CHICKEN, BREAST, MEAT & SIN, CKD, ROASTED	3	OUNCE	85.1	168	0	25	7
5044	CHICKEN, DARK MEAT, MEAT ONLY, CKD, FRIED	3	OUNCE	85.1	203	2	25	10
5045	CHICKEN, DARK MEAT, MEAT ONLY, CKD, ROASTED	3	OUNCE	85.1	174	0	23	8
5036	CHICKEN, DARK MEAT, MEAT & SKIN, CKD, FRIED, FLR	3	OUNCE	85.1	242	3	23	14
5037	CHICKEN, DARK MEAT, MEAT & SKIN, CKD, ROASTED	3	OUNCE	85.1	215	0	22	13
5072	CHICKEN, DRUMSTICK, MEAT ONLY, CKD, FRIED	3	OUNCE	85.1	166	0	24	7
5073	CHICKEN, DRUMSTICK, MEAT ONLY, CKD, ROASTED	3	OUNCE	85.1	146	0	24	5
5068	CHICKEN, DRUMSTICK, MEAT & SKIN CKD, FRIED, FLR	3	OUNCE	85.1	208	1	23	12
5069	CHICKEN, DRUMSTICK, MEAT & SKIN, CKD, ROASTED	3	OUNCE	85.1	184	0	23	9
5081	CHICKEN, LEG, MEAT ONLY, CKD, FRIED	3	OUNCE	85.1	177	1	24	8
5082	CHICKEN, LEG, MEAT ONLY, CKD, ROASTED	3	OUNCE	85.1	162	0	23	7
5077	CHICKEN, LEG, MEAT & SKIN, CKD, FRIED, FLR	3	OUNCE	85.1	216	2	23	12
5078	CHICKEN, LEG, MEAT & SKIN, CKD, ROASTED	3	OUNCE	85.1	197	0	22	11
5097	CHICKEN, THIGH, MEAT ONLY, CKD, FRIED	3	OUNCE	85.1	185	1	24	9
5098	CHICKEN, THIGH, MEAT ONLY, CKD, ROASTED	3	OUNCE	85.1	178	0	22	9
5093	CHICKEN, THIGH, MEAT & SKIN, CKD, FRIED, FLR	3	OUNCE	85.1	223	3	23	13
5094	CHICKEN, THIGH, MEAT & SKIN, CKD, ROASTED	3	OUNCE	85.1	210	0	21	13
5106	CHICKEN, WING, MEAT ONLY, CKD, FRIED	3	OUNCE	85.1	179	0	26	8
5107	CHICKEN, WING, MEAT ONLY, CKD, ROASTED	3	OUNCE	85.1	173	0	26	7
5102	CHICKEN, WING, MEAT & SKIN, CKD, FRIED, FLR	3	OUNCE	85.1	273	2	22	19
5103	CHICKEN, WING, MEAT & SKIN, CKD, ROASTED	3	OUNCE	85.1	247	0	23	175
16058	CHICKPEAS, CND	½	CUP	120.0	143	27	6	1
16059	CHILI W/BEANS, CND	½	CUP	127.5	143	15	7	7
19183	CHOCOLATE PUDDING	1	CUP	298.1	396	68	8	12
15158	CLAMS, CKD, BREADED AND FRIED	3	OUNCE	85.1	172	9	12	9
15160	CLAMS, CND, DRAINED SOLIDS	3	OUNCE	85.1	126	4	22	2
19219	COCONUT CREAM PUDDING	1	CUP	280.0	291	50	9	7
15016	COD, ATLANTIC, CKD, DRY HEAT	3	OUNCE	85.1	89	0	19	1
15017	COD, ATLANTIC, CND	3	OUNCE	85.1	89	0	19	1

Saturated Fat (g)	Monounsaturated Fat (g)	Polyunsaturated Fat (g)	Fiber (g)	Cholesterol (g)	Folate (g)	Vitamin A (RE)	Vitamin B$_6$ (mg)	Vitamin B$_{12}$ (µg)	Vitamin C (mg)	Vitamin E (mg)	Riboflavin (mg)	Thiamin (mg)	Calcium (mg)	Iron (mg)	Magnesium (mg)	Niacin (mg)	Phosphorus (mg)	Potassium (mg)	Sodium (mg)	Zinc (mg)
0	-	-	0	0	-	40	-	-	0	-	-	-	120	0	-	-	-	18	310	-
0	-	-	0	0	-	40	-	-	0	-	-	-	120	0	-	-	-	18	310	-
6	2	0	0	38	14	54	.2	.7	0	-	.4	.1	209	.3	8	.4	143	26	475	1.2
10	3	0	-	45	2	663	0	.1	0	-	.5	.1	381	.8	23	1	310	20	147	.7
6	2	0	0	20	5	578	.1	.1	0	-	.2	0	60	.8	7	.2	109	11	156	.4
7	3	0	0	48	9	74	0	.7	0	-	.1	0	298	.1	12	0	232	51	348	1.7
8	4	0	0	38	8	108	0	.4	0	-	.2	0	317	.3	11	0	189	34	228	1.3
4	2	0	0	25	4	75	0	.3	0	-	.1	0	275	.1	10	0	197	36	198	1.2
6	3	0	0	33	3	102	0	.3	0	-	.1	0	220	.1	8	0	158	29	159	.9
2	3	1	0	0	5	186	0	.3	0	-	.2	0	259	.2	17	.1	248	193	291	.8
1	0	0	0	4	0	9	0	.1	0	-	0	0	69	0	3	-	40	5	93	.2
7	3	0	0	29	4	112	0	.6	0	-	.1	0	321	.2	12	.1	211	59	372	1.4
2	1	0	0	13	6	48	0	.1	0	-	.1	0	116	.2	6	0	78	53	53	.6
4	2	0	0	22	5	57	0	.1	0	-	.1	0	88	.2	5	0	67	44	36	.5
7	3	0	0	44	3	60	0	.5	0	-	.2	0	452	.3	17	0	323	37	510	1.1
8	3	0	0	39	3	108	0	.7	0	-	.2	0	409	.1	15	0	257	47	111	1.7
9	4	0	0	48	3	130	0	.7	0	-	.2	0	438	.3	17	0	432	122	777	2
6	3	1	2	34	14	79	0	.2	0	-	.2	.1	138	.4	15	.4	187	169	304	.4
0	0	0	1	0	5	16	0	0	3	-	0	0	17	.7	15	.5	27	164	4	.1
0	0	0	2	0	3	15	0	0	5	-	0	0	11	.3	8	.3	14	162	0	0
0	0	0	1	0	5	25	0	0	1	-	.1	0	16	.5	13	.2	21	258	1	.1
3	7	3	1	0	10	-	.1	0	1	-	0	0	15	.6	10	.3	36	101	308	.2
-	-	-	-	0	0	6	.7	5.3	20	-	.2	.7	15	10.5	27	7.2	80	114	432	.9
3	3	5	0	26	4	36	.1	.3	1	-	.1	0	9	.5	9	1.4	28	156	321	.9
4	5	3	0	79	8	25	.3	.3	0	-	.2	.1	22	1.4	21	6.5	150	213	84	2.4
3	4	3	0	77	6	24	.3	.3	0	-	.2	.1	20	1.2	19	6	140	202	82	2.3
5	7	4	-	76	7	31	.3	.2	0	-	.2	.1	20	1.4	20	6.2		192	77	2.1
5	7	4	0	75	5	84	.2	.2	0	-	.2	.1	18	1.2	17	5.7	131	179	74	1.9
1	1	1	0	77	3	6	.5	.3	0	-	.1	.1	14	1	26	12.6	209	235	67	.9
1	1	1	0	72	3	5	.5	.3	0	-	.1	.1	13	.9	25	11.7	194	218	63	.9
2	3	2	-	76	3	13	.5	.3	0	-	.1	.1	14	1	26	11.7	198	220	65	9
2	3	1	0	71	3	23	.5	.3	0	-	.1	.1	12	.9	23	10.8	182	208	60	.9
3	4	2	0	82	8	20	.3	.3	0	-	.2	.1	15	1.3	21	6	159	215	82	2.5
2	3	2	0	79	7	19	.3	.3	0	-	.2	.1	13	1.1	20	5.6	152	204	79	2.4
4	6	3	-	78	7	26	.3	.3	0	-	.2	.1	14	1.3	20	5.8	150	196	76	2.2
4	5	3	0	77	6	49	.3	.2	0	-	.2	.1	13	1.2	19	5.4	143	187	74	2.1
2	3	2	0	80	8	15	.3	.3	0	-	.2	.1	10	1.1	20	5.2	158	212	82	2.7
1	2	1	0	79	8	15	.3	.3	0	-	.2	.1	10	1.1	20	5.2	156	209	81	2.7
3	5	3	-	77	7	21	.3	.3	0	-	.2	.1	10	1.1	20	5.1	150	195	76	2.5
3	4	2	0	77	7	26	.3	.3	0	-	.2	.1	10	1.1	20	5.1	149	195	77	2.4
2	3	2	0	84	8	17	.3	.3	0	-	.2	.1	11	1.2	21	5.7	164	216	82	2.5
2	3	2	0	80	7	16	.3	.3	0	-	.2	.1	10	1.1	20	5.4	156	206	77	2.4
3	5	3	-	80	7	24	.3	.3	0	-	.2	.1	11	1.2	20	5.6	155	198	75	2.3
3	4	3	0	78	6	33	.3	.3	0	-	.2	.1	10	1.1	20	5.3	148	191	74	2.2
2	3	2	0	87	8	18	.3	.3	0	-	.2	.1	11	1.2	22	6.1	169	220	81	2.4
3	4	2	0	81	7	17	.3	.3	0	-	.2	.1	10	1.1	20	5.5	156	202	75	2.2
3	5	3	-	82	7	25	.3	.3	0	-	.2	.1	12	1.3	21	5.9	159	202	75	2.1
4	5	3	0	79	6	41	.3	.2	0	-	.2	.1	10	1.1	19	5.4	148	189	71	2
2	3	2	0	71	3	15	.5	.3	0	-	.1	0	13	1	18	6.2	139	177	77	1.8
2	2	2	0	72	3	15	.5	.3	0	-	.1	0	14	1	18	6.2	141	179	78	1.8
5	8	4	-	69	3	32	.3	.2	0	-	.1	0	13	1.1	16	5.7	128	151	65	1.5
5	6	4	0	71	3	40	.4	.2	0	-	.1	0	13	1.1	16	5.7	128	156	70	1.5
0	0	1	5	0	80	2	.6	0	5	-	0	0	38	1.6	35	.2	108	206	359	1.3
3	3	0	6	22	29	43	.2	0	2	-	.1	.1	60	4.4	57	.5	196	465	666	2.6
2	5	4	3	9	9	33	.1	0	5	-	.5	.1	268	1.5	63	1	238	537	385	1.3
2	4	2	-	52	15	77	.1	34.2	9	-	.2	.1	54	11.8	12	1.8	160	277	310	1.2
0	0	0	0	57	24	145	.1	84.1	19	-	.4	.1	78	23.8	15	2.9	287	534	95	2.3
5	1	0	-	20	11	140	.4	.7	2	-	.4	.1	316	.6	45	.3	249	445	456	1
0	0	0	0	47	7	12	.2	.9	1	-	1	.1	12	.4	36	2.1	117	208	66	.5
0	0	0	0	47	7	12	.2	.9	1	-	.1	.1	18	.4	35	2.1	221	449	185	.5

Code	Name	Amount	Unit	Grams	Kilocalories	Carbohydrates (g)	Protein (g)	Fat (g)
18104	COFFEECAKE	1	SLICE	63.0	263	29	4	15
11159	COLESLAW	½	CUP	64.0	44	8	1	2
11162	COLLARDS, CKD	½	CUP	64.0	17	4	1	0
11161	COLLARDS, FRESH	1	CUP	36.0	11	3	1	0
11164	COLLARDS, FRZ. CHOPPED, CKD	½	CUP	85.0	31	6	3	0
20092	CORN, CKD	½	CUP	70.0	88	20	2	1
11901	CORN, SWEET, WHITE, CKD	½	CUP	82.0	89	21	3	1
11905	CORN, SWEET, WHITE, CND	½	CUP	82.0	66	15	2	1
11906	CORN, SWEET, WHITE, CND, CREAM STYLE	½	CUP	128.0	92	23	2	1
11900	CORN, SWEET, WHITE, FRESH	½	CUP	77.0	66	15	2	1
11168	CORN, SWEET, YELLOW, CKD	½	CUP	82.0	89	21	3	1
11174	CORN, SWEET, YELLOW, CND, CREAM STYLE	½	CUP	128.0	92	23	2	1
11167	CORN, SWEET, YELLOW, FRESH	½	CUP	77.0	66	15	2	1
15137	CRAB, ALASKA KING, CKD, MOIST HEAT	3	OUNCE	85.1	82	0	16	1
15138	CRAB, ALASKA KING, IMITATION	3	OUNCE	85.1	87	9	10	1
18216	CRACKERS, CRISPBREAD, RYE	1	EACH	10.0	37	8	1	0
18217	CRACKERS, MATZO, PLAIN	1	EACH	28.4	112	24	3	0
18219	CRACKERS, MATZO, WHOLE-WHEAT	1	EACH	28.4	100	22	4	0
18220	CRACKERS, MELBA TOAST, PLAIN	1	EACH	5.0	20	4	1	0
18229	CRACKERS, RITZ	1	EACH	3.0	15	2	0	1
18226	CRACKERS, RYE, WAFERS, PLAIN	1	EACH	25.0	84	20	2	0
18228	CRACKERS, SALTINES	1	EACH	3.0	13	2	0	0
18232	CRACKERS, WHEAT, REGULAR	1	EACH	2.0	9	1	0	0
9078	CRANBERRIES, FRESH	½	CUP	47.5	23	6	0	0
9080	CRANBERRY JUICE BOTTLED	¾	CUP	189.4	108	27	0	0
14240	CRANBERRY-APRICOT JUICE DRINK, BOTTLED	¾	CUP	183.4	117	30	0	0
15243	CRAYFISH, FARMED, CKD, MOIST HEAT	3	OUNCE	85.1	74	0	15	1
18238	CREAM PUFFS, SHELL, W/ CUSTARD FILLING	1	EACH	130.0	335	30	9	20
1067	CREAM SUBSTITUTE, NONDAIRY, LIQUID	1	TBSP.	15.0	20	2	0	1
1069	CREAM SUBSTITUTE, NONDAIRY, POWERED	1	TSP.	2.0	11	1	0	1
1049	CREAM, HALF AND HALF, CREAM AND MILK	1	TBSP.	15.0	20	1	0	2
1053	CREAM, HEAVY WHIPPING	1	TBSP.	15.0	52	0	0	6
1052	CREAM, LIGHT WHIPPING	1	TBSP.	15.0	44	0	0	5
1050	CREAM, LIGHT, COFFEE OR TABLE	1	TBSP.	15.0	29	1	0	3
1054	CREAM, WHIPPED, PRESSURIZED	1	TBSP.	3.0	8	0	0	1
18239	CROISSANTS, BUTTER	1	MEDIUM	57.0	231	26	5	12
18242	CROUTONS, PLAIN	1	CUP	30.0	122	22	4	2
18243	CROUTONS, SEASONED	1	CUP	40.0	186	25	4	7
11205	CUCUMBERS, FRESH	½	CUP	52.0	7	1	0	0
18245	DANISH PASTRY, CHEESE	1	EACH	71.0	266	26	6	16
18246	DANISH PASTRY, FRUIT	1	EACH	71.0	263	34	4	13
18247	DANISH PASTRY, NUT	1	EACH	65.0	280	30	5	16
9087	DATES, DOMESTIC, NATURAL AND DRY	½	CUP	89.0	245	65	2	0
18251	DOUGHNUTS, CHOCOLATE, SUGARED OR GLAZED	1	EACH	42.0	175	24	2	8
18253	DOUGHNUTS, FRENCH CRULLERS, GLAZED	1	EACH	41.0	169	24	1	8
18255	DOUGHNUTS, GLAZED	1	EACH	60.0	242	27	4	14
18248	DOUGHNUTS, PLAIN	1	EACH	47.0	198	23	2	11
18249	DOUGHNUTS, PLAIN, CHOCOLATE-COATED OR FROSTED	1	EACH	43.0	204	21	2	13
18250	DOUGHNUTS, PLAIN, SUGARED OR GLAZED	1	EACH	45.0	192	23	2	10
18254	DOUGHNUTS, W/ CREME FILLING	1	EACH	85.0	307	26	5	21
18256	DOUGHNUTS, W/ JELLY FILLING	1	EACH	85.0	289	33	5	16
18257	ECLAIRS, CUSTARD-FILLED W/ CHOCOLATE GLAZE	1	EACH	62.0	162	15	4	10
19168	EGG CUSTARDS	1	CUP	282.0	296	30	14	13
1142	EGG SUBSTITUTE, FROZEN	1	CUP	240.0	384	8	27	27
1143	EGG SUBSTITUTE, LIQUID	1	CUP	251.0	211	2	30	8
1057	EGGNOG	1	CUP	254.0	342	34	10	19
11210	EGGPLANT, CKD	½	CUP	48.0	13	3	0	0
11209	EGGPLANT, FRESH	½	CUP	41.0	11	2	0	0
1128	EGGS, CHICKEN, WHOLE, CKD, FRIED	1	LARGE	46.0	92	1	6	7
1129	EGGS, CHICKEN, WHOLE, CKD, HARD-BOILED	1	LARGE	50.0	78	1	6	5

Saturated Fat (g)	Monounsaturated Fat (g)	Polyunsaturated Fat (g)	Fiber (g)	Cholesterol (g)	Folate (g)	Vitamin A (RE)	Vitamin B6 (mg)	Vitamin B12 (μg)	Vitamin C (mg)	Vitamin E (mg)	Riboflavin (mg)	Thiamin (mg)	Calcium (mg)	Iron (mg)	Magnesium (mg)	Niacin (mg)	Phosphorus (mg)	Potassium (mg)	Sodium (mg)	Zinc (mg)
4	8	2	2	20	20	18	0	.1	0	-	.1	.1	34	1.2	14	1.1	68	77	221	.5
0	0	1	-	5	17	52	.1	0	21	-	0	0	29	.4	6	.2	20	116	15	.1
-	-	-	1	0	4	175	0	0	8	-	0	0	15	.1	4	.2	5	84	10	.1
-	-	-	1	0	4	120	0	0	8	-	0	0	10	.1	3	.1	4	61	7	0
-	-	-	-	0	65	508	.1	0	22	-	.1	0	179	1	26	.5	23	213	43	.2
0	0	0	3	0	4	4	0	0	0	-	0	0	1	.2	25	.4	53	22	0	.4
0	0	0	5	0	38	0	0	0	5	-	.1	.2	26	1.3	84	204	14	.4	
0	0	0	2	0	57	0	.1	0	6	-	.1	0	4	.5	22	1.2	65	172	365	.7
0	0	0	2	0	35	0	0	0	5	-	0	.2	2	.4	28	1.3	69	208	12	.3
0	0	0	2	0	38	18	0	0	5	-	.1	.2	2	.5	26	1.3	84	204	14	.4
0	0	0	2	0	40	13	0	0	7	-	.1	0	4	.7	16	1	53	160	265	.3
0	0	0	2	0	57	13	.1	0	6	-	.1	0	4	.5	22	1.2	65	172	365	.7
0	0	0	2	0	35	22	0	0	5	-	0	.2	2	.4	28	1.3	69	208	12	.3
0	0	0	0	45	43	8	.2	9.8	6	-	0	0	50	.6	54	1.1	238	223	912	6.5
0	0	1	0	17	1	17	0	1.4	0	-	0	0	11	.3	37	.2	240	77	715	.3
0	0	0	2	0	2	0	0	0	0	-	0	0	3	.2	8	.1	27	32	26	.2
0	0	0	1	0	4	0	0	0	0	-	.1	.1	4	.9	7	1.1	25	32	1	.2
0	0	0	3	0	10	0	0	0	0	-	.1	.1	7	1.3	38	1.5	86	90	1	.7
0	0	0	0	0	1	0	0	0	0	-	0	0	5	.2	3	.2	10	10	41	.1
0	0	0	0	0	0	0	0	0	0	-	0	0	4	.1	1	.1	7	4	25	0
0	0	0	-	0	11	1	.1	0	0	-	.1	.1	10	1.5	30	.4	84	124	199	.7
0	0	0	0	0	1	0	0	0	0	-	0	0	4	.2	1	.2	3	4	39	0
0	0	0	0	0	0	0	0	0	0	-	0	0	1	.1	1	.1	4	4	16	0
-	-	-	2	0	1	2	0	0	6	-	0	0	3	.1	2	0	4	34	0	.1
-	-	-	-	0	0	0	0	0	67	-	0	0	6	.3	4	.1	4	34	4	.1
0	-	-	0	0	1	84	0	0	0	-	0	0	17	.3	6	.2	9	112	4	.1
0	0	0	0	117	9	13	.1	2.6	0	-	.1	0	43	.9	28	1.4	205	202	82	1.3
5	8	5	-	174	20	259	.1	.5	0	-	.4	.2	86	1.5	16	1.1	142	150	443	.8
0	1	-	0	0	1	0	0	0	0	-	0	0	1	0	0	0	10	29	12	.1
1	0	0	0	0	0	0	0	0	0	-	0	0	0	0	0	0	8	16	4	0
1	0	0	0	6	0	16	0	0	0	-	0	0	16	0	2	0	14	19	6	.1
3	2	0	0	21	1	63	0	0	0	-	0-	0	10	0	1	0	9	11	6	0
3	1	0	0	17	1	44	0	0	0	-	0	0	10	0	1	0	9	15	5	0
2	1	0	0	10	0	27	0	0	0	-	0	0	14	0	1	0	12	18	6	0
0	0	0	0	2	0	6	0	0	0	-	0	0	3	0	0	0	3	4	4	0
7	3	1	2	43	16	78	0	.2	0	-	.1	.2	21	1.2	9	1.2	60	67	424	.4
0	1	0	2	0	7	0	0	0	0	-	.1	.2	23	1.2	9	1.6	34	37	209	.3
2	4	1	2	1	16	2	0	0	0	-	.2	.2	38	1.1	17	1.9	56	72	495	.4
0	0	0	0	0	7	11	0	0	3	-	0	0	7	.1	6	.1	10	75	1	.1
5	8	2	-	32	18	44	0	.2	0	-	.2	.1	25	1.1	11	1.4	77	70	320	.6
3	7	2	1	15	11	11	-	.1	3	-	.2	.2	33	1.3	11	1.4	63	59	251	.4
4	8	4	1	30	18	9	.1	.1	1	-	.2	.1	61	1.2	21	1.5	72	62	236	.6
-	-	-	7	0	11	4	.2	0	0	-	.1	.1	28	1	31	2	36	580	3	3
2	5	1	1	24	7	11	0	.1	0	-	0	0	89	1	14	.2	68	50	143	.2
2	4	1	-	5	3	-	0	0	0	-	.1	.1	11	.6	5	.6	50	32	141	.1
3	8	2	1	4	13	-	0	.1	0	-	.1	.2	26	1.2	13	1.7	56	65	205	.5
2	5	4	1	17	4	8	0	.1	0	-	.1	.1	21	.9	9	.9	126	60	257	.3
4	7	2	1	25	7	13	0	.2	0	-	0	.1	15	1.1	17	.6	87	49	184	.3
2	5	1	-	14	5	1	0	.1	0	-	.1	.1	27	.5	8	.7	53	46	181	.2
6	11	3	-	20	12	7	0	.1	0	-	.1	.3	21	1.6	17	1.9	65	68	263	.7
4	9	2	-	22	14	7	0	1	1	-	.1	.3	21	1.5	17	1.8	72	67	249	.6
3	4	2	-	79	9	118	0	.2	0	-	.2	.1	39	.7	9	.5	66	73	209	.4
7	4	1	-	245	28	169	.1	.9	1	-	.6	.1	316	.8	39	.2	319	431	217	1.5
5	6	15	0	5	39	324	.3	.8	1	-	.9	.3	175	4.8	36	.3	172	512	479	2.4
2	2	4	0	3	37	542	0	.7	0	-	.8	.3	133	5.3	22	.3	304	828	444	3.3
11	6	1	0	149	2	203	.1	1.1	4	-	.5	.1	330	.5	47	.3	278	420	138	1.2
0	0	0	1	0	7	3	0	0	1	-	0	0	3	.2	6	.3	11	119	1	1
0	0	0	1	0	8	3	0	0	1	-	0	0	3	.1	6	.2	9	89	1	.1
2	3	1	0	211	17	114	.1	.4	0	-	.2	0	25	.7	5	0	89	61	612	.5
2	2	1	0	212	22	84	.1	.6	0	-	.3	0	25	.6	5	0	86	63	62	.5

Code	Name	Amount	Unit	Grams	Kilocalories	Carbohydrates (g)	Protein (g)	Fat (g)
1131	EGGS, CHICKEN, WHOLE, CKD, POACHED	1	LARGE	50.0	75	1	6	5
1132	EGGS, CHICKEN, WHOLE, CKD, SCRAMBLED	½	CUP	110.0	183	2	12	13
18260	ENGLISH MUFFINS, MIXED-GRAIN (INCLUDES GRANOLA)	1	EACH	66.0	155	31	6	1
18258	ENGLISH MUFFINS, PLAIN	1	EACH	57.0	134	26	4	1
18264	ENGLISH MUFFINS, WHEAT	1	EACH	57.0	127	26	5	1
18170	FIG BARS	1	EACH	16.0	56	11	1	1
15027	FISH FILLETS AND STICKS, FRIED	3	OUNCE	85.1	231	20	13	10
15029	FOUNDER, CKD, DRY HEAT	3	OUNCE	85.1	100	0	21	1
18269	FRENCH TOAST, MADE W/ LOWFAT (2%) MILK	1	SLICE	65.0	149	16	5	7
9103	FRUIT SALAD JUICE PACK	½	CUP	124.5	62	16	1	0
9102	FRUIT SALAD, WATER PACK	½	CUP	122.5	37	10	0	0
18173	GRAHAM CRACKERS, PLAIN OR HONEY	1	EACH	70	30	5	0	1
19015	GRANOLA BARS, HARD, PLAIN	1	EACH	28.4	134	18	3	6
19020	GRANOLA BARS, SOFT, PLAIN	1	EACH	28.4	126	19	2	5
9135	GRAPE JUICE, CND OR BOTTLED, UNSWEETENED	¾	CUP	189.4	116	28	1	0
9124	GRAPEFRUIT JUICE, CND, SWEETENED	¾	CUP	187.0	86	21	1	0
9123	GRAPEFRUIT JUICE, CND, UNSWEETENED	¾	CUP	185.2	70	17	1	0
9404	GRAPEFRUIT JUICE, PINK, FRESH	¾	CUP	185.3	72	17	1	0
9128	GRAPEFRUIT JUICE, WHITE, FRESH	¾	CUP	185.3	72	17	1	0
9116	GRAPEFRUIT, FRESH, WHITE	1	MEDIUM	136.0	45	11	1	0
9120	GRAPEFRUIT, SECTIONS, CND, JUICE PACK	½	CUP	124.5	46	11	1	0
9119	GRAPEFRUIT, SECTIONS, CND, WATER PACK	½	CUP	122.0	44	11	1	0
9131	GRAPES, AMERICAN TYPE, FRESH	½	CUP	46.0	29	8	0	0
6114	GRAVY, AU JUS, CND	¼	CUP	59.6	10	1	1	0
6527	GRAVY, UNSPECIFIED TYPE	¼	CUP	65.4	22	4	1	0
15032	GROUPER, CKD, DRY HEAT	3	OUNCE	85.1	100	0	21	1
15037	HALIBUT, CKD, DRY HEAT	3	OUNCE	85.1	119	0	23	3
15196	HALIBUT, GREENLAND, CKD, DRY HEAT	3	OUNCE	85.1	203	0	16	15
7032	HAM AND CHEESE LOAF (OR ROLL), LUNCH MEAT	1	SLICE	28.4	73	0	5	6
7031	HAM SALAD SPREAD	1	TBSP.	15.0	32	2	1	2
7028	HAM, EXTRA LEAN, APPX 5% FAT	1	SLICE	28.4	37	0	5	1
62626	HAMBURGER PATTY, MEATLESS	1	EACH	90.0	140	8	18	4
20030	HOMINY, CND, WHITE	½	CUP	80.0	58	11	1	1
20330	HOMINY, CND, YELLOW	½	CUP	80.0	58	11	1	1
19296	HONEY	1	TBSP.	21.0	64	17	0	0
7022	HOT DOG, BEEF	1	EACH	57.0	180	1	7	16
7024	HOT DOG, CHICKEN	1	EACH	45.0	116	3	6	9
62605	HOT DOG, FAT FREE	1	EACH	50.0	40	2	7	0
7025	HOT DOG, TURKEY	1	EACH	45.0	102	1	6	8
16137	HUMMUS, FRESH	½	CUP	123.0	210	25	6	10
18270	HUSH PUPPIES	1	EACH	22.0	74	10	2	3
19270	ICE CREAM, CHOCOLATE	½	CUP	66.0	143	19	3	7
19090	ICE CREAM, FRENCH VANILLA, SOFT-SERVE	½	CUP	66.5	143	15	3	9
19271	ICE CREAM, STRAWBERRY	½	CUP	66.0	127	18	2	6
19095	ICE CREAM, VANILLA	½	CUP	66.0	133	16	2	7
19088	ICE MILK, VANILLA	½	CUP	66.5	92	15	3	3
19096	ICE MILK, VANILLA, SOFT SERVE	½	CUP	66.5	84	14	3	2
62547	ICED TEA, BOTTLED, ALL FLAVORS	1	CUP	236.6	118	29	0	0
19297	JAMS AND PRESERVES	1	TBSP.	20.0	48	13	0	0
19300	JELLIES	1	TBSP.	19.0	51	13	0	0
9148	KIWIFRUIT, FRESH	1	MEDIUM	76.0	46	11	1	0
17225	LAMB, GROUND, CKD, BROILED	3	OUNCE	85.1	241	0	21	17
17002	LAMB, MEAT AND FAT, CKD	3	OUNCE	85.1	250	0	21	18
4002	LARD	¼	CUP	51.3	462	0	0	51
11247	LEEKS, CKD	½	CUP	5.20	16	4	0	0
11246	LEEKS, FRESH	½	CUP	52.0	32	7	1	0
19380	LEMON PUDDING	1	CUP	298.1	373	75	0	9
9150	LEMONS, FRESH, W/O PEEL	1	MEDIUM	58.0	17	5	1	0
11252	LETTUCE, ICEBERG, FRESH	1	CUP	56.0	7	1	1	0
11253	LETTUCE, LOOSELEAF, FRESH	1	CUP	56.0	10	2	1	0

Saturated Fat (g)	Monounsaturated Fat (g)	Polyunsaturated Fat (g)	Fiber (g)	Cholesterol (g)	Folate (g)	Vitamin A (RE)	Vitamin B6 (mg)	Vitamin B12 (µg)	Vitamin C (mg)	Vitamin E (mg)	Riboflavin (mg)	Thiamin (mg)	Calcium (mg)	Iron (mg)	Magnesium (mg)	Niacin (mg)	Phosphorus (mg)	Potassium (mg)	Sodium (mg)	Zinc (mg)
2	2	1	0	212	18	95	.1	.4	0	-	.2	0	25	.7	5	0	89	60	140	.6
4	5	2	0	387	33	215	.1	.8	0	-	.5	.1	78	1.3	13	.1	187	152	308	1.1
0	1	0	-	0	23	1	.1	0	0	-	.2	.3	129	2	29	2.4	98	103	275	.6
0	0	1	-	0	21	0	0	0	0	-	.2	.3	99	1.4	12	2.2	76	75	264	.4
0	0	0	-	0	22	0	.1	0	0	-	.2	.2	101	1.6	22	1.9	66	106	218	.6
0	1	0	1	0	2	1	0	0	0	-	0	0	10	.5	4	.3	10	33	56	.1
3	4	3	0	95	15	26	.1	1.5	0	-	.2	.1	17	.6	21	1.8	154	222	495	.6
0	0	0	0	58	8	9	.2	2.1	0	-	.1	.1	15	.3	49	1.9	246	293	89	.5
2	3	2	-	75	15	86	0	.2	0	-	.2	.1	65	1.1	11	1.1	76	87	311	.4
0	0	0	-	0	3	756	0	0	4	-	0	0	14	.3	10	.4	17	1454	6	.2
0	0	0	-	0	3	54	0	0-	2	-	0	0	9	.4	6	.5	11	96	4	.1
0	0	0	0	0	1	0	0	0	0	-	0	0	2	.3	2	.3	7		42	.1
1	1	3	2	0	7	4	0	0	0	-	0	.1	17	.8	27	.4	79	95	83	.6
2	1	2	1	0	7	0	0	.1	0	-	0	.1	30	.7	21	.1	65	92	79	.4
0	0	0	0	0	5	2	.1	0	0	-	.1	0	17	.5	19	.5	21	250	6	.1
0	0	0	0	0	19	0	0	0	50	-	0	.1	15	.7	19	.6	21	303	4	.1
0	0	0	0	0	19	2	0	0	54	.1	0	.1	13	.4	19	.4	20	283	2	.2
0	0	0	-	0	19	82	.1	0	70	-	0	.1	17	.4	22	.4	28	300	2	.1
0	0	0	0	0	19	2	.1	0	70	-	0	.1	17	.4	22	.4	28	300	2	.1
0	0	0	1	0	14	1	.1	0	45	-	0	.1	16	.1	12	.4	11	201	0	.1
0	0	0	0	0	11	0	0	0	42	-	0	0	19	.3	14	.3	15	210	9	.1
0	0	0	0	0	11	0	0	0	27	-	0	0	18	.5	12	.3	12	161	2	.1
0	0	0	1	0	2	5	.1	0	2	-	0	0	6	.1	2	.1	5	88	1	0
0	0	0	-	0	1	0	0	.1	1	-	0	0	2	.4	1	.5	18	48	30	.6
0	0	0	-	0	1	0	0	0	0	-	0	0	9	.1	3	.2	12	16	356	.1
0	0	0	0	40	9	43	.3	.6	0	-	0	.1	18	1	31	.3	122	404	45	.4
0	1	1	0	35	12	46	.3	1.2	0	-	.1	.1	51	.9	91	6.1	242	490	59	.5
3	9	1	0	50	1	15	.4	.8	0	-	.1	.1	3	.7	28	1.6	179	293	88	.4
2	3	1	0	16	1	7	.1	.2	.7	-	.1	.2	16	.3	5	1	72	83	381	.6
1	1	0	0	6	0	0	0	.1	1	-	0	.1	1	.1	2	.3	18	22	137	.2
0	1	0	0	13	1	0	.1	.2	7	-	.1	.3	2	.2	5	1.4	62	99	405	.5
2	-	1	5	0	-	0	-	-	0	-	-	.3	96	1.5	-	4	-	-	380	7.5
0	0	0	2	0	1	0	0	0	0-	0	0	0	8	.5	13	0	28	7	168	.8
0	0	0	-	0	1	9	0	0	0	-	0	0	8	.5	13	0	28	7	168	.8
-	-	-	0	0	0	0	0	0	0	-	0	0	1	.1	0	0	1	11	1	0
7	8	1	0	35	2	0	.1	.9	14	-	.1	0	11	.8	2	1.4	50	95	585	1.2
2	4	2	0	45	2	17	.1	.1	0	-	.1	0	43	.9	5	1.4	48	38	617	.5
0	0	0	0	15	-	0	-	-	0	-	-	-	0	.2	-	-	-	-	460	-
3	3	2	0	48	4	0	.1	.1	0	-	.1	0	48	.8	6	1.9	60	81	642	1.4
2	4	4	6	0	73	2	.5	0	10	-	.1	.1	61	1.9	36	.5	138	214	300	1.4
0	1	2	1	10	4	9	0	0	0	-	.1	.1	61	.7	5	.6	42	32	147	.1
4	2	0	-	22	11	79	0	.2	0	-	.1	0	72	.6	19	.1	71	164	50	.4
5	2	0	-	61	6	102	0	.3	1	-	.1	0	87	.1	8	.1	77	118	41	.3
-	-	-	-	19	8	51	0	.2	5	-	.2	0	79	.1	9	.1	66	124	40	.2
4	2	0	0	29	3	77	0	.3	0	-	.2	0	84	.1	9	.1	69	131	53	.5
2	1	0	0	9	4	31	0	.4	1	-	.2	0	92	.1	10	.1	72	140	57	.3
1	1	0	0	8	4	19	0	.3	1	-	.1	0	104	0	9	.1	80	147	47	.4
0	-	-	0	0	-	0	-	-	0-	-	-	-	0	0	-	-	-	-	10	-
0	0	0	0	0	7	0	0	0	2	-	0	0	4	.1	1	0	2	15	8	0
-	-	-	0	0	0	0	0	0	0	-	0	0	2	0	1	0	1	12	7	0
-	-	-	3	0	-	14	-	0	74	-	0	0	20	.3	23	.4	30	252	4	-
7	7	1	0	82	16	0	.1	2.2	-	.1	.2	.1	19	1.5	20	5.7	171	288	69	4
8	8	1	0	82	15	0	.1	2.2	0	-	.2	.1	14	1.6	20	5.7	160	264	61	3.8
20	23	6	0	49	0	0	0	0	0	.6	0	0	0	0	0	0	0	0	0	.1
0	0	0	-	0	13	3	.1	0	2	-	0	0	16	.6	7	.1	9	45	5	0
0	0	0	1	0	33	5	.1	0	6	-	0	0	31	1.1	15	.2	18	94	10	.1
1	4	3	-	0	0	0	0	0	0	-	0	0	6	.2	3	0	15	3	417	.1
0	0	0	2	0	6	2	0	0	31	-	0	0	15	.3	5	.1	9	80	1	0
0	0	0	1	0	31	18	0	0	2	-	0	0	11	.3	5	1	11	88	5	.1
0	0	0	1	0	28	106	0	0	10	-	0	0	38	.8	6	.2	14	148	5	.2

Code	Name	Amount	Unit	Grams	Kilocalories	Carbohydrates (g)	Protein (g)	Fat (g)
11251	LETTUCE, ROMAINE, FRESH	1	CUP	56.0	9	1	1	0
15148	LOBSTER, NORTHERN, CKD, MOIST HEAT	3	OUNCE	85.1	83	1	17	1
62533	MACARONI AND CHEESE	1	CUP	111.9	360	44	1	13
20100	MACARONI, CKD, ENRICHED	1	CUP	140.0	197	40	7	1
20400	MACARONI, CKD, UNENRICHED	1	CUP	140.0	197	40	7	1
20106	MACARONI, VEGETABLE, CKD, ENRICHED	1	CUP	134.0	172	36	6	0
20108	MACARONI, WHOLE-WHEAT, CKD	1	CUP	140.0	174	37	7	1
62535	MANGO JUICE	¾	CUP	179.9	66	16	-	0
9176	MANGOS, FRESH	½	CUP	82.5	54	14	0	0
4128	MARGARINE, IMITATION (APPX 40% FAT)	1	TSP.	4.8	17	0	0	2
4132	MARGARINE, REGULAR, W/ SALT ADDED	1	TSP.	4.7	34	0	0	4
4130	MARGARINE, SOFT, W/ SALT ADDED	1	TSP.	4.7	34	0	0	4
11256	MARINARA SAUCE	½	CUP	125.0	85	13	2	4
19303	MARMALADE, ORANGE	1	TBSP.	20.0	49	13	0	0
19116	MARSHMALLOWS	1	CUP	46.0	146	37	1	0
4018	MAYONNAISE	1	TBSP.	14.7	57	4	0	5
62610	MAYONNAISE, FAT FREE	1	TBSP.	15.0	10	3	0	0
62609	MAYONNAISE, LIGHT	1	TBSP.	15.0	25	1	0	2
9181	MELONS, CANTALOUPE, FRESH	1	WEDGE	80.0	28	7	1	0
9183	MELONS, CASABA, FRESH	1	WEDGE	164.0	43	10	1	0
9184	MELONS, HONEYDEW, FRESH	1	WEDGE	129.0	45	12	1	0
19120	MILK CHOCOLATE	1	BAR	44.0	226	26	3	13
19126	MILK CHOCOLATE COATED PEANUTS	1	OUNCE	28.4	147	14	4	9
19127	MILK CHOCOLATE COATED RAISINS	1	OUNCE	28.4	111	19	1	4
19132	MILK CHOCOLATE W/ ALMONDS	1	BAR	41.0	216	22	4	14
1110	MILK SHAKES, THICK CHOCOLATE	1	CUP	345.4	410	73	11	9
1111	MILK SHAKES, THICK VANILLA	1	CUP	345.4	386	61	13	10
1088	MILK, BUTTERMILK	1	CUP	245.0	99	12	8	2
1103	MILK, CHOCOLATE DRINK, LOWFAT, 2% FAT	1	CUP	250.0	179	26	8	5
1102	MILK, CHOCOLATE DRINK, WHOLE	1	CUP	250.0	208	26	8	8
1095	MILK, CND, CONDENSED, SWEETENED	¼	CUP	76.3	245	42	6	7
1082	MILK, LOWFAT, 1% FAT	1	CUP	244.0	102	12	8	3
1079	MILK, LOWFAT, 2% FAT	1	CUP	244.0	121	12	8	5
1085	MILK, SKIM	1	CUP	245.0	86	12	8	0
1077	MILK, WHOLE, 3.3% FAT	1	CUP	244.0	150	11	8	8
1078	MILK, WHOLE, 3.7% FAT	1	CUP	244.0	157	11	8	9
18274	MUFFINS, BLUEBERRY	1	LARGE	65.0	180	31	4	4
18279	MUFFINS, CORN	1	LARGE	65.0	198	33	4	5
18283	MUFFINS, OAT BRAN	1	LARGE	65.0	176	31	5	5
18273	MUFFINS, PLAIN	1	LARGE	65.0	192	27	4	7
18287	MUFFINS, WHEAT BRAN	1	LARGE	65.0	184	27	5	8
11261	MUSHROOMS, CKD	½	CUP	78.0	21	4	2	0
11264	MUSHROOMS, CND, DRAINED SOLIDS	½	CUP	78.0	19	4	1	0
11260	MUSHROOMS, FRESH	½	CUP	35.0	9	2	1	0
20113	NOODLES, CHINESE, CHOW MEIN	½	CUP	22.5	119	13	2	7
20310	NOODLES, EGG, CKD, ENRICHED	½	CUP	80.0	106	20	4	1
20510	NOODLES, EGG, CKD, UNENRICHED	½	CUP	80.0	106	20	4	1
20112	NOODLES, EGG, SPINACH, CKD, ENRICHED	½	CUP	80.0	106	19	4	1
20115	NOODLES, JAPANESE, SOBA, CKD	½	CUP	57.0	56	12	3	0
15058	OCEAN PERCH, ATLANTIC, CKD, DRY HEAT	3	OUNCE	85.1	103	0	20	2
4053	OIL, OLIVE	1	TBSP.	13.5	119	0	0	14
4042	OIL, PEANUT	1	TBSP.	13.5	119	0	0	14
4058	OIL, SESAME	1	TBSP.	13.6	121	0	0	14
4044	OIL, SOYBEAN	1	TBSP.	13.6	121	0	0	14
4034	OIL, SOYBEAN, (HYDR)	1	TBSP.	13.6	121	0	0	14
4543	OIL, SOYBEAN, (HYDR) & CTTNSD	1	TBSP.	13.6	121	0	0	14
4518	OIL, VEGETABLE, CORN	1	TBSP.	13.6	121	0	0	14
4582	OIL, VEGETABLE, CANOLA	1	TBSP.	13.6	121	0	0	14
4501	OIL, VEGETABLE, COCOA BUTTER	1	TBSP.	13.6	121	0	0	14
4502	OIL, VEGETABLE, COTTONSEED	1	TBSP.	13.6	121	0	0	14

Saturated Fat (g)	Monounsaturated Fat (g)	Polyunsaturated Fat (g)	Fiber (g)	Cholesterol (g)	Folate (g)	Vitamin A (RE)	Vitamin B6 (mg)	Vitamin B12 (µg)	Vitamin C (mg)	Vitamin E (mg)	Riboflavin (mg)	Thiamin (mg)	Calcium (mg)	Iron (mg)	Magnesium (mg)	Niacin (mg)	Phosphorus (mg)	Potassium (mg)	Sodium (mg)	Zinc (mg)
0	0	0	1	0	767	146	0	0	13	-	.1	.1	20	.6	3	.3	25	162	4	.1
0	0	0	0	61	9	22	.1	2.6	0	-	.1	0	52	.3	30	.9	157	299	323	2.5
8	-	-	16	40	-	100	-	-	0	-	-	-	240	1.5	-	-	-	-	1029	-
0	0	0	2	0	10	0	0	0	0	-	.1	.3	10	2	25	2.3	76	43	1.	.7
0	0	0	2	0	10	-	0	0	0	-	0	0	10	.7	25	.6	76	43		.7
0	0	0	6	0	8	7	0	0	0	-	.1	.2	15	.7	25	1.4	67	42	8	.6
0	0	0	6	0	7	0	.1	0	0	-	.1	.2	21	1.5	42	1	125	62	4	1.1
-	-	-	-	0	-	0	-	-	30	-	-	-	0	0	-	-	-	-	18	-
0	0	0	1	0	-	321	.1	0	23	.9	0	0	8	.1	7	.5	9	129	2	0
0	1	1	0	0	48	0	0	0	0	.2	0	0	1	0	0	0	1	1	46	0
1	2	1	0	0	0	47	0	0	0	.4	0	0	1	0	0	0	1	2	44	0
1	1	2	0	0	0	47	0	0	0	.3	0	0	1	0	0	0	1	2	51	0
1	2	1	-	0	17	120	.3	0	16	-	.1	.1	22	1	30	2	44	530	786	.3
-	-	-	0	0	7	1	0	0	1	-	0	0	8	0	0	0	1	7	11	0
-	-	-	0	0	0	0	0	0	0	-	0	0	1	.1	1	0	4	2	22	0
1	1	3	0	4	1	12	0	0	0	.6	0	0	2	0	0	0	4	1	104	0
0	-	-	0	0	-	0	-	-	0	-	-	-	0	0	-	-	-	1	105	-
0	-	-	5	0	-	0	-	-	0	-	-	-	0	0	-	-	-	5	130	-
-	-	-	1	0	14	258	.1	0	34	.1	0	0	9	.2	9	.5	14	247	7	.1
-	-	-	1	0-	-	5	-	0	26	-	0	.1	8	.7	13	.7	11	344	20	-
-	-	-	1	0	-	5	.1	0	32	-	0	.1	8	.1	9	8	13	350	13	-
8	4	0	2	10	3	21	0	.2	0	-	.1	0	84	.6	26	.1	95	169	36	.6
4	4	1	1	3	2	0	.1	.1	0	-	0	0	29	.4	26	1.2	60	142	12	.5
2	1	0	1	1	2	0	.1	0	0	-	0	0	24	.5	13	.1	41	146	10	.2
7	6	1	3	8	5	6	0	.2	0	-	.2	0	92	.7	37	.3	108	182	30	.5
6	3	0	1	36	17	73	.1	1.1	0	-	.8	.2	456	1.1	55	.4	435	774	383	1.7
7	3	0	0	41	23	97	.1	1.8	0	-	.7	.1	505	.3	41	.5	398	631	330	1.3
1	1	0	0	9	12	20	.1	.5	2	-	.4	.1	285	.1	27	.1	219	371	257	1
3	1	0	4	17	12	142	.1	.8	2	-	.4	.1	284	.6	33	.3	254	422	150	1
5	2	0	4	30	12	72	.1	.8	2	-	.4	.1	280	.6	33	.3	251	417	149	1
4	2	0	0	26	9	62	0	.3	2	-	.3	.1	216	.1	20	.2	193	284	97	.7
2	1	0	0	10	12	144	.1	.9	2	-	.4	.1	300	.1	34	.2	235	381	123	1
3	1	0	0	18	12	139	.1	.9	2	-	.4	.1	297	.1	33	.2	232	377	122	1
0	0	0	0	4	13	149	.1	.9	2	-	.3	.1	302	.1	28	.2	247	406	126	1
5	2	0	0	33	12	76	.1	.9	2	-	.4	.1	291	.1	33	.2	228	370	120	.9
6	3	0	0	35	12	83	.1	.9	4	-	.4	.1	290	.1	33	.2	227	368	119	.9
1	2	1	2	20	10	-	0	.4	1	-	.1	.1	37	1	10	.7	128	80	291	.3
1	2	2	-	33	22	23	.1	.1	0	-	.2	.2	48	1.8	24	1.3	185	45	339	.5
1	1	3	5	0	12	-	.1	0	0	-	.1	.2	41	2.7	102	.3	244	330	255	1.2
1	2	4	2	25	8	26	0	.1	0	-	.2	.2	130	1.6	11	1.5	99	79	304	.4
1	2	4	-	21	34	163	.2	.1	5	-	.3	.2	122	2.7	51	2.6	185	207	382	1.8
0	0	0	2	0	14	0	.1	0	3	-	.2	.1	5	1.4	9	3.5	68	278	2	.7
0	0	0	2	0	10	0	0	0	0	-	0	.1	9	.6	12	1.2	51	101	332	.6
0	0	0	0	0	7	0	0	0	1	-	.2	0	2	.4	4	1.4	36	130	1	.3
1	2	4	1	0	5	2	0	0	0	-	.1	.1	5	1.1	12	1.3	36	27	99	.3
0	0	0	-	26	6	5	0	.1	0	-	.1	.1	10	1.3	15	1.2	55	22	132	.5
0	0	0	-	26	6	5	0	.1	0	-	0	0	10	.5	15	.3	55	22	132	.5
0	0	0	2	26	17	11	.1	.1	0	-	.1	.2	15	.9	19	1.2	46	30	10	.5
0	0	0	-	0	4	0	0	0	0	-	0	.1	2	.3	5	.3	14	20	34	.1
0	1	0	0	46	9	12	.2	1	1	0	.1	.1	117	1	33	2.1	236	298	82	.5
2	10	1	0	0	0	0	0	0	0	1.6	0	0	0	.1	0	0	0	0	0	0
2	6	4	0	0	0	0	0	0	0	1.6	0	0	0	0	0	0	0	0	0	0
2	5	6	0	0	0	0	0	0	0	.2	0	0	0	0	0	0	0	0	0	0
2	3	8	0	0	0	0	0	0	0	1.5	0	0	0	0	0	0	0	0	0	0
2	6	5	0	0	0	0	0	0	0	1.1	0	0	0	0	0	0	0	0	0	0
2	4	7	0	0	0	0	0	0	0	1.7	0	0	0	0	0	0	0	0	0	0
2	3	8	0	0	0	0	0	0	0	2	0	0	0	0	0	0	0	0	0	0
1	8	4	0	-	0	0	0	0	0	-	0	0	0	0	0	0	0	0	0	0
8	4	0	0	0	0	0	0	0	0	.2	0	0	0	0	0	0	0	0	0	0
4	2	7	0	0	0	0	0	0	0	4.8	-	0	0	0	0	0	0	0	0	0

Code	Name	Amount	Unit	Grams	Kilocalories	Carbohydrates (g)	Protein (g)	Fat (g)
405	OIL, VEGETABLE, PALM	1	TBSP.	13.6	121	0	0	14
4513	OIL, VEGETABLE, PALM KERNEL	1	TBSP.	1.6	118	0	0	14
4510	OIL, VEGETABLE, SAFFLOWER, LINOLEIC	1	TBSP.	13.6	121	0	0	14
4511	OIL, VEGETABLE, SAFFLOWER, OLEIC	1	TBSP.	13.6	121	0	0	14
4584	OIL, VEGETABLE, SUNFLOWER	1	TBSP.	13.6	121	0	0	14
11279	OKRA, CKD	½	CUP	80.0	26	6	1	0
11278	OKRA, FRESH	½	CUP	50.0	19	4	1	0
11281	OKRA, FRZ, CKD	½	CUP	92.0	34	8	2	0
11280	OKRA, FRZ, UNPREPARED	½	CUP	71.3	21	5	1	0
10161	OLIVE LOAF, LUNCH MEAT	1	SLICE	28.4	67	3	3	5
9194	OLIVES, RIPE, CANNED (JUMBO-SUPER COLLOSSAL)	1	JUMBO	8.3	7	0	0	1
9193	OLIVES, RIPE CANNED (SMALL-EXTRA LARGE)	1	SMALL	3.2	4	0	0	0
11282	ONIONS, FRESH	½	CUP	79.9	30	7	1	0
9206	ORANGE JUICE, FRESH	¾	CUP	186.0	84	19	1	0
9215	ORANGE JUICE, FROM CONCENTRATE	¾	CUP	186.4	84	20	1	0
9200	ORANGES, FRSH	1	MEDIUM	131.0	62	15	1	0
15168	OYSTER, EASTERN, BREADED AND FRIED	3	OUNCE	85.1	168	10	7	11
15170	OYSTER, EASTERN, CND	3	OUNCE	85.1	59	3	6	2
18390	PANCAKES, BUTTERMILK	1	4 IN.	9.5	22	3	1	1
18293	PANCAKES, PLAIN	1	4 IN.	9.5	22	3	1	1
18300	PANCAKES, WHOLE-WHEAT	1	4 IN.	44.0	92	13	4	3
9226	PAPAYAS, FRESH	1	MEDIUM	304.0	119	30	2	0
11808	PARSNIPS, CKD, W/SALT	½	CUP	78.0	63	15	1	0
11299	PARSNIPS, CKD, W/O SALT	½	CUP	78.0	63	15	1	0
11298	PARSNIPS, FRESH	½	CUP	66.5	50	12	1	0
20321	PASTA, CKD, ENRICHED, W/ADDED SALT	½	CUP	70.0	99	20	3	0
20121	PASTA, CKD, ENRICHED, W/O ADDED SALT	½	CUP	73.0	99	20	3	0
20094	PASTA, FRESH-REFRIGERATED, PLAIN, CKD	½	CUP	73.0	96	18	4	1
20096	PASTA, FRESH-REFRIGERATED, SPINACH, CKD	½	CUP	73.0	95	18	4	1
20097	PASTA, HOMEMADE, MADE W/EGG, CKD	½	CUP	73.6	96	17	4	1
20098	PASTA, HOMEMADE, MADE W/O EGG, CKD	½	CUP	73.6	91	18	3	1
20127	PASTA, SPINACH, CKD	½	CUP	70.0	91	18	3	0
20125	PASTA, WHOLE-WHEAT, CKD	½	CUP	70.0	87	19	4	0
9251	PEACH NECTAR, CND/W/O ADDED VIT C	¾	CUP	186.4	101	26	1	0
9238	PEACHES, CND, JUICE PACK	½	CUP	124.0	55	14	1	0
9240	PEACHES, CND, LIGHT SYRUP PACK	½	CUP	125.5	68	18	1	0
9237	PEACHES, CND, WATER PACK	½	CUP	122.0	29	7	1	0
9246	PEACHES, DRIED, SULFURED	¼	CUP	40	96	25	1	0
9236	PEACHES, FRESH	1	MEDIUM	87.0	37	10	1	0
9250	PEACHES, FROZEN, SLICED, SWEETENED	½	CUP	125.0	118	30	1	0
16097	PEANUT BUTTER, CHUNK STYLE, W/SALT	2	TBSP.	32.3	190	7	8	16
16098	PEANUT BUTTER, SMOOTH STYLE, W/SALT	2	TBSP.	32.3	190	7	8	16
16088	PEANUTS, ALL TYPES, CKD, BOILED, W/SALT	½	CUP	31.5	100	7	4	7
16090	PEANUTS, ALL TYPES, DRY-ROASTED, W/SALT	½	CUP	73.0	427	16	17	36
16390	PEANUTS, ALL TYPES, DRY-ROASTED, W/O SALT	½	CUP	73.0	427	16	17	36
16087	PEANUTS, ALL TYPES, FRESH	½	CUP	73.0	414	12	19	36
16089	PEANUTS, ALL TYPES, OIL-ROASTED, W/SALT	½	CUP	72.0	418	14	19	35
16389	PEANUTS, ALL TYPES, OIL-ROASTED, W/O SALT	½	CUP	72.0	418	14	19	35
9340	PEARS, ASIAN, FRESH	1	MEDIUM	122.0	51	13	1	0
9254	PEARS, CND, JUICE PACK	½	CUP	124.0	62	16	0	0
9253	PEARS, CND, WATER PACK	½	CUP	122.0	35	10	0	0
9252	PEARS, FRESH	1	MEDIUM	166.0	98	25	1	1
11300	PEAS, EDIBLE-PODDED, FRESH	½	CUP	72.5	30	5	2	0
11305	PEAS, GREEN, CKD	½	CUP	80.0	67	13	4	0
11308	PEAS, GREEN, CND	½	CUP	85.0	59	11	4	0
11304	PEAS, GREEN, FRESH	½	CUP	72.5	59	10	4	0
11313	PEAS, GREEN, FRZ, CKD	½	CUP	80.0	62	11	4	0
12142	PECANS, DRIED	½	CUP	54.0	360	10	4	37
11329	PEPPERS, HOT CHILI, GREEN, CND	1	EACH	73.0	18	4	1	0
11670	PEPPERS, HOT CHILI, GREEN, FRESH	1	EACH	45.0	18	4	1	0

Saturated Fat (g)	Monounsaturated Fat (g)	Polyunsaturated Fat (g)	Fiber (g)	Cholesterol (g)	Folate (g)	Vitamin A (RE)	Vitamin B6 (mg)	Vitamin B12 (µg)	Vitamin C (mg)	Vitamin E (mg)	Riboflavin (mg)	Thiamin (mg)	Calcium (mg)	Iron (mg)	Magnesium (mg)	Niacin (mg)	Phosphorus (mg)	Potassium (mg)	Sodium (mg)	Zinc (mg)
7	5	1	0	0	0	0	0	0	0	2.6	0	0	0	0	0	0	0	0	0	-
11	2	0	0	0	0	0	0	0	0	-	0	0	0	0	0	0	0	0	0	-
1	2	10	0	0	0	0	0	0	0	4.7	0	0	0	0	0	0	0	0	0	0
1	10	2	0	0	0	0	0	0	0	4.7	0	0	0	0	0	0	0	0	0	0
1	11	1	0	-	0	0	0	0	0	-	0	0	0	0	0	0	0	0	0	0
0	0	0	2	0	37	46	.1	0	13	-	0	.1	50	.4	46	7	45	258	4	.4
0	0	0	1	0	33	33	.1	0	11	-	0	.1	41	.4	29	.5	32	152	4	.3
0	0	0	3	0	134	47	.1	0	11	-	.1	.1	88	.6	47	.7	42	215	3	.6
0	0	0	2	0	105	33	0	0	9	-	.1	.1	58	.4	31	.5	30	150	2	.4
2	2	1	0	11	1	6	.1	.4	.2	-	.1	.1	31	.2	5	.5	36	84	421	.4
0	0	0	-	0	0	3	0	0	0	-	0	0	8	.3	0	0	0	1	75	0
0	0	0	-	0	0	1	0	0	0	-	0	0	3	.1	0	0	0	0	28	0
0	0	0	1	0	15	0	.1	0	5	.2	0	0	16	.2	8	.1	26	125	2	.2
0	0	0	0	0	56	37	.1	0	93	.1	.1	2	20	.4	20	.7	32	372	2	.1
0	0	0	0	0	82	15	0	0	73	-	0	.1	17	.2	19	.4	30	354	2	.1
0	0	0	3	0	40	28	.1	0	70	.3	.1	.1	52	.1	13	.4	18	237	0	.1
3	4	3	-	69	12	77	.1	13.3	3	-	.2	.1	53	5.9	49	1.4	135	208	355	74.1
1	0	1	0	47	8	77	.1	16.3	4	-	.1	.1	38	5.7	46	1.1	118	195	95	77.4
0	0	0	-	6	1	3	0	0	0	-	0	0	15	.2	1	.1	13	14	50	.1
0	0	0	-	6	1	5	0	0	0	-	0	0	21	.2	2	.1	15	13	42	.1
1	1	1	-	27	9	28	-	.1	0	-	.2	.1	110	1.4	20	1	164	123	252	.5
0	0	0	5	0	116	85	.1	0	188	-	.1	.1	73	.3	30	1	15	781	9	.2
0	0	0	-	0	45	0	.1	0	10	-	0	.1	29	.5	23	.6	54	286	192	.2
0	0	0	-	0	45	0	.1	0	10	-	0	.1	29	.5	23	.6	54	286	8	.2
0	0	0	3	0	44	0	.1	0	11	-	0	.1	24	.4	19	.5	47	249	7	.4
0	0	0	-	0	5	-	0	0	0	-	.1	.1	5	1	13	1.2	38	22	70	.4
0	0	0	0	0	5	-	0	0	0	-	.1	.1	5	1	13	1.2	38	22	1	.4
0	0	0	-	24	5	4	0	.1	0	-	.1	.2	4	.8	13	.7	46	18	4	.4
0	0	0	-	24	13	10	.1	.1	0	-	.1	.1	13	.8	18	.7	42	27	4	.5
0	0	0	-	30	14	13	0	.1	0	-	.1	.1	7	.9	10	.9	38	15	61	.3
0	0	0	-	0	13	0	0	0	0	-	.1	.1	4	.8	10	10	29	14	54	.3
0	0	0	-	0	8	11	.1	0	0	-	.1	.1	21	.7	43	1.1	76	41	10	.8
0	0	0	3	0	4	0	.1	0	0	-	0	.1	11	.7	21	.5	62	31	2	.6
0	0	0	1	0	3	48	0	0	10	-	0	0	9	.4	7	.5	11	75	13	.1
0	0	0	1	0	4	47	0	0	4	-	0	0	7	.3	9	.7	21	159	5	.1
0	0	0	1	0	4	44	0	0	3	-	0	0	4	.5	6	.7	14	122	6	.1
0	0	0	1	0	4	65	0	0	4	-	0	0	2	.4	6	.6	12	121	4	.1
0	0	0	3	0	0	86	0	0	2	-	.1	0	11	1.6	17	1.8	48	398	3	.2
0	0	0	2	0	3	47	0	0	6	-	0	0	4	.1	6	.9	10	171	0	.1
0	0	0	2	0	4	35	0	0	118	-	0	0	4	.5	6	.8	14	162	7	.1
3	8	5	2	0	30	0	.1	0	0	-	0	0	13	.6	51	4.4	102	241	157	.9
3	8	5	2	0	25	0	.1	0	0	-	0	0	11	.5	51	4.2	104	233	154	.8
1	3	2	3	0	23	0	0	0	0	-	0	.1	17	.3	32	1.7	62	57	237	.6
5	18	11	6	0	106	0	.2	0	0	5.7	.1	.3	39	1.6	128	9.9	261	480	593	2.4
5	18	11	6	0	106	0	.2	0	0	-	.1	.3	39	1.6	128	9.9	251	480	4	2.4
5	18	11	6	0	175	0	.3	0	0	6.1	.1	.5	67	3.3	123	8.8	274	515	13	2.4
5	18	11	7	0	91	0	.2	0	0	5	.1	.2	63	1.3	133	10.3	372	491	312	4.8
5	18	11	7	0	91	0	.2	0	0	-	.1	.2	63	1.3	133	10.3	372	491	4	4.8
0	0	0	4	0	10	0	0	0	5	-	0	0	5	0	10	.3	13	148	0	0
0	0	0	2	0	1	1	0	0	2	-	0	0	11	.4	9	.2	15	119	5	.1
0	0	0	2	0	1	0	0	0	1	-	0	0	5	.3	5	.1	9	65	2	.1
0	0	0	4	0	12	3	0	0	7	-	.1	0	18	.4	10	.2	18	208	0	.2
0	0	0	2	0	30	10	.1	0	44	-	.1	.1	31	1.5	17	.4	38	145	3	.2
0	0	0	4	0	51	48	.2	0	11	-	.1	.2	22	1.2	31	1.6	94	217	2	1
0	0	0	3	0	38	65	.1	0	8	-	.1	.1	17	.8	14	.6	57	147	186	.6
0	0	0	4	0	47	46	.1	0	29	.1	.1	.2	18	1.1	24	1.5	78	177	4	.9
0	0	0	4	0	47	54	.1	0	8	-	.1	.2	19	1.3	23	1.2	72	134	70	.8
3	23	9	4	0	21	7	.1	0	1	-	.1	.5	19	1.2	69	.5	157	212	1	3
0	0	0	1	0	7	45	.1	0	50	-	0	0	5	.4	10	.6	12	137	856	.1
0	0	0	1	0	11	35	.1	0	109	-	0	0	8	.5	11	.4	21	153	3	.1

Code	Name	Amount	Unit	Grams	Kilocalories	Carbohydrates (g)	Protein (g)	Fat (g)
11820	PEPPERS, HOT CHILI, RED, CND	1	EACH	73.0	18	4	1	0
11819	PEPPERS, HOT CHILI, RED, FRESH	1	EACH	45.0	18	4	1	0
11632	PEPPERS, JALAPEÑO, CND	¼	CUP	34.0	8	2	0	0
11333	PEPPERS, SWEET, GREEN, FRESH	1	MEDIUM	74.0	20	5	1	0
11821	PEPPERS, SWEET, RED, FRESH	1	MEDIUM	74.0	20	5	1	0
11951	PEPPERS, SWEET, YELLOW, FRESH	1	MEDIUM	74.0	20	5	1	0
11945	PICKLE RELISH, SWEET	1	TBSP.	15.0	29	5	0	0
11941	PICKLE, CUCUMBER, SOUR	1	SLICE	7.0	1	0	0	0
11937	PICKLE, CUCUMBER, DILL	1	SLICE	6.0	1	0	0	0
11940	PICKLE, CUCUMBER, SWEET	1	SLICE	6.0	7	2	0	0
9273	PINEAPPLE, JUICE, CND	¾	CUP	187.6	105	26	1	0
9268	PINEAPPLE, CND, JUICE PACK	½	CUP	125.0	75	20	1	0
9267	PINEAPPLE, CND, WATER PACK	½	CUP	123.0	39	10	1	0
9266	PINEAPPLE, FRESH	1	SLICE	84.0	41	10	0	0
12652	PISTACHIO, DRY ROASTED	½	CUP	64.09	388	18	10	34
9282	PLUMS, CND, PURPLE, JUICE PACK	½	CUP	126.0	73	19	1	0
9281	PLUMS, CND, PURPLE, WATER PACK	½	CUP	124.5	51	14	0	0
9279	PLUMS, FRESH	1	MEDIUM	66.0	36	9	1	0
19034	POPCORN, AIR-POPPED	1	CUP	8.0	31	6	1	0
19036	POPCORN, CAKES	1	CAKE	10.0	38	8	1	0
19038	POPCORN, CARAMEL-COATED, W/PEANUTS	1	CUP	35.2	141	28	2	3
19039	POPCORN, CARAMEL-COATED, W/O PEANUTS	1	CUP	35.2	152	28	1	5
19040	POPCORN, CHEESE-FLAVOR	1	CUP	11.0	58	6	1	4
19035	POPCORN, OIL-POPPED	1	CUP	11.0	55	6	1	3
19408	PORK SKINS, BARBECUE-FLAVOR	1	OUNCE	28.4	153	0	16	9
19041	PORK SKINS, PLAIN	1	OUNCE	28.4	155	0	17	9
10193	PORK, BACKRIBS	3	OUNCE	85.1	315	0	21	25
10127	PORK, BRAUNSCHWEIGER	3	OUNCE	85.1	305	3	11	27
10220	PORK, GROUND, CKD	3	OUNCE	85.1	253	0	22	18
10154	PORK, HAM AND CHEESE LOAF OR ROLL	3	OUNCE	85.1	220	1	14	17
10147	PORK, HAM PATTIES, GRILLED	3	OUNCE	85.1	291	1	11	26
10148	PORK, HAM SALAD SPREAD	3	OUNCE	85.1	184	9	7	13
10185	PORK, HAM, CND, EXTRA LEAN AND REG, ROASTED	3	OUNCE	85.1	142	0	18	7
10140	PORK, HAM, CND, REGULAR (APPROX 13% FAT), ROASTED	3	OUNCE	85.1	192	0	17	13
10134	PORK, HAM, EXTRA LEAN (5% FAT), ROASTED	3	OUNCE	85.1	123	1	18	5
10133	PORK, HAM, EXTRA LEAN (5% FAT), UNHEATED	3	OUNCE	85.1	111	1	16	4
10183	PORK, HAM, EXTRA LEAN AND REG, ROASTED	3	OUNCE	85.1	140	0	19	7
10182	PORK, HAM, EXTRA LEAN AND REG, UNHEATED	3	OUNCE	85.1	138	2	16	7
10151	PORK, HAM, MEAT AND FAT, ROASTED	3	OUNCE	85.1	207	0	18	14
10153	PORK, HAM, MEAT ONLY, ROASTED	3	OUNCE	85.1	134	0	21	5
10136	PORK, HAM, REGULAR (11% FAT), ROASTED	3	OUNCE	85.1	151	0	19	8
10135	PORK, HAM, REGULAR (11% FAT), UNHEATED	3	OUNCE	85.1	155	3	19	9
10172	PORK, SMOKED LINK SAUSAGE, GRILLED	3	OUNCE	85.1	331	2	19	27
10089	PORK, SPARERIBS, MEAT AND FAT, CKD, BRAISED	3	OUNCE	85.1	338	0	25	26
10221	PORK, TENDERLOIN, MEAT AND FAT, CKD, BROILED	3	OUNCE	85.1	171	0	25	7
10223	PORK, TENDERLOIN, MEAT ONLY, CKD, BROILED	3	OUNCE	85.1	159	0	26	5
19042	POTATO CHIPS, BARBECUE-FLAVOR	1	OUNCE	28.4	139	15	2	9
19421	POTATO CHIPS, CHEESE-FLAVOR	1	OUNCE	28.4	141	16	2	8
19422	POTATO CHIPS, LIGHT	1	OUNCE	28.4	134	19	2	6
19411	POTATO CHIPS, PLAIN, SALTED	1	OUNCE	28.4	152	15	2	10
19811	POTATO CHIPS, PLAIN, UNSALTED	1	OUNCE	28.4	152	15	2	10
19043	POTATO CHIPS, SOUR-CREAM-AND-ONION-FLAVOR	1	OUNCE	28.4	151	15	2	10
11672	POTATO PANCAKES, HOME-PREPARED	1	OUNCE	28.4	77	8	2	4
11414	POTATO SALAD	½	CUP	125.0	179	14	3	10
19415	POTATO STICKS	1	OUNCE	28.4	148	15	2	10
11843	POTATOES, AU GRATIN, HOME-PREPARED	½	CUP	122.5	162	14	6	9
11363	POTATOES, BAKED, W/O SKIN	1	MEDIUM	202.0	188	44	4	0
11674	POTATOES, BAKED, W/SKIN	1	MEDIUM	202.0	220	51	5	0
11365	POTATOES, BOILED, CKD IN SKIN	1	MEDIUM	202.0	176	41	4	0
11367	POTATOES, BOILED, CKD, W/O SKIN	1	MEDIUM	202.0	174	40	3	0

Saturated Fat (g)	Monounsaturated Fat (g)	Polyunsaturated Fat (g)	Fiber (g)	Cholesterol (g)	Folate (g)	Vitamin A (RE)	Vitamin B6 (mg)	Vitamin B12 (μg)	Vitamin C (mg)	Vitamin E (mg)	Riboflavin (mg)	Thiamin (mg)	Calcium (mg)	Iron (mg)	Magnesium (mg)	Niacin (mg)	Phosphorus (mg)	Potassium (mg)	Sodium (mg)	Zinc (mg)
0	0	0	1	0	7	868	.1	0	50	-	0	0	5	.4	10	.6	12	137	856	.1
0	0	0	1	0	11	484	.1	0	109	-	0	0	8	.5	11	.4	21	153	3	.1
0	0	0	-	0	5	58	.1	0	4	-	0	0	9	1	4	.2	6	46	497	.1
0	0	0	1	0	16	422	.2	0	141	.5	0	0	7	.3	7	.4	14	131	1	.1
0	0	0	2	0	16	422	.2	0	141	.5	0	0	7	.3	7	.4	14	131	1	.1
-	-	-	-	0	19	18	.1	0	136	-	0	0	8	.3	9	.7	18	157	1	.1
0	0	0	-	0	0	2	0	0	0	-	0	0	0	.1	1	0	2	4	122	0
0	0	0	0	0	0	1	0	0	0	-	0	0	0	0	0	0	1	2	85	0
0	0	0	0	0	0	2	0	0	0	-	0	0	1	0	1	0	1	7	77	0
0	0	0	0	0	0	1	0	0	0	-	0	0	0	0	0	0	1	2	56	0
0	0	0	0	0	43	0	.2	0	20	-	0	.1	32	.5	24	.5	15	251	2	.2
0	0	0	1	0	6	5	.1	0	12	-	0	.1	17	.3	17	.4	7	152	1	.1
0	0	0	1	0	6	1	.1	0	9	-	0	.1	18	.5	20	.4	9	132	1	.2
0	0	0	1	0	6	2	.1	0	9	-	0	.1	18	.5	22	.4	5	156	1	.1
4	23	5	7	0	38	15	.2	0	5	-	.2	.3	45	2	83	.9	305	621	499	.9
0	0	0	1	0	3	127	0	0	4	-	.1	0	13	.4	10	.6	19	194	1	.1
0	0	0	1	0	3	113	0	0	3	-	.1	0	9	.2	6	.5	16	157	1	.1
0	0	0	1	0	1	21	.1	0	6	-	.1	0	3	.1	5	.3	7	114	0	.1
0	0	0	1	0	2	2	0	0	0	-	0	0	1	.2	10	.2	24	24	0	.3
0	0	0	0	0	2	1	0	0	0	-	0	0	1	.2	16	.6	28	33	29	.4
0	1	1		0	6	2	.1	0	0	-	0	0	23	1.4	28	.7	45	125	104	.4
1	1	2	2	1	4	0	0	0		-	0	0	15	.6	12	.8	29	38	73	.2
1	1	2	1	1	1	5	0	.1	0	-	0	0	12	.2	10	.2	40	29	98	.2
1	1	1	1	0	2	2	0	0	0	-	0	0	1	.3	12	.2	27	25	97	.3
3	4	1	-	33	9	52	0	0	0	-	.1	0	12	.3	0	1	62	51	756	.2
3	4	1	-	27	0	11	0	.2	0	-	.1	0	9	.2	3	.4	24	36	521	.2
9	11	2	-	100	3	3	.3	.5	0	-	.2	.4	38	1.2	18	3	166	268	86	2.9
9	13	3	0	133	37	3589	.3	17.1	8	-	1.3	.2	8	8	9	7.1	143	169	972	2.4
7	8	2	0	80	5	2	.3	.5	1	-	.2	.6	19	1.1	20	3.6	192	308	62	2.7
6	8	2	0	48	3	20	.2	.7	21	-	.2	.5	49	.8	14	2.9	215	250	1142	1.7
9	12	34	0	61	3	0	.1	.6	0	-	.2	.3	8	1.4	9	2.8	86	208	904	1.6
4	6	2	0	31	1	0	.1	.6	5	-	.1	.4	7	.5	9	1.8	102	128	776	.9
2	3	1	0	35	4	0	.3	.7	19	-	.2	.8	6	.9	17	4.3	188	299	908	2
4	6	2	0	53	4	0	.3	.9	12	-	.2	.7	7	1.2	14	4.5	207	304	800	2.1
2	2	0	0	45	3	0	.3	.6	18	-	.2	.6	7	1.3	12	3.4	167	244	1023	2.4
1	2	0	-	40	3	0	.4	.6	22	-	.2	.8	6	.6	14	4.1	185	298	1215	1.6
2	3	1	0	48	3	0	.3	.6	19	-	.2	.6	7	1.2	16	4.5	211	308	1178	2.2
2	3	1	0	45	3	0	.3	.7	23	-	.2	.8	6	.8	15	4.3	201	253	1087	1.7
5	7	2	0	53	3	0	.3	.5	-	-	.2	.5	6	.7	16	3.8	182	243	1010	2
2	2	1	0	47	3	0	.4	.6	-	-	.2	.6	6	.8	19	4.3	193	269	1129	2.2
3	4	1	0	50	3	0	.3	.6	19	-	.3	.6	7	1.1	19	5.2	239	348	1276	2.1
3	4	1	0	48	3	0	.3	.7	24	-	.2	.7	6	.8	16	4.5	210	282	1120	1.8
10	12	3	0	58	4	0	.3	1.4	2	-	.2	.6	26	1	16	3.9	138	286	1276	2.4
9	11	2	0	103	3	3	.3	.9	2	-	.3	.3	40	1.6	20	4.7	222	272	79	3.9
2	3	1	-	80	5	2	.4	.8	1	-	.3	.8	4	1.2	30	4.3	247	378	54	2.5
2	2	0	-	80	5	2	.4	.9	1	-	.3	.8	4	1.2	31	4.4	251	384	55	2.5
2	2	5	1	0	24	6	.2	0	10	-	.1	.1	14	.5	21	1.3	53	357	213	.3
2	2	3	-	1	0	2	.1	0	15	-	0	0	20	.5	21	1.4	85	433	213	.3
1	1	3	-	0	8	0	.2	0	7	-	.1	.1	6	.4	25	2	55	494	139	0
3	3	3	1	0	13	0	.2	0	9	-	.1	0	7	.5	19	1.1	47	361	168	.3
3	3	3	-	0	13	0	.2	0	9	-	.1	0	7	.5	19	1.1	47	361	2	.3
3	2	5	1	2	18	6	.2	.3	11	-	.1	.1	20	.5	21	1.1	50	377	177	.3
1	1	2	1	27	7	4	.1	.1	6	-	0	0	7	.4	9	.6	31	223	144	.2
2	3	5	-	85	8	41	.2	0	12	-	.1	.1	24	.8	19	1.1	65	317	661	.4
3	2	5	1	0	11	0	.1	0	13	-	0	0	5	.6	18	1.4	49	351	71	.3
4	3	1	-	18	10	47	.2	0	12	-	.1	.1	146	.8	24	1.2	138	485	530	.8
0	0	0	3	0	18	0	.6	0	26	-	0	.2	10	.7	51	2.8	101	790	10	.6
0	0	0	5	0	22	0	.7	0	26	-	.1	.2	20	2.7	55	3.3	115	844	16	.6
0	0	0	4	0	20	0	.6	0	26	-	0	.2	10	.6	44	2.9	89	766	8	.6
0	0	0	4	0	18	0	.5	0	15	-	0	.2	16	.6	40	2.7	81	663	10	.5

Code	Name	Amount	Unit	Grams	Kilocalories	Carbohydrates (g)	Protein (g)	Fat (g)
11370	POTATOES, HASHED BROWN	½	CUP	78.0	119	6	2	11
11657	POTATOES, MASHED, HOME-PREPARED	½	CUP	105.0	81	18	2	1
11671	POTATOES, O'BRIEN, HOME-PREPARED	½	CUP	97.0	79	15	2	1
11844	POTATOES, SCALLOPED	½	CUP	122.5	105	13	4	5
19047	PRETZELS, HARD, PLAIN, SALTED	1	OUNCE	28.4	108	22	3	1
19814	PRETZELS, HARD, PLAIN, UNSALTED	1	OUNCE	28.4	108	22	3	1
19050	PRETZELS, HARD, WHOLE-WHEAT	1	OUNCE	28.4	103	23	3	1
9294	PRUNE JUICE, CND	¾	CUP	191.8	136	33	1	0
9289	PRUNES, DEHYDRATED	¼	CUP	33.0	112	29	1	0
9293	PRUNES, DRIED, STEWED, W/ADDED SUGAR	¼	CUP	59.5	74	20	1	0
9292	PRUNES, DRIED, STEWED, W/O ADDED SUGAR	¼	CUP	53.0	57	15	1	0
9291	PRUNES, DRIED, UNCOOKED	¼	CUP	40.3	96	25	1	0
11429	RADISHES, FRESH	½	CUP	58.0	10	2	0	0
11431	RADISHES, ORIENTAL, CKD	½	CUP	73.5	12	3	0	0
11432	RADISHES, ORIENTAL, DRIED	½	CUP	58,0	157	37	5	0
11430	RADISHES, ORIENTAL, FRESH	½	CUP	44.0	8	2	0	0
9297	RAISINS, GOLDEN SEEDLESS	½	CUP	72.5	219	58	2	0
9299	RAISINS, SEEDED	½	CUP	72.5	215	57	2	0
9298	RAISINS, SEEDLESS	½	CUP	72.5	218	57	2	0
9302	RASPBERRIES, FRESH	½	CUP	61.5	30	7	1	0
9306	RASPBERRIES, FROZEN RED, SWEETENED	½	CUP	125.0	129	33	1	0
62536	RAVIOLI, BEEF	1	CUP	243.9	230	36	9	5
62537	RAVIOLI, CHEESE	1	CUP	243.9	220	38	9	3
62557	RED BEANS AND RICE	2	OUNCE	56.7	189	40	8	1
19051	RICE CAKES, BROWN RICE, PLAIN	1	CAKE	9.0	35	7	1	0
19816	RICE CAKES, BROWN RICE, PLAIN, UNSALTED	1	CAKE	9.0	35	7	1	0
19193	RICE PUDDING	1	CUP	298.1	486	66	6	22
20037	RICE, BROWN, LONG-GRAIN, CKD	½	CUP	97.5	108	22	3	1
20045	RICE, WHITE, LONG-GRAIN, CKD	½	CUP	79.0	103	22	2	0
20049	RICE, WHITE, LONG-GRAIN, INSTANT, ENRICHED	½	CUP	82.5	81	18	2	0
20053	RICE, WHITE, SHORT-GRAIN, CKD	½	CUP	93.0	121	27	2	0
20057	RICE, WHITE, W/PASTA, CKD	½	CUP	101.0	123	22	3	3
15232	ROUGHY, ORANGE, CKD, DRY HEAT	3	OUNCE	85.1	76	0	16	1
62541	SALAD DRESSING, BLUE CHEESE	2	TBSP.	32.0	90	5	1	7
62542	SALAD DRESSING, BLUE CHEESE, FAT FREE	2	TBSP.	35.0	50	12	1	0
4120	SALAD DRESSING, FRENCH	2	TBSP.	31.3	134	5	0	13
62545	SALAD DRESSING, FRENCH, FAT FREE	2	TBSP.	35.0	50	12	0	0
4020	SALAD DRESSING, FRENCH, LO FAT	2	TBSP.	32.5	44	7	0	2
4114	SALAD DRESSING, ITALIAN	2	TBSP.	29.4	137	3	0	14
62543	SALAD DRESSING, ITALIAN, FAT FREE	2	TBSP.	31.0	10	2	0	0
4021	SALAD DRESSING, ITALIAN, LO CAL	2	TBSP.	30.0	32	1	0	3
62539	SALAD DRESSING, RANCH	2	TBSP.	29.0	170	2	0	18
62540	SALAD DRESSING, RANCH, FAT FREE	2	TBSP.	35.0	50	11	0	0
4015	SALAD DRESSING, RUSSIAN	2	TBSP.	30.7	151	3	0	16
4022	SALAD DRESSING, RUSSIAN, LOW CAL	2	TBSP.	32.5	46	9	0	1
4016	SALAD DRESSING, SESAME SEED	2	TBSP.	30.7	136	3	1	14
4017	SALAD DRESSING, THOUSAND ISLAND	2	TBSP.	31.3	118	5	0	11
4023	SALAD DRESSING, THOUSAND ISLAND, LO CAL	2	TBSP.	30.7	49	5	0	3
62544	SALAD DRESSING, THOUSAND ISLAND, FAT FREE	2	TBSP.	35.0	45	11	0	0
4135	SALAD DRESSING, VINEGAR AND OIL	2	TBSP.	31.3	140	1	0	16
15209	SALMON, ATLANTIC, WILD, CKD, DRY HEAT	3	OUNCE	85.1	155	0	22	7
15212	SALMON, PINK, CKD, DRY HEAT	3	OUNCE	85.1	127	0	22	4
62546	SALSA	2	TBSP.	33.0	20	5	0	0
15088	SARDINE, ATLANTIC, CND IN OIL	3	OUNCE	85.1	177	0	21	10
6313	SAUCE, WHITE	½	CUP	131.9	120	11	5	7
11439	SAUERKRAUT, CND, SOL & LIQ	½	CUP	118.0	22	5	1	0
7003	SAUSAGE, BEERWURST, PORK	1	SLICE	23.0	55	0	3	4
7006	SAUSAGE, BOCKWURST	1	LINK	65.0	200	0	9	18
7013	SAUSAGE, BRATWURST	1	LINK	85.0	256	2	12	22
7089	SAUSAGE, ITALIAN, CKD	1	LINK	83.0	268	1	17	21

Saturated Fat (g)	Monounsaturated Fat (g)	Polyunsaturated Fat (g)	Fiber (g)	Cholesterol (g)	Folate (g)	Vitamin A (RE)	Vitamin B6 (mg)	Vitamin B12 (µg)	Vitamin C (mg)	Vitamin E (mg)	Riboflavin (mg)	Thiamin (mg)	Calcium (mg)	Iron (mg)	Magnesium (mg)	Niacin (mg)	Phosphorus (mg)	Potassium (mg)	Sodium (mg)	Zinc (mg)
4	5	1	2	-	6	0	.2	0	4	-	0	.1	6	.6	16	1.6	33	250	19	.2
0	0	0	2	2	9	20	.2	0	7	-	0	.1	27	.3	19	1.2	50	314	318	.3
1	0	0	-	4	8	55	.2	0	16	-	.1	.1	35	.5	17	1	49	258	210	.3
2	2	1	-	7	11	23	.2	0	13	-	.1	.1	70	.7	23	1.3	77	463	410	.5
0	0	0	1	0	24	0	0	0	0	-	.2	.1	10	1.2	10	1.5	32	41	486	.2
0	0	0	1	0	24	0	0	0	0	-	.2	.1	10	1.2	10	1.5	32	41	82	.2
0	0	0	-	0	15	-0	.1	0	0	-	.1	.1	8	.8	9	1.9	35	122	58	.2
0	0	0	2	0	1	0	.4	0	8	-	.1	0	23	2.3	27	1.5	48	529	8	.4
0	0	0	-	0	1	58	.2	0	0	-	.1	0	24	1.2	21	1	37	349	2	.2
0	0	0	2	0	0	17	.1	0	2	-	.1	0	12	.6	11	.4	20	186	1	.1
0	0	0	3	0	0	16	.1	0	2	-	.1	0	12	.6	11	.4	19	177	1	.1
0	0	0	3	0	1	80	.1	0	1	-	.1	0	21	1	18	.8	32	300	2	.2
0	0	0	1	0	16	1	0	0	13	-	0	0	12	.2	5	.2	10	135	14	.2
0	0	0	1	0	13	0	0	0	11	-	0	0	12	.1	7	.1	18	209	10	.1
0	0	0	-	0	171	0	.4	0	0	-	.4	.2	365	3.9	99	2	118	2027	161	1.2
0	0	0	1	0	12	0	0	0	10	-	0	0	12	.2	7	.1	10	100	9	.1
0	0	0	3	0	2	3	.2	0	2	-	.1	0	38	1.3	25	.8	83	541	9	.2
0	0	0	5	0	2	0	.1	0	4	-	.1	.1	20	1.9	22	.8	54	598	20	.1
0	0	0	3	0	2	1	.2	0	2	-	.1	.1	36	1.5	24	.6	70	544	9	.2
0	0	0	4	0	16	8	0	0	15	.2	.1	0	14	.4	11	.6	7	93	0	.3
0	0	0	5	0	32	7	0	0	21	-	.1	0	19	.8	16	.3	21	142	1	.2
2	-	-	4	20	-	150	-	-	2	-	-	-	0	1.5	-	-	-	-	1150	-
1	-	-	4	15	-	60	-	-	1	-	-	-	24	1.5	-	-	-	-	1280	-
0	-	-	7	0	-	99	-	-	6	-	-	.2	48	1.5	-	2.8	-	-	786	-
0	0	0	0	0	2	0	0	0	0	-	0	0	1	.1	12	.7	32	26	29	.3
0	0	0	0	0	2	0	0	0	0	-	0	0	1	.1	12	.7	32	26	2	.3
3	10	8	-	3	9	104	.1	.6	1	-	.2	.1	155	.9	24	.5	203	179	253	1.5
0	0	0	2	0	4	0	.1	0	0	-	0	.1	10	.4	42	1.5	81	42	5	.6
0	0	0	0	0	2	0	.1	0	0	-	0	.1	8	.9	9	1.2	34	28	1	.4
0	0	0	0	0	3	0	0	0	0	-	0	.1	7	.5	4	.7	12	3	2	.2
0	0	0	-	0	2	0	.1	0	0	-	0	.2	1	1.4	7	1.4	31	24	0	.4
1	1	1	4	1	7	0	.1	.1	0	-	.1	.1	8	.9	12	1.8	37	42	574	.3
0	1	0	0	22	7	20	.3	2	0	-	.2	-	-	-	-	-	-	-	30	-
4	-	-	0	10	-	0	-	-	0	-	-	-	24	0	-	-	-	-	470	-
0	-	-	0	0	-	0	-	-	0	.4	-	-	0	0	-	-	-	-	340	-
3	3	7	0	18	1	6	0	0	0	1.6	0	0	3	.1	0	0	4	25	428	0
0	-	-	0	0	-	100	-	-	0	-	-	-	0	0	-	-	-	-	300	-
0	0	1	0	2	0	0	0	0	0	.3	0	0	4	.1	0	0	5	26	256	.1
2	3	8	0	0	1	7	0	0	0	1.5	0	0	3	.1	0	0	1	4	231	0
0	-	-	0	0	-	0	-	-	0	-	-	-	0	0	-	-	-	-	290	-
0	1	2	0	2	0	0	0	0	0	.3	0	0	1	.1	0	0	2	5	236	0
3	-	-	0	5	-	0	-	-	0	.6	-	-	0	0	-	-	-	-	270	-
0	-	-	0	0	-	0	-	-	0	.6	-	-	0	0	-	-	-	-	310	-
2	4	9	0	6	3	63	0	.1	2	1.8	0	0	6	.2	0	.2	11	48	266	.1
0	0	1	0	2	1	5	0	0	2	.1	0	0	6	.2	0	0	12	51	282	0
2	4	8	-	0	1	63	0	0	0	1.5	0	0	6	.2	0	0	11	48	307	0
2	3	6	1	8	2	30	0	.1	0	1.3	0	0	3	.2	1	0	5	35	219	0
0	1	2	0	5	2	29	0	.1	0	.3	0	0	3	.2	0	0	5	35	307	0
0	-	-	0	0	-	0	-	-	0	-	-	-	0	0	-	-	-	-	300	-
3	5	8	0	0	0	0	0	0	0	1.3	0	0	0	0	0	0	0	2	0	0
1	2	3	0	60	25	11	.8	2.6	0	-	.4	.2	13	.9	31	8.6	218	534	48	.7
1	1	1	0	57	4	35	.2	2.9	0	-	.1	.2	14	.8	28	7.3	251	352	73	.6
0	-	-	0	0	-	80	-	-	4	-	-	-	0	0	-	-	-	-	240	-
1	3	4	0	121	10	57	.1	7.6	0	-	.2	.1	325	2.5	33	4.5	417	338	430	1.1
3	2	1	-	17	8	46	0	.5	1	-	.2	0	212	.1	132	.3	128	222	398	.3
0	0	0	3	0	28	2	.2	0	17	-	0	0	35	1.7	15	.2	24	201	780	.2
1	2	1	0	14	1	0	.1	.2	7	-	0	.1	2	.2	3	.7	24	58	285	.4
7	8	2	0	38	4	4	.1	.5	0	-	.1	.3	10	.4	12	2.7	95	176	718	1
8	10	2	0	51	2	0	.2	.8	1	-	.2	.4	37	1.1	13	2.7	127	180	473	2
8	10	3	0	65	4	0	.3	1.1	2	-	.2	.5	20	1.2	15	3.5	141	252	765	2

Code	Name	Amount	Unit	Grams	Kilocalories	Carbohydrates (g)	Protein (g)	Fat (g)
7037	SAUSAGE, KIELBASA, KOLBASSY	1	LINK	85.0	264	2	11	23
7038	SAUSAGE, KNOCKWURST	1	LINK	68.0	209	1	8	19
7075	SAUSAGE, LINK, PORK AND BEEF	1	LINK	68.0	228	1	9	21
16107	SAUSAGE, MEATLESS	1	LINK	25.0	64	2	5	5
7057	SAUSAGE, PEPPERONI	1	SLICE	5.5	27	0	1	2
7059	SAUSAGE, POLISH-STYLE	1	EACH	227.0	740	4	32	65
7064	SAUSAGE, PORK, LINKS OR BULK, CKD	1	LINK	13.0	48	0	3	4
7072	SAUSAGE, SALAMI, BEEF AND PORK, DRY	1	SLICE	10.0	42	0	2	3
7068	SAUSAGE, SALAMI, BEEF, CKD	1	SLICE	23.0	60	1	3	5
7074	SAUSAGE, SMOKED LINK, PORK	1	LINK	68.0	265	1	15	22
15092	SEA BASS, CKD, DRY HEAT	3	OUNCE	85.1	105	0	20	2
12036	SEEDS, SUNFLOWER, DRIED	½	CUP	72.0	410	14	16	36
12537	SEEDS, SUNFLOWER, DRY ROASTED, W/SALT ADDED	½	CUP	64.0	372	15	12	32
12538	SEEDS, SUNFLOWER, OIL ROASTED, W/SALT ADDED	½	CUP	67.5	415	10	14	39
12539	SEEDS, SUNFLOWER, TOASTED, W/SALT ADDED	½	CUP	67.0	415	14	12	38
14346	SHAKE, CHOCOLATE	1	CUP	226.4	288	46	8	8
14428	SHAKE, STRAWBERRY	1	CUP	226.4	256	43	8	6
14347	SHAKE, VANILLA	1	CUP	226.4	251	41	8	7
11640	SHALLOTS, FREEZE-DRIED	½	CUP	7.2	25	6	1	0
11677	SHALLOTS, FRESH	½	CUP	79.9	58	13	2	0
19097	SHERBET, ALL FLAVORS	1	CUP	192.0	265	58	2	4
15150	SHRIMP, CKD, BREADED AND FRIED	3	OUNCE	85.1	206	10	18	10
15151	SHRIMP, CKD, MOIST HEAT	3	OUNCE	85.1	84	0	18	1
15149	SHRIMP, FRESH	3	OUNCE	85.1	90	1	17	1
15102	SNAPPER, CKD, DRY HEAT	3	OUNCE	85.1	109	0	22	1
62599	SORBET, ALL FLAVORS	½	CUP	90.0	100	25	0	0
6474	SOUP, BEAN W/BACON	1	CUP	264.9	106	16	5	2
6007	SOUP, BEAN W/HAM	1	CUP	243.0	231	27	13	9
6406	SOUP, BEAN W/HOT DOGS	1	CUP	250.0	187	22	10	7
6404	SOUP, BEAN W/PORK	1	CUP	253.0	172	23	8	6
6008	SOUP, BEEF BROTH OR BOUILLON	1	CUP	240.0	17	0	3	1
6547	SOUP, BEEF MUSHROOM	1	CUP	244.0	73	6	6	3
6409	SOUP, BEEF NOODLE	1	CUP	244.0	83	9	5	3
6070	SOUP, BEEF, CHUNKY	1	CUP	240.0	170	20	12	5
6402	SOUP, BLACK BEAN	1	CUP	247.0	116	20	6	2
6478	SOUP, CAULIFLOWER	1	CUP	256.1	69	11	3	2
6411	SOUP, CHEESE	1	CUP	247.0	156	11	5	10
6480	SOUP, CHICKEN BROTH OR BOUILLON	1	CUP	244.0	22	1	1	1
6417	SOUP, CHICKEN GUMBO	1	CUP	244.0	56	8	3	1
6549	SOUP, CHICKEN MUSHROOM	1	CUP	244.0	132	9	4	9
6419	SOUP, CHICKEN NOODLE	1	CUP	241.0	75	9	4	2
6018	SOUP, CHICKEN NOODLE, CHUNKY	1	CUP	240.0	175	17	13	6
6485	SOUP, CHICKEN RICE	1	CUP	252.8	61	9	2	1
6022	SOUP, CHICKEN RICE, CHUNKY	1	CUP	240.0	127	13	12	3
6425	SOUP, CHICKEN VEGETABLE	1	CUP	241.0	75	9	4	3
6024	SOUP, CHICKEN VEGETABLE, CHUNKY	1	CUP	240.0	166	19	12	5
6412	SOUP, CHICKEN W/DUMPLINGS	1	CUP	241.0	96	6	6	6
6423	SOUP, CHICKEN W/RICE	1	CUP	241.0	60	7	4	2
6015	SOUP, CHICKEN, CHUNKY	1	CUP	251.0	178	17	13	7
6426	SOUP, CHILI BEEF	1	CUP	250.0	170	21	7	7
6027	SOUP, CLAM CHOWDER, MANHATTAN STYLE	1	CUP	240.0	134	19	7	3
6230	SOUP, CLAM CHOWDER, NEW ENGLAND	1	CUP	248.0	164	17	9	7
6034	SOUP, CRAB	1	CUP	244.0	76	10	5	2
6201	SOUP, CREAM OF ASPARAGUS	1	CUP	248.0	161	16	6	8
6210	SOUP, CREAM OF CELERY	1	CUP	248.0	164	15	6	10
6216	SOUP, CREAM OF CHICKEN	1	CUP	248.0	191	15	7	11
6243	SOUP, CREAM OF MUSHROOM	1	CUP	248.0	203	15	6	14
6246	SOUP, CREAM OF ONION	1	CUP	248.0	186	18	7	9
6253	SOUP, CREAM OF POTATO	1	CUP	248.0	149	17	6	6
6256	SOUP, CREAM OF SHRIMP	1	CUP	248.0	164	14	7	9

Saturated Fat (g)	Monounsaturated Fat (g)	Polyunsaturated Fat (g)	Fiber (g)	Cholesterol (g)	Folate (g)	Vitamin A (RE)	Vitamin B6 (mg)	Vitamin B12 (μg)	Vitamin C (mg)	Vitamin E (mg)	Riboflavin (mg)	Thiamin (mg)	Calcium (mg)	Iron (mg)	Magnesium (mg)	Niacin (mg)	Phosphorus (mg)	Potassium (mg)	Sodium (mg)	Zinc (mg)
8	11	3	0	57	4	0	.2	1.4	18	-	.2	.2	37	1.2	14	2.4	126	230	915	1.7
7	9	2	0	39	1	0	.1	.8	18	-	.1	.2	7	.6	7	1.9	67	135	687	1.1
7	10	2	0	48	1	0	.1	1	13	-	.1	.2	7	1	8	2.2	73	129	643	1.4
1	1	2	1	0	7	16	.2	0	0	-	.1	.6	16	.9	9	2.8	56	58	222	.4
1	1	0	0	4	0	0	0	.1	0	-	0	0	1	.1	1	.3	7	19	112	.1
23	31	7	0	159	5	0	.4	2.2	2	-	.3	1.1	27	3.3	32	7.8	309	538	1989	4.4
1	2	0	0	11	0	0	0	.2	0	-	0	.1	4	.2	2	.6	24	47	168	.3
1	2	0	0	8	0	0	.1	.2	3	-	0	.1	1	.2	2	.5	14	38	186	.3
2	2	0	0	15	0	0	0	.7	4	-	0	0	2	.5	3	.7	26	52	270	.5
8	10	3	0	46	3	0	.2	1.1	1	-	.2	.5	20	.8	13	3.1	110	228	1020	1.9
1	0	1	0	45	5	54	.4	.3	0	-	.1	.1	11	.3	45	1.6	211	279	74	.4
4	7	24	8	0	164	4	.6	0	1	-	.2	1.6	84	4.9	255	3.2	508	496	2	3.6
3	6	21	4	0	152	0	.5	0	1	-	.2	.1	45	2.4	83	4.5	739	544	499	3.4
4	7	26	5	0	158	3	.5	0	1	-	.2	.2	38	4.5	86	2.8	769	326	407	3.5
4	7	25	-	0	159	0	.5	0	1	-	.2	.2	38	4.6	86	2.8	776	329	411	3.6
5	2	0	-	29	8	52	.1	.8	1	-	.6	.1	256	.7	38	.4	231	453	220	.9
4	-	-	-	25	7	66	.1	.7	2	-	.4	.1	256	.2	29	.4	226	412	188	.8
4	2	0	-	25	7	72	.1	.8	2	-	.4	.1	276	.2	27	.4	231	394	186	.8
0	0	0	-	0	8	404	.1	0	3	-	0	0	13	.4	7	.1	21	119	4	.1
0	0	0	-	0	27	998	.3	0	6	-	0	0	30	1	17	.2	48	267	10	.3
2	1	0	-	10	8	27	.1	.2	8	-	.1	0	104	.3	15	.2	77	184	88	.9
2	3	4	-	151	7	48	.1	1.6	1	-	.1	.1	57	1.1	34	2.6	185	191	293	1.2
0	0	0	0	166	3	56	.1	1.3	2	-	0	0	33	2.6	29	2.2	117	155	191	1.3
0	0	1	0	129	3	46	.1	1	2	-	0	0	44	2	31	2.2	174	157	126	.9
0	0	1	0	40	5	30	.4	3	1	-	0	0	34	.2	31	.3	171	444	48	.4
0	-	-	1	0	-	0	-	-	12	-	-	-	0	0	-	-	-	-	10	-
1	1	0	9	3	8	5	0	0	1	-	.3	.1	56	1.3	29	.4	90	326	927	.7
3	4	1	11	22	29	396	.1	.1	4	-	.1	.1	78	3.2	46	1.7	143	425	972	1.1
2	3	2	-	12	30	87	.1	.1	1	-	.1	.1	87	2.3	47	1	165	477	1092	1.2
2	2	2	9	3	32	89	0	.1	2	-	0	.1	81	2	46	.6	132	402	951	1
0	0	0	0	0	5	0	0	.2	0	-	.1	0	14	.4	5	1.9	31	130	782	0
1	1	0	-	7	10	0	0	.2	5	-	.1	0	5	.9	10	1	34	154	942	1.5
1	1	0	1	5	4	63	0	.2	0	-	.1	.1	15	1.1	5	1.1	46	100	952	1.5
3	2	0	1	14	13	262	.1	.6	7	-	.2	.1	31	2.3	5	2.7	120	336	866	2.6
0	1	0	4	0	25	49	.1	0	1	-	.1	.1	44	2.1	42	.5	106	274	1198	1.4
0	1	1	-	0	3	0	0	.2	3	-	.1	.1	10	.5	3	.5	51	105	843	.3
7	3	0	-	30	5	109	0	0	0	-	.1	0	141	.7	5	.4	136	153	958	.6
0	0	0	0	0	2	12	0	0	0	-	0	0	15	.1	5	.2	12	24	1484	0
0	1	0	2	5	5	15	.1	0	5	-	0	0	24	.9	5	.7	24	76	954	.4
2	4	2	-	10	0	112	0	0	0	-	.1	0	29	.9	10	1.6	27	154	942	1
1	1	1	1	7	2	72	0	.1	0	-	.1	.1	17	.8	5	1.4	36	55	1106	.4
1	3	2	4	19	5	122	0	.3	0	-	.2	.1	24	1.4	10	4.3	72	108	850	1
0	1	0	1	3	1	0	0	.1	0	-	0	0	8	0	0	.4	10	10	981	.1
1	1	1	1	12	4	586	0	.3	4	-	.1	0	34	1.9	10	4.1	72	108	888	1
1	1	1	1	10	5	265	0	.1	1	-	.1	0	17	.9	7	1.2	41	154	945	.4
1	2	1	-	17	12	600	.1	.2	6	-	.2	0	26	1.5	10	3.3	106	367	1068	2.2
1	3	1	1	34	2	53	0	.2	0	-	.1	0	14	.6	5	1.8	60	116	860	.4
0	1	0	1	7	1	65	0	.1	0	-	0	0	17	.7	0	1.1	22	101	815	.3
2	3	1	2	30	5	131	.1	.3	1	-	.2	.1	25	1.7	8	4.4	113	176	889	1
3	3	0	9	12	17	150	.2	.3	4	-	.1	.1	42	2.1	30	1.1	147	525	1035	1.4
2	1	0	3	14	9	329	.3	7.9	12	-	.1	.1	67	2.6	19	1.8	84	384	1001	1.7
3	2	1	1	22	10	40	.1	10.2	3	-	.2	.1	186	1.5	22	1	156	300	992	.8
0	1	0	1	10	15	51	.1	.2	0	-	.1	.2	66	1.2	15	1.3	88	327	1235	1.5
3	2	2	1	22	30	84	.1	.5	4	-	.3	.1	174	.9	20	.9	154	360	1042	.9
4	2	3	1	32	8	67	.1	.5	1	-	.2	.1	186	.7	22	.4	151	310	1009	.2
5	4	2	0	27	8	94	.1	.5	1	-	.3	.1	181	.7	17	.9	151	273	1047	.7
5	3	5	0	20	10	37	.1	.5	2	-	.3	.1	179	.6	20	.9	156	270	1076	.6
4	3	2	1	32	12	67	.1	.5	2	-	.3	.1	179	.7	22	.6	154	310	1004	.6
4	2	1	0	22	9	67	.1	.5	1	-	.2	.1	166	.5	17	.6	161	322	1061	.7
6	3	0	0	35	10	55	.4	1	1	-	.2	.1	164	.6	22	.5	146	248	1037	.8

Code	Name	Amount	Unit	Grams	Kilocalories	Carbohydrates (g)	Protein (g)	Fat (g)
6501	SOUP, CREAM OF VEGETABLE	1	CUP	260.1	107	12	2	6
6036	SOUP, GAZPACHO	1	CUP	244.0	56	1	9	2
6037	SOUP, LENTIL W/HAM	1	CUP	248.0	139	20	9	3
6440	SOUP, MINESTRONE	1	CUP	241.0	82	11	4	3
6039	SOUP, MINESTRONE, CHUNKY	1	CUP	240.0	127	21	5	3
6493	SOUP, MUSHROOM	1	CUP	253.0	96	11	2	5
6445	SOUP, ONION	1	CUP	241.0	58	8	4	2
6249	SOUP, PEA, GREEN	1	CUP	254.0	239	32	13	7
6451	SOUP, PEA, SPLIT W/HAM	1	CUP	253.0	190	28	10	4
6050	SOUP, PEA, SPLIT W/HAM, CHUNKY	1	CUP	240.0	185	27	11	4
6359	SOUP, TOMATO	1	CUP	248.0	161	22	6	6
6461	SOUP, TOMATO BEEF W/NOODLE	1	CUP	244.0	139	21	4	4
6463	SOUP. TOMATO RICE	1	CUP	247.0	119	22	2	3
6499	SOUP, TOMATO VEGETABLE	1	CUP	253.0	56	10	2	1
6465	SOUP, TURKEY NOODLE	1	CUP	244.0	68	9	4	2
6466	SOUP, TURKEY VEGETABLE	1	CUP	241.0	72	9	3	3
6064	SOUP, TURKEY, CHUNKY	1	CUP	236.0	135	14	10	4
6500	SOUP, VEGETABLE BEEF	1	CUP	253.1	53	8	3	1
6067	SOUP, VEGETABLE, CHUNKY	1	CUP	240.0	122	19	4	4
6468	SOUP, VEGETARIAN VEGETABLE	1	CUP	241.0	72	12	2	2
1056	SOUR CREAM	1	TBSP.	12.0	26	1	0	3
62556	SOUR CREAM, FAT FREE	1	TBSP.	16.0	13	3	1	0
1074	SOUR CREAM, IMITATION, NONDAIRY, CULTURED	1	TBSP.	14.4	30	1	0	3
62555	SOUR CREAM, LIGHT	1	TBSP.	16.0	16	1	1	1
6134	SOY SAUCE	1	TBSP.	18.0	10	2	1	0
11455	SPAGHETTI SAUCE	½	CUP	124.5	136	20	2	6
11458	SPINACH, CKD	½	CUP	90.0	21	3	3	0
11461	SPINACH, CND, DRAINED SOLIDS	½	CUP	107.0	25	4	3	1
11457	SPINACH, FRESH	1	CUP	56.0	12	2	2	0
11464	SPINACH, FRZ, CKD	½	CUP	95.0	27	5	3	0
11642	SQUASH, SUMMER, CKD	½	CUP	90.0	18	4	1	0
11641	SQUASH, SUMMER, FRESH	½	CUP	65.0	13	3	1	0
11644	SQUASH, WINTER, BAKED	½	CUP	102.5	40	9	1	1
11643	SQUASH, WINTER, FRESH	½	CUP	58.0	21	5	1	0
11953	SQUASH, ZUCCHINI, BABY, FRESH	1	MEDIUM	11.0	2	0	0	0
9316	STRAWBERRIES, FRESH	½	CUP	74.5	22	5	0	0
9320	STRAWBERRIES, FROZEN, SWEETENED	½	CUP	127.5	122	33	1	0
9318	STRAWBERRIES, FROZEN, UNSWEETENED	½	CUP	74.5	26	7	0	0
11508	SWEET POTATOES, BAKED IN SKIN	½	CUP	100.0	103	24	2	0
11510	SWEET POTATOES, BOILED, W/O SKIN	½	CUP	164.0	172	40	3	0
11659	SWEET POTATOES, CANDIED	½	CUP	113.4	155	32	1	4
11514	SWEET POTATOES, MASHED	½	CUP	127.5	129	30	3	0
11511	SWORDFISH, CDK, DRY HEAT	3	OUNCE	85.1	132	0	22	4
19348	SYRUP, CHOCOLATE, FUDGE-TYPE	1	TBSP.	21.0	73	12	1	3
19349	SYRUP, CORN, DARK	1	TBSP.	20.0	56	15	0	0
19351	SYRUP, CORN, HIGH-FRUCTOSE	1	TBSP.	19.0	53	14	0	0
19350	SYRUP, CORN, LIGHT	1	TBSP.	20.0	56	15	0	0
19353	SYRUP, MAPLE	1	TBSP.	20.0	52	13	0	0
19128	SYRUP, PANCAKE, LO CAL	1	TBSP.	20.0	33	9	0	0
19360	SYRUP, PANCAKE, W/2% MAPLE	1	TBSP.	20.0	53	14	0	0
19113	SYRUP, PANCAKE, W/BUTTER	1	TBSP.	20.0	59	15	0	0
18360	TACO SHELLS, BAKED	1	MEDIUM	13.0	61	8	1	3
9221	TANGERINE JUICE, FRESH	¾	CUP	185.2	80	19	1	0
9219	TANGERINES, CND, JUICE PACK	½	CUP	124.5	46	12	1	0
9220	TANGERINES, CND, LIGHT SYRUP PACK	½	CUP	126.0	77	20	1	0
9218	TANGERINES, FRESH	1	MEDIUM	84.0	37	9	1	0
19218	TAPIOCA PUDDING	1	CUP	298.1	355	58	6	11
6112	TERIYAKI SAUCE	1	TBSP.	18.0	15	3	1	0
16126	TOFU, FRESH, FIRM	1	OUNCE	28.4	41	1	4	2
16127	TOFU, FRESH, REGULAR	1	OUNCE	28.4	22	1	2	1

Saturated Fat (g)	Monounsaturated Fat (g)	Polyunsaturated Fat (g)	Fiber (g)	Cholesterol (g)	Folate (g)	Vitamin A (RE)	Vitamin B6 (mg)	Vitamin B12 (µg)	Vitamin C (mg)	Vitamin E (mg)	Riboflavin (mg)	Thiamin (mg)	Calcium (mg)	Iron (mg)	Magnesium (mg)	Niacin (mg)	Phosphorus (mg)	Potassium (mg)	Sodium (mg)	Zinc (mg)
1	3	1	1	0	8	3	0	.1	4	-	.1	1.2	31	.5	10	.5	55	96	1170	.3
0	1	1	4	0	10	20	.1	0	3	-	0	0	24	1	7	.9	37	224	1183	.2
1	1	0	-	7	50	35	.2	.3	4	-	.1	.2	42	2.7	22	1.4	184	357	1319	.7
1	1	1	1	2	16	234	.1	0	1	-	0	.1	34	.9	7	.9	55	313	911	.7
1	1	0	2	5	31	434	.2	0	5	-	.1	.1	60	1.8	14	1.2	110	612	864	1.4
1	2	2	1	0	5	0	0	.3	1	-	.1	.3	66	.5	5	.5	76	200	1020	.1
0	1	1	1	0	15	0	0	0	1	-	0	0	27	.7	2	.6	12	67	1053	.6
4	2	1	3	18	8	58	.1	.4	3	-	.3	.2	173	2	56	1.3	239	376	1046	1.8
2	2	1	-	8	3	46	.1	.3	2	-	.1	.1	23	2.3	48	1.5	213	400	1007	1.3
2	2	1	4	7	5	487	.2	.2	7	-	.1	.1	34	2.1	38	2.5	178	305	965	3.1
3	2	1	0	17	21	109	.2	.4	68	-	.2	.1	159	1.8	22	1.5	149	449	932	.3
2	2	1	1	5	7	54	.1	.2	0	-	.1	.1	17	1.1	7	1.9	56	220	917	.8
1	1	1	1	2	14	77	.1	0	15	-	0	.1	22	.8	5	1.1	35	331	815	.5
0	0	0	1	0	10	20	.1	0	6	-	0	.1	8	.6	20	.8	30	104	1146	.2
1	1	0	1	5	2	29	0	.1	0	-	.1	.1	12	1	5	1.4	49	76	815	.6
1	1	1	0	2	5	243	0	.2	0	-	0	0	17	.8	5	1	41	176	906	.6
1	2	1	-	9	11	715	.3	2.1	6	-	.1	0	50	1.9	24	3.6	104	361	923	2.1
1	0	0	1	0	8	23	.1	.3	1	-	0	0	13	.9	23	.5	35	76	1002	.3
1	2	1	1	0	17	588	.2	0	6	-	.1	.1	55	1.6	7	1.2	72	396	1010	3.1
0	1	1	0	0	11	301	.1	0	1	-	0	.1	22	1.1	7	.9	34	210	822	.5
2	1	0	0	5	1	23	0	0	0	-	0	0	14	0	1	0	10	17	6	0
0	-	-	-	3	-	30	-	-	0	-	-	-	36	0	-	-	-	-	18	-
3	0	0	0	0	0	0	0	0	0	-	0	0	0	.1	1	0	6	23	15	.2
1	-	-	5	-	18	-	-	-	0	-	-	-	22	0	-	-	-	27	9	-
0	0	0	0	0	3	0	0	0	0	-	0	0	3	.4	6	.6	20	32	1029	.1
1	3	2	4	0	27	153	.4	0	14	-	.1	.1	35	.8	30	1.9	45	478	618	.3
0	0	0	2	0	131	737	.2	0	9	-	.2	.1	122	3.2	78	.4	50	419	63	.7
0	0	0	-	0	105	939	.1	0	15	-	.1	0	136	2.5	81	.4	47	370	29	.5
0	0	0	2	0	109	376	.1	0	16	-	.1	0	55	1.5	44	.4	27	312	44	.3
0	0	0	3	0	102	739	.1	0	12	-	.2	.1	139	1.4	66	.4	46	283	82	.7
0	0	0	1	0	18	26	.1	0	5	-	0	0	24	.3	22	.5	35	173	1	.4
0	0	0	1	0	17	13	.1	0	10	-	0	0	13	.3	15	.4	23	127	1	.2
0	0	0	3	0	29	365	.1	0	10	-	0	.1	14	.3	8	.7	21	448	1	.3
0	0	0	1	0	13	235	0	0	7	-	0	.1	18	.3	12	.5	19	203	2	.1
0	0	0	-	0	2	5	0	0	4	-	0	0	2	.1	4	.1	10	50	0	.1
0	0	0	2	0	13	2	0	0	42	.1	0	0	10	.3	7	.2	14	124	1	.1
0	0	0	2	0	19	3	0	0	53	-	.1	0	14	.8	9	.5	17	125	4	.1
0	0	0	2	0	13	3	0	0	31	.2	0	0	12	.6	8	.3	10	110	1	.1
0	0	0	3	0	23	2182	.2	0	25	-	.1	.1	28	.4	20	.6	55	348	10	.3
0	0	0	4	0	18	2796	.4	0	28	-	.2	.1	34	.9	16	1	44	302	21	.4
2	1	0	-	9	13	475	0	0	8	-	0	0	29	1.3	12	.4	29	214	79	.2
0	0	0	-	0	14	1929	.3	0	7	-	.1	0	38	1.7	31	1.2	66	268	96	.3
1	2	1	0	43	2	35	.3	1.7	1	-	.1	0	5	.9	29	10	287	314	98	1.3
1	1	1	0	3	1	5	0	.1	0	-	0	0	21	.3	10	0	36	45	27	.2
-	-	-	0	0	0	0	0	0	0	-	0	0	4	.1	2	0	2	9	31	0
-	-	-	0	0	0	0	0	0	0	-	0	0	1	0	0	0	0	1	24	0
-	-	-	0	0	0	0	0	0	0	-	0	0	13	.2	3	0	0	41	2	.8
-	-	-	0	0	0	0	0	0	0	-	0	0	0	0	0	0	9	1	40	0
-	-	-	0	0	0	0	0	0	0	-	0	0	1	0	0	0	2	1	12	0
0	0	0	-	1	0	3	0	0	0	-	0	0	0	0	0	0	2	1	20	0
0	1	1	1	0	1	5	0	0	0	-	0	0	21	.3	14	.2	32	23	48	.2
0	0	0	0	0	9	78	.1	0	57	-	0	.1	33	.4	15	.2	26	330	2	.1
0	0	0	1	0	6	106	.1	0	43	-	0	.1	14	.3	14	.6	12	166	6	.6
0	0	0	1	0	6	106	.1	0	25	-	.1	.1	9	.5	10	.6	13	98	8	.3
0	0	0	2	0	17	77	.1	0	26	-	0	.1	12	.1	10	.1	8	132	1	.2
2	5	4	0	3	12	0	.3	.3	2	-	.3	.1	250	.7	24	.9	236	310	352	.8
0	0	0	0	0	4	0	0	0	0	-	0	0	5	.3	11	.2	28	41	690	0
0	1	1	1	0	8	5	0	0	0	-	0	0	58	3	27	.1	54	67	4	.4
0	0	1	0	0	4	3	0	0	0	-	0	0	30	1.5	29	.1	27	34	2	.2

Code	Name	Amount	Unit	Grams	Kilocalories	Carbohydrates (g)	Protein (g)	Fat (g)
16129	TOFU, FRIED	1	OUNCE	28.4	77	3	5	6
11954	TOMATILLOS, FRESH	1	MEDIUM	34.0	11	2	0	0
11540	TOMATO JUICE, CND, W/ SALT	¾	CUP	183.0	31	8	1	0
11886	TOMATO JUICE, CND, W/O SALT	¾	CUP	183.0	31	8	1	0
11533	TOMATOES, CND, STEWED	½	CUP	127.5	33	8	1	0
11537	TOMATOES, CND, W/ GREEN CHILIES	½	CUP	120.5	18	4	1	0
11531	TOMATOES, CND, WHOLE, REG PK	½	CUP	120.0	24	5	1	0
11529	TOMATOES, FRESH	1	MEDIUM	123.0	26	6	1	0
11527	TOMATOES, GREEN, FRESH	1	MEDIUM	123.0	30	6	1	0
11955	TOMATOES, SUN-DRIED	¼	CUP	13.5	35	8	2	0
11956	TOMATOES, SUN-DRIED, PACKED IN OIL	¼	CUP	27.5	59	6	1	4
62538	TORTELLINI, BEEF	1	CUP	257.9	230	46	5	1
19057	TORTILLA CHIPS, NACHO-FLAVOR	1	OUNCE	28.4	141	18	2	7
19424	TORTILLA CHIPS, NACHO-FLAVOR, LIGHT	1	OUNCE	28.4	126	20	2	4
19056	TORTILLA CHIPS, PLAIN	1	OUNCE	28.4	142	18	2	7
19058	TORTILLA CHIPS, RANCH-FLAVOR	1	OUNCE	28.4	139	18	2	7
18363	TORTILLAS, CORN	1	MEDIUM	25.0	56	12	1	1
18364	TORTILLAS, FLOUR	1	MEDIUM	35.0	114	19	3	2
15219	TROUT, CKD, DRY HEAT	3	OUNCE	85.1	162	0	23	7
15241	TROUT, RAINBOW, FARMED, CKD, DRY HEAT	3	OUNCE	85.1	144	0	21	6
15116	TROUT, RAINBOW, WILD, CKD, DRY HEAT	3	OUNCE	85.1	128	0	19	5
15128	TUNA SALAD	3	OUNCE	85.1	159	8	14	8
15183	TUNA, LIGHT MEAT, CND IN OIL	3	OUNCE	85.1	168	0	25	7
15184	TUNA, LIGHT MEAT, CND IN WATER	3	OUNCE	85.1	111	0	25	0
15185	TUNA, WHITE MEAT, CND IN OIL	3	OUNCE	85.1	158	0	23	7
15186	TUNA, WHITE MEAT, CND IN WATER	3	OUNCE	85.1	116	0	23	2
15221	TUNA, YELLOWFIN, CKD, DRY HEAT	3	OUNCE	85.1	118	0	25	1
5297	TURKEY, BOLOGNA	1	SLICE	21.0	42	0	3	3
7079	TURKEY BREAST MEAT	1	SLICE	21.0	23	0	5	0
5287	TURKEY LUNCH MEAT	1	SLICE	28.4	36	0	5	1
5296	TURKEY ROAST, ROASTED	3	OUNCE	85.1	132	3	18	5
5291	TURKEY ROLL, LIGHT AND DARK MEAT	3	OUNCE	85.1	127	2	15	6
5290	TURKEY ROLL, LIGHT MEAT	3	OUNCE	85.1	125	0	16	6
5299	TURKEY SALAMI	1	SLICE	28.4	56	0	5	4
5294	TURKEY THIGH, PREBASTED, MEAT & SKIN, CKD, ROASTED	3	OUNCE	85.1	134	0	16	7
5190	TURKEY, BACK, MEAT & SKIN, CKD, ROASTED	3	OUNCE	85.1	207	0	23	12
5192	TURKEY, BREAST, MEAT & SKIN, CKD, ROASTED	3	OUNCE	85.1	161	0	24	6
5188	TURKEY, DARK MEAT, CKD, ROASTED	3	OUNCE	85.1	159	0	24	6
5184	TURKEY, DARK MEAT, MEAT & SKIN, CKD, ROASTED	3	OUNCE	85.1	188	0	23	10
5306	TURKEY, GROUND, CKD	3	OUNCE	85.1	200	0	23	11
5194	TURKEY, LEG, MEAT & SKIN, CKD, ROASTED	3	OUNCE	85.1	177	0	24	8
5186	TURKEY, LIGHT MEAT, CKD, ROASTED	3	OUNCE	85.1	134	0	25	3
5182	TURKEY, LIGHT MEAT, MEAT & SKIN, CKD, ROASTED	3	OUNCE	85.1	168	0	24	7
5168	TURKEY, MEAT ONLY, CKD, ROASTED	3	OUNCE	85.1	145	0	24	4
5166	TURKEY, MEAT & SKIN, CKD, ROASTED	3	OUNCE	85.1	177	0	24	8
5288	TURKEY, THIN SLICED	3	OUNCE	85.1	94	0	19	1
5196	TURKEY, WING, MEAT & SKIN, CKD, ROASTED	3	OUNCE	85.1	195	0	23	11
11565	TURNIPS, CKD	½	CUP	78.0	14	4	1	0
11564	TURNIPS, FRESH	½	CUP	65.0	18	4	1	0
18328	VANILLA CREAM PIE	1	SLICE	126.0	350	41	6	18
19201	VANILLA PUDDING	1	CUP	298.1	388	65	7	11
17089	VEAL, MEAT AND FAT, CKD	3	OUNCE	85.1	196	0	26	10
17091	VEAL, MEAT ONLY, CKD	3	OUNCE	85.1	167	0	27	6
11578	VEGETABLE JUICE CND	¾	CUP	181.5	34	8	1	0
11581	VEGETABLES, MIXED, CND	½	CUP	81.5	38	8	2	0
11584	VEGETABLES, MIXED, FRZ	½	CUP	91.0	54	12	3	0
18392	WAFFLES, BUTTERMILK	1	EACH	75.0	217	25	6	10
18367	WAFFLES, PLAIN	1	EACH	75.0	218	25	6	11
18403	WAFFLES, PLAIN, FROZEN, TOASTED	1	EACH	33.0	87	13	2	3
15223	WHITEFISH, CKD, DRY HEAT	3	OUNCE	85.1	146	0	21	6

Saturated Fat (g)	Monounsaturated Fat (g)	Polyunsaturated Fat (g)	Fiber (g)	Cholesterol (g)	Folate (g)	Vitamin A (RE)	Vitamin B6 (mg)	Vitamin B12 (µg)	Vitamin C (mg)	Vitamin E (mg)	Riboflavin (mg)	Thiamin (mg)	Calcium (mg)	Iron (mg)	Magnesium (mg)	Niacin (mg)	Phosphorus (mg)	Potassium (mg)	Sodium (mg)	Zinc (mg)
1	1	3	1	0	8	0	0	0	0	-	0	0	105	1.4	17	0	81	41	5	.6
-	-	-	1	0	2	4	0	0	4	-	0	0	2	.2	7	.6	13	91	0	.1
0	0	0	1	0	36	102	.2	0	33	-	.1	.1	16	1.1	20	1.2	35	403	661	.3
0	0	0	1	0	36	102	.2	0	33	+	.1	.1	16	1.1	20	1.2	35	403	18	.3
0	0	0	+	0	7	70	0	0	17	+	0	.1	42	.9	.15	.9	26	305	324	.2
0	0	0	-	0	11	47	.1	0	7	-	0	0	24	.3	13	.8	17	129	483	.2
0	0	0	1	0	9	72	.1	0	18	-	0	.1	31	.7	14	.9	23	265	196	.2
0	0	0	1	0	18	76	.1	0	23	.4	.1	.1	6	.6	14	.8	30	273	11	.1
0	0	0	2	0	11	79	.1	0	29	-	0	.1	16	.6	12	.6	34	251	16	.1
0	0	0	2	0	9	12	0	0	5	-	.1	.1	15	1.2	26	1.2	48	463	283	.3
1	2	1	-	0	6	35	.1	0	28	-	.1	.1	13	.7	22	1	38	430	73	.2
0	-	-	9	15	-	150	-	-	4	-	-	-	96	1.5	-	-	-	-	770	-
1	4	1	2	1	4	12	.1	0	1	-	.1	0	42	.4	23	.4	69	61	201	.3
1	3	1	-	1	7	12	.1	0	0	-	.1	.1	45	.5	27	.1	90	77	284	-
1	4	1	2	0	3	6	.1	0	0	-	.1	0	44	.4	25	.4	58	56	150	.4
1	4	1	-	0	5	8	.1	0	0	-	.1	0	40	.4	25	.4	68	69	174	.4
0	0	0	1	0	4	6	.1	0	0	-	0	0	44	.4	16	.4	79	39	40	.2
0	1	1	1	0	4	0	0	0	0	-	.1	.2	44	1.2	9	1.3	43	46	167	.2
1	4	2	0	63	13	16	.2	6.4	0	-	.4	.4	47	1.6	24	4.9	267	394	57	.7
2	2	2	0	58	20	73	.3	4.2	3	-	.1	.2	-	.3	27	7.5	226	375	36	.4
1	1	2	0	59	16	13	.3	5.4	2	-	.1	.1	-	.3	26	4.9	229	381	48	.4
1	2	4	0	11	6	23	.1	1	2	-	.1	0	14	.9	16	5.7	151	151	342	.5
1	3	2	0	15	5	20	.1	1.9	0	-	.1	0	11	1.2	26	10.5	265	176	43	.8
0	0	0	0	15	4	20	.3	1.9	0	-	.1	0	10	2.7	25	10.5	158	267	43	.4
1	2	3	0	26	4	20	.4	1.9	0	-	.1	0	3	.6	29	9.9	227	283	43	.4
1	1	1	0	36	3	20	.4	1.9	0	-	0	0	3	.5	29	4.9	227	241	43	.4
0	0	0	0	49	2	17	.9	.5	1	-	0	.4	18	.8	54	10.2	208	484	40	.6
1	1	1	0	21	1	0	0	.1	0	-	0	0	18	.3	3	.7	28	42	184	.4
0	0	0	0	9	1	0	.1	.4	0	-	0	0	1	.1	4	1.7	48	58	301	.2
0	0	0	0	16	2	0	.1	.1	0	-	.1	0	3	.8	5	1	54	92	282	.8
2	1	1	0	45	4	0	.2	1.3	-	-	.1	0	4	1.4	19	5.3	208	253	578	2.2
2	2	2	0	47	4	0	.2	.2	0	-	.2	.1	27	1.1	15	4.1	143	230	498	1.7
2	2	1	0	36	3	0	.3	.2	0	-	.2	.1	34	1.1	14	6	156	213	416	1.3
1	1	1	0	23	1	0	.1	.1	0	-	0	0	6	.5	4	1	30	69	285	.5
2	2	2	0	53	5	0	.2	.2	0	-	.2	.1	7	1.3	14	2	145	205	372	3.5
4	4	3	0	77	7	0	.3	.3	0	-	.2	0	28	1.9	19	2.9	161	221	62	3.3
2	2	2	0	63	5	0	.4	.3	0	-	.1	0	18	1.2	23	5.4	179	245	54	1.7
2	1	2	0	72	6	0	.3	.3	0	-	.2	.1	27	2	20	3.1	174	247	67	3.8
3	3	3	0	76	8	0	.3	.3	0	-	.2	0	28	1.9	20	3	167	233	65	3.5
3	4	3	0	87	6	0	.3	.3	0	-	.1	0	21	1.6	20	4.1	167	230	91	2.4
3	2	2	0	72	8	0	.3	.3	0	-	.2	.1	27	2	20	3	169	238	65	3.6
1	0	1	0	59	5	0	.5	.3	0	-	.1	.1	16	1.1	24	5.8	186	259	54	1.7
2	2	2	0	65	5	0	.4	.3	0	-	.1	.1	16	1.1	24	5.8	186	259	54	1.7
1	1	1	0	65	6	0	.4	.3	0	-	.2	0	18	1.2	22	5.3	177	242	54	1.7
2	3	2	0	70	8	0	.3	.3	0	-	.2	.1	21	1.5	22	4.6	181	253	60	2.6
0	0	0	0	35	3	0	.3	1.7	0	-	.1	0	22	1.5	21	4.3	173	238	58	2.5
3	4	3	0	69	5	0	.4	.3	0	-	.1	0	6	.3	17	7.1	195	236	1217	1
0	0	0	2	0	7	0	.1	0	9	-	0	0	20	1.2	21	4.9	168	226	52	1.8
0	0	0	1	0	9	0	.1	0	14	-	0	0	17	.2	6	.2	15	105	39	.2
5	8	4	-	78	14	107	.1	.4	1	-	.3	0	25	.4	4	.1	220	45	197	.1
2	5	4	0	21	0	18	0	.3	0	-	.4	.2	113	1.3	16	1.2	131	159	328	.7
4	4	1	0	97	13	0	.3	1.3	0	.3	.3	.1	19	1	22	6.8	203	276	74	4
2	2	1	0	100	14	0	.3	1.4	0	.4	.3	.1	20	1	24	7.2	213	287	76	4.3
0	0	0	1	0	38	212	.3	0	50	-	.1	.1	20	.8	20	1.3	31	350	662	.4
0	0	0	-	0	19	949	.1	0	4	-	0	0	22	.9	13	.5	34	237	121	.3
0	0	0	5	0	17	389	.1	0	3	-	.1	.1	23	.7	20	.8	46	154	32	.4
2	3	5	-	50	11	26	0	.2	0	-	.3	.2	137	1.6	14	1.5	124	128	451	.6
2	3	5	-	52	11	49	0	.2	0	-	.3	.2	191	1.7	14	1.6	143	119	383	.5
0	1	1	-	8	12	120	.3	.8	0	-	.2	.1	77	1.5	7	1.5	139	42	260	.2
1	2	2	0	65	14	33	.3	.8	0	-	.1	.1	28	.4	36	3.3	294	345	55	1.1

Code	Name	Amount	Unit	Grams	Kilocalories	Carbohydrates (g)	Protein (g)	Fat (g)
15131	WHITEFISH, SMOKED	3	OUNCE	85.1	92	0	20	1
20089	WILD RICK, CKD	½	CUP	82.0	83	17	3	0
62552	YOGURT, FROZEN, FAT FREE	½	CUP	67.0	100	22	4	0
62604	YOGURT, FRUIT, FAT FREE	1	CUP	248.0	233	48	10	0
62627	YOGURT, FRUIT, FAT FREE, LIGHT	1	CUP	248.0	110	19	10	0
1121	YOGURT, FRUIT, LOWFAT, 10 G PROTEIN PER 8 OZ.	1	CUP	227.0	231	43	10	2
62603	YOGURT, PLAIN, FAT FREE	1	CUP	248.0	120	17	13	0
1119	YOGURT, VANILLA, LOWFAT, 11 G PROTEIN PER 8 OZ.	1	CUP	227.0	194	31	11	3

RESTAURANTS, INCLUDING FAST FOOD (QUICK SERVICE)

Code	Name	Amount	Unit	Grams	Kilocalories	Carbohydrates (g)	Protein (g)	Fat (g)
32391	ARBY'S-BEEF'N CHEDDAR SANDWICH	1	EACH	194.0	443	30	35	20
32400	ARBY'S-CHICKEN BREAST FILLET SANDWICH	1	EACH	204.0	547	53	26	28
32413	ARBY'S-CURLY FRIES	1	EACH	99.2	337	43	4	18
32405	ARBY'S-FISH FILLET SANDWICH	1	EACH	221.0	526	50	23	27
32411	ARBY'S-FRENCH FRIES	1	EACH	70.9	246	30	2	13
32406	ARBY'S-HAM'N CHEESE SANDWICH	1	EACH	170.1	411	38	24	19
32390	ARBY'S-REGULAR ROAST BEEF	1	EACH	155.9	388	25	16	16
32393	ARBY'S-SUPER ROAST BEEF	1	EACH	241.0	516	51	26	23
32410	ARBY'S-TURKEY SUB	1	EACH	277.0	599	54	33	28
34858	BURGER KING-BACON DOUBLE CHEESEBURGER	1	EACH	202.0	613	29	34	40
34856	BURGER KING-CHEESEBURGER	1	EACH	134.7	360	35	18	16
34857	BURGER KING-DOUBLE CHEESEBURGER	1	EACH	191.4	537	32	33	30
34855	BURGER KING-HAMBURGER	1	EACH	122.9	310	35	16	12
34841	BURGER KING-SALAD W/HOUSE DRESSING	1	EACH	176.0	159	8	3	13
34846	BURGER KING-SALAD W/REDUCED-CALORIE ITALIAN	1	EACH	176.0	42	7	2	1
34859	BURGER KING-WHOPPER	1	EACH	283.5	684	54	28	39
21002	FAST FOOD-BISCUIT W/EGG	1	EACH	136.0	316	24	11	20
21003	FAST FOOD-BISCUIT W/EGG AND BACON	1	EACH	150.0	458	29	17	31
21004	FAST FOOD-BISCUIT W/EGG AND HAM	1	EACH	192.0	442	30	20	27
21005	FAST FOOD-BISCUIT W/EGG AND SAUSAGE	1	EACH	180.0	581	41	19	39
21007	FAST FOOD-BISCUIT W/EGG, CHEESE, AND BACON	1	EACH	144.0	477	33	16	31
21008	FAST FOOD-BISCUIT W/HAM	1	EACH	113.0	386	44	13	18
21009	FAST FOOD-BISCUIT W/SAUSAGE	1	EACH	124.0	485	40	12	32
21010	FAST FOOD-BISCUIT W/STEAK	1	EACH	141.0	455	44	13	26
21001	FAST FOOD-BISCUIT, PLAIN	1	EACH	74.0	276	34	4	13
21027	FAST FOOD-BROWNIE	1	EACH	60.0	243	39	3	10
21060	FAST FOOD-BURRITO W/BEANS	1	EACH	108.5	224	36	7	7
21061	FAST FOOD-BURRITO W/BEANS AND CHEESE	1	EACH	93.0	189	27	8	6
21062	FAST FOOD-BURRITO W/BEANS AND CHILI PEPPERS	1	EACH	102.0	206	29	8	7
21063	FAST FOOD-BURRITO W/BEANS AND MEAT	1	EACH	115.5	254	33	11	9
21064	FAST FOOD-BURRITO W/BEANS, CHEESE, AND BEEF	1	EACH	101.5	165	20	7	7
21065	FAST FOOD-BURRITO W/BEANS, CHEESE, AND CHILI PEPPERS	1	EACH	167.0	329	42	17	11
21066	FAST FOOD-BURRITO W/BEEF	1	EACH	110.0	262	29	13	10
21067	FAST FOOD-BURRITO W/BEEF AND CHILI PEPPERS	1	EACH	100.5	213	25	11	8
21068	FAST FOOD-BURRITO W/BEEF, CHEESE, AND CHILI PEPPERS	1	EACH	152.0	316	32	20	12
21069	FAST FOOD-BURRITO W/FRUIT (APPLE OR CHERRY)	1	EACH	74.0	231	35	3	10
21100	FAST FOOD-CHEESEBURGER, LARGE, DOUBLE PATTY	1	EACH	258.0	704	40	38	44
21098	FAST FOOD-CHEESEBURGER, LARGE, SINGLE PATTY	1	EACH	219.0	563	38	28	33
21097	FAST FOOD-CHEESEBURGER, LARGE, SINGLE PATTY W/BCN & COND	1	EACH	195.0	608	37	32	37
21096	FAST FOOD-CHEESEBURGER, LARGE, SINGLE PATTY, PLAIN	1	EACH	185.0	609	47	30	33
21095	FAST FOOD-CHEESEBURGER, REGULAR, DOUBLE PATTY	1	EACH	228.0	650	53	30	35
21091	FAST FOOD-CHEESEBURGER, REGULAR, SINGLE PATTY	1	EACH	154.0	359	28	18	20
21089	FAST FOOD-CHEESEBURGER, REGULAR, SINGLE PATTY, PLAIN	1	EACH	102.0	319	32	15	15
21011	FAST FOOD-CHEESEBURGER, TRIPLE PATTY, PLAIN	1	EACH	304.0	796	27	56	51
21103	FAST FOOD-CHICKEN FILLET SANDWICH W/CHEESE	1	EACH	228.0	632	42	29	39

Saturated Fat (g)	Monounsaturated Fat (g)	Polyunsaturated Fat (g)	Fiber (g)	Cholesterol (g)	Folate (g)	Vitamin A (RE)	Vitamin B6 (mg)	Vitamin B12 (µg)	Vitamin C (mg)	Vitamin E (mg)	Riboflavin (mg)	Thiamin (mg)	Calcium (mg)	Iron (mg)	Magnesium (mg)	Niacin (mg)	Phosphorus (mg)	Potassium (mg)	Sodium (mg)	Zinc (mg)
0	0	0	0	28	6	48	.3	2.8	0	-	.1	0	15	.4	20	2	112	360	867	.4
0	0	0	1	0	21	0	.1	0	0	-	.1	0	2	.5	26	1.1	67	83	2	1.1
0	-	-	-	0	-	20	-	-	0	-	-	-	96	0	-	-	-	-	70	-
0	0	0	0	7	-	0	-	-	0	-	-	-	438	0	-	-	-	-	423	153	-
0	0	0	0	5	-	0	-	-	15	-	-	-	420	.2	-	-	-	-	510	160	-
2	1	0	0	10	21	25	.1	1.1	1	-	.4	.1	345	.2	33	.2	271	442	133	1.7
0	0	0	0	5	-	0	-	-	4	-	.2	-	480	0	-	-	0	600	170	-
2	1	0	0	11	24	30	.1	1.2	2	-	.5	.1	389	.2	37	.2	306	498	149	1.9
10	4	4	1	85	45	64	.4	2.3	1	.4	.5	.4	202	5.6	44	6.5	442	380	1801	6
6	11	11	2	101	35	17	.7	.4	0	2.9	.4	.5	123	3.9	51	16.4	322	366	1130	1.9
7	8	2	-	0	-	-	-	-	-	-	.1	.1	16	.8	-	1.9	-	724	167	-
7	9	11	-	44	-	-	-	-	1	-	.3	.3	72	2.1	-	5.3	-	450	872	-
3	6	5	-	0	-	-	-	-	4	-	-	.1	-	.6	-	1.9	-	240	114	-
7	8	2	1	68	83	112	.2	.6	3	1.3	.6	.4	151	3.8	19	3.1	177	338	899	1.6
4	8	2	1	58	45	71	.3	1.4	2	.2	.3	.4	61	4.7	35	6.6	268	354	888	3.8
9	8	6	2	41	42	0	.5	4.4	0	.4	.6	.6	118	6.6	60	9.7	414	518	822	11
6	7	8	-	82	-	-	-	-	-	-	.4	.5	94	3.2	-	9.4	-	-	1432	-
17	15	6	1	115	32	74	.4	3.4	8	1.6	.4	.3	162	4.1	39	8.4	386	480	833	6.6
-	-	-	-	-	-	-	-	-	-	-	-	-	-	-	-	-	-	-	705	-
14	12	2	2	111	34	111	.3	2	7	2	.3	.2	210	3.3	34	5.5	339	383	947	4.5
-	-	-	-	-	-	-	-	-	-	-	-	-	-	-	-	-	-	-	560	-
-	-	-	-	11	-	-	-	-	25	-	0	0	352	.1	95	.2	592	402	293	.1
-	-	-	-	0	-	-	-	-	25	-	0	0	320	.1	105	.2	472	390	430	.1
18	15	2	3	113	34	209	.3	3.1	14	4.2	0	0	113	6.5	54	5.6	339	565	1075	5.8
6	8	4	-	233	30	178	.1	.7	0	-	.3	.3	154	3.1	20	.7	185	160	654	1.1
10	13	6	-	353	30	53	.1	1	3	-	.2	.1	189	3.7	24	2.4	239	251	999	1.6
8	11	5	-	300	33	240	.3	1.2	0	-	.6	.7	221	4.6	31	2	317	319	1382	2.2
15	16	4	-	302	40	164	.2	1.4	0	-	.5	.5	155	4	25	3.6	490	320	1141	2.2
11	14	3	-	261	37	166	.1	1.1	2	-	.4	.3	164	2.5	20	2	459	230	1260	1.5
11	5	1	-	25	8	34	.1	0	0	-	.3	.5	160	2.7	23	3.5	554	197	1433	1.6
14	13	3	1	35	9	14	.1	.5	0	-	.3	.4	128	2.6	20	3.3	446	198	1071	1.6
7	11	6	-	25	11	16	.2	.9	0	-	.4	.4	116	4.3	27	4.2	204	234	795	2.7
9	3	1	-	5	6	24	0	.1	0	-	.2	.3	90	1.6	9	2	260	87	584	.3
3	4	3	-	10	4	2	0	.2	3	-	.1	.1	25	1.3	16	.6	88	83	153	.6
3	2	1	-	2	59	16	.2	.5	1	-	.3	.3	56	2.3	43	2	49	327	493	.8
3	1	1	-	14	41	119	.1	.4	1	-	.4	.1	107	1.1	40	1.8	90	248	583	.8
4	3	0	-	16	59	10	.1	.6	1	-	.4	.2	50	2.3	36	2.2	57	290	522	1.7
4	4	1	-	24	37	32	.2	.9	1	-	.4	.3	53	2.4	42	2.7	70	328	668	1.9
4	2	1	-	62	30	75	.1	.5	3	-	.4	.2	65	1.9	25	1.9	70	205	495	1.2
6	4	1	-	78	72	190	.2	1	3	-	.6	.3	144	3.8	48	3.8	142	402	1024	3
5	4	0	-	32	20	14	.2	1	1	-	.5	.1	42	3	41	3.2	87	370	746	2.4
4	3	0	-	27	18	23	.2	.6	1	-	.4	.2	43	2.2	30	2.5	70	249	558	2.2
5	5	1	-	85	29	56	.2	1	2	-	.6	.3	111	3.9	35	4.2	158	333	1046	4
5	3	1	-	4	4	37	.1	.5	1	-	.2	.2	16	1.1	7	1.9	15	104	212	.4
18	17	5	-	142	49	54	.4	3.4	1	-	.5	.4	240	5.9	52	7.2	395	596	1148	6.7
15	13	2	-	88	28	129	.3	2.6	8	1.2	.5	.4	206	4.7	44	7.4	311	445	1108	4.6
16	14	3	-	111	33	80	.3	2.3	2	-	.4	.3	162	4.7	45	6.6	400	332	1043	6.8
15	13	2	-	96	39	148	.3	2.5	0	-	.6	.5	91	5.5	39	11.2	422	644	1589	5.6
13	13	6	-	93	34	84	.3	2.1	3	2	.4	.6	169	4.7	36	8.3	349	390	921	4.1
9	7	1	-	52	22	71	.2	1.2	2	-	.2	.3	182	2.6	26	6.4	216	229	976	2.6
6	6	2	-	50	27	37	.1	1	0	-	.4	.4	141	2.4	21	3.7	196	164	500	2.4
22	22	3	-	161	52	85	.6	5.9	3	-	.6	.6	283	8.3	61	11.5	541	821	1213	10.9
12	14	10	-	78	46	128	.4	.5	3	-	.5	.4	258	3.6	43	9.1	406	333	1238	2.9

Code	Name	Amount	Unit	Grams	Kilocalories	Carbohydrates (g)	Protein (g)	Fat (g)
21101	FAST FOOD-CHICKEN FILLET SANDWICH, PLAIN	1	EACH	182.0	515	39	24	29
21037	FAST FOOD-CHICKEN NUGGETS PLAIN	1	EACH	17.0	48	3	3	3
21038	FAST FOOD-CHICKEN NUGGETS, W/BARB. SAUCE	1	EACH	17.0	43	3	2	2
21039	FAST FOOD-CHICKEN NUGGETS, W/HONEY	1	EACH	17.0	49	4	2	3
21040	FAST FOOD-CHICKEN NUGGETS, W/MUST. SAUCE	1	EACH	17.0	42	3	2	2
21041	FAST FOOD-CHICKEN NUGGETS W/SWEET AND SOUR	1	EACH	17.0	45	4	2	2
21042	FAST FOOD-CHILI CON CARNE	1	CUP	253.0	256	22	25	8
21070	FAST FOOD-CHIMICHANGA, W/BEEF	1	EACH	174.0	425	43	20	20
21071	FAST FOOD-CHIMICHANGA, W/BEEF AND CHEESE	1	EACH	183.0	443	39	20	23
21030	FAST FOOD-CHOCOLATE CHIP COOKIES	1	BOX	55.0	233	36	3	12
21043	FAST FOOD-CLAMS, BREADED AND FRIED	3	OUNCE	85.1	333	29	9	20
21128	FAST FOOD-CORN ON THE COB W/BUTTER	1	EACH	146.0	155	32	4	3
21045	FAST FOOD-CRAB, SOFT-SHELL, FRIED	1	EACH	125.0	334	31	11	18
21011	FAST FOOD-CROISSANT W/EGG AND CHEESE	1	EACH	127.0	368	24	13	25
21012	FAST FOOD-CROISSANT W/EGG, CHEESE, AND BACON	1	EACH	129.0	413	24	16	28
21013	FAST FOOD-CROISSANT W/EGG, CHEESE AND HAM	1	EACH	152.0	474	24	19	34
21014	FAST FOOD-CROISSANT W/EGG, CHEESE, AND SAUSAGE	1	EACH	160.0	523	25	20	38
21015	FAST FOOD-DANISH PASTRY, CHEESE	1	EACH	91.0	353	29	6	25
21016	FAST FOOD-DANISH PASTRY, CINNAMON	1	EACH	88.0	349	47	5	17
21017	FAST FOOD-DANISH PASTRY, FRUIT	1	EACH	94.0	335	45	5	16
21104	FAST FOOD-EGG AND CHEESE SANDWICH	1	EACH	146.0	340	26	16	19
21018	FAST FOOD-EGG, SCRAMBLED	2	EGGS	94.0	199	2	13	15
21074	FAST FOOD-ENCHILADA W/CHEESE	1	EACH	163.0	319	29	10	19
21075	FAST FOOD-ENCHILADA W/CHEESE AND BEEF	1	EACH	192.0	323	30	12	18
21076	FAST FOOD-ENCHIRITO W/CHEESE, BEEF, AND BEANS	1	EACH	193.0	344	34	18	16
21019	FAST FOOD-ENG. MUFFIN W/BUTTER	1	EACH	63.0	189	30	5	6
21020	FAST FOOD-ENG. MUFFIN W/CHEESE AND SAUSAGE	1	EACH	115.0	393	29	15	24
21021	FAST FOOD-ENG. MUFFIN W/EGG, CHEESE, AND CAN. BACON	1	EACH	146.0	383	31	20	20
21022	FAST FOOD-ENG. MUFFIN W/EGG, CHEESE, AND SAUSAGE	1	EACH	165.0	487	31	22	31
21047	FAST FOOD-FISH FILLET, BATTERED AND FRIED	1	EACH	91.0	211	15	13	11
21105	FAST FOOD-FISH SANDWICH W/TARTAR SAUCE	1	EACH	158.0	431	41	17	23
21106	FAST FOOD-FISH SANDWICH W/TARTAR SAUCE AND CHEESE	1	EACH	183.0	523	48	21	29
21023	FAST FOOD-FRENCH TOAST W/BUTTER	1	SLICE	67.5	178	18	5	9
21031	FAST FOOD-FRIED PIE, FRUIT (APPLE, CHERRY, OR LEMON)	1	EACH	85.0	266	33	2	14
21077	FAST FOOD-FRIJOLES W/CHEESE	3	OUNCE	85.1	115	15	6	4
21116	FAST FOOD-HAM AND CHEESE SANDWICH	1	EACH	146.0	352	33	21	15
21117	FAST FOOD-HAM, EGG, AND CHEESE SANDWICH	1	EACH	143.0	347	31	19	16
21114	FAST FOOD-HAMBURGER, DOUBLE PATTY W/COND AND VEG	1	EACH	226.0	540	40	34	27
21111	FAST FOOD-HAMBURGER, DOUBLE PATTY W/CONDIMENTS	1	EACH	215.0	576	39	32	32
21110	FAST FOOD-HAMBURGER, DOUBLE PATTY, PLAIN	1	EACH	176.0	544	43	30	28
21113	FAST FOOD-HAMBURGER, LARGE, SINGLE PATTY W/COND & VEG	1	EACH	218.0	512	40	26	27
21112	FAST FOOD-HAMBURGER, LARGE, SINGLE PATTY, PLAIN	1	EACH	137.0	426	32	23	23
21108	FAST FOOD-HAMBURGER, SINGLE PATTY W/CONDIMENTS	1	EACH	107.0	275	33	14	10
21107	FAST FOOD-HAMBURGER, SINGLE PATTY, PLAIN	1	EACH	90.0	275	31	12	12
21115	FAST FOOD-HAMBURGER, TRIPLE PATTY W/CONDIMENTS	1	EACH	259.0	692	29	50	41
21119	FAST FOOD-HOT DOG W/CHILI	1	EACH	114.0	296	31	14	13
21120	FAST FOOD-HOT DOG W/CORN FLOUR COATING (CORNDOG)	1	EACH	175.0	460	56	17	19
21118	FAST FOOD-HOT DOG, PLAIN	1	EACH	98.0	242	18	10	15
21028	FAST FOOD-ICE MILK, VANILLA, SOFT-SERVE W/CONE	1	EACH	103.0	164	24	4	6
21078	FAST FOOD-NACHOS W/CHEESE	3	OUNCE	85.1	260	27	7	14
21079	FAST FOOD-NACHOS W/CHEESE AND JALAPENO PEPPER	3	OUNCE	85.1	253	25	7	14
21080	FAST FOOD-NACHOS W/CHEESE, BEANS, GROUND BEEF	3	OUNCE	85.1	190	19	7	10
21081	FAST FOOD-NACHOS W/CINNAMON AND SUGAR	3	OUNCE	85.1	462	49	6	28
21130	FAST FOOD-ONION RINGS, BREADED AND FRIED	1	EACH	10.0	33	4	0	2
21048	FAST FOOD-OYSTERS, BATTERED OR BREADED, AND FRIED	3	OUNCE	85.1	225	24	8	11
21025	FAST FOOD-PANCAKES W/BUTTER AND SYRUP	1	EACH	74.0	166	29	3	4
21049	FAST FOOD-PIZZA W/CHEESE	1	SLICE	63.0	140	21	8	3
21050	FAST FOOD-PIZZA W/CHEESE, SAUSAGE, AND VEGETABLES	1	SLICE	79.0	184	21	13	5
21051	FAST FOOD-PIZZA W/PEPPERONI	1	SLICE	71.0	181	20	10	7
21131	FAST FOOD-POTATO, BAKED W/CHEESE SAUCE	1	EACH	296.0	474	47	15	29

Saturated Fat (g)	Monounsaturated Fat (g)	Polyunsaturated Fat (g)	Fiber (g)	Cholesterol (g)	Folate (g)	Vitamin A (RE)	Vitamin B6 (mg)	Vitamin B12 (µg)	Vitamin C (mg)	Vitamin E (mg)	Riboflavin (mg)	Thiamin (mg)	Calcium (mg)	Iron (mg)	Magnesium (mg)	Niacin (mg)	Phosphorus (mg)	Potassium (mg)	Sodium (mg)	Zinc (mg)
9	10	8	-	60	29	31	.2	.4	9	-	.2	.3	60	4.7	35	6.8	233	353	957	1.9
1	1	0	0	10	2	5	.1	.1	0	-	0	0	3	.2	3	1.1	34	42	90	.2
1	1	0	-	8	4	6	0	0	0	-	0	0	3	.2	3	.9	28	42	108	.1
1	1	0	-	9	2	4	0	0	0	-	0	0	3	.2	3	1	30	38	79	.2
1	1	0	-	8	2	4	0	0	0	-	0	0	3	.2	3	.9	29	37	103	.1
1	1	0	-	8	2	10	0	0	0	-	0	0	3	.2	3	.9	28	36	89	.1
3	3	1	-	134	30	167	.3	1.1	2	-	1.1	.1	68	5.2	46	2.5	197	691	1007	3.6
9	8	1	-	9	31	16	.3	1.5	5	-	.6	.5	63	4.5	63	5.8	124	586	910	5
11	9	1	-	51	33	126	.2	1.3	3	-	.9	.4	238	3.8	60	4.7	187	203	957	3.4
5	5	1	-	12	16	15	0	.1	1	.4	.2	.1	20	1.5	17	1.4	52	82	188	.3
5	8	5	-	65	7	27	0	.8	0	-	.2	.2	15	2.3	23	2.1	176	196	617	1.2
2	1	1	-	6	44	96	.3	0	7	-	.1	.2	4	.9	41	2.2	108	359	29	.9
4	8	5	-	45	20	4	.2	4.5	1	-	.1	.1	55	1.8	25	1.8	131	163	1118	1.1
14	8	1	-	216	37	255	.1	.8	0	-	.4	.2	244	2.2	22	1.5	348	174	551	1.8
15	9	2	-	215	35	120	.1	.9	2	-	.3	.3	151	2.2	23	2.2	276	201	889	1.9
17	11	2	-	213	36	117	.2	1	11	-	.3	.5	144	2.1	26	3.2	336	272	1081	2.2
18	14	3	-	216	38	109	.1	.9	0	-	.3	1	144	3	24	4	290	283	1115	2.1
5	16	2	-	20	15	13	.1	.2	3	-	.2	.3	70	1.8	15	2.5	80	116	319	.6
3	11	2	-	27	14	5	.1	.2	3	-	.2	.3	37	1.8	14	2.2	74	96	326	.5
3	10	2	-	19	15	24	.1	.2	2	-	.2	.2	22	1.4	14	1.8	69	110	333	.5
7	8	3	-	291	37	181	.1	1.1	1	-	.6	.3	225	3	22	2.1	302	188	804	1.6
6	6	2	0	400	53	252	.2	.9	3	.9	.5	.1	54	2.4	13	.2	227	138	211	1.6
11	6	1	-	44	34	186	.4	.7	1	-	.4	.1	324	1.3	51	1.9	134	240	784	2.5
9	6	1	-	40	192	142	.3	1	1	-	.4	.1	228	3.1	83	2.5	167	574	1319	2.7
8	7	0	-	50	253	133	.2	1.6	5	-	.7	.2	218	2.4	71	3	224	560	1251	2.8
2	2	1	-	13	17	33	0	0	1	.1	.3	.3	103	1.6	13	2.6	85	69	386	.4
10	10	3	-	59	18	86	.1	.7	1	-	.3	.7	168	2.3	24	4.1	186	215	1036	1.7
9	7	2	-	234	44	158	.2	.8	1	.6	.5	.5	207	3.3	34	3.9	320	213	784	1.8
12	13	3	-	274	54	172	.2	1.4	1	-	.5	.8	196	3.5	30	4.5	287	294	1135	2.4
3	2	6	-	31	51	11	.1	1	0	-	.1	.1	16	1.9	22	1.9	156	291	484	.4
5	8	8	-	55	44	30	.1	1.1	3	.9	.2	.3	84	2.6	33	3.4	212	340	615	1
8	9	9	-	68	31	97	.1	1.1	3	1.8	.4	.5	185	3.5	37	4.2	311	353	939	1.2
-	-	-	-	58	15	73	0	.2	0	-	.2	.3	36	.9	8	2	73	88	257	.3
7	6	1	-	13	4	33	0	.1	1	.4	.1	.1	13	.9	8	1	37	51	325	.2
2	1	0	-	19	57	36	.1	.3	1	-	.2	.1	96	1.1	43	.8	89	308	449	.9
6	7	1	-	58	72	76	.2	.5	3	.3	.5	.3	130	3.2	16	2.7	152	291	771	1.4
7	6	2	-	246	43	149	.2	1.2	3	-	.6	.4	212	3.1	26	4.2	346	210	1005	2
11	10	3	-	122	27	11	.5	4.1	1	-	.4	.4	102	5.9	50	7.6	314	570	791	5.7
12	14	3	-	103	45	4	.4	3.3	1	-	.4	.3	92	5.5	45	6.7	284	527	742	5.8
10	12	2	-	99	37	0	.3	2.9	0	1.3	.4	.3	86	4.6	37	8.3	234	363	554	5.7
10	11	2	-	87	37	33	.3	2.4	3	-	.4	.4	96	4.9	44	7.3	233	480	824	4.9
8	10	2	-	71	32	0	.2	2.1	0	-	.3	.3	74	3.6	27	6.2	175	267	474	4.1
4	4	2	-	43	17	13	.1	.8	3	.4	.3	.3	51	2.5	22	4.7	110	215	564	2.1
4	5	1	-	35	25	0	.1	.9	0	.5	.3	.3	63	2.4	19	3.7	103	145	387	2
16	18	3	-	142	31	16	.6	4.9	1	-	.5	.3	65	8.3	54	11	394	785	712	10.7
5	7	1	-	51	50	6	0	.3	3	-	.4	.3	19	3.3	10	3.7	192	166	480	.8
5	9	3	-	79	60	37	.1	.4	0	-	.7	.3	102	6.2	18	4.2	166	263	973	1.3
5	7	2	-	44	29	0	0	.5	0	-	.3	.2	24	2.3	13	3.6	97	143	670	2
4	2	0	-	28	5	52	.1	.2	1	.4	.3	.1	153	1.2	15	.3	139	169	92	.6
6	6	2	-	14	8	69	.2	.6	1	-	.3	.1	205	1	42	1.2	208	129	614	1.3
6	6	2	-	35	8	196	.2	.4	0	-	.2	.1	259	1	45	1.2	164	122	724	1.2
4	4	2	-	7	13	156	.1	.3	2	-	.2	.1	128	.9	32	1.1	129	151	600	1.2
14	9	3	-	31	6	9	.1	1.3	6	-	.3	.1	66	2.3	15	3.1	26	61	343	.5
1	1	0	-	2	1	0	0	0	0	0	0	0	9	.1	2	.1	10	16	52	0
3	4	3	-	66	8	66	0	.6	.3	-	.2	.2	17	2.7	14	2.7	120	111	414	9.6
2	2	1	-	19	11	22	0	.1	1	.4	.2	.1	41	.8	16	1.1	152	80	352	.3
2	1	0	-	9	59	74	0	.3	1	-	.2	.1	117	.6	16	2.5	113	110	336	.8
2	3	1	-	21	27	101	.1	.4	2	-	.2	.2	101	1.5	18	2	131	179	382	1.1
2	3	1	-	14	53	55	.1	.2	2	-	.2	.1	65	.9	9	3	75	153	267	.5
11	11	6	-	18	27	228	.7	.2	26	-	.2	.2	311	3	65	3.3	320	1166	382	1.9

Code	Name	Amount	Unit	Grams	Kilocalories	Carbohydrates (g)	Protein (g)	Fat (g)
21132	FAST FOOD-POTATO, BAKED W/CHEESE SAUCE AND BACON	1	EACH	299.0	451	44	18	26
21133	FAST FOOD-POTATO, BAKED W/CHEESE SAUCE AND BROCCOLI	1	EACH	339.0	403	47	14	21
21134	FAST FOOD-POTATO, BAKED W/CHEESE SAUCE AND CHILI	1	EACH	395.0	482	56	23	22
21135	FAST FOOD-POTATO, BAKED W/SOUR CREAM AND CHIVES	1	EACH	302.0	393	50	7	22
21136	FAST FOOD-POTATO, FRENCH FRIED IN BEEF TALLOW	1	LARGE	115.0	359	44	5	19
21137	FAST FOOD-POTATO, FRENCH FRIED IN BEEF TALLOW AND VEG OIL	1	LARGE	115.0	358	44	5	19
21138	FAST FOOD-POTATO, FRENCH FRIED IN VEGETABLE OIL	1	LARGE	115.0	355	44	5	19
21139	FAST FOOD-POTATOES, MASHED	½	CUP	120.0	100	19	3	1
21026	FAST FOOD-POTATOES, HASHED BROWN	½	CUP	72.0	151	16	2	9
21122	FAST FOOD-ROAST BEEF SANDWICH W/CHEESE	1	EACH	176.0	473	45	32	18
21121	FAST FOOD-ROAST BEEF SANDWICH, PLAIN	1	EACH	139.0	346	33	22	14
21052	FAST FOOD-SALAD, W/O DRESSING	½	CUP	69.3	11	2	1	0
21053	FAST FOOD-SALAD, W/O DRESSING, W/CHEESE AND EGG	½	CUP	72.3	34	2	3	2
21054	FAST FOOD-SALAD, W/O DRESSING, W/CHICKEN	½	CUP	72.7	35	1	6	1
21055	FAST FOOD-SALAD, W/O DRESSING, W/PASTA AND SEAFOOD	½	CUP	139.0	126	11	5	7
21056	FAST FOOD-SALAD, W/O DRESSING, W/SHRIMP	½	CUP	78.7	35	2	5	1
21058	FAST FOOD-SCALLOPS, BREADED AND FRIED	1	EACH	24.0	64	6	3	3
21059	FAST FOOD-SHRIMP, BREADED AND FRIED	1	OUNCE	28.4	79	7	3	4
21123	FAST FOOD-STEAK SANDWICH	1	EACH	140.0	315	36	21	10
21124	FAST FOOD-SUBMARINE SANDWICH W/COLDCUTS	1	EACH	228.0	456	51	22	19
21125	FAST FOOD-SUBMARINE SANDWICH W/ROAST BEEF	1	EACH	216.0	410	44	29	13
21126	FAST FOOD-SUBMARINE SANDWICH W/TUNA SALAD	1	EACH	256.0	584	55	30	28
21032	FAST FOOD-SUNDAE, CARAMEL	1	EACH	155.0	304	49	7	9
21033	FAST FOOD-SUNDAE, HOT FUDGE	1	EACH	158.0	284	48	6	9
21034	FAST FOOD-SUNDAE, STRAWBERRY	1	EACH	153.0	268	45	6	8
21082	FAST FOOD-TACO	1	LARGE	263.0	568	41	32	32
21083	FAST FOOD-TACO SALAD	½	CUP	66.0	93	8	4	5
21084	FAST FOOD-TACO SALAD W/CHILI CON CARNE	½	CUP	87.0	97	9	6	4
21088	FAST FOOD-TOSTADA, W/GUACAMOLE	1	OUNCE	28.4	39	3	1	3
21085	FAST FOOD-TOSTADA, W/BEANS AND CHEESE	1	EACH	144.0	223	27	10	10
21086	FAST FOOD-TOSTADA, W/BEANS, BEEF, AND CHEESE	1	EACH	225.0	333	30	16	17
21087	FAST FOOD-TOSTADA, W/BEEF AND CHEESE	1	EACH	163.0	315	23	19	16
40349	HARDEE'S-BIG CHEESE	1	EACH	141.8	495	28	30	30
40350	HARDEE'S-BIG DELUXE	1	EACH	248.1	675	46	31	41
40356	HARDEE'S-BIG FISH SANDWICH	1	EACH	191.4	514	49	20	26
40353	HARDEE'S-BIG ROAST BEEF	1	EACH	163.0	365	39	22	13
40351	HARDEE'S-BIG TWIN	1	EACH	141.8	369	28	19	20
40358	HARDEE'S-BISCUIT	1	EACH	78.0	275	35	5	13
40348	HARDEE'S-CHEESEBURGER	1	EACH	100.6	335	29	17	17
40357	HARDEE'S-CHICKEN FILLET	1	EACH	191.4	510	42	27	26
40347	HARDEE'S-HAMBURGER	1	EACH	100.1	305	29	17	13
40354	HARDEE'S-HOT DOG	1	EACH	50.0	346	26	11	22
40355	HARDEE'S-HOT HAM & CHEESE	1	EACH	141.8	376	37	23	15
40352	HARDEE'S-ROAST BEEF SANDWICH	1	EACH	141.8	323	39	19	11
44118	JACK IN THE BOX-BACON CHEESEBURGER	1	EACH	242.0	705	41	35	45
44101	JACK IN THE BOX-BREAKFAST JACK	1	EACH	126.0	313	29	19	14
44141	JACK IN THE BOX-CHEESECAKE	1	EACH	99.0	309	29	8	18
44115	JACK IN THE BOX-JUMBO JACK	1	EACH	222.0	497	41	25	26
44116	JACK IN THE BOX-JUMBO JACK W/CHEESE	1	EACH	242.0	559	40	28	31
44136	JACK IN THE BOX-REGULAR FRENCH FRIES	1	EACH	109.0	351	45	4	17
44135	JACK IN THE BOX-SMALL FRENCH FRIES	1	EACH	68.0	219	28	3	11
47265	K.F.C.-COLONEL'S CHICKEN SANDWICH	1	EACH	166.0	482	39	21	27
47261	K.F.C.-FRENCH FRIES	1	EACH	77.0	244	31	3	12
47260	K.F.C.-MASHED POTATOES AND GRAVY	1	EACH	98.0	71	12	2	2
47239	K.F.C.-ORIGINAL RECIPE CENTER BREAST	1	EACH	103.0	261	9	25	15
47240	K.F.C.-ORIGINAL RECIPE DRUMSTICK	1	EACH	57.0	169	5	12	12
47241	K.F.C.-ORIGINAL RECIPE THIGH	1	EACH	95.0	324	11	16	24
47237	K.F.C.-ORIGINAL RECIPE WING	1	EACH	53.0	172	5	12	11
48204	MCDONALD'S-BACON, EGG AND CHEESE BISCUIT	1	EACH	153.0	432	32	18	26
48174	MCDONALD'S-BIG MAC	1	EACH	215.0	560	43	25	32

Saturated Fat (g)	Monounsaturated Fat (g)	Polyunsaturated Fat (g)	Fiber (g)	Cholesterol (g)	Folate (g)	Vitamin A (RE)	Vitamin B_6 (mg)	Vitamin B_{12} (µg)	Vitamin C (mg)	Vitamin E (mg)	Riboflavin (mg)	Thiamin (mg)	Calcium (mg)	Iron (mg)	Magnesium (mg)	Niacin (mg)	Phosphorus (mg)	Potassium (mg)	Sodium (mg)	Zinc (mg)
10	10	5	-	30	30	173	.7	.3	29	-	.2	.3	308	3.1	69	4	347	1178	972	2.2
9	8	4	-	20	61	278	.8	.3	48	-	.3	.3	336	3.3	78	3.6	346	1441	485	2
13	7	1	-	32	51	174	.9	.2	32	-	.4	.3	411	6.1	111	4.2	498	1572	699	3.8
10	8	3	-	24	33	278	.8	.2	34	-	.2	.3	106	3.1	69	3.7	184	1383	181	.9
9	8	1	-	21	38	3	.3	.1	6	-	0	.2	18	1.6	38	2.6	153	819	187	.6
8	8	2	-	16	38	3	.3	.1	6	-	0	.2	18	1.6	38	2.6	153	819	187	.6
6	9	3	-	0	38	3	.3	.1	6	-	0	.2	18	1.6	38	2.6	153	819	187	.6
1	0	0	-	2	10	12	.3	.1	0	-	.1	.1	25	.6	22	1.4	66	353	272	.4
4	4	0	-	9	8	3	.2	0	5	.1	0	.1	7	.5	16	1.1	69	267	290	.2
9	4	4	-	77	40	46	.3	2.1	0	-	.5	.4	183	5.1	40	5.9	401	345	1633	5.4
4	7	2	-	51	40	21	.3	1.2	2	-	.3	.4	54	4.2	31	5.9	239	316	792	3.4
0	0	0	-	0	26	79	.1	0	16	-	0	0	9	.4	8	.4	27	119	18	.1
1	1	0	-	33	28	38	0	.1	3	-	.1	0	33	.2	8	.3	44	124	40	.3
0	0	0	-	24	23	32	.1	.1	6	-	0	0	12	.4	11	2	57	149	70	.3
1	2	3	-	17	33	213	.1	.6	13	-	.1	.1	24	1.1	17	1.2	68	200	524	.6
0	0	0	-	60	29	26	0	1.3	3	-	.1	0	20	.3	13	4	53	135	163	.4
1	2	0	-	18	7	7	0	.1	0	-	.1	0	3	.3	5	0	49	49	153	.2
1	3	0	-	35	8	6	0	0	0	-	.2	0	14	.5	7	0	60	32	250	.2
3	4	2	-	50	62	31	.3	1.1	4	-	.3	.3	63	3.5	34	5	204	360	547	3.1
7	8	2	-	36	55	80	.1	1.1	12	-	.8	1	189	2.5	68	5.5	287	394	1651	2.6
7	2	3	-	73	45	50	.3	1.8	6	-	.4	.4	41	2.8	67	6	192	330	845	4.4
5	13	7	-	49	56	41	.2	1.6	4	-	.3	.5	74	2.6	79	11.3	220	335	1293	1.9
5	3	1	0	25	12	68	0	.6	3	.9	.3	.1	189	.2	28	.9	217	318	195	.8
5	2	1	0	21	9	57	.1	.6	2	.7	.3	.1	207	.6	33	1.1	228	395	182	.9
4	3	1	0	21	18	58	.1	.6	2	.8	.3	.1	161	.3	24	.9	155	271	92	.7
17	10	1	-	87	37	226	.4	1.6	3	-	.7	.2	339	3.7	108	4.9	313	729	1233	6
2	2	1	-	15	13	26	.1	.2	1	-	.1	0	64	.8	17	.8	48	139	254	.9
2	2	1	-	2	21	71	.2	.2	1	-	.2	.1	82	.9	17	.8	51	130	295	1.1
1	1	0	-	4	12	24	0	.1	0	-	.1	0	46	.2	8	.2	25	71	87	.4
5	3	1	-	30	75	85	.2	.7	1	-	.3	.1	210	1.9	59	1.3	117	403	543	1.9
11	4	1	-	74	97	173	.2	1.1	4	-	.5	.1	189	2.5	68	2.9	173	491	871	3.2
10	3	1	-	41	15	96	.2	1.2	3	-	.6	.1	217	2.9	64	3.1	179	572	897	3.7
-	-	-	-	-	-	-	-	-	-	-	-	-	-	-	-	-	-	-	1251	-
-	-	-	-	-	-	-	-	-	-	-	-	-	-	-	-	-	-	-	1063	-
-	-	-	-	-	-	-	-	-	-	-	-	-	-	-	-	-	-	-	314	-
6	6	2	1	55	29	0	.3	3	0	.2	.4	.4	80	4.5	40	6.6	280	389	1071	7.4
9	7	4	1	45	28	14	.2	1.9	2	.7	.3	.2	66	3.3	29	5.5	161	229	475	3.8
-	-	-	-	-	-	-	-	-	-	-	-	-	-	-	-	-	-	-	650	-
-	-	-	-	-	-	-	-	-	2	-	.3	.5	-	-	-	5.5	-	-	789	-
-	-	-	-	-	-	-	-	-	-	-	-	-	-	-	-	-	-	-	360	-
-	-	-	-	-	-	-	-	-	2	-	.6	.6	-	-	-	6.4	-	-	682	-
-	-	-	-	-	-	-	-	-	-	-	-	-	-	-	-	-	-	-	744	-
-	-	-	-	-	-	-	-	-	-	-	-	-	-	-	-	-	-	-	1067	-
5	5	2	1	44	25	0	.3	2.6	0	.2	.4	.3	70	3.9	35	5.7	244	323	908	6.5
15	16	9	-	113	-	70	-	-	8	-	.5	.2	200	2.8	-	8.4	-	-	1240	-
5	5	3	-	190	-	138	.1	1.1	3	-	.5	.4	184	2.6	25	5.3	323	198	1080	1.9
9	7	2	-	63	-	-	-	-	-	-	.2	0	88	.3	-	1.9	-	-	2.8	-
10	11	2	-	72	-	67	.3	2.4	4	-	.3	.4	121	4.1	40	10.5	236	444	1023	3.8
13	11	2	-	98	-	196	.3	2.7	4	-	.3	.5	243	4.1	44	10.1	366	444	1482	4.3
4	7	-	-	0	-	-	-	-	26	-	0	.2	-	.7	-	3.6	-	-	194	-
3	7	-	-	0	-	-	-	-	16	-	-	.1	-	.4	-	2.3	-	-	121	-
6	4	9	1	47	29	14	.6	.3	0	2.3	.3	.4	100	3.1	41	10.6	261	297	1060	1.5
3	7	1	-	2	-	-	-	-	16	-	.1	.2	-	.3	-	1.9	-	-	139	-
1	0	0	-	-	-	-	-	-	-	-	0	-	16	.2	-	1.1	-	-	339	-
4	4	2	0	87	4	15	.6	.4	0	.5	.1	.1	16	1.2	31	14	238	265	603	1.1
2	3	2	-	59	5	14	.2	.2	0	.4	.1	0	7	.7	13	3.4	99	130	268	1.7
6	6	3	0	103	8	28	.3	.3	0	.5	.2	.1	13	1.4	23	6.5	176	224	549	2.4
3	6	2	-	59	-	-	-	-	-	-	.1	0	24	.3	-	2.9	-	-	383	-
8	16	2	1	248	18	157	.2	.6	0	1.5	.3	.4	181	2.6	30	2.5	442	232	1206	1.7
10	20	2	-	103	21	106	.3	1.8	2	-	.4	.5	256	4	38	6.8	314	237	950	4.7

Code	Name	Amount	Unit	Grams	Kilocalories	Carbohydrates (g)	Protein (g)	Fat (g)
48205	MCDONALD'S-BISCUIT W/SPREAD	1	EACH	75.0	260	32	5	13
48170	MCDONALD'S-CHEESEBURGER	1	EACH	116.0	310	30	15	13
48187	MCDONALD'S-CHEF SALAD	1	EACH	265.0	215	7	20	12
48181	MCDONALD'S-CHICKEN MCNUGGETS	1	EACH	18.5	45	3	3	3
48226	MCDONALD'S-CHOCOLATE LOWFAT MILK SHAKE	1	EACH	294.1	321	66	11	2
48189	MCDONALD'S-CHUNKY CHICKEN SALAD	1	EACH	255.0	143	5	23	3
48198	MCDONALD'S-EGG MCMUFFIN	1	EACH	135.0	284	27	18	11
48201	MCDONALD'S-ENGLISH MUFFIN W/SPREAD	1	EACH	58.0	170	26	5	4
48175	MCDONALD'S-FILET O' FISH	1	EACH	141.0	437	38	14	26
48188	MCDONALD'S-GARDEN SALAD	1	EACH	189.0	50	6	4	2
48169	MCDONALD'S-HAMBURGER	1	EACH	102.0	255	30	12	9
48209	MCDONALD'S-HASH BROWN POTATOES	1	EACH	53.0	130	15	1	7
48210	MCDONALD'S-HOTCAKES W/MARGARINE AND SYRUP	1	EACH	174.0	440	74	8	12
48180	MCDONALD'S-LARGE FRENCH FRIES	1	EACH	122.0	400	46	6	22
48176	MCDONALD'S-MCCHICKEN	1	EACH	187.0	415	39	19	20
48223	MCDONALD'S-MCDONALDLAND COOKIES	1	EACH	56.7	290	47	4	9
48179	MCDONALD'S-MEDIUM FRENCH FRIES	1	EACH	97.0	320	36	4	17
48171	MCDONALD'S-QUARTER POUNDER	1	EACH	166.0	410	34	23	20
48207	MCDONALD'S-SAUSAGE BISCUIT	1	EACH	118.0	420	32	12	28
48203	MCDONALD'S-SAUSAGE BISCUIT W/EGG	1	EACH	175.0	505	33	19	33
48199	MCDONALD'S-SAUSAGE MCMUFFIN	1	EACH	135.0	345	27	15	20
48200	MCDONALD'S-SAUSAGE MCMUFFIN W/EGG	1	EACH	159.0	430	27	21	25
48208	MCDONALD'S-SCRAMBLED EGGS	1	EACH	100.0	140	1	12	10
48190	MCDONALD'S-SIDE SALAD	1	EACH	106.0	30	4	2	1
48178	MCDONALD'S-SMALL FRENCH FRIES	1	EACH	68.0	220	26	3	12
48227	MCDONALD'S-STRAWBERRY LOWFAT MILK SHAKE	1	EACH	294.1	320	67	11	1
48225	MCDONALD'S-VANILLA LOWFAT MILK SHAKE	1	EACH	294.1	320	60	11	1
52366	PIZZA HUT-CHEESE PIZZA, HAND TOSSED	1	SLICE	70.0	259	28	17	10
52359	PIZZA HUT-CHEESE PIZZA, PAN	1	SLICE	70.0	246	29	15	9
53322	PIZZA HUT-CHEESE PIZZA, THIN'N CRISPY	1	SLICE	70.0	199	19	14	9
52363	PIZZA HUT-PEPPERONI PIZZA, THIN'N CRISPY	1	SLICE	70.0	207	18	13	10
52370	PIZZA HUT-PEPPERONI PERSONAL PAN PIZZA	1	EACH	250.0	675	76	37	29
52367	PIZZA HUT-PEPPERONI PIZZA, HAND TOSSED	1	SLICE	70.0	250	25	14	12
52360	PIZZA HUT-PEPPERONI PIZZA, PAN	1	SLICE	70.0	270	31	15	11
52365	PIZZA HUT-SUPER SPRM PIZZA, THIN'N CRISPY	1	SLICE	70.0	232	22	15	11
52362	PIZZA HUT-SUPER SUPREME PIZZA, PAN	1	SLICE	70.0	282	27	17	13
52369	PIZZA HUT-SUPER SUPREME, HAND TOSSED	1	SLICE	70.0	278	27	17	13
52371	PIZZA HUT-SUPREME PERSONAL PAN PIZZA	1	EACH	250.0	647	76	33	28
52368	PIZZA HUT-SUPREME PIZZA, HAND TOSSED	1	SLICE	70.0	270	25	16	13
52361	PIZZA HUT-SUPREME PIZZA, PAN	1	SLICE	70.0	295	27	16	15
52364	PIZZA HUT-SUPREME PIZZA, THIN'N CRISPY	1	SLICE.	70.0	230	21	14	11
62559	SUBWAY-BMT, ON ITALIAN ROLL	1	12 IN.	213.0	982	83	44	55
62561	SUBWAY-CLUB SANDWICH, ON ITALIAN ROLL	1	12 IN.	213.0	693	83	46	22
62562	SUBWAY-COLD CUT COMBO, ON ITALIAN ROLL	1	12 IN.	184.0	853	83	46	40
62564	SUBWAY-HAM AND CHEESE, ON ITALIAN ROLL	1	12 IN.	184.0	643	81	38	18
62565	SUBWAY-MEAT BALL SANDWICH, ON ITALIAN ROLL	1	12 IN.	215.0	918	96	42	44
62567	SUBWAY-ROAST BEEF, ON ITALIAN ROLL	1	12 IN.	184.0	689	84	42	23
62569	SUBWAY-SEAFOOD, ON ITALIAN ROLL	1	12 IN.	210.0	986	94	29	57
62571	SUBWAY-SPICY ITALIAN, ON ITALIAN ROLL	1	12 IN.	213.0	1043	83	42	63
62572	SUBWAY-STEAK AND CHEESE, ON ITALIAN ROLL	1	12 IN.	213.0	765	83	43	32
58318	TACO BELL-BEAN BURRITO	1	EACH	206.0	387	63	15	14
58319	TACO BELL-BEEF BURRITO	1	EACH	206.0	431	48	25	21
58321	TACO BELL-BURRITO SUPREME	1	EACH	198.0	440	55	20	22
62585	TACO BELL-LIGHT 7-LAYER BURRITO	1	EACH	276.0	440	67	19	9
62583	TACO BELL-LIGHT BEAN BURRITO	1	EACH	198.0	330	55	14	6
62586	TACO BELL-LIGHT BURRITO SUPREME	1	EACH	248.0	350	50	20	8
62584	TACO BELL-LIGHT CHICKEN BURRITO	1	EACH	170.0	290	45	12	6
62587	TACO BELL-LIGHT CHICKEN BURRITO SUPREME	1	EACH	248.0	410	62	18	10
62582	TACO BELL-LIGHT CHICKEN SOFT TACO	1	EACH	120.0	180	26	9	5
62575	TACO BELL-LIGHT SOFT TACO	1	EACH	99.0	180	19	13	5

Saturated Fat (g)	Monounsaturated Fat (g)	Polyunsaturated Fat (g)	Fiber (g)	Cholesterol (g)	Folate (g)	Vitamin A (RE)	Vitamin B6 (mg)	Vitamin B12 (µg)	Vitamin C (mg)	Vitamin E (mg)	Riboflavin (mg)	Thiamin (mg)	Calcium (mg)	Iron (mg)	Magnesium (mg)	Niacin (mg)	Phosphorus (mg)	Potassium (mg)	Sodium (mg)	Zinc (mg)
3	9	1	1	1	6	0	0	.1	0	1.8	.1	.2	75	1.3	14	1.5	168	100	730	.7
5	8	1	-	50	18	118	.1	.9	2	.5	.2	.3	199	2.3	21	3.9	177	223	750	2.1
6	6	1	-	120	-	385	-	-	13	-	.3	.3	240	1.4	-	3.4	-	-	459	-
1	2	0	-	9	-	-	-	-	-	-	0	0	-	.1	-	1.3	-	-	97	-
1	1	0	-	10	-	92	-	-	0	-	.5	.1	333	.8	-	.4	-	-	241	-
1	2	1	1	80	28	373	.6	.6	20	11	.2	.2	35	1	38	8.7	262	445	235	3
4	6	1	1	221	43	147	.2	.8	1	1.8	.3	.5	250	2.7	32	3.6	312	208	724	1.8
2	2	1	2	9	51	37	.1	-	0	.1	.1	.3	151	1.6	12	2.5	60	74	285	.4
5	10	11	1	50	20	44	.1	.8	-	-	.1	.3	164	1.8	27	2.7	227	149	1023	.9
1	1	0	-	65	-	900	-	-	21	-	.1	.1	32	.8	-	.4	-	-	70	-
3	5	1	-	37	-	40	-	-	2	-	.2	.3	80	1.5	-	3.8	-	-	490	-
1	4	2	-	0	-	-	-	-	1	-	-	.1	-	-	-	.8	-	-	330	-
2	5	5	-	8	-	40	-	-	-	-	.3	.3	80	1	-	2.9	-	-	685	-
5	15	2	-	0	-	-	-	-	15	-	-	.2	-	.6	-	2.9	-	-	20	-
4	9	7	-	50	-	20	-	-	2	-	-	.2	.9	120	1.5	-	8.6	-	-	830	-
1	7	1	-	0	-	-	-	-	-	-	.2	.2	-	1	-	1.9	-	-	300	-
4	12	2	-	0	-	-	-	-	12	-	-	.2	-	.4	-	2.9	-	-	150	-
8	11	1	-	84	-	40	-	-	4	-	.3	.4	120	2	-	6.7	-	-	645	-
8	17	3	-	44	-	-	-	-	-	-	.2	.5	64	1	-	3.8	-	-	1040	-
10	20	3	-	260	-	60	-	-	-	-	.3	.5	80	2	-	3.8	-	-	1210	-
7	11	2	-	57	-	40	-	-	-	-	.3	.5	160	1.5	-	4.8	-	-	770	-
8	14	3	-	270	-	100	-	-	-	-	.4	.5	200	2	-	4.8	-	-	920	-
3	5	2	-	425	-	100	-	-	-	-	.3	.1	48	1	-	-	-	-	290	-
0	1	0	-	33	-	800	-	-	12	-	.1	.1	16	.4	-	-	-	-	35	-
3	8	1	-	0	-	-	-	-	9	-	-	.2	-	.2	-	1.9	-	-	110	-
1	1	0	-	10	-	60	-	-	-	-	.5	.1	280	-	-	.4	-	-	170	-
1	1	0	-	10	-	60	-	-	-	-	.5	.1	280	-	-	-	-	-	170	-
7	3	-	-	28	-	50	-	.3	5	-	.2	.2	300	1.5	32	2.6	220	198	638	2.3
5	5	-	-	17	-	45	-	.3	4	-	.3	.3	252	1.5	26	2.5	188	160	470	2
5	3	-	-	17	-	35	-	.3	2	-	.2	.2	264	.9	21	2.3	188	131	434	1.8
5	5	-	-	23	-	35	-	.3	3	-	.2	.2	180	.9	19	2.5	148	144	493	1.7
13	17	-	-	53	-	120	-	.4	10	-	.7	.6	584	3.2	53	7.8	360	408	1335	3.8
6	5	-	-	25	-	50	-	.3	4	-	.3	.3	176	1.4	26	2.7	156	208	634	1.9
5	7	-	-	21	-	50	-	.3	4	-	.2	.3	208	1.8	25	2.6	176	203	564	2.1
5	5	-	-	28	-	50	-	.4	4	-	.2	.3	184	1.4	26	2.6	168	232	668	2.3
6	7	-	-	28	-	60	-	.4	5	-	.3	.4	216	1.9	32	3	188	266	724	2.7
7	6	-	-	27	-	55	-	.4	6	-	.3	.4	176	1.9	33	3.5	168	258	824	2.4
11	17	-	-	49	-	120	-	.5	11	-	.7	.6	416	3.7	53	7.6	320	487	1313	3.8
6	7	-	-	28	-	55	-	.4	6	-	.3	.3	192	2.3	35	3.4	184	289	735	2.9
7	8	-	-	24	-	60	-	.4	5	-	.4	.4	200	1.4	33	2.9	184	290	832	2.8
6	6	-	-	21	-	50	-	.3	5	-	.2	.3	172	1.7	30	2.6	160	272	664	2.3
20	24	7	5	133	63	67	.5	2.3	5	5.1	.3	.3	64	4.3	66	5.1	308	917	3139	6.1
7	8	4	5	84	47	74	.6	1	20	1.3	.3	.5	58	3.1	66	12.5	384	971	2717	2.5
12	15	10	5	166	39	87	.2	1.2	17	.9	.3	.4	227	2.9	28	3.8	315	876	2218	2.7
7	8	4	5	73	45	174	.3	.8	17	3.8	.4	.5	304	2.2	50	3.6	527	834	1710	2.8
17	17	4	3	88	35	72	.4	3.2	19	1	.4	.4	78	5	47	9.4	263	1210	2022	6.2
8	9	4	5	83	54	58	.4	2	5	4.4	.3	.2	55	3.7	57	4.4	266	910	2288	5.3
11	15	28	-	56	91	107	.3	6.5	5	2.5	.4	.5	230	4.4	32	7	336	641	2027	5.3
23	28	7	5	137	-	-	-	-	-	-	-	-	-	-	-	-	-	880	2282	-
12	12	4	6	82	36	119	.4	2.5	6	.8	.5	.3	231	4.2	43	5.1	456	909	1556	6.8
4	-	2	3	9	-	-	-	-	53	-	2	.4	190	4	-	2.8	-	495	1148	-
8	-	2	2	57	-	-	-	-	2	-	.3	.4	150	3	-	3.2	-	380	1311	-
8	-	2	3	33	-	-	-	-	26	-	2.1	.4	190	4	-	3.6	-	501	1181	-
-	-	-	-	5	-	350	-	-	5	-	-	-	300	2.5	-	-	-	-	1130	-
-	-	-	-	5	-	300	-	-	2	-	-	-	120	2	-	-	-	-	1340	-
-	-	-	-	25	-	600	-	-	9	-	-	-	96	1.5	-	-	-	-	1160	-
-	-	-	-	30	-	200	-	-	4	-	-	-	72	1.5	-	-	-	-	900	-
-	-	-	-	65	-	250	-	-	5	-	-	-	72	1.5	-	-	-	-	1190	-
-	-	-	-	30	-	150	-	-	5	-	-	-	48	.8	-	-	-	-	570	-
4	-	1	2	25	-	40	-	-	0	-	.2	.4	48	.6	-	2.8	-	196	554	-

Code	Name	Amount	Unit	Grams	Kilocalories	Carbohydrates (g)	Protein (g)	Fat (g)
62581	TACO BELL-LIGHT SOFT TACO SUPREME	1	EACH	128.0	200	23	14	5
62574	TACO BELL-LIGHT TACO	1	EACH	78.0	140	11	11	5
62588	TACO BELL-LIGHT TACO SALAD	1	EACH	464.0	330	35	30	9
62580	TACO BELL-LIGHT TACO SUPREME	1	EACH	106.0	160	23	14	5
58328	TACO BELL-MEXICAN PIZZA	1	EACH	223.0	575	40	21	37
58325	TACO BELL-NACHOS	1	EACH	106.0	346	37	7	18
58323	TACO BELL-NACHOS BELL GRANDE	1	EACH	287.0	649	61	22	35
58329	TACO BELL-PINTOS' N CHEESE	1	EACH	128.0	190	19	9	9
58337	TACO BELL-SALSA	1	EACH	10.0	18	4	1	0
58314	TACO BELL-SOFT TACO	1	EACH	92.0	225	18	12	12
58313	TACO BELL-TACO	1	EACH	78.0	183	11	10	11
58332	TACO BELL-TACO SALAD	1	EACH	575.0	905	55	34	61
58333	TACO BELL-TACO SALAD W/O SHELL	1	EACH	520.0	484	22	28	31
58316	TACO BELL-TOSTADO	1	EACH	156.0	243	27	9	11
61273	WENDY'S-BIG CLASSIC	1	EACH	251.0	480	44	27	23
62322	WENDY'S-BKD POTATO W/BACON AND CHEESE	1	EACH	380.0	510	75	17	17
61287	WENDY'S-BKD POTATO W/BROCCOLI AND CHEESE	1	EACH	411.0	450	77	9	14
62524	WENDY'S-BKD POTATO W/CHEESE	1	EACH	383.0	550	74	14	24
61281	WENDY'S-CHICKEN CLUB SANDWICH	1	EACH	220.0	520	44	30	25
61285	WENDY'S-FRENCH FRIES, BIGGIE	1	EACH	170.0	450	62	6	22
61284	WENDY'S-FRENCH FRIES, MEDIUM	1	EACH	136.0	360	50	5	17
61283	WENDY'S-FRENCH FRIES, SMALL	1	EACH	91.0	240	33	3	12
61301	WENDY'S-FROSTY DAIRY DESSERT, MEDIUM	1	EACH	321.8	460	76	12	13
61271	WENDY'S-PLAIN SINGLE	1	EACH	133.0	350	31	25	15
61272	WENDY'S-SINGLE W/EVERYTHING	1	EACH	219.0	440	36	26	23

Saturated Fat (g)	Monounsaturated Fat (g)	Polyunsaturated Fat (g)	Fiber (g)	Cholesterol (g)	Folate (g)	Vitamin A (RE)	Vitamin B6 (mg)	Vitamin B12 (µg)	Vitamin C (mg)	Vitamin E (mg)	Riboflavin (mg)	Thiamin (mg)	Calcium (mg)	Iron (mg)	Magnesium (mg)	Niacin (mg)	Phosphorus (mg)	Potassium (mg)	Sodium (mg)	Zinc (mg)
-	-	-	-	25	-	100	-	-	2	-	-	-	48	.6	-	-	-	-	610	-
4	-	1	1	20	-	40	-	-	0	-	.1	.1	0	0	-	1.2	-	159	276	-
-	-	-	-	50	-	1200	-	-	27	-	-	-	120	1.5	-	-	-	-	1610	-
-	-	-	-	20	-	100	-	-	2	-	-	-	0	0	-	-	-	-	340	-
11	-	10	3	52	-	-	-	-	31	-	.3	.3	257	4	-	3	-	408	1031	-
6	-	2	1	9	-	-	-	-	2	-	.2	-	191	1	-	.6	-	159	399	-
12	-	3	4	36	-	-	-	-	58	-	.3	.1	297	3	-	2.2	-	674	997	-
4	-	1	2	16	-	-	-	-	52	-	.2	.1	156	1	-	.4	-	384	642	-
0	-	0	0	0	-	-	-	-	-	-	.1	-	36	1	-	-	-	376	376	-
5	-	1	2	32	-	-	-	-	1	-	.2	.4	116	2	-	2.8	-	196	554	-
5	-	1	1	32	-	-	-	-	1	-	.1	.1	84	1	-	1.2	-	159	276	-
19	-	12	4	80	-	-	-	-	75	-	.6	.5	320	6	-	4.8	-	673	910	-
14	-	2	3	80	-	-	-	-	74	-	.4	.2	290	4	-	3.2	-	612	680	-
4	-	1	2	16	-	-	-	-	45	-	.2	.1	180	2	-	.6	-	401	596	-
7	8	7	-	75	-	60	-	-	12	-	.3	.5	120	3.5	-	6.7	-	500	850	-
4	3	8	-	15	-	100	-	-	36	-	.2	.5	80	2.5	-	6.7	-	1370	1170	-
2	3	7	-	0	-	200	-	-	60	-	.1	.3	80	2.5	-	4.8	-	1310	450	-
8	6	7	-	30	-	150	-	-	36	-	.2	.3	240	2	-	3.8	-	1210	640	-
6	7	9	-	75	-	20	-	-	9	-	.4	.6	80	8	-	15.2	-	470	980	-
5	15	1	-	0	-	-	-	-	12	-	.1	.3	16	.8	-	3.8	-	950	280	-
4	12	1	-	0	-	-	-	-	9	-	0	.2	16	.6	-	2.9	-	760	220	-
2	8	1	-	0	-	-	-	-	6	-	0	.2	-	.4	-	1.9	-	510	150	-
7	3	1	-	55	-	100	-	-	-	-	1	.2	320	.8	-	.8	-	830	260	-
6	7	2	-	70	-	-	-	-	-	-	.2	.4	80	3	-	5.7	-	280	510	-
7	7	7	-	75	-	60	-	-	9	-	.2	.4	80	3	-	6.7	-	430	850	-

Glossary

abstinence to refrain completely from engaging in a particular behavior.

acesulfame nonnutritive sweetener that is 200 times sweeter than sucrose and marketed as "sunette" in many food products.

Acquired Immunodeficiency Syndrome (AIDS) viral destruction of the immune system, causing loss of ability to fight infections.

acute illness an illness that occurs suddenly, often has no identifiable cause, is usually treatable, and often disappears in a short time.

addiction a pathological need for a substance that has life-damaging potential.

addictive behavior behavior that is excessive, compulsive, and psychologically and physically destructive.

adipose cells fat cells.

adrenocorticotropic hormone (ACTH) hormone released by the hypothalamus during periods of stress that initiates various physiological responses.

aerobic literally "with oxygen"; when applied to exercise, refers to activities in which oxygen demand can be supplied continuously by individuals during performance.

aerobic capacity maximum oxygen consumption.

alcohol socially acceptable drug.

alcoholism disease in which an individual loses control over drinking; inability to refrain from drinking.

alternative medicine body of therapies that are not taught in the U.S. medical schools and are generally unavailable from doctors or hospitals.

amenorrheic cessation of menstruation.

amino acid chemical structures that form protein.

anabolic steroids drugs closely related to testosterone that increase muscle mass in humans.

anaerobic literally "without oxygen"; when applied to exercise, refers to high-intensity physical activities in which oxygen demand is greater than the amount that can be supplied during performance.

android deposition of fat that is characteristic of men; fat tends to accumulate in the abdomen and upper body.

aneurysm weak spot in an artery that forms a balloonlike pouch that can rupture

angina chest pain that is the result of ischemia (see **ischemic**).

anorexia nervosa serious illness of deliberate self-starvation with profound psychiatric and physical components.

antioxidants compounds that block the oxidation of substances in food or the body (vitamins C and E and beta-carotene are examples).

arthritis inflammatory disease of the joints.

asymptomatic without symptoms.

atherosclerosis slow, progressive disease of the arteries characterized by the deposition of plaque on the inner lining of arterial walls.

ATP adenosine triphosphate, the actual unit of energy used for muscular contraction.

atrophy a decrease in the size of organ, muscles, and body tissues from disease or disuse.

autogenics form of suggestion that precipitates relaxation.

autoimmune disease disease in which the immune system fails to recognize its own body parts and produces antibodies against them to the point of causing injury.

autonomic nervous system part of the nervous system that is concerned with control of involuntary bodily functions.

avoidance a behavioral strategy that emphasizes eliminating circumstances associated with undesirable behavior.

ballistic stretching repetitive contractions of agonist muscles to produce very quick, rapid stretches of antagonist muscles.

balloon angioplasty surgical procedure that involves the insertion of a catheter with a balloon at the tip used to compress fatty deposits and plaque against the walls of the artery.

basal cell carcinoma the most common type of skin cancer. It grows slowly and usually does not metastasize (spread).

basal metabolic rate (BMR) number of calories needed to sustain life.

behavior assessment process of counting, recording, observing, measuring, and describing behavior.

behavior substitution lifestyle change technique in which an incompatible behavior is substituted for a behavior being altered.

behavioral contract a written agreement in a lifestyle-change program.

benign noncancerous; refers to a growth that is unable to spread.

binge drinking consuming five or more drinks in a single session at least once during the previous two weeks, with the intent to become intoxicated.

binge-eating disorder practice of eating large amounts of food in a short period of time.

biofeedback educational tool used to provide information about an individual's physiological actions.

blood alcohol concentration (BAC) percentage of alcohol content in the blood.

body composition amount of lean versus fat tissue in the body.

body dysmorphic disorder (BDD) a psychiatric disorder characterized by a preoccupation with perceived imperfections in physical appearance that cause the person to withdraw from social activities.

body mass index (BMI) the ratio of body weight in kilograms to height in meters squared.

botanicals plants that are thought to have medicinal properties (also called *herbs* and *phytomedicinals*).

bulimia eating disorder characterized by episodes of secretive binge eating and purging.

Caesarean section delivery surgical removal of the fetus through the abdominal wall.

caffeine a stimulant that increases the heart rate.

caloric expenditure calories expended by physical activity and metabolism.

caloric intake calories supplied by food.

calorie short for *kilocalorie*, which is the unit of measurement for food energy. A calorie is the amount of heat required to raise the temperature of 1 gram of water 1 degree Centigrade.

cancer group of diseases characterized by uncontrolled, disorderly cell growth.

cannabinoids chemicals found only in marijuana.

cannabis sativa Indian hemp plant from which marijuana and hashish are derived.

carbon monoxide a colorless, tasteless, odorless gas that is the product of incomplete combustion of carbon-containing fuels.

carcinogens substances that cause cancer or enable the growth of cancer cells; cancer-causing agents.

carcinoma cancer of a body surface or body cavity, such as cancer of the breast, lung, skin, stomach, testis, or uterus.

cariogenic refers to the promotion of dental caries, or cavities.

cardia dysrhythmia irregular heart rate that is sometimes intractable.

cardiac output amount of blood ejected by the heart in 1 minute.

cardiorespiratory endurance ability to take in, deliver, and extract oxygen for physical work.

catheterization the process of examining the heart by introducing a thin tube (catheter) into a vein or an artery and passing it into the heart.

cause and effect in medical research, the type of a relationship in which one variable is scientifically proved to cause a certain effect.

cerebral hemorrhage bursting of a blood vessel in the brain.

chemoprevention nutritional intervention to prevent diseases, such as cancer, by bolstering the immune system.

chemotherapy use of drugs and hormones to treat various cancers.

child abuse physical, emotional, or sexual mistreatment of a child.

chlamydia one of the most common sexually transmitted diseases.

cholesterol steroid that is an essential structural component of neural tissue and cell walls and is required for the manufacture of hormones and bile.

chronic disease a disease that usually begins gradually and persists for an indefinite period of time, usually months or years.

chronic effects of exercise the physiological changes that result from cardiorespiratory training.

circuit resistance training a total of 8 to 15 exercises are usually used in a circuit. The exerciser goes through the circuit three times with minimum rest between exercise stations.

cocaine a stimulant used in powdered form.

cognitive dissonance an internal conflict that occurs when a person's behaviors are inconsistent with his or her beliefs, values, or knowledge.

communicable diseases diseases that can be transmitted from one person to another.

complete protein protein that contains all the essential amino acids.

complex carbohydrates polysaccharides, including starch and fiber.

concentric contraction shortening of the muscle as it develops the tension to overcome an external resistance.

condyloma warts on the genitalia.

contraindication reason for not prescribing a drug or treatment.

control group in health research, the group receiving no treatment.

coping effort(s) made to manage or deal with stress.

coronary artery bypass surgery procedure involving the removal of a leg vein that is used as a shunt around the blocked area in the coronary artery.

countering the substitution of a new behavior for an undesirable one.

crack smokable form of cocaine that is extremely dangerous and very addictive.

Crohn s disease a type of inflammatory bowel disease whose cause is unknown. Crohn's disease is characterized by frequent and intense diarrhea, abdominal pain, gas, fever, and rectal bleeding.

cross-training the attainment of physical fitness by participating in a variety of activities regularly.

crude fiber residue of plant food following chemical treatment in the laboratory.

cunnilingus oral sex performed on the female genitalia.

daily reference values (DRV) provides nutritional guidelines for ingestion of carbohydrate, fat, saturated fat, cholesterol, sodium, potassium, and dietary fiber.

deceptive advertising advertising that misleads consumers by overstating or exaggerating the performance of a product.

deductible amount paid by a patient before being eligible for benefits from an insurance company.

defensive medicine practice of prescribing medical tests to protect doctors against malpractice lawsuits.

dehydration excessive loss of body water.

delta-9-tetrahydrocannabinol (THC) major psychoactive drug found in marijuana.

depressants known as sedatives and tranquilizers; these agents slow the central nervous system.

designer drugs illegally manufactured drugs that mimic controlled substances.

diabetes mellitus metabolic disorder involving the pancreas and the failure to produce insulin; a risk factor for cardiovascular disease.

diagnostic laboratory tests tests conducted for specific symptoms during a physical examination.

dietary fiber residue of plant food after digestion in the human body. One gram of crude fiber equals 2 to 3 grams of dietary fiber.

diet resistance the inability to lose weight by dieting.

disability insurance insurance that pays for income lost because of the inability to work due to an illness or injury.

distress form of stress that results in negative responses.

diuretics substances that increase water output and body's need for water.

diverticulitis infection of the diverticula of the intestines.

diverticulosis condition of having saclike swellings (diverticula) in the walls of the intestines.

double-blind study type of health research in which neither the researcher nor the subjects know who is receiving an experimental treatment.

drug chemical substance that has the potential to alter the structure and functioning of a living organism.

eccentric contraction the lengthening of a muscle as the weight or resistance is returned to the starting position.

echocardiography noninvasive technique that uses sound waves to determine the shape, texture, and movement of the valves of the heart.

ectomorph body shape characterized by thin body frame.

elderly abuse physical, emotional, sexual, or medical abuse of an elderly person. Most often the abuser is an adult child of the victim.

electrocardiograph (ECG) device for recording electrical variations in action of the heart muscle.

embolus mass of undissolved matter in the blood or lymphatic vessels that detaches from the vessel walls.

endomorph body shape characterized by rounded physical features and large body frame.

endorphins mood-elevating, pain-killing substances produced by the brain.

energy nutrients nutrients, such as carbohydrates, fat, and protein, that provide a source of energy for the body.

environmental dimension of wellness comprises aspects of wellness that improve quality of life in the community, including laws and agencies that safeguard the physical environment.

epidemiological studies population studies that observe the health habits and diseases of large numbers of people.

epinephrine hormone produced by the adrenal medulla that speeds up body processes.

essential fat fat that is indispensable for individuals to function biologically and necessary to support life.

essential hypertension high blood pressure caused by unknown reasons.

essential nutrients nutrients that cannot be made by the body and must be supplied in the diet.

ethyl alcohol intoxicating agent in alcoholic drinks; colorless liquid with a sharp, burning taste.

eustress stress judged as "good"; positive stress or stress that contributes to positive outcomes.

exclusion medical services that are not covered by an insurance policy.

experimental group in health research, the group receiving some form of experimental treatment.

false negative test results that incorrectly show a person is healthy when an abnormality actually exists.

false positive test results that incorrectly show an abnormality when a person is actually healthy.

family practitioner medical doctor who serves as a general practitioner for an individual or a family.

fasting complete starvation; avoidance of food consumption.

fat mixture of triglycerides.

fellatio oral sex performed on the male genitalia.

fiber substances in food that resist digestion; formerly called *roughage.*

fight-or-flight syndrome initial phase of the general adaptation syndrome (GAS); when a stressor is encountered, the body responds by preparing to stand and fight or run away depending on the situation; also called the *alarm phase* of the GAS.

fixed indemnity benefits specified amounts that are paid by an insurance company for particular medical procedures.

flexibility range of motion at a joint.

fraternal twins twins who emanate from separate eggs and do not have identical genes.

freebasing smoking liquefied cocaine.

free radicals naturally produced chemicals that arise from cell activity.

fructose fruit sugar.

general adaptation syndrome (GAS) series of physiological changes that occur when a stressor is encountered; the GAS is conceived of as having three phases: alarm, resistance, and exhaustion.

genital warts warts on the genitalia.

glucose primary source of energy used by the body; blood sugar.

glyceride general term for fat compounds, including triglyceride, monoglyceride, and diglyceride.

Golgi tendon organ a proprioceptor that responds to muscle stretch and tension.

goniometer a protractor-like instrument used to measure the flexibility of various joints.

gonorrhea bacterial disease that is sexually transmitted and can lead to serious complications if left untreated, including sterility and scarring of the heart valves.

gynoid fat deposition characteristic of females, in whom fat tends to accumulate on the hips and thighs.

hardiness label used in describing a particular type of personality that tends to remain healthy even under extreme stress; the three components of hardiness are challenge, commitment, and control.

hashish resin from the *cannabis sativa* plant that can be smoked to alter mood; a frequently abused drug.

hate crimes crimes directed at individuals or groups solely because of their racial, ethnic, or religious background, sexual orientation, or other differences from the perpetrator.

headache a common discomfort that is often caused by distress, tension, and anxiety; may be the result of injury or brain disease.

health balancing of the physical, emotional, social, and spiritual components of personality in a manner that is conducive to optimal well-being and a higher quality of existence.

health behavior gap discrepancy between what people know and what they actually do regarding their health.

health care providers people and facilities such as physicians and hospitals that provide health care services.

health fatalism in health information the view that new information cannot be believed or trusted because it will inevitably be refuted.

health insurance a contract between an insurance company and an individual or a group for the payment of medical care costs.

health maintenance organization (HMO) prepaid group insurance program that provides a full range of medical services.

health-promoting behaviors things done to maintain and improve one's level of wellness.

health promotion art and science of helping people change their lifestyle to move toward a higher state of wellness.

health-related fitness components of fitness that include cardiorespiratory endurance, muscular strength, muscular endurance, flexibility, and body composition.

health risk appraisals questionnaires used to provide information about health habits, lifestyle, and medical history.

heat exhaustion serious heat-related condition characterized by dizziness, fainting, rapid pulse, and cool skin.

heat stroke heat-related medical emergency characterized by high temperature (106° F or higher) and dry skin and accompanied by some or all of the following: delirium, convulsions, and loss of consciousness.

hemoglobin substance in blood that carries oxygen.

hepatitis B one of five types of viral hepatitis. Hepatitis B is the most serious type and can be transmitted sexually.

herbs see *botanicals.*

herpes simplex virus (HSV) virus responsible for herpes genitalis, a sexually transmitted disease.

highly polyunsaturated fat fatty acid composed of triglycerides in which the carbon chain has room for many hydrogen atoms.

homeostasis state of balance or constancy; the body is continually attempting to maintain homeostasis.

homicide the intentional taking of another person's life; murder.

homocysteine amino acid that is thought to increase the risk of heart disease.

homogeneous group group of subjects with similar characteristics.

hypertrophy increase in the size of organs and muscle tissue.

human immunodeficiency virus (HIV) virus that is the source of AIDS.

human papilloma virus (HPV) causative agent of condyloma (genital warts).

hydrogenation process of adding hydrogen to unsaturated fatty acid to make it more saturated.

hyperglycemia high blood sugar.

hyperplasia increase in the number of cells.

hypertension high blood pressure.

hyperthermia excessive buildup of heat in the body.

hyperthyroidism disease caused by an overactive thyroid gland.

hypertrophy increase in the size of a cell.

hypokinesis physical inactivity.

hypothalamus part of the limbic system that contains the center for many bodily functions; in stressful situations the hypothalamus releases specific hormones to elicit appropriate bodily responses.

hypothermia cold weather-related condition that results in abnormally low body temperature.

hypothyroidism disease caused by an underactive thyroid gland.

iatrogenic disease condition caused as a result of receiving medical care.

identical twins twins who emanate from the same egg.

immunization a vaccine or other preparation administered to prevent disease.

immunotherapy in relation to cancer, technique for stimulating the body's immune system to destroy cancer cells.

implied consent nonverbal authorization of a medical procedure such as a cooperation during the administration of tests.

incomplete protein protein that does not contain all the essential amino acids in the proportions needed by the body.

infarction death of heart muscle tissue.

inflammatory bowel disease a variety of diseases that cause inflammation of the intestines. The two most common types are Crohn's disease and ulcerative colitis.

influenza commonly called *flu;* caused by a virus.

informed consent legal provision requiring patient's authorization of any medical procedure, therapy, or treatment.

inhalants substances that cause druglike effects when inhaled.

insoluble fiber fiber that does not dissolve in water; comes from wheat bran and vegetables.

insulin hormone secreted by the pancreas that increases the use of glucose by the tissues of the body.

intensity degree of vigorousness of a single bout of exercise.

internist medical doctor specializing in internal medicine and sometimes serving as a primary care physician.

ischemic diminished supply of blood to the heart muscle.

isoflavones Phytoestrogens in soybeans that are thought to help prevent breast cancer by blocking natural estrogens.

isokinetic method for developing muscular strength that involves a constant rate of speed and changes in the amount of weight resistance.

isometric use of static contractions to develop strength.

isotonic method for developing muscular strength that involves a variable rate of speed and a constant weight resistance.

lactic acid metabolite formed in muscles as a result of incomplete breakdown of sugar.

lactose simple sugar; milk sugar.

lactovegetarian a person who eats plant foods and dairy products but excludes eggs, fish, poultry, and meat from their diet.

leptin a protein made in fat cells that controls weight gain and loss.

leukemia cancer of the blood-forming tissues, including the bone marrow and spleen.

life insurance insurance that pays a death benefit.

limbic system large, C-shaped area that contains the centers for emotions, memory storage, learning relay, and hormone production (the pituitary gland, thalamus, and hypothalamus).

lipid class of nutrients more commonly referred to as *fat.*

lipoprotein fat-carrying protein.

locus-of-control perspective from which an individual views life. Individuals with an *internal* locus-of-control believe that their decisions make a difference and that they have control over their lives. People with *external* locus-of-control see themselves as "victims" and consider other people, situations, and conditions as being the controlling factors in their lives.

low-calorie diet diet that limits intake to 800 to 1000 calories a day; results in atrophy of heart muscle.

lymphoma cancer that develops in the lymphatic system, including the neck, armpits, groin, and chest.

macronutrients nutrients required by the body in large amounts. Usually refers to the energy nutrients: protein, fat, and carbohydrates.

mainstream smoke smoke that is inhaled and exhaled by smoker.

major minerals those minerals required in large amounts (more than 5 grams a day).

malignant cancerous; refers to a growth that has the ability to spread to other areas of the body.

mammography x-ray examination of the breast to detect cancer.

marijuana comes from the cannabis plant.

megadose large doses, usually in the form of supplements.

melanoma a dangerous form of skin cancer that has a strong tendency to spread to other areas of the body.

mesomorph body shape characterized by a muscular, athletic body build.

metabolism all chemical reactions that occur within the cells of the body.

metastasis process by which cancerous cells spread from their original location to another location in the body.

micronutrients nutrients required by the body in small amounts. Usually refers to vitamins and minerals.

migraine headaches headaches characterized by throbbing pain that can last for hours or days, sometimes accompanied by nausea and vomiting. Migraines are thought to be the result of dilation of blood vessels in the head.

minerals inorganic compounds in food necessary for good health.

mitochondria the cell's "powerhouse."

moderate calorie diet diet that limits caloric intake to 1300 to 1600 calories a day.

monounsaturated fat fatty acid composed of triglycerides in which the carbon chain has room for two hydrogen atoms.

morbidity incidence of disease and/or sickness.

mortality incidence of death.

muscular endurance application of repeated muscular force developed by many repetitions against resistances considerably less than maximum.

muscular strength maximal force that a muscle or muscle group can exert in a single contraction.

myocardial infarction heart attack; death of heart muscle tissue.

narcotics powerful painkillers.

negative reinforcers avoidance of something unpleasant.

neoplasm abnormal mass of cells; also called a *tumor*; can be benign or malignant.

neutraceuticals natural ingredients intended to promote and maintain health.

newsgroup a location on the internet where electronic messages related to a medical topic are posted.

nicotine addictive substance and alkaloid poison found in tobacco.

nucleoside analogs a combination of drugs (AZT& ddl) that seems to prevent the development of opportunistic infections associated with AIDS.

nutrient substance found in food that is required by the body.

nutrient density ratio of nutrients to calories; also called the *index of nutritional quality*.

nutrition science that deals with the study of nutrients and the way the body ingests, digests, absorbs, transports, metabolizes, and excretes these nutrients.

obesity excessive amount of storage fat.

ob gene a gene found in fat cells that produces leptin. Also called the "fat gene."

occupational dimension of wellness comprises aspects of wellness that help achieve a balance between work and leisure in a way that promotes health and a sense of personal satisfaction.

Olestra a synthetic fat that has the flavor and taste of real fat but yields no calories.

omega-3 fatty acids type of fatty acid found in cold-water seafood and thought to lower the risks of heart disease.

oncogene cancer-causing gene.

osteoarthritis most common form of arthritis characterized by the deterioration of articular cartilage that covers the gliding surfaces of the bones in certain joints.

osteophyte another name for a bone spur.

osteoporosis progressive decrease in the mineral content of bone, making bones brittle.

overcompensatory eating an eating pattern characterized by over-consumption of low-fat foods, which causes an increase in total caloric intake.

overfat may or may not be within normal guidelines for weight but with an excessive ratio of fat compared with lean tissue.

overweight excessive weight for one's height without regard for body composition.

ovolactovegetarian a person who eats plant foods, eggs, and dairy products but excludes fish, poultry, and meat from the diet.

partner abuse physical or emotional abuse committed by an adult against his or her partner.

passive smoking inhalation of environmental cigarette smoke by a nonsmoker.

pathogen disease-producing organism.

pelvic inflammatory disease (PID) chronic condition of infection in the uterus, fallopian tubes, and upper reproductive areas; the leading cause of infertility in women.

performance-related fitness sports fitness; composed of speed, power, balance, coordination, agility, and reaction time.

periodic examination physical exam in which tests and assessments are prescribed according to risk factors.

pescovegetarian a person who eats plant foods, eggs, dairy products, and fish but excludes red meat from the diet.

phytochemical plant chemicals that exist naturally in foods.

phytoestrogen plant hormone (estrogen) that exists naturally in foods.

phytomedicinals see *botanicals*.

placebo inactive substance, such as a fake drug.

pollovegetarian a persons who eats plant foods, eggs, dairy products, fish, and poultry but excludes red meat.

polyunsaturated fat fatty acid composed of triglycerides in which the carbon chain has room for four or more hydrogen atoms.

positive reinforcers rewards earned for achieving goals in a lifestyle-change program.

preferred providers organization (PPO) a group of private practitioners who sell their services at reduced rates to insurance companies.

preventive health behaviors health practices associated with the promotion of wellness and the prevention of sickness and death.

primary care physician medical doctor who is responsible for an individual's overall health.

primary site (reference to cancer) original site of cancer cell formation.

proprioceptive neuromuscular facilitation (PNF) consists of several stretching techniques that involve some combination of contraction and static stretching and holding agonist and antagonist muscle groups.

prospective study an epidemiological study in which researchers predict possible disease relationships and patterns among groups of people.

protease inhibitor inhibits the enzyme protease, which allows HIV to develop.

protein complementing practice of combining plant protein with cereal/grain protein to provide complete protein.

psychoactives drugs that can alter feelings, moods, and/or perceptions.

psychosomatic disease diseases (physical symptoms) caused by psychological and emotional stressors.

psychoneuroimmunology a medical discipline whose philosophy rests on the connections among brain function, the nervous system, and the body's response to infection and abnormal cell division.

radiotherapy use of radiation to either destroy cancer cells or destroy their reproductive mechanism so they cannot replicate.

RDA acronym for recommended dietary allowances.

reactance motivation a behavioral response to force or coersion in which behavior is the opposite of that intended (e.g., a child refuses to eat a particular food because of parental force).

recidivism the tendency to revert to original behaviors/conditions after completing a behavioral change program.

recommended dietary allowances (RDA) daily recommended intakes of nutrients for normal, healthy people in the United States.

reference daily intakes (RDI) represents minimum standards for essential nutrients and replaces the U.S. recommended daily allowance established in 1968.

relaxation techniques techniques used in coping with and managing stress.

reliability extent to which health studies yield consistent results.

reminders a behavioral strategy used to formulated action goals.

residual volume amount of air remaining in the lungs after expiration.

retrospective study an epidemiological study in which researchers review previously gathered data to identify possible disease relationships and patterns among groups of people.

reward deficiency syndrome a variety of disorders that have in common the traits of impulsiveness, addiction, and compulsiveness.

rheumatoid arthritis most crippling form of arthritis, characterized by inflammation of the joints, pain, swelling, and deformity.

risk factors conditions that threaten wellness and increase the chances of contracting a disease.

road rage overly aggressive driving that includes physical or verbal assault against another driver after a traffic dispute.

saccharides refers to sugars (general term).

safer sex a pattern of behavior in which steps are taken to protect oneself and one's partner from pregnancy and infection with HIV and sexually transmitted diseases. These steps can include using condoms or dental dams and having periodic medical tests and examinations.

sarcoma cancer of a connective tissue, such as bone and muscle.

saturated fat fatty acid composed of triglycerides in which all the fatty acids contain the maximum number of hydrogen atoms.

scientifically controlled study a study conducted in a controlled setting that involves a treatment (experimental) group and a placebo (control) group.

secondary site refers to the location of cancer cells after they have spread from the primary site.

sedentary physically inactive

selective health examination specific test used in response to specific symptoms or for diagnosing a specific problem.

self-care movement toward individuals taking increased responsibility to prevent or manage certain health conditions.

self-efficacy people's belief in their ability to accomplish a specific task or behavior; that belief then affects the outcome of the task or behavior; the theory that individuals who expect to succeed tend to succeed and those who expect to fail tend to fail.

self-help   approach to lifestyle change that assumes individuals can plan and execute their own plans.

setpoint theory   theory that the body has a preference for maintaining a certain amount of weight and defends that weight quite vigorously.

sexually transmitted diseases (STDs)   diseases spread through sexual contact, such as AIDS, chlamydia, gonorrhea, and herpes.

shaping up   a behavioral strategy in which a person acclimates to desired behaviors in small increments

sidestream smoke   smole given off by burning tobacco products.

skinfold measures   method for determining the amount of body fat by using skin calipers.

sleep apnea   a condition characterized by loud snoring and brief periods during which breathing ceases.

soluble fiber   fiber that dissolves in water; comes from fruit pectins and oat bran.

squamous cell carcinoma   the second most common type of skin cancer. It rarely spreads to other areas, but it grows more quickly than basal cell carcinoma.

starch   plant polysaccharides composed of glucose and digestible by humans.

static stretching   passive stretching of antagonist muscles by slowly stretching and holding a position for 15 to 30 seconds.

statistical relationship   an association between two or more variables or events.

statistical significance   the probability that a study's findings are reliable and are not due to chance.

stimulants   drugs that speed up the central nervous system.

stimulus control   technique in lifestyle management involving the elimination and/or manipulation of stimuli related to a specific behavior.

stress   nonspecific response of the body to any demands made on it.

stressor   any physical, psychological, or environmental event or condition that initiates the stress response.

stretch reflex   the myotatic reflex.

stroke volume   amount of blood that the heart can eject in one beat.

subliminal advertising   technique in which messages, words, and symbols are embedded or hidden in advertisements.

sucrose   table sugar.

syndrome X   combination of high blood pressure, high blood sugar, high blood lipids, and abdominal obesity.

syphilis   a sexually transmitted disease.

tar   black, sticky, dark fluid composed of thousands of chemicals and found in tobacco.

tension headaches   most common kind of headache; caused by involuntary contractions of the scalp, head, and neck muscles and may be precipitated by anxiety, stress, and allergic reactions.

thermogenic effect of food   the amount of energy required by the body to digest, absorb, metabolize, and store nutrients.

thrombus   stationary blood clot; can occlude an artery supplying the brain.

trace minerals   those minerals required in small amounts.

transfatty acids   saturated fat found in processed food that has been hydrogenated.

transmit time   the time it takes food to move through the body.

triglyceride   compound composed of carbon, hydrogen, and oxygen with three fatty acids.

tropical oils   oils that come from the fruit of coconut and palm trees.

ulcerative colitis   chronic inflammation of the colon lining. The symptoms are the same as those of Crohn's disease, but the only area affected is the colon lining.

unintentional injury   any injury that occurs as a result of an accident or reckless behavior.

unsaturated fat   fatty acid composed of triglycerides in which the carbon chain has room for more hydrogen atoms.

validity   extent to which the research design of a health study permits the assertion of certain health claims.

variable resistance   provides increasing resistance as a weight is lifted through the full range of motion.

vegan   a person whose diet is limited to plant foods. Also called a *strict vegetarian.*

viral hepatitis   inflammination of the liver caused by one or more viruses.

visualization   a form of meditation that makes use of the imagination.

vital capacity   amount of air that can be expired after a maximum inspiration.

vitamin supplements   natural and synthetic compounds taken orally to supplement the vitamins consumed in food.

vitamins   organic compounds in food necessary for good health.

weight cycling   potentially harmful pattern of repeated weight loss and weight gain.

wellness   engaging in activities and behaviors that enhance quality of life and maximize personal potential.

Credits

Index

A

Abdominal crunch, 104
Abdominal fat, and risk of illness, 217–218, 236–237
Abdominal muscular endurance, assessment of, 123
Accidents, death from, 7
Achilles tendon stretch, 136
Acquaintance rape, 316–317
  prevention guidelines, 317
Acquired immunodeficiency virus (AIDS). *See* HIV and AIDS
Action stage, self-help approach, 17–18
Acute illness, meaning of, 7
Addiction
  causes of, 334
  meaning of, 333
Adenosine triphosphate (ATP), and cardiorespiratory training, 69
Advertising, subliminal advertising, 12
Aerobic capacity
  and cardiorespiratory training, 69
  genetic factors, 215
  limitations to, 69
  meaning of, 67
Aerobic exercise. *See also* Cardiorespiratory training
  health benefits, 72
African Americans
  and hypertension, 46–47
  prostate cancer risk, 394
Age. *See also* Children; Older adults
  and cardiovascular disease, 38
  and chronic disease, 406
  and weight gain, 239, 253
Aggression, road rage, 313–314
Agonists, 133
Alcoholics Anonymous (AA), 340
Alcoholism, 338–340
  assessment for, 353
  binge drinking, 339–340
  fetal alcohol syndrome (FAS), 339
  treatment of, 338
  treatment resources, 340
  and women, 339
Alcohol use, 335–340
  blood alcohol concentration (BAC), 336–337

Alcohol use—*Cont.*
  and HDL levels, 44
  health benefits, 184
  health risks from, 184, 380
  long-term effects of, 336
  reactions to alcohol, variables in, 337–338
  responsible drinking guidelines, 337
  short-term effects of, 336
Alternative medicine, 434, 438
  cancer treatment, 395
  common elements of therapies, 438
  criticisms of, 434, 436
  proponents of, 434
Amino acids, 156
Anabolic-androgenic steroids, negative health effects, 115
Anaerobic exercise. *See also* Resistance training
  meaning of, 99
Aneurysm, and stroke, 38
Angel dust, 348
Anger, health effects of, 5–6
Anorexia nervosa, 255–256
  diagnostic criteria for, 256
Antabuse, 340
Antagonists, 136
Antioxidants, 162–163
Arteries, and circulation, 34
Arthritis, 407–408
  and exercise, 407–408
  osteoarthritis, 407–408
  rheumatoid arthritis, 408
Art therapy, and health, 5
Aspirin, heart disease prevention, 55
Asthma
  exercise-induced, 411
  extrinsic and intrinsic, 410
  management assessment, 419
  treatment of, 410–411
Atherosclerosis
  and cholesterol level, 36, 43–44
  lipid oxidation theory, 43
  progression of, 36, 44
Autogenics, steps in, 285, 286
Automated teller machines (ATMs), safety precautions, 315–316
Automobile safety, 311–314
  and accidents with SUVs, 312

Automobile safety—*Cont.*
  car phone use, 313
  drowsiness prevention, 312
  pedestrian safety, 315
  restraint systems, 313
  road rage, 313–314

B

Baby boomers, 406
Back extension, 105
Back pain
  causes of, 139
  prevention of, 139–141
Back stretch, 135
Ballistic stretching, 139
Balloon angioplasty, 55–56
Basal cell carcinoma, 387
Basal metabolic rate (BMR)
  and age, 253
  exercise effects, 252
B complex vitamins, 163, 164, 166
  food sources of, 164
  functions of, 164
  recommended intake, 163
Behavior
  influences on, 12
  resistance motivation, 12
Behavior change
  assessment for, 16
  contracting, 18
  countering strategies for problem behaviors, 18
  goal setting for, 17
  resistance to, 12, 15–16
  self-help approach, 15–19
  shaping up, 18
Bench press, 103–104
Bench step test, 91
Benign tumors, 379
Beta carotene, 165
Biceps curl, 101, 102
Bicycling, safety guidelines, 308–309
Bilberry, 172
Binge drinking, 339–340
Binge-eating disorder, 257–258
  diagnostic criteria for, 258
Bioelectrical impedance analysis (BIA), 221–222

Biofeedback
   health uses of, 5
   stress management, 286
Birth defects, reducing with folate, 166, 185
Blood
   circulation of, 34–35
   components of, 35
Blood alcohol concentration (BAC), 336–337
Blood glucose test, 442
Blood pressure, 45–48
   high/low readings, 46, 441
   hypertension, 46–48
   measurement of, 46, 441
Blood tests, routine tests, 440
Blood volume, and cardiorespiratory
      training, 68
Boating, safety guidelines, 310–311
Body composition
   meaning of, 214
   obesity, 214
   overfat, 216
   overweight, 214, 216
   regional fat distribution, 216–218
Body composition assessment
   bioelectrical impedance analysis (BIA),
      221–222
   skinfold measurements, 222–225
   underwater weighing, 219, 221
Body dysmorphic disorder, 234, 235
Body fat
   and children/adolescents, 220
   desirable weight calculated from, 226, 231
   recommendations for men, 215
   recommendations for women, 214
Body fat distribution, 216–218
   feminine pattern of, 216–217, 218
   masculine pattern of, 217
   and risk of illness, 217–218
   waist-to-hip ratio, 217
Body image
   assessment of, 265
   negative image, factors in, 234
Body mass index (BMI), 218–219
   assessment of, 229
   for overweight and obesity, 235
   table for calculation of, 220
Body shape, genetic factors, 240
Body weight
   American preoccupation with, 234–235
   caloric intake/caloric expenditure
      balance, 234
   desirable weight calculation, 226, 231
   genetic factors, 215
   increases for adult Americans, 235–236
Body weight assessment
   body mass index (BMI), 218–219
   direct measurement, 219
   height/weight tables, 218
Bone density test, 442
Bone loss, osteoporosis, 408–410
Brain
   and addiction, 334
   stress response, 278
Breast, self-examination, 392–393
Breast cancer, 389, 391
   drug treatment, 389

Breast cancer—*Cont.*
   early detection, 389
   exercise as prevention, 384
   genetic factors, 389
   signs of, 389
Breathing
   deep breathing, 284
   and resistance training, 114
Bulimia, 256–257
   diagnostic criteria for, 257
B vitamins, cardiovascular disease
   prevention, 54

C
Caffeine
   and bone loss, 409
   headache remedy, 412
   overuse problem, 335
Calcium, 168–169
   food sources of, 168
   functions of, 168
   for osteoporosis, 409
   supplements, 168
Calf stretch, 136
Calisthenic exercises, muscular strength
      assessment, 125–127
Caloric deficit, and weight loss, 243
Calories
   burning and weight loss, 250–252
   caloric cost and common activities, 252
   caloric cost and common activities
      assessment, 271
   definition of, 155
   expenditure through exercise
      assessment, 267
   recommended intake, 155
Campylobacter jejuni, cause and signs
      of, 188
Canadian trunk strength test, 123
Cancer
   breast cancer, 389, 391
   causes of, 380–382
   and cigarette smoking, 341, 380
   colorectal cancer, 384–385
   dietary strategies for, 190
   early detection inventory, 399–400
   and HIV and AIDS, 362
   leukemia, 386
   liver cancer, 385
   lung cancer, 384
   lymphoma, 386–387
   malignant tumor, 379
   and obesity, 236
   oral cancer, 388–389
   ovarian cancer, 391
   pancreatic cancer, 385–386
   prostate cancer, 394
   skin cancer, 387–388
   stomach cancer, 385
   testicular cancer, 393
   types/sites for, 380, 383
   uterine cancer, 391
Cancer prevention
   checkup guidelines, 390
   dietary guidelines, 379
   and exercise, 382–384

Cancer prevention—*Cont.*
   self-assessment, 401
Cancer treatments
   alternative treatment, 395
   chemotherapy, 394
   immunotherapy, 394–395
   radiotherapy, 394
   surgery, 394
Candidiasis, 369
Carbohydrates, 155–156
   assessing intake, 199
   complex, 156
   pre-exercise meals, 186–187
   recommended intake, 156
   simple, 155
Carbon monoxide
   cigarette smoke, 341
   detection in home, 307
Carcinogens, types/cancer sites, 380
Carcinoma, 380
Cardiac catheterization, 55
Cardiac output, and cardiorespiratory
      training, 67–68
Cardiorespiratory endurance, 67–76
   definition of, 67
   and wellness, 70
Cardiorespiratory training, 67–70
   and blood volume, 68
   and cardiac output, 67–68
   and heart rate, 67
   and heart volume, 68
   metabolic responses to, 68–70
   respiratory responses to, 68
   and stroke volume, 67
Cardiovascular disease
   coronary heart disease, 36–37
   diagnosis of, 54–55
   medical treatment of, 55–57
   statistics on, 34
   stroke, 37–38
Cardiovascular disease prevention
   B vitamins, 54
   diet, 53–54, 189–190
   iron-enriched blood, 54
   lipoprotein (a), 54
Cardiovascular disease risk, 36, 38–53
   and abdominal fat deposition, 217
   age, 38
   blood pressure, 45–48
   cholesterol level, 40–45
   cigarette smoking, 48–49
   diabetes mellitus, 51–53
   genetic factors, 40
   homosyteine, 54
   male gender, 38, 40
   obesity, 51, 236
   physical inactivity, 49–51
   stress, 53
   very low fat diets, 160
Cardiovascular system
   circulation, 34–35
   heart, 34–35
Car jacking, safety precautions, 316
Carotenoids, 165
Car phones, safety tips, 313
Cell abnormalities, cancer, 381

Cerebral hemorrhage, and stroke, 38
Cervical cancer
and sexual behavior, 391
signs of, 391
Challenge, meaning of, 282
Chancroid, 369
Chemotherapy, cancer treatment, 394
Chest press, 108
Chest stretch, 135
Chest X-ray, 442
Children
body fat, 220
common cancers in, 378, 386
lifestyle of, 37
obesity, 237
Type I diabetes, 404
China white, 348
Chlamydia, 367–368
complications of, 368
signs of, 368
treatment, 368
Cholesterol, 40–45
and atherosclerosis, 36, 43–44
and coronary heart disease, 41
dietary sources of, 42
lowering, strategies for, 42, 190
suggested daily consumption, 40
transport of, 41, 43
Chromium picolinate, 114–115
Chronic disease
and age, 406
arthritis, 407–408
diabetes, 404–407
meaning of, 7
osteoporosis, 408–410
Cigarette smoking
and bone loss, 409
cardiovascular disease risk, 48–49
cardiovascular effects of, 49
death from, 10
health risks, 341, 380
passive smoking, 49, 342
and women, 339
Cigarette smoking cessation, 49, 343–344
health benefits of, 343, 345
nicotine-containing products for, 344
tips for, 343
Cigar smoking, 49, 50, 342–343
Circuit resistance training, 110–111
Circulation, 34–35
Cities, exercise tips, 82
Clinical trials, 425
Clostridium botulinum, cause and signs
of, 188
Clove cigarettes, 343
Cocaine, 345–346
effects of use, 345–346
Cognitive dissonance, meaning of, 15
Colds
signs of, 411
treatment of, 411
Cold sores, 365
Cold temperature and exercise, 82–83
frostbite, 82
hypothermia, 82–83
precautions, 82–83

College students, binge drinking, 339–340
Colorectal cancer, 384–385
dietary prevention, 385
exercise as prevention, 383–384
risk factors, 385
screening for, 385
signs of, 385
Commitment, meaning of, 282
Communication
patient-physician communication, 432,
434, 447
in relationships, 319
about safe sex, 360
Concentric muscle contraction, 100,
101, 107
Condoms, effective use guidelines, 360
Congenital heart defects, 36, 70
Congestive heart failure, 36
Contemplation stage, self-help
approach, 15
Contracting, behavior change, 18
Cool down, exercise, 77
Coping. See also Stress management
coping style assessment, 297–298
guidelines for, 283
Coronary artery bypass surgery, 55
Coronary heart disease, 36–37
and childhood behavior patterns, 37
forms of, 36
heart attack, 37–38
risk factors, 36
Crack, 346
Crank, 347
Creatine supplementation, 114
Crime. See Violence
Crohn's disease, 413
Cross-training, benefits of, 76
Cycling, weight cycling, 243–244

D

Daily log, resistance training, 115–116, 129
Daily Values (DV), food labels, 190, 191
Dance therapy, and health, 5
Date rape, 316–317
prevention guidelines, 317
Rohypnol, 318
Death, leading causes of, 7, 10
Deep breathing, for relaxation, 284
Defensive medicine, 439
Dehydration, prevention and exercise,
80–82
Depressant drugs
actions of, 334
types of, 334
Depression, and illness, 52
Designer drugs, 334–335
types of, 335, 348
Diabetes mellitus
and abdominal fat deposition,
217–218
cardiovascular disease risk, 51–53
causes of, 404–405
complications of, 52, 404, 407
dietary strategies for, 190, 405–406
exercise effects, 406
and obesity, 236, 405

Diabetes mellitus—Cont.
physiological events of, 404
prevention of, 405
risk assessment, 417
screening guidelines, 405
signs of, 404
stress, and illness, 52
Type I, 51–52, 404
Type II, 52–53, 404
Diagnostic laboratory tests, 439–442
false positives/false negatives, 439
most common tests, 440–442
reference range of tests, 449–450
Diet. See also Nutrients; Nutrition
cancer-prevention diet, 379, 385
disease prevention strategies, 189–190
nutritional assessment, 193–194
prepackaged convenience foods, 193
small adjustments, value of, 194
snacking, 192–193
Dietary fat, 157–162
assessing intake, 201, 209–210
and athletic activity, 187
cancer risk from, 380
and cholesterol, 158
fat content of foods, chart of, 159
fish oils, 158
high-fat theory of obesity, 241–242
monounsaturated fat, 158
oils, fat content comparison, 161
polyunsaturated fat, 158, 162
recommended intake, 160–162
saturated fat, 158, 160–162
stress effects on, 281
synthetic fat, 158
transfatty acids, 158, 159, 162
Dietary Guidelines for Americans, 174,
184, 194
Diet drugs, 247
Dieting, 243–247
diet-only programs, 243–244
fad diets, 246–247
low-fat diets, 244–245
and overcompensatory eating, 245
and oversized food portions, 245–246
popular diets, listing of, 248–249
very-low-calorie diets, 244
Diet resistance, 241
Disaccharides, 155
Distress, definition of, 274
Disulfiram, 340
Domestic violence, 318–320
elder abuse, 320
partner abuse, 319–320
Double-blind study, 424–425
Drugs. See also Illegal drugs
caffeine, 335
drug use assessment, 355
over-the-counter (OTC) drugs, 349
pain relievers, types of, 441
reasons for use, 332–333
terminology related to, 333
Duration
aerobic exercise, 74–75
resistance training, 113
Dynamic contractions, muscle, 100

E

Eating behaviors
    assessment of, 211
    changing, strategies for, 255
Eating disorders, 235
    anorexia nervosa, 255–256
    binge-eating disorder, 257–258
    bulimia, 256–257
    underweight, 258
Eccentric muscle contraction, 100, 101, 107
Echinacea, 172
Echocardiography, 55
E. coli, cause and signs of, 188
Ecstasy, 348
Elder abuse, 320
Elderly. *See* Older adults
Electrocardiograms (ECGs), 442
ELISA, HIV testing, 365
Embolus, and stroke, 37–38
Emotional arousal, meaning of, 15
Emotional problems, cancer risk, 381
Emotional wellness, and physical health, 4–6
Endometrial cancer, 391
Endorphins, 278
Energy, stress effects on, 281
Energy nutrients, 155
Environment, impact on wellness, 6–7
Epidemiological studies, 424
    prospective and retrospective studies, 424
Epinephrine, stress response, 278
Ergogenic aids
    anabolic-androgenic steroids, 115
    chromium picolinate, 114–115
    creatine supplementation, 114
    ginseng, 114
    protein supplementation, 113
Essential nutrients. *See* Nutrients
Estrogen
    and body fat distribution, 216–217
    cancer risk, 380
    heart disease prevention, 40
Ethnic foods, traditional compared to
        Americanized, 182
Eustress, meaning of, 274
Exercise
    and arthritis, 407–408
    and basal metabolic rate (BMR), 252
    and cancer prevention, 382–384
    and cold weather, 82–83
    and control of diabetes, 406
    cool down, 77
    cross-training, 76
    effects on hypertension, 48
    energy and nutrition, 186–187
    fitness equipment, 79
    and fluid consumption, 81–82
    fun, importance of, 254
    health benefits of, 52
    and hot weather, 79–82
    motivational tips, 76
    and osteoporosis prevention, 410
    overtraining, 74
    safety tips, 71
    sports activities, 78
    for stress management, 288

Exercise—*Cont.*
    types of activities, 77–79
    in urban environment, 82
    warm up, 76–77
    and weight loss, 250–254
Exercise principles, 70–76
    duration, 74–75
    frequency, 74
    intensity, 70, 73–74
    overload, 75
    specificity, 75–76
Experiments, double-blind study, 424–425
Extrinsic asthma, 410
Eye examination, 442

F

Fad diets, 246–247
False negatives, lab tests, 439
False positives, lab tests, 439
Fasting, and weight loss, 250
Fat-soluble vitamins, 162, 163, 164
Fen-phen, 247
Fetal alcohol syndrome (FAS), 339
Feverfew, 172
Fiber, 173–174
    health benefits, 174–175
    insoluble fiber, 173–174
    recommended intake, 174
    soluble fiber, 173
    sources of, 173, 174
Fight of flight, stress response, 53, 275
Fire detection devices, 306–307
Fish oils, 158, 162
Fitness assessment
    bench step test, 91
    and exercise program design, 95
    heart rate calculation, 93
    1.5–mile run/walk test, 89
    Rockport Fitness Walking Test, 85–87
Fitness equipment, buying guidelines, 79
Flexibility assessment
    goniometer, 139
    shoulder flexion test, 147
    sit-and-reach test, 145
    sling test, 149
    trunk extension, 151
Flexibility training. *See also* Stretching
        exercises
    benefits of, 132
Fluid consumption, and exercise,
        81–82, 187
Folate
    food sources of, 164, 166
    functions of, 164, 166
    in pregnancy, 166, 185
Foodborne illness, 187–189
    cooking guidelines, 189
    prevention of, 188–189
    types of, 188
Food Guide Pyramid, 175–176
    illustration of, 176
    serving size, 175, 177
Food labels
    claims allowed on, 190–191
    Daily Values (DV), 190, 191

Food labels—*Cont.*
    example of, 191
    FDA information specification, 192
Free radicals
    antioxidant protection, 162–163
    formation of, 162
Free-weight training, 109
Frequency
    aerobic exercise, 74
    resistance training, 113
Frostbite, 82

G

Gallbladder disease, and obesity, 236
Garlic, 172
Gateway drugs, 347
Gender differences
    cardiovascular disease risk, 38, 40
    fat deposition, 216–217, 237
General adaptation syndrome, phases of,
        275–276
Genetic factors
    aerobic capacity, 215
    body shape, 240
    body weight, 215
    breast cancer, 389
    cancer, 380–381
    cardiovascular disease risk factors, 40
    colorectal cancer, 385
    diabetes mellitus, 405
    obesity, 239–240
    ovarian cancer, 391
Genital warts, 367
Ginger, 172
Ginkgo, 172
Ginseng, 114, 172
Glaucoma test, 442
Goal setting
    as coping strategy, 283
    realistic goals, 17
    weight loss, 215
Goniometer, 139
Gonorrhea, 368
    complications of, 368
    signs of, 368
    treatment of, 368
Granola inguinale, 369
Groin stretch, 135
Gum, nicotine-containing, 344

H

Half-squat, 106
Hamstring curl, 107
Hamstring stretch, 136
Hardy personality, assessment of, 299
Hate crimes, 320
Headaches
    management of, 413
    migraine headaches, 412
    and stress, 279
    tension headaches, 412
    triggers for, 412
Health behavior, assessment of, 31
Health care
    alternative medicine, 434, 438

Health care—*Cont.*
hospitalization, 429–431
immunizations, 442
laboratory/diagnostic tests, 440–442
physical examination, 438–439
visits to doctor, times for, 428–429
Health care professionals
information sources on, 432
patient-physician communication, 432, 434, 447
primary-care physician, 432
for second opinion, 434, 437
types of specialties, 433
Health care terminology, listing of, 435–436
Health disparities
Healthy People 2010 on, 8–9
and population groups, 7
Health fatalism, meaning of, 422
Health information
evaluation of, 422–423
headlines, 423
and Internet, 425–427
telephone services for, 427–428
Health insurance
health maintenance organizations
(HMOs), 443
indemnity plans, 443
Medicare and Medicaid, 443–444
point of service (POS), 443
preferred provider organizations
(PPO), 443
Health maintenance organizations
(HMOs), 443
Health-related fitness, meaning of, 66
Health-related studies
double-blind study, 424–425
epidemiological studies, 424
population in, 425
reliability, 423
risk factors, 424
statistical relationship, 424
statistical significance, 423–424
validity, 423
Healthy People 2000, 8
Healthy People 2010, on health disparities,
8–9
Heart
anatomy of, 34–35
and circulation, 35
Heart attack, 37–38
estrogen as protection, 40
heart damage from, 36
risk assessment, 61–63
silent, 37
after strenuous exercise, 70
warning signs, 37
Heart rate
calculation of, 73–74, 93
and cardiorespiratory training, 67
Heart transplant, 56–57
Heart volume, and cardiorespiratory
training, 68
Hearty personality, characteristics of, 282
Height/weight tables, 218
Hemoccult tests, 440

Hepatitis A, cause and signs of, 188
Hepatitis B, signs of, 367
Hepatitis vaccinations, 442
Herbs, 171–173
listing of common herbs, 172
precautions in use, 171–173
weight loss remedies, 247, 250
Heroin, 347
increase in use, 347
Herpes, 365–367
cold sores/fever blisters, 365
drug treatment, 366–367
genital type, 366–367
High-density lipoproteins, 43–44
guidelines for levels of, 45
increasing, 44
protective effects of, 44
and very low fat diet, 160
HIV and AIDS, 361–365
infections/cancers related to, 362
information sources on, 366
prevention of, 364, 365
signs of, 361
tests for, 365, 442
transmission of, 363–364
treatment approaches, 365
types of HIV, 363
Homeostasis, 275
Home safety, 306–307
assessment of, 323–324
carbon monoxide detection, 307
fire detection devices, 306–307
guidelines, 306
Homicide, FBI statistics, 318
Homosysteine
cardiovascular disease risk, 54, 166
reduction of levels, 166, 190
Hormone-replacement therapy, for
osteoporosis, 409–410
Hospitalization, 429–431
and informed consent, 430
patient decisions related to, 429–431
patient rights, 430
Hot weather and exercise, 79–82
heat loss, types of, 80
prevention of, 80–82
Human immunodeficiency virus (HIV). *See*
HIV and AIDS
Hydrogenation, 158
Hyperglycemia, 404
Hyperplasia, fat cells, 237
Hypertension, 46–48
and abdominal fat deposition, 218
and cardiovascular system damage, 46
dietary strategies for, 190
essential hypertension, 46
and obesity, 218, 236
risk factors, 45–47
treatment of, 47–48
Hypertrophy
fat cells, 237
muscle, 113
Hypnosis
autogenics, 285, 286
health uses of, 5

Hypothalamus, and stress response, 278
Hypothermia, 82–83

I

ILISA, HIV testing, 365
Illegal drugs
classification of, 334–335
cocaine, 345–346
designer drugs, 334–335, 348
drug use prevention, 348
heroin, 347
LSD (lysergic acid diethylamide), 347
marijuana, 346–347
methamphetamine, 347
PCP (phencyclidine), 348
Imagery, and health, 5
Immune system, and stress, 278–280
Immunizations, for adults, 442
Immunotherapy, cancer treatment, 394–395
Indemnity plans, 443
Inflammatory bowel disease
Crohn's disease, 413
ulcerative colitis, 413
Influenza, 411–412
prevention of, 412
signs of, 412
Informed consent, 430
Inhalants
actions of, 334
types of, 334
In-line skating, safety guidelines, 309–310
Intellectual wellness, importance of, 6
Intensity
aerobic exercise, 70, 73–74
resistance training, 112–113
Interferon, 395
Interleukin-2, 395
Internet
health information, quality of, 425–427
health sites, listing of, 426–427
wellness sites, 14
Intrinsic asthma, 410
Iron, 168, 169
deficiency, 169
food sources of, 168, 169
functions of, 168
levels and cardiovascular disease, 54
Ischemia, 37
Isoflavones, 156
Isokinetic training, 109–110
Isometric exercises, 100–107
limitations of, 100
Isotonic training, 107–108

J

Joint disease, arthritis, 407–408

K

Karvonen formula, heart rate
calculation, 73

L

Lactic acid, 77
Lactovegetarians, 180
Lateral supine raises, 108

Leg press, 106
Legumes, 156–157
  nutritional benefits of, 156–157
Leukemia, 380, 386
Lifestyle
  assessment inventory, 23–29
  of children and adolescents, 37
Lifting objects, guidelines for, 140
Limbic system, functions of, 277–278
Lipid oxidation theory, 43
Lipoprotein (a), cardiovascular disease
      prevention, 54
Listeria monocytogenes, cause and signs
      of, 188
Liver cancer, 385
Locus of control, health locus of control
      assessment, 29
Low-density lipoproteins, 43
  safe/unsafe levels, 43, 45
Low-fat diet, 181–183
  fat content in, 160
  fat reduction tips, 181–183, 251
  heart disease risk, 160
  and overcompensatory eating, 245
  and weight loss, 244–245
LSD (lysergic acid diethylamide), 347
Lung cancer, 384
  and cigarette smoking, 384
  prevention of, 384
Lycopene, 165
Lymphoma, 380, 386–387
  signs of, 387

M
Macronutrients, 155
Maintenance stage, self-help approach, 19
Malignant melanoma, 387–388
  identification of, 387–388
  prevention of, 388
  risk factors, 387
Mammography, 441
Marijuana, 346–347
  long-term effects, 346–347
  and reproduction, 347
  short-term effects, 346
Massage therapy, stress management, 286
Medicaid, 443–444
Medical history, 438–439
Medical records, patient access to, 430
Medical telephone services, listing of, 428
Medicare, 443–444
  Parts A and B, 443–444
Medicine chest, essential items for, 440
Meditation
  and health, 5
  steps in, 285
  stress management, 285
Mediterranean diet, 161–162
Men, and cardiovascular disease risk, 38, 40
Meridia, 247
Metabolic syndrome, 218
Metabolism, exercise effects, 252
Methamphetamine, 347
Micronutrients, 155
Middle age, life satisfaction survey, 281

Minerals, 167–169
  and athletic activity, 187
  calcium, 168–169
  iron, 168, 169
  major minerals, 167–168
  in pregnancy, 185
  sodium, 168
  trace minerals, 168
  zinc, 169
Monogamy
  as safe sex choice, 358
  serial type, 358
Monosaccharides, 155
Monounsaturated fat, 158
  diabetes control diet, 406
  recommended intake, 161
Moonrock, 347
Motivation, tips for exercise, 76
Motorcycle safety, 314–315
  guidelines for, 314–315
Movement meditation, benefits of, 133
Muscle contractions
  agonists and antagonists, 136
  concentric and eccentric, 100, 101, 107
  dynamic contractions, 100
  static contractions, 100
Muscles
  fiber types, 110
  front/rear views of, 109
  hypertrophy, 113
Muscle soreness, and strength training, 108
Muscular endurance
  assessment of, 121
  best exercises for, 111
Muscular strength, development of, 99–100
Muscular strength assessment
  abdominal muscular endurance, 123
  with calisthenic exercises, 125–127
  for muscular endurance, 121
  strength/body weight ratio, 119–120
Music
  music therapy, 5
  stress management, 286–287
Myocardial infarction, 36. *See also*
      Heart attack

N
Narcotic drugs
  actions of, 334
  heroin, 347
  types of, 334
Nautilus equipment, 109
Neck pain, prevention of, 139–141
Neck stretches, 134
Nicotine, cardiovascular effects of, 49
Nicotrol inhaler, 344
Nongonococcal urethritis, 369
Nucleoside analogs, 365
Nutrient intake assessment, 203–205
Nutrients
  and calories, 155
  carbohydrates, 155–156
  dietary fat, 157–162
  excessive consumption, examples of, 178
  fiber, 173–174

Nutrients—*Cont.*
  and food variety, 174–175
  herbs, 171–173
  minerals, 167–169
  nutrient density, 177, 179
  phytochemicals, 170–171
  protein, 156–157
  vitamins, 162–167
  water, 169–170
Nutrition
  and alcohol consumption, 184
  essential nutrients, 154–155
  Food Guide Pyramid, 175–176
  low-fat diet, 181–183
  moderation and healthy diet, 177–178
  in pregnancy, 185
  relationship to physical activity, 185–187
  salt, 184
  stress effects on, 281
  sugar, limiting intake, 183
  and variety of foods, 174–175, 176
  vegetarian diet, 179–181
Nutritional assessment
  carbohydrate intake, 199
  dietary fat, 201, 209–210
  eating behaviors, 211
  nutrient intake, 203–205
  protein intake, 199
  for recommended dietary intakes, 207–208

O
Obesity
  and age, 239
  cardiovascular disease risk, 51, 236
  classification of, 238
  definition of, 214
  development of, 237
  and diabetes, 405
  diet resistance, 241
  genetic factors, 239–240
  health risks of, 236–237
  high-fat theory of, 241–242
  and physical inactivity, 242–243
  set point theory, 240–241
Occupational wellness, importance of, 6
Oils, fat content of, 161
Older adults
  flexibility guidelines for, 138
  malnutrition of, 177
  nutritional requirements of, 177
  protein intake, 157
  and resistance training, 100
  and self-care, 437
Olestra, 158, 245
Omega-3 fatty acids, 158, 162
Omega-6 fatty acids, 162
Oncogenes, 381
1.5–mile run/walk test, 89
Opportunistic infections, and HIV and
      AIDS, 362
Oral cancer, 388–389
Osteoarthritis, 407–408
Osteoporosis, 408–410
  causes of bone loss, 409
  dietary strategies for, 190

Osteoporosis —cont'd
  high risk groups, 408
  prevention of, 409–410
Outdoor recreation injuries, types of, 308
Outdoor recreation safety, 307–311
  assessment of, 325–326
  bicycling, 308–309
  boating, 310–311
  guidelines, 307–308
  in-line skating, 309–310
  skateboarding, 309
  snowmobiling, 311
Ovarian cancer, 391
  cure rates, 391
  genetic factors, 391
  signs of, 391
Overcompensatory eating, and dieting, 245
Overfat, meaning of, 216
Overhead press, 102–103
Overload
  aerobic exercise, 75
  resistance training, 113
Over-the-counter (OTC) drugs, 349
  safety guidelines, 349
Overtraining, signs of, 74
Overweight, definition of, 214, 216
Ovolactovegetarians, 180

P
Pain relievers, types of, 441
Pancreatic cancer, 385–386
Pap smear, 391, 441–442
Parasites, foodborne, 188
Partner abuse, 319–320
Passive smoking, 49, 342
PCP (phencyclidine), 348
Pediculosis, 369
Pelvic examination, 441–442
Pelvic inflammatory disease (PID), 368
  signs of, 369
  treatment of, 369
Perfectionism, problem of, 287
Performance-related fitness, meaning of, 66
Personality traits
  and addiction, 334
  hardy personality, 299
Pescovegetarians, 180
Physical activity. *See also* Exercise
  benefits of, 13, 50–51
  caloric cost of common activities, 252
  relationship to nutrition, 185–187
  use of term, 51
Physical Activity and Health, 11
Physical examination, 438–439
  components of, 438–439
  diagnostic laboratory tests, 439–442
  frequency of, 438
Physical fitness
  cardiorespiratory endurance, 67–76
  health-related fitness, 66
  performance-related fitness, 66
Physical inactivity
  cardiovascular disease risk, 49–51
  and colon cancer, 383–384
  and obesity, 242–243

Phytochemicals, 170–171
  food sources of, 171
  health benefits, 171
  types of, 171
Phytoestrogens, 156, 171
Placebo, meaning of, 425
Point of service (POS), 443
Pollovegetarians, 180
Polysaccharides, 156
Polyunsaturated fat, 158, 162
  recommended intake, 162
  types of, 162
Population, in health-related studies, 425
Potentiating effect, meaning of, 333
Prayer, and health, 5
Precontemplation stage, self-help
    approach, 15
Preferred provider organizations
    (PPO), 443
Pregnancy
  diet and nutritional needs in, 185
  folate in, 166, 185
  HIV-infected mothers, 363
  vitamins/minerals in, 185
  weight gain in, 185
Prepackaged convenience foods, 193
  supersized portions, 246
Preparation stage, self-help approach, 16–17
Primary-care physician, 432
Procrastination, problem of, 287
Progression
  aerobic exercise, 75
  resistance training, 113
Progressive muscle relaxation, 284–285
  steps in, 285
Proprioceptive neuromuscular facilitation
    (PNF), 137–139
  guidelines for, 138
Prospective studies, 424
Prostate cancer, 394
  at-risk groups, 394
  exercise as prevention, 384
  screening for, 394, 442
  signs of, 394
Protease inhibitor, 365
Protein, 156–157
  amino acids, 156
  assessing intake, 199
  complete and incomplete, 156
  legumes, 156–157
  and older adults, 157
  recommended intake, 157
  stress effects on, 281
Protein supplementation, 113, 186–187
Proto-oncogenes, 381
Psychoactive drugs
  actions of, 334
  LSD (lysergic acid diethylamide), 347
  marijuana, 346–347
  types of, 334
Psychoneuroimmunology (PNI)
  and cancer research, 395
  study of, 279
Psychotherapy, and health, 5
Pulse rate, normal, 441

Q
Quadriceps stretch, 136
Quality of life, meaning of, 332

R
Radiotherapy, cancer treatment, 394
Rape, 316–318
  acquaintance rape, 316–317
  date rape, 316–317
  post-rape actions, 318
  rape trauma syndrome, 317–318
Recidivism, meaning of, 16
Recommended dietary allowances
    (RDAs), 154
Recreation safety. *See* Outdoor
    recreation safety
Redux, 247
Relationships, effective communication in, 319
Relaxation methods, 283–285
  deep breathing, 284
  and hypertension, 47
  progressive muscle relaxation, 284–285
Reliability, health-related studies, 423
Repetition, in resistance training, 99,
    112–113
Resistance motivation, meaning of, 12
Resistance training
  circuit resistance training, 110–111
  daily log, 115–116, 129
  exercises, illustrations of, 101–108
  free-weight training, 109
  health benefits of, 98–99
  increasing effectiveness, tips for, 114
  isokinetic training, 109–110
  isometric exercises, 100–107
  isotonic training, 107–108
  muscle soreness, 108
  and older adults, 100
  performance aids. *See* Ergogenic aids
  variable resistance training, 108–109
Resistance training principles
  duration, 113
  frequency, 113
  intensity, 112–113
  overload, 113
  progression, 113
  specificity, 113
Retrospective studies, 424
Reward deficiency syndrome, and
    addiction, 334
Rheumatic heart disease, 36
Rheumatoid arthritis, 408
Risk factors, meaning in health
    information, 424
Ritalin, and attentional problems, 332
Road rage, 313–314
  reducing, tips for, 314
  self-assessment, 327
Rockport Fitness Walking Test, 85–87
Rohypnol, 318

S
Safe sex, 358–360
  communication with partner, 360
  condom use, 360

Safe sex—*Cont.*
  relationship-oriented choices, 358
  safe sex practices, 358–359
  unsafe practices, 359–360
Safety
  automobile safety, 311–314
  home safety, 306–307
  motorcycle safety, 314–315
  outdoor recreation safety, 307–311
  violence, 315–320
St. John's wort, 172
Salmonella infections, cause and signs of, 188
Salt intake
  and hypertension, 47
  limiting, tips for, 184
Sarcoma, 380
Saturated fat, 158, 160–162
  recommended intake, 160
Saw palmetto, 172
Seat belts, 313
Second opinion, about health status,
    434, 437
Self-blame, rape victim, 317–318
Self-care
  and older adults, 437
  self-assessment, 451
Self-efficacy
  and health, 6
  meaning of, 6
Self-esteem
  components of, 280
  and stress, 280
Self-help approach, 12–19
  action stage, 17–18
  basis of, 13
  contemplation stage, 15
  maintenance stage, 19
  precontemplation stage, 15
  preparation stage, 16–17
  termination stage, 19
Serial monogamy, 358
Serum triglycerides, and heart disease, 45
Serving size
  examples of, 178
  meaning of, 175, 177
Set point theory, obesity, 240–241
Sexual experiences
  decision making about, 359, 375–376
  safe sex, 358–360
Sexually transmitted disease (STD)
  chlamydia, 367–368
  genital warts, 367
  gonorrhea, 368
  hepatitis B, 367
  herpes, 365–367
  HIV and AIDS, 361–365
  incidence of, 361
  risk assessment, 373
  safe sex, 358–360
  syphilis, 368–369
Shaping up, behavior change, 18
Shin splints, causes of, 71
Shoes, athletic, 71
Shoulder flexion test, 147
Shoulder stretch, 134
Side stitches, causes of, 71

Sidestream smoke, 342
Sigmoidoscopy, 442
Single-use diagnostic system (SUDS), 365
Sit-and-reach test, 145
Skateboarding, safety guidelines, 309
Skin cancer, 387–388
  basal cell carcinoma, 387
  malignant melanoma, 387–388
  squamous cell carcinoma, 387
  visual test for, 442
Skinfold measurements, 222–225
Sleep apnea, and obesity, 236
Sling test, 149
Smokeless tobacco, 49, 343, 380
Snacking, 192–193
  healthful snacks, 193
Snowmobiling, safety guidelines, 311
Social health, importance of relationships, 4
Social isolation, and cancer, 381
Sodium
  functions of, 168
  limiting intake, 47, 184
Soybeans, health benefits, 156–157
Specificity
  aerobic exercise, 75–76
  resistance training, 113
Spine, vertebral column, illustration
    of, 142
Spirituality
  aspects of, 3–4
  and physical health, 5
Sports, fitness rating for, 78
Spotting, and resistance training, 114
Squamous cell carcinoma, 387
Staphylococcus, cause and signs of, 188
Static contractions, muscle, 100
Static stretching, 136–137
  guidelines for, 137
Statistical relationship, health-related
    studies, 424
Statistical significance, health-related studies,
    423–424
Stimulant drugs
  actions of, 334
  cocaine, 345–346
  methamphetamine, 347
  types of, 334
Stomach cancer, 385
Strength assessment. *See* Muscular strength
    assessment
Strength training. *See* Resistance training
Stress
  assessment of, 291–295
  and cancer, 381
  cardiovascular disease risk, 53
  dealing with. *See* Stress management
  definition of, 274
  general adaptation syndrome phases,
    275–276
  good stress, 274
  and immune system, 278–280
  negative effects of, 276–277
  and nutrition, 281
  physiological effects of, 53, 275, 277–278
  and self-esteem, 280
  stressful situations, categories of, 276

Stress—*Cont.*
  stress-related personality types, 282
  stress style, 295
Stress management
  autogenics, 285
  biofeedback, 286
  coping tips, 283
  exercise, 288
  massage therapy, 286
  meditation, 285
  music, 286–287
  pleasurable experiences as, 289
  relaxation methods, 283–285
  time management, 287–288
  visualization, 285–286
Stressors
  definition of, 274
  individual reactions to, 274
  life stressor assessment, 291–292
  types of, 53, 274
Stress tests, 55, 442
Stretching exercises, 67
  ballistic stretching, 139
  for cooldown, 77
  illustrations of, 134–136
  proprioceptive neuromuscular facilitation
    (PNF), 137–139
  static stretching, 136–137
Stretch reflex, 136
Stroke, 37–38
  causes of, 37–38, 46
  prevention of, 38
  warning signs, 38
Stroke volume, and cardiorespiratory
    training, 67
Subliminal advertising, 12
Sugar, limiting intake, 183
Sun exposure
  and cancer, 380, 381, 388
  tanning devices, dangers of, 388
Support groups
  cancer survivors, 395
  value of, 5
Syndrome X, 51, 218
Synergistic effect, meaning of, 333
Syphilis, 368–369
  diagnostic difficulty, 368
  stages of, 368–369
  treatment of, 369

T
Tai chi, benefits of, 133
Tanning devices, dangers of, 388
Tapeworms, foodborne, 188
Telephone services, for health information,
    427–428
Termination stage, self-help
    approach, 19
Testicles, self-examination, 393
Testicular cancer, 393
  signs of, 393
Therapeutic index, meaning of, 333
Thermogenic effect of food, 241
Thrombus, and stroke, 37–38
Thyroid gland, and body weight, 239
Time juggling, problem of, 287

Time management, 287–288
  guidelines, 287–288
  time robbers, 287
  use of time analysis, 303–304
  worksheet for, 301–302
Tolerance, to alcohol, 338
Tonometry, 442
Transdermal patches, nicotine, 344
Transfatty acids, 158, 159, 162
Transtheoretical Model of Behavior Change,
  and self-help approach, 13
Trauma, rape trauma syndrome,
  317–318
Treadmill test, 55
Trichomoniasis, 369
Trunk extension test, 151
Tumors
  benign, 379
  malignant. *See* Cancer
Type A personality, 282
Type B personality, 282

U

Ulcerative colitis, 413
Underwater weighing, 219, 221
Underweight, 258
Universal Gym, 109
Uterine cancer, 391
  risk factors, 391

V

Valerian, 172
Validity, health-related studies, 423
Variable resistance training, 108–109
Vegans, 179
Vegetarian diet, 179–181
  deficiency problems of, 180
  dietary strategies, 179, 181
  food pyramid for, 180
  forms of, 180
  health benefits, 181
  in pregnancy, 185
Very-low-calorie diets, 244
Violence, 315–320
  at automated teller machines (ATMs),
    315–316
  car jacking, 316
  domestic violence, 318–320

Violence—*Cont.*
  hate crimes, 320
  homicide, 318
  rape, 316–318
  self-assessment for risk of, 329–330
Virginity, secondary virginity, 359
Viruses, and cancer, 381–382
Visualization, stress management, 285–286
Vitamin A
  carotenoids, 165
  food sources of, 164
  recommended intake, 163
Vitamin C
  food sources of, 164
  functions of, 163–164, 164
  recommended intake, 163, 164
Vitamin D
  and calcium, 168
  functions of, 164
  recommended intake, 163
Vitamin E
  food sources of, 164
  functions of, 164, 165
  recommended uses, 165
Vitamin K
  food sources of, 164
  functions of, 164
  recommended intake, 163
Vitamins, 162–167. *See also* individual
    vitamins
  antioxidants, 162–163
  and athletic activity, 187
  deficiency and vegetarian diet, 180
  fat-soluble vitamins, 162, 163, 164
  functions of, 162
  for older adults, 177
  in pregnancy, 185
  shopping tips, 167
  stress effects on, 281
  supplements, recommended use, 166–167
  water soluble vitamins, 162, 163, 164

W

Waist-to-hip ratio, body fat
    distribution, 217
Warm up, exercise, 76–77
Water, 169–170
  and exercise, 81–82, 187

Water—*Cont.*
  functions of, 169
  recommended intake, 170
Water soluble vitamins, 162, 163, 164
Weight cycling, 243–244
Weight gain
  and high fat intake, 160
  and pregnancy, 185
  and quitting smoking, 49
Weight loss
  and caloric deficit, 243
  and calories burned, 250–252
  cycling, 243–244
  diet drugs, 247
  dieting, 243–247
  estimation of, 216
  fasting, 250
  herbal remedies, 247, 250
  and physical activity, 250–254
  predictors of success, 252, 254–255,
    258–260
  realistic goal setting, 215
Wellness
  benefits of, 2
  and cardiorespiratory endurance, 70
  challenges to, 9–11
  components of, 3–7
  self-help approach, 12–19
  steps in, 9
Women
  and AIDS, 361, 363
  alcohol and tobacco use, 339
  and cigarette smoking, 339
  coping with work/home stress, 280
  estrogen, protective effects, 40
Workaholism, 287

Y

Yesism, problem of, 287
Yoga
  benefits of, 133
  and health, 5

Z

Zinc, 169
  stress effects on, 281

7